WOMEN AS
INTERPRETERS
OF THE
VISUAL ARTS,
1820-1979

Recent titles in
Contributions in Women's Studies

WOMEN AS INTERPRETERS OF THE VISUAL ARTS, 1820-1979

Edited by CLAIRE RICHTER SHERMAN
with Adele M. Holcomb

Contributions in Women's Studies, Number 18

Greenwood Press

WESTPORT, CONNECTICUT • LONDON, ENGLAND

Grateful acknowledgment is given to the following:

Roberta M. Capers for permission to quote passages from her unpublished memoirs.

Anne C. Eagles for permission to quote passages from a letter from Ann H. Zwinger.

Ingeborg C. Sachs for permission to quote excerpts from "Autobiography of a Female Scholar" by Margarete Bieber.

Christopher Tietze for permission to quote passages from Erica Tietze-Conrat's unpublished memoirs.

Library of Congress Cataloging in Publication Data
Main entry under title:

Women as interpreters of the visual arts, 1820-1979.

    (Contributions in women's studies ; no. 18 ISSN 0147-104X.
    Bibliography: p.
    Includes index.
    1. Women art critics. 2. Women art historians.
3. Women art teachers. 4. Art criticism—History.
5. Art, Modern—19th century—History. 6. Art,
Modern—20th century—History. I. Sherman, Claire
Richter. II. Holcomb, Adele M. III. Series.
N7476.W65   709'.2'2 [B]   80-785
ISBN 0-313-22056-5 (lib. bdg.)

Library of Congress Catalog Card Number: 80-785
ISBN: 0-313-22056-5
ISSN: 0147-104X

First published in 1981

Greenwood Press
A division of Congressional Information Service, Inc.
88 Post Road West, Westport, Connecticut 06881

Printed in the United States of America

10 9 8 7 6 5 4 3 2 1

Women are supposed to be very calm generally: but women feel just as men feel; they need
exercise for their faculties, and a field for their
efforts as much as their brothers do; they suffer from too rigid a restraint, too absolute a
stagnation, precisely as men would suffer;
and it is narrow-minded in their more privileged fellow-creatures to say that they ought
to confine themselves to making puddings
and knitting stockings, to playing on the piano
and embroidering bags. It is thoughtless to
condemn them, or laugh at them, if they seek
to do more or learn more than custom has
pronounced necessary for their sex.

Charlotte Brontë, *Jane Eyre*

CONTENTS

ILLUSTRATIONS

PREFACE

The initial impulse for this book came from a group of women meeting informally to discuss the historical role of women in the visual arts. This contemporary version of the salon began in 1973 as the Study Group of Washington Women Art Professionals. WWAP, as it was called, had been formed as the result of the seminal conference on Women in the Visual Arts held in April 1972 at the Corcoran Gallery in Washington, D.C. WWAP flourished from 1973 until 1975, when its functions were gradually absorbed by the Women's Caucus for Art and the Washington Women's Art Center. The Women's Caucus for Art had been launched in January 1972 in San Francisco as the Women's Caucus of the College Art Association.

In the course of its discussions, the WWAP Study Group, led by Claire Sherman, realized that little attention had been given in current art historical literature to the past and present contributions of women scholars in the field. To remedy this situation, the Study Group originally agreed to develop an anthology of writings by women critics and scholars for use in college courses. In October 1973, when the Study Group decided to enlist the aid of additional colleagues, the focus of the book shifted. Adele Holcomb, who had independently become interested in the presence of women in art scholarship, joined Claire Sherman to collaborate on the project. In the course of their discussions they concluded that a series of biographical and critical essays on the careers of individual women scholars, followed by bibliographies of their writings, would yield more significant kinds of information about women's participation in the field than would an anthology. A substantial introductory section was planned to place the essays within a wider frame of reference.

The preliminary stage of matching contributors with specialized know-

ledge of a field or subjects for essays took over a year. Helpful suggestions
came from colleagues who responded to requests for information. Among
them, Alessandra Comini, Meyer Schapiro, and Kathleen Weil-Garris
provided advice and encouragement. As the project involved a type of
biographical and critical essay that did not have many precedents in the
field, additional advice from various consultants was sought. A guide to
biographical methods and sources was compiled by Luree Miller, now the
author of two books on modern women. Susan Cardinale, a librarian at
the University of Maryland, provided a bibliography on women in the
professions. Because most of the contributors concerned with more recent
history had never conducted personal interviews, in June 1975 Claire
Sherman attended a workshop on oral history held at George Washington
University. With the cooperation of Mary Jo Deering of the Audio-Visual
Section of the George Washington University Library and of Roberta
Greene, a member of the Robert and John F. Kennedy oral history project
of the National Archives, instructions on conducting interviews were
developed and sent to contributors. Ruth W. Spiegel, now an editor for the
Smithsonian Institution Press, compiled a series of editorial guidelines.
Professor Robert Ginsberg of Pennsylvania State University, editor of
The Critique of War: Contemporary Philosophical Explorations, gave
much practical advice on other aspects of launching a collaborative project.

To promote the sense of common goals and to inform contributors on the
progress of the book, three newsletters were sent during the initial stages of
the project. Grants from the Women's Caucus for Art helped to defray
initial expenses. At two meetings in Washington, local and visiting contributors discussed issues and problems they had encountered in writing
their essays. On 2 February 1976, during the annual meeting of the College
Art Association in Chicago, a panel discussion sponsored by the Women's
Caucus for Art, entitled "Women Scholars in the Arts: A Progress Report"
promoted valuable discussion among the contributors and members of the
audience. Later that year, after first drafts of the essays were submitted,
Michelle Cliff, a professional editor, made useful comments on them. Jean
Sutherland Boggs, Emily Vermeule, Ann Sutherland Harris, Elly Miller,
and Winifred Needler read and commented on the first draft of the introduction and, in some cases, on individual essays as well. In 1978, when the
book was substantially complete, Mary Laing, an experienced editor in fine
arts publications, evaluated the entire manuscript and made helpful suggestions on the steps necessary for completing the project.

In April 1979, when the decision was made to enlarge the biographical
scope of the introductory chapters of the book, various individuals and
institutions helped in finding essential sources. Professor Pamela Askew of
Vassar College supplied additional information on the late Agnes Rindge
Claflin. Avis Berman, who has written on women in American art museums,

generously shared her knowledge of the subject. Maureen Robinson and Ellen Hicks of the American Association of Museums furnished needed materials. For their responses to requests for information, Claire Sherman thanks the following archivists: Patricia K. Ballou, Barnard College; Jane S. Knowles, Radcliffe College; Wilma R. Slaight, Wellesley College; Marilyn Ghausi, Detroit Institute of Arts; Patricia Pellegrini, Metropolitan Museum of Art; and Merle Chamberlain, Philadelphia Museum of Art. The librarians of the following institutions were also helpful: Annette Masling, Albright-Knox Art Gallery; John W. Teahan, Wadsworth Atheneum; and Blanche Cooney, Smith College. Roberta M. F. A. Capers graciously gave permission to publish excerpts from her unpublished memoir on the education department of the Metropolitan Museum of Art.

Adele Holcomb wishes to acknowledge the help received from the following individuals. Dame Janet Vaughan, former principal of Somerville College, provided information about the college. She also shared her reminiscences of Gisela Richter and answered queries, as did Marcel Roethlisberger and Mary and Colin Allsebrook. Mrs. Allsebrook, daughter of Harriet Boyd Hawes, recalled her mother's work and personality in conversation with Adele Holcomb, as did her brother, Alexander Boyd Hawes, with Claire Sherman. Winifred Needler talked about her work and her experience in entering the field of Egyptology in Canada during the 1930s. Helen Lowenthal discussed some aspects of the presence of women in art history and her memories of Dorothy Miner. Eckhard Rothe, reference librarian at Bishop's University, provided bibliographic assistance.

Claire Sherman wishes to acknowledge her great indebtedness to the superb collections and the facilities for scholarly research provided by the Library of Congress. She has received unusual help from many staff members in the Library's various divisions; in particular, she benefited from the assistance of Myron Weinstein of the Hebraic Section and that of Sarah Pritchard, a reference librarian specializing in women's studies. Peter Petcoff, the Library's reference specialist in biography, has rendered exceptional service in locating materials on this and other subjects. Many colleagues among the scholarly community at the Library of Congress, including Mary Garrard, Dorothy Ross, Shirley Schwarz, Hilda Smith, Ellen Ginsberg, and Elke P. Frederiksen, have offered advice and information. For such help and for their continued support, Claire Sherman wishes to express heartfelt gratitude to Jane Bond Howard, Luree Miller, and J. B. Ross.

Claire Sherman also wishes to acknowledge the help of her husband, Stanley M. Sherman. Although his assistance has taken many forms, none was more vital than his typing of large portions of the manuscript, including the first three chapters and the final section of the bibliography. His understanding and encouragement throughout the project have meant a great deal. Her son Daniel J. Sherman found the epigraph for the book and helped with editorial revisions. Ruth W. Spiegel has continued to give valued editorial advice and personal support. Diane Russell and Eugenia Kaledin provided wise counsel on many subjects.

The contributors have shown great patience in seeing the project through to a successful conclusion. Despite delays and discouragements, their commitment has fostered a rewarding and unusual collegiality.

Washington, D.C./Sherbrooke, P.Q.
January 1980

INTRODUCTORY NOTE

This book begins with the premise that women have made significant contributions as interpreters of the visual arts. The term interpreter signifies here the public and professional roles of women as published critics and historians of art, archaeologists, educators, facilitators of research about art, curators, and administrators in museums and other institutions. Such activities by steadily increasing numbers of European and American women begin in the early-nineteenth century with published writings on art and parallel the development of art history as an intellectual discipline with defined professional and institutional relationships. Despite the quality of their attainments and their presence in substantial numbers, in the existing art historiographic literature women's achievements as interpreters of the visual arts have largely been ignored or relegated to marginal notes on masculine achievements.

This volume attempts to repair the neglect of women's attainments as interpreters of the visual arts. First, twelve biographical and critical essays on representative European and American women reveal the range of their contributions to the field. These essays are preceded by three introductory chapters that review the careers of about a hundred other women who, from 1820 until 1979, made important contributions as interpreters of the visual arts. Although by no means a complete record, this volume will serve as a companion to other studies of women's professional achievements in fields like medicine or science, in which they have been far less numerous.

What are the possible explanations for the virtual omission of women's contributions from current art historiographic literature? First of all, the general literature on the theoretical and institutional aspects of art history leaves a lot to be desired. Aside from published lectures, ill-digested synopses in anthologies, or brief discussions in encyclopedias, a full-scale treatment of the conceptual foundations of art history on an international basis remains to be written. Nor have questions of methodology and the relationship of art history to allied disciplines such as anthropology and archaeology received adequate attention. As to academic art history, a particularly lamentable instance of the gaps in the literature involves the inadequate documentation of American developments. The one exception is the indispensable reference source written by Priscilla Hiss and Roberta Fansler for the Carnegie Corporation in 1934, *Research in Fine Arts in the Colleges and Universities of the United States*. Similar weaknesses characterize most books on the history of museums. General surveys of the subject tend to obscure the importance of these institutions in modern cultural life by a preference for anecdotal narratives about wealthy or eccentric benefactors, directors, and personnel. Some major museums lack institutional histories; few of the existing ones supply such necessary factual information as a chronological listing of the professional staff. In short, the literature on the theory and institutions of art history is notably inadequate. Nevertheless, even in the present unsatisfactory state of art historiography, women's participation in the field calls for further investigation. Some explanations for its neglect will emerge from both the introductory chapters and the essays themselves.

In the course of documenting the records of women's attainments as interpreters of the visual arts, certain other issues arise. Among them is the validity of isolating female from male achievements. The method followed here does not proceed from any simple belief that women's intellectual processes, writing, or scholarship differ inherently from men's. Such considerations involve complex problems for which no easy or definitive answers exist. Yet, as the biographical and bibliographic evidence will indicate, one can say that the differences between the social status and cultural roles of men and women of similar professional aspirations have greatly influenced the range and scope of their achievements. Such disparities affected not only the opportunities for education and employment open to women but also the psychological preconditions for creative intellectual efforts. In fact, the ways in which women entered the field in substantial numbers derive from certain assumptions about their social and cultural roles in nineteenth-century Europe and America.

In structure as well as content this book seeks to correct the present neglect of women's contributions as interpreters of the visual arts and to show how their achievements were shaped by changing social, cultural, and historical factors. For these reasons, the first three chapters, which together form Part I of this volume, provide an extensive historical introduction to the twelve essays presented in three groups of four chapters each in Parts II, III, and IV. Without any specific mention of women's contributions, each of the first three introductory chapters begins with a short preliminary account of the developments in the field as a whole. There next follows a separate consideration of women's contributions, beginning with their writings because publication is generally viewed as the most important criterion of achievement in the field. Because both publications by women and the general level of their attainment were fundamentally affected by the opportunities available to them for education and employment, these topics are explored in separate sections within each of the first three chapters, which conclude by discussing the effects of professional aspirations and achievements on women's lifestyles. Evidence is drawn both from the biographies of the twelve subjects of essays and from the careers of about a hundred women discussed in these introductory chapters.

More specifically, the first three chapters correspond historically to the periods in which the twelve subjects of essays were active. Their placement is determined by the dates of their first professional activity, rather than simply by birth dates. Of course, some careers extended to the next period. The dates of the periods themselves signify important historical or professional landmarks. Thus, Chapter 1, *Precursors and Pioneers*, covers the period from 1820 to 1890, when the first four subjects of essays in Part II, *Nineteenth-Century Writers on the Arts*, produced their most important works. The beginning date of 1820 was chosen because that decade marked the publication in England and Germany of books by women on specifically art-historical topics. By the terminal date of 1890, women's status outside official institutions characteristic of this period began to change significantly.

In Chapter 2, *Widening Horizons*, which covers the period from 1890 to 1930, women take their places in various institutional settings as archaeologists, art historians, and art educators, although non-affiliated writers continue to make important contributions. The work of the next four subjects of essays—Georgiana Goddard King, Margarete Bieber, Gisela Richter, and Erica Tietze-Conrat—in Part III, *Art Historians and Archaeologists of the Late-Nineteenth and Early-Twentieth Centuries*, corresponds to this period from 1890 to 1930.

Except for King, who died in 1939, Bieber, Richter, and Tietze-Conrat continued their activity well into the third historical period, from 1930 to 1979. These years are covered in Chapter 3, entitled *The Tradition Continues*, which presents the historical background for the last group of essays in Part IV, *Scholars Active from the Early-Twentieth Century to 1979*. The 1930s witnessed several important art-historical developments that resulted from the turbulence of this decade. Among them was the emergence in the United States of government sponsorship of art in federal programs that responded to the hardships of the Great Depression. A second was the flight from Hitlerism of distinguished refugee scholars to various European countries and America. The women discussed in Chapter

3 and the four subjects of essays in Part IV represent the generation born before World War I. Extension of the discussion to younger women, who have been drawn to the field in ever-increasing numbers, would call for another book almost as long as this one. An epilogue following the essays examines in summary fashion the past and present condition of women as interpreters of the visual arts and the possible effects of the women's movement on future developments.

The twelve subjects of these biographical and critical essays—as well as the women mentioned in the introductory chapters—have been selected as representative of the kinds of professional careers open to women as interpreters of the visual arts in the three separate periods just described. The term professional indicates here a recognized public function involving the presentation and interpretation of information about the visual arts in various forms and settings. These activities include publication, employment by or association with academic institutions, museums, research or other organizations, and libraries that engage in the study, collection, and teaching of art from an educational, critical, or historical point of view. By these criteria, with rare exceptions, patrons, collectors, and *salonières* who have not been publicly active in the listed senses are not included. This decision results from restrictions of space rather than from any failure to recognize the powerful influence of such women on the institutionalized art world.

Practical limitations of resources have also restricted coverage of the over-all subject of women as interpreters of the visual arts mainly to developments in the English-speaking world, particularly the United States. Most regrettably, the essays do not include women who have contributed to the study of Oriental art and non-literate cultures. Although the work of several women art educators in museums is mentioned, this topic has not been thoroughly explored. Nor has it been possible to discuss women's important contributions as registrars and conservators in art museums. In some cases, lack of sufficient or accessible biographical materials has prevented the undertaking or completion of essays on likely subjects such as Maud Cruttwell or Belle da Costa Greene. In other instances, either a prominent subject or the most appropriate author declined invitations to participate in the project. The basis of criteria for the selection of women for the introductory chapters included the representative character of their careers and the availability of biographical and bibliographic material. The documentation assembled here represents only the first step in the recovery of a vital and extensive tradition.

A few methodological procedures need clarification here. The first concerns the vexing problem of references to women's names in the first three chapters. Unlike a man's, a woman's identity does not remain fixed if she marries, remarries, or is divorced. The older method of referring to women by their husbands' Christian, or simply family, name is not followed here. Instead, a woman's Christian name is always given: for example, Mary Philadelphia Merrifield, not Mrs. Merrifield; or Eugénie Sellers Strong, not Mrs. Arthur Strong. In the first three chapter, a woman's maiden and married names are both given, particularly when both are used professionally. If a woman's professional activities occur before her marriage, she is called by her maiden name in the text; if afterwards, by her married name. In instances where women have been married more than once, their various names are given if necessary to establish professional identity or authorship. For reference purposes, however, women are listed under the names by which they appear in library catalogues. Because of its widespread use, the system employed by the Library of Congress is adopted here.

Furthermore, it should be noted that the capitalization of the first important reference to a woman's name in the first three chapters indicates that further biographical information about her will be found in the last section of the bibliography. In many cases, this biographical information in the bibliography serves also as documentation for the first three chapters, which in a more specialized work would take the form of individual footnotes. Although footnotes follow the first three chapters, they have been kept to a minimum. For more specific information the reader is referred again to the various sections of the bibliography.

C. R. S.

ABBREVIATIONS

These abbreviations are used primarily for the footnotes in Chapters 1-3 and for the biographical section of the bibliography.

AAA	*American Art Annual*
AJ	*Art Journal*
AR	*Architectural Review*
BM	*Burlington Magazine*
CA	*Contemporary Authors*, Detroit
CB	*Current Biography*, New York
DAB	*Dictionary of American Biography*, New York
DNB	*Dictionary of National Biography*, London
GBA	*Gazette des Beaux-Arts*
Hiss and Fansler, *Research*	Priscilla Hiss and Roberta Fansler, *Research in Fine Arts in the Colleges and Universities of the United States*. New York, 1934.
Kleinbauer, *Modern Perspectives*	W. Eugene Kleinbauer, *Modern Perspectives in Western Art History: An Anthology of 20th-Century Writings on the Visual Arts*. New York, 1971.
LDF	*Lexikon der Frau*. 2 vols. Zurich, 1953-54.

NAW	*Notable American Women: A Biographical Dictionary*. Edited by Edward T. James, Janet W. James, and Paul S. Boyer. 3 vols. Cambridge, Mass., 1971.
NAW (supp.).	*Notable American Women: The Modern Period. A Biographical Dictionary*. Edited by Barbara Sicherman and Carol Hurd Green. Cambridge, Mass., 1980.
NCAB	*National Cyclopedia of American Biography*, New York
NY Times	*New York Times*
Panofsky, "Three Decades of Art History"	Erwin Panofsky, "Three Decades of Art History in the United States: Impressions of a Transplanted European." In *Meaning in the Visual Arts*. Garden City, New York, 1955.
QR	*Quarterly Review*
Salerno, "Historiography"	Luigi Salerno, "Historiography." In *Encyclopedia of World Art*, 10. New York, 1965.
WWAA	*Who's Who in American Art*, New York
WWAW	*Who's Who of American Women*, Chicago

PART I   *WOMEN AS INTERPRETERS OF THE VISUAL ARTS*

CHAPTER 1
PRECURSORS AND PIONEERS (1820-1890)

Claire Richter Sherman
with the assistance of Adele M. Holcomb

GENERAL BACKGROUND OF ART HISTORY

The work of the four subjects of the essays in Part II of this book, the nineteenth-century writers on the arts Anna Jameson (1794-1860), Margaret Fuller (1810-1850), Emilia Francis Strong Pattison, Lady Dilke (1840-1904), and Mariana Griswold Van Rensselaer (1851-1934) was produced outside the university and the art museum—the two main institutional forms of the new discipline of art history.[1] The nineteenth century saw the development of this field in its modern form, although Western art history begins with the Italian Renaissance, particularly in Giorgio Vasari's *Lives of the Most Eminent Italian Painters, Sculptors and Architects* (second Italian edition, 1568). Although Vasari's focus was artistic biography, his work contained many strands of future art-historical study such as the concept of style, distinct historical periods, reference to the existing literature of art, and the idea of cyclical development based on progress toward an ideal standard of artistic value. The first work to use the term history of art in the title was Johann Joachim Winckelmann's *Geschichte der Kunst des Altertums (History of Ancient Art)*, published in 1764. A crucial feature of Winckelmann's work was the focus on individual works of art (in relation to their historical context), not individual artists. This emphasis on the analysis of the individual work of art as the primary source for study characterizes modern art history. Art-historical analysis includes examination of the physical character of the art object (including material and technique), the

Author's note: The first three chapters are in part based on two preliminary drafts for an introduction by Adele M. Holcomb. Her assistance, particularly with Chapter 1, is gratefully acknowledged.

identification of its creator, and the place and date of creation. The paramount orientation is thus the location of works of art in a historical matrix. The distinctive style, subject, and expressive content of individual works of art are related to other works of art by the same artist and to larger units—regional group or school, period, country, and culture. Art criticism, which in many cases overlaps art history in the analysis of the formal or expressive character of works of art, may place less importance on historical aspects, emphasize moral and aesthetic values, and present a subjective point of view rather than the supposedly objective standards characteristic of the art historian.

Two main strands of thought contributed to the development of art history in the nineteenth century. The first of these was Romanticism, a complex international literary, philosophical, and artistic movement, itself shaped by such great historical forces as the French revolution and the age of Napoleon. In the realm of art criticism, one contribution of Romanticism was rejection of the traditional theory that art imitates nature. Instead, Romanticism contended that the highest function of the visual arts is the creation of symbols of human experience and the world of nature to which it is allied. Also of great importance was the loosening in Romantic criticism of the position of classical Greek and Italian High Renaissance art—and the standard of ideal beauty realized in them—as the sole touchstones of aesthetic value. More relative standards of taste in evaluating works of art arose from the realization (already evident in the eighteenth century) that works of art formed part of larger cultural identities embodied in the traditions of separate countries or regions. One consequence of Romantic thinking was the reevaluation of the art of such non-classical periods and regions as the Middle Ages and northern Europe.[2] Later in the century, writing that emphasized the interpretation of art in terms of the total cultural expression of an era was derived in part from the new historical consciousness. The most famous model for this approach is Jacob Burckhardt's *The Civilization of the Renaissance in Italy* (first published in English in 1878), although it scarcely discusses the visual arts. Related also to the idea that works of art express the culture in which they were produced is iconography, the identification and analysis of the meaning of subject matter. Inspired particularly by the new interest in the Middle Ages, the study of Christian symbolism in relationship to medieval culture flourished in this period.[']

Burckhardt's writing also reflected a second nineteenth-century moving force in historiography: the search for a scientific method. Borrowing from philology and allied disciplines of history like numismatics and paleography, art scholars began to investigate documents that would locate precisely the historical circumstances in which works of art were produced, commissioned, and sold. A pioneering work in this field was Karl Friedrich von

Rumohr's *Italienische Forschungen* ("Italian Researches")* of 1827-1831. In order to test the accuracy of writings on Italian art, beginning with Vasari's *Lives*, Rumohr conducted intensive examinations of original documents in the archives of Florence, Siena, and other cities. Rumohr's analysis of written sources was combined with close firsthand knowledge of works of art. Rumohr's contemporary Johann David Passavant introduced a new concern for exhaustive research in his monograph on Raphael (1839). Passavant examined virtually everything previously written on the master, meticulously scrutinizing all Raphael's surviving works and maintaining a critical attitude toward his sources.

Both Rumohr and Passavant strove for objectivity in discussing works of art. That goal was reflected in Franz Kugler's *Handbuch der Geschichte der Malerei* . . . of 1837, familiar to English readers as *A Handbook of the History of Painting*. . . . The notion that art was a single entity with some kind of common essence was manifest in his impartial and impersonal treatment of the material. Because Kugler had so much ground to cover, he offers not insightful analysis of individual works but generalities about style. Kugler's deficiences still prevail in many current introductory survey texts of art history intended for beginning students of the subject.

Early in the nineteenth century, the history of art became an academic subject taught at universities and colleges. The first chairs were founded in universities of Germany and present-day Austria, the countries where modern art history first developed.[3] The first professor to teach the subject was Johann Dominic Fiorillo, named to a chair at Göttingen in 1813, who was followed by Gustav Waagen in Berlin (1844) and Rudolf von Eitelberger in Vienna (1851). Academic teaching of art history divorced from studio practice did not take place in England until the twentieth century. In the United States, despite earlier abortive efforts, the 1870s and 1880s marked the real beginnings of sustained undergraduate instruction.[4] A landmark in this regard was Charles Eliot Norton's lectureship at Harvard that began in 1874-1875 on "The History of Fine Arts as Connected with Literature."[5] In Germany and Austria the teaching of the history of art as an academic discipline encouraged specialized studies based on rigorous documentary research. Outstanding examples are the series of studies on the written sources of Renaissance and later art undertaken by scholars at the University of Vienna.

A second aspect of ascertaining historical facts about works of art concerns their dating, localization, attribution, and history when no written documents exist. This kind of study, based on extensive firsthand examina-

---

*Translations of titles of foreign-language works for which no English published editions exist are set off by quotation marks; published English translations are italicized.

tion of original works of art, is known as connoisseurship. Connoisseurship
was not invented in the nineteenth century; the collection and sale of works
of art had long created a need for experts who advised those involved in the
contemporary art market. In the nineteenth century the creation of public
art museums and collections gave new importance to connoisseurship as a
means of gathering reliable information on works of art accessible to the
public. In the seventeenth and eighteenth centuries, private collections of
art gradually opened to the public on a limited basis in various European
countries. The great impetus for making collections of royal art treasures
the property of the people came from the French revolution. In 1793 the
Louvre, the royal palace containing the art collections acquired by the kings
of France, was opened as a public art museum.[6] The victorious campaigns
of the French revolutionary armies, capped by Napoleon's conquests,
brought priceless treasures from the defeated countries to Paris and under
the Empire resulted in a centralized art administration system for France
and its satellites. Although some of the art works taken as booty were
returned after Waterloo, many remained in France, divided between Paris
and the provincial museums. In reaction to Napoleon's cultural imperialism,
museums were founded in various European countries as symbols of
national pride.

The national support of museums in Europe did not provide a precedent
for American developments in the nineteenth century. With the exception
of a few city and university museums, the first encyclopedic art institutions,
beginning with the Metropolitan Museum in New York and the Boston
Museum of Fine Arts, were not founded until 1870. Private philanthropy
and local municipalities afforded sources of financial support.[7] Education
of the broad public by various programs and of craftsmen and artists in
museum schools were particular features of American museums.

The collection, organization, and exhibition of works of art in public
museums encouraged research and publication. In Europe some academic
art historians directed public museums: Waagen was first director of the
Berlin Gallery from 1830; Passavant headed the Städel Art Institute in
Frankfurt in 1840. Close ties between museums and the art historians of the
University of Vienna began very early. Academic scholarship benefited
from the study of works of art increasingly accessible in museums. Connoisseurship in museums focused on studying the objects already collected,
classifying them according to technique or chronology, and then publishing
catalogues based on these findings. Connoisseurship was also crucial in the
purchase of new works for museums, especially in distinguishing original
works from forgeries and in establishing correct attributions to specific
artists; the monetary value attached to a work of art was directly affected by
its history and evidence of its creation by a famous master.

Sometimes connoisseurs criticized museum policies by questioning purchases and attributions. Such objections were voiced in the important *New History of Painting in Italy from the Second to the Sixteenth Century* by Joseph Archer Crowe and Giovanni Battista Cavalcaselle (1864-1866). Their attributions were in turn challenged by the Italian politician and statesman Giovanni Morelli (1816-1891), trained first in Berlin in comparative anatomy and medicine. Morelli tried to develop a scientific and objective method of connoisseurship based on a study of an artist's rendering of small but revealing details, such as fingernails or ear shapes, that would reveal autograph works of major artists and distinguish them from lesser hands and forgeries. Instead of inexact engravings or drawings, Morelli introduced photography as a more exact tool for studying and comparing works of art. His theories, controversial at the time because they challenged established museum practice, won the day; his method was clearly superior in establishing orderly systems of attribution and in recognizing works by major artists formerly ascribed to minor masters.

In addition to art-historical research sponsored by universities or encouraged by museum activities, older national antiquarian societies continued to flourish. They were joined by governmental agencies that supported studies of classical and national monuments, a sponsorship that encouraged the development of architectural history. The great national libraries were also influential in publishing research on illuminated manuscripts, printed books, and prints and drawings in their collections. Specialized periodicals supported by these organizations, universities, and museums encouraged dissemination by articles and reviews of the newest developments in scholarship.

Art criticism, closely allied to literature for most of this period, attracted a wide public. Both specialized art periodicals and more general journals addressed a new public for art drawn from the growing urban populations of both Europe and the United States.[8] Although John Ruskin's art criticism cannot easily be summarized, his insistence that art should have a redeeming moral and social value had wide influence, and in England at least, tended to delay the development of a historical point of view. Among his compatriots, Walter Pater reacted against Ruskin's equation of the value of architecture and art with the moral health of the artist or society that produced them, in his writings such as *The Seven Lamps of Architecture* (1849). In *The Renaissance; Studies in Art and Poetry* (1873), Pater defined literary and artistic beauty as independent of non-aesthetic criteria. In France, literary and art criticism written by poets, novelists, and journalists created a climate favorable to contemporary art and to art of other eras spurned by official taste and institutions.

This short summary of developments in art history and criticism between 1820 and 1890 indicates that fundamental patterns establishing the field as a scholarly discipline in academic institutions and museums had formed, while art criticism attracted a wide audience interested in both art and literature. While women were for the most part excluded from employment in museums and universities in this period, their activity was directed to writing on art for a general audience.

WOMEN WRITERS AND WRITINGS ON ART

The careers of the first two subjects of essays in this book, Anna Jameson and Margaret Fuller, were greatly influenced by the Romantic movement. In turn, they and their sisters became influential disseminators of Romantic viewpoints on literature and art. Women writers also exerted an important influence on artistic taste by their works on late medieval and early Renaissance masters of Italy and northern Europe, known as "primitives" because their styles antedated the naturalism and classicism of Italian Renaissance art. Romanticism, as Susan Conrad has pointed out, also encouraged women's intellectual engagement with the arts by its emphasis on certain qualities associated with women's nature: intuition, imagination, and perception of symbolic relationships. Romanticism also fostered women's sense of a separate emotional and spiritual identity, which served as a stimulus to creative intellectual activity.[9]

The life and writings of MADAME DE STAËL* (1766-1817) served as emblems for women seeking visible models of personal and literary achievements.[10] Born Germaine Necker in Paris, she was the daughter of a wealthy Geneva banker who became finance minister of Louis XVI in the years before the French revolution. She took an important and public role in the events of the revolutionary and Napoleonic periods. Her brilliant salon and conversation, as well as her emancipated lifestyle, marked her as a heroic woman of unique genius. Her major literary work, De l'Allemagne (Germany), completed in 1810 and published in England in 1813, explored the characteristic aspects of northern European literature as an expression of a culture distinct from the classical orientation of France and Italy. For women, her most influential publication was her novel Corinne (1807), whose heroine—identified with Madame de Staël herself—became the embodiment of the creative and inspirational ideals and activity of women like Anna Jameson and Margaret Fuller. Among the important themes in Corinne are friendships between women and the heroine's active role as a guide to Italian sites and monuments.

In 1803 Madame de Staël's travels in Germany introduced her to prominent figures in German Romanticism. Women played important roles in

---

*The capitalization indicates that further biographical sources, which also serve as documentation, will be found in the last section of the bibliography.

presiding over salons that served as intellectual and social centers for Romantic literature and thought.[11] In Berlin, the salons of two brilliant Jewish women were instrumental in founding the cult of Goethe. These women were Henriette Herz (1764-1867) and RAHEL VARNHAGEN (1771-1833). Indeed, Varnhagen's brilliance and charismatic personality earned for her the title of the German Madame de Staël. The publication of her voluminous correspondence and journals, a collection of her aphorisms, and the various biographies written about her attest to the lasting impression left by her personality and ideas. A recent study indicates that Varnhagen's letters and journals contain many prophetic and prescriptive comments on the need for educational and social reforms of women's condition.[12] Although not known as a feminist, Henriette Herz translated in 1832 Mary Wollstonecraft's *A Vindication of the Rights of Woman* of 1792. DOROTHEA MENDELSSOHN SCHLEGEL (1763-1839), who in 1804 married the influential literary critic Friedrich Schlegel, translated *Corinne* into German shortly after its publication. Originally part of the Berlin circle of Herz and Varnhagen, she was a prolific writer on literary subjects for Schlegel's journal *Europa*. All these women were radical in creating independent identities for themselves and in their emancipated lifestyles. Their published correspondence with one another was important in ending their isolation and providing models for friendships between intellectual women.

Also the leader of a salon, in Weimar, was another admirer of Goethe, JOHANNA SCHOPENHAUER (1766-1838). Mother of a noted son and daughter, Schopenhauer's varied career included writing guidebooks, novels, and articles on art and other subjects for various journals, as well as writing a biography of the amateur Karl Ludwig Fernow (1810). In *Johann van Eyck und seine Nachfolger* ("Jan Van Eyck and His Followers") of 1822, Schopenhauer produced the first book on the Flemish master and his school. Despite some historical errors and a frequently overwrought style, the book, which used the meager source materials available at the time, received contemporary recognition. The main importance of Schopenhauer's monograph lay in its reevaluation of northern European painting of the late Gothic period, fostered by Romantic historiography and criticism.

The career of WILHELMINE VON CHÉZY (1783-1856), another literary and artistic critic associated with German Romanticism, illustrates a path women writers frequently travelled in establishing an independent career. The first step often involved translations—in Chézy's case, of texts in old French she made for Friedrich Schlegel when she became associated with his circle. Although translations do not express independent creative effort, they established women's credentials and gave needed self-confidence. Linguistic skills, mastered at home or as the result of travel, gave women "their first intellectual opportunities" and "opened exclusively male intellectual milieus to them out of necessity."[13] Chézy took on various kinds of literary jobs to maintain herself. She wrote a successful guidebook, *Gemälde von Heidelberg, Mannheim, usw (Manual for Travellers to Heidelberg and Its Environs)*, published in 1816. Chézy also wrote critiques of contemporary exhibitions for periodicals, another genre of journalistic activity in which women became prominent. For Schlegel's *Europa*, published from 1803 to 1805, and other periodicals, she wrote critiques of the Paris salons that are full of incisive observation.

In England, too, writing guidebooks was for women an important step towards interpreting the visual arts. Travel, like knowledge of foreign languages, was an essential prerequisite for the study of art.[14] Travel was at the same time a symbol of freedom from confinement at home and greatly relished for the possibilities of adventure that it afforded.

MARIANA STARKE (1762?-1838), who grew up in India, drew upon her experience to write several successful plays for the London stage. Her residence in Italy led her to publish accounts of her life in that country during the turbulent 1790s. These *Travels in Italy* (1802) became the basis for best-selling guidebooks to the continent published between 1820 and 1838. They combined practical advice with descriptions of works of art ranked by a system of exclamation marks, the forerunner of Baedeker's or Michelin's stars.[15]

Writing in 1845, Elizabeth Rigby (later LADY EASTLAKE)—a successful practitioner of the genre—claimed the preeminence of English women in travel literature, a type of writing that she highly valued. She speaks of the "peculiar powers inherent in ladies' eyes," by which she means "that power of observation, which, so long as it remains at home counting canvass stitches by the fireside, we are apt to consider no shrewder than our own, but which once removed from the familiar scene, and returned to us in the shape of letters or books, seldom fails to prove its superiority." Rigby cites women's abilities to pick out telling details of the travel experience and communicate them in a lively, easy manner and their superior knowledge "of human nature and modern languages."[16] Of course, power of observation, linguistic and verbal skills, and responsiveness to both the individual details and the overall patterns of a foreign culture have direct application to writing criticism on art.

Maria Dundas Graham (1785-1842)—later LADY CALLCOTT—wrote in 1820 the first monograph in English on the French Baroque artist Nicholas Poussin. As the wife of a naval captain, she had earlier published accounts of her travels in India and Italy, followed by books on Brazil and Chile. Lady Callcott, as she became, had advanced tastes in art. Her appreciation of the fourteenth-century north-Italian artist Altichiero is an early example of a preference for the Italian primitives in England, which probably encouraged the collecting interests of the first director of England's

National Gallery, Sir Charles Eastlake. Her enthusiasm for Giotto, acquired on her wedding trip in Italy with her second husband, the painter Augustus Callcott, led to the first publication of the Florentine artist's famous Paduan fresco cycle, the *Description of the Chapel of the Annunziata dell'Arena* (1835). Her husband provided the illustrations of this great work, reproduced for the first time.

LADY MORGAN (1783?-1859), born Sydney Owenson, was the daughter of an Irish actor. Brought up in the theater, she worked briefly as a governess before making a living by writing best-selling novels. A lively and dramatic personality with an individual style not always appreciated in England, Lady Morgan travelled to France and Italy immediately after the Napoleonic wars. Influenced by Madame de Staël, her more journalistic accounts of developments in these countries are now valued as important sources for intellectual and social history. In 1824, Lady Morgan brought out a notable biography of an Italian Baroque artist, *The Life and Times of Salvator Rosa*. Although the work tends to embrace the legend that the painter had woven for himself, in the spirit of Romanticism, it attempts to reconstruct the physical surroundings and imaginative world of the artist.

As Adele Holcomb indicates in her essay, Anna Jameson's first publications reflect the importance of travel as a theme affirming individual independence and engagement in literary and artistic activity. Anna Jameson's continental journeys as a governess formed the basis of her experience in *Diary of an Ennuyée* (1826). Strongly influenced by the tour guide activity of Madame de Staël's Corinne, the *Diary* offers Jameson's perceptive observations of and responses to works of art. In *Visits and Sketches at Home and Abroad* (1834), she shows her appreciation of contemporary German art and of the Italian and German "primitives." Jameson and Lady Callcott were soon joined by other women writers in promoting in England a taste for these hitherto unfashionable periods. Also widely influential was Jameson's *Winter Studies and Summer Rambles in Canada* (1838), significant as the account of a woman's travel in remote areas of Ontario, an appreciation of landscape, and a sensitivity to the status of the Indian women whom she encountered.

Margaret Fuller also discovered in *Corinne* a model of female achievement and action. Susan Conrad has illuminated the role of Romanticism in providing the symbolic and philosophical touchstones of Fuller's search for an intellectual and feminine identity.[17] In turn, she became one of the chief interpreters of German Romanticism in the United States. She too began her literary career with a translation: *Eckermann's Conversations with Goethe* (1839). In 1842 she produced another translation, the record of a friendship between two German women, a quintessential expression of Romantic sensibility, the *Correspondence of Fräulein Günderode and Bettina von Arnim*. Fuller's travels to the Middle West inspired her

lyrical *Summer on the Lakes* (1844). As Corlette Walker and Adele
Holcomb indicate in their essay, Fuller's sympathy with spiritual and
aesthetic qualities in nature also inspired her warm response to the landscape paintings of Washington Allston in her first piece of published criticism on the visual arts dating from 1840. Her dispatches from Europe as a
correspondent for the *New York Tribune* (1846-1848), later published as *At
Home and Abroad* (1856), continue in the vein of travel literature. Her
accounts of artistic developments in Europe are remarkably perceptive,
including a description of Turner's late synthetic style of landscape
painting.

Anna Jameson was also a pioneer in the study of religious iconography.
Her *Sacred and Legendary Art* (1848) and succeeding volumes reflect an
understanding of the sources of Christian imagery within a historical
context. Her knowledge was based on a firsthand acquaintance with German developments in art scholarship and criticism. The historical and
objective view she took of her subject matter contrasted sharply with the
contemporary moralizing views of Ruskin or Lord Lindsay. In France, a
remarkable pioneering figure in this field was FÉLICIE D'AYZAC (1801-
1891). D'Ayzac first published in 1833 a collection of poetry, *Soupirs
poétiques* ("Poetic Sighs"). She received her education, taught, and then
served as adjunct librarian and wardrobe mistress of the boarding school at
Saint-Denis founded by Napoleon for female relatives of holders of the
Legion of Honor. At the time she began her iconographic work on French
Gothic sculpture in 1846, the study of medieval art was flourishing in
France as a branch of the Gothic revival. D'Ayzac was, however, original in
pointing out the symbolic nature of medieval imagery and in calling attention to the derivation of visual formulas from specific textual sources like
the Fathers of the Church and Vincent of Beauvais. From 1846 she wrote
articles on iconography for leading journals such as A.-N. Didron's
Annales archéologiques and published a *Histoire de Saint-Denis* (1860-1861)
based on her firsthand study over many years of the abbey and its monuments.

For the rest of the nineteenth century, Christian iconography remained
something of a woman's field. LOUISA TWINING (1820-1911), one of a
notable line of women artists who became social reformers, wrote *Symbols
and Emblems of Early and Mediaeval Christian Art* (1852), presenting the
"chronological" order of Christian symbols. Twining's book is representative of many such works written by women. In America, the most notable
book in this genre was perhaps the *Handbook of Christian Symbols and
Stories of the Saints as Illustrated in Art* (1886) by CLARA ERSKINE
CLEMENT WATERS (1834-1916), known also for her travel books and
her work *Women in the Fine Arts* (1904).

Two earlier books on women artists were written by ELIZABETH

ELLET (1812?-1877), an American, and Ellen C. Clayton (1834-1900), born in Dublin. Ellet's book *Women Artists in All Ages and Countries* (1859) is more ambitious in scope than Clayton's two-volume work on *English Female Artists* of 1876. Both authors came to the subject of women artists from their interest in the history of women. Ellet had previously published pioneering works that for the first time considered the role of women in American history. Clayton, a contributor to popular London journals, wrote on such varied topics as female vocalists and women warriors.

Another important area in the development of art history to which women made lasting contributions was the recovery and publication of essential documents. In England, MARY PHILADELPHIA MERRIFIELD (1804/05-1889), who also wrote guidebooks to Brighton, published in 1849 a two-volume collection of *Original Treatises Dating from the XIIth to the XVIIIth Centuries on the Arts of Painting in Oil, Miniature, Mosaic and on Glass; of Gilding, Dyeing and Preparation of Colours and Artificial Gems.* She reproduced with facing translations the original texts, selected for their information about actual studio working procedures. In 1844 she had translated Cennino Cennini's early fifteenth-century *A Treatise on Painting* recently discovered and published in 1821 by an Italian antiquarian Giuseppe Tambroni. Commissioned by the Royal Commission on the Fine Arts, in 1846 Merrifield published *The Art of Fresco Painting*, another collection of original texts related to the history of this medium. Merrifield's work on fresco painting is still used today. Documents in the form of the artist's letters and journals known at the time were an important feature of *The History of the Life of Albrecht Dürer*, the first biography published in English (1870) by MARY MARGARET HEATON (1836-1883).

These contributions to the documentary history of art obviously rested on the skills of Merrifield and Heaton as translators. Translations, like travel books, continued to serve as passports for women's publications in the arts. Translations, however, could be done at home, an important consideration at a time when women's work in public places was still restricted. Translations of contemporary and earlier writings on art by women writers also played a significant part in broadening public taste and understanding of new currents. Such a role was performed by Elizabeth Rigby, later LADY EASTLAKE (1809-1893). Rigby profited by her travels to the Baltic to write two books on her experiences and by a two-year stay in Heidelberg, where she learned German. She translated various works by German art historians. Among them is Passavant's *Tour of a German Artist in England with Notices of Private Galleries, and Remarks on the State of Art* (1836; original German edition, 1833). Sometimes the tradition of "anonymous was a woman" applied to translators. The announcement that the English version of Kugler's *Handbook of the History of Painting* (1842) was by a

"Lady" falls into this pattern, although she is elsewhere identified as Margaret Hutton. Hutton's successor for the second edition of the book in 1851 was Lady Eastlake. Lady Eastlake also undertook the translation in three volumes of Gustav Waagen's important *Treasures of Art in Great Britain* (1854) and a supplemental volume, *Galleries and Cabinets of Art in Great Britain* (1857). In 1883 the translation by LOUISE SCHWAB RICHTER of *Italian Masters in German Galleries* promoted the dissemination in England of Giovanni Morelli's controversial ideas.

The popularizing function of women's writings on art is also evident in their general histories of the subject. Indicating a continued interest among women writers in Netherlandish art, Mary Margaret Heaton in 1869 wrote *Masterpieces of Flemish Art*. In 1873 her *Concise History of Painting* had a successful reception. Heaton's career shows another enduring dimension of women's professional involvement with the arts: that of contributors of "tools of research." Heaton prepared a new edition of Allan Cunningham's *Lives of the Most Eminent British Painters* and wrote important entries for a new edition of Bryan's *Dictionary of Painters and Engravers*. Like translating or editing, such work is poorly paid and yields little prestige.

Women's contributions to connoisseurship are more difficult to establish in this period when museum employment was closed to them. Even as independent scholars—the category to which Morelli belonged—women seldom commanded independent resources for the necessary mobility to study at firsthand works of art in scattered and sometimes obscure locations. Moreover, women's lack of an acknowledged public role made it almost unimaginable for them to challenge openly the opinions of male professionals. Nevertheless, Anna Jameson's catalogues of the London public galleries (1842) and of private collections in and near London (1844) contain tactfully general remarks on the common practice by which works of followers and copyists were assigned to leading masters.

Lady Eastlake developed substantial skills and knowledge as a connoisseur while pursuing her interests as a writer on art and while travelling with her husband Sir Charles Eastlake on his searches for pictures for the London National Gallery. Her quality as a connoisseur is, however, difficult to assess because it is not directly reflected in her publications. Her writings do reveal, though, that she was an early partisan of Morelli's scientific method of connoisseurship and of the use of photography.[18] Furthermore, she was credited with equal partnership in Sir Charles's work by him and other contemporaries. Her acumen as a connoisseur was praised by Morelli, Jean Paul Richter, and Bernard Berenson.[19] Mary Smith Costelloe (later MARY BERENSON) recalls how on a visit she and Berenson were stimulated by Lady Eastlake's account of joint discoveries with her husband when they "turned pictures to the light from the lumber room of the Uffizi and whispered incredulously to each other 'Botticelli—Fra Filippo.'" Costelloe concludes: "Bernhard and I looked at each other with shining eyes that confirmed each of our secret resolutions to follow in our humbler way the example of Lady Eastlake.''[20]

An example of independent connoisseurship in a field considered appropriate for women—the decorative arts—is the catalogue (1885) by LADY CHARLOTTE SCHREIBER (1812-1895) of almost two thousand objects from her ceramics collection, which she gave to the Victoria and Albert Museum in 1884. Born Lady Charlotte Bertie, she became an English collector of ceramics and decorative objects after her second marriage in middle age to Charles Schreiber. By her first marriage to Sir John Guest, the owner of a large ironworks in Wales, Lady Charlotte had ten children. She taught herself Welsh in order to edit and translate from a manuscript the medieval Celtic legends called *The Mabinogion*. Her translation (1849), complete with authoritative notes on English and European scholarship, opened a new field of study and became a standard work. For several years after her first husband died, Lady Charlotte, who had enjoyed keeping its financial records, ran the ironworks herself. Her later passion for collecting took her to all parts of Europe in constant search of treasures, for which she had an extremely keen eye. She also wrote the catalogue for her collection of fans (1888-1890) and playing cards (1892-1895) given to the British Museum, although she did not live to complete the latter work.

By the time Emilia F. S. Pattison (Lady Dilke) and Mariana Griswold Van Rensselaer—the third and fourth subjects of essays in Part II—began in the 1870s and 1880s to publish on the arts, women's contributions to the field were substantial. Van Rensselaer's career as the first American woman to produce extensive work as an art critic had a precedent in Margaret Fuller's journalistic criticism. Like many of her sisters, Van Rensselaer thought briefly of a literary career before turning in 1876 to writing for various American journals on art topics. She was a perceptive critic of contemporary developments in American art in her exhibition reviews. Her particular subject was architectural criticism; her most outstanding work, a monograph on the life and work of Henry Hobson Richardson (1888), was the first written on an American architect and is still in print today. Van Rensselaer also wrote a successful book on *English Cathedrals* (1892), followed by *Art Out-of-Doors: Hints on Good Taste in Gardening* (1893). Both were developed from series of magazine articles and represent her last serious writings on the arts. From this point, her interests turned toward literature, history, and social involvement. As Cynthia Kinnard's essay points out, there did not yet exist enough support for serious, specialized journals appropriate to Van Rensselaer's type of art criticism, nor did the expected social roles of wealthy upper-class women promote a sense of professionalism.

Colin Eisler's essay stresses the emotional conflicts that also confronted Emilia F. S. Pattison, Lady Dilke. She too started out writing on literary and philosophical topics for various English journals before turning to the arts. Like Van Rensselaer, she cultivated a new field of study and interpretation. Lady Dilke's books examine both the major and the minor arts in France from the Renaissance to the eighteenth century in their relationship to French history and culture. Like Lady Eastlake, who in 1856 attacked Ruskin's assumption that art was primarily valuable as a vehicle of thought, she rejected the powerful influence of Ruskin's moralizing approach. Lady Dilke's monograph on the seventeenth-century French painter Claude Lorrain (1888), published in France, was based on fresh archival research, including the publication of the artist's will. Her misnamed *Art in the Modern State* (1884) reviewed the institutional art world of the seventeenth century in France and encompassed analyses of the Royal Academy and related systems of patronage used for political propaganda. Like her first monograph of 1879 on *The Renaissance of Art in France, Art in the Modern State* still holds up today in viewing the interaction of all forms of art within a well-developed social and historical context. The same qualities of research inform her last four books on various aspects of French eighteenth-century art published from 1889 until 1902.

In the period 1820 to 1890 women writers made important contributions to art criticism and history. One area in which women made their mark was travel literature, a useful but not highly regarded literary genre. Both in guidebooks and in periodical articles, women's travel reports led to, and sharpened, skills in writing about the arts. As a means of developing professional credentials, translations by women often opened possibilities for more independent and creative work. Valuable but poorly paid and little esteemed, translations and other tools of research produced by women enabled new ideas about art to reach a wider public. Women also contributed to identifiable genres of art-historical research, including the study of architecture, connoisseurship of the decorative arts, biographies of artists, iconographic studies, and the cultural and documentary history of art. Women writers supported contemporary art; by their books and publications in widely read journals they influenced taste and patterns of collecting. They were remarkable too for their initiative in taking up a number of unexplored or neglected areas of research. Although for obvious reasons women cannot be numbered among the founding fathers or theorists of academic art history, their record of lasting and innovative writing on the arts in this period can stand on its own merit.

SOCIAL AND CULTURAL CONDITIONS OF WOMEN'S INVOLVEMENT WITH THE VISUAL ARTS

The extent of women's writings on the arts in this period raises the question of why women could achieve so notably even while they stood outside the gates of professional advancement in the field. One reason surely is that authorship, the only professional avenue open to them, was a socially accepted occupation for middle-class women. Unlike law or medicine, which required public contact and training and admission by institutional bodies, women writers on the arts, working in private, could by various means acquire enough skills to make their work eligible for publication. Languages could be learned at home or by travel. Because of limited economic resources and social taboos, travel was a more difficult proposition; but women grasped the opportunities available: Mariana Starke while caring for a sick relative; Anna Jameson during her employment as a governess; Elizabeth Rigby on visits to married sisters; and Maria Graham on voyages with her seafaring husband. Of course, it took individuals of exceptional personality and force of character like Margaret Fuller to travel as a full-time correspondent just as journalism became a profession opening up to women in this period. Teaching and librarianship, two professions that would welcome women, were also developing at this time. Their importance for women in the fine arts belongs to a slightly later period.

The tradition of women as amateur practitioners of the arts, mentioned earlier, certainly paved the way for the acceptance of women as interpreters of the visual arts. Lady Trevelyan's portrait of Emilia F. S. Pattison painting (Figure 6) conveys a sense of the sometimes decorative, genteel nature of the enterprise. Feminine practice of the arts is shown as a socially acceptable accomplishment of middle- and upper-class women. As is well known, in the nineteenth century the teaching of drawing, painting, and needlework were features of the curricula of fashionable American and European seminaries or academies for young ladies. The "ornamental branches," as instruction in art and needlework was called, were taught even in progressive institutions like Emma Willard's famous seminary in Troy, New York, where in the 1830s educational reforms, including the study of mathematics, had been introduced. At Oberlin College, which awarded the first American bachelor's degrees to women in 1841, instruction in painting and drawing was offered for extra fees in the Young Ladies' Preparatory Program. In the first women's colleges, separate schools of art in which painting and drawing were taught were special features of Vassar, Wellesley, and Smith.[21]

Although female amateurism has certainly had negative effects, the tradition also served to attract women to the criticism and scholarship of the visual arts. To take just a few examples, Lady Callcott, Lady Eastlake, and Louisa Twining were trained in painting and drawing, while Lady Charlotte Schreiber was an accomplished etcher. It almost goes without saying that practical study of design and techniques is an extremely valuable foundation for critical and scholarly writing on the visual arts. Women trained as artists would play vital roles in all areas of future professional involvement.

Associated with female amateurism in fostering engagement with the visual arts were certain widely-held views of women's traditional social roles. For much of the nineteenth century, both in Western Europe and the United States, the exclusion of middle-class women from public life was justified on the grounds that home and family constituted a positive and proper scope for their activities. By their separation from the contaminating effects of political and commercial endeavors, proponents of such arguments maintained, women could by virtue of their innate, superior spiritual qualities play within the domestic sphere the traditional part of guardian of culture: a role in which females transmit through the child-rearing process prevailing moral principles and related cultural values. Implicit also in the guardian of culture concept during the nineteenth century were such notions of women's inborn characteristics of sensitivity, intuition, sympathy, and self-sacrifice. During this period, as social and economic conditions changed and the basis of morality gradually shifted from a religious to a secular set of ethical values, such ideas about women's character and their roles as guardians of culture encouraged first on an amateur, and later on a professional basis, both aesthetic and philanthropic activities outside the home.

As the visual arts gained respectability in the United States, feminine identification with aesthetic values was justified on several levels. First of all, a woman's interest in art and architecture had practical value in creating a harmonious and healthy domestic environment. Women were informed by other women writing in the popular "etiquette" books and ladies' magazines on how to improve the decor and architecture of the home. A milestone in this kind of publication was *The American Woman's Home* (1869), written by the celebrated novelist Harriet Beecher Stowe and her sister Catharine Beecher, advocate of women's role as guardians of culture and a prominent educational reformer.[22]

In the United States a second aspect of the concept of women's roles as guardians of culture also justified their involvement with art. As the connections between the visual arts and individual and social morality were forged by American clergymen before the Civil War, women's cultivation of aesthetic interests gradually became associated with and assimilated to their moral responsibilities in forming the character of the young.[23] Initially this nurturant function related to maternal responsibilities within the home. Its broadened application provided a justification for general reform in women's education in the 1830s on the grounds that broader academic opportunities for females would make them better wives and mothers. In addition, when unmarried women began to leave the home to work as public-school teachers, their responsibilities as moral guardians were carried into this new realm as an extension of their maternal function. The acceptability of aesthetic interests for feminine self-cultivation and its subsequent application to women as art educators would have profound consequences.

THE BEGINNINGS OF FORMAL EDUCATION
IN THE VISUAL ARTS

The Civil War, which brought women into prominent roles in public life, intensified the pressure for reforms in education that had begun in the 1830s. Not only secondary but higher education for women advanced significantly. The founding of the women's colleges was a highlight of the post-Civil War period. Their early programs and distinctive institutions reflected the strength of the association of women's role as the guardians of culture and their cultivation of aesthetic interests. Vassar was the earliest of the women's colleges to introduce art courses, doing so in 1867, two years after the college opened. The professor of painting and drawing was Henry Van Ingen, an artist who lectured to juniors and seniors on art theory and history. Reminiscences of an alumna reveal that more emphasis was placed on practical than on theoretical studies: "In the late Spring, he would take some of his pupils to sightly spots overlooking the Hudson in the near neighborhood of Poughkeepsie. They carried luncheon with them and spent the day in sketching under his supervision."[24] Nevertheless, the first graduate thesis in fine arts in the United States was written by a Vassar woman in 1876; Elizabeth R. P. Coffin received the M.A. for her thesis on the "Progress of Art in Ancient Times."

Vassar's commitment to art in the college curriculum also had another basis. The founding of its Art Gallery, one of the earliest fine arts museums in the United States, was recommended as soon as the college opened because of an identification of art with women's cultural responsibilities. It was entirely appropriate that the "Report of the Committee on the Art Gallery of Vassar Female College," dated 1864, was written by the Reverend E. L. Magoon, a Baptist minister who zealously stressed the moral values of art. In urging the establishment of a gallery of original works of art—largely based on the purchase of Magoon's own collection—he stressed that "Art is diviner than science. . . ." He states also that "the legitimate use of sanctified art is to visit every recess of our complex nature, that it may search and purify it with celestial fire." The Board was reminded that "no worthy monument was ever built, or enduring thought conceived, that was not inspired by and dedicated to woman—Minerva or Mary."[25] Despite Magoon's self-interest in this matter, his advice was sound. The Vassar Art Gallery became a distinguished college museum that also served as a valuable teaching resource.

At Wellesley and Smith, both founded in 1875, art museums were built soon after their opening. The Smith College Museum of Art was established in 1881; at Wellesley the Farnsworth Art Museum (now the Wellesley College Museum in the Jewett Art Center) was begun in 1889, and the Dwight Hall Museum at Mount Holyoke in 1901. At Smith, formal instruction in the history and theory of the fine arts began in 1877 and was given by J. Wells Champney, an artist who also gave practical instruction. All students were supposed to receive instruction in the history and principles of the fine arts. A separate art school continued until 1902/03, when an academic department combining practical and historical teaching was established. At Wellesley, by 1884 "theoretical instruction covered lectures in Egyptian and Greek art, Italian art, and the art of Germany, France, and England. In 1887 a department of the history of art was established with courses in early Christian and Renaissance art. The courses in drawing and modelling were still continued."[26] At Mount Holyoke, the first lectures in art were given in 1874 by members of the Amherst faculty. Later, Elizabeth Blanchard, principal of the Mount Holyoke Seminary, as it was called until 1888 when it became a college, taught the course in the history of art required for seniors. Its orientation was philosophical rather than practical. Fine arts instruction began in 1881/82 at what later became a coordinate branch of Harvard University, the Society for the Collegiate Instruction for Women, later Radcliffe College, founded in 1879. From the beginning, separate instruction was given by Harvard faculty members who repeated their lectures at the nearby Radcliffe campus. For many years, Charles Moore offered courses on the principles, practice, and appreciation of art, which were augmented by those given by Charles Eliot Norton on Greek, Roman, and medieval art. Bryn Mawr College, founded in 1885, began, ten years later, programs in archaeology and the fine arts of the greatest importance to women's professional opportunities in these fields.

In this early period, without intending to prepare students for professional careers in the arts, practical courses were more often offered in women's colleges than in men's or in coeducational institutions. Certainly the strong association of aesthetic interests with woman's role as the guardian of culture helps to explain the emphasis on the study and teaching of art in the women's colleges. This connection also accounts for the prominence of these institutions in the development of the field at a time when both art museums and the sustained teaching of art history were just getting under way in the United States.

Of course, the women's colleges were not alone in offering courses on the history of art. Colleges and universities of the Midwest, to which women were gradually admitted as a result of the first feminist movements of the 1840s, also developed instruction in the visual arts. At Oberlin College, a member of the class of 1856, Adelia A. Field Johnston, returned in 1870 as a teacher of history and as head of the Women's Department. She later offered the first course in art (on Italian painting) and by 1898 taught three of the courses offered at Oberlin in the field.[27]

In England, among the women's colleges founded from 1848 on, Royal Holloway College, established in 1886 and affiliated with the University of London, was unusual in having its own art gallery and collection.[28] As in the United States, British reforms in women's education resulted from the expansion of public primary and secondary education and the consequent need for teachers. Queen's College for Women in London was initially opened in 1848 as a response to the need for a program of more professional training for governesses. Queen's College in turn became a training ground for women who established pioneering secondary schools for women that prepared them for university examinations. Bedford College was founded in 1849; and the University of London, of which it is an affiliate, became the first British university to admit women to degrees in 1878. At the separate women's colleges founded at Cambridge, Girton (1869) and Newnham (1871), and at Oxford, Lady Margaret Hall and Somerville (1879), St. Hugh's (1886), and St. Hilda's (1893), the absence of a history of art program reflected the general situation already noted at English universities. Yet the excellent instruction women received in the classics paved the way for the training of the first generation of archaeologists. Women did not, however, receive Oxford or Cambridge degrees until after World War I. In Germany and Austria, centers of art-historical studies in Europe, women were not admitted to universities until the 1890s. In general, although American women undergraduates were taught art history and archaeology earlier than their European sisters, advanced study did not begin in the United States until the 1890s.

LIFESTYLES OF WOMEN WRITERS ON THE ARTS

Despite their varied backgrounds, women writers on the arts confronted obstacles common among middle- and upper-class women in the nineteenth century who sought professional achievement. Paid work outside the domestic sphere was not sanctioned for married women. For unmarried women who had to support themselves, opportunities for paid employment were limited and involved a loss of social status. In both cases, the search for a personal identity—a necessary condition of intellectual attainment—presented real difficulties because of the absence of social and institutional support for such endeavors.

Among the most severe handicaps that intellectual women faced was their lack of formal education. Still, as the careers of Jameson, Fuller, Dilke, and Van Rensselaer indicate, self-educated women could accomplish a great deal. Studies at home, sometimes with a governess or with a brother's tutor, began the process of instruction. Learning foreign languages was a primary requirement for women writers on the arts, and one that all of them mastered. Parental encouragement, particularly by fathers, was crucial for girls seeking the equivalent of their brothers' education. The case of Margaret Fuller presents a perhaps egregious example of a girl pushed by her father to painful intellectual precocity.

To educate themselves, middle- and upper-class women had long devised various informal systems for interaction with one another which favored learning about literature and art. In Europe—particularly in France—beginning in the seventeenth century, salons presided over by upper-class and aristocratic women had allowed them to become acquainted with, and in turn encourage, new cultural developments through discussions with the leading intellectuals of the day. Madame de Staël brilliantly carried on the French tradition in which influential women served as "sponsors and creators of high culture."[29] As already noted, middle-class German women, such as Henriette Herz and Rahel Varnhagen in Berlin and Johanna Schopenhauer in Weimar, presided over salons that were instrumental as centers for the meeting of leading personalities and the diffusion of the ideas of early Romanticism. In London during the 1820s and 1830s, Lady Callcott and her artist husband conducted an informal salon that had important effects on English taste and collecting. Lady Eastlake, together with her husband, the first director of the National Gallery, occupied a central position in official London intellectual and artistic life that affected English taste even more markedly than did the Callcotts.[30] In a different vein, Anna Jameson presided over a feminist salon in the 1850s that became a rallying point for the emerging women's rights movement in England.

This European tradition hardly existed in the United States. Romanticism was important in encouraging feminist consciousness and friendships, the first steps towards creating informal networks among women seeking intellectual companionship. In 1827, Margaret Fuller and her friend Lydia Marie Francis (later Child) found the writings and ideas of Madame de Staël a common bond of interest.[31] After a successful stint as a teacher at a girls' school in Providence, Rhode Island, Fuller began her informal salon for the intellectually inclined women of Boston, known as the "Conversations." Beginning in 1839, women paid a fee to participate in weekly discussions led by Margaret Fuller on such topics as "ancient mythology, the fine arts, ethics, education, and the influence of women."[32]

Their own struggles and their concern for other women's social and economic disadvantages prompted Fuller, Jameson, and Lady Dilke to work for legal and social reform. Anna Jameson, affected by her own experience as a governess, lobbied for improvement in the status of women in the only profession then open to middle-class women who had to earn their own living. Lady Eastlake and Lady Morgan also supported such efforts. Jameson courageously lectured in public in the 1850s on the need to open a wide variety of trades and occupations to women. She was active, too, in the campaign to change the laws regarding married women's right to hold property. Jameson's protegees, including Barbara Leigh Smith Bodichon (a founder of Girton College) and Bessie Parkes, carried on her campaigns for educational and social reforms.

In the United States, Margaret Fuller's *Woman in the Nineteenth Century* (1845) made her a celebrity as she called for the intellectual and emotional emancipation of women in the decade that saw the beginnings of the feminist movement. In this period, not all women writers expressed feminist viewpoints separately from their critical and scholarly writings. In 1844, SARAH WORTHINGTON KING PETER (1800-1877), a cultured society woman with both a deep interest in the arts and a sympathy for women who needed to earn a living, founded the first American school for training women in commercial and industrial art, the Philadelphia School of Design, now the Moore Institute.[33] Another facet of her dual interest in art and women's groups was the founding of the future Cincinnati Art Museum and the Cincinnati Fine Arts Academy by the Women's Museum Association. Peter's activities were among the earliest in a long chain linking women's personal interests in art with cultural philanthropy, education, and social reform.

Emilia F. Strong's training at the South Kensington Art School may have inspired her engagement with social issues. As Colin Eisler points out in his essay, there existed a connection between social reform and the contemporary art criticism of John Ruskin and William Morris. While still married to Mark Pattison, the future Lady Dilke espoused the cause of women's suffrage before attempting to improve the conditions of women working in industrial and craft trades. She became associated with the Women's Trade Union League and spoke often at the annual Trades Union Congress. The radicalism of her social views contrasts strongly with the fashionable social world in which she moved after her second marriage and with her intellectual interests in French court art.

As many women writers on the arts, including Lady Dilke and Mariana Van Rensselaer, came from well-to-do backgrounds, their desire for a vocation did not stem from any pressure to make a living. Anna Jameson, however, had to support herself and assist her parents and sisters from an early age, as her father's income as a miniature painter was uncertain. Sydney Owenson, later Lady Morgan, the daughter of an actor, who also had to support herself, established herself as a successful novelist before her marriage. The family of Margaret Fuller was more comfortably situated, although its economic status deteriorated after the father died in 1835. Margaret Fuller began teaching the following year in order to help out at home. Interestingly enough, the aristocratic and comfortably-off Van Rensselaer felt that she had to justify the continuation of her career on the grounds of economic necessity after her husband's death.

Whatever their backgrounds, these nineteenth-century figures are more colorful than their professionally oriented successors. In their search for personal identities, as well as in the heroic scale of their activities, they seem larger than life. Margaret Fuller became almost instantly a romantic legend, as did Rahel Varnhagen. In Anna Jameson there emerges the self-made woman of the nineteenth century, one whose circumstances render her generosity and adherence to principle all the more remarkable. Her literary executrix, Lady Eastlake, was a commanding presence. About six feet tall, her strong personal and intellectual influence was generally acknowledged by her contemporaries. Lady Charlotte Schreiber—scholar, businesswoman, connoisseur, and matriarch—represents a life of protean energy and varied levels of accomplishment. Tenaciously pursuing a career in widow's weeds, Van Rensselaer had to confront the opposition of her social class to a woman's intellectual attainment. The achievement of Emilia F. S. Pattison Dilke seems all the more remarkable in view of her unhappy first marriage, the scandal surrounding her second husband, and the paradox concerning her social situation and political concerns.

Most of the women discussed here, including the four subjects of essays, were married at some point in their lives, thus reflecting in one sense what was considered the proper condition for women. Marriage in the cases of Lady Callcott and Lady Eastlake brought real advantages of social, financial, and intellectual support. Even a happy marriage, with a congenial mate—like the Eastlakes'—could mean loss of an independent professional identity. For Anna Jameson and others, unhappy alliances brought emotional and financial disasters. Of the four subjects, Fuller and Van Rensselaer had one child each. With the notable exception of Lady Charlotte Schreiber, most of the married women writers on art mentioned here did not have large families; a few had no children at all. None of these women had to face an externally imposed choice between marriage and work. This absence of conflict in turn reflected the outsider status in this period of women writers on art. They had neither the opportunities nor the disadvantages of accommodation to institutional employment.

Along with their striking force of character, women writers on the arts stand out because of the breadth of their literary and cultural interests. Lady Callcott wrote a popular children's history of England; Lady Morgan, plays, songs, and best-selling novels; Mary Margaret Heaton, children's poetry. Elizabeth Rigby, Lady Eastlake, was the first woman to write on a variety of artistic, literary, and social topics for the prestigious *Quarterly Review*. With her edition and translation of *The Mabinogion*, Lady Charlotte Guest (later Schreiber) inspired interest in Celtic folklore and Arthurian romances. Addressed to wide audiences, their writings reflect the outlook of a generation unconcerned by considerations of professional correctness.

In short, women made substantial contributions as writers on the arts in this period, despite their virtual exclusion from museum and university employment. Their attainments in both popular and scholarly genres of art criticism and history and their ventures into untried or neglected areas of taste and research are all the more striking in view of their educational and professional disadvantages. Yet these women ingeniously found ways to learn languages, travel, and seek out female exemplars and companionship that provided necessary intellectual and emotional support. Sensible to the only too visible evidence of women's inferior economic and social position, some joined or promoted practical and theoretical efforts to remove these disabilities. The personal examples and reputations forged by these pioneers and precursors helped to open the door for the next generation of women seeking wider professional opportunities.

NOTES

1. For general accounts of developments in art history during this period, see Salerno, "Historiography," and Kleinbauer, *Modern Perspectives*, pp. 1-105.

2. For nineteenth-century interest in northern European and medieval art, see Francis Haskell, *Rediscoveries in Art: Some Aspects of Taste, Fashion and Collecting in England and France* (London, 1976); and David Robertson, *Sir Charles Eastlake and the Victorian Art World* (Princeton, N.J., 1978).

3. For the German role in the development of art history, see Wilhelm Waetzoldt, *Deutscher Kunsthistoriker*, 2 vols. (Leipzig, 1921); and Udo Kultermann, *Geschichte der Kunstgeschichte* (Vienna, 1966).

4. For the development of academic art history in the United States until 1930, the best source is Hiss and Fansler, *Research*.

5. Ibid., pp. 20-25. See also Kermit Vanderbilt, *Charles Eliot Norton: Apostle of Culture in a Democracy* (Cambridge, Mass., 1959).

6. For a convenient summary of the origins of the art museum, see Edward P. Alexander, *Museums in Motion: An Introduction to the History and Functions of Museums* (Nashville, Tenn., 1979).

7. For an excellent analysis of the cultural and social foundations of American art museums, see Daniel M. Fox, *Engines of Culture: Philanthropy and Art Museums* (Madison, Wis., 1963).

8. See Trevor Fawcett and Clive Philpot, eds., *The Art Press: Two Centuries of Art Magazines* (London, 1976).

9. Susan P. Conrad, *Perish the Thought: Intellectual Women in Romantic America 1830-1860* (New York, 1976), pp. 9-11.

10. For the influence of Madame de Staël, see ibid., pp. 18-20; and Ellen Moers, *Literary Women: The Great Writers* (Garden City, N.Y., 1977), pp. 263-319.

11. For excellent background on the subject, see *LDF*, "Romantik" and "Salon"; on Henriette Herz and others, see Mary Hargrave, *Some German Women and their Salons* (London, n.d.); Bertha Meyer, *Salon Sketches: Biographical Studies of Berlin Salons of the Emancipation* (New York, 1938); and Ingeborg Drewitz, *Berliner Salons* (Berlin, 1965). See also Margarete Susman, *Frauen der Romantik* (Jena, 1931).

12. Doris Starr-Guilloton, "Rahel Varnhagen und die Frauenfrage in der deutschen Romantik: Eine Untersuchung ihrer Briefe und Tagebuchnotizen," *Monatshefte*, 69/4 (Winter 1977), 391-403.

13. Conrad, *Perish the Thought*, p. 187.

14. For the theme of travel in women's literature, see Moers, *Literary Women*, Ch. 7.

15. Haskell, *Rediscoveries in Art*, pp. 107-8.

16. Elizabeth Rigby (Lady Eastlake), "Lady Travellers," *QR*, 76 (June 1845), 98-99.

17. Conrad, *Perish the Thought*, Ch. 2.

18. Lady Eastlake, "Photography," *QR*, 101 (April 1857), 465-67; idem, "Giovanni Morelli: The Patriot and Critic," *QR*, 173 (July 1891), 235-52.

19. See Bernard Denvir, "The Eastlakes," *QR*, 295 (Jan. 1957), 85-97; John Steegman, *Victorian Taste: A Study of the Arts and Architecture from 1830-1870* (Cambridge, Mass., 1970), p. 7. See also *Italienische Malerei der Renaissance im Briefwechsel von Giovanni Morelli und Jean Paul Richter 1876-1891*, eds. Irma Richter and Gisela Richter (Baden-Baden, 1960).

20. Ernest Samuels, *Bernard Berenson: The Making of a Connoisseur* (Cambridge, Mass., 1979), pp. 120-21.

21. For the teaching of the "ornamental branches," see Louise Boas, *Women's Education Begins: The Rise of the Women's Colleges* (Norton, Mass., 1935), p. 18; For Oberlin, see Sophia Jex-Blake, *A Visit to Some American Schools and Colleges* (London, 1867; reprint ed., Westport, Conn., 1976), pp. 60-61. For early programs at Vassar and Smith, see Hiss and Fansler, *Research*, pp. 18, 150, and 158. See also the bibliography at the end of this book.

22. For women's domestic involvement with art and architecture, see Doris Cole, *From Tipi to Skyscraper: A History of Women in Architecture* (Boston, 1973), pp. 34-48. In *Catharine Beecher: A Study in American Domesticity* (New York, 1976, pp. 155-63), Kathryn K. Sklar emphasizes the importance of the guardian of culture concept in Beecher's thought.

23. For clergymen as promoters of art, see Neil Harris, *The Artist in American Society: The Formative Years 1790-1860* (New York, 1966), pp. 300-313. For a fruitful exploration of the interaction of American middle-class women and Protestant clergymen, see Ann Douglas, *The Feminization of American Culture* (New York, 1977). For the relationship between teaching and women's roles as guardians of culture, see Dee Garrison, "The Tender Technicians: The Feminization of Public Librarianship, 1876-1905," in *Clio's Consciousness Raised: New Perspectives on the History of Women*, eds. Mary Hartman and Lois W. Banner (New York, 1974), pp. 160-61.

24. Hiss and Fansler, *Research*, p. 18; see ibid., p. 195, for the Coffin thesis.

25. For the text of Magoon's speech, see *Vassar College Art Gallery*, (Poughkeepsie, N.Y., 1939), pp. 19-24; the citations appear on pp. 19, 20, and 24.

26. Hiss and Fansler, *Research*, p. 163. For Smith and Mt. Holyoke, see ibid., pp. 150 and 115-16. For Radcliffe College, see The Society for the Collegiate Instruction of Women [later Radcliffe College], *Reports of the Treasurer and Secretary for 1882, Third Year* (Cambridge, Mass., 1882), p. 6. Further information is contained in the annual *Courses of Instruction*.

27. For Oberlin, see Laurine Bongiorno, "The Fruits of Idealism," *Apollo*, 103 (Feb. 1976), 91.

28. For Royal Holloway College, see David Owen, *English Philanthropy 1660-1960* (Cambridge, Mass., 1964), pp. 399-400. For a brief account of the women's colleges at Oxford and Cambridge, see Phyllis Stock, *Better than Rubies: A History of Women's Education* (New York, 1978), pp. 179-83.

29. Catherine B. Silver, *"Salon, Foyer, Bureau:* Women and the Professions in France," in *Clio's Consciousness Raised*, p. 77.

30. Haskell, *Rediscoveries in Art*, pp. 48-49.

31. Conrad, *Perish the Thought*, p. 55.

32. Ibid., p. 64

33. For a recent discussion of Peter's educational role, see Anthea Callen, *Women Artists of the Arts and Crafts Movement 1870-1914* (New York, 1979), p. 45; see also Ch. 1, "Design Education for Women."

CHAPTER 2

WIDENING HORIZONS
(1890-1930)
Claire Richter Sherman

DEVELOPMENTS IN ARCHAEOLOGY AND ART HISTORY

The lives of the four subjects of essays in Part III—Georgiana Goddard King (1871-1939), Margarete Bieber (1879-1978), Gisela Marie Augusta Richter (1882-1972), and Erica Tietze-Conrat (1883-1958)—overlap all three sections of this book. Their careers, however, developed in the first years of the twentieth century. In contrast to the subjects of Part II, these four women all had university educations and three of them were affiliated with a college, a university, or a museum. These important changes in educational and professional status indicate that association with established institutions in this period had become possible for women scholars of the visual arts. This widening sphere of participation resulted from the reforms in the status of women mentioned in Chapter 1, most notably in the educational and political arenas. One effect of this continued pressure came after World War I, when women were granted the vote in many countries.

Margarete Bieber and Gisela Richter were among the first generation of women to enter the developing disciplines of classical archaeology and Egyptology.[1] The study of the material remains of these Mediterranean cultures had long existed in humanistic circles of the Renaissance and received renewed impetus in the eighteenth century, when amateur antiquarians examined ancient sites and monuments. The growth of a scientific method of archaeological excavation by the end of the nineteenth century involved a complex series of developments. Among the most important were the influence of the historical sciences, a non-religious theory of human evolution, and techniques for scientific dating of material remains. Academic and national institutes for research and exploration sponsored excavations, published their findings, and displayed objects in museum collections. The scientific and scholarly archaeological establishment grew so rapidly that the amateur status of Heinrich Schliemann, a German businessman, caused a somewhat hostile reception to his discoveries of Troy and Mycenae in the 1870s. Important for his excavations of Cretan civilization was Sir Arthur Evans, who excavated Minoan sites in the 1890s. Sir William Flinders Petrie, who excavated in Egypt between 1880 and 1924, evolved a system of sequence-dating, the assignment of relative dates based on pottery types and stratification, that first made possible a chronology of Egyptian civilization. This scheme proved applicable to prehistoric settlements in Egypt and to other Mediterranean civilizations.

At the beginning of this period Europe remained in the forefront of art-historical developments.[2] French scholars continued to excel in the study of medieval art, including illuminated manuscripts, architecture, and sculpture; their research tended to maintain an archaeological and antiquarian focus. Distinguished scholarship in Christian iconography, most notably of the Gothic period, was carried out by Emile Mâle. French art historians were also prominent in the new field of Byzantine art, a subject encompassing the medieval art of Eastern Greek-speaking Christianity centered in Constantinople.

German scholars in museums and universities expanded the whole range of knowledge of different periods and genres in Western art. They produced surveys, monographs, catalogues of museum collections, and studies of art theory and literature. Such studies employed rigorous standards of documentary research, connoisseurship, and allied techniques of historical method.

The history of art as a central dimension of the history of civilization extended in several directions. The study of iconography was considerably broadened and deepened by the German art historian Aby Warburg, who approached the creation of images as part of the process of historical change. Like Burckhardt, he took note of every kind of historical evidence, however ephemeral or humble, as possible clues to the ambiguities and complexities of the symbolic and expressive content of individual images. Among the brilliant scholars at the University of Vienna around the turn of the century was Max Dvořák.[3] In his writings he analyzed the forms and content of the art of a given period as an expression of the intellectual and spiritual ideals common to that era.

Cultural history was one element in the influential synthesis of the Swiss-born Heinrich Wölfflin, a student of Burckhardt. Wölfflin focused on psychological and visual responses in examining the formal qualities of works of art. He constructed abstract schemes that accounted for patterns and sequences of style different from those of the traditional cyclical models, in that they allowed for fundamental differences of psychology, and hence of purpose, in historical styles. The influential work of Alois

Riegl, also of the Vienna School, examined and eliminated the idea of decadence previously associated with such non-naturalistic styles as late Roman and early Christian art. Riegl also stressed the importance of the so-called minor arts for the process of stylistic evolution and the social context of art. At about the same time, Franz Wickhoff, who held the chair of art history at the University of Vienna, broke new ground in viewing Roman art not as an inferior imitation of Greek art but as a positive and independent development.

The enlarged perspective on the value of periods of art formerly considered decadent, like the sixteenth-century style called Mannerism, or inferior because of a non-naturalistic mode of representation, like archaic Greek art, was extended to "primitive" and non-Western art. The art of non-literate peoples, so-called primitive art, increasingly exhibited at ethnological museums, in turn influenced artists in the avant-garde of twentieth-century art before World War I. The English critics Clive Bell and Roger Fry, who stressed the paramount importance of the formal elements of the individual work of art, supported the claims of twentieth-century modernism. In Europe, the period from 1890 until World War I saw major developments in the methods and scope of art history and archaeology.

In the United States sustained graduate education in art-related fields began in the 1890s. Princeton had the largest number of the earliest doctorates in art history awarded before World War I, although other American universities had awarded Ph.D.s in archaeology even earlier.[4] Indeed, it was the application of the methods of classical archaeology to other periods that gradually brought about rigorous standards of art historical scholarship in American universities. The American scholars at Harvard and Princeton were particularly strong in architectural studies that used excavation and photographic methods to document the history of medieval monuments. In 1906, Charles Rufus Morey—originally trained as a classicist—joined the art department at Princeton. Morey played a seminal role in encouraging the study of art history, particularly of medieval art, in the United States. He was a founder in 1913 of the College Art Association of America and its scholarly publication, the *Art Bulletin*. Ten years later, the *Art Bulletin* attained a level of serious scholarly inquiry considered the equal of European work in the field.[5] This coming of age of American art history coincided with a considerable expansion in the 1920s of doctoral programs in art history, as distinguished from archaeology. In 1929 the founding of the New York University Institute of Fine Arts marked another milestone in the emergence of the United States as an important center of art-historical scholarship.

This new academic distinction was related to a tremendous growth of American art museums in this period, both in the foundation of new, and the enlargement of existing, institutions. Buying lavishly with fortunes

made in industry and finance, around 1900, private collectors actively
entered the art market.[6] These individuals leaned heavily on the advice of
connoisseurs like Bernard Berenson, who in this period became the leading
authority on Italian painting. Museum directors and curators vied with one
another to appoint influential collectors and businessmen to their boards of
trustees and acquire important collections for their institutions. Sometimes,
as did Henry Walters, Henry Clay Frick, or Isabella Stewart Gardner,
collectors founded their own museums. American museums were influenced
by other cultural philanthropic institutions with the same mission of educating and uplifting the lives of broad segments of the public. For example,
Henry W. Kent, trained as a librarian, organized the accession, registration,
and photographing of the Metropolitan's collections according to the
methods of library science developed by Melvil Dewey.[7] Kent also began
systematic publication and educational programs at the Metropolitan.
Education and service to the community rather than acquisition of precious
objects were the primary goals of Kent's friend and fellow librarian, John
Cotton Dana. Dana founded the Newark Museum in 1909 as an outgrowth
of the municipal library.[8] In order to handle growing collections, the need
for professionally trained museum staffs became obvious. The most
famous, if not the first, class to train museum administrators and curators,
was initiated in 1921 by Paul Sachs at Harvard.[9] After World War I, new
installation and exhibition techniques, as well as broader cultural programs,
showed that American museums were seriously trying to encourage wider
community engagement in meaningful educational and aesthetic experiences.
A model for such involvement existed in the settlement houses founded in
American cities around 1890.[10] At a time when archaeology and art history
were rapidly expanding, particularly in the United States, improvements in
women's educational, social, and political status from 1890 to 1930 gradually permitted some women to gain professional affiliation with new and
existing institutions.

WOMEN ARCHAEOLOGISTS
AND HISTORIANS OF CLASSICAL ART

In 1890, travel continued to attract middle- and upper-class women as an
escape from a still confined social role. The discoveries of lost civilizations
in the nineteenth century made journeys to the Mediterranean and the Near
East especially desirable as goals of romantic pilgrimage. The lure of a life
spent in independent physical activity outdoors was also extremely attractive to women like GERTRUDE BELL (1868-1926), the future mountaineer
and desert explorer, amateur archaeologist, and diplomat. Virginia Woolf
reports that as a young woman Bell was not allowed to "go out in London
without a female friend, or failing that, a maid."[11] As precedents, women

archaeologists seeking adventure in remote and exotic locales could cite the experiences of their sisters who were sent abroad as missionaries.[12]

A more exact parallel was the field work carried out in the 1870s and 1880s by various pioneering American women anthropologists and ethnologists. In Germany, Johanna Mestorf (1829-1909) came to know the pioneering Scandinavian archaeologists of the day, some of whose works she translated. She then became a field archaeologist in her native region of Schleswig-Holstein, an area bitterly contested by Germany and Denmark. Mestorf published on the rich prehistory and ethnology of the region during the 1870s and 1880s. Most exceptionally for the period, she was made a curator and later director of the Kiel Mueum of National Antiquities, a post she held until her death. In 1899, on her seventieth birthday, she received the singular honor for a woman of being created a professor by the Prussian government.[13]

The cause and course of Egyptology in England were greatly advanced by two remarkable women. The older of these was AMELIA ANN BLAND-FORD EDWARDS (1831-1892), who had made her living as a journalist and writer of popular history, novels, and travel books. A trip to Egypt in 1873/74 inspired her to devote the rest of her life to studying and promoting the cause of Egyptology. In addition to many articles, her books *A Thousand Miles Up the Nile* (1877) and collected lectures published as *Pharoahs, Fellahs, and Explorers* (1891) were an important means of arousing public interest in the need for scientific exploration methods and preservation of historic monuments. Edwards also founded the Egypt Exploration Fund to support the work of Sir Flinders Petrie. To University College, London, she bequeathed her library, her collection of Egyptian antiquities, and funds for the first chair in Egyptology in Britain, which was held by Petrie for forty years. Edwards's lecture tour of the United States in 1889/90 created great enthusiasm, and her contributions to the field were recognized by awards of honorary degrees from three American colleges and universities.

Another Englishwoman who made valuable contributions to Egyptology was MARGARET ALICE MURRAY (1863-1963), who celebrated her centenary by the publication of her autobiography *My First Hundred Years* and a book on the *Genesis of Religion*. One of the first English women field archaeologists, she was trained at University College by Petrie and others beginning in 1894, although at this time, except for a purely linguistic program, there was no formal curriculum in Egyptology at any English university. Murray opened the field for women, after facing stiff opposition from university faculty who believed that anthropology and archaeology contained "many things a woman ought not to know."[14] In 1907 she organized the first systematic program of training in archaeology at University College, where she received her doctorate and served as assistant professor until her retirement in 1950. Murray worked with Petrie in the field in Egypt and Palestine, contributing greatly to his archaeological reports and supplying plates for them. She contributed more than eighty books and articles on Egyptian subjects, including the *Osireion* (1904), *Handbook of Egyptian Sculpture* (1930), and *The Splendour That Was Egypt* (1949). She was also an authority in the fields of witchcraft and folklore.

The extraordinary career of SARA YORKE STEVENSON (1847-1921), an American society woman born and educated in France, included valuable services to anthropology and archaeology. Beginning in the 1890s, her publications in the field focus on Egyptian history, religion, and mythology. She reportedly was the first woman to lecture at the Peabody Museum of Harvard University in 1894 and at the University of Pennsylvania, where she was also the first of her sex to receive an honorary Sc.D. A resident of Philadelphia, Stevenson was a founding member of the Archaeological Association of the University of Pennsylvania; she was instrumental in establishing the department of archaeology in 1891 and launching the University Museum. As secretary and president of the museum's board of managers, she became one of the first women to head the board of trustees of an American museum. From 1895 to 1905 she served as the curator of the museum's Egyptian and Mediterranean section. In 1897/98, she made trips to Rome and Egypt for the city of Philadelphia and the American Exploration Society, which she founded. Elected to membership in the American Philosophical Society, she served as president of the Pennsylvania branch of the American Archaeological Institute of America from 1899 to 1903. The public and professional scope of Stevenson's activities was recognized as a significant gain in the status of women. Stevenson also made notable contributions in the later phase of her career at the Pennsylvania (now Philadelphia) Museum, which will be discussed shortly.

Sara Stevenson was a generation older than the first group of academically trained American women who became pioneers in classical archaeology. In order to attain the equivalent of men's education, the women's colleges stressed the study of Latin and Greek; at Bryn Mawr, knowledge of Greek was a prerequisite for graduation. M. Carey Thomas, president of Bryn Mawr from 1894 to 1922, with a keen interest in archaeology, was influential in securing permanent residency for women at the American School of Classical Studies in Athens. In 1896, Harriet Boyd, later HARRIET BOYD HAWES (1871-1945), who had enrolled at the American School, heard reports of Sir Arthur Evans's discoveries in Crete. Boyd had graduated from Smith in 1892, having majored in classics. After teaching in two private girls' schools for four years, she resolved to go to Crete, locate a site, and take responsibility herself for its excavation. Despite initial opposition to this scheme from the American School, Boyd and a friend travelled to eastern Crete with Evans's encouragement. Her initial findings at Kavousi provided the material for her M.A. thesis from Smith. With the support of the American Exploration Society of Philadelphia—founded by Sara Yorke Stevenson—she excavated from 1901 to 1904 the bronze-age town of Gournia, the "solitary well-preserved urban site of the Minoan Age to have been uncovered in the course of three-quarters of a century's work on Crete."[15] Harriet Boyd was the first woman of any nationality to have charge of an excavation and to publish the results. Newspaper accounts of Boyd's accomplishments recognized that they were unprecedented for a woman.

Edith Hall (later EDITH HALL DOHAN) (1877-1943), a graduate student in archaeology at Bryn Mawr who also received her B.A. from Smith, served as one of Boyd's assistants at Gournia. Hall sent lively reports to her family in Woodstock, Connecticut. In a letter of 14 April 1904, she asked her sister to:

Imagine sleeping the other side of a sheet from a gentleman like Mr. Seager [Richard P. Seager, another Boyd assistant and later a prominent archaeologist], and of having six people gazing at you from outside the door, and following you if you made a motion to depart! But as Miss Boyd says it is bad taste to write home about such things instead of about the glorious mountains, the fine ruins and the fast gallops we had.[16]

Hall stayed on to gather material for a dissertation, "The Decorative Art of Crete in the Bronze Age," for which she received the first Ph.D. in archaeology awarded by Bryn Mawr, in 1908. Her later career, distinguished for scholarship in early Greek and Etruscan studies, unfolded at the University Museum in Philadelphia.

In 1911 another pair of Americans were the first women to direct an archaeological expedition on the Greek mainland. They were HETTY GOLDMAN (1881-1972), a Bryn Mawr graduate, and Alice Leslie Walker (1885-1954), a Vassar alumna. Goldman, then at the beginning of a distinguished career in classical and Anatolian archaeology, had come to Greece in 1910 on a Harvard fellowship. Between 1911 and 1914, under the auspices of the American School of Classical Studies in Athens, they excavated the classical site of Halae, a seaport town on the east coast of Greece. In the 1920s and 1930s, Goldman directed excavations in Greece, Yugoslavia, and Turkey sponsored by various American academic and archaeological associations.

Less spectacular, but very solid, were the contributions to Roman archaeology of ESTHER BOISE VAN DEMAN (1862-1937). Van Deman was one of the first women admitted to graduate study at the University of Michigan, where she received the M.A. in 1892. In 1898 she was awarded a doctorate by the newly founded University of Chicago. After teaching at Mt. Holyoke and Goucher, she spent the rest of her life in research work conducted largely at the American School in Rome, later the American Academy. As a Carnegie Fellow in 1906, Van Deman was the first woman to enter the Classical School, followed the next year by the Bryn Mawr Fellow in Latin, Lily Ross Taylor. Van Deman devised a method for dating concrete structures in Roman architecture and published a magisterial study of Roman aqueducts (1934). This work represented the results of thirty years of field work, during which she and Dr. Thomas Ashby, former director of the British School at Rome, tirelessly tracked down and plotted the building history and sources of the ancient aqueducts around Rome. Van Deman was famous not only for her ability to tell the age of a wall by looking at it but also as "the only archaeologist in Rome who could date a brick by the *taste* of the mortar."[17] Van Deman's unpublished work on Roman construction provided the basis and starting-point for a book by Marion Elizabeth Blake (1892-1961), who had heard her lecture at Mt. Holyoke. Over the years Van Deman had agreed to leave her notes to Blake, who published *Roman Construction in Italy from the Prehistoric Period to Augustus* (1947). In turn, Blake's work on *Roman Construction in Italy from Nerva through the Antonines* (1973) was edited and compiled after her death by Doris Taylor Bishop. This three-generation undertaking by women archaeologists is a basic work in the field.

The convergence of gifted women in the field of archaeology at the turn of the century certainly constitutes a striking chapter in the annals of women's contributions to art scholarship. During the first decade of the twentieth century that brought Boyd and Hall to Crete, Murray to Egypt, Van Deman to Rome, and Goldman and Walker to Greece, two subjects of essays in Part III, Gisela Richter and Margarete Bieber, found their vocations in archaeology and classical art. Richter received her training in classics at Girton College before studying for a year at the British School of Archaeology in Athens, where she completed a study of classical vases. In 1906 Margarete Bieber finished her dissertation on a Greek relief in Dresden, and the next year she received her doctorate from the University of Bonn. As the first woman to receive a travelling fellowship from the German Archaeological Institute, she studied classical art in Greece, Italy, and the Near East from 1909 to 1914.

This impressive record of female achievement did not take place without initially arousing opposition. With characteristic candor, Margarete Bieber describes the ostracism she faced as a fellow of the German Archaeological Institute, as well as her stratagems for overcoming it. Harriet Boyd's project for an excavation of her own was opposed by the director of the American School in Athens, Rufus B. Richardson, who believed that:

"women cannot well travel in the interior of Greece, nor share in the active work of excavation." Hetty Goldman is reported to have stated that the location of the dig at Halae was determined by a later director's desire to have her and Alice Walker occupied at a site distant from Athens. These early obstacles to women's participation in the field were the reason for the establishment in 1898 of the Agnes Hoppin Memorial Fellowship. A stipend of a thousand dollars annually was provided by Mrs. Cortlandt Hoppin and her family for women students at the American School because "the activity of the School for women students was limited to a certain degree."[18] Harriet Boyd used part of the Hoppin Fellowship she received in 1899/1900 to sponsor her first excavation in Crete. Edith Hall was the last person to hold the Hoppin, in 1903/04; after that time the fellowship was withdrawn because the sponsors believed that the obstacles to women's participation had been removed. The brilliant records achieved by women, as well as the newness and rapid growth of the field, offered favorable conditions for the pioneering women archaeologists. Attracted both by opportunities for freedom of movement and on an imaginative level by romantic traditions associated with lost civilizations, women showed that they could live and work under arduous conditions that disturbed conventional notions of social propriety. When, to the utter amazement of the inhabitants, Harriet Boyd rode about Athens on a bicycle in the late 1890s, she exhibited an independence emblematic of a growing emancipation in women's lives.

Women historians of classical art in this period were trained in the new methods of archaeology and incorporated the latest findings in their work. They were, however, not primarily field archaeologists. Moreover, their writings emphasize wider problems of connoisseurship, style, and iconography than is generally the case in strictly archaeological scholarship. In her essay, Larissa Bonfante gives a clear idea of the diversity and richness of Margarete Bieber's scholarship in this period, including studies of mosaics representing theater scenes, the medallions of the arch of Constantine, a catalogue of Greek sculpture in the museum at Kassel, and her book on Greek dress, published in 1928. The next year saw the publication of a book that has remained the standard authority in the field, *Ancient Painting*, by MARY HAMILTON SWINDLER (1884-1967), who received her Ph.D. from Bryn Mawr in 1912 and became a distinguished member of the college's department of archaeology.

Another woman who was concerned with art-historical problems in writing her authoritative books on Roman art was EUGÉNIE SELLERS STRONG (1860-1943). Born in London and educated in France and Spain, Eugénie Sellers was one of the early graduates of Girton College. The example of the classicist Jane Harrison, who lectured at the British Museum in the 1880s, had suggested that she might make a similar career for herself.

Sellers is reported to have adapted Morellian methods in her lectures on Greek sculpture at the British Museum around 1890. Sylvia Sprigge, who knew her in the 1920s, has described Strong's handsome appearance—with appropriately Roman imperial features—and magnetic lecturing style.[19] After a brief spell as a teacher in a girls' school, she went to Germany for graduate study, working in Munich with a famous scholar of Greek art, Adolf Furtwängler. Following a now familiar pattern, her earliest publications were translations, beginning in 1891 with an account of Schliemann's excavations. With her contemporary at Girton, Katharine Jex-Blake, who provided the translation of the text, Sellers wrote the introduction and commentary for *The Elder Pliny's Chapters on the History of Art* (1896), a rare source for Hellenistic theory and practice of painting and sculpture. Strong provided the entire translation for Franz Wickhoff's seminal study on the manuscript called the Vienna Genesis, *Roman Art, Some of Its Principles and Their Application to Early Christian Painting* (1900). Married to Sandford Arthur Strong in 1897, she succeeded him as librarian (with general charge of the collections) at Chatsworth, the estate of the Duke of Devonshire, after her husband's death in 1904. Her main sphere of activity subsequently shifted to Rome, where she served as assistant director of the British School of Archaeology (founded 1901) from 1909 to 1925. In 1907, she published *Roman Sculpture from Augustine to Constantine*, still considered an authoritative text and recently reprinted. The book begins with a positive reevaluation of Roman art, a position introduced earlier in the works of Wickhoff and Riegl. From that time on, her life's work was the affirmation of the art of imperial Rome. Always interested in symbolism and religion, she focuses in *Apotheosis and Afterlife* (1915) on the connections between the compositions and iconography of late antique and early Christian art. Strong brought out a two-volume expanded edition of her 1907 book in Italian, *La scultura romana da Augusto a Costantino* (1923-26), and contributed many articles on Roman art to learned journals and two chapters on the subject to the *Cambridge Ancient History*. Her reports on archaeological discoveries in Italy appeared in the *Times Literary Supplement*.

WOMEN ART HISTORIANS

In this period, the publications by women art historians on later periods of Western art generally reflect academic standards of scholarship acquired by study in colleges and universities. Many of them continued to work in the various genres of scholarship established earlier in the nineteenth century. But others, like their predecessors, opened new areas of research and tackled previously unexplored problems.

Eugénie Strong was aided in casting the set of lectures delivered at American colleges and universities into the book *Apotheosis and Afterlife* by KATHARINE ADA ESDAILE (1881-1950). Esdaile had studied classical archaeology at one of the first women's colleges at Oxford, Lady Margaret Hall, and then turned to the totally uncultivated subject of British sculpture. Her *English Monumental Sculpture since the Renaissance* (1927) is the pioneering book in the field and her work on eighteenth-century sculpture, in studies of Louis François Roubiliac (1928) and John Michael Rysbrack (1932) and in *English Church Monuments, 1510 to 1840*, written in 1946, long preceded the current interest of art historians in the eighteenth century. Indeed, women writers seem to have been extremely interested in this period, including Lady Dilke and Erica Tietze-Conrat in her early work on Georg Raphael Donner.

Iconographic studies by women in this period were not always separate works on religious symbolism but were increasingly integrated with a wider approach to art-historical problems. For example, although Erica Tietze-Conrat was primarily concerned with connoisseurship, she was alert to the relevance of iconographic issues, and devoted various articles to such subjects as Renaissance myth and allegory. The expatriate English scholar EVELYN SANDBERG-VAVALÀ (1888-1961) also joined the concerns of the connoisseur with a penetrating study of iconography in *La croce dipinta italiana e l'iconografia della passione* ("Italian Painted Crucifixes and the Iconography of the Passion"). This book, published in 1929, deals with a large and important category of medieval panel painting and remains the definitive work on the subject. In 1934 Sandberg-Vavalà also produced a short study on an iconographic subject, *L'iconografia della Madonna col bambino nella pittura del dugento* ("The Iconography of the Madonna and Child in Italian Painting of the Thirteenth Century"). The redoubtable Georgiana Goddard King, who hired Aby Warburg's nephew to teach at Bryn Mawr, as we learn from Susanna Saunders's essay, emphasized iconography in the classroom and in her publications on Spanish art.

Georgiana Goddard King was also a distinguished contributor to the field of medieval architectural history, a strongpoint of the American school of art history. Like her contemporaries, she loved travel and adventure and delighted in finding remote and unknown sites. She has ties, too, with the earlier generation of women writers on the arts, in the wealth of historical and literary reference in her work. A devoted reader of Anna Jameson, whose books she knew by heart, King organized her most popular study, *The Way of Saint James* (1920), according to the routes followed by medieval pilgrims to the shrine of Spain's patron saint. This scheme, while based on the medieval itinerary, has obvious affinities with nineteenth-century travel literature.

In the initial stages of his career, Bernard Berenson, the most famous connoisseur of modern times, was substantially aided by his wife MARY SMITH COSTELLOE BERENSON (1864-1945). Recent publications have revealed the extent of her personal and professional role in launching Berenson's career. A dynamic and forceful American woman who attended Smith and Radcliffe Colleges, Mary Pearsall Smith came from a distinguished Philadelphia family of Quakers. Her wealthy parents were well-known preachers; her mother, Hannah Smith, an ardent feminist. Married at an early age to an English barrister, Frank Costelloe, Mary took up the feminist cause prior to her meeting with Berenson. She began to publish on Italian art before Berenson did; her *Guide to the Italian Pictures at Hampton Court* (1894) corrected mistaken attributions of paintings in the gallery. It was she who urged Berenson to write, and from 1891 to 1892 she kept records of the paintings and drawings she and Berenson identified. These descriptions became a principal source for his early publications. She helped Berenson find publishers for his first writings and wrote favorable reviews of them. After their marriage, on their important tour of America in 1903-1904, she served as his public voice, lecturing with great success to large audiences, including those at various women's colleges. So impressive was Mary's performance that she was reportedly offered a "chair" at the University of Chicago at the handsome annual salary of three thousand dollars.[20] Because she did not establish an independent identity for herself as a scholar of art, her contributions have been all the more easily ignored.

A rare example of a husband-and-wife team in which the woman kept a distinct identity is that of Erica Tietze-Conrat and her husband Hans Tietze. In her essay, Madlyn Kahr gives a persuasive account of their working method. Their work on Albrecht Dürer, *Kritisches Verzeichnis der Werke Albrecht Dürers* ("A Critical Catalogue of the Work of Albrecht Dürer"), published in two volumes between 1929 and 1938, shows the Morellian method of connoisseurship learned from their teacher Franz Wickhoff and informed by the breadth of vision of the Vienna school. The Tietzes' later work *Drawings of the Venetian Painters* (1944) is a counterpart of Berenson's volumes on the *Drawings of the Florentine Painters*. The Tietzes' work is again infused with a wider point of view, one that considers the function, patronage, and creative intention underlying the drawings.

Until her retirement as curator of the department of Greek and Roman art at the Metropolitan Museum, Gisela Richter's scholarship also involved connoisseurship within the museum context of attributing and dating new acquisitions, publishing them separately in museum publications, or considering them as groups in catalogues raisonnés. As a girl, Richter was taught the methods of Morellian connoisseurship by her father, the well-known art historian Jean Paul Richter. As the essay by Ingrid Edlund, Anna Marguerite

McCann, and Claire Sherman brings out, Richter remained loyal through-out her career to applying Morellian criteria to the analysis of classical art.

In this period, the tradition in which women produced histories of art for a wide public was carried on by HELEN GARDNER (1878-1946). A classics major at the University of Chicago, she became a teacher of the history of art at the School of the Art Institute of Chicago. Gardner wrote *Art Through the Ages* (1926) in response to her classroom needs. Her revised second (1936) and third (1948) editions reflect the popularity of the work and her own broadening perspectives. In its concern for design and aesthetic considerations, the book shows its origins in teaching students with immediate concern for studio practice.

Related to this popularizing function was the continued presence of women as translators. In the case of Eugénie Sellers Strong, her translation of Wickhoff's book on Roman art provided not only professional creden-tials but also the starting point of her life's work. For LOUISE SCHWAB RICHTER (1852-1938), mother of Gisela and Irma Richter, her translation of Morelli's *Italian Masters in German Galleries* (1883) was part of the family's long personal and professional identification with the influential connoisseur. Louise Richter's translation also launched her career as a writer on art, via the traditional genre of the art guide, starting with a solid book on Siena (1901) in German. The second, on Chantilly (1913), is the first work in English on the history and architecture of the château and the marvelous collections of the Musée Condé. Richter's lengthy descrip-tions of the French and northern European paintings, drawings, and illuminated manuscripts extend beyond the dimensions of guidebook treatment.

Women also continued to write monographs on the lives of artists that were enriched by various developments in art historiography. For example, Erica Tietze-Conrat contributed a whole series of short monographs on northern Baroque artists. Maud Cruttwell, an English art historian and friend of the Berensons, published still valuable monographs on Italian Renaissance artists including Luca Signorelli (1899), Verrocchio (1904), and Antonio Pollaiuolo (1907). Contemporary with Cruttwell's books is Laura Ragg's *Women Artists of Bologna* (1907), a rare example of collective treat-ment of female artists.

From this limited sample, it becomes obvious that women's scholarship in art history in this period continued to add to knowledge of the field both in specialized studies and in more popular works. Among the genres to which they contributed are iconographic studies, catalogues raisonnés, artistic biographies, architectural history, art guides, translations, and general surveys. Although these books generally reflect academic standards of research, almost none of their authors held a university appointment. Women also continued to cultivate new or previously neglected areas of scholarship. In this respect, women writing art history seem to have retained their outsider status to a greater extent than in archaeology, a field which demands organized and collaborative effort. This lack of institutional employment for women in prestigious European universities, coupled with discriminatory social attitudes, may at least partially account for their absence among the theoreticians in academic art history mentioned earlier, who were active before World War I. Before 1918, women were not allowed to teach in German universities and only to do so on a very limited basis at the University of Vienna. Although the evidence is scanty, it is possible that the marginal position of women in these centers of academic art history discouraged women from taking new or controversial positions.

WOMEN AS ART CRITICS

During the period from 1890 to 1930 women maintained a high level of activity in art criticism, a field in which they had so early excelled. In the area of journalism, they followed the paths indicated by Margaret Fuller and Mariana Van Rensselaer, who lived until 1934. LEILA MECHLIN (1874-1949), for forty-five years an art critic for newspapers in Washington, D.C., advocated a point of view also held by Van Rensselaer that it was the critic's responsibility to guide public taste. Her colleague, writing for the *New York Times*, was ELISABETH LUTHER CARY (1867-1936), similarly concerned with fostering a wider understanding of art. Cary's literary career began with translations of French authors and studies of Tennyson and Browning. Cary was chosen in 1908 as the *Times*'s first art critic on the basis of the literary skill and judgment displayed in an art magazine she started, wrote, and edited. By that date she had published biographies of the Rossettis (1900) and of William Morris (1902) that still figure in bibliographies on these artists.

Several women art critics of the period addressed their writing to a more cultivated, educated audience. Inevitably they responded in various ways to the ideas of leading male critics of the nineteenth century, among whom Ruskin was a prominent and inescapable presence. Such Ruskinian concepts as his connection of Gothic architecture with an ideal of social harmony were perceived by some late nineteenth-century critics as denials of the primarily sensuous reality of the work of art. One of the most brilliant and original of these critics was VIOLET PAGET (1856-1935), whose pseudonym was VERNON LEE. Her early works show the influence of Walter Pater. In an essay of 1881, "The Child in the Vatican" (reprinted from the collection *Belcaro: Being Essays on Sundry Aesthetical Questions*), Lee mentally reconstructs the classical group of Niobe statues in Florence, imagining their formal aspect and the interrelationships of the figures as they would originally have appeared as an ensemble on a temple pediment. Her emphasis on the separation of the narrative dimensions of the tragic subject from the principles by which the sculptor has composed the forms stands diametrically opposed to Ruskin's assumption of continuity between the idea or sentiment of an artist's theme and its realization as form.

Raised to be a writer, "another Madame de Staël for choice," Vernon Lee grew up as a member of an expatriate English family that settled in Italy in 1873. It was Mary Singer Sargent, mother of the painter, who initiated her into the "cult of the *genius loci*, the numinous guardian of places," encouraging the development of a remarkable gift for evoking the atmosphere and texture of localities.[21] Vernon Lee wrote on a wide range of subjects in art, history, and aesthetics. On this last topic, she and her companion Clementina Anstruther-Thomson (1857-1921) entered into a bitter dispute with her neighbor in Florence, Bernard Berenson, in 1897 about which party could claim priority in arriving at theories closely related to the famous "tactile values" aesthetic of Berenson. But the lasting value of Lee's writing resides in such works as her pioneering *Studies of the Eighteenth Century in Italy* (1880), which created the neglected Settecento as a period in somewhat the sense that Burckhardt had created the Renaissance. *Renaissance Fancies and Studies* (1895) includes "Loves of the Saints," an essay of impressive range and vigor, which shows how the Franciscan movement of the thirteenth century wrought a profound change throughout European civilization, and particularly in the arts, beginning with Nicola Pisano.

The work of Vernon Lee decisively influenced EDITH WHARTON (1862-1937), who became a best-selling writer on interior design some years before she established herself as a novelist. Descended from an aristocratic family of "old New York" (like Van Rensselaer), Wharton was educated at home. In her father's library she read Anna Jameson, Ruskin, and Kugler's *Handbook of Italian Painting*. As a young woman, she carried Vernon Lee's books with her on annual trips to Italy. In Lee's books Wharton found guides to her own taste in seventeenth- and eighteenth-century architecture. When Wharton had the chance to meet the author in 1894, she discovered in Vernon Lee "the first highly cultivated and brilliant woman I had ever known."[22] Curiously, in view of Wharton's interest in the eighteenth century and in interior decoration—the subject of her first book—she does not seem to have known the work of Lady Dilke.

The Decoration of Houses (1897) was written by Wharton in collaboration with a Boston architect, Ogden Codman, Jr., who shared her revulsion against the suffocating clutter of contemporary interiors. Recommending the architectural treatment of rooms with elegant, simple proportions and clear linear division of interior space, the book invokes French practice, especially that of the eighteenth century, as a model of fitness and practicality. In the course of their argument, Wharton and Codman attack Ruskin's analogy between artistic integrity and the higher moral imperatives. The point is similar to Vernon Lee's in that the arrangement of interiors, like the realm of sculptural forms, follows principles of its own. A new tendency congenial to Wharton's ideas had been noted earlier by Mariana Van Rensselaer in an 1885 article in the *Century Magazine* that called attention to the involvement of architects with interiors in the recent work of McKim, Mead, and White.[23] Persuasively and lucidly written, the unexpected success of *The Decoration of Houses* expressed a reaction against Victorian taste in favor of Italian Renaissance and French classical restraint and elegance.

Seven years later, Wharton published a study of a subject on which very little had been written—Italian garden architecture. Wharton reported that in order to gather material for *Italian Villas and Their Gardens* (1904), Vernon Lee "took me to nearly all the villas I wished to visit near Florence." Lee also provided introductions to residences elsewhere in Italy.[24] Avoiding the great palatial gardens, Wharton discussed architecture of a social stratum roughly similar to the haut bourgeois audience addressed in *The Decoration of Houses*. Treating some eighty examples of villa architecture, Wharton's work combines graceful writing with a background of solid historical research. Interestingly enough, her editor, Richard Watson Gilder, who had objected to Van Rensselaer that the content of her articles was overly serious, made the same complaint about Wharton.[25] Although Wharton's two books were successful, she soon wrote only fiction.

Wharton's work on *Italian Villas and Their Gardens* was followed ten years later by a history of landscape architecture, apparently the first of its kind. A German woman, MARIE LUISE GOTHEIN (1863-1931), published in two volumes the *Geschichte der Gartenkunst* (1914), (*History of Garden Art*, English edition, 1928). The wife of Eberhard Gothein, professor at the University of Heidelberg, she translated and wrote extensively about Wordsworth, Keats, and Elizabeth Barrett Browning before beginning to work for ten years on her *History of Garden Art*. International in scope, the first volume begins with Egyptian gardens and proceeds historically through antiquity, the Middle Ages, and the English Renaissance; the second one continues till the end of the nineteenth century. Gothein considers patronage, social and environmental functions, the architectural framework, and the use of plant materials in individual gardens and the period as a whole. The almost seven hundred illustrations are drawn, wherever possible, from contemporary sources, including works of art. Despite the encyclopedic nature of the undertaking, the book is delightful to read, incorporating contemporary literary references that enliven the historical framework. Gothein's book, like a number of others by women mentioned in this chapter, is still recognized as an authoritative work in its field.

The writings by women art critics in this period continued to address wide audiences on both journalistic and more serious levels. Like their counterparts in Chapter 1, they were largely self-educated and had broad interests. They possessed genuine literary talent and, drawing on the tradition of travel literature, revealed a remarkable ability to evoke the quality of a scene and the relation of monuments to their milieu. With memorable results, Vernon Lee and Edith Wharton blended in their work originality, understanding of the past, and a graceful style.

EDUCATION IN THE VISUAL ARTS

Unlike the subjects of Part II of this book, those of Part III—King, Richter, Bieber, and Tietze-Conrat—were all university educated, and the last two received doctorates from the Universities of Bonn and Vienna respectively. Moreover, all four attended secondary schools for girls, three of which had specific ties with feminist or reform groups. Although less is known about Leache-Wood School (later Seminary), which Georgiana Goddard King attended, the principals were women of developed aesthetic interests who encouraged King to attend Bryn Mawr College. In turn, King founded the art history department at Bryn Mawr, the first independent woman's college to offer doctorates in that subject.

On both the undergraduate and graduate levels the women's colleges played significant roles in the development of art history in the United States. As was true of the discipline in general, advanced instruction in archaeology came first. Harriet Boyd (later Hawes), an early graduate of Smith College, introduced the study of archaeology there in 1900, and received her M.A. from the same school the next year on the basis of her excavations at Kavousi. The first woman awarded an M.A. from Smith, Mary Louise Nicols (1898), was also the first recipient of a Hoppin Fellowship. Between 1893 and 1920 eight Vassar women received the M.A. in classical archaeology. Not surprisingly, Bryn Mawr, which from the beginning had supported a graduate school, awarded the first archaeology doctorates given by a woman's college, beginning with Edith Hall (later Dohan) in 1908. In 1916 Hetty Goldman, a Bryn Mawr B.A., received her Ph.D. in archaeology from Radcliffe, the administrator of advanced degrees to women from Harvard. She was followed in 1922 by Kate Denny McKnight, who had received an M.A. from Vassar two years earlier.[26]

The significant role of women in archaeology is reflected also in the early dates and numbers in which they received doctorates from coeducational institutions. Esther Boise Van Deman was apparently the first woman to receive a Ph.D. in archaeology from the University of Chicago in 1898,

followed by Caroline L. Ransom in 1905. The year before (1904) Henrietta
J. Muter received her doctorate from the University of Pennsylvania, while
in 1905 Ida Thallon was awarded a Ph.D. from Columbia. Eight out of
seventeen doctorates in archaeology from Johns Hopkins awarded between
1911 and 1930 were given to women.

The women's colleges also promoted art historical studies in this period.
While continuing to offer practical courses, between 1890 (at Vassar) and
1902/1903 (at Smith and Goucher), separate departments or schools stressing
studio art and design at the women's colleges were abandoned for academic
departments in which historical courses were offered. The women's colleges
were sensitive to the opinion that these separate schools and their connection with the female amateur tradition somehow diminished the academic
respectability of their institutions.[27] This course of action also typified the
general movement in the United States toward greater academic rigor in the
teaching of art history.

Because of the ramifications of its programs, Wellesley provides an
instructive example of the innovative roles performed by the women's
colleges in expanding the teaching of art history. In 1897 ALICE VAN
VECHTEN BROWN (1862-1949) became head of Wellesley's art department. Brown came from a New England family prominent as educators and
theologians. She studied painting from 1881 to 1885 at the Art Students'
League in New York. In 1894 she became director of the Norwich, Connecticut, Art School (affiliated with the Norwich Free Academy), where she
attracted attention for "her method of teaching art history, which included
drawing and modeling from photographs or casts of the works being
studied, as a means of developing and sharpening observation, thus serving
a purpose analogous to that of laboratory experimentation in science." As
head of the Wellesley art department, she saw that the "laboratory method" was integrated with the study of art history. Brown's reforms attracted
a growing enrollment and led to an expansion of faculty and facilities. After
1897 Wellesley pioneered in offering graduate study not only in archaeology
but also in art history. In 1899-1900 Wellesley became the first college in the
country to offer an undergraduate major in art history. The curriculum
gradually broadened to include new subjects; in 1927 Alfred H. Barr, Jr.,
gave the first college course in the United States on modern art. Brown also
reorganized the Farnsworth Art Museum, acquiring objects of superior
quality, rearranging them to serve as aids to teaching, and beginning in
1899-1900 arranged a series of loan exhibitions.[28] The museum training
program begun at Wellesley in 1910-1911 was the earliest of its kind given
in a college, and will be discussed shortly.

Thus, art instruction, begun in the 1860s at Vassar and developed in the
1870s at other women's colleges in the United States as a result of the identification of women's aesthetic interests with their roles as guardians of culture,

became increasingly academic rather than practical in this period. This is true of the enrichment of the art history curricula and museums at Smith, Vassar, and Mt. Holyoke. The art department at Barnard College, the coordinate institution for women affiliated with Columbia University, was not established until 1923. In her essay, Susanna Saunders has described in detail the development of the art department at Bryn Mawr under Georgiana Goddard King.

The important role of the women's colleges in the academic development of American art history before 1920 is clear. Another sign of women's extensive participation in the field is their substantial presence in the ranks of the College Art Association, founded in 1913. By 1917, women constituted almost 50 percent of the individual membership of this organization, which became the professional voice of the discipline.[29] In one sense, women's continued participation in the field was assured in the 1920s, the decade when art history became a fully respectable academic discipline. Women were admitted to several of the most prestigious universities that now began regularly to award doctorates in art history, as distinguished from anthropology or archaeology. Although women continued to be excluded from Princeton until the 1960s, they were admitted to the graduate programs of other all-male institutions like Columbia and Harvard. Radcliffe College, which administered all advanced degrees awarded by Harvard to women, produced the first twelve women doctorates in the history of art between 1925 and 1931. Although Bryn Mawr theoretically granted doctoral degrees in art history, none was awarded until the 1930s, as women students preferred the more developed curriculum offered at Harvard and elsewhere. It is worth noting that in almost all cases women were granted full admission to the new doctoral programs when leadership in professional training came from all-male or male-dominated institutions. Although these universities were willing to accept women as graduate students and award them degrees equivalent to those received by their masculine counterparts, it did not follow that these institutions considered women with equal credentials qualified to become members of their faculties. This contradiction, which still exists virtually unchanged fifty years later, rests on widely held (if not openly voiced) cultural beliefs about women's proper place in society.

PROFESSIONAL OPPORTUNITIES FOR WOMEN

The barriers that prevented women from teaching in exclusively male or coeducational American universities in this period were social ones, rather than the legal obstacles that prevented women like Margarete Bieber from teaching at a German university until the Weimar Republic abolished them after World War I. The main source of academic employment for the early degree-holders in archaeology and art history in the United States was the women's colleges, although the faculties of these institutions were not all female. Esther Van Deman found teaching positions at Mt. Holyoke and Goucher, Harriet Boyd (later Hawes) at Smith and Wellesley, and Mary Swindler at Bryn Mawr. Before she joined the staff of the University of Pennsylvania Museum, Edith Hall (later Dohan) taught at Mt. Holyoke. For women archaeologists the one thorough triumph in gaining admission to a male stronghold apparently was Hetty Goldman's appointment to the Institute for Advanced Study in Princeton at a somewhat later date, in 1936. The scope of a career in the women's colleges in the early decades of the twentieth century is suggested by the biography of Georgiana Goddard King, who held no degrees in art and whose colorful presence as first head of the art department at Bryn Mawr emerges in the essay presented here.

The notion of women as guardians of culture was one underlying rationale of their employment as teachers in the pre-Civil War period; but the role of women as educators broadened in the period 1890 to 1930 to include a variety of institutional settings, all defined by the goals of cultural philanthropy. Settlement houses, libraries, and museums were all institutions in which art and culture were considered to have the moral and spiritual potential to improve the quality of life of the growing and ethnically diverse populations of American cities. The association of women with aesthetic culture and moral education helps to account for their presence in settlement houses, libraries, and museums as acceptable public environments for the first generation of college-trained women.

In her sensitive and moving autobiography, *Twenty Years at Hull-House* (1910), JANE ADDAMS (1860-1935) describes her disillusionment with the ideal of fashionable aesthetic cultivation as an acceptable pastime for upper-class women. She describes her growing dissatisfaction with the social ritual of the Grand Tour of Europe, while she reaffirms the spiritual and moral value of Dürer's art or the choir stalls of Ulm cathedral.[30] Yet for Addams European travel had the unexpected result of suggesting a positive solution for her inability to take part in remedying the ills of urban society. With the support of her friend from Rockford Seminary (later College), ELLEN GATES STARR (1859-1940), Addams founded Hull-House, a settlement house on Chicago's West End modelled after Toynbee Hall in London. Starr, who had taught art appreciation in a girls' school in Chicago, had herself been inspired by her aunt, the noted art educator and lecturer Eliza Allan Starr (1824-1901). Ellen Starr was extremely influential in emphasizing the role of art in the early days of Hull-House. She and Addams believed that in various ways art could brighten the drab lives of the laboring classes living in Chicago. Both women were influenced by the ideas of John Ruskin and William Morris. Starr was particularly close to the ideals of the arts and crafts movement, travelling to London in the late 1890s to study bookbinding.[31] Starr was instrumental in raising the funds for the first addition to Hull-House in 1891, the Butler Art Gallery, patterned after the Whitechapel Art Gallery in London's East End, founded by Canon Samuel and Henrietta Barnett of Toynbee Hall.[32] Exhibitions, art classes, literary programs, and drama were features of life at Hull-House. In its early days the settlement house became a center of intellectual and cultural life in Chicago, not only for the community of women who lived there but also for faculty members of the newly established University of Chicago and representatives of the city's social and cultural élite. Although Starr and Addams soon realized that a knowledge of art could not cure poverty and its attendant ills and turned to serious issues of labor and political reform, the art and other cultural programs continued at Hull-House. In addition, Starr founded in 1894 the Chicago Public Art Society to establish programs of art education for school children.[33] Such programs, which reached out to involve the community, became an important model for the education departments of museums, in which women have played strategic roles.

A second cultural institution in which the education of the public was a major goal is the municipal library. Even before the Civil War, women were influential as the clientele and leading pressure group for the organization of public libraries. But it was in the 1880s, when librarianship first became a profession taught in separate schools, that women were attracted in great numbers to the field. Dee Garrison has shown that the notion of women as guardians of culture served to justify the employment of women as librarians, as had been the case earlier with respect to teaching. Stereotypes of women's nature as nurturant, "refining, and spiritualizing" connected women's work in the profession with the educational function of libraries and their mission to bring "moral uplift to the masses." Melvil Dewey, the founder of library science in the United States, urged educated women to enter the field on the grounds that the library was less taxing than the schoolroom and offered a more genteel, refined environment. Employment in libraries provided a welcome enlargement of opportunities for the first generation of college-educated women, whose knowledge of languages was particularly valued. Libraries, with their limited budgets, gladly hired women who were willing to accept lower salaries than those paid to male librarians.[34]

A connection between librarianship and art scholarship emerges in the career of MYRTILLA AVERY (1868-1959), an early associate of Melvil Dewey. A Wellesley graduate (class of 1891), Avery majored in Greek and Latin and taught these subjects before receiving a Bachelor of Library Science degree from the New York State Library School. In 1901 she and

Dewey devised the first mobile library system, which included art reproductions. Apparently this exposure to art aroused her interest in the subject
and led her to return to Wellesley, where she received an M.A. in 1913 after
writing her thesis on a medieval subject, the frescoes in the nave of the
upper church of Saint Francis at Assisi. From that time on, Avery's
career unfolded at Wellesley, where in addition to teaching she worked on
the reorganization of the Farnsworth Art Museum. In 1925 she made an
important contribution to the study of early Christian art in an *Art Bulletin*
article, "The Alexandrian Style at Santa Maria Antiqua, Rome." She
became one of the first group of women awarded a Radcliffe doctorate in
art history in 1927. Her dissertation on "The Exultet Rolls of South
Italy"—published in 1936—reflected the new American scholarship on
medieval manuscript illumination encouraged by the writings and teachings
of Charles Rufus Morey. Avery assumed the responsibility of chairing the
Wellesley art department in 1929, succeeding Alice Van Vechten Brown.

For certain women, librarianship provided an entrée to employment as
curators in museums. Museums, like libraries, were institutions with a
physical environment and identification with culture that provided another
appropriately genteel work setting for women. Among women who were
first trained as librarians before entering the art field was Susan A. Hutchinson, employed in a dual capacity as librarian and curator of prints at the
Brooklyn Museum from 1899 to 1934. Hutchinson attended the Pratt
Institute School of Library Science. Isabel Weadock, who served first as
librarian, became curator of prints at the Detroit Institute of Arts in 1924.
She supplemented her initial training by study with Fitzroy Carrington,
curator of prints at the Boston Museum of Fine Arts. The examples of
Hutchinson and Weadock suggest that book illustration may have provided
the link between librarianship and their specialization in prints.[35]

The idea that museums, like libraries, could furnish suitable employment
for college-educated women with a knowledge of art history was clear to
Myrtilla Avery, who had a firsthand working knowledge of both institutions. Beginning in 1910-1911 the Wellesley art department set up at the
Farnsworth Museum a one-year course for "the training of Art Museum
assistants." Students were graduates of Wellesley and other colleges with a
knowledge of art history. The course included art library and office training, as well as the care of objects, exhibit design and installation, and
methods of museum instruction. Students also received instruction from the
staff at various museums in the area and visited art dealers.[36]

Another woman of vision, Sara Yorke Stevenson, had established in 1910
a very similar museum training program at the School of Industrial Art of
the Pennsylvania Museum, where she was employed as an assistant curator
beginning in 1908. The Philadelphia course took two years to complete and

focused mainly on problems of connoisseurship relating to the decorative and applied arts. Stevenson taught the course until shortly before her death in 1921. These two programs established by women preceded Paul Sachs's famous Harvard course for training museum curators and directors, which began in 1921. Sachs wrote to ask Avery for printed material and advice about the course drawn from her own experience. Sachs was familiar with the Wellesley program because he had briefly taught there and, according to Agnes Abbot, actually had served as an instructor in the museum course.[37]

Women were also prominent in a less elitist museum training course inaugurated at the Newark Museum in 1925 by its imaginative director, John Cotton Dana. The one-year course, designed for college graduates or others with equivalent qualifications interested in entering museum work, emphasized the practical aspects of running a museum. The student's rotation through the various departments of the Newark Museum was related to that institution's goal of establishing "a direct relation with the daily life and activities of the city." The eight graduates of the first class in 1926 were all women, some of whom like DOROTHY MILLER went on to important careers in American museums. After Dana's death, the program was carried on by KATHERINE COFFEY, whose work is discussed in Chapter 3. By 1935, the Newark Museum program had placed twenty-seven students in fifteen American museums.[38]

Long before these museum courses had been established, women had entered museum employment without special qualifications or training. In 1895, Florence Virginia Paull, later FLORENCE PAULL BERGER (1871–1967), who had no college education, began to work at the Boston Museum of Fine Arts as a secretarial assistant to the director. Paull stayed on, working on the museum registration system, and in 1909 was named "Assistant in Charge of Other Collections in the Department of Western Art."[39] In this capacity she organized exhibitions of American silver and musical instruments. After her marriage in 1918, Berger became general curator—an administrative position—at the Wadsworth Atheneum in Hartford, Connecticut. She held this post until 1951 when she was named curator of textiles and costumes; she became curator emerita in 1966 and died the next year after a museum career of fifty-eight years. Among her achievements at the Wadsworth Atheneum was the organization of the large collection of decorative art objects left to the museum by J. Pierpont Morgan. Berger also put on many exhibitions, lectured, and started the publication of the museum bulletin.

Another early woman museum professional was FRANCES MORRIS (1865/66-1955), whose career also centered on musical instruments and the decorative arts. Morris began to work at the Metropolitan Museum from 1897 to 1905 as an employee of Mrs. John Crosby Brown, who was donat-

ing her collection of musical instruments to that institution with the stipula-
tion that she could work on its arrangement. From 1905 Morris became a
full-time employee of the Metropolitan when the first part of the Crosby
Brown catalogue was finished. Little is known of Morris's background,
except that she worked as a secretary and had a knowledge of musical
instruments. Her next job was to organize the collection of lace at the
Metropolitan, a task that called for collaboration with mostly female
collectors, who served as volunteer curators. By 1910, she was in charge of
the textile study room, which was opened to the public. In the same year
Morris was named assistant curator in the department of decorative arts
and, in 1921, became associate curator in charge of textiles. Morris continued to oversee the collection of musical instruments and completed a
second volume of the catalogue in 1913. She later coauthored a catalogue of
the Ballard collection of oriental rugs in the Metropolitan and a five-volume
work on the history of lace. At the Metropolitan, Morris also lectured on
textiles and musical instruments between 1915 and 1920 and later spoke
before concerts about the musical instruments used for the performances.
She was also active as an organizer at the Metropolitan of the employees'
association and of the Ladies' Lunch Club, initially composed of female
staff members who gathered together in her office to eat their midday meal
out of sight of the first director, General di Cesnola, who did not care for
women employees.[40] Morris worked at the Metropolitan until her resignation in 1929.

The careers of Berger and Morris suggest a tendency in this period of
women in museums to be confined to the so-called minor arts, especially
textiles and the decorative arts. To take a few further examples, Bessie
Bennett, the first woman curator at the Art Institute of Chicago, from 1915
to 1939, was curator of decorative arts. GERTRUDE UNDERHILL (1874-
1954), a Wellesley graduate, came to the Cleveland Museum in a clerical
capacity shortly after it opened. She served as assistant to the director and
worked in the education department before being named assistant in textiles
in January, 1924. She was promoted to the rank of curator in 1944, three
years before she retired. It appears probable that women's prominence in
the field came not only from an identification of textiles and decorative arts
as appropriate female concerns, but also from their ability to work with
collectors, who in many cases were women.

One of the few women who became curators in fields other than prints,
textiles, and decorative arts in this period was Gisela Richter, at the time
the most prominent woman curator in a major American museum. She was
hired at a salary of five dollars a day by the Metropolitan in 1905, through
the good offices of her friend Harriet Boyd, in order to catalogue a collection of jewelry. In 1906 Richter joined what became the department of

Greek and Roman art at the Metropolitan at a moment when it was beginning a period of great growth. Working energetically and effectively, she aided in the acquisitions, installations, exhibitions, and publications of the department. For a woman, she had the unusual advantages of training in connoisseurship and acquaintance with the world of collecting. Promoted to full curator in 1925, her dedicated labors at the Metropolitan until her retirement in 1948 added greatly to the museum's stature in the important field of classical art.

A final example of a woman's career in a museum in this period is that of Sara Yorke Stevenson. Her influence at the University Museum and later at the Pennsylvania (now Philadelphia) Museum grew partly from her volunteer promotional, administrative, and social activities. Her expertise in archaeology and her superb administrative abilities led, however, to an increasingly professional status. Between 1890 and 1905 she acted as (apparently unpaid) curator of the Egyptian and Mediterranean section of the University Museum, while serving in various executive capacities on the board of managers. At the Pennsylvania Museum, her activity also showed this dual aspect. From 1908 until 1918, she was assistant curator; and, from 1918 until 1921, she was curator of the museum. At the same time, she served as a member and chairman of the Associate Committee of Women. Her salary as curator at the Pennsylvania Museum was paid from a special subscription fund. Her activities included the founding and teaching of the first known museum training course, organizing exhibitions, selecting acquisitions, and standing in for the director in an administrative capacity.[41] Stevenson's museum career typifies the fluidity of administrative and professional organization in museums of this period.

Both the lack of an accepted public role for women and the administrative structures of museums explain why, with few exceptions, women did not become directors of large art museums. Originally private philanthropic benefactions, the large municipal museums were run by boards of trustees mainly composed of wealthy businessmen. Because securing gifts of money and works of art donated by collectors were primary goals of directors and curators, social connections on equal terms with the wealthy were often determinants of employment. Most women were considered ignorant of money matters and operating budgets and not able to "wheel and deal" on equal terms with collectors and trustees. Women fared better in American university museums, in which less money was involved and greater interest in research prevailed. Although in general most European museums were state supported and so favored the importance of scholarly criteria rather than social credentials, bitter resistance to women by civil service bureaucracies in many cases prevented advancement.

The first woman head of a U.S. art museum was Cornelia Bentley Sage (1876-1936) (later CORNELIA BENTLEY SAGE QUINTON), who became director of the Albright Art Gallery of the Buffalo Fine Arts Academy in 1910. Daughter of a socially prominent local family, Sage was a practising artist. Sage organized innovative exhibitions of the Photo-Secession Movement (1910), American painting, and American sculpture (1916), while keeping up the high quality of the museum publication, *Academy Notes*. In 1924, she was appointed first director of the San Francisco Palace of the Legion of Honor.

Another American art museum director of this period was FLORENCE LEVY (1870-1947), who helped shape the Baltimore Museum, where she served on a part-time basis as its first director from 1922 to 1926. Levy had considerable experience as an art administrator and educator, having founded in 1898 the *American Art Annual*, a comprehensive account of events in the art world, a directory of its institutions, and a biographical listing of artists. This publication has proved invaluable in tracing many of the early women museum curators and staff, as have its offshoots, the *American Art Directory* and *Who's Who in American Art*. Levy was also active in the field of art education and prepared a series of catalogues on American artists for exhibitions held at the Metropolitan. Although not a museum director, Leila Mechlin also created organizations for promoting American art. She was a founder of the American Federation of Arts and editor of its official publication, the *American Magazine of Art*.

Among the very few women who became directors of museums in this period were two librarians. BEATRICE WINSER (1869-1947) succeeded John Cotton Dana as director of the Newark Museum in 1929, serving in that post until her death in 1947. As Dana himself was a librarian and the museum was an outgrowth of the Newark Library, Winser's background and enthusiastic endorsement of the educational and community outreach policy begun by her predecessor were particularly appropriate qualifications. Although she did not attend college or library school, BELLE DA COSTA GREENE (1883-1950) became J. P. Morgan's librarian in 1905 and director of the Morgan Library when it opened to the public in 1924. Greene developed her reputation as a noted scholar and connoisseur of illuminated manuscripts and rare books through her acquisitions, catalogues, and exhibitions.

In short, women's professional opportunities expanded considerably in the period under review in the interconnected areas of art education, librarianship, and museums. Although these widening horizons represented real advances, women were far from reaching equal status with their male colleagues. This is certainly true in college teaching, where the new women doctorates in archaeology and art history were largely confined to employment in the women's colleges which, except for Bryn Mawr and Radcliffe, did not offer Ph.D.s. These distinctions became crucial beginning in the 1920s, when art history became a fully respectable academic discipline. The situation was similar in museum employment. Usually women worked for long periods at lower ranks and at lower pay without promotion in less prestigious fields like textiles, decorative arts, and prints, which at that time had not become major areas of collecting. At the Metropolitan Museum, twenty-three women joined the curatorial ranks between 1905 and 1945, just over half the number of male appointees in this category. Only Gisela Richter advanced to full curatorial rank in this period, as compared with nineteen of her male colleagues. In other major American art museums like Boston, Chicago, Detroit, Cleveland, and Philadelphia, women who attained full curatorial rank were limited in number (less than ten in all); and they were employed in departments of decorative arts, lace, textiles, and prints.[42]

WOMEN'S CHANGING LIFESTYLES

The professional affiliation of women with museums and universities substantially affected their lifestyles. One area of conspicuous change was the socially imposed choice between marriage and career. Nearly all of the women mentioned in this section who held long-term museum or academic positions remained single: Avery, Bieber, Brown, Gardner, Greene, King, Levy, Richter, Murray, Van Deman, and Winser. Eugénie Sellers Strong had married, but she was widowed before accepting her one continuous appointment at the British School at Rome. Edith Hall Dohan and Harriet Boyd Hawes, who both married and had children, temporarily retired before returning to work. Sara Yorke Stevenson's professional and public activities did not begin until almost twenty years after her marriage, while Cornelia Benton Sage Quinton's marriage occurred after her appointment as director of a museum. Perhaps professionally minded women did not wish to marry, but the evidence suggests that institutional status discouraged the idea that women could have both marriage and a career. This situation contrasts sharply with that of nineteenth-century figures, who often combined writing on art with marriage and whose publication efforts were sometimes encouraged by their husbands. Conversely, unmarried women with careers had to show a single-minded devotion to work and to the institutions with which they were affiliated. The loneliness of single life was creatively countered by Margarete Bieber in adopting a child, a solution daring at the time. Gisela Richter found support, emotional and professional, in her sister Irma. All four subjects of essays had wide-ranging friendships in the scholarly world.

For these professional women the pressure to succeed must have been great; women like King, Bieber, Tietze-Conrat, and Richter achieved a record of prodigious scholarly publication. Professional women in museums or colleges remained in one institution for all their working lives. Interestingly enough, many women of this generation were long-lived. Among them were Myrtilla Avery, Alice Van Vechten Brown, Margarete Bieber, Florence Berger, Frances Morris, and Gisela Richter. A woman without institutional status who married a man in her own field had great difficulty in maintaining a separate identity as a scholar. The marriage of Erica Tietze-Conrat is a rare instance of a union that did not submerge the wife's independence in the role of factotum to the husband.

During this period, as earlier in the nineteenth century, examples of female achievement stimulated the aspirations of younger women. In this generation, schools run by feminists to provide a basis for higher education for women were important to all four subjects of essays in Part III. Georgiana Goddard King's literary interests had her mother's extensive involvement in this area as a precedent. Louise Schwab Richter's writings on art subjects offered an example to her daughter Gisela. When Eugénie Sellers saw the possibility of a career for herself in the study of ancient art, she had Jane Harrison as a model, while Vernon Lee cherished the notion that she would be another Madame de Staël. Edith Wharton in turn was crucially influenced as a writer on art by qualities she found in the work of Vernon Lee, the first woman of distinguished intellect she had ever met. Of course, women were also significantly affected by male teachers and colleagues, such as Georg Loeschcke in Bieber's case and Franz Wickhoff in the formation of Erica Tietze-Conrat and Eugénie Sellers Strong, to say nothing of the effect of Jean Paul Richter's ideas and activities as an art historian on his daughter Gisela. Yet the presence and examples of women who had gone before and "cast light upon the path"—to borrow Margaret Fuller's words—nourished the imagination of their juniors with particular force.

Both in England and the United States, the residence of women faculty in the women's colleges provided these scholars with a nucleus of intellectual companionship missing for most of the nineteenth century and with the potential for serving as role models for their students. For critics and writers without this kind of affiliation, traditional methods of finding intellectual stimulation in more informal situations continued. At Hull-House Jane Addams created a "salon in the slums" that became a center of intellectual life in Chicago.[43] The brilliance of social occasions organized by Edith Wharton and Mary Costelloe Berenson for members of an international social and intellectual elite reflected their considerable, and commanding, stature. In Rome, Eugénie Sellers Strong, although living on a more modest income (including her emoluments as a lifetime fellow of Girton College), provided distinguished entertainments for her guests. The home of Marie Luise and Eberhard Gothein was a gathering place for the intellectual lights of pre-1914 Heidelberg.

In general, the female networks of support revealed in these essays did not have the cohesiveness of the remarkable group of women living in Hull-House. Instead, help was extended on an individual basis, such as Boyd's introduction of Gisela Richter to the United States and to a job at the Metropolitan Museum. The work of Boyd and Edith Hall at Gournia was supported by the American Exploration Society founded by Sara Yorke Stevenson. Bieber, like other single women, was ingenious in finding female recruits to support her efforts. Her woman Friday, Fraülein Freytag, was a creative solution to the need for various kinds of help available to masculine colleagues from wives and secretaries.

Unlike Fuller, Jameson, and Dilke the four subjects of essays in Part III did not take part in feminist causes or social reform movements. Although biographical data about the other women mentioned is incomplete, only one, Sara Yorke Stevenson, took an active part in the suffrage campaign as founder and first president of the Equal Franchise Society of Pennsylvania. Several explanations of this dramatic change of attitude are possible. The attainment of educational opportunities and professional status may have satisfied these women with their station in life. Furthermore, institutional affiliation and the conformity it promoted may have discouraged association with what were then considered radical and controversial causes. With the exception of a few leaders like Carey Thomas at Bryn Mawr, the women's colleges—students included—until late in the struggle took a dim view of the agitation for women's suffrage.[44] For another thing, the academic and rarified atmosphere that had come to surround art-historical studies may have discouraged an interest in social issues and reforms like those so fruitfully undertaken by the group at Hull-House and other settlements. Exceptions to the rule were Harriet Boyd Hawes, who remained an ardent fighter against social injustice, and Hetty Goldman, who undertook refugee work abroad after World War I.

One channel for the social conscience of women interpreters of the visual arts was their work in settlement houses and as educators in museums. This connection is suggested by the career of Louise M. Dunn, who had worked in a settlement house (and in a public library) before joining the department of education at the Cleveland Museum.[45] Roberta Murray Fansler (later Alford, now Capers)—coauthor with Priscilla Hiss of the indispensable *Research in the Fine Arts in the Colleges and Universities of the United States*— relates that in 1927, when she was hired in the department of education at the Metropolitan by Henry W. Kent, he knew that "as an undergraduate at Bryn Mawr I had been very much interested in

Workers' Education, and as a kind of latter day follower of William Morris and of Ruskin, I longed to bring the delights of art to the masses." In addition to her work at the Metropolitan, Capers notes that she lectured to the Women's Trade Union League, stressing in a course "What Workers Have Wrought through the Ages."[46]

A common characteristic of the subjects of the essays in Part III was a commitment to professional achievement, not unexpectedly accompanied by very different personal styles. The dramatic persona cultivated by Georgiana Goddard King was surely sustained by innate flair; it also addressed the pinched, asexual stereotype of the learned woman. In this regard King's assertion, "I've done everything known to man," sounds like a direct challenge to such a stereotype. Madlyn Kahr's essay reveals that Erica Tietze-Conrat contrived to prevail through an imperial manner accompanied by daunting frankness. Also known as commanding presences were Vernon Lee, Belle Greene, and Mary Costelloe Berenson. For some women, cultivation of distinctive, even eccentric, personalities was a means of escaping from conventional ideas of female behavior.

Women's support of contemporary art and literature, noted earlier in the careers of Margaret Fuller and Mariana Van Rensselaer, continued in this period with important consequences for the future. Erica Tietze-Conrat and her husband championed contemporary Austrian artists by their writings and lectures. Georgiana Goddard King's encouragement of Gertrude Stein's writing and her advocacy of modern art are striking examples of independent critical judgments. At Wellesley, the first course on modern art in the United States was given in 1927. The involvement of women as annalists and critics of modern art developed even more markedly after 1930.

The period from 1890 to 1930 was dramatic in the expansion of women's employment in higher education, museums, and libraries as interpreters of the visual arts. Women trained as artists played important roles as educators and museum administrators. Despite the significant increase in college-educated and professionally affiliated women, valuable art criticism was produced by women who had no higher education; and art-historical writing was produced by independent research scholars. This "widening sphere" may have encouraged a false sense that all doors were open to women on a level equal with men. Women were restricted from teaching in male institutions with graduate departments and were not greatly welcomed either in the most prestigious coeducational faculties. In museums, women did not achieve the highest professional ranks and seem to have clustered in less prestigious departments. The women's colleges were the most receptive to employing female degree-holders, and they offered intellectual and social support networks. Socially, women's affiliation with established institutions generally called for a choice between marriage and a career. Allegiance to feminist causes seems to have taken second place to professional status, at least on an overt basis. The next generation would benefit from the professional standing gained by women between 1890 and 1930, but they would also be faced with many of the same choices.

NOTES

1. For developments in archaeology, see "Archaeology: Research and Discoveries," in *Encyclopedia of World Art*, 1 (New York, 1959); Jacquetta Hawkes, ed., *The World of the Past*, 2 vols. (New York, 1963); John D. Wortham, *The Genesis of British Egyptology 1549-1906* (Norman, Okla. 1971).

2. For a summary of developments in art history, see Salerno, "Historiography." See also Kleinbauer, *Modern Perspectives*, for Aby Warburg and the Warburg School, pp. 61-65; for Heinrich Wölfflin, pp. 27-30 and 154-55; and for Clive Bell and Roger Fry, p. 7.

3. For the Vienna School of art history, see Kultermann, *Geschichte der Kunstgeschichte*, Ch. 15. For Max Dvořák and Alois Riegl, see Kleinbauer, *Modern Perspectives*, pp. 397-98 and 124-26.

4. Hiss and Fansler, *Research*, pp. 6-7, 35-36, 144-48, and 193-94; Kleinbauer, *Modern Perspectives*, pp. 57-61; and Rensselaer W. Lee, "Art History at Princeton," *Princeton Alumni Weekly*, 64/3 (8 Oct. 1968), 6-8 and 13.

5. For American art history, see James S. Ackerman, *Art and Archaeology* (Englewood Cliffs, N. J., 1963), pp. 187-95; and Panofsky, "Three Decades of Art History," pp. 321-46.

6. For a scholarly account of American collecting in this period, see René Brimo, *L'évolution du goût aux Etats-Unis d'après l'histoire des collections* (Paris, 1938). For an excellent analysis of the implications of museum philanthropy, see Fox, *Engines of Culture*, Chs. 1 and 2.

7. See also Henry W. Kent, *What I am Pleased to Call My Education* (New York, 1949), Ch. 10. For Kent's work, see Calvin Tomkins, *Merchants and Masterpieces: The Story of the Metropolitan Museum of Art* (New York, 1970), pp. 115-19.

8. Richard Grove, "John Cotton Dana," *Museum News*, 56/5 (May-June 1978), 33-39 and 86-88.

9. For two recent assessments of Sachs's career and the museum course, see Ada V. Ciniglio, "Paul J. Sachs," *Museum News*, 55/1 (Sept.-Oct. 1976), 48-51 and 68-71; and Karl E. Meyer, *The Art Museum: Power, Money, Ethics* (New York, 1979), pp. 40-43.

10. For the connections between museums, libraries, and settlement houses, see Fox, *Engines of Culture*, pp. 52-58.

11. Virginia Woolf, *Three Guineas* (New York, 1938), p. 76, citing *The Earlier Letters of Gertrude Bell*, ed. Elsa Richmond (London, 1937).

12. See Barbara Welter, "She Hath Done What She Could: Protestant Women's Missionary Careers in Nineteenth-Century America," *American Quarterly* 30/5 (1978), 624-38.

13. For an interesting discussion, see Nancy O. Lurie, "Women in Early American Anthropology," in *Pioneers of American Anthropology*, ed. June Helm (Seattle and London, 1966), pp. 29-81. For Mestorf, see ibid., 32, n. 4, citing Alexander F. Chamberlain, "Miss Johanna Mestorf," *American Anthropologist*, N.S. 11 (1909), 536-37.

14. Jacquetta Hawkes, Review of Margaret Murray, *My First Hundred Years*, *Antiquity*, 37 (1963), 312.

15. Phyllis W. Lehmann, "Introductory Remarks," in *A Land Called Crete: A Symposium in Memory of Harriet Boyd Hawes* (Smith College Studies in History, 45) (Northampton, Mass., 1968), p. 12.

16. Edith Hall (later Dohan), "Memoirs of an Archaeologist in Crete," ed. Katharine Page, *Archaeology*, 31/2 (March-April 1978), ll.

17. For women at the American Academy in Rome, see Lucia Valentine and Alan Valentine, *The American Academy in Rome, 1894-1969* (Charlottesville, Va., 1973), p. 50. For photos of and by Van Deman, see the catalogue of the interesting exhibition held at the American Academy in Rome, *Fotografia archeologica 1865-1914*, ed. Karin Bull-Simonsen Einaudi [Rome, 1978?]. For Van Deman's and Ashby's explorations, see Paul MacKendrick, *The Mute Stones Speak: The Story of Archaeology in Italy* (New York, 1976), pp. 317-19; for the quote, ibid., p. 320.

18. For conditions at the American School in Athens, see Louis E. Lord, *A History of the American School of Classical Studies at Athens, 1882-1942* (Cambridge, Mass., 1947), p. 94. For Hetty Goldman's choice of Halae as an excavation site, see Homer Thompson, "Introductory Remarks," in Institute for Advanced Study, *A Symposium in Honor of Hetty Goldman, 1881-1972* (Princeton, N.J., 1974), p. viii.

19. For Jane Harrison's influence on Eugénie Sellers (later Strong), see Gladys S. Thomson, *Mrs. Arthur Strong: A Memoir* (London, 1949), p. 24; for Strong's appearance and use of Morellian methods, see Sylvia Sprigge, *Berenson: A Biography* (London, 1960), pp. 176-77.

20. Samuels, *Berenson*, p. 425.

21. For the ideal of Madame de Staël, see Peter Gunn, *Vernon Lee: Violet Paget, 1856-1935* (London, 1964; reprint ed., New York, 1975), p. 48; for Sargent's influence, see ibid., p. 33.

22. Edith Wharton, *A Backward Glance* (New York, 1934), pp. 132-34.

23. William A. Coles, "The Genesis of a Classic," introduction to the 1978 edition of *The Decoration of Houses*, p. xxxv. For the career of another pioneer in interior design, see *NAW*, "Candace Thurber Wheeler (1827-1923)"; and Callen, *Women Artists of the Arts and Crafts Movement*, pp. 128-35 and 173-75.

24. Wharton, *Backward Glance*, pp. 134-35.

25. Ibid., p. 138.

26. The data on programs and degrees in archaeology comes from Hiss and Fansler, *Research*. Although the authors state that the information is incomplete, the book furnishes the most reliable data available thus far.

27. For changes in the art curriculum of various women's colleges, see ibid., pp. 150 and 158; Anna H. Knipp and Thaddeus P. Thomas, *The History of Goucher College* (Baltimore, 1938), pp. 64-66; and Dorothy A. Plum and George B. Dowell, comps., *The Magnificent Enterprise: A Chronicle of Vassar College*, (Poughkeepsie, N.Y., 1961), p. 31.

28. Agnes A. Abbot, "The Department of Art at Wellesley College," *AJ*, 21/4 (Summer 1962), 264-65; idem, *NAW*, "Alice Van Vechten Brown."

29. For membership figures, see *Bulletin of the College Art Association* (Nov. 1917), 6-8.

30. See *Twenty Years at Hull-House* (New York, 1910; Signet Edition, 1960), pp. 66-67 and 71.

31. Callen, *Women Artists of the Arts and Crafts Movement*, pp. 198-99.

32. John A. R. Pimlott, *Toynbee Hall: Fifty Years of Social Progress, 1884-1934* (London, 1935), pp. 165-73.

33. For additional information on the art program at Hull-House, see *Eighty Years at Hull-House*, eds. Allen F. Davis and Mary L. McCree (Chicago, 1969); and Helen L. Horowitz, *Culture and the City: Cultural Philanthropy in Chicago from the 1880s to 1917* (Lexington, Ky., 1976), Ch. 6.

34. Dee Garrison, "The Tender Technicians: The Feminization of Public Librarianship, 1876-1905," in *Clio's Consciousness Raised*, pp. 158-78; the quotations, from ibid., p. 161.

35. For Susan Hutchinson, see *AAA*, 23 (1926), 472, and *The Brooklyn Museum Handbook* (Brooklyn, 1967), p. 542 and Fig. 18; for Isabel Weadock, see *AAA*, 23 (1926), 485, and *Bulletin of the Detroit Institute of Arts*, 31/2 (1951-52), 39.

36. The Wellesley museum training course is described in various college announcements and newspapers, including Farnsworth Museum of Art, Wellesley College, "Museum Training Course," 1913-14; and *Wellesley Alumnae Magazine*, 11/6 (Aug. 1927), 343. For another description, see *Museum News*, 13 (1 Sept. 1935), 8. This last source states the course was given in 1911-1917, 1927-1928, and 1930-1932. Its later history is not clear; it does not seem to be mentioned after 1941.

37. For Sara Stevenson's career at the University of Pennsylvania Museum, see the egregiously titled volume by Percy Madeira, *Men in Search of Man* (Philadelphia, 1964); for the course she gave at the School of Industrial Art of the Pennsylvania (now Philadelphia) Museum in 1910/11, see "Circular of the Art Department," School of Applied Art, 34th Season. See also Paul J. Sachs to Myrtilla Avery, 14 July 1921, Wellesley College Archives, Unprocessed Acquisition A 77-48. See also Abbot, "Department of Art, Wellesley," 264.

38. Beatrice Winser, "Newark Museum Completes Ten Years of Apprentice Training," *Museum News*, 13 (15 Sept. 1935), 8; and Groves, "John Cotton Dana," 34 and 88.

39. Walter M. Whitehill, *Museum of Fine Arts, Boston: A Centennial History* (Cambridge, Mass., 1970), I, p. 393.

40. Patricia Pellegrini, Archivist of the Metropolitan Museum, supplied additional information about Morris's career, especially about the dates of her full-time employment. See also Emmanuel Winternitz, "The Crosby Brown Collection of Musical Instruments: Its Origin and Development," *Metropolitan Museum Journal*, 3 (1970), 337-56. For the history of the Ladies' Lunch Club, see Winifred E. Howe, *A History of the Metropolitan Museum of Art* (New York, 1946), II, pp. 201-03, and Chapter 10 of this volume.

41. Information on Stevenson's career at the Pennsylvania (now Philadelphia) Museum and the School of Industrial Art was obtained from the Archives of the Philadelphia Museum, courtesy of Merle Chamberlain, Archivist.

42. Figures on employment at the Metropolitan were derived from Howe, *Metropolitan Museum*, II, pp. 235-40. Information on the other museums was obtained through inquiries to librarians, archivists, and other staff of these institutions.

43. For "salon in the slums," see Jill Conway, "Jane Addams, an American Heroine," in *The Woman in America*, ed. Robert J. Lifton (Boston, 1964), p. 252.

44. Mabel Newcomer, *A Century of Higher Education for American Women* (New York, 1959), p. 18.

45. Fox, *Engines of Culture*, p. 56 and nn. 11, 57; and Thomas Munro and Jane Grimes, *Educational Work at the Cleveland Museum of Art* (2d ed. rev., Cleveland, 1952), pp. 36-37.

46. Roberta M. Fansler Alford Capers, "Recollections of the Education Department of the Metropolitan Museum of Art between 1927 and 1945," unpublished memoir.

CHAPTER 3
THE TRADITION CONTINUES (1930-1979)
Claire Richter Sherman

DEVELOPMENTS IN ART HISTORY

The four subjects of essays in Part IV, Sirarpie Der Nersessian (b. 1896), Dorothy Burr Thompson (b. 1900), Dorothy Miner (1904-1973), and Agnes Mongan (b. 1905), began their careers around 1930, the opening of a decade dominated by the Great Depression and the rise of Fascism. Despite these bleak developments, these women achieved exceptional distinction in their respective fields and as research scholars. Except for Miner, who died in 1973, as of this writing the other three continue their professional activity as scholars. Also of continued importance well into this period was the prodigious output of Erica Tietze-Conrat (d. 1958), Gisela Richter (d. 1972), and Margarete Bieber (d. 1978). A reflection of expanding opportunities, the increased numbers of women in the generation born before World War I who became interpreters of the visual arts have made the selection of subjects for inclusion in Part IV even more difficult than for the earlier periods.

As the experiences of Bieber, Tietze-Conrat, and many others attest, Fascism tore apart the fabric of European art scholarship. The emigration of many distinguished scholars from Germany and other European countries and their subsequent employment in American and English colleges and universities greatly enriched the development of the discipline in these countries.[1] Among the most far-reaching events was the removal to London of the Warburg Institute, which had been formed as a research center in Hamburg by Fritz Saxl during Aby Warburg's prolonged illness after World War I. In 1930 the first center for graduate studies in art history was founded in England when Samuel Courtauld's offer to finance such an institute was accepted by the University of London. Courtauld also offered support to the Warburg Institute in 1933. By the time Anthony Blunt became director in 1947, the Courtauld Institute had achieved a fusion of English university teaching, museum connoisseurship, and continental art history.[2] Since World War II the teaching of art history in English universities has increased to the extent that, by the early 1960s, twelve institutions offered degrees in the field. With the development of the polytechnic institutes in the 1970s, a new era opened up for the expansion of the history of art. Recently a Ph.D. program has been inaugurated in Canada, at the University of Toronto, and at this writing one has been approved at the University of British Columbia.

In the same period, the arrival of refugee scholars occurred at a time when the number of newly created, and the size of existing, departments of art history in the United States were beginning to grow enormously. A 1978 survey by the College Art Association indicates that forty-four American colleges or universities offered doctorates in art history. In the 1930s, the recently founded Institute of Fine Arts of New York University became a particularly important center for the employment of distinguished refugee scholars. The Institute's ambience in this period has been affectionately evoked by Erwin Panofsky (1892-1968), who came to the United States permanently in 1933. One of the most learned, imaginative, and gifted art historians of any period, Panofsky has exerted an immense influence as both a teacher and a scholar.[3] Panofsky had been associated with the Warburg Institute while it was located in Hamburg and later became a professor at the new University of Hamburg. After an initial appointment at the Institute of Fine Arts, he joined the Institute for Advanced Study at Princeton. Although his work has many facets, including seminal studies of *The Life and Work of Albrecht Dürer* (3rd ed., 1948), and *Early Netherlandish Painting* (1953), he is best known for elucidating the scope and method of iconology. This term connotes a further level beyond the descriptive and identifying function of iconographic investigation—one that embraces many dimensions of cultural meaning in a given image. *Studies in Iconology: Humanistic Themes in the Art of the Renaissance* (1939), which describes his methodology, has had great impact in all fields of humanistic scholarship.

Rudolf Wittkower was another German scholar associated with the Warburg Institute and the University of London before coming to the United States in 1956 to accept an appointment at Columbia, where he was known as an inspiring teacher and served as chairman of the department. Although the wide range of his interests also prevents a summary characterization, two fields in which he made outstanding contributions are those of Renaissance architecture and Italian Baroque art, especially in studies of the Italian master, Bernini.

Ernst Gombrich, an Austrian scholar who received his Ph.D. at the University of Vienna, settled in London and later became director of the Warburg Institute and author of a biography of its founder (1972). Combining the interests of the Warburg and Vienna schools, he has enriched and extended several of the main traditions of art history of the past hundred years in his writings on medieval and Renaissance art. In *Art and Illusion: A Study in the Psychology of Pictorial Representation* (1960) and subsequent books on theories of visual representation he has challenged traditional assumptions about the sources of artistic styles.

Among the distinguished art historians trained at the University of Vienna was Richard Offner, who came to New York in 1923. Offner was an important exponent of connoisseurship in the study of fourteenth- and fifteenth-century Italian painting. His interests show the continuing influence of Bernard Berenson notably in Offner's multivolume work, *A Critical and Historical Corpus of Florentine Painting*, begun in 1931.

Among the many outstanding art historians trained in the United States during the 1920s was the late Millard Meiss. Meiss, who received his doctorate from the Institute of Fine Arts of New York University, taught at Harvard, Columbia, and Princeton before his appointment as Panofsky's successor at the Institute for Advanced Study. Meiss's writings combine connoisseurship, iconography, and attention to the social context of Italian and northern European medieval and Renaissance art. His last series of books focused on the complex field of French late-medieval manuscript illumination.

Meyer Schapiro, whose writings are currently being published in four volumes, had a brilliant teaching career at Columbia. Now retired, he is famous for his gifts as a lecturer and the breadth of his culture. A medievalist, his special fields are early Christian and Romanesque art; but his writings on modern art and aesthetic theory have also become classics in these areas.

Apart from the publications of the figures just discussed, there have been few major breakthroughs in the methods and theories of art history. A more innovative and integrated approach to aesthetic, psychological, and social concerns is evident in critical and historical writing on modern architecture and art. In addition to Schapiro's work, the writings of Lewis Mumford, Sigfried Giedion, and Nikolaus Pevsner on architecture have greatly expanded both the method and knowledge of the field.

The private collecting of modern art was an important motivation for the opening of three major American museums in New York City around 1930: the Museum of Modern Art (1929), the Whitney Museum of American Art (1930), and the Guggenheim Museum (1939).[4] The founding of the Whitney Museum also marked a turning point in the positive reevaluation

of American art and culture in the thirties. Beginning in 1934, for almost
ten years, American art, past and contemporary, was greatly stimulated by
the federal government's patronage of the visual arts. As a means of employing artists who were suffering unusual hardships caused by the Depression, the Federal Arts projects sponsored a wide range of innovative programs in the arts that profoundly affected many areas of intellectual and
cultural life.[5]

Another aspect of the federal government's concern with art patronage
was signalled by the founding in 1937 of the National Gallery of Art in
Washington, D.C. As part of the Smithsonian Institution, the Freer
Gallery (1921), devoted to Oriental art, antedated the National Gallery.
Under dynamic leadership since 1964, the Smithsonian has greatly increased
the federal art presence in Washington by founding or sponsoring five
art galleries or museums. In 1978, a second building of the National Gallery
of Art was opened, an example of the continued expansion of this group
of American art museums.

A study conducted in 1971-1972 indicates that there are now 340 art
museums in the United States. These institutions have become in many
instances cultural centers for the performing as well as the visual arts. The
educational function of museums has become even more prominent and has
been expanded to reach out to attract wider community participation.
Museums still pursue an active acquisitions policy by seeking donations or
by purchases on the art market. The staging of spectacular loan exhibitions,
often from abroad, are designed to attract large audiences. Institutions
compete for grants now offered by various government agencies for
museum support. As operating funds have been affected by inflationary
pressures, additional income has been sought by increasing the scope of
museum gift shops specializing in reproductions of objects from the
institution's collections. Amid these expanding spheres of museum opera-
tions, the traditional museum functions of conservation, publication, and
research on objects already in collections demand their share of scarce
financial resources.[6]

In academe, art history is also facing an uncertain future in the face of
projected declines in enrollments and budgetary pressures. The era of
expansion of American art history, which flourished despite the Depression
and the upheavals of World War II, may be drawing to a close. During the
fifty years spanned by this third chapter, women's activities as interpreters
of the visual arts have greatly enriched the achievements in the field as a
whole.

Both the expansion of the field and the extent of women's contributions
to it are reflected in the growing volume of their publications during the
period from 1930 to 1979. For this reason, writings by women art historians

and critics have been somewhat arbitrarily divided in this chapter by period and institutional activity. The discussion of publications by archaeologists and historians of ancient art precedes the section on post-classical Western art. A separate section is devoted to a discussion of works by women on American and modern art. There follow references to important books by women on the art of various periods in the context of their activity as educators or curators in museums. In this, as in earlier periods, some women work in accepted genres of criticism and scholarship while at the same time others seek out new areas of research.

WOMEN ARCHAEOLOGISTS AND HISTORIANS OF ANCIENT ART

Classical art and archaeology continued to attract women scholars. In their active retirements, Gisela Richter (b. 1882) and Margarete Bieber (b. 1879) kept up their prodigious publication records until shortly before their deaths in 1972 and 1978 respectively. During the twenty years following her retirement from the Metropolitan, Richter produced a series of books on Greek art that reached both unusually large general and scholarly audiences. Bieber's works on *The Sculpture of the Hellenistic Age* (1955, 2d ed. 1961) and *The History of the Greek and Roman Theater* (1961) also gained a wide readership. The generosity and encouragement offered by these internationally known scholars to two generations of students also remain a vital part of their achievements.

The legacy of women's early participation in the field was important for the next generation. Christine Havelock's essay on Dorothy Burr (later Thompson) discovers one source of her subject's early interest in archaeology in the lectures she heard as a girl in Philadelphia. On these occasions Edith Hall Dohan described her work with Harriet Boyd Hawes on the Gournia excavation. In 1924, after four years at Bryn Mawr, where she studied with Mary Swindler and Rhys Carpenter, Burr found an opportunity to assist another pioneer archaeologist, Hetty Goldman, on a dig at Eutresis in Greece. The following year she went on to her own discovery of a Mycenean beehive tomb. In 1932, she became the first woman to be named a Fellow of the Agora, the ancient Athenian marketplace excavated under the auspices of the American School of Classical Studies. She gradually developed as her specialty the study of small-scale terra-cotta sculpture of the Hellenistic period. In the 1940s, Thompson held both museum and teaching posts in Toronto. Since that time, her career has been devoted to research.

Following in the paths of Edith Hall Dohan and Gisela Richter, DOROTHY KENT HILL (b. 1907), a Vassar graduate who received her Ph.D. from Johns Hopkins, pursued the career of a museum curator of ancient art. Like her colleague Dorothy Miner, Hill was one of the five professional staff members who came in 1934 to the Walters Art Gallery, Baltimore, to transform the private collection of William and Henry Walters into a public museum. There she remained for forty-three years until her retirement in 1977. Not only did Hill bring order to the Walters collection of almost four thousand objects from Greece, Egypt, Rome, and the Near East, she made significant acquisitions in many areas, invited other scholars to study the collections, and published extensively in many areas of ancient art. Hill belongs to the generation of scholars in small museums who performed simultaneously various research, educational, and editorial jobs with professional skill and unflagging personal devotion.

Although PHYLLIS WILLIAMS LEHMANN (b. 1912) began her career at the Brooklyn Museum, her major affiliation was with Smith College, where she had a distinguished teaching career from 1946 until her retirement in 1977 and also served as dean of the college from 1965 to 1970. As a student at Wellesley, Lehmann studied with Harriet Boyd Hawes, whose influence she acknowledges in her introductory remarks to *A Land Called Crete*, the publication of a symposium she organized at Smith in 1967 in Hawes's honor. Holder of a Ph.D. from the Institute of Fine Arts of New York University, Lehmann has written on a wide range of topics in Greek and Roman art. She is especially well known for her excavations and writings on the art of Samothrace, on which she collaborated with her late husband, Karl Lehmann. Her concern with the revival and survival of antique themes in Renaissance art is the theme of two essays collected in *Samothracian Reflections: Aspects of the Revival of the Antique* (with Karl Lehmann), published in 1973. The book is dedicated to the memory of her long-time Smith colleague, RUTH WEDGWOOD KENNEDY, with whom she taught a seminar on the relationship between antiquity and the Italian Renaissance. In turn, Lehmann's contributions as a teacher and scholar were honored in the exhibition (with catalogue) held at Smith in 1978 on the appropriate theme of *Antiquity in the Renaissance*.

In England, JOCELYN M. C. TOYNBEE (b. 1897), a graduate of Newnham (the second women's college founded at Cambridge) and recipient of a doctorate from Oxford, carried on the legacy of Eugénie Sellers Strong in making valuable contributions to the study of Roman art. In her published dissertation, *The Hadrianic School* (1934), Toynbee saw the public monuments erected by the emperor as evidence for regarding Roman art as part of a larger continuity within the Greek tradition. In her masterly survey, *The Art of the Romans* (1965), dedicated to Strong, Toynbee acknowledges the scholarly and personal inspiration and encouragement she received from the older scholar.

Toynbee's compatriot KATHLEEN KENYON (1906-1978) made spectacular finds as a field archaeologist. Kenyon, educated at another early women's institution, Somerville College, Oxford, excavated from 1929 at a wide range of sites in England, Africa, and the Near East. In 1952 she undertook for the British School of Archaeology in Jerusalem the excavation of the biblical town of Jericho. During the course of six years' work, she found the ruins of the "Joshua Wall" where Joshua waged his famous battle. She went on to discover twenty-nine walls at successively lower levels of the site. By the late 1950s she had found houses dating from the first half of the eighth millennium B.C., remnants of the oldest known urban development. Kenyon served as director of the British School of Archaeology in Jerusalem from 1951 to 1966. In addition to publications directed to archaeologists, she has written accounts of her work for the general reader in *Digging Up Jericho* (1957) and *The Bible and Recent Archaeology* (1978).

These American and English archaeologists and historians of ancient art represent a limited sample of the impressive record of excavations and publications produced by women in these fields. Both their educations in women's colleges and the examples of the pioneer generation stimulated their achievements.

WOMEN ART HISTORIANS AND CRITICS

One field that attracted women scholars in this period was the study of medieval illuminated manuscripts, which constitute an indispensable source for the history of medieval painting and culture. Manuscript studies had developed from the systematic cataloguing of the collections of various European national libraries as they became accessible to the public. In this country, two great private collections of manuscripts acquired by J. P. Morgan and William and Henry Walters became available for study when the Morgan Library was opened in New York in 1924, followed ten years later by the Walters Art Gallery in Baltimore. Charles Rufus Morey was a crucial figure in making the study of illuminated manuscripts part of the graduate curriculum in American universities. As a graduate student at Columbia, Dorothy Miner, the future keeper of manuscripts and rare books at the Walters Gallery, took the first seminar in this subject offered there by Meyer Schapiro. Among the first women Ph.D.s in art history, several wrote their doctoral dissertations on manuscript subjects. In addition to Myrtilla Avery, Helen Woodruff published her dissertation on an influential group of manuscripts by Prudentius, an early Christian writer. His subject, a combat between the virtues and vices called the *Psychomachia*, began a long line of literary and visual treatment of the subject in medieval art. ELEANOR PATTERSON SPENCER (b. 1895) wrote a Radcliffe dissertation on a late-fifteenth-century French illuminator, "Maître François and His Atelier." Sirarpie Der Nersessian's books of the 1930s were the published forms of her dissertations, on Byzantine and Armenian subjects, for the Sorbonne, and reflect her lifelong preoccupation with medieval manuscripts. Indeed, as Jelisaveta Allen's essay indicates, Der Nersessian, a French scholar of Armenian origin, was among the first art historians to work extensively on the cataloguing and interpretation of manuscripts from the eastern sphere of medieval Christendom. Der Nersessian's study of Armenian illuminated manuscripts of the twelfth to the fourteenth centuries, published in 1937, was the earliest substantial investigation of the subject, and it led to discoveries of the important relationship between Armenian art and that of Byzantium. Her book *Armenia and the Byzantine Empire* (1945) is a pioneer and authoritative summary of the complex interconnections between two highly developed traditions of medieval culture.

In the same period MARGUERITE DEVIGNE (1884-1965?) undertook to define the contributions of a distinctive region of northern Europe. *La sculpture mosane du XIIe au XVIe siècle* (1932), which discusses the flowering and dissemination of the art of the Meuse valley beginning in the twelfth century, is still respected as a scholarly work in the field. In 1912 Devigne became the first student to receive a doctoral diploma from the University of Liège, which had only recently begun to offer instruction in the history of art. Named professor at the Royal Academy of Fine Arts in Brussels in 1919, Devigne encountered opposition as one of the first women appointed to a Belgian art institution.

Women were also pioneers in scholarship associating Judaic culture with the dominant Christian tradition in medieval art. The study of Jewish illuminated manuscripts, ritual objects, and religious architecture became an important subject of research in this period. A distinguished Polish art historian, ZOFJA AMEISENOWA (1897-1967) published works on Jewish iconography and manuscripts. A professor at the University of Cracow, where she received her doctorate, and head of the graphics collection at the Jagellonian Library, Ameisenowa began publishing in the 1920s on manuscipts and incunabula (books printed before 1500) in that institution. In a study of 1929 on an illuminated fourteenth-century Hebrew Bible in Cracow, she posited a preexisting Jewish Biblical cycle in manuscripts as a prototype for the earliest extant Christian representations of Old Testament scenes. This hypothesis was confirmed three years later when the fresco cycle in the synagogue at Dura-Europos in Syria was excavated. Ameisenowa travelled widely in Europe before World War II and enjoyed close ties with various members of the Warburg Institute. It was in the *Journal of the Warburg and Courtauld Institutes* (1949) that she published an extremely important article clarifying connections between pictorial motives in Christian art and Jewish, Islamic, and Near Eastern religions entitled "Animal-headed Gods, Evangelists, Saints, and Righteous Men."

RACHEL BERNSTEIN WISCHNITZER (b. 1885) has also written on Jewish iconography, ritual objects, architecture, and medieval manuscripts. Born in Russia and educated there, in Warsaw, Belgium, and Germany, she was among the first European women to receive a diploma in architecture, from the Ecole Spéciale d'Architecture in Paris in 1907. Her first articles on Jewish art in Russia and Poland were published in 1914 in a book on the history of the Jews in those countries. In Berlin, where she and her husband lived in the 1920s, they published the first periodicals devoted to Jewish art. In this decade Wischnitzer also published on Jewish illuminated manuscripts in English libraries. Several major books, written after her immigration to the United States, are fundamental studies in English of European and American synagogue architecture. The strength of her architectural training is apparent in her book *The Messianic Theme in the Paintings of the Dura Synagogue*, published in 1948.

A third scholar who has written extensively on Jewish art is HELEN ROSENAU (b. 1900). Rosenau was born in Monte Carlo and educated in France and Germany, where she received her doctorate from the University of Hamburg. She has long lived in England, where she taught at various institutions. Rosenau's publications on Jewish art include a general history, works on iconography, illuminated manuscripts, and studies of synagogue architecture. She is also noted for her works on Western architecture, including those on the medieval period, the visionary eighteenth-century designer Boullée, and criticism on such themes as the social function of architecture. A brilliant exploration that draws on concepts from philosophy, sociology, and other disciplines is Rosenau's book *The Ideal City in Its Architectural Evolution* (1959). In it she traces the history of the concept of an ideal urban entity in terms of the aspirations of a particular culture or period. The scope of the book extends from Plato's ideal city through the medieval antitypes of good and evil cities embodied in Jerusalem and Babylon, to more recent forms like the nineteenth-century garden city. Rosenau has also published on the eighteenth-century French painter Jacques-Louis David (1948) and, most exceptionally for the time, in 1944, on *Woman in Art*.

Less scholarly and addressed to a broad, educated audience are two books on architecture and gardens that carry on the tradition of Edith Wharton's writings on these subjects. In *Italian Villas and Palaces* (1959) and *Italian Gardens* (1961) the English writer GEORGINA MASSON (b. 1912) displays a mastery of Italian history, culture, and artistic styles in the mode of gracefully written and informative travel literature. Although classed as guidebooks, the two volumes by EVELYN SANDBERG-VAVALÀ, *Uffizi Studies* (1948) and *Sienese Studies* (1953), are as valuable to serious students of Italian art as to tourists. These books by Masson and Sandberg-Vavalà continue a genre of writing in which women have traditionally excelled.

Analysis of the contemporary scene was the focus of the writings and teaching of architectural critic SIBYL MOHOLY-NAGY (1903-1971). Born in Dresden, she attended the universities of Leipzig and Frankfurt before entering the world of theatre and films. While working as an experimental filmmaker, she met and collaborated with the Bauhaus painter Laszlo Moholy-Nagy, whom she married in 1932. Her career as a writer began in 1950 with the publication of a biography of her husband, who died in 1946. She went on to establish a reputation as an outspoken architectural critic with *Native Genius in Anonymous Architecture* (1957). Astringently critical of current architectural practice, she set forth her views of architecture and city planning as a multileveled influence on social life in *Matrix of Man: An Illustrated History of Urban Environment* (1969). Moholy-Nagy was also active as a lecturer and taught architectural history at Pratt Institute from 1951 to 1969.

Women's activities as connoisseurs generally continued in the context of their work as museum curators. In her essay, Claire Sherman points out that Dorothy Miner's writings reflect her constant exposure to the Walters' outstanding collection of manuscripts. Miner's responsiveness to the physical evidence and the over-all design of the medieval book resulted not only from her keen eye but from long study over the years. As Diane Bohlin indicates in her essay, Agnes Mongan's judgment of old master drawings is also informed by a sensitive vision cultivated by prolonged firsthand study of the objects in the Fogg Museum and elsewhere. Connoisseurship, while a central element in both Mongan's and Miner's work, was fused with their broad background in both history and literature, in which they had extensive training.

The connoisseurship of Italian painting was the life work of KLARA STEINWEG (1902-1972). Steinweg, born and trained in Germany, produced in 1929 a doctoral dissertation on the style of Andrea Orcagna, an important Florentine painter of the fourteenth century. Just about that time, Steinweg became an associate of Richard Offner in compiling the monumental *Critical and Historical Corpus of Florentine Painting*, of which the first volume appeared in 1931. Her whole life was spent on the research and publication of this project. Although she was named coauthor after World War II and took charge of the project after Offner's death in 1965, the nature and design of the undertaking meant that her numerous discoveries in Trecento painting were not identified as such in its volumes, nor apparently were they published elsewhere.

Among the many possible contributions by women to other traditional genres of art historical scholarship, it is possible to mention only a few examples. In the area of the documentary history of art, Elizabeth Gilmore Holt (b. 1908) has rendered valuable services to students and teachers in her two-volume anthology of original source materials. Originally published as a single book in 1947, *Literary Sources of Art History: An Anthology of Texts from Theophilus to Goethe* was later expanded to include a second volume on the nineteenth century.

Although for the most part iconography tended to be integrated with other types of studies, Dorothy C. Shorr (1896-1969) produced a valuable separate work on a subject that had interested Evelyn Sandberg-Vavalà. In 1954 Shorr published *The Christ Child in Devotional Images in Italy during the XIV Century*. Trained at the Institute of Fine Arts of New York University, Shorr studied with Richard Offner. Shorr's work in rare-book rooms and print departments of several libraries and museums indicates another link in the relationship between art scholarship, printed books, and librarianship already noted in Chapter 2.

Another student of Richard Offner at the Institute of Fine Arts was GERTRUDE ACHENBACH COOR (1915-1962), whose monograph on the fifteenth-century Sienese artist *Neroccio de'Landi 1447-1500* (1961) was published shortly before her untimely death. Born in Germany, she came to the United States about 1940 and received a fellowship for graduate study at Bryn Mawr, where she received her M.A. before going on to New York University. A leading authority in the field of late medieval and Renaissance Sienese painting, she became in 1959 a research associate at the Institute of Advanced Study in Princeton and assisted Millard Meiss with the preparation of his early volumes on late medieval manuscript illumination.

A second and final example of a distinguished artistic biography is *Recherches sur Claus Sluter* (1936), a published dissertation of Aenne Liebreich. This monograph is an outstanding contribution to the literature on an important Netherlandish sculptor who worked in France around 1400. Liebreich, who already held one doctorate from the University of Bonn, apparently did not survive World War II.

Published writings by women on post-classical art maintained high standards of excellence in various genres of scholarship. Several pioneered in studies of ethnic traditions that had not previously been considered influences on the mainstream culture and art of the Middle Ages. The study of illuminated manuscripts was a field that attracted many women scholars and presented them with opportunities to produce valuable contributions to a developing branch of medieval studies. As most of these women were trained in art history on the graduate level, their works reflect academic standards of scholarship. Many, but not all, produced their scholarship while employed in colleges, museums, libraries, or research institutes. With few exceptions, their writings were addressed to specialized audiences.

WOMEN AS INTERPRETERS OF AMERICAN ART AND EUROPEAN MODERNISM

Women made important contributions to public understanding of past and contemporary American and modernist European art when these fields were unfashionable or controversial. Publications by women in those areas continued after public acceptance was won. Earlier instances of women's support of contemporary art were Margaret Fuller's appreciation of Washington Allston and Van Rensselaer's appreciation of H. H. Richardson. More recently, Erica Tietze-Conrat and her husband took up the cause of contemporary Austrian Expressionist art, and Georgiana Goddard King recognized Gertrude Stein and avant-garde French developments.

ELIZABETH McCAUSLAND (1899-1965), a Smith College graduate and art critic for the *Springfield Republican* and other journals, did a great deal to stimulate interest in American painting. With great enthusiasm for what was identifiably American, she organized exhibitions of American art in galleries and museums across the country. In 1939, for a Federal Art Project program, she wrote the short text of *Changing New York* (recently republished as *New York in the Thirties*, 1973) featuring the fine photographs of Berenice Abbott. McCausland also published biographies and monographs on such painters as the landscapist George Inness, Alfred H. Maurer, and Marsden Hartley, early modernists of the American school.

American and contemporary art were explored in various aspects by ALINE BERNSTEIN LOUCHEIM SAARINEN (1914-1972), who published critical articles and reviews in the United States and abroad. As a student at Vassar, Aline Bernstein was strongly influenced by Agnes Rindge (later Claflin) to choose a career in art. After completing an M.A. at the Institute of Fine Arts at New York University in 1941, she wrote for and became managing editor of *Art News*. A decade after the retirement of Elizabeth Cary as art critic for the *New York Times*, she took up that position. In 1962 she brought art criticism to television. Saarinen, who expressed a desire to be another Madame de Staël, thought of her television program as "a poor girl's salon."[7] Among her publications, *The Proud Possessors* (1958) contains valuable information about the history of American collecting in the nineteenth and early-twentieth centuries enlivened by amusing stories about imperious or eccentric personalities like Isabella Stewart Gardner and Edward Root.

ELLEN JOHNSON (b. 1910) has been an eloquent historian and critic of modern art, as well as an influential educator at Oberlin College. In both spheres of activity, she has enhanced the distinguished tradition of art-historical scholarship at that institution. In her volume of collected essays, *Modern Art and the Object: A Century of Changing Attitudes* (1976), Johnson has focussed on the artist's relation to nature, exemplified by his or her approach to the representation of individual objects as a means of distinguishing the essential character of various developments in modern art. The book's broad scope is matched by its clear presentation, informed by Johnson's sensitivity and lifelong study of the field.

In Europe, three German women who later became refugees were interpreters of different phases of modernism. The German art historian ROSA SCHAPIRE (1874-1954) was an early and lifelong champion of

German Expressionism. As a female doctoral candidate at the University of Zurich, Schapire experienced difficulties that prompted the subject of her first publication in 1897, "A Word on the Emancipation of Women," which appeared in the *Sozialistische Monatshefte*. An early admirer of Emil Nolde, she wrote about his work in 1907 and soon joined the Dresden Expressionist group *Die Brücke* (The Bridge) on Nolde's invitation. Visual evidence of her three decades of publication and other activities on behalf of German Expressionist artists remains in their many portraits of Schapire. She was particularly attracted to the art of Karl Schmidt-Rottluff, and in 1924 she brought out a book on his graphic work. Schapire was forced to emigrate in 1939; her moving account of her arrival in England, her new country of residence, states that she retrieved from the wreckage of her life the sum of ten marks and, astonishingly, her collection of paintings by Schmidt-Rottluff. She bequeathed part of her collection to English museums in gratitude for the hospitality she received.

Another German scholar who espoused the cause of modern art was HERTA KAUERT WESCHER (1899-1971). Although she received a doctorate from Freiburg in 1923 on sixteenth-century German painting and later worked in Berlin as an (unpaid) assistant to Max Friedländer and Ludwig Burchard, her interests soon turned to modern art as a friend and defender of the Bauhaus. She immigrated to France shortly after Hitler declared the work of the Bauhaus "degenerate art." Wescher wrote for many international art periodicals and organized exhibitions on what became a special interest, the medium of collage, which has developed extensively in the twentieth century. The term refers to a composition of fragments of printed matter and/or other materials affixed to a surface. She published the first of what was intended as a two-volume study in 1968, *Die Collage, Geschichte eines künstlerischen Ausdrucksmittels* ("Collage: History of an Artistic Means of Expression," translated into English as *Collage*, n.d.). Wescher surveyed the history and roots of the medium, giving a detailed account of the modern development before World War II, and sketching its renewed popularity in the 1950s and 1960s. Beautifully illustrated and extremely well documented, her book is a valuable contribution to the literature on the subject, including many references to the works of women artists, who showed a notable affinity for the medium.

A third German woman refugee scholar who became an interpreter of twentieth-century art is KATE TRAUMAN STEINITZ (1889-1975), though she later developed into a Renaissance scholar as well. As a young woman in Berlin, she had studied art with Käthe Kollwitz and art history with Heinrich Wölfflin. From 1918 she worked in Hanover as an artist and writer, frequently under the name of Annette Nobody, and collaborated with the Dadaist artist Kurt Schwitters on a lively range of publications. Long after, she wrote the book *Erinnerungen und Gespräche mit Kurt*

Schwitters (1963), translated as *Kurt Schwitters: A Portrait from Life* (1968). In 1936 Kate Steinitz immigrated to New York with her family. Installed as librarian of the Belt collection of Vinciana at the University of California at Los Angeles in 1945, she transformed herself into a Leonardo specialist, developing the library and publishing on Leonardo manuscripts and on such topics as Poussin's relations to the work of the Renaissance master.

The writings by women on American art and European modernism played a considerable role in making these subjects known to and understood by the general public. As critics and journalists, McCausland and Saarinen addressed wide audiences. Although Schapire and Wescher had written doctoral dissertations on the art of earlier periods, they soon became involved with contemporary art and artists, as did Steinitz. With the exception of Ellen Johnson, none of these women seems to have held regular academic appointments. The writings by women interpreters of American art and European modernism were of course not the only means by which these movements achieved public and scholarly acceptance. But they had a signal share in that development.

WOMEN AND MUSEUMS

The tremendous expansion in the number of American museums after 1930 created new employment opportunities for women. Getting in on the ground floor of an institutional enterprise before fixed social hierarchies develop has proved advantageous for many women just beginning their careers. For example, Dorothy Miner and Dorothy Kent Hill began their curatorial work at the Walters Art Gallery on the recommendation of their mentors when the formerly private collection was opening as a public museum. Agnes Mongan started at the Fogg Museum at a time when the cataloguing of the drawing collections was getting under way. It is not surprising, then, to find women actively involved in organizing and promoting the causes of modernism and American art, two fields that in the 1930s were struggling to achieve institutional recognition.

The Museum of Modern Art was founded in 1929 by three women collectors, Abby Aldrich Rockefeller, Lizzie P. Bliss, and MARY JOSE-PHINE QUINN SULLIVAN (1877-1939). Before her marriage to Cornelius J. Sullivan, Mary Quinn had had an independent career as an art teacher in the New York public schools and as a faculty member of the Pratt Institute. Women were also prominent in the life of the Museum of Modern Art in the 1930s under the directorship of Alfred H. Barr, Jr. Barr had conceived of the museum's program when he taught the first undergraduate course on modern art at Wellesley in 1927. One of Barr's carefully selected students in the Wellesley course was Ernestine Fantl, who joined the Museum of Modern Art as secretary to Philip Johnson, advanced to head of publications, and then served briefly as curator of architecture and design from November 1935 to February 1937. From 1936 to 1947, Elodie Courter, another Wellesley alumna, ran the department of circulating exhibitions and thereby took an important part in introducing modern art to the American public. Shortly after she was hired, Sarah Newmeyer, director of public relations from 1933 to 1948, was responsible for publicizing to great effect the museum's borrowing from the Louvre of Whistler's famous painting of his mother and an exhibition of Van Gogh paintings. Iris Barry played a highly influential role as creator and curator of the museum's pioneer film library.[8]

The most lasting career among these influential women was that of DOROTHY C. MILLER (b. 1904), who was associated with the museum from 1934 to 1969. Miller, an alumna of Smith College, was a graduate of the first class in the apprentice museum course started in 1925 by John Cotton Dana at the Newark Museum and continued by his successor Beatrice Winser under the direction of KATHERINE COFFEY. After two years at Newark, Miller worked in the Montclair Museum before moving to New York. She assisted Holger Cahill, whom she married in 1938, with the first Municipal Art Exhibition held at Rockefeller Center in 1934. Shortly thereafter she met Alfred Barr and came to the Museum of Modern Art as his assistant. Miller rose to the position of senior curator of painting and sculpture. She made a crucial contribution to advancement of the cause of American art by organizing a series of landmark exhibitions. Among them in 1936 was *New Horizons in American Art*, which surveyed the first year of the Works Project Administration/Federal Art Project (hereafter WPA/-FAP), of which Holger Cahill was national director. Miller evolved a close working partnership with Barr based on a similarity of outlook and sharp critical discernment on her part. Together they were influential in discovering and promoting the careers of many contemporary American artists like Mark Rothko. Miller also made signal discoveries on her own in the course of group exhibitions that helped make many reputations and in themselves became events in the history of American art.

Another important interpreter of modern art is KATHARINE KUH (b. 1904). Kuh, a Vassar graduate, has had a varied career as journalist, critic, educator, gallery owner, and art consultant. Kuh was curator of the gallery of art interpretation and of painting and sculpture at the Art Institute of Chicago, where she worked from 1937 to 1959. *Looking at Modern Art* (1955) grew out of an adult education program on the subject. It is an imaginative guide, in which individual works form the basis for wider discussions of the formal and social character of modern art. Kuh is also well known for the effective exhibits she organized as curator of the Art Institute's gallery of interpretation on such themes as "How Real is Realism" and on the explication of Cézanne's composition.

Of the few women born before 1914 who became museum directors, three
were active supporters of American art and of European modernism.
JULIANA FORCE (1876-1948) became the first director of the Whitney
Museum of American Art. Force came from a family of limited financial
resources and was working as a secretary when she met her employer's
sister-in-law, Gertrude Vanderbilt Whitney. Force was recruited by Whitney to help manage the Whitney Studio, a center organized in 1914 to assist
young artists. The two women established a close friendship and working
association. When the Whitney was founded in 1930 as a permanent
museum that would "have a vital relation to the art and to the artists of its
own country and period," Force became its director and continued in that
role until her death.[9] Force was a vibrant personality and gifted administrator, responsible for an exhibition program that encompassed annual shows
and exhibitions on special themes and for initiating a series of publications
on American art. Force also participated in organizing the first federal art
program of the Depression, the Public Works of Art Project (1933-1934).

The first director of another new institution devoted to modern art was
HILLA REBAY, Hilla Rebay von Ehrenwiesen (1890-1967). Rebay
achieved her appointment as head of the Guggenheim Museum through a
rare conjunction of circumstances. The force of her personality and her
enthusiasm for the art she admired persuaded Solomon R. Guggenheim to
assume the novel role of a patron of non-objective art and form a collection
on her recommendations. Rebay was herself a painter who ardently believed
in her duty to foster creative genius when she found it in others. Capricious,
certainly, in her taste, she gave undue amounts of museum space to her own
paintings and those of a favorite, Rudolf Bauer. Yet Rebay had a significant impact in introducing many artists and the American public to European abstract art. The Kandinskys, whose purchase she recommended,
along with works by Klee, Kokoschka, and members of the Dutch De Stijl
group, are a legacy of lasting importance.

A third woman museum director who actively supported the cause of
modern art is GRACE McCANN MORLEY (b. 1900). As first director of
the San Francisco Museum of Art (in 1935), Morley is credited with making
that institution "a vital champion of modern art."[10] Unlike Force and
Rebay, who became museum directors by virtue of their relationships with
the museum's patron, her appointment seems to have rested on outstanding
ability backed by an impressive list of academic credentials. Still, Morley's
experience indicates the importance of coming in at the beginning of an
enterprise and of making do with extremely limited resources. In her
twenty-three-year administration, Morley developed the museum as an
exhibition center to the acclaim of its constituency and created a substantial
permanent collection where originally there had been almost nothing. After
leaving the San Francisco Museum, she served for a year as assistant direc-

tor of the Guggenheim and then moved to India to become director of the National Museum in New Delhi.

Although the service of ADELYN DOHME BREESKIN (b. 1896) as director of the Baltimore Museum had many notable dimensions, none was more outstanding than her acquisition of the famous collection of modern art assembled by the Cone sisters, Dr. Claribel and Etta Cone. Breeskin, appointed in 1942 as acting director and subsequently in 1947 as director of the Baltimore Museum of Art, obtained those positions because of the difficulty of finding a male replacement for director Leslie Cheek, Jr., when he resigned to join the army during World War II. At that time, Breeskin had been a pillar (or caryatid) of the museum for twelve years, serving with distinction as curator of prints from 1938 and then as general curator. The opportunity provided by the directorship gave full range to her administrative abilities. With distinguished results, she guided the dedicated and overworked staff of an institution with fine collections but limited financial resources.

Under KATHERINE COFFEY (1900-1972), who in 1949 succeeded Beatrice Winser as director of Newark Museum, that institution's venturesome collections of both popular and contemporary avant-garde American art championed by John Cotton Dana were prominently displayed in the new building opened in 1925. In fact, Coffey, a Barnard graduate who began working at the museum around 1923, took charge of the management and equipment of this structure. For a time Coffey headed the exhibition department when such innovative shows as *American Primitives* (1930), *American Folk Sculpture* (1931), and *Aviation in Newark Industry* (1932) were organized by Holger Cahill. Appointed general curator in 1931, Coffey enthusiastically endorsed the community-outreach and educational missions of the museum and for a time served as head of the Junior Museum. She also headed the apprentice museum program begun in 1925 by Dana, which placed many young people in museum posts. Within the museum itself, she favored continuing and expanding programs of practical instruction for adults and children. Coffey's career offers another example of a woman professional who spent her entire working life in one museum.

Agnes Mongan's devotion to the Fogg Museum of Art at Harvard University is a major theme of Diane Bohlin's essay. Her accession, two years before her retirement, to the directorship of the Fogg after forty years of dedicated service seems a conspicuously belated recognition of a very distinguished career. Bohlin's account also shows the difficulties encountered by a woman making her professional way through the exclusive male hierarchies of the oldest university in the United States.

Women's employment as curators of art museums in this period continued in traditional female specialties like textiles, decorative arts, and prints. At the same time a few women entered more prestigious "mainstream" departments. As for textiles, the work of members of the first generation like GERTRUDE UNDERHILL (1874-1954) at Cleveland and Mildred Davison at Chicago carried over well into this period. At the Boston Museum of Fine Arts GERTRUDE TOWNSEND (1892-1979), who began as an assistant in 1919, became the first woman to attain full curatorial rank at that venerable institution in 1929. Townsend, who formed the museum's distinguished costume collections, held that position until 1959. Although on her retirement Townsend's job did not fall to another woman, Underhill's successor in Cleveland is Dorothy Shepherd. Another outstanding authority in this field was ADELE COULIN WEIBEL (1880-1963), who developed the textile collections of the Detroit Institute of Arts. Born in Switzerland, she was educated in English and classics at Oxford and in art history at the University of Berne. She studied also in Vienna with Josef Strzygowski and came with him to the United States as his assistant. Like Riegl, Strzygowski was interested in ornament as a touchstone of stylistic change and also of intercultural assimilation in the history of art. In 1927, Weibel accepted the invitation of W. R. Valentiner, director of the Detroit Institute, to join its staff. She has published extensively, locating her subjects within the broader context of cultural history. With the appearance of her *Two Thousand Years of Textiles* (1952), the first publication of comparable scope in the field for fifty years, she achieved international recognition.

Her somewhat younger contemporary, the Belgian MARTHE CRICK-KUNTZIGER (1891-1963), achieved eminence as an authority on tapestries, a highly significant branch of the history of Flemish art. As the recipient of a doctoral degree at the University of Liège in 1919, she completed her studies in the history of art and archaeology there shortly after Marguerite Devigne. Crick-Kuntziger entered the Royal Museum of Art and History in Brussels as an *attachée*, approximately equivalent to "assistant" in 1921 and was promoted to *conservateur* (curator) in 1936. Like Weibel, she was a thorough scholar of her subject and completed a catalogue raisonné of the Brussels collection, drawing on her previous publications on particular aspects of the tapestries. Through the choice of works for display and through catalogue contributions, she participated in major exhibitions, such as the 1953 *Exposition Bruxelles au XVᵉ siècle* ("Brussels in the Fifteenth Century").

In departments of prints, sometimes combined with drawings, women continued to hold important positions in major museums. At Cleveland, Leona Prasse was succeeded as curator by Louise Richards. From 1929 to 1934, Mildred Prentiss served as acting curator of prints and drawings at the Art Institute of Chicago, followed from 1934 to 1941 by Lilian Combs, who held the same title. From 1936 to 1969, also at the Art Institute, Margaret

O. Gentles (d. 1969) was associate curator of Oriental art and keeper of the distinguished Buckingham collection of Japanese prints. Gentles produced the second and finished the first volume of the catalogue raisonné of the Buckingham collection begun by Helen C. Gunsaulus (1886-1954), who was assistant curator of Oriental art and keeper of the same collection from 1926 to 1943. At the Boston Museum of Fine Arts, Eleanor Sayre, who joined the staff in 1945, became curator of prints and drawings in 1967. She is the second woman after Townsend to achieve that rank in this institution.[11]

Agnes Mongan's work as a curator of drawings is well known. Her publications of catalogues raisonnés of the Fogg and other collections reveal the extensive growth of American holdings in this area since World War I. The exhibitions which she put on in the 1930s and 1940s, like those organized by Dorothy Miner for the Walters on medieval manuscripts and bookbinding, served to acquaint both the general public and scholars with the range of American holdings in these areas.

Adelyn Breeskin's work in the print department of the Baltimore Museum in 1930 followed a brief period at the Metropolitan's print room ten years earlier. After her marriage ended, she started work in Baltimore, where she developed the print collection from its beginning. Her interest in Mary Cassatt, who was little known at the time, led to an exhibition of her prints and drawings in the mid-1930s and ultimately to Breeskin's definitive catalogue of the artist's graphic work (1948). In one respect the "discovery" of Cassatt reflected the growing attention to American art that was a hallmark of the 1930s. From another point of view, Breeskin's work is a notable—and rare—instance of the scholarly establishment of a woman artist's reputation by a woman curator.

While Adelyn Breeskin headed the Baltimore Museum, a series of outstanding exhibitions was organized by GERTRUDE ROSENTHAL (b. 1903), who held curatorial posts there between 1945 and 1969. A German refugee, Rosenthal first worked in Baltimore as a lecturer and art librarian at Goucher College, where Eleanor Spencer chaired the art department. Rosenthal brought distinguished scholarly credentials to her work as director of research at the Baltimore Museum. In her curatorial capacity she organized such shows as *The Age of Elegance: The Rococo and Its Effects* (with Adelyn Breeskin) in 1959 and *Four Paris Painters: Manet, Degas, Morisot, and Mary Cassatt* (1962).

Women born before World War I gradually became curators in more prestigious fields in major American art museums in this period. The new field of modern art has proved hospitable to such talented women as Katherine Kuh at the Art Institute of Chicago and Dorothy Miller at the Museum of Modern Art. At the Philadelphia Museum, Jean Gordon Lee became curator of the department of Far Eastern art in 1955. Gertrude Rosenthal at the Baltimore Museum and Dorothy Kent Hill at the Walters

Gallery offer two further examples drawn from distinguished but smaller institutions. The younger generation of women curators born after 1930 has advanced even further into fields formerly reserved for men. Yet progress in this direction at major museums has been relatively slow in view of the many capable women with the proper training, credentials, and publications.

WOMEN AS FACILITATORS OF RESEARCH AND ART ADMINISTRATORS

From the earliest stages of their involvement with the visual arts, women have played important—if often unrecognized and poorly paid—roles in facilitating research and scholarship by translations, compilations of indexes and bibliographies, collections of documents, and the like. Founding and editing scholarly or museum publications also belongs in this category of endeavor. In the nineteenth century, such work by women writers on the arts was done privately at home. As women took on more public roles, their activities as facilitators of research involved institutional and administrative functions. In this regard, Sara Yorke Stevenson's work in behalf of the archaeology department and museum of the University of Pennsylvania in the 1890s was considered precedent-shattering. The connection between facilitating research and art administration emerges in Florence Levy's publication of the *American Art Annual* and Leila Mechlin's editing of the magazine of the American Federation of the Arts, while she served as the secretary of that organization. From 1930 to the present time, women in museums have undertaken several of those functions in addition to their curatorial duties. Dorothy Miner's responsibilities as editor of publications, librarian, and keeper of manuscripts and rare books at the Walters Art Gallery are currently divided among three people. In this period, women's dual functions as facilitators of research and art administrators were to take on new dimensions in response to two great crises of the 1930s, the rise of Fascism and the Great Depression.

In other settings as well, women continued to work on scholarly enterprises as facilitators of research. An important tool of research for medievalists is the Index of Christian Art founded by Charles Rufus Morey in 1917. The Index is an iconographic index of subjects and individual works of art with pertinent bibliography extending from the early Christian era to about 1400. Organization of the Index underwent a decisive phase in the 1930s, when Helen Woodruff, one of the first women Ph.D.s in art history, became its director. Previously women volunteers worked on the Index until regular funding was found at Princeton in the late 1920s. Moreover, Morey credited Myrtilla Avery, a professionally trained librarian, with important help in correcting the early weaknesses in the system. It is rather ironic that in its formative stages the Index was maintained by women volunteers and later directed by women in an institution that did not even admit female students until the 1960s.[12]

In the 1930s, the rise of Fascism violently disrupted the centers of European scholarship. Among the institutions immediately threatened by Hitler's accession as chancellor was the Warburg Institute in Hamburg. The need to remove the Institute was recognized by Warburg's institutional legatees, Fritz Saxl (1890-1948) and GERTRUD BING (1892-1964). Under difficult conditions it was Bing who organized the actual removal of Warburg's great research library, which was received and established in London in 1933/ 1934 with the financial support of the Warburg family and Samuel Courtauld. One of the most brilliant traditions of German art history was thus transplanted to the English-speaking world and maintained through the research program of the Institute and its *Journal*, associated from 1944 with the University of London. During the Warburg Institute's early years in London, Bing's small room in the improvised library became a humane refuge for many traumatically displaced scholars.

As a young woman, Bing had studied literature and philosophy. She received a doctorate from the newly founded University of Hamburg with a dissertation on "Lessing's Concept of Necessity," written under the supervision of Ernst Cassirer, whose interest in the philosophy of symbolic forms remained a lifelong intellectual legacy. A decisive step in her life came when she joined the Warburg Institute as a librarian in 1922. She became Aby Warburg's assistant in 1927, and after his death in 1929 assumed the task of editing his collected works, published in 1932. Her profound knowledge of Warburg's ideas, evident in her scholarly emendations, were contributions of lasting importance. After Fritz Saxl's untimely death, Bing performed similar editorial labors in preparing his *Lectures* for publication. In addition to her editorship of various volumes of *Studies of the Warburg Institute*, she wrote an important article on "The Apocalypse Block— Books and Their Manuscript Models" for the *Warburg Journal* (1942) and a valuable memoir of Fritz Saxl in *Fritz Saxl: A Volume of Memorial Essays* (ed. D. J. Gordon, 1957). Bing assumed an increasingly responsible administrative role in the life of the institute, becoming vice-director (from 1944) and director (1955-1959) as well as Professor of the Classical Tradition at the University of London. Her article in the 1963 *Journal of the Warburg and Courtauld Institute* conveys her ideas about the Warburg heritage, which she did so much to preserve.

Women were also prominent in creating new institutions designed to counter the threats to artistic and intellectual life in the United States posed by another crisis of the 1930s, the Great Depression. The various programs undertaken by the Federal Art Project had several overlapping goals: offering financial and social support to artists and writers and making art an

integral part of democratic culture by increasing community participation
in art. Juliana Force's role as an organizer of the first federally funded
project (December 1933-June 1934), the Public Works of Art Project, has
already been noted. Even earlier, the College Art Association had undertaken "the first relief work program for artists in December, 1932."[13] The
president of the organization, John Shapley, gave his permission for such
actions to two women staff members, Frances Pollak and AUDREY
McMAHON (b. 1900?). McMahon had done graduate work in fine arts and
social work before becoming director of the College Art Association and
editor of its publications. McMahon and Pollak, first with private and then
with state and federal funds, set up and administered imaginative programs
that set art teachers and muralists to work in municipal and community
institutions. When the WPA/FAP program got under way in 1935, Audrey
McMahon became the head of the important New York State region and
devised and administered many influential and far-sighted programs in art
education, the commission of art works for public buildings, art therapy in
hospitals and prisons, and the establishment of community art centers.
These innovations had lasting effects on American cultural life, well after
the WPA/FAP was liquidated in 1943. After this time, McMahon worked
for various social agencies. Her career illustrates the continued connection
between social reform and art education observed earlier in the careers of
Jane Addams and Ellen Gates Starr.

Women played an important role in another WPA/FAP project, the
Index of American Design, a vital research and pictorial tool for the study
of American decorative and folk arts. Beginning in 1935, Romana Javitz,
head of the New York Public Library's Picture Library, and Ruth Reeves, a
New York textile designer, saw the necessity for a project to record in
pictorial form the American heritage in the decorative, applied, and
popular arts. The idea of the Index was approved by Holger Cahill, national
head of the WPA/FAP, who had long been interested in American folk art.
After the project was adopted by the WPA/FAP, Reeves became national
coordinator and later field expert of the project. Also taking an important
part in the project, first as national editor and later as coordinator of
research, was Constance Mayfield Rourke (1885-1941), noted writer on
American folklore and humor. Frances Lichten, Pennsylvania supervisor of
the Index, published in 1946, on the basis of the material she collected, a
book on *Folk Art of Rural Pennsylvania*. The Index, housed in the National
Gallery of Art in Washington since 1944, brought American folk art to the
attention of a large public and made its inheritance a visible part of American culture.[14]

A third aspect of the WPA/FAP programs in which women took a
decisive role was related to the development of community arts centers.
Among these vital neighborhood associations the Harlem Community Arts

Center was outstanding. As the result of the Harlem Renaissance of the 1920s, black artists had gained a sense of their common cultural identity. Encouraged also by the Harmon Foundation exhibitions of the work of Afro-American artists held from 1928 to 1933, a group of black artists formed the Harlem Artists' Guild. This organization requested that the FAP sponsor an art center in Harlem. AUGUSTA SAVAGE (1892-1962), a gifted black sculptor, had set up an art school in Harlem that provided excellent training for black artists. Savage also helped many black artists with enrollment in the WPA programs by documenting their accomplishments. Savage aided the work of GWENDOLYN BENNETT (b. 1902), a painter who was director of the Harlem Community Arts Center from 1937 to 1940. From its opening, attended by Eleanor Roosevelt, the Harlem center became an important focus for art education, innovative exhibitions on art and psychotherapy, and a visible symbol of the aspirations and accomplishments of black culture.[15]

Another black woman artist, the noted painter LOIS MAILOU JONES (b. 1905), who taught painting and design at Howard University for about forty years, has supported and promoted the cause of Afro-American art by her research, publications, and organization of exhibitions. Beginning in the 1960s, Jones received a series of research grants from Howard University to collect visual materials and biographical data on the Afro-American art heritage. She has travelled to Haiti, Jamaica, and various African countries to interview artists and gather visual and biographical documentation that she presented to the archives of the Howard University Art Gallery. The results of Jones's project on Caribbean and Afro-American women artists, soon to be published by the Howard University Press, will include slides of their work that she made.[16]

The achievements and contributions of women as facilitators of research and art administrators in the period under review illustrate only a small sample of such activities. These examples indicate, however, that women's roles as guardians and preservers of culture have taken on new dimensions as their public roles increased. Women's contributions in this area, whether in the private or public spheres, have rarely received the recognition they deserve.

ART EDUCATORS IN THE WOMEN'S COLLEGES

In this period, women's education in the visual arts largely followed the pattern established by the preceding generation, except that graduate study was carried on in a greatly expanded number of universities. Bryn Mawr was still the only independent women's college to offer the doctorate in art history and archaeology. Beginning in 1963, women studying in the fine arts department at Harvard received the Ph.D. from that institution, rather than from Radcliffe, which had awarded it previously. The other women's colleges continued to offer excellent undergraduate programs led by an outstanding group of female scholars. One interesting development which occurred at Barnard and Goucher Colleges was the addition of practical studio courses in art to the curriculum. As a historian of Barnard College put it:

For many years the leading women's institutions had avoided like the plague any suspicion of those ladylike accomplishments which the girls' schools of a former century had taught—painting, piano playing, ballroom dancing, and the like. But now, having proved that women could do exactly the same work as was required of men in the sciences and the classics, women's colleges dared to interest themselves in some of these arts and amenities.[17]

At two new women's colleges founded around 1930, Sarah Lawrence and Bennington, the studio and performing arts were stressed at the expense of structured art history programs offered by the more traditional women's schools.

At Wellesley, 1929 marked the changing of the guard as Myrtilla Avery took over the direction of the art department upon the retirement of Alice Van Vechten Brown, who had served in that capacity for thirty-three years. Avery added new courses on Far Eastern, Islamic, Roman, and Byzantine art. To teach this last subject for the first time at a women's college, Avery persuaded Sirarpie Der Nersessian to come to Wellesley. Jelisaveta S. Allen's essay gives a full account of Der Nersessian's contribution to the department, both before and after 1937, when, on Avery's retirement, she succeeded her as chairperson.

After Agnes Mongan graduated from Bryn Mawr, where Georgiana Goddard King's teaching had deeply impressed her, she went to Europe to study with the Smith College Graduate Program in a seminar led by RUTH WEDGWOOD KENNEDY (1896-1968) and her husband Clarence. Mongan credits the intensive study of original works of art in the seminar with having provided an excellent foundation for her achievements in connoisseurship. Ruth Wedgwood Kennedy, who received her B.A. from Radcliffe in economics and a diploma from Oxford in the same subject, turned to art history after her marriage. She made distinguished contributions to the study and teaching of her special field, the Italian Renaissance, in her monograph on Baldovinetti (1938) and in *The Renaissance Painter's Garden* (1948). Clarence Kennedy, a noted photographer, prepared the typography and illustrations for these and other publications. Ruth Kennedy's influence as a colleague and teacher of Italian Renaissance art has been acknowledged by Phyllis Williams Lehmann; her students deeply valued the memories of Kennedy's love of Italy and of Renaissance culture that her classes and family hospitality evoked.

At Barnard, MARION LAWRENCE (1901-1978), after teaching at Bryn Mawr and Wellesley, chaired the art department from 1938 to 1967. Lawrence, a Bryn Mawr alumna (class of 1923), was one of the first Radcliffe Ph.D.s in art history. She would have preferred to receive her degree from Princeton, as she was a student of Charles Rufus Morey. As Princeton remained closed to women until the 1960s, Lawrence "made do" with Radcliffe, as Morey taught there as a visiting professor. Morey introduced her to the field of Early Christian art, and she became a specialist in the sarcophagi of that period. Her monograph on *The Sarcophagi of Ravenna* (1945) and other publications in this area remain standard works in the field. Lawrence helped Margarete Bieber to find a job at Barnard and was a firm supporter of her students, who regarded her character and achievements as models for their professional aspirations.

At Vassar College AGNES RINDGE, later AGNES RINDGE CLAFLIN (1900-1977), a Radcliffe B.A. and Ph.D. in art history (1928), had a notable career as professor and head of the art department and director of the Art Gallery. Her book *Sculpture* (1929), based on her dissertation, recalls the aesthetic rather than the historical approach characteristic of an earlier era in fine arts instruction. Yet her attention to recent developments in twentieth-century art reflects a new interest on the part of scholars. At Harvard, Rindge had met Alfred Barr and others who would have decisive parts in founding the Museum of Modern Art, where she later served as an administrative officer in 1943/44. She maintained a lifelong interest in contemporary art and established friendships with famous artists. Claflin also fostered the collection and study of modern art at the Vassar College Art Gallery, and in 1939 compiled a catalogue of the entire collection. She taught at Vassar from 1923, serving as the head of the department from 1943 to 1965. Claflin was instrumental in bringing to Vassar several outstanding German refugee scholars of the first rank, including Richard Krautheimer and Adolf Katzenellenbogen, whose presence added luster to the department. Claflin launched many of her students and supported them along the path to outstanding careers in the arts as critics, journalists, teachers, and museum professionals.

In short, the tradition of women teaching women at the colleges mentioned here, as well as at other institutions, continued to bear fruit in providing excellent training and role models for new generations of students. These are considerable accomplishments in themselves. Yet it must be recognized that distinguished work at women's colleges did not result in the appointment of women of the high academic caliber of those just mentioned to prestigious graduate faculties of art history in American universities. In fact, Sirarpie Der Nersessian, named Henri Focillon professor of art and archaeology at Harvard in 1953, is the only woman discussed here to receive such an appointment.

CRISES, CHANGE, AND CONTINUITY
IN WOMEN'S LIFESTYLES

In the nineteenth century, the ability to travel was both a requirement for professional achievement and a means of asserting independence for women writers on the arts and archaeologists. But in the 1930s travel became a prerequisite for survival for many European women scholars, and knowledge of foreign languages essential for new lives in alien lands. The attempted genocide of the Armenian people by the Turks in 1915, prefiguring Hitler's attempt to eradicate the Jews, forced the young Der Nersessian sisters to flee Constantinople; but it was the fury of Hitlerian persecution that had the most profound effect on the lifestyles of European women scholars.

In the removal of the Warburg Institute, Gertrud Bing's courage and resourcefulness helped sustain her colleagues; and she in turn had the support of her Warburg associates. For Margarete Bieber, a single woman with an adopted child, the triumph of Hitler was particularly traumatic for several reasons. It came, first of all, at a time when she had finally arrived at the top of the academic hierarchy; and in addition, Bieber, like many German scholars a member of a converted Jewish family, did not consider herself subject to Hitler's anti-Semitic edicts. After her dismissal from Giessen in 1933, she was first offered academic positions in England and the United States that would not permit her to lecture. After an initial appointment at Barnard, she became a member of the faculty of the department of art and archaeology at Columbia. Her position there reflected the prevailing discrimination against women in such prestigious universities: although a scholar of the first rank internationally, she was never made a full professor and achieved associate rank only in 1947, a year before her retirement.

Erica Tietze-Conrat had not previously held a teaching or museum post. Her acceptance of occasional teaching assignments suggests, however, that she might have welcomed such a position, but one never materialized. Even more surprising was the inability of Hans Tietze to secure a permanent teaching or museum post. Colin Eisler suggests in his lively and moving chronicle "*Kunstgeschichte* American Style" that a pervasive anti-Semitism in American museums may have proved an obstacle to employment for Tietze and other German refugees. The Russian-born Rachel Wischnitzer, who had always maintained her Jewish affiliation, was already a much-published scholar of Jewish art before her arrival in New York in 1940, but she felt that her immigration called for the acquisition of American academic credentials. In her mid-fifties she began studying at the Institute of Fine Arts at N.Y.U., where she worked with Karl Lehmann and Richard Offner and received her M.A. in 1944. But, shortly before taking her Ph.D. examinations in 1944, the shocking news of her father's death at the hands of the Nazis two weeks before the liberation of Paris discouraged her from pursuing her academic goals. She did, however, eventually achieve an academic career as a professor at Stern College of Yeshiva University in New York City, while adding an array of English-language publications to those she had written in Russian, German, and French.

Of course, both men and women shared the ordeal of the refugee scholar. By and large, the American academic community was sensitive to their plight and, in the difficult circumstances of the Depression, tried to find employment for them. The women's colleges also played a part in this effort. Margarete Bieber's initial appointment at Barnard received the support of Marion Lawrence and of Gisela Richter and Hetty Goldman. Agnes Rindge Claflin's role at Vassar in hiring refugee scholars has been noted. Gertrude Rosenthal was hired as art librarian at Goucher by Eleanor Spencer, and Gertrude Achenbach (later Coor) received a fellowship for graduate study at Bryn Mawr.

Certainly the upheavals of the 1930s, foreign and domestic, gave rise to a new concern with social problems on the part of women art professionals. Audrey McMahon's relief work for contemporary artists signalled the kinds of programs initiated by the WPA/FAP; for example, the Harlem Community Arts Center and the Index of American Design, in which women took active roles. Educational programs within museums also took note of the needs of the unemployed (as at Newark) and of the newly arrived refugees. Roberta M. Fansler Alford Capers recalls that at the Metropolitan:

Our refugee friends were the first to tell us clearly what our program meant to them: a place where lonely people could come together around a common interest which tended to knit them together; where a solitary person could at least call the lecturer by name and count on a friendly response and possibly an interesting after-lecture conversation.[18]

As in the 1890 to 1930 period, female networks flourished on an informal rather than on an organized basis. Among the subjects of essays in Part IV, Agnes Mongan, who acknowledged the influence of Georgiana Goddard King, saw through the press King's collection of unpublished essays, *Heart of Spain*. Dorothy Miner's editorship of *Studies in Art and Literature for Belle da Costa Greene* similarly honors the memory of her mentor and friend. Sirarpie Der Nersessian, in turn, dedicated her catalogue of *Armenian Manuscripts in the Walters Art Gallery* to Miner's memory, reflecting a collaboration and friendship going back almost forty years. Dorothy Burr Thompson remembers accounts of the excavations of Harriet Boyd (Hawes) and Edith Hall (Dohan) she heard as a girl and values her studies with Mary Swindler. Hawes was certainly an inspiration for her Wellesley student Phyllis Williams Lehmann. Agnes Rindge (later Claflin) influenced Aline Bernstein Saarinen's choice of art as a career and launched many other young women as well. The same holds true of Marion Lawrence, Ruth Wedgwood Kennedy, Myrtilla Avery, Eleanor Spencer, and Sirarpie Der Nersessian. Indeed, the large number of women interpreters of the visual arts who graduated from women's colleges demonstrates the importance of female role models as examples of professional achievement.

Even earlier in their development, the subjects of essays in Part IV received encouragement from their families, which were of the middle or professional classes. Sirarpie Der Nersessian found a model of intellectual and cultural associations in the life and writings of her uncle, a Patriarch of the Armenian Church, while enjoying the advantages of a superior educational and artistic training provided by her parents. Dorothy Burr (Thompson) noted that her novelist mother's writing was a serious pursuit that could not be disturbed, while her lawyer father fostered her verbal and critical abilities. Dorothy Miner was introduced to the classics and to the museum world by her father, a distinguished marine biologist. Both Burr and Miner were as children and young women interested in drawing and painting. Agnes Mongan's father, a doctor, wanted his daughters to have the best possible education for women, while her mother passed on to her children an interest in literature and taught them how to distinguish between visual forms in nature. Dorothy Miner, like Der Nersessian and Mongan, attended a female preparatory school where she was encouraged in her artistic and intellectual pursuits.

The unmarried subjects of essays found additional support of different kinds from family members. Agnes and Betty Mongan and Sirarpie and Arax Der Nersessian are closely identified sisters, as were Gisela and Irma Richter and, in their later years, Georgiana Goddard King and her sisters, Margaret King and Ella Adams. Dorothy Miner remained close to her family, including her twin brother, Dwight.

Women continued to find intellectual and social stimulation in entertaining friends and colleagues in distinctive settings, domestic or otherwise, that reflected their tastes and interests. The apartments of Margarete Bieber in New York and of Gisela Richter in Rome and the Der Nersessians' quarters at Dumbarton Oaks are examples of gatherings and environments fondly remembered by their guests, including young people who were welcomed by these distinguished women.

Der Nersessian, Miner, and Mongan never married. Other women of this generation prominent at the women's colleges generally remained single or married late in life. Dorothy Burr Thompson gave up her career for some years in order to raise her children. Like Erica Tietze-Conrat, she has maintained a separate professional identity, while benefiting from the support and opportunities offered by her husband's career as an archaeologist. In the museum world, too, only a minority of married women, and particularly of those with children, enjoyed uninterrupted professional careers. The choice between marriage and professional achievement, although often not expressly formulated, continued until the advent of the women's movement in the early 1970s prompted a rethinking of social attitudes. Until that time —and even today—the old justification of women's involvement with the visual arts on a nonprofessional level continued with the survival of their identification as guardians and transmitters of culture.

The remarkable productivity of the four subjects in this chapter continues the records of their predecessors. However, their bibliographies, impressive as they are, are not the only tangible evidence of their achievements. As teachers, editors, and administrators of various scholarly enterprises, each assumed, and completed with distinction, a range of work seemingly impossible for one individual to accomplish in a single lifetime. Their record is all the more remarkable in view of the continuing social disadvantages faced by women in the academic and museum worlds. If on the basis of scanty evidence it appears that women have not become theoreticians or leaders of schools of academic art history, the history of the limitations on their social and professional positions may explain their absence from these categories. Surely recognition of the dimensions of human and professional achievements by these and other women as interpreters of the visual arts is long overdue.

NOTES

1. See Colin Eisler, *"Kunstgeschichte* American Style: A Study in Migration,"* in *The Intellectual Migration: Europe and America 1930-1960,* eds. Bernard Bailyn and Donald Fleming (Cambridge, Mass., 1969), pp. 544-629. See Kleinbauer, *Modern Perspectives,* for further information on Giedion, 40; Gombrich, 72-73 and 271-73; Mumford, 11-12; Offner, 47 and 107-08; and Schapiro, 11, 74-75, and 93-94.

2. Peter Lasko, "L'Institut Courtauld et l'histoire de l'art en Grande-Bretagne," *Revue de l'art,* 30 (1975), 87-91; English text, 114-15.

3. For Panofsky's own account of his experiences, see "Three Decades of Art History." See also Kleinbauer, *Modern Perspectives,* 62-63 and 193-94; and Eisler, *"Kunstgeschichte,"* 582-83.

4. For the founding of the Whitney Museum, see B. H. Friedman, *Gertrude Vanderbilt Whitney* (New York, 1978); for the Museum of Modern Art, Russell Lynes, *Good Old Modern: An Intimate Portrait of the Museum of Modern Art* (New York, 1973); and for the Guggenheim, John H. Davis, *The Guggenheims: An American Epic* (New York, 1978).

5. For a useful survey of the Federal Art Project, see Richard D. McKinzie, *The New Deal for Artists* (Princeton, N.J., 1973). For a convenient bibliography, see Francis V. O'Connor, ed., "The New Deal Art Projects," *Federal Art Patronage Notes,* 3/3 (Summer, 1979).

6. For a study of American museums, see National Endowment for the Arts, *Museums USA: Art, History, Science, and Other Museums* (Washington, D.C., 1974). For a review of problems facing American museums, see Meyer, *The Art Museum*; and Alexander, *Museums in Motion.*

7. Marion Marzolf, *Up from the Footnote: A History of Women Journalists* (New York, 1977), p. 169.

8. For the women staff members at the Museum of Modern Art, see Lynes, *Good Old Modern*, especially 108-21.

9. Juliana Force, "The Whitney Museum of American Art," *Magazine of Art*, 39/7 (Nov. 1946), 271 and 328.

10. Nathaniel Burt, *Palaces for the People: A Social History of the American Art Museum* (Boston, 1977), p. 392.

11. The Boston Museum of Fine Arts, the Art Institute of Chicago, the Philadelphia Museum, and the Cleveland Museum of Art provided information about women curators. For Helen Gunsaulus and Margaret Gentles, see *Art Institute of Chicago Quarterly*, 49/1 (Feb. 1955), 6-8. For an obituary of Gentles, see *GBA*, 75 (Jan. 1970), 28.

12. For Avery's help, including training Woodruff and two staff members of the Index, see Morey's tribute in Florence Converse, *A History of Wellesley College: A Chronicle of the Years 1875-1938* (Wellesley, Mass., 1939), p. 252. See also Helen Woodruff, *The Index of Christian Art at Princeton University, A Handbook* (Princeton, N.J., 1942), pp. vii-ix.

13. The Gallery Association of New York State; Marlene Park and Gerald E. Markowitz, exhibition catalogue, *New Deal for Art: The Government Art Projects of the 1930s with Examples from New York City and State* (Hamilton, N.Y., 1977), p. xii.

14. See Holger Cahill, "Introduction," in Erwin O. Christensen, *The Index of American Design* (New York, 1950), pp. ix-xvii; and William F. McDonald, *Federal Relief Administration and the Arts: The Origins and Administrative History of the Arts Projects of the Works Progress Administration* (Columbus, Ohio, 1969), pp. 441-58.

15. See Gwendolyn Bennett, "The Harlem Community Art Center," in *Art for the Millions: Essays from the 1930s by Artists and Administrators of the WPA Federal Art Project*, ed. Francis V. O'Connor (Greenwich, Conn., 1973), pp. 213-15. See also McDonald, *Federal Relief Administration*, 410-15.

16. Interview with Lois Mailou Jones, 26 November 1979.

17. Marian C. White, *A History of Barnard College* (New York, 1954), pp. 132-33. See also Barbara Jones, *Bennington College: The Development of an Educational Idea* (New York 1946); and on Sarah Lawrence, Constance Warner, *A New Design for Women's Education* (New York, 1940).

18. Capers, "Recollections of the Education Department of the Metropolitan Museum," unpublished memoir.

PART II   *NINETEENTH-CENTURY WRITERS ON THE ARTS*

CHAPTER 4

ANNA JAMESON
(1794-1860): SACRED ART AND SOCIAL VISION

Adele M. Holcomb

Actively possessing the foreground in D. O. Hill's calotype portrait, the likeness of Anna Jameson is that of a writer on art in the midst of her labors (Figure 1). One arm leans on a volume beside a paisley shawl; the right hand holds spectacles that have apparently just been removed, and a magnifying glass for the closer inspection of engravings hangs from a ribbon around her neck. Like the study of "Mr. Bryson, horologer," who fingers a watch in the same Hill-Adamson Series of 1843-1848, or of the Newhaven "Fisher-woman" bending over a wicker basket, the image of Anna Jameson belongs to the genre of the occupational portrait. Her morning cap and the informal setting recall working portraits of eighteenth-century writers, while her seriousness seems attuned to the current Victorian discussion of the significance of human work.

Jameson's definition by professional attributes and her nearly magisterial presence are exceptional among Hill's photographs of women. At the same time, suggestions of reticence and fatigue qualify the authorial persona. She had by this point in the mid-1840s been active for two decades as a writer of works ranging from instructional books for children to travel literature and social criticism in the vein of Madame de Staël. Her course was marked by the gradual acquisition of reputation against resistances that had to do with her gender, Irish background, and modest family circumstances. Jameson did not announce her specialization as a writer on art until 1842, with *A Handbook to the Public Galleries of Art in and near London*. The commitment came relatively late, then, in her career, though it drew on an extensive earlier knowledge of and interest in art; it would occupy the remaining eighteen years of her life. During this comparatively brief span, she produced two catalogues of London galleries that are indispensable records

Figure 1. Portrait of Anna Brownell Jameson, by D. O. Hill and R. Adamson, ca. 1845. From album *Calotype Studies* (II, 10) presented by the photographers to the Royal Academy in London in 1848. (*Courtesy of the Trustees of the National Portrait Gallery, London*)

of the history of taste, a widely influential account of Italian painting from the thirteenth to the sixteenth centuries, six volumes (two published post-humously) that comprise the first systematic study of Christian iconography in English, and other significant publications.

For whatever its value might have been to a student of the visual arts, university education was not available to women in Anna Jameson's life-time. Like Jane Marcet and Harriet Martineau, contemporaries who similarly laid claim to a specialized expertise, she was substantially self-educated. Her professional opportunities lay solely in publication, such curatorial posts as existed at the time not being accessible to women. Even the exceptional possibility of public lecturing came late in Jameson's career and was then connected not with art, but with her advocacy of improved employment prospects for women. Finally, she had to contend with severe disappointment and exacting responsibility in her personal life, as can be seen in the circumstances of her family background and private history.

Anna Brownell Murphy was born in Dublin in 1794, the first child of a miniature painter, Denis Murphy, and his English wife, whose name is not recorded. The Murphys emigrated to England in 1798, opportunely in view of Denis Murphy's adherence to the cause of the United Irishmen; they took Anna with them, leaving two younger daughters to be sent for later. The family settled in Whitehaven, where a fourth daughter was born, and in 1803 moved permanently to London.

Traits of her inner life between ages five and ten that Anna Jameson later remembered were the obstinacy of a strong personality and a corrosive vindictiveness. In retrospect she thought that the latter very disturbing quality was dispelled only by a developing sense of her own powers. In this and kindred dilemmas of feeling, she was not helped by the religious teach-ings to which she had been exposed. The absence of any doctrinal bias in Jameson's later interpretation of Christian art may indeed be related to her early experience: "though no pains were spared to *indoctrinate* me," her understanding of Bible lessons was extremely "confused and heterodox."[1] Hannah More's tracts she considered positively malignant, with their insistence on the risk of being found out as the main objection to wrong-doing. In her affections, Anna suffered severe anxiety that the love she invested in others might not be returned. Sturdy independence was a salient characteristic of her personality as a child, in the recollection of a younger sister, Camilla. Anna's reveries were variations on a leading theme:

. . . that I was always a princess heroine in the guise of a knight, a sort of Clorinda or Britomart, going about to redress the wrongs of the poor, fight giants, and kill dragons; or founding a society in some far-off solitude or desolate island, which would have rivalled that of Gonsalez, where there were to be no tears, no tasks, and no laws,—except those which I made myself. . . .[2]

Anna's early occasions for "heroinism"* were largely confined to the nursery where, for several years after the move to London, she supervised her sisters' lessons. Little is known of her preparation for this role except that for a time, from 1802 or 1803, she had been taught by the governess who accompanied Anna's younger sisters from Dublin. Anna's first literary efforts were stories written for the younger girls' instruction and amusement. With particular encouragement from her father, she was resourceful as well in advancing her own education, notably in the acquisition of languages. Denis Murphy knew only a modest success in his work,[3] and from an early age Anna shared her parents' anxiety about money. Partly to help out at home, she accepted a position as governess to the Marquess of Winchester in, probably, 1810, serving for a period of four years. In 1821 she was in the employ of the Rowles family of Bradbourne Park and with them made her first trip to the continent. From 1822 until her marriage in 1825, the Littletons of Teddesley engaged her in what would be her last stint as a governess.

Her experience in what Margaret Maison has called the genteel slave trade must mainly be inferred from indirect evidence. In 1846 Jameson wrote a pamphlet for the Governesses' Benevolent Institution in which she explored with deep feeling the anomalous expectations and difficult conditions of work in what was almost the only form of remunerative employment for educated women. But while forming her opinions she had the wit to profit from occasional opportunities in a generally unsatisfactory calling. Service with the Rowles family took her on a Grand Tour itinerary of sites she had known only from engravings and written descriptions, and she recorded her impressions at length in a journal. These would furnish *A Lady's Diary*, anonymously published in 1826 and reissued in the same year as *The Diary of an Ennuyée*.

The heroine of the *Diary* travels not as the appendage of a household but at her own pleasure, fulfilling a hunger for independence such as that which had been noticed in her creator as a child. An unhappy love affair causes the *Ennuyée* to sigh and languish at intervals throughout the account, which closes with her suicide. In between what one feels to be the real enterprise of the book goes forward: an enthusiastic encounter with the monuments of ancient Roman, Renaissance, and Baroque art. Ellen Moers has recently pointed out the resemblance of this combined novel and Baedeker to Madame de Staël's *Corinne* (1807), illuminating the extent to which Jameson's response to the work of her elder contemporary epitomized that of a generation of women writers.[4] What has not been noticed in the *Diary* is the evidence of close and thoughtful scrutiny of works of art. It is exampled in a disquisition resulting from the heroine's practice of taking her

*For this term, see Ellen Moers, *Literary Women: The Great Writers*, New York, 1976.

portable seat to the Pitti to "minutely study and compare the styles of the different masters." She is at pains to distinguish in her idea of style between the artist's conception of subject—essentially the interpretation of human character and emotion—and the manner of execution; the former belongs to the mind, while the latter is simply mechanical.[5] Another instance of her seriousness is the sustained comparison she makes between Raphael's *Transfiguration* and Domenichino's *Communion of St. Jerome* in the Vatican.[6]

The plot of the *Ennuyée* had a basis, however embellished, in Anna Murphy's broken engagement to Robert Jameson, a young barrister and would-be poet from Ambleside who shared her literary interests. They met and became engaged in 1821. Misgivings on her part seem to have been responsible for the termination of the engagement before she left for the continent in the same year. However, they married in 1825 and set up housekeeping in Bloomsbury.

Early on there were signs that the marriage would not be successful; apparently it was never consummated.[7] Anna complained of Robert's "coldness" and bizarre lapses of courtesy towards her. He did urge her to write, and his encouragement was possibly crucial in her resolve to work up the materials of her travel diary with a view to publication. Even so, her diffidence is clear in the decision to publish anonymously and in the fact that she bartered away her right to any profits from the *Ennuyée* in return for a Spanish guitar.

After attempting for four years to establish himself in London, Robert Jameson renounced the effort and left for a position as puisne (junior) judge in Dominica. His letters from the West Indies attest to his wretchedness there. For his deliverance from this cul-de-sac he would be indebted to the patronage of the writer and legal reformer Basil Montagu,[8] assisted by the influence of Anna, who was friendly with the Montagus in London. His next appointment was far more advantageous: in 1833 he went to Toronto as attorney-general of Upper Canada.

With the vaguely defined intention that they would be reunited once Robert was appropriately established, Anna remained in London. She had begun to earn money from her writing with *The Loves of the Poets* (1829). Whatever was forthcoming from her work was needed to supplement remittances from her husband. She was contributing to the support of her parents' household, which included two unmarried daughters at this period.

Loves of the Poets, followed by *Memoirs of Celebrated Female Sovereigns* (1831) and *Characteristics of Women* (1832), mark Jameson's transformation from a hesitant amateur to a critic commanding serious respect in English and, subsequently, German literary circles. They are of interest in the present context because they register her growing professionalism and because they anticipate certain directions of her later writing on art.

Published as by the unnamed author of the *Ennuyée*, *Loves of the Poets* is introduced by a quotation in which Madame de Staël characterizes her pursuit of celebrity as compensation for disappointment in love. Reference to the idea that fame for a woman is "love generalised" is of course an allusion to Jameson's situation and to her hope for literary reputation. At first glance *Loves of the Poets*, which proposes to examine "the influence which the beauty and virtue of women have exercised over the characters and writings of men of genius,"[9] would perhaps seem a frothy support for such aspirations. But the character of the book, a well-written exposition of cultural history based on extensive reading, rather belies its introduction. In addition its view of the far-reaching impact of chivalry on attitudes towards women—"in the ages called gothic and barbarous . . . the sex began to take their true station in society"[10]—is one that would play a shaping role in Jameson's work on Christian symbolism.

"Heroinism" found broader scope in the subject of *Celebrated Female Sovereigns*. Its theme is justified by the desire to elucidate "how far the feminine character may be so modified by education, as to render its inseparable defects as little injurious to society, and its peculiar virtues as little hurtful to herself, as possible."[11] In the event, Jameson glories in such achievements as the building programs of Zenobia of Palmyra and the Latin oratory of Joanna I of Naples; we hear no more of "inseparable defects." With this work the author further defined her genre as social and cultural history directed by an interest in the personality traits and attainments of women.

As though to close a sequence, *Characteristics of Women* set out to analyze the types of female character in a comprehensive manner. In assuming that psychological actualities in some normative sense could be fruitfully approached through the study of Shakespeare's characters, Jameson endorsed the Romantic belief that Shakespeare's imagination in its scope and richness was coterminous with Nature itself. Her sympathy with the situation of women in society channeled and deepened her appreciation of the vividness, nobility, and moral energy of a Helena or a Portia. Invoking a classical conception of biographical types, the author ordered her female subjects as they exemplify leading qualities of intellect, of passion, or of affection. The warmth and intelligence of her interpretation elicited an enthusiastic response and brought Jameson new confidence as a writer.

Vital to this success were the grace and fluency of her style and a remarkable skill in creating persuasive "entrances" to her subjects. Jameson's manner is entirely unpretentious and tentative, so far from the pontifical tone frequent among male writers of the Victorian period as to seem virtually a criticism of their certitude. At the same time, her sustained rhetorical flights have affinities with those of contemporaries like Carlyle, while they almost certainly influenced Ruskin's style. Her passage on the German painter Julie von Egloffstein in a work of 1834 should, for example, be compared with Ruskin on Turner's Yorkshire drawings.[12] Jameson's tact in the proportioning of her materials and in the relation of illustration to argument and the engaging interest of her illustrations are exemplary. From the standpoint of content, her concentration on qualities of mind and character in the early work announced her commitment as a writer on art to those fundamental principles of Renaissance and Baroque theory concerned with the *istoria* or subject of painting or sculpture, dramatically represented to display an action and the ideas or passions associated with it. Finally, that Jameson's early writings were explicitly addressed to a female audience is a fact of importance for her later work, even though she did not direct herself solely to women from 1834 on. With a single exception that will be noted, she spoke as a woman from what she regarded as a distinctively female point of view. Her conception of those qualities that were characteristically womanly affected her views of history and of the history of art, as well as her ideas of a balance between male and female influences essential to social harmony.

Visits and Sketches at Home and Abroad (1834) was directed to "English and German friends—particularly the artists," by whom Jameson hoped to be read with indulgence. As Madame de Staël's *De l'Allemagne* had sought to explain German society and culture in the face of French chauvinism, so did her admirer hope to challenge English insularity. Indeed, the precedent of Madame de Staël prompted Jameson to claim this ambassadorial role for women, in the conviction that their breadth of sympathy especially suited them for the requirements of diplomacy. Within a very much more miscellaneous framework than that of Madame de Staël's work, Jameson placed predominant emphasis on the traits and tendencies of German art. She thus gave scope to the interest in painting demonstrated in the *Ennuyée*, while avoiding too close a comparison with her model.

The immediate basis for Jameson's interpretation of Germany to the British was furnished by journeys she made in 1829 and in 1833, when she traveled with letters of introduction from her friend Robert Noel, a relative of Lady Byron. She met the poet and novelist Ludwig Tieck in Dresden and the renowned literary critic A. W. Schlegel in Bonn. At Weimar she formed an ardent and lasting friendship with Ottilie von Goethe (the daughter-in-law of the great man, recently deceased), whose circle included such highly cultivated women as Johanna and Adèle Schopenhauer, and the gifted amateur archaeologist Sybille Mertens. Among artists she became acquainted with Moritz Retsch and Julie von Egloffstein (a rare instance, she notes, of a German woman who persevered in following painting as a profession), while in Frankfurt she met the sculptor J. H. Dannecker and in Munich toured the new Royal Palace with its architect, Leo von Klenze. Berlin was not on the itinerary of these trips, and Jameson apparently did not meet the connoisseur and gallery director Dr. G. F. Waagen until a later date. But the historical principles on which he had recently organized and catalogued the contents of the Berlin Royal Gallery had elsewhere been applied, as she notes in comments on the Städel Museum in Frankfurt, the Munich Glyptothek, and the Dresden Gallery.

Fertile, in some cases even prophetic, in its choice of topics, *Visits and Sketches* takes up such themes as the revival of mural painting in Germany and the problem of "trickery in art." Cornelius's frescoes in the Munich Glyptothek are examined at length with regard to their program and their effect as an ensemble of monumental designs. She is moved by Schnorr von Carolsfeld's Nibelungen murals in the Munich Royal Palace to lament the absence of similar opportunities for artists in England: "Alas! . . . such men as Hilton and Etty illustrate annuals, and the genius of Turner shrinks into a vignette!"[13] In another vein, she complains of an arrangement by which a kind of stained-glass window shade could be lowered to cast a "crimson tint" on Dannecker's statue of Ariadne. Long in advance of Ruskin's strictures, she objected in principle to what she regarded as dishonesty in art.[14]

But most significant in this work is its evidence of the author's growth in discernment and appreciation. She came to terms with Rubens on this occasion, via the Munich Pinakothek, by a process she would retrace in her introduction to the English translation of Waagen's life of the artist in 1840. Most striking is the expansion of her sympathies where she encountered works by artists whose forms and manner fell outside her preferred Italianate modes. The Boisserée Gallery and contemporary German enthusiasm for the "Gothic" (that is, late medieval Flemish and German art) impelled her to speculate on the basis for this interest. "It arises," she suggests, "from a perception of the *mind* they brought to bear upon their subjects, the simplicity and integrity of feeling with which they worked, and the elaborate marvellous beauty of the execution of the parts." She finds that their "conception and painting of *countenance*" beggars description.[15]

These observations are significant early contributions to that later phase of the Gothic Revival that reversed prevailing opinion on the merits of the primitives. (The term primitive was applied to painters before Raphael because their work was considered deficient in knowledge and skill.) Since Flemish, German, and Italian painting was at issue here, the nationalism of the early nineteenth century that fostered British enthusiasm for Gothic architecture as a national style was not an encouraging factor. Nevertheless, in a writer and *salonière* like Maria Callcott, as well as in collectors of the discernment of William Roscoe and Samuel Rogers, England produced notable pioneers of a taste that would remain exceptional at least through the 1840s. With Maria (later Lady) Callcott, Jameson was influential in stimulating interest in the primitives among a widening section of the public and on the part of literary women like Elizabeth Rigby (later Lady Eastlake) and Mary P. Merrifield, the translator of Cennini. In a sense they were pursuing the implications of Madame de Staël's respect for variety of idiom as a revelation of national character.

Personal crises unhappily interrupted Jameson's expanding social and intellectual life in Germany. She went home in November 1833 when her father suffered a stroke, one that would leave him permanently incapacitated. Having provided for her parents, she returned to Germany in the summer of 1834 to stay for nearly two years. In the meantime, Robert Jameson became a candidate for the vice-chancellorship of Upper Canada and considered it desirable that his wife join him in Toronto. His insistence and her own concern to reach some kind of resolution of their relationship decided her on the dreaded transatlantic voyage. She left for Canada in October 1836.

Desolation of spirit marked Jameson's journey from the outset. At the end of a month at sea, there was no one to meet her when she disembarked in New York, and the rest of the trip was equally cheerless. Any hope that the marriage might yet be viable was conclusively dispelled. On her husband's advancement to the vice-chancellorship in 1837 she wrote: "He now possesses the highest dignity to which he can aspire in his profession and has only to be content for the rest of his life. . . . We go on quite peaceably together with a perfect understanding that I remain independent."[16] When she sailed for England in 1838, it was with a formal agreement that she live independently and that Robert pay her an allowance of £300 a year.

Anna Jameson's resourcefulness had otherwise turned her year in Canada to good account. In the summer of 1837 she set forth on a journey unprecedented for a European woman, one that took her west to Port Talbot and Detroit, by steamer to Mackinaw Island, and thence by small boat to Sault Ste. Marie. "I wish to see, with my own eyes, the condition of women in savage life," she explained in a letter to her family.[17] On Manitoulin Island she witnessed the annual distribution of presents to the Indians by a representative of the British Crown; she next enjoyed an exhilarating four-day trip by *bateau* down Lake Huron. On her return to Toronto in mid-August she was received with astonishment and enthusiasm.

All of this was to furnish the splendidly vital travel account that figures in *Winter Studies and Summer Rambles in Canada* (1838). One critic likened some of its descriptions to passages in Mary Wollstonecraft's *Letters from Norway:* "there is a pensive mellowness of colouring in both, which recalls to us the tone of certain leafy forest-landscapes, by Gaspar Poussin."[18] Invoking concepts that were indeed derived from Mary Wollstonecraft, ideas of the shaping role of education and of the "artificial" (i.e., conventional) nature of social relationships, she used the situation of Indian women to expose the anomalies she found in civilized life. Although the duties performed by Indian women were heavy, the rational nature of the arrangements was in contrast to European hypocrisy that exempted some women from useful work while exploiting others without regard to any humane consideration. "If women are to be exempted from toil in reverence to the sex, and as *women*, I can understand this, though I think it unreasonable; but if it be merely a privilege of station, and confined to a certain set, while the great primeval penalty is doubled on the rest, then I do not see where is the great gallantry and consistency of this our Christendom," she wrote.[19] The protest against the gross contradiction between official pieties and the realities of social existence for women would inform Jameson's activism in the 1840s and 1850s as a spokesperson for the employment of women.

Critical acclaim for *Winter Studies*, in spite of some hostility to its feminist argument, gained its author an expanded readership and enhanced authority. In her introduction to the London publication of G. F. Waagen's *Peter Paul Rubens* (1840), she launched an astute attack on the prevailing philistinism of art criticism in England. "Neither our English artists nor our English public are as yet accustomed to that *many-sided* and elevated spirit in criticism with which the Germans have long been familiar," she noted, and this despite the excellence of British art and the wealth of the national collections. A narrow ability to discern *"what* a picture represents, and with what degree of propriety and success it is represented," adequate only to the most routine productions, is helpless before those of greatly gifted artists.[20] With Dr. Waagen, Jameson denied that the work of art is a fortuitous result of circumstances, affirming that it is a synthetic expression of the artist's mind or soul. In urging the fitness of Rubens to illustrate this principle, she was apparently opposing a widespread distaste for his work in England. She conceived that Rubens gives different degrees of pleasure depending on one's sympathy and understanding of the man but that there cannot be a question of his merits as a painter. Her readers were thus challenged to confront Rubens's artistic personality. Jameson also contributed substantially to Waagen's text through her extensive and learned annotations, prefaced by a ritual denial that these might be of value to any but "the mere amateur."

In a letter to Ottilie von Goethe of April 1840, Jameson wrote that she had begun a new project, a guide to the public galleries of art in London. She had also started "another work of a far more important nature, which I have been meditating for some years. . . . It is the Biography of female Artists, and their social position philosophically and morally considered."[21] In the event, the project on the lives of women artists was not realized, and the task devolved on her American follower, Clara Clement Waters. But the

Public Galleries (1842) was to be a far more substantial effort than this allusion would suggest. With its sequel, the *Companion to the Most Celebrated Private Galleries of Art in London* (1844), it is a major assessment of the history of collecting in England. Its value as an historical account is further enhanced by Jameson's urbane commentary on a wide spectrum of issues related to her subject. *Public Galleries* is concerned with the National Gallery, the pictures in Windsor Castle and at Hampton Court, the Dulwich Gallery, James Barry's cycle in the Society of Arts, and the Soane Museum, in that order. To provide the greatest ease of reference, Jameson catalogued pictures by the arrangement in which they were hung.

The difficulties of producing this work to a rigorous standard of accuracy and completeness were enormous and of a nature for which the author's previous career as a writer did not provide any specific preparation. Protesting as usual the modesty of her goals, she admitted nevertheless that "the task has so extended itself under my hand as to fill double the space at first assigned to it, while the labour required and the responsibility incurred have both proved infinitely greater than I anticipated."[22] These exertions were not expected or understood by an exacting public or by reviewers sophisticated in the arts; if anything, her scrupulousness risked inviting the charge of affectation that greeted Lady Dilke's announcement in 1884 of a book on Claude Lorrain based on unpublished documents. In both cases, scholarly standards were self-imposed.

Addressed to the novice, *Public Galleries* is introduced by an illuminating discussion of such terms as "invention," "manner," "design," and "motive" (recently adopted from the German, Jameson explains). In the *Ennuyée*, "manner" had to do only with execution; here she stipulates that when it "is the manifestation of the individual mind, it is a great interest and charm." When imitated or exaggerated, it becomes an affectation: "Thus, the *manner* of Correggio became in Parmigiano [sic] *mannerism*."[23] For Jameson in the 1840s, the assimilation of concepts of style to the artist's qualities of mind was vital to understanding works of art in the context of a greatly broadened range of sympathies. Further, she urged a new seriousness in the study of art in England, where the status of artists lagged behind that of their counterparts on the continent and the equation of art with manual skill was extremely widespread. Jameson's argument immediately preceded and in all likelihood influenced Ruskin's contention in *Modern Painters*, the first volume of which appeared in 1843, that the language of painting is valuable as the vehicle of thought; it was also pertinent somewhat later to his characterization of Gothic style in relation to the architect's mental or psychological predispositions in *The Stones of Venice* (1851-1853).

The nature of the collection and unresolved issues facing its administration made Jameson's comments on the National Gallery especially consequential. As she observed, no provision had been effected in the plan of the National Gallery for the historical arrangement of paintings by schools and no purchase fund allotted to it at the time of writing. She speculated: "As to the effect that would be produced here by the exhibition of an old Greek or Siennese Madonna, I can imagine it all;—the sneering wonder, the aversion, the contempt; for as yet we are far from that intelligence which would give to such objects their due relative value as historic monuments."[24] The educational role that Jameson performed in her very favorably received catalogues was no doubt a factor in the changing direction of the National Gallery. Her work offered vital support for policies initiated by Charles Eastlake as an officer of the institution in the 1840s. As it happened, Jameson was in correspondence with Sir Robert Peel about her catalogue of his collection for the *Private Galleries* in 1843 when Peel exerted his influence to have Eastlake named Keeper of the National Gallery, and she dedicated the book to the Prime Minister.[25]

The *Private Galleries* addressed no questions of public policy, and here the author could point most affirmatively to English priority among private collectors in the case of the Earl of Arundel and to the distinction of the country's early collections—those of Arundel, the Duke of Buckingham, Charles I, and Sir Peter Lely. Equally proud was the record of private owners' generosity in granting access to their treasures. In this volume the founding and growth of the Queen's Gallery, the Bridgewater, Sutherland, and Grosvenor Galleries, and the collections of the Marquess of Lansdowne, Sir Robert Peel, and Samuel Rogers offered the most congenial materials for Jameson's skills as a writer. Even the spectacular Bridgewater speculation on Italian pictures in the Orleans collection gains in interest from her exposition. Procedures are carefully explained: she has changed attributions

where I could have *no* doubt. . . . We must take it for granted that in many cases, a Titian, a Paul Veronese, &c., means simply a Venetian picture, of the style and time of Titian or Veronese. I firmly believe, for instance, that half the pictures which bear Titian's name, were painted by Bonifazio, or Girolamo de Tiziano, or Paris Bordone, or some other of the *Capi* of the Venetian school. . . .[26]

In *Private Galleries*, Jameson improved on her previous organization by hanging arrangements with a division of each collection into national schools and the alphabetical entry of artists within those categories. The first entry for each name is preceded by a general introduction to the painter's work. In scale her task was virtually encyclopedic, and it was managed with exemplary grace and cogency. Evidence of her growth as a critic is found, for example, in a characterization of the Spanish School as portraying the mysteries of faith and the deepest human feeling "in forms the most familiar, which yet are redeemed from all vulgar association by the intensity and propriety of the expression. . . ."²⁷ In spite of the vogue for Murillo in England, she had the discernment to call Velasquez the greatest of Spanish painters. Gaspard Poussin finds his most articulate admirer of the period in Anna Jameson. Of his Tivoli landscape in the Grosvenor Gallery, she wrote: "Such woods were haunted of old by Hypolitus and Meleager; such glades were the haunt of the antique Sylvans, lurking Satyr, or peeping Faun. None ever painted solitude like Gaspar—the solitude that invites to thought as well as to repose."²⁸ Her comments on Rogers's Giotto fragments (now attributed to Spinello Aretino) mark a further acceptance of the primitives: "these heads have a peculiar value, not as curiosities merely, but as giving an idea of that earnest and devout feeling in art, which makes amends for all mechanical deficiencies."²⁹

By the time this judgment appeared, Jameson had developed her view of the expressive qualities of "early" art as a leading theme in articles for the *Penny Magazine*. These came out as forty-three installments on Italian painters from Cimabue to Bassano, between 1843 and 1845. Charles Knight, the magazine's editor, later pointed proudly to her contributions as indicative of his effort to improve the quality of the journal's work in mass education. They also boosted the circulation of the *Penny Magazine* and were republished as a book, *Memoirs of the Early Italian Painters* (1845), that rivalled *Characteristics of Women* in public favor. Jameson's "indispensable primer" encouraged the *Athenaeum*'s reviewer to assert: "Criticism does make some progress among our compatriots, and many of its first steps have been accomplished with her aid."³⁰ Moreover, the *Memoirs* maintained a large readership throughout the nineteenth century, evidenced in the dozen editions issued in Britain by the early 1890s, followed by numerous reprintings in the United States.

The *Memoirs* is an urbane and tactfully proportioned synthesis of the existing knowledge of Italian painting. Drawing on a wide range of sources from Vasari's *Lives* to Kugler's *Handbuch der Geschichte der Malerei* (1837), it makes substantially complete though not systematic acknowledgment to them. Wherever the author finds evidence disproving a popular tradition, like that of Leonardo's death in the arms of Francis I, she calls attention to it with an expression of courteous regret. Her work has some affinities with A.-F. Rio's *De la Poésie chrétienne* (1836), a tendentious panorama of the role of faith in Western art from the catacombs to the school of Giovanni Bellini. Closely linked with the program of the Catholic Revival in France, Rio celebrated the simplicity and integrity of the primitives as Jameson had earlier done in connection with late Gothic painters in the Boisserée Gallery. She was too much the historian, and perhaps disinclined from her own lack of doctrinal commitment, to attach any absolute value to Christian faith as a determinant of art history. Nor did she share

Rio's exclusive taste for the earlier periods that resulted in an "advanced" position on Raphael that caused him to drop consideration of Raphael's work after the *Disputà* fresco (1509) on the grounds of its decadence. Her sympathy with Christian faith as an influence on the history of art belonged to her grasp of the distinctive spiritual contextures of past epochs. This respect for the integrity of historical phenomena is reflected in Jameson's scholarly scrupulousness. In her work the rigor of a Waagen or a Kugler is joined with rare qualities of sympathetic imagination.

In the midst of these labors, Jameson resumed the role of women's advocate that she had taken up in *Winter Studies and Summer Rambles*. Written anonymously in a male voice, her review of the Royal Commission's Report on the Employment of Women and Young People appeared in the *Athenaeum* in 1843. It confronted such facts as the hours worked by London milliners—upwards of eighteen hours a day in the "regulated" houses—and the Commission's conclusion, which was to blame "voluptuous London's" love of finery. It confronted, too, the Commission's assignment of responsibility to working mothers for widespread opium poisoning among the children of Nottingham lacemakers. Her fury with the investigators' incomprehension approached more closely to a bellow of despair than anything in her previous or later writings, though it remained controlled. In the lower middle class, she noted, two-thirds of the women must work: the necessity was not one in her opinion that they would regret in the long run. Meanwhile, their choices of employment, as compared with those of men, were as one to ten. Apart from the exceptional career in literature or art, women could become governesses or milliners—and even in those areas opportunities were deteriorating. Efforts at reform founder, Jameson observed, because every legislative attempt to improve the situation of women is thought to interfere with the privileges of husbands or fathers.

It is characteristic of her thinking on social questions at this time that she did not advance specific remedies; she addressed herself rather to those attitudes of arrogance or complacency that made reform unthinkable. Her pamphlet of 1846, *On the Relative Social Position of Mothers and Governesses*, similarly posed a dilemma, that of the educated middle-class woman restricted to governessing as a vocation. She found that the role itself was devalued by the inferior status of women, by their usually inadequate training (itself an outcome of attitudes towards female education), and even by antique precedent: "Female arts were taught by female slaves: the liberal arts by men."[31] The disadvantages of the position were in inverse proportion to the demands laid upon it by employers seeking a saintly character, superior intellectual competence, and total dedication to duty. But there is no one-sided casting of blame at parents concerned for the welfare of their children. The pamphlet is an exploration of the inherent anomalies of the role in a social framework of severe limitations on the employment of women.

With the *Athenaeum* review, *Mothers and Governesses* helped furnish *Memoirs and Essays Illustrative of Art, Literature, and Social Morals*, published in 1846. The most distinguished contribution on art in this miscellany is "The House of Titian," a consideration of the painter's art in relation to its Venetian setting. From scene and locale, the author proceeded to an assessment of contemporary attitudes towards the past. Rejecting a sentimental nostalgia over the transience of all institutions, the advocate of seamstresses and teachers affirmed: "Well is it for us that some things are transitory!" In the arts those creations that deserve to live enjoy an earthly immortality. The value of "old art" lies in its *"truth*, as embodying the spirit of a particular age. We have not so much outlived that spirit, as we have comprehended it in a still larger sphere of experience and existence."[32] The art of the past speaks to us through the irreversible medium of historical time. So misguided in her view was the prevailing revivalism of period styles that she concluded the present age is not expressed in the fine arts but instead, perhaps, in the design of machinery or the perfecting of social institutions.

The rigor of this judgment is somewhat exceptional in Jameson's work, however. Elsewhere she stressed the possibility of fruitful contact with the spirit of earlier art from the standpoint of its possible relevance to contemporary experience. A passage in *Visits and Sketches* states, for example, that Dannecker in his statue of Christ had "worked in the antique spirit" while avoiding the imitation of antique models.[33] *In Sacred and Legendary Art* she would suggest that artists could extract and translate into new forms those elements of Christian tradition that held meaning for the present.

"Ye too must fly before a chasing hand,/Angels and Saints, in every hamlet mourned!" To recall the "radiant shapes" lamented in Wordsworth's sonnet and to explain their character and function in Christian iconography was the purpose of Jameson's largest undertaking, *The Poetry of Sacred and Legendary Art* (Figure 2). She had planned this work and negotiated for its publication by 1842. Issued in two volumes in 1848, following serialization in the *Athenaeum*, it would be expanded into what the author called a "series," a tetralogy completed by *Legends of the Monastic Orders* (1850), *Legends of the Madonna* (1852), and *The History of Our Lord* (1864). Jameson's magnum opus is the first in English to interpret both systematically and genetically the symbolism of Christian art. The sole work by an English writer to which it has an affinity is Lord Lindsay's *Sketches of the History of Christian Art* (1847), which relates the character of post-antique art to a process of historical development conceived in Hegelian terms. *Sacred and Legendary Art* is quite different in

scope and point of view, as can be demonstrated by a closer examination of
its text than has been applied in the present essay to Jameson's other writings. Its encyclopedic structure is closer to that of A.-N. Didron's *Iconographie chrétienne* (1843), from which it nevertheless diverges as a work of
responsive intelligence rather than archaeological inquiry in its organization
and in its readability. Jameson's purview—the iconography of the angels,
evangelists, apostles, Church doctors, and saints, in that order—may on the
other hand have been negatively influenced by Didron in the wish to avoid
duplication or rivalry with his subject, the "history of God."

Didron's plan for the organization of his book involved the "immutable"
sequence of Nature, Science, Ethics, and History found in Vincent of
Beauvais's *Speculum Universale*; the French scholar considered that he was
following this scheme in beginning with the Creation and proceeding on to
the Apocalypse. Jameson claimed no "formal, nor technical" plan for her
work but rather proposed to lead the reader through successive perspectives, as one subject opened upon another. The manner in which one vein of
discussion is succeeded by a topic related through the association of ideas—
as where an account of various "fallen women" in Christian tradition is
suggested by the story of Mary Magdalene—adds to the appeal of her work.
Jameson's professed lack of system is part of her usual insistence on the
modesty of her ambitions and should not obscure the fact that the associa-
tive principle is developed in a well-considered and coherent manner in
Sacred and Legendary Art.

She situates the study of Christian imagery in a perspective that takes into
account the prejudices of her audience. With mistressly diplomacy,
Jameson observes that it is as though these once popular Catholic legends
belonged to remote antiquity rather than having connection "with the faith
of our forefathers and the history of civilisation and Christianity."[34] A
reviving interest in medieval art, she notes, brings with it a desire to understand the states of feeling from which this art sprang and the traditions on
which it was based. Not solely the product of "the brains of dreaming
monks," its source in the legendary literature of the Middle Ages was
informed by popular feeling. This emphasis differs diametrically from
Didron's insistence on the responsibility of the Church in sponsoring
imagery to educate the illiterate masses. For Jameson the extravagance of
many legends of the saints reflects the conditions in which they were
formed, but even the wildest contain some kernel of truth. By "truth" she
meant principally the ethical implications of Christian "hero-worship": the
celebration of charity and self-sacrifice, of the heroism of women and of
pacific virtues opposed to war, violence, and slavery. "If we have not much
sympathy with modern imitations of Mediaeval Art, still less should we
sympathise with that narrow puritanical jealousy which holds the monuments of a real and earnest faith in contempt. All that God has permitted

170.   Laus Deo.

Introduction.

I. OF THE ORIGIN AND GENERAL SIGNIFICANCE OF THE LEGENDS
REPRESENTED IN ART.

WE cannot look round a picture gallery — we cannot turn to a
portfolio of prints after the old masters — we cannot even look
over the modern engravings which pour upon us daily, from Paris,
Munich, or Berlin, without perceiving how many of the most
celebrated productions of Art, more particularly those which have
descended to us from the early Italian and German schools, represent incidents and characters taken from the once popular legends of
the Catholic Church.   This form of *" Hero-Worship"* has become,
since the Reformation, strange to us — as far removed from our
sympathies and associations as if it were antecedent to the fall of
Babylon, and related to the religion of Zoroaster, instead of being
left but two or three centuries behind us, and closely connected with
the faith of our forefathers and the history of civilization and Christianity.   Of late years, with a growing passion for the works of Art
of the Middle Ages, there has arisen among us a desire to com-
prehend the state of feeling which produced them, and the legends
and traditions on which they are founded; — a desire to understand,
and to bring to some surer critical test, representations which have
become familiar without being intelligible.   To enable us to do this,

Figure 2. Initial page of Introduction to *The Poetry of Sacred and
Legendary Art*, by Anna Jameson. With wood-engraved vignette,
Laus Deo, after Liberale di Verona, 1848. (*By permission of the
Trustees of the British Library*)

once to exist in the past should be considered as the possession of the present; sacred for example or warning. . . ."[35]

There were also the prejudices of connoisseurship to affront, the indifference of this science to the context in which works of art were created and to their connections with history. Given the animus against "Popery," perhaps it was as well, the author says, that amateurs dwelt harmlessly on draperies, tints, and attributions. Still, how can one do justice to the work without knowing "what was *intended* as to incident, expression, character?"[36] Incomprehension of Christian subjects prevails among persons whose liberal education has ensured them an acquaintance with classical themes.

Having established this rationale, Jameson sets forth in an illuminating manner some broad considerations bearing on her subject. The first of these is a distinction of fundamental utility between devotional and historical images, one that she had earlier rehearsed in discussing Correggio's works in Dresden.[37] The difference between images presented as objects of devotion and those representing an action had largely been obscured in Renaissance and Baroque art theory by Alberti's emphasis on the *istoria*, the dramatic depiction of a suitably important event in sacred or secular history. Recognition of the devotional function is requisite not only to an understanding of a major class of images in medieval art but also to the study of the Renaissance, as Jameson illustrates in explaining the *sacra conversazione:* "a group of sacred personages where no action is represented."[38] She notes further that an event may be so treated as to suggest a theme for contemplation. Certain subjects, such as the Crucifixion and the Last Supper, lend themselves to either devotional or narrative interpretation, in Jameson's view, while others such as the Marriage of St. Catherine are entirely visionary or devotional in nature.

Further laying the foundation of her subject, she accounts for the introduction of donor figures, rules of precedence in the portrayal of devotional subjects, and factors bearing on the presence of local or patron saints. The possibility of "anachronisms" in the timeless realm of the devotional image is laid to rest. Jameson points to the ahistorical outlook of the Middle Ages in its congeries of classical, Jewish, and Christian worthies and to the desire to embrace all phases of culture within the compass of Christianity—"most Catholic," she thinks, "as well as in the most poetical, spirit."[39]

From this vantage point, she weighs with judgment and tact characteristic Protestant objections to the anthropomorphic portrayals of Deity, to miraculous episodes in the lives of the saints, and to grisly martyrdoms. Description of the imagery of patron saints follows, with a register of names, localities, and attributes. An explanation of the most common "emblems" of Christian art then brings the reader to the main threshold of Jameson's subject, the triumphant vista of the angelic ranks. In splendor and energy of rhetoric, joined with intellectual substance, this evocation has few parallels in the art literature of the nineteenth century.

Priority of the angels in the introduction of sacred *personae* was a well-considered decision. Ministering angels are an ubiquitous motif in Victorian culture, with precedents in earlier neoclassical funerary sculpture and in the art of William Blake. The sympathetic character of these beings, their rapport with human needs and suffering, were profoundly congenial to a mid-nineteenth century audience and to the author's own distinctive emphasis on humane values in the Christian ethos. The observation that angelic existence had long been a popular article of faith, despite theologians' views that their bodily forms were allegorical, announced the author's orientation toward her theme as a whole. She was exploring from the inside, as it were, a world of belief which she certainly did not share in a literal sense; her work is an act of imaginative reconstruction in the sense posited by Giambattista Vico as a means of understanding remote historical climates of thought and feeling.[40]

In this important respect, Jameson's outlook is utterly divergent from that of Christian revivalists like A.-F. Rio, Pugin, or the Ruskin of 1846 who exalted Christian art as an absolute standard of excellence in the second volume of *Modern Painters*.[41] In *Sacred and Legendary Art* and its sequels, Jameson maintained so consistently this measure of historical distance that it is impossible to determine where she stands in relation to any tenet of Christian dogma. Nowhere in her writings did she express belief in such doctrines as the immortality of the soul, and her emphasis on the human and social dimensions of religious feeling may indicate a lack of orthodox commitment. Discretion would have precluded any avowals of personal skepticism, however. Her urbanity is instanced in the good-humored observation that popular faith could as well accommodate eleven thousand martyred virgins in St. Ursula's company as conceive of eleven; she is amused by attempts to read this legend so as to yield the lower figure. In the main this distancing element in Jameson's view of religious imagery was an advantage in defusing passions that a partisan attitude could have provoked, though *Blackwood's* reviewer reproved her for saying *Catholic* rather than *Romish* Church and for not expressing a positive quality of religious belief.[42]

Sacred and Legendary Art drew on a wide range of source material. Didron had considered the thirteenth-century *Golden Legend* of Jacopo da Voragine adequate for the nonscriptural components of Christian iconography; Jameson consulted at least six compendia of lives of the saints which she supplemented with extensive readings in the history of Christianity and of Western civilization, as well as in the literature of art. The extent of her sources reflects the assumption that it was necessary to examine all dimensions of the meaning of symbols. She brought to bear on Christian iconography a knowledge of Jewish customs, of Old Testament imagery, of Greco-Roman sources of Christian tradition, of the writings of the Church Fathers, and even of fossil remains (for their possible relation to the form of dragons) that is magisterial in scope and yet free of pedantry.

Anna Jameson's work was universally well received despite its price at two guineas, the competition of Lord Lindsay's volumes on Christian art, and the circumstances of Chartist agitation in London and revolutionary uprisings on the continent. Its author was urged by the *Edinburgh Review* to take up the legends of the Virgin and of monasticism. In 1850 the latter project was realized with publication of *Legends of the Monastic Orders.* The apology with which it was offered differs somewhat from that of the 1848 volumes. "Monachism is not the consecration of the beautiful, even in idea; it is the apotheosis of deformity and suffering," in Jameson's severe judgment.[43] Solitude, which she tended to identify with the monastic calling, was repugnant to her personally and because it eschewed the active ministry that she had associated with egalitarian ideals in *Sacred and Legendary Art.* But she found redeeming values in the monastic nurture of learning and of art, as well as in the fact that it offered educational and administrative opportunities to women. *Monastic Orders* also advanced a strong argument for its subject in terms of the historical interest attached to an influential development of human culture. Familiarity with the traditions of the orders is necessary, she urged, to an understanding of the art sponsored by these establishments.

Specifying her sources as before, Jameson sets forth some relevant considerations: the importance of knowing dates of canonization for the identification of figures in monastic art, practices respecting the tonsure of monks, the color and form of the habit, and some common symbols such as the stag, "the general emblem of solitude." Without being forced or arbitrary, the book's organization is directed to national and local interest in the history of the topic. Growth of monasticism in the British Isles thus precedes an account of continental developments. In this perspective, one sees in insular terms the imposition of the Normans' alien hagiology on indigenous traditions.

Sacred and Legendary Art contains only scattered suggestions that its thesaurus of Christian imagery is a usable resource for contemporary artists, though *Blackwood's* stressed its utility for the "resumption of sacred art" in England. More frequent and more warmly urged recommendations occur in *Monastic Orders.* The whole of Thomas à Becket's life is rich in materials for the historical painter, according to Jameson, and many other "capital" subjects are adduced. But she proposed the creative interpretation of these themes rather than imitation of their portrayal in earlier art. Her idea of thematic invention that would make free use of Christian tradition in its relation to contemporary concerns is remarkably close to what the Pre-Raphaelites attempted at this time. Holman Hunt avowed that he had learned "not a little" from Jameson's articles in the *Penny Magazine*,[44] and the likelihood that her writings were influential for the whole Early Christian phase of the Pre-Raphaelite Brotherhood is very great. Millais's painting, *Christ in the House of his Parents* (1850), and Hunt's *Hireling Shepherd* (1851) exemplify the free adaptation of Christian imagery for its current didactic relevance that she championed. The significance of her work in its own right, however, rests on the application of its central historical, and art-historical, rationale for the study of Christian traditions.

"You may imagine my astonishment when on the book-stall of the Railway Station at Birmingham I found the 'Legends of the Madonna,'" Jameson exclaimed in a letter of 13 December 1852 to Ottilie von Goethe.[45] Published earlier in the year, her volume on Marian iconography would seem to be the first extensive study of the imagery of the Virgin in the literature of art. The subject had been touched on only incidentally under such headings as "The Nimbus" or "The Trinity" in Didron's *Iconographie chrétienne*, nor had it received substantial consideration in historical works such as Kugler's *Handbuch* or Rio's *Poésie chrétienne*.

The topic was a likely, but not necessary, extension of Jameson's "series." One probable encouragement to her choice of subject was the quickening of interest in the Madonna's cult that preceded Pius IX's proclamation of the doctrine of the Immaculate Conception in 1854. But a more fundamental circumstance perhaps was the wide-ranging debate initiated in England around 1850 on the nature and value of woman's role. Discussion was stimulated with the advent of organized feminism, announced by Harriet Taylor in her 1851 article on the first national women's rights convention in Massachusetts (1850) and carried forward in Britain by Barbara Leigh Smith's committee on married women's property rights. Participation in this debate was very far from being limited to those who agreed, for example, with Taylor or with Harriet Martineau on the suffrage question. (Jameson did not herself believe that it was prudent to insist on a "political existence" for women.) But from the feminists at one pole, to women like Florence Nightingale and George Eliot, who combined unconventional careers with traditional views, to Queen Victoria at the most conservative terminus of opinion, there was effective agreement that "woman's sphere" was an issue.

The informing viewpoint of *Legends of the Madonna* is one that admits certain fundamental distinctions between the male and the female character. In examining the historical impact of the cult of the Virgin, Jameson points to the civilizing agency of feminine influence as epitomized in the imagery of the Madonna. The scope of the female contribution to development of European society has been of a special nature and it has been crucial, the book claims. This is not to suggest that *Legends* is a polemic, but that a synthesizing historical vision has been joined with a close study of the genesis and character of Marian iconography.

As a prologue to discussing the types of Madonna images in medieval and Renaissance art, Jameson traces the cult to the Council of Ephesus, which in 431 established that Mary was the Mother of God, rather than simply of Christ in his human aspect. In support of this dogma, the Madonna and Child image multiplied, nourished by such pagan antecedents as the Egyptian type of Isis nursing the god Horus. It was in Egypt that the first effigies of the Virgin and Child originated, she notes. The earliest notice of worship of the Madonna is found in St. Epiphanius (d. 403), who mentions a sect of women who made ritual offerings of cakes to the Virgin, thus transferring to her the honors formerly rendered to Ceres.

These and other pagan sources of the cult coincided with the emergence in Christianity of what Jameson discerned as new ideas of the moral responsibility of women, ideas which challenged "Hebrew and classical prejudices concerning the whole sex."[46] She stresses throughout those tendencies of the faith that gave support to ideas of the dignity and value of women. Thus, she dwells on aspects of cult and imagery that exemplify the Madonna's energy, initiative, and intellectual competence, while also noting her more commonly celebrated virtues of humility and obedience. For Jameson, Mary's decisiveness and fortitude in undertaking the journey to Elizabeth while pregnant are salient features of the subject of the Visitation and she finds that the intellectual faculties of the Madonna are honored in the type of the *Virgo Sapientissima*, the exponent of Divine Wisdom.

But this emphasis occurs within a framework of systematic consideration of the historical and devotional images of the Madonna. Their analysis extends the principles of iconographical classification and interpretation applied in the preceding volumes of the sequence, and as before the author interweaves through her plan a wealth of acute judgments on works of art. We find, for example, an appreciation of Jan van Eyck's *Madonna of the Chancellor Rolin* that criticizes the current identification in it of St. Joseph adoring the Christ Child; she also expresses a pioneering admiration for Botticelli. Her exposition of the history of the Annunciation as a subject is extremely lucid. Very apt, too, is her perception of the Venetian origins— "pastoral and lyrical"—of the *Sacra conversazione*.

Jameson's numerous imitators most often reduced the complexity of her material to dictionary format, while renouncing the interpretative dimensions of her work. In *Emblems of Saints* (London, 1850), for example, the Reverend F. C. Husenbeth gives a tabular listing of saints and attributes. Less skeletal, Clara Clement Waters's *Handbook of Christian Symbols* (Boston, 1886) remains an iconographical dictionary, while Margaret

Tabor's *The Saints in Art* (London, 1908) is the barest listing of symbols and attributes. However, Jameson had at least one follower of imaginative vision in Henry Adams, a measure of her profound impact on American thinking about the visual arts. The premise of *Legends of the Madonna*, that medieval and Renaissance art have "bequeathed to us . . . one prevailing idea: it is that of an impersonation in the feminine character of beneficence, purity, and power, standing between an offended Deity and poor, sinning, suffering humanity, and clothed in the visible form of Mary, the Mother of our Lord," underlies the conception of *Mont-Saint-Michel and Chartres*. It informs the entire symbolic contrast drawn by Adams between martial severity in the Norman fortress and the benign grace of the cathedral, inspired by and dedicated to the Virgin.

Jameson's life in the 1840s was marked by widening appreciation of her work and personal satisfaction in a range of friends that included Catherine Sedgwick, Lady Byron, Elizabeth Barrett, and Robert Browning. Her ties with Ottilie von Goethe remained very close. In 1842, Denis Murphy died after a long illness; his daughter continued to support her mother and unmarried sisters in their home at Ealing as she had done for some time and would continue to do for the rest of her life. She was never entirely free of worries about money. These became acute when Robert Jameson compulsorily retired in 1851 from the vice-chancellorship in Toronto, having become incapacitated by alcoholism, and ceased paying his wife's yearly allowance. Through the efforts of Anne Procter and other friends, Jameson was nominated for and awarded a pension by the Queen. It was not equivalent to Jameson's £300 a year, however. She sustained a blow to both her finances and her dignity in 1854, when Robert died leaving a will that excluded his wife from any claim on his estate. Again she was helped by friends, who raised funds to buy her an annuity. In the same year, Mrs. Murphy died at an advanced age, and Anna Jameson's friendship with Lady Byron foundered on a painful misunderstanding.

Up to this point in the mid-1850s, Jameson had maintained an extraordinary level of productivity as a writer. In addition to the four volumes of her "series," she wrote articles for the *Art Journal* and *Edinburgh Review* and contributed *A Hand-book to the Courts of Modern Sculpture* to a series of guides to art exhibitions in the new Crystal Palace (1854). She had always been more attracted to contemporary sculpture than to painting, and the *Hand-book* provided an occasion to expatiate on the varying perception of classical models in the work of Canova, Flaxman, and Thorvaldsen. Finally, at mid-decade she published *A Commonplace Book of Thoughts, Memories, and Fancies*, a work that contains many sensitive and penetrating observations on a variety of topics; among the more memorable are reflections on childhood suggested by her own early experience.

In this period Jameson presided over a salon at her family's cottage in Ealing, where a group of young women gathered weekly for discussions of the "Woman Question." From this circle came some of the leading catalysts of British feminism in the 1850s and 1860s: the poet Adelaide Procter, Bessie Parkes, Emily Faithfull, and Barbara Leigh Smith, one of the founders of Girton College. Jameson was the respected senior adviser of these women, initiators of the first organized feminist movement in Britain around the Married Women's Property Bill, introduced in Parliament in 1857. Bessie Parkes, in her tribute to Jameson as a women's advocate, recalled that her name was first "of all the many thousands" on petitions claiming for wives the right to their own earnings. Jameson's influence was most conspicuous in her disciples' concentration on the employment issue, the chief focus of their "Ladies' Circle" and of *The English Woman's Journal*, the latter launched in 1858. These efforts addressed not only the problem of "educated destitution" among middle-class women but also the necessity to open up skilled trades such as printing and clerical occupations. With great vision, Jameson argued for the creation of a vast field for women in the expanding area of social services. In the mid-1850s she lectured on the social benefits to be expected from employing women in the workhouses, prisons, and hospitals. Published as *Sisters of Charity* (1855) and *The Communion of Labour* (1856), her lectures called on Parliament to recognize "that women do exist as a part of the community, whose responsibilities are to be acknowledged, and whose capabilities are to be made available" in the public interest.[47]

During the last five years of her life, Jameson made extended visits to Rome, where her niece and biographer, Gerardine MacPherson, was resident. The Brownings' presence, indeed that of the whole Anglo-American colony that included W. W. Story, John Gibson, and Harriet Hosmer, also drew her to Italy. She had for some time been collecting material for the final two volumes of *Sacred and Legendary Art*, and in 1859 at age 65 began to write *The History of Our Lord*. Describing Jameson at this juncture, A.-F. Rio stated:

One may say that she has fulfilled her mission with truly heroic perseverance, for twenty years after having begun it in London, she continued it in Florence with an ardor that the progress of age was unable to chill, and in seeing her so indefatigable in pursuing her task, I discovered more energy for the accomplishment of mine. . . .[48]

She was in fact suffering from arthritis and from failing eyesight, worn out by the habit of writing half through the night. Early in the following year Jameson returned to London to continue her work in the British Museum. These labors were cut short when she contracted bronchial pneumonia and died, after a brief illness, on 17 March 1860.

The Eastlakes had long been admirers of Jameson's work; Sir Charles in his notes to an 1869 edition of Kugler stated that studies he previously had consulted on the iconography of the saints may "be now considered superseded by Mrs. Jameson's 'Poetry of Sacred and Legendary Art.'"[49] Lady Eastlake took upon herself the arduous task of completing *The History of Our Lord*. By far the larger part of the text remained to be written, and the ordering of its topics was indicated only by the briefest outline. This order Lady Eastlake saw fit to change in favor of a strictly chronological development of the subject. In spite of these difficulties and the differences in point of view that might have produced a disjointed effect, *The History of Our Lord* presents a remarkable cohesiveness. Once past the un-Jamesonian stipulations of the preface ("For no philosophy, 'falsely so called,' intrudes into the domain of Christian art—no subtleties on His human nature. . . ," etc.), the work is coherent in its outlook, highly readable and rich in interest. This is so despite the fact that Lady Eastlake very properly declined to recast Jameson's fragments, but incorporated them, with designation of authorship, where they fit topically within the adopted sequence. Lady Eastlake had learned a great deal from her predecessor with regard to didactic clarity and the methodology of art-historical reconstruction; she similarly stresses the significance of the function of works of art, the relevance of locale to iconography, the importance of pagan traditions, and so on. Indeed, she preserves Jameson's feminist tendency of interpretation. In its integrity and as a conclusion to *Sacred and Legendary Art*, the work is a tribute by Lady Eastlake to the elder writer.

Lady Eastlake's role as her literary executrix should have precluded some dismissive judgments that have been passed on Jameson's contributions to the history of art criticism and scholarship. John Steegman's *Consort of Taste*, for example, makes the curious statement that Elizabeth Eastlake could evidently "have felt no fear of intellectual rivalry" from Anna Jameson.[50] This would be comprehensible if "social" were substituted for "intellectual" rivalry—assuming that rivalry were in question. There were considerable differences of social background between these women, as well as divergences in personal style that may be related to the more reticent English inheritance of Lady Eastlake in contrast to Jameson's Irish candor of emotional expression. In some contemporary and later opinions (Henry Crabb Robinson's would be an earlier example[51]), snobbishness towards the self-made woman—the former governess—seems essentially to be involved. It is inconceivable that Lady Eastlake would have undertaken the disciple's task of completing the work of a woman who was not at least her peer intellectually.

We have Lady Eastlake's explicit assessment on the occasion of Anna Jameson's death: "excellent in judgement and advice . . . profound and conscientious in all she did. . . . We shall not see her likes again. Sir Charles laments her deeply.''[52] A.-F. Rio asserted the preeminence of her contributions to the aesthetic education of the English public: ''I can affirm without fear of contradiction that this education, whatever its import may be, has been more her work than that of all the other English writers who in various forms have treated the same subject.''[53] Frank Herrmann has called attention to Jameson's effectiveness as a writer, in contrast to contemporaries such as William Buchanan and G.F. Waagen, observing that she, with Lady Eastlake and Lady Charlotte Schreiber, dominated the nineteenth-century collecting scene ''because of their remarkable intellectual capacity, their scholarship and their fantastic energy.''[54] Finally, Bernard Berenson proposed her art-historical niche in placing Anna Jameson with Lanzi, Schnaase, Lord Lindsay, and Ruskin, ''among the pioneers and creators of the universe into which people like myself were born.''[55]

NOTES

The principal published sources for the biography of Anna Jameson are her *A Commonplace Book of Thoughts, Memories, and Fancies, Original and Selected*, London, 1854; Gerardine MacPherson, *Memoirs of the Life of Anna Jameson*, London, 1878; Beatrice C. Erskine, ed., *Anna Jameson: Letters and Friendships, 1812-1860*, London, 1915; G.H. Needler, ed., *Letters of Anna Jameson to Ottilie von Goethe*, London, 1939; and Clara Thomas, *Love and Work Enough: The Life of Anna Jameson*, Toronto, 1967. In addition to these titles, the following manuscript sources have been consulted for the present essay: British Library, correspondence of Anna Jameson and Sir Robert Peel, and letter to editors of *Handbook of Contemporary Biography*; New York Public Library, sixteen letters to and from Anna Jameson; Rush Rhees Library, University of Rochester, two letters to and from Anna Jameson. For an extensive bibliography listing published biographical sources, manuscript collections, critical publications, and first editions of Jameson's books, the reader is referred to Professor Thomas's study.

1. Anna Jameson, *A Commonplace Book of Thoughts, Memories, and Fancies, Original and Selected*, New York, 1855, p. 127.

2. Jameson, *Commonplace Book*, p. 121.

3. Denis Brownell Murphy (b?-1842) was active as a miniaturist in Dublin before his emigration to England, where he exhibited at the Royal Academy and British Institution between 1800 and 1827. He was sufficiently esteemed to attract some sitters of distinction, e.g., Charles Bicknell (Solicitor to the Admiralty), Wordsworth, and John Crome. Appointed Miniature Painter in Ordinary to Princess Charlotte in 1810, he was commissioned to make miniatures after portraits by Lely at Windsor. The series was incomplete when Charlotte died in 1818, and Prince Leopold declined to buy it. After a long search for a purchaser, engravings after the portraits were published with a text by Anna Jameson as *Memoirs of the Beauties of the Court of Charles II*, London, 1831. For Murphy's career, see Daphne Foskett, *A Dictionary of British Miniature Painters*, London, 1972.

4. Ellen Moers, *Literary Women: The Great Writers*, New York, 1976, pp. 187-88.

5. *The Diary of an Ennuyée*, London, 1826, pp. 313-23.

6. *Diary*, pp. 176-78.

7. Clara Thomas (*Love and Work Enough*, Toronto, 1967, p. 196) states that Anna Jameson told her mother the marriage had not been consummated, though I have not been able to locate this assertion in the source cited. But there are various indications that would

tend to support it, e.g., Anna's observation in a letter to Robert of February 1836 that "a union such as ours is, and has been ever, is a real mockery of the laws of God and man." (Quoted in Gerardine MacPherson, *Memoirs of the Life of Anna Jameson*, London, 1878, p. 108.)

8. According to a contemporary witness, the diarist H. Crabb Robinson (1775-1867), who practiced law between 1813 and 1828, in *On Books and Their Writers* I, London, 1938, 442. A later source stresses Robert Jameson's patronage by the chancellor Lord Eldon, in whose court he had served as reporter (David B. Read, *The Lives of the Judges of Upper Canada and Ontario from 1791 to the Present Time*, Toronto, 1888, p. 189). Beatrice C. Erskine states that his post was obtained through the influence of Mrs. Basil Montagu (née Benson) in *Anna Jameson: Letters and Friendships, 1812-1860*, London, 1915, pp. 94-95.

9. *Loves of the Poets* I, London, 1829, vii-viii; in fact, some of the poets are female, e.g., Vittoria Colonna and Veronica Gambara, and thus do not fit this formula.

10. *Loves of the Poets* I, 14.

11. *Memoirs of Celebrated Female Sovereigns* I, London, 1831, xi.

12. Of the Countess von Egloffstein, Jameson wrote that she "shows a decided predilection for the picturesque in humble life, and seems to have turned to simple nature in perfect simplicity of heart. . . . there is nothing mannered or conventional in her style. . . . In this little bit of natural poetry [a coast scene with peasants] there was no seeking after effect, no prettiness, no pretension; but a quiet genuine simplicity of feeling. . . ." (*Visits and Sketches* I, London, 1834, 367-68.) Nine years later in the first volume of *Modern Painters*, Ruskin declared that of all Turner's drawings, "those of the Yorkshire series have the most heart in them, the most affectionate, simple, unwearied, serious finishing of truth. There is in them little seeking after effect, but a strong love of place; little exhibition of the artist's own powers or peculiarities, but intense appreciation of the smallest local minutiae." *The Works of Ruskin* III, E. T. Cook and A. Wedderburn, eds., London, 1903, 233.

13. *Visits and Sketches at Home and Abroad* I, London, 1834, 300.

14. *Visits and Sketches* I, 95.

15. *Visits and Sketches* I, 262.

16. G. H. Needler, ed., *Letters of Anna Jameson to Ottilie von Goethe*, London, 1939, p. 83.

17. Erskine, *Letters and Friendships*, p. 154.

18. [John Kemble] Review of *Winter Studies and Summer Rambles in Canada*, *The British and Foreign Review*, 8 (1839), 148.

19. *Winter Studies and Summer Rambles in Canada*, Toronto, 1923, p. 416.

20. G. F. Waagen, *Peter Paul Rubens*, London, 1840, pp. vi and vii.

21. Needler, *Letters*, p. 124.

22. *A Handbook to the Public Galleries of Art in and near London*, London, 1842, pp. v-vi.

23. *Public Galleries*, p. xx.

24. *Public Galleries*, p. 14.

25. On the beginning of Jameson's and Eastlake's friendship in Rome in 1822, see David Robertson, *Sir Charles Eastlake and the Victorian Art World*, Princeton, 1978, p. 19. Chapters V, VII, and VIII in this study treat Eastlake's contributions to the shaping of the National Gallery.

26. *Companion to the Most Celebrated Private Galleries of Art in London*, London, 1844, p. xviii.

27. *Private Galleries*, p. 173.

28. *Private Galleries*, p. 241.

29. *Public Galleries*, p. 396.

30. Review of *Memoirs of the Early Italian Painters*, *The Athenaeum* 18 (1845), 817.

31. [Reprinted in] *Memoirs and Essays Illustrative of Art, Literature, and Social Morals*, London, 1846, p. 252.

32. *Memoirs and Essays*, pp. 26-29.

33. *Visits and Sketches* I, 115-16.

34. *Sacred and Legendary Art* I, London, 1905, 1.

35. *Sacred and Legendary Art* I, 6.

36. *Sacred and Legendary Art* I, 8.

37. *Visits and Sketches* II, 110.

38. *Sacred and Legendary Art* I, 11.

39. *Sacred and Legendary Art* I, 15.

40. The Italian philosopher Vico (1668-1744) studied myth as the key to establishing a rational theory of human origins.

41. An aspect of the relation of Jameson's work to Ruskin's is discussed in Adele M. Holcomb, "A.-F. Rio, Anna Jameson and Some Sources of the Second Volume of *Modern Painters* by Ruskin (1846)," *Gazette des Beaux-Arts* 91 (1978).

42. Review of *Sacred and Legendary Art, Blackwood's Magazine* 65 (1849), 186.

43. *Legends of the Monastic Orders*, London, 1850, p. xviii.

44. William Holman Hunt in *Pre-Raphaelitism and the Pre-Raphaelite Brotherhood* (2 vols., London, 1905) observes that "in the forties there was no systematic education to be obtained from the leaders of art" (I, 46) and that his reading of Reynolds and other standard works, joined "with what I already knew—not a little of this from the *Penny Magazine*—put me into a position to follow up clues when larger opportunities presented themselves" (I, 24). In the period of the early to mid-1840s to which Hunt alludes, the Jameson essays were the only source of such education in the *Penny Magazine*.

45. Needler, *Letters*, p. 188.

46. *Legends of the Madonna*, Boston, 1885, p. 23.

47. *Sisters of Charity, Catholic and Protestant, and the Communion of Labour*, Boston, 1857, p. 68.

48. Mary Camille Bowe, *François Rio: Sa Place dans le Renouveau catholique en Europe, 1797-1874*, Paris, n.d., p. 179. Translation by author.

49. Franz Kugler, *Handbook of Painting, I: The Italian Schools*, ed. by Sir Charles L. Eastlake, London, 1869, p. xiv.

50. John Steegman, *Consort of Taste, 1830-1870*, London, 1950, p. 185.

51. Robinson's depreciatory statements have often been quoted despite his own admission that an irrational association prevented him from trusting Jameson's good qualities. See his *Books and Their Writers* I, London, 1938, 441.

52. Lady Eastlake, *Journals and Correspondence* II, London, 1895, 137.

53. Bowe, *François Rio*, p. 180.

54. Frank Herrmann, *The English as Collectors: A Documented Chrestomathy*, New York, 1972, p. 329.

55. Undated letter to Mary Camille Bowe, quoted in her *François Rio*, p. 245.

SELECTED BIBLIOGRAPHY OF ANNA JAMESON

The present bibliography lists first editions of those books by Anna Jameson that are discussed or referred to in this essay and a selection of her periodical publications, which are not listed in Clara Thomas's bibliography.

Books, First Editions

A First or Mother's Dictionary for Children. London [1825].

A Lady's Diary. London 1826. Republished as *The Diary of an Ennuyée*. London, 1826.

The Loves of the Poets. 2 vols. London, 1829.

Memoirs of Celebrated Female Sovereigns. 2 vols. London, 1831.

Characteristics of Women, Moral, Poetical, and Historical. 2 vols. London, 1832.

Visits and Sketches at Home and Abroad. 4 vols. in 2. London, 1834.

Winter Studies and Summer Rambles in Canada. 3 vols. London, 1838.

Introduction and annotations to *Peter Paul Rubens: His Life and Genius*, by G. F. Waagen. London, 1840.

A Handbook to the Public Galleries of Art in and Near London. London, 1842.

Companion to the Most Celebrated Private Galleries of Art in London. London, 1844.

Memoirs of the Early Italian Painters. 2 vols. London, 1845.

On the Relative Position of Mothers and Governesses. London, 1846. Reprinted in *Memoirs and Essays*, 1846.

Memoirs and Essays Illustrative of Art, Literature, and Social Morals. London, 1846.

The Poetry of Sacred and Legendary Art. 2 vols. London, 1848.

Legends of the Monastic Orders, as Represented in the Fine Arts. London, 1850.

Legends of the Madonna, as Represented in the Fine Arts. London, 1852.

A Commonplace Book of Thoughts, Memories, and Fancies, Original and Selected. London, 1854.

A Hand-book to the Courts of Modern Sculpture in *The Fine Arts' Courts in the Crystal Palace.* London, 1854.

Sisters of Charity, Catholic and Protestant. London, 1855.

The Communion of Labour: A Second Lecture on the Social Employments of Women. London, 1856.

The History of Our Lord as Exemplified in Works of Art. Completed by Lady Eastlake, 2 vols. London, 1864.

Periodical Publications

Note: Page numbers have been omitted for the appearance in periodicals of work subsequently published in book form.

"Report of the Commissioners on the Employments of Children, &c: Condition of the Women and the Female Children." *The Athenaeum* 16 (1843). Reprinted in *Memoirs and Essays* as " 'Woman's Mission' and Woman's Position."

"Essays on the Lives of Remarkable Painters." *The Penny Magazine of the Society for the Diffusion of Useful Knowledge*, new series, 12 (1843): 19 installments; 13 (1844): 15 installments; 14 (1845): 11 installments. Reprinted as *Memoirs of the Early Italian Painters*.

"Washington Allston." *The Athenaeum* 17 (1844), 15-16; 39-41.

Excerpts from *Companion to the Most Celebrated Private Galleries of Art in London.* *The Athenaeum* 17 (1844).

Excerpts from *Sacred and Legendary Art.* *The Athenaeum* 18 (1845): 12 installments; 19 (1846): 6 installments.

"Some Thoughts on Art. Addressed to the Uninitiated." *The Art-Journal* 2 (1849), 69-71.

"John Gibson." *The Art-Journal* 2 (1849), 139-41.

Review of Tom Taylor, *The Life of Benjamin Robert Haydon, Historical Painter, with His Autobiography and Journals* (London, 1853), *Edinburgh Review*, 98 (1853), 518-66.

CHAPTER 5
MARGARET FULLER (1810-1850): HER WORK AS AN ART CRITIC

Corlette R. Walker
and Adele M. Holcomb[1]

Renowned as the brilliant and egocentric Corinne of New England transcendentalism, as editor, journalist and, ultimately, as partisan in the struggle
for Italian independence, Margaret Fuller has been more copiously written
about than any other female intellectual of early nineteenth-century America. Her presence as the only non-British subject of Edith Sitwell's *English
Eccentrics*, and Ralph Waldo Emerson's perplexed confession that "her
strength was not my strength,—her powers were a surprise"[2] suggest something of the ambivalence, mockery, and incomprehension with which
Fuller has been viewed. Recently she has become more credible, and more
compelling, as a result of studies by Ann Douglas, Susan Conrad, and
Paula Blanchard.[3] These writers have reconstructed sympathetically the
contradictory pressures of Fuller's education, the stratagems necessitated
by a social setting hostile to her self-realization, and the evidence of
integrity in the way she lived out the implications of her ideas. She is in the
process of being recovered as one of the "genuine heroines" of American
history, to use a phrase applied to Fuller by Ann Douglas.[4]

It seems partly understandable that Fuller's interest in the visual arts and
in the consideration of aesthetic questions has scarcely been noticed in the
recent literature. Paula Blanchard's generally excellent biography actually
deplores the art criticism Fuller "had the temerity to write for the *Dial*," the
result of what she takes to have been inadequate instruction; she cites with
disapproval tendencies in Fuller's writing on art, such as an interest in
physiognomy, that were in fact widely characteristic of art criticism at the
time.[5] Yet Fuller's concept of artistic creation as the highest form of human
knowledge and of spiritual realization was central to an important phase of
her thought. It was, to be sure, an idea she shared with other members of

the transcendentalist movement, but one which she characteristically developed so as to emphasize the active, symbol-forming function of the artist's mind. Despite limited firsthand acquaintance with art prior to her years in Europe (from 1846), she applied herself assiduously to all that could be learned from engravings, casts, books, and the tutelage of a friend, Samuel Ward, who had had the advantage of several years' study abroad. That these efforts were fruitful is attested by the superior penetration of her writings on aesthetic topics. Although they are limited in certain respects by the very character of transcendentalist belief, they register an altogether more serious level of engagement than that of contemporaries like Emerson and Thoreau, who did not recognize an obligation of close study of the visual arts. If not the first, she was certainly one of the earliest American critics to achieve a measure of competence in this field. As the first woman in her country to publish art criticism of any significance, she helped define a new area of intellectual opportunity beyond the limited domain (chiefly fiction) that women had entered.

Like most of her female contemporaries, Fuller (Figure 3) was educated primarily at home. Born in Cambridgeport, Massachusetts, in 1810, Sarah Margaret was the eldest child of Timothy and Margaret Crane Fuller. Her family was Unitarian. A man of unbending principle, Timothy Fuller had entered Harvard in 1797, where he was outspoken on behalf of unpopular causes such as opposition to slavery. Subsequently, he read law, set up practice in Boston, and ran successfully for the state legislature. In 1818 Fuller was elected to the first of four terms in the U.S. Senate. His intellectual ambitions for Sarah Margaret strongly marked her childhood to the detriment, she later claimed, of her health. From the age of three when her unusual intelligence was noticed, he worked out strenuous lesson plans for his daughter and would regularly hear her recite in the evening when he came home from his office. In this way she received an education, thoroughly grounded in the classics, that was normally restricted to sons who would enter the ministry or the law. While very young she mastered Latin; and her early acquaintance with the Greek myths, which antedated instruction in Christian tenets, influenced her imaginative life in a particularly vivid and lasting manner. She also learned several modern languages and read widely in English and French literature. It was part of the contradictions of Timothy Fuller's character that while he honored the traditional feminine virtues in his gentle and amiable wife, he demanded the highest standards of intellectual rigor in his articulate eldest daughter.

Paula Blanchard has pointed out that the educational regime imposed on Margaret (as she preferred to be called) was overlaid during adolescence by pressures of an opposite kind.[6] By this time, Timothy Fuller considered Margaret's imperfect grasp of feminine requirements to be regrettable and an obstacle to her success as an adult. Feminine requirements were of course

Figure 3. Margaret Fuller, ca. 1845. Photographed in 1870 by Purdy and Frear, Ithaca, New York, from a daguerreotype. (*Courtesy the Schlesinger Library, Radcliffe College*)

incompatible with the uncompromising candor she practiced out of principle as Timothy Fuller's daughter. Her attendance in 1824-1825 at a school
for young ladies in Groton was intended to temper her forthrightness and
also her physical awkwardness in society. Academic content at Miss
Prescott's establishment reflected prevailing opinions of what girls needed
to know and offered the wildest possible contrast to Timothy Fuller's
tuition at home. Margaret's experience of the disjunctive "masculine" and
"feminine" phases of her upbringing posed very sharply the problem of
reconciling her intellectual and sexual energies with strategies that would
gain her acceptance as a woman.

   Her mother was surely important to a sense of her female identity that
Margaret consistently cherished. They were mutually devoted, and Mrs.
Fuller relied heavily on her daughter for advice and assistance following
Timothy Fuller's sudden death in 1835. Margaret's feeling about the
maternal tie is suggested in one of her contributions to the *Dial*, "The
Magnolia of Lake Pontchartrain." In this fictional piece the magnolia, who
clearly speaks for the writer, laments, "Ceaselessly they [man and nature]
called on me for my beautiful gifts. . . . yet never sought to aid me." Overcome by an entire absence of sympathy, she falls over, "black, stiff, and
powerless."[7] She is "taken home" and consoled by the queen and guardian
of the flowers, who is "secret, radiant, profound ever. . . . Like all such
beings she was feminine. All the secret powers are 'Mothers.' There is but
one paternal power."[8] Fuller's image of one of the "secret powers"
conforms with a widespread tendency in nineteenth-century religious
thought to posit or exalt a female divinity in some form,[9] but the loyalties
from which it derived were rooted in personal experience.

   Another female influence in Margaret's early life was that of a young
Englishwoman, Ellen Kilshaw, who became a friend of the Fullers in 1818.
She was an amateur painter, and part of her glamor for Margaret may have
been associated with her artistic interests. But Ellen Kilshaw's entire being
was eloquent in Margaret's view; her very presence seemed to her young
admirer to be consummately expressive and graceful. Shortly after Ellen's
American visit, her father in Liverpool lost his fortune. The Fullers, including Margaret, were informed by correspondence of the excruciating dilemmas into which Ellen was then plunged. Although horrified to do so, she
was forced to hire out as a governess.

   Margaret was deeply responsive to natural beauty and later in her
writings would frequently invoke images of the world of nature as meta-
phors of human growth or states of mind. The magnolia of her *Dial* piece
not only was typical of the flower symbolism she identified with the
feminine psyche but also was part of a view of nature as the fundamental
medium through which the human spirit confronts itself and receives
intimations of a larger whole, or divine presence. Characteristically, the

resolution of a spiritual crisis she experienced in 1831 was associated with a natural setting, that of a secluded pool in woods near Cambridge, where the sun suddenly shone out with a "transparent sweetness" and she was "taken up into God," thus becoming reconciled with the conditions of her life.[10] Her feeling for nature was no less profound because it did not elicit the renunciatory devotion of a Thoreau, for whom the attainment of oneness depended in part on sustained retirement and sexual continence.

Endowed with a generous capacity for friendship, with ebullient sexual energies and a dazzling talent for conversation, Margaret Fuller's gifts directed her towards society. Talk was more her medium than written expression, and the problem of finding, or creating, an appropriate audience in provincial New England exceeded the analogous difficulty of defining a readership through publication. Of her powers as a conversationalist, William Henry Channing wrote: "She was at once impressible and creative, impulsive and deliberate. . . . By the vivid intensity of her conceptions, she brought out in those around their own consciousness, and, by the glowing vigor of her intellect, roused into action their torpid powers."[11]

Her conversation attracted many young men, as well as women, to her circle. In instances that occurred over a period of fifteen years, passionate attachment on her side developed under the name of friendship. The earliest of these, an attraction to her cousin George Davis, set the pattern for such relationships. In 1832 he abruptly announced his engagement to another woman and left town to establish himself elsewhere. Margaret suffered deeply from this rejection as she had done, less intensely, from the defections of other young men who enjoyed her company but finally chose quiet girls with no intellectual attainments. She must have sympathized with the comment of one of her favorite writers, Madame de Staël, on the common male preference for women of limited understanding: "It's a matter of taste; and anyway, as the number of distinguished women is very small, those who don't want one have a wide choice."[12]

The year 1832 brought another disappointment when Timothy Fuller lost his hopes of an ambassadorship under John Quincy Adams, who was defeated in the presidential election of that year. Timothy Fuller decided to retire from politics and in 1833 moved his family to rural solitude on a farm at Groton. Removed from friends in Cambridge and Boston, to her utter dismay, Margaret also had to give up hopes of a trip to Europe, as family finances were straitened. Instead, she helped with the work of a farm household. There were now six younger Fuller children, and Margaret assumed the task of teaching her sister and brothers. She resolved that her free time would be entirely devoted to study of the German language and literature. In this decision, she was one of the earliest and most assiduous among students of German letters in New England at the time.

Fuller had become aware of the new currents in German philosophy and literature by way of publications by Coleridge and Carlyle and through the work of Madame de Staël, whose example as an intellectual she would later praise in *Woman in the Nineteenth Century*. Published in 1813 in London, *De l'Allemagne* introduced German culture to the outside world, that is, essentially, to France. Madame de Staël's achievement in interpreting German literature and art as an expression of national character suggested to Fuller the possible scope of criticism as a vocation for women. *De l'Allemagne* also offered an introduction to recent German thought through a luminous exposition of the leading ideas of Kant's *Critique of Pure Reason* (1781) and of the revolution in German philosophy that it engendered. Kant's analysis of the ordering processes of the mind as a shaping factor in sensory perception would have a bearing on ideas about art that Fuller worked out in the late 1830s.

With her friend James Freeman Clarke, she had begun in 1830 to read systematically in German literature. Fuller's characteristic intensity of engagement led to study of the German language, which she had not mastered in infancy. She did so in three months in 1831 or 1832. With the Unitarian minister Frederick Henry Hedge and Elizabeth Palmer Peabody, Fuller's senior by six years and fluent in German since the mid-1820s, she became one of a small minority in New England who could read German writers in the original. If Fuller's attraction to German thought came to be shared generally by the intellectuals of her circle, it was in good part as a result of her initiative. When Emerson was first introduced to the work of Goethe, he expressed indifference. It was only after Fuller had borrowed his edition of Goethe, made notes on it, and discussed these notes with Emerson that his interest was engaged.[13] Although the importance of German ideas to Emerson's thought has been questioned,[14] they undoubtedly had a catalytic effect on American Romanticism. Fuller's contributions to this development were essential, especially with regard to the interpretation of Goethe. While gathering materials for a life of the writer (deceased in 1832), Fuller produced a translation of *Eckermann's Conversations with Goethe* (1839). Her urbanity of mind is evident in the preface to this work. Against such charges as Goethe's lack of Christian piety, recently levelled by *Blackwood's Magazine* but in any case prevalent in the United States, she argues for the assessment of Goethe by his own law. He should be measured, Fuller claims, against his belief in creative activity, by his powers of observation and sympathy, and by his search for an underlying unity of phenomena in nature and the human realm. Finally, he should be judged by his quality as a writer and as a critic of art and literature.

Goethe's art criticism, which even today has been insufficiently examined and appreciated, encouraged Margaret Fuller's attention to the visual arts in the later 1830s. Another circumstance favoring an interest in art was her friendship from 1835 with Samuel Gray Ward. Ward was a student at

Harvard who wanted to be a landscape painter. In August 1835 he joined a party with Fuller, her Cambridge friend Eliza Farrar, and others to tour the upper Hudson and Mohawk Valley. Sites in the Catskills recalled Byron's evocation of the Rhine in *Childe Harold* and Turner engravings of Drachenfels and Ehrenbreitstein; members of the excursion admired scenes that were being celebrated just then by Thomas Cole and other painters of the Hudson River School. To Fuller's enjoyment of the beauty of nature, deepened by the poetry of Goethe, Ward contributed the point of view of an enthusiast of landscape painting.

Soon after their friendship was formed, Ward left for Europe and did not return till 1838. He brought back with him a large collection of engravings after Raphael, Leonardo, Michelangelo and Guercino, among others; his architectural prints included engravings after Greek architecture, Palladio's *Four Books of Architecture* and the etchings of Piranesi's *Vedute di Roma* and *Carceri* series. Ward regaled Fuller with his discovery of art history and she applied herself to learn all that she could about the visual arts. During long conversations in the Athenaeum with Rafaello, as she called him, Fuller conceived a fervent attraction to Ward that was masked by an insistence on the claims of friendship. Though her self-awareness in general was remarkable, it is unlikely that she recognized the ambiguity of her behavior in such an instance. But it also seems apparent that none of the men she knew in New England were capable of accepting her as a woman— a very different situation indeed from that of Madame de Staël and her male admirers. Ward backed off for a time and finally announced he was in love with someone else, who disconcertingly proved to be a mutual friend, Anna Barker. Fuller struggled to surmount her pain in a spirit of stoical renunciation.

In the early 1830s, Fuller had begun to earn some money by giving evening lessons to women in language and literature. Advertising these sessions, which were organized as twelve-week courses, she offered to help reduce the obstacles and discouragement women faced in their attempts at self-education. She was impelled by concern for the problem as well as by the need to become financially self-sustaining. The devoted following of female pupils that Fuller began to form at that time was later extended with the success of her "Conversations for Women" in Boston, initiated in 1839. One participant wrote that "In no way was Margaret's supremacy so evident as in the impulse she gave to the minds of younger women."[15]

She was much less fond of teaching children but saw no alternative to accepting a position at Bronson Alcott's school in Boston after Timothy Fuller's death in 1835. Alcott was the benign and improvident father of Louisa May and an exponent of educational ideas that were far in advance of their time. Wishing to encourage rather than stifle the spontaneity of childhood, he used a conversational method wherever the nature of the subject matter permitted. Fuller loyally defended him when charges of blasphemy and obscenity greeted the publication in 1837 of *Conversations on the Gospels*, an account of proceedings at Alcott's school. By then funds were insufficient to pay her salary. She next taught for two years at the Greene Street School in Providence. But Providence had no intellectual life, and in leaving two years later she confessed to her girl pupils that she had been "oppressed while teaching them" because of "false impressions which were given me of the position I should there occupy."[16] Surviving letters indicate that she inspired respect and admiration despite the unfavorable conditions.[17]

Margaret Fuller's most congenial experience as a teacher came with the opening of her Boston Conversations in 1839. The earlier evening lessons for women helped suggest the idea, as did her experience of Alcott's method and the example of Elizabeth Peabody's "historical conferences." These seminars on history for adult women had been introduced by Peabody in 1832. It was in Peabody's front parlor that Fuller held the initial session of her Conversations on 6 November 1839.[18] The participants were women of prominence in Boston, who paid a fee to attend: Eliza Quincy; Elizabeth Bancroft; the three Peabody sisters, Elizabeth, Sophia Hawthorne, and Mary Mann; Maria White, the abolitionist; Lydia Cabot Parker; and others. Proceeding "to open all the great questions of life," these women took as their point of departure Fuller's allegorical concepts of the Greco-Roman gods—of Jupiter, for example, as an embodiment of the will and Mercury of understanding.[19] In the discussions, she "depicted what she had gained from art," according to Caroline Healey Dall.[20] For instances of the representation of pagan deities, Fuller referred to casts that since 1823 had comprised a museum of reproductions in the Boston Athenaeum. It included the Apollo Belvedere, the Laocoon, the Diana of Versailles, the Belvedere Torso and other traditionally venerated examples of ancient sculpture. Classical subjects also figured in engravings after works in European museums which were part of the Brimmer donation to the Athenaeum in 1838.

Margaret and her Friends, or Ten Conversations with Margaret Fuller upon the Mythology of the Greeks and its Expression in Art, by Caroline Dall, is the only full transcript of a sequence of Fuller's conversations. It records evening sessions for men and women that she held in 1841. That such a program was launched at the substantial price of twenty dollars for ten conversations indicates how lively an interest had been generated by the women's series. Yet Margaret "never enjoyed this mixed class," according to Caroline Dall.[21] Emerson, Bronson Alcott, the scholarly minister F. H. Hedge, and the sculptor William W. Story were among the male participants who attended more or less regularly. They were joined by many of the women from the previous group and, incidentally, by the beautiful but not remarkably bright Anna Barker to whom Fuller had lost Samuel Ward.

Caroline Dall reports Margaret's presentation of a theme for each evening and the talk that ensued. Elaborating her concept of myth as a key to the emergence of civilization, she proposed at the first session that Saturn devouring his children "depicts" the slow evolution of human faculties, when time absorbed the sum of human energies; Rhea, or productive energy, finally puts an obstacle in his way in the form of Jupiter, personification of the will, who usurps the rule of time.[22] And so on; the development of ideas is rich and ingenious. Most members of the class were well able to discuss the ideas, but very little prepared to relate them to works of art. Fuller nevertheless would revert to that aspect of her topic. On the third evening she avowed that all her ideas of Greek myth "were deduced from Art," rather than from literary sources.[23]

Caroline Dall's account decidedly shows that the men dominated the discussions, and Margaret must have felt that an opportunity to draw the women out was largely lost. Dall also reveals (and deplores) a male propensity to wander from the point. Alcott, for example, might wonder if a "purer mythology" could not arise from a mixture of Persian, Greek, and Christian myths and deflect the evening's plan into "confusing and tiresome talk,"[24] though Fuller's guidance was rarely frustrated to that extent.

Most of the participants in the conversations were associated with the transcendentalist movement. In 1836, transcendentalism had assumed a casually organized form as a discussion group of liberal Unitarian ministers and, in its subsequent phases, most of the adherents were, or had been, Unitarians.[25] Among the original members were Emerson, F. H. Hedge, George Ripley, and Theodore Parker. The Transcendental Club was soon opened to nonclergymen and in 1837 admitted four women: Margaret Fuller, Sarah Alden Ripley, Elizabeth Hoar, and Lidian Emerson. Transcendentalism reached general public awareness in 1838, when Emerson delivered his Divinity College address in Cambridge describing religious experience as a private intuition of self-executing moral laws. Essentially a movement in religious thought, transcendentalism drew on the impetus of German Romanticism in its opposition to the empiricism of John Locke, in its faith in knowledge that "transcended" the evidence of sense data, and in its resistance to institutional forms of authority. The transcendentalist idea was at least potentially a liberating impulse for women because it affirmed that women as human beings had the right to full development of their God-given capacities.[26]

As a movement, transcendentalism found its most significant expression in the publication between 1840 and 1844 of *The Dial*, a quarterly "Magazine for Literature, Philosophy, and Religion." During its first two years Margaret Fuller edited the journal on what proved to be a meagerly remunerated basis. Throughout its span she contributed to it articles on art and literature, as well as poetry and works of fiction. She was largely responsible for the remarkable degree to which *Dial* contributors wrote on the visual arts, though there clearly was a general fund of interest in the subject. It was connected with a tendency in transcendentalism to celebrate vision as the most crucial faculty in attaining a deeper insight into the divine presence in nature. Besides Fuller's pieces, the *Dial* included such items as James Freeman Clarke's "Nature and Art, or the Three Landscapes" (Oct. 1840), invoking typical works by Gaspard Poussin, Domenichino, and Washington Allston; it offered Emerson's "Thoughts on Art" (January 1841), "Painting and Sculpture" by Sophia Ripley (July 1841), and Samuel Ward's "Notes on Art and Architecture" (July 1843).

In transcendentalist belief the phenomenal world was seen as a manifestation, necessarily limited under any aspect in which it was physically perceived, of divine coherence in the universe. The implications of this view for art included a dismissive attitude towards the material means of the plastic arts. This was a serious deficiency if not offset by a willingness to learn, where poverty of artistic culture was the prevailing circumstance. The transcendental idea also led to inordinate demands on art as revelation, and this expectation is perhaps involved in the sharp disappointment Fuller expressed with aspects of the work of Allston and Canova. On the other hand, the nature of art as a visual medium equipped it to deal with the most important category of divine signals and to suggest realities that lay beyond what was immediately given. Such indeed was the power of the great contemporary masters of Romantic landscape, J. M. W. Turner and Caspar David Friedrich.

The direction taken by Emerson in his "Thoughts on Art" was to assert expansively that art is "the conscious utterance of thought, by speech or action, to any end."[27] He considered that there was a distinction in purpose of use and beauty between the applied and the fine arts. The useful arts were totally subservient to Nature, while the fine arts admitted the presence of "Art, which resides in the model or plan on which the genius of the artist is expended."[28] His conclusion is that "the power of Nature predominates over the human will in all works of even the fine arts. . . . Nature paints the best part of the picture; carves the best part of the statue; builds the best part of the house; and speaks the best part of the oration."[29]

Recalling her view of the origins of civilization as a triumph of the human will, one would not expect Margaret Fuller to endorse Emerson's notion of the artist as comparatively passive before the spectacle or forces of Nature. In her "Essay on Critics" (July 1840) she distinguished art and Nature as comprising separate spheres. "Nature is the literature and art of the divine mind; human literature and art the criticism on that,"[30] and she insisted on judging each by its own standard. Imitation was not the purpose of art. Because the artist's concern was actively to grasp and give form to transcendent truth, artistic creation was in her view the loftiest type of human existence. The criticism of art was yet another sphere, and its relation to that of the artist engaged her all the more because she doubted that women could be creators in the full sense. Reasons for this failure of confidence are not far to seek in Romantic notions of the artist's god-like powers. Even so, she seized on what evidence she could find of women's achievement as artists; a later issue of the *Dial* contained her translation of a romance based on traditions about the Dutch painter Maria von Oosterwyck, in whose work "all the flowers of the field have lived again."[31] In the meantime, the criticism of art had its legitimate function. The critic is a mediator between artist and public and must have qualities of the poet, the philosopher, and the observer.[32]

Fuller did not claim for herself as an art critic the "comprehensive" mental powers that she associated with the highest standard of criticism, represented to her by Goethe. Not many contemporaries, with better opportunities than hers, could have done so. In presenting her article on an exhibition of Washington Allston's pictures (July 1840), she stated that her "eye and taste" had not been sufficiently formed by study of "the best works of art" to produce criticism of the level she admired.[33] Among members of her circle she was unusual in holding any such concept of the requirements. Fuller proposed rather to fill a breach, as almost no published commentary had appeared since the exhibition was held in 1839. Admitted- ly she was disappointed with the work, which she had mostly seen before, because in the ensemble it did not match the idea she had formed of the artist's mind. Time and place were not propitious to pursuit of the grand manner, but in any event Allston was not adequate to his purpose. Her criticism of his thirteen-by-eleven-foot canvas, *The Dead Man Revived by Touching the Bones of the Prophet Elisha* (1811-1813), shows a firm grasp of traditional principles of dramatic concentration in the depiction of an action and of the requirements of decorum. Fuller might have been con- trasting the work with its Renaissance model, Sebastiano del Piombo's *Resurrection of Lazarus*, in pointing out that subjects like the miracles of Christ depend for plausibility on the "moral dignity" of the main actor: "He is the natural centre of the picture, and the emotions of all present grade from and cluster round him."[34] There is no "natural centre" in the *Dead Man*, where a miracle occurs through the agency of relics and the corpse—so "offensive to the sensual eye"—cannot register the expression essential in a principal figure.

The "beautiful" rather than the "grand historical style" is Allston's domain, Fuller concludes. Referring to pictures of single figures, which are almost always in attitudes of repose, she observes: "A certain bland delicacy enfolds all these creations as an atmosphere."[35] Her full enthusiasm is reserved for his landscapes, of which the *Moonlit Landscape* of 1819 (Figure 4) is a fine example. In no other "department" does he display in such high degree

Figure 4. *Moonlit Landscape*, by Washington Allston, 1819. Boston, Museum of Fine Arts. (*Courtesy Museum of Fine Arts, Boston; Gift of William Sturgis Bigelow*)

the attributes of the master. A power of sympathy, which gives each landscape a perfectly individual character. [sic] Here the painter is merged in his theme, and these pictures affect us as parts of nature, so absorbed are we in contemplating them. . . . How the trees live and breathe out their mysterious souls! . . . Dear companions of my life, whom yearly I know better, yet into whose heart I can no more penetrate than see your roots, while you live and grow. I feel what you have said to this painter; I can in some degree appreciate the power he has shown in repeating here the gentle oracle.[36]

Fuller thought of sculpture as corresponding "both from the material used and the laws of the art, to the highest state of the mind."[37] Sculpture portrayed the heights of human potentiality, as the ancient Greeks recognized in representing the human form in that medium to express divinity. Painting, on the other hand, was prosaic in its tendency to represent "more objects"; in the use of color, painting "worked more by illusion" and inclined towards the commonplace. Important for Fuller was the greater scope given the interpretation of character, especially heroic character, in the traditions of sculpture, notably those of the public monument and the Roman portrait bust. In her *Dial* review of an Athenaeum exhibition of painting and sculpture (October 1840), she hurries past copies of Raphael and Guido to the newly opened Sculpture Hall. Discussing the works (which were casts or copies), she does not employ the language of formal analysis, nonexistent at the time, but responds to the treatment of character. This was a central consideration of neoclassical portraits that invoked antique precedent not only in their form but in the gravity and truthfulness with which they interpreted male subjects. The direction of her comments on a head of Napoleon, probably one by Canova that was widely disseminated in copies, is therefore pertinent. Her observations on the two styles available to the portrait sculptor explore sensitively the prevailing modes by which male and female subjects were characterized:

A head must be of a style either very stern or very chaste, to make a deep impression on the beholder; there must be a great force of will and withholding of resources, giving a sense of depth below depth, which we call sternness; or else there must be that purity, flowing as from an inexhaustible fountain through every lineament, which drives far off or converts all baser natures. Napoleon's head is of the first description; it is stern, and not only so, but ruthless. Yet the ruthlessness excites no aversion. . . .[38]

When Fuller had an opportunity to see an exhibition in Boston of copies of Canova's work by his pupils, she found that it did not live up to her expectations of the most celebrated sculptor of recent times. But her *Dial* review (April 1843) states that after recognizing there was no question of finding a genius, "we have learnt to value him as a man of taste, and to understand why he filled such a niche in the history of his time."[39] This review contains a notable protest against the philistinism of a commercial society, one in which it seemed doubtful that citizens might be willing to spare time for the contemplation of sculpture. She protests that the arts are not a luxury extraneous to the real business of life, but the "magic mirror by whose aid all its phases are interpreted. . . ."[40]

Fuller's article on Canova was followed shortly in the *Dial* by her essay of July 1843: "The Great Lawsuit: Man versus Men. Woman versus Women." In expanded form it appeared two years later as a book, *Woman in the Nineteenth Century*. As George Eliot recognized in her essay "Margaret Fuller and Mary Wollstonecraft," Fuller's work was lineally related to that of the eighteenth-century feminist.[41] Attacking the social conventions that stifle the development of female intellect, she argues that women must have an education to equip them as independent and effective members of society. For Fuller this is nothing less than a sacred claim: "A being of infinite scope must not be treated with an exclusive view to any one relation."[42] She considered the male and female elements of personality to be two sides of what she called the great radical dualism and that constraints on women's development diminished the quality of any union of the sexes. "Therefore," she wrote:

. . . I would have Woman lay aside all thought, such as she habitually cherishes, of being taught and led by men. I would have her, like the Indian girl, dedicate herself to the Sun, the Sun of Truth, and go nowhere if his beams did not make clear the path. I would have her free from compromise, from complaisance, from helplessness, because I would have her good enough and strong enough to love one and all beings from the fullness, not the poverty of being.[43]

During the summer of 1843, Fuller travelled to Niagara with her friend Sarah Clarke, who was a landscape painter, a pupil of Washington Allston. In Buffalo they embarked on a Great Lakes steamboat to Chicago. Their circuitous excursion was followed by journeys in northern Illinois and into Wisconsin as far as Milwaukee. From her notes, Fuller wrote *Summer on the Lakes*, a travel book of remarkable graphic power, sharp social analysis, and good humor. It vividly describes her dilating apprehension of space before the "sublime distances" of the western prairies. Fuller's pictorial sense is deployed with arresting effect in passages that evoke some phase of human activity that takes on color and particularity from its location in a larger scene; immediacy and breadth of spatial reference are intimately joined. The book shows a certain bilateral symmetry, from topographical and thematic points of view, with the travel part of Anna Jameson's *Winter Studies and Summer Rambles in Canada* (1838). Jameson had noted the discontent of most women she encountered in Canada and their poor preparation for life under frontier conditions. Fuller similarly found that

American women, reared to pursue decorative accomplishments, were meagrely equipped mentally and physically to support the hardships of life as settlers. In one notable respect, however, she differed with Jameson's opinions. While acknowledging the eloquence of her argument, Fuller rejected the claim that the status of Indian women was less disadvantaged than that of their European counterparts.

Correspondences between Fuller's interests and those of Anna Jameson extend well beyond the affinities displayed on this occasion. Jameson's German travels and friendships and the role she created for herself as a critic of literature and art aroused Fuller's admiration. They may have met when Jameson was in Boston in 1837; certainly they did in the later 1840s when Jameson presented Margaret Fuller to Ottilie von Goethe at St. Peter's in Rome.[44] Respectful allusions to the elder woman's work are scattered throughout Fuller's writings. Indeed, the Indian girl who dedicated herself to the sun in *Woman in the Nineteenth Century* is an acknowledged reminiscence of Jameson's account of a Chippewa woman who chose to remain single and devote herself to sun worship.[45]

In 1844 Fuller left Boston to begin a new career as journalist and critic for the *New York Tribune*. Horace Greeley was then developing the mass readership of a paper that would later rally public opinion behind Lincoln's conduct of the war and the Emancipation Proclamation. In New York, Fuller was responsible for the literary and art criticism of a daily newspaper, and she also read the foreign press to select items of interest for the *Tribune*. She began to see herself as a journalist in relation to the example of her English contemporary Harriet Martineau, with whom she had become acquainted in Boston in 1835. Fuller's purview included music criticism, poetry, travel literature, children's books, and commentary on a wide range of topics such as the condition of the blind, Swedenborgianism, and clairvoyance. Weekly translations of articles from the *Schnellpost* and the *Courrier des Etats-Unis* were also part of her assignment. It is an index of the prevailing respect for Fuller's work that reviews in the *Tribune* were collected and published in 1846 under the title *Papers on Literature and Art*. Edgar Allan Poe praised her criticism as "forcible, thoughtful, suggestive, brilliant and to a certain extent scholar-like." He thought her style "one of the very best with which I am acquainted. In general effect, I know of no style which surpasses it. It is singularly piquant, vivid, terse, bold, luminous —leaving details out of sight, it is everything that a style should be."[46]

As in her *Dial* article on Canova, Fuller's art criticism for the *Tribune* offered judgments that were related to the nature of the artist's claims. She distinguished three categories of creative power: the work of genius, the work of scholars or interpreters of genius, and the work of vigorous minds with something to say to their own generation. Her reviews indicate that she valued the suggestive power of visual imagery, its possible resonance of association. At the same time, a respect for clarity and propriety of expression that had been implanted by Fuller's classical education led her to insist on the adequacy of means to the requirements of communication. In this period, she had still not had the opportunity to study art in Europe.

An occasion to do so materialized at last when Fuller's New York friends Rebecca and Marcus Spring invited her to accompany them on a trip to England, France, and Italy. The journey became financially feasible with the help of a loan and an understanding that she would work as foreign correspondent for the *Tribune*, at the rate of eight dollars per report. She thus was the first American woman to work as a foreign correspondent and one of the first among her compatriots generally to work in that capacity. Fuller's dispatches to the *Tribune* form the bulk of her surviving writings from 1846 until her death in 1850. A number of these were published under the title *At Home and Abroad* in 1856.

As a correspondent, her reports took the diarist's form characteristic of travel writing of the period. Fuller relished the latitude for wide-ranging commentary in this expansive genre. Gratefully absorbed in her first encounter with societies other than her own and, especially, in recognition of the sources of tradition in Italy, she wrote of the "joy here that is experienced by the colonist in returning to the parent home. What was but picture to us becomes a reality; remote allusions and derivations trouble us no more: we see the pattern of the stuff and understand the whole tapestry. . . ."[47] Like herself, she imagined that the ideal traveller ought to have "a poetic sensibility to what is special and individual both in nations and men" and should entertain "no special object in traveling beyond the delight of new and various impressions."[48]

She was consistently open and responsive to new ideas. Admiring the new strictness of method in art scholarship as exemplified in the work of G. F. Waagen, director of the Berlin Gallery, she praised his *Art and Artists in England and Paris* (1838) after studying its subject at firsthand. "Dr. Waagen's book," she advised her readers, "is merely a list of these treasures, but a list made out and marked as only a virtuoso of diamond-pure virtue could do it. In him we see concentrated, refined, and arranged, the best knowledge, the last analyses of taste, so that each word he says *tells*, and all his plain remarks are keys to regions of thought."[49]

Her own account of Turner's current work is a splendid instance of her receptivity and discernment as a critic, confronted for the first time with Turner's paintings. Introducing her readers to the controversy in England over the master's late style, she notes that according to one group "it is impossible to make out the design, or find what Turner is aiming at by those strange blotches of color," while the other side acclaims him as divine.[50] Her observations are based on a visit to a private collection in London in 1846, possibly that of H. A. J. Munro, where she might have seen watercolors like the *Lucerne: Moonlight* (Figure 5):

Figure 5. *Lucerne: Moonlight*, by Joseph Mallord William Turner, 1843. London, British Museum. (*By permission of the Trustees of the British Museum*)

The later pictures . . . were mysterious-looking things,—hieroglyphics of picture, rather than picture itself. Sometimes you saw a range of red dots, which, after long looking, dawned on you as the roofs of houses,—shining streaks turned out to be most alluring rivulets, if traced with patience and a devout eye. Above all, they charmed the eye and the thought. Still, these pictures, it seems to me, cannot be considered fine works of Art. . . . A great work of Art demands a great thought, or a thought of beauty adequately expressed. . . . But in a transition state, whether of Art or literature, deeper thoughts are imperfectly expressed because they cannot yet be held and treated masterly. This seems to be the case with Turner. . . . He has become awake to what is elemental, normal in Nature,—such, for instance, as one sees in the working of water on the sea-shore. He tries to represent these primitive forms. In the drawings of Piranesi, in the pictures of Rembrandt, one sees this grand language exhibited more truly. It is not picture, but certain primitive and leading effects of light and shadow, or lines and contours, that captivate the attention.[51]

While such defenders as Ruskin and C. R. Leslie in the mid-1840s justified Turner's "indistinctness" on the grounds of its truth to nature, Fuller perceived the presence of a pictorial language that sought to convey depth and richness of thought. If it imperfectly succeeded in doing so, the transitional state of art (or Turner's relation to the process itself?) did not admit a vantage point from which such contents might be firmly seized and articulated. Despite her impression of an inchoate character in his work, Fuller's sensitivity to the potency of suggestion in Turner—his intimations of what is primordial and incessant in nature—marks her review as one of the most candid and thoughtful among contemporary judgments.

While in England, Fuller was a guest of Harriet Martineau at Ambleside and, with the Springs, visited Wordsworth at Rydal Mount. Through an introduction from Emerson, she met Carlyle in London and, as she did not challenge his dominance of the conversation, he decided that she was "not nearly such a bore as I expected."[52] Far more significant was the friendship she formed with Giuseppe Mazzini, who was then living in exile in England and working tirelessly on behalf of Italian liberation from Austrian rule. Her interest in the cause of Italian independence was engaged then, before the period of her residence in Rome.

During the fall and winter of 1846-1847, Fuller visited Paris, where she did not have the kind of entrée into intellectual circles that she had enjoyed in London. Insufficiently prepared to appreciate the traditions of French art, she was also out of sympathy with the new realist tendencies, considering that "Art can only be truly art by presenting an adequate outward symbol of some fact in the interior life." She continues: "But then it is a symbol that Art seeks to present, and not the fact itself. These French painters seem to have no idea of this; they have not studied the method of Nature."[53] Her objections to the representation of suffering in French painting by "streams of blood,—wickedness by the most ghastly contortions" anticipate a salient theme in English critical response to French art during the 1850s and 1860s.[54]

But in Paris she had the great satisfaction of meeting George Sand, whom she considered one of the three leading French novelists of the day (with Balzac and Eugène Sue). To a friend, she described how heartily she "enjoyed the sense of so rich, so prolific, so ardent a genius. I liked the woman in her, too, very much. . . ."[55] She was also rewarded by meeting Adam Mickiewicz, the Polish patriot and poet, just prior to her departure. Their friendship continued in correspondence in which he encouraged her to break away from the trammels of New England puritanism and take stock of her sexual needs and capabilities. Mickiewicz's appreciation of her as a woman and as a human being helped to prepare the personal transformation that Fuller experienced in Italy.

It was in Italy that Fuller found her true spiritual and aesthetic home at last. Arriving in Rome in April 1847, she found Italy "worthy to be loved and embraced, not talked about"[56] and "that one cannot pass the time better than by quietly *looking* one's fill. . . ."[57] Yet she was thoroughly immersed in the social and political struggle that was then tending towards its culmination in the revolutions of 1848. Two months before the workers' rising in Paris of June 1848, she had announced that "the political is being merged in the social struggle," and she was equally sibylline in pronouncing on the fall of Metternich: "the seed of the woman has had his foot on the serpent."[58] The fervent hunger for self-transformation, for transcendence, that had marked Fuller's personal quest had its deepest fulfilment in her presence at the festival of European revolution in 1848. She wrote to W. H. Channing that it was "a time such as I always dreamed of" and that when she returned, she "would be possessed of a great history."[59]

Her feeling that Italy was a truer home to her than the one she had left was subsequently reinforced by her liaison with Giovanni Ossoli, the youngest son of an ancient and aristocratic, though not affluent, Roman family. They became lovers in the autumn of 1847. The only surviving evidence as to their marriage (and many papers were destroyed by the Fuller family because marriage after the birth of Margaret's child was considered scandalous) has been published by Joseph Jay Deiss.[60] It consists of a letter from Ossoli's sister Angela to Fuller's sister Ellen in which Angela refers to her brother's marriage in Florence, where he and Margaret lived after their departure from Rome in September 1849. Besides sexual attraction, their union was based on an unusual quality of personal sympathy and a shared commitment to the goal of Italian independence.

Though her life in Italy was extraordinarily eventful in its private and public dimensions, Fuller managed to visit the studios of nearly all the notable English, American, and European artists in Rome and Florence. She was not enthusiastic about the work of her compatriots, Horatio

Greenough, Thomas Crawford, and Hiram Powers. Of the latter's *Greek Slave*, one of the most widely acclaimed statues of the nineteenth century, she wrote that much of its reputation depended on "drawing-room rapture and newspaper echo."[61] The fairest opportunity for American artists seemed to lie in the direction of landscape. "Prodigality of subject" in the American scene "seems to give us a hint not to be mistaken," she urged. In the painters Christopher Cranch and Jasper Cropsey, she found promise of a national school:

Nature, it seems to me, reveals herself more freely in our land; she is true, virgin and confiding,—she smiles upon the vision of a true Endymion. I hope to see, not only copies upon canvas of our magnificent scenes, but a transfusion of the spirit which is their divinity.[62]

But the sense that American landscape had qualities of innocence and splendor to reveal through its painters was in contrast to Fuller's perception of her country's fading value as a political example to the rest of the world. In her opinion, the movement that brought down the monarchy of Louis Philippe in France held a lesson for the American people in the meaning of fraternity and equality.

After an extremely difficult and anxious pregnancy, Fuller gave birth to a son in country retirement at Rieti on 5 September 1848. By complicated arrangements, Ossoli saw to the essential step of having the baby baptized with his name as Angelo Eugenio Ossoli. Fuller discovered an intense and unlooked for happiness in the presence of little Angelo. She and Ossoli drew together more closely in their joint concern for the infant's welfare. But both were caught up shortly after in the events surrounding establishment of the Roman Republic in February 1849. While Ossoli fought in the defense of Rome, Fuller accepted the responsibility offered her by Princess Cristina Belgioioso to direct the hospital of the Fate Bene Fratelli throughout the period of resistance. The capitulation of the city to the French under General Oudinot, who entered Rome on 4 July, prompted her to write that "private hopes of mine are fallen with the hopes of Italy."[63]

Before and after the debacle, Fuller collected materials for a history of the Italian revolution that she thought would be her most important work. Elizabeth Barrett Browning, who met Fuller and Ossoli in the autumn of 1849 in Florence, stated that the book "would probably have been more equal to her faculty" than anything Fuller had previously written, but that if completed its socialist views "would have drawn the wolves on her . . . both in England and America."[64] Though her mother was prepared to welcome her back, consternation filled her relatives and friends at home when rumors circulated early in 1850 that the marriage consisted of a Fourierist ceremony without legal status.[65] It was in these inauspicious circumstances that she embarked for America with Ossoli and their child on 17 May 1850. As they neared New York two months later, a storm drove the ship into sands off Fire Island. There the vessel broke up within sight of the shore and Fuller, Ossoli, and their son perished.

Margaret Fuller's gifts as an interpreter of the visual arts were deployed partly through her conversations, of which there is record of only one series, one that she did not consider especially successful. Her achievement in this dimension is obviously difficult to measure, yet her brilliance in spontaneous talk was widely recognized; it was largely directed to defining qualities embodied in the plastic arts and in examining themes she thought had their most compelling expression in sculpture and painting. That she was able to create an audience for such talk among people who had seen almost nothing besides engravings and casts, and without having herself had the benefit of European travel, is by any standard remarkable. Her seriousness in seizing what means were available to her in New England for the study of art "transcended" indeed the habit of lofty generalization on the subject with which most intellectuals in her circle were satisfied.

Fuller's written work as an art critic consists entirely of journal or newspaper pieces. The obstacles to inventing a vocation for herself in a setting that did not offer the encouragement she needed, along with the very urgent need of finding money to live on, divided her energies among teaching, editorship, and journalism. Finally, she was directed to the writing of history by her experiences in Rome. Her attraction to art had its importance in each of the phases of her career—even at the height of her involvement with the Roman struggle, she grieved for the irreparable damage done to the city's fabric as a result of the siege—but she did not have the leisure or means for sustained writing on art.

Her significance lies in the audacity, and the quality, of her efforts to introduce an understanding of art in a provincial scene. Fuller went against the grain of a society increasingly obsessed with money-getting in her assertion that "the arts are no luxury, no mere ornament and stimulus to a civic and complicated existence," but rather the "magic mirror" by which all phases of life may be understood.[66] It is no small thing to have published such a statement in Boston in 1843. Her commentary on landscape painting and her evocation of prairie landscapes in *Summer on the Lakes* identified what was probably the most crucial aspect of aesthetic experience in nineteenth-century America, that associated with the land and the potentialities suggested by its distances and its immediacies of texture. Fuller's exploration of recent German literature, especially that of Goethe, helped provide a framework within which new requirements could be formulated and the interrelationships of the arts examined. But most suggestive and valuable in her art criticism is the quality of personal encounter in her scrutiny of works of art, in the intentness of her questioning, and in her willingness to pursue the implications of what she saw.

For Americans who wrote on art in the nineteenth century, Margaret Fuller's example was fruitful. The most immediate sequel to her work was that of her friend Elizabeth Peabody, who published the first (and, unfortunately, the only) issue of her journal, *Aesthetic Papers*, in 1849. Elizabeth Ellet took up the subject of women artists (1859), addressing in some degree the question of women's capacity as artists that had tormented Fuller. She had another follower in Mariana Van Rensselaer, who created a career for herself in a mode that Fuller had prepared, that of criticism for mass periodicals. Finally, her interests were taken up by novelists and historians whose relation to the visual arts was important in their work, by Nathaniel Hawthorne, Henry Adams, Henry James, and Edith Wharton.

NOTES

The chief published sources for the biography of Margaret Fuller are Ralph Waldo Emerson, W. H. Channing, James Freeman Clarke, eds., *Memoirs of Margaret Fuller Ossoli*, 2 vols., Boston, 1852, reprint 1972; Julia Ward Howe, *Margaret Fuller*, Boston, 1883; T. W. Higginson, *Margaret Fuller Ossoli*, Boston, 1884; Katharine Anthony, *Margaret Fuller: A Psychological Inquiry*, New York, 1920; Mason Wade, *Margaret Fuller: Whetstone of Genius*, New York, 1940; Faith Chippenfield, *In Quest of Love: The Life and Death of Margaret Fuller*, New York, 1957; Arthur W. Brown, *Margaret Fuller*, New York, 1964; Joseph Jay Deiss, *The Roman Years of Margaret Fuller*, New York, 1969; and Paula Blanchard, *Margaret Fuller: From Transcendentalism to Revolution*, New York, 1978. From the standpoint of interpretation, Blanchard's life has been most helpful for the biographical aspects of the present essay. An account of Fuller's life is combined with a useful selection from her writings in Bell Gale Chevigny, *The Woman and the Myth: Margaret Fuller's Life and Writings*, Old Westbury, N.Y., 1976. Stimulating discussions of Fuller's career and its implications for developments in American cultural history are found in Susan P. Conrad, *Perish the Thought: Intellectual Women in Romantic America, 1830-1860*, New York, 1976; and Ann Douglas, *The Feminization of American Culture*, New York, 1977. Conrad's study gives a bibliography on Fuller (to 1976), including periodical literature.

1. Acknowledgments are due to Claire Sherman for assistance in gathering materials used in the preparation of this essay, and to Eugenia Kaledin for helpful suggestions from her background in American studies.

2. Ralph Waldo Emerson, W. H. Channing, James Freeman Clarke, eds., *Memoirs of Margaret Fuller Ossoli*, Boston, 1852, I, 228.

3. Cited in headnote of biographical sources.

4. Ann Douglas, *The Feminization of American Culture*, New York, 1977, p. 259.

5. Blanchard, *Margaret Fuller*, New York, 1978, pp. 134 and 160. Blanchard seems to have been influenced by an earlier pejorative opinion, that of Helen Neill McMaster in *Margaret Fuller as a Literary Critic*, Buffalo, N.Y., 1928, pp. 89-90.

6. Blanchard, *Fuller*, pp. 34-35, 40-43, and 47.

7. *The Dial*, I (Jan. 1841), 303.

8. *The Dial*, I (Jan. 1841), 304.

9. See Barbara Welter, "The Feminization of American Religion: 1800-1860" in *Clio's Consciousness Raised*, Mary Hartman and Lois W. Banner, eds., New York and London, 1974, pp. 137-57.

10. *Memoirs*, I, 141.

11. *Memoirs*, II, 21.

12. From the 1814 preface to *Letters on Rousseau*, as quoted in Ellen Moers, *Literary Women: The Great Writers*, New York, 1976, p. 190.

13. McMaster, *Margaret Fuller as a Literary Critic*, p. 51.

14. See René Wellek, "Emerson and German Philosophy," *New England Quarterly*, XVI (March 1943), 41-62. In "The Minor Transcendentalists and German Philosophy," *New England Quarterly*, XV (Dec. 1942), 677-79, Wellek separates Fuller's "obvious" interest in aesthetic questions from a general interest in philosophy and finds little evidence of the latter.

15. Caroline W. Healey (Dall), *Margaret and Her Friends, or Ten Conversations with Margaret Fuller upon the Mythology of the Greeks and Its Expression in Art*, Boston, 1895, p. 13.

16. As quoted in Chevigny, *The Woman and the Myth*, p. 174.

17. Excerpts quoted in Blanchard, *Fuller*, p. 121.

18. *Memoirs*, I, 328.

19. Healey (Dall), *Margaret and Her Friends*, p. 6.

20. *Margaret and Her Friends*, p. 7.

21. *Margaret and Her Friends*, p. 13.

22. *Margaret and Her Friends*, pp. 25-26.

23. *Margaret and Her Friends*, p. 74.

24. *Margaret and Her Friends*, p. 105.

25. On transcendentalism, see Octavius Brooks Frothingham, *Transcendentalism in New England*, New York, 1876; and Clarence Louis Frank Gohdes, *The Periodicals of American Transcendentalism*, Freeport, N.Y., 1970 (orig. pub. 1931).

26. Male attitudes were rich in contradictions on this point. See Blanchard, *Fuller*, pp. 160-62 and 119-20.

27. *The Dial*, I (Jan. 1841), 367.

28. *The Dial*, I (Jan. 1841), 370.

29. *The Dial*, I (Jan. 1841), 372.

30. *The Dial*, I (July 1840), 7.

31. "Marie Von Oosterwich," *The Dial*, II (April 1842), 439.

32. "A Short Essay on Critics," *The Dial*, I (July 1840), 7.

33. "A Record of Impressions Produced by the Exhibition of Mr. Allston's Pictures in the Summer of 1839," *The Dial*, I (July 1840), 73.

34. *The Dial*, I (July 1840), 76.

35. *The Dial*, I (July 1840), 79.

36. *The Dial*, I (July 1840), 82.

37. "Canova," *The Dial*, III (April 1843), 454.

38. *The Dial*, I (Oct. 1840), 262.

39. "Canova," *The Dial*, III (April 1843), 455-56.

40. *The Dial*, III (April 1843), 454.

41. "Margaret Fuller and Mary Wollstonecraft," *The Leader*, VI (13 Oct. 1855), 988-99.

42. *Woman in the Nineteenth Century*, New York, 1971, p. 96.

43. *Woman in the Nineteenth Century*, pp. 119-20.

44. G. H. Needler, ed., *Letters of Anna Jameson to Ottilie von Goethe*, London and New York, 1939, p. 186.

45. *Winter Studies and Summer Rambles in Canada*, Toronto, 1923, p. 283.

46. As quoted in Mason Wade, *Margaret Fuller: Whetstone of Genius*, New York, 1940, p. 154.

47. Margaret Fuller, *At Home and Abroad*, Boston, 1875, p. 250.

48. As quoted in Russell E. Durning, *Fuller: Citizen of the World*, Heidelberg, 1969, p. 127. 1969, p. 127.

49. As quoted in Durning, *Margaret Fuller*, p. 128.

50. *At Home and Abroad*, p. 198.

51. *At Home and Abroad*, pp. 199-200.

52. As quoted in Blanchard, *Margaret Fuller*, p. 257.

53. *At Home and Abroad*, p. 198.

54. See Howard D. Rodee, "France and England: Some Mid-Victorian Views of One Another's Painting," *Gazette des Beaux-Arts*, XCI (Jan. 1978). 39-48.

55. *Memoirs*, I, 197.

56. *At Home and Abroad*, p. 220.

57. As quoted in Blanchard, *Margaret Fuller*, p. 265.

58. *At Home and Abroad*, p. 306.

59. *Memoirs*, II, 235.

60. *The Roman Years of Margaret Fuller*, New York, 1969, pp. 291-92.

61. *At Home and Abroad*, p. 250.

62. *At Home and Abroad*, p. 369.

63. Letter to Richard Fuller, as quoted in Chevigny, *The Woman and the Myth*, p. 390.

64. F. G. Kenyon, ed., *The Letters of Elizabeth Barrett Browning*, I, New York, 1898, 460.

65. Chevigny, *The Woman and the Myth*, p. 393.

66. "Canova," *The Dial*, III (April 1843), 454.

SELECTED BIBLIOGRAPHY OF MARGARET FULLER

Books, including volumes of collected papers:

Trans. *Eckermann's Conversations with Goethe*. Boston, 1839.

Trans. *Correspondence of Fräulein Günderode and Bettina von Arnim*. Boston, 1842.

Summer on the Lakes, in 1843. Boston and New York, 1844.

Woman in the Nineteenth Century. New York, 1845. Reprint, New York: W. W. Norton, 1971.

Papers on Literature and Art. 2 vols. New York, 1846.

At Home and Abroad: or, Things and Thoughts in America and Europe. A. B. Fuller, ed., Boston, 1856.

Life Without and Life Within; or, Reviews, Narratives, Essays, and Poems. A. B. Fuller, ed., Boston and New York, 1859.

The Writings of Margaret Fuller. Mason Wade, ed., New York, 1941 (contains bibliography of Fuller's periodical publications).

Selected List of Articles and Reviews in *The Dial*:

"A Short Essay on Critics," I (July 1840), 5-11.

"A Record of Impressions Produced by the Exhibition of Mr. Allston's Pictures in the Summer of 1839," I (July 1840), 73-84.

"The Athenaeum Exhibition of Painting and Sculpture," I (October 1840), 260-64.

"The Magnolia of Lake Pontchartrain," I (January 1841), 299-305.

"Menzel's *View of Goethe*," I (January 1841), 340-47.

"Goethe," II (July 1841), 1-41.

"Bettina Brentano and her Friend Günderode," II (January 1842), 313-57.

"Marie van Oosterwich" (trans.), II (April 1842), 437-48.

"Canova," III (April 1843), 454-83.

"The Great Lawsuit: Man versus Men. Woman versus Women," IV (July 1843), 1-47.

CHAPTER 6

LADY DILKE (1840-1904): THE SIX LIVES OF AN ART HISTORIAN
Colin Eisler[1]

On her Roman honeymoon, Dorothea Casaubon, heroine of *Middlemarch*, is described as belonging to a time "more ignorant of good and evil by forty years than it is at present. Travellers did not often carry full information on Christian art in their heads or their pockets." An outstanding art historian of the generation following George Eliot's, Francis Pattison was a friend of the novelist and, despite her access to books on Christian iconography, is often viewed as the model for Dorothea Casaubon.[2] The resemblance is not associated with Francis Pattison's active career as a writer and art scholar. As such she produced innumerable book reviews and articles on European politics for the leading liberal journals and prepared several major monographs and many articles on art in France from the later fifteenth to the end of the nineteenth century. To this day no other scholar can be said to have been so profoundly cognizant of five hundred years of French art as this Englishwoman, who was largely self-educated in the fields of her professional activity.

The *Middlemarch* connection has rather to do with the circumstances of Francis Pattison's married life. Like Dorothea Casaubon, she married a man very much her senior. Both Mark Pattison and Casaubon were trained as ministers; both were difficult, demanding, and unusually self-centered men. But while neither was appealing, Pattison, the Rector of Lincoln College, was far from the narrow-minded, conceited fool that was Eliot's Casaubon. Only the latter's domineering, stingy manner corresponded to Mark Pattison's worst habits. Like his young wife, he was a person of principle—his contribution to *Essays and Reviews* (1860) presented unfashionable views on the growth of rationalism and other aspects of English religious thought in the eighteenth century, a period virtually omitted from history by High Church Anglicans. Beauty, idealism, self-righteousness, and a certain lack of humor were traits shared by Dorothea and Francis. Shafts and shadows of the miserable union of the Edward Casaubons do suggest the dismal, destructive flatness of the Pattisons' *mésalliance*, but it would be wrong to translate these largely glancing correspondences into a major mimesis. Curiously, the closest parallels between the heroine of *Middlemarch* and Francis Pattison were to be realized after Eliot's death, when Francis' second husband, Sir Charles Dilke, would bear a striking similarity to Will Ladislaw, whom Dorothea married after Casaubon's death. Both Dilke and Ladislaw began as art students, were compellingly attractive, as young or younger than their wives, and were motherless at an early age. Audacious, impulsive, and romantic, Dilke was chairman of the Royal Commission on Working Class Housing, a driving concern of Dorothea Casaubon and of Ladislaw. All in all, *Middlemarch* may be seen more as a prophecy than as an imitation of Francis' life.

EARLY LIFE

Emily Francis Strong (1840-1904) was the daughter of Emily (née Weedon) and Henry Strong, a bank manager in Iffley, the lovely ancient town on Oxford's outskirts. A retired Indian army officer, an amateur musician and painter, Strong was the son of a Georgia Loyalist and a friend of John Everett Millais. It was a favorite family story that on seeing that Pre-Raphaelite master's sketches for *The Battle of Stirling*, the pugnacious little Emily had urged the artist to paint "more dead bodies."

Forceful and independent, Emily Strong was intensely proud of her Georgia Loyalist ancestry. From an early age she referred to herself as E. Francis Strong, stressing the active aspects of her second and masculine given name, that of her godfather, killed during the Indian Mutiny at Cawnpore. Her first major purchase, made at the age of eleven, was the incisive *Essays on the Anatomy of Expression in Painting* by Sir Charles Bell, the anatomist and artist who analyzed the way in which nerves and muscles communicate feeling from mind to matter, inner thought to exterior expression, as delineated through art. It was the role of art as a reflection of governing ideas, whether seen in the furniture of a boudoir or the supervision of urban design, that was often to be the subject of Emily's future works and a topic of lifelong concern. The girl placed her new name, with Francis given precedence over her mother's Christian name, now reduced to an initial, on Bell's book.[3]

The intense Anglo-Catholic pietism of Edward Pusey's mid-nineteenth-century Oxford Movement was a major element in Emily Weedon's faith and in her daughter's early life. For all her precocious independence of thought and action, Francis was subject to extremes of religious obsession and a sense of guilt, going through terrible physical self-punishments in her youth.⁴ Perhaps she visited these upon herself because her powerful impulse to self-assertion was in such painful conflict with contemporary religious and social concepts of woman's place. Francis's first husband, a clergyman's son, was ordained in 1830; her second husband, like Francis herself, had an extremely devout mother. The most important records of her early life, a memoir based on what she told of these years to her second husband, Sir Charles Dilke, are to be found in a book entitled *The Book of the Spiritual Life* (1905), wherein he wrote that she had a "habit of doing penance for the smallest fault, imaginary or real, lying for hours on the bare floor or on the stones with her arms in the attitude of the Cross."⁵ Such concern with the Imitation of Christ accompanied her creativity in the visual arts and may have led to the history of art, so much of which is devoted to religious imagery and to the concept of imitation.

Subject to hallucinations for much of her life, Francis wrote that she converted such experience into "a powerful unconscious ally in the strong visual memory, which I have cultivated for purposes of my own convenience."⁶ It is hard to appreciate today just how crucial a role memory played in scholarship in the time before affordable photographs. Theaters of memory and other mnemonic devices meant much in the education of artists and scholars. When Francis Strong was a girl, photography was still very costly. Horace Lecoq de Boisbaudran's *L'Education de la mémoire pittoresque*, later translated as *Training of the Memory in Art and the Education of the Artist*, a forceful factor in the education of the sculptor Auguste Rodin, was a central agent in Francis' training in art as it was to be in her self-education and work as an art historian.⁷

At eighteen, having had an excellent education from her governess Miss Bowditch, she decided to leave on her own for London to study painting at the South Kensington School of Art, so advised by the Aclands, friends of John Ruskin and of the Dilkes, a liberal, prosperous London family of publishers and parliamentarians. She first met Charles Dilke at South Kensington as a fellow art student. He recalled that "Her great talent and power of expression in speech and writing made her rather a terrible person to a boy of sixteen when she was nineteen and she seemed altogether to belong to an older generation than myself and I classed her with people of a greater age and rank, but still worshipped from afar and she was very kind to me and used to talk to me a great deal."⁸

Decades before Eakins fought (and lost) the battle to have his women students draw from the nude, Francis Strong insisted upon and won this opportunity so essential to the training of an artist in her final year of studies. She was popular with her fellow art students. A favorite guest at Little Holland House, where G. F. Watts lived, she was addressed by the venerable, celebrated painter as Francesca. Living up to this quaint Italianism, she often dressed in the romantic recreation of Renaissance garb favored by the Pre-Raphaelites.[9] Sir Edward Burne-Jones was another acquaintance among artists, introduced to Francis by George Eliot, who, twenty-one years her senior, addressed Francis as "Figliuolina," using the equally maternal signature of "Madre."

The painter William Bell Scott described Francis Strong as "one of the most perfectly lovely women in the world"—her golden hair and high coloring accentuated by picturesque dress.[10] She is shown wearing a green brocade gown as she paints a pilaster-shaped canvas of sunflowers in a portrait by Lady Trevelyan of 1863 (National Portrait Gallery, London, Figure 6). Both the curtain drawn aside to reveal her at work and her dress are strewn with fleurs-de-lis, emblem of the country whose art she was to study to such advantage for almost forty years. Later, when her articles on the painting of the eighteenth century appeared, Francis' attire was such that "she seemed to impart a reminiscence of the canvases of Boucher and Van Loo, which she celebrated as the types of the *Grand siècle* when the highest forms of feminine intelligence were not divorced from exterior signs of feminine grace."[11] All in all, this may strike the reader as an oddly fe-Maileresque Advertisement for Herself as Art Historian, a dicey equation of subject with self.

In 1861, a few months after her return from London art study, Francis married Mark Pattison. Twenty-seven years her senior and thus more than twice her age, he had just been appointed Rector of Lincoln College. A disciple of Newman, Pattison was ordained in 1843, two years before his master's conversion to Roman Catholicism. His was a grim childhood, as the sole surviving son among the eight daughters of a banker's daughter and her crazed, seemingly impoverished country clergyman husband who insisted upon tutoring his son at their dismal home. Pattison remained locked in family life before coming to Oxford. Such non-attendance of boarding school was radically unorthodox among the English educated classes. As a result young Mark was utterly unprepared for any aspect of university life excepting the least important—the academic. Ugly, humorless, poor, brave, pious, hugely intelligent, Pattison was also defensively graceless. When he finally succeeded to the deserved Rectorship of Lincoln College that honor came far too late for true satisfaction.

Pattison had a dream of Oxford radically transformed into a new university along rigorous German lines, far removed from the three-year camp of cultivated languor between public school and independent maturity that it provided in his day. Still medieval, the college system was to be reorganized towards mastery of an "ideal order of intellect," which Pattison conceived as "a scaffolding on which is built up the grand conception of the universe as a totality governed by fixed laws."[12] The Rector's sympathy for German

Figure 6. Francis Pattison, later Lady Dilke, at Wallington, Northumberland, by Pauline Trevelyan, 1863. London, the National Portrait Gallery. (*Courtesy of the Trustees of the National Portrait Gallery*)

method and language could well have guided his bride toward the new fusion of art and history, that concern with the look and the fact of the past art known as *Kunstgeschichte*. The work of German art historians, especially that of Jacob Burckhardt, would provide a substructure for the pioneering English writings of Francis Pattison, enabling her to move away from Ruskin's sometimes sentimental morality and Walter Pater's exquisite aestheticism toward a new objectivity. Mark Pattison's conversion to the positivist philosophy of Auguste Comte, in which Francis joined him, also allowed for a newly dispassionate scrutiny of culture.

The Pattisons' was to be among the worst of the many miserable marriages in nineteenth-century literature, recorded first in Hector Malot's *Vices français*, and, most memorably, by George Eliot. *Middlemarch* was published in 1872, eleven years after the Pattison wedding. It is striking that the unusual name of Casaubon was that of the Huguenot humanist Isaac Casaubon, the subject of one of Pattison's best books. Written in 1875, it was a biography of a refugee from the same world Francis Pattison would address in her first book, *The Art of the Renaissance in France* (1879).

The couple professed to see no connection between themselves and Eliot's protagonists and maintained their friendship with the novelist. Francis even claimed never to have read the book! Her recent, admirably thorough biographer, Betty Askwith, has cited passages from *Middlemarch* in which the resemblance between Dorothea Brooke and Francis Strong seems closest:

Young, ardently theorist, longing to find meaning and some great purpose in life, rejecting the petty standards of everyday, she (Francis Strong) perhaps looked on him (Pattison) as Dorothea looked on Edward Casaubon as a "winged messenger." Like Dorothea she longed to make her life "greatly effective" and perhaps even more ardently than Dorothea she wanted to justify this longing "by the completest knowledge. . . . " Into this soul-hunger, as yet unfulfilled, all her youthful passion was poured; the union which attracted her was one that would free her from her girlish subjection to her own ignorance, and give her the freedom of voluntary submission to a guide who would take her along the grandest path.[13]

Everything Mr. Casaubon "said seemed like a specimen from a mine or the inscription on the door of a museum which might open on the treasures of past ages . . . marriage to him would be like marrying Pascal." Mark Pattison actually approximated the exalted character that Dorothea Brooke initially attributed to Casaubon. Not only the key to the past through his forceful, informed scholarship, Pattison *was* the past, a museum of intellectual method and a very strange but probably crucial helpmeet toward the realization of Francis Strong's gifts.

FINDING A VOCATION

During Francis' girlhood, England had gone through an extraordinary period of "consciousness-raising" in the arts, centered around the good works of the German-born Prince Consort, which included founding the South Kensington Art School.[14] Major art exhibitions, unparalleled in their scope and brilliance, took place in Manchester and Birmingham. The vast Crystal Palace displays stressed the world of arts and crafts and industrial design. Sir Charles Wentworth Dilke (father of Francis' second husband) had furthered the Prince's plans for the Great Exposition and was knighted for the success of his vast organizational efforts.

From the complementary perspectives of Darwin's theory and Comte's belief in the perfectibility of society, faith in the progress of the arts was affirmed, despite the contrary beliefs of the German painters known as the Nazarenes, who upheld the supremacy of medieval art, and their British followers, the Pre-Raphaelites. The story of *Kunstgeschichte* could be seen by the optimistic as a positive study in creative evolution, from its beginnings with the "Primitives" to the fullest spectrum of illusion first attained in the photographic arts of the mid-nineteenth century.

For all the attention given to the arts, both the invention of photography and the other ingenuities of the industrial revolution undermined the opportunities of most painters for patronage. A few artists were to amass unparalleled fortunes, but increasingly art became a genteel female pastime. Removed from real power, restricted to polite Culture's feeble realm, Prince Albert's own position may unwittingly have encouraged such "feminization." June Wayne's recent "The Male Artist as Stereotypical Female" and Ann Douglas' *Feminization of American Culture* have hit upon ugly truths in the world of the beaux-arts.[15] (The period of Douglas' study precedes that of Lady Dilke's career, the last third of the nineteenth century.) For most women practitioners, the creative, inspired madness of *furor poeticus* was approached no more closely than through the cultivated impotence of amateur standing. The precarious economic position of most professional artists, romanticized in the operatic version of Murger's *Scènes de la vie de Bohême* made the creation of art a socially marginal occupation, analogous in character to the even more gratuitous situation of female amateurs.

The practice of art and authorship on the subject were among the very few areas to be considered at all acceptable as lady's work. Such eighteenth-century court portraitists as Rosalba Carriera, Elisabeth Vigée-Lebrun, and Angelica Kauffmann had achieved fame unprecedented for women painters. Later, Rosa Bonheur won wealth and reputation as an artist of powerful "beastly subjects," freed from the portraitist's need to flatter a sitter's

vanity. Women writers of the earlier nineteenth century concerned themselves with artists in the realm of drama: Carolin Bernstein wrote a com-
edy, *Rembrandts Meisterstück* (1834), and Charlotte Birch-Pfeiffer's
Rubens appeared in 1839.[16] Lady Sydney Morgan brought out a biography
of that important, enigmatic artist-playwright, Salvator Rosa, as early as
1824. Maria Dundas Graham's memoir of the life of Nicholas Poussin was
printed four years earlier. In 1835 and 1836 the same writer, now married to
Augustus Wall Callcott, R.A., published her *Description of the Chapel of
the Annunziata dell'Arena; or Giotto's Chapel in Padua* and *Essays
towards the History of Painting*.[17] Several internationally recognized
publications such as Mary P. Merrifield's *Original Treatises . . . on the Arts
of Painting* (1849) and the many works of Lady Eastlake and Anna Jameson had shown British women to be outstandingly expert in the study of art,
following and improving upon the lead provided by Johanna Schopenhauer, whose criticism and whose book on the Van Eycks (1822) were
widely read by the generation of the Nazarenes. Mary Merrifield's compilation and annotation of Greek, Latin, and medieval texts on techniques in
the arts has never been superseded and is still available in paperback
editions today.

Just as actresses and singers were invariably listed as "Mrs.," so were the
authors of the day, such as Mary Merrifield and Anna Jameson, as though
they could write, and be published, only under husbandly aegis. Yet Lady
Eastlake's reputation as an author had been firmly established before her
marriage, when she wrote as Elizabeth Rigby, and the even more successful
career of Anna Jameson was also independently founded.

Mark Pattison may well have had Jameson or Graham in mind when he
urged his young wife to specialize. "It was put before me," she recalled,
"that if I wished to command respect I must make myself *the* authority
on some one subject which interested me. I was told, and it was good
counsel, not to take hack-work, and to reject even well-paid things that
would lead me off the track."[18]

Francis Pattison's early articles are marked by evidence of great breadth
of study and knowledge and by unwillingness, almost Benthamite in its
obstinacy, to take anything for granted, according to Charles Dilke.[19]
"From 1861 for many years she signed "E.F.S. Pattison," the "S," which
stood for her family name of Strong, being introduced by her to mark her
wish for some recognition of the independent existence of the woman, and
in some resistance to the old English doctrine of complete merger in the
husband."[20] Dilke went on to describe, in chilling fashion, how in her
young married days Francis' "mind and learning deserved the surrender of
the educational direction of a young girl, however gifted, to his [Pattison's]
mental and philosophical control; and he obtained it. Although full of love
of personal liberty, she had an unusually disciplined reverence for Author-

ity as represented by those she thought really competent in ability and learning."[21]

Her article "The Idealist Movement and Positive Science: An Experience" for an American magazine, *Cosmopolis*, in 1897, was described as "a fragment of self-history," a remarkably modern term. She portrays the stringent moral environment into which, as a young woman, she had married. In this setting she "forsook the exact observance of Church practice . . .whilst still holding fast to its ethical system," as set forth in the preface of Comte's *Catéchisme positiviste* (1852). But she soon recognized that Comte's ethics required an "abnegation as complete as that enacted by the Imitatio Christi," and they "brought no change" in her conception of duty. She went on to write that

as my powers and character matured . . .my whole nature fought against the self-imposed yoke. I became aware of an intense desire for the enjoyment of life—not in any limited or common sense, but a desire for knowledge and experience in every direction, utterly incompatible with the ideal of self-renunciation with which I was striving to bring myself into conformity; but I regarded the protest of my own nature as immoral, and strove yet more earnestly to suppress it.[22]

Art was the way out and the way in. It had served this need in Francis Pattison's London studies and would continue to do so in much of her literary career. Ambiguity between reality and illusion, often the essence of art, provided special appeal to women, as it paralleled their often tenuous situation where the self-assertive, the educated, and the professional were seen as the denial of their sex. Obstacles women encountered in the scholarly world can be glimpsed in the critical reception of the first, and still valuable, biography in English of Albrecht Dürer, by Mary Margaret Heaton. Published in 1870, it was accompanied by her exemplary translation of all the German master's writings then known. Heaton's unusually objective and documentary work was characterized by William Bell Scott, author of a Dürer monograph appearing later in the year, as "hysterical and prejudiced," traits which he said could only be expected in a work by a woman. Such condemnation did not prevent Scott from helping himself generously to her invaluable translations, without, of course, crediting their source. Undeterred, Heaton's publishers brought out her *Masterpieces of Flemish Art* (1869), *Life of Leonardo da Vinci* (1872), and *A Concise History of Painting* (1873).[23]

Francis Pattison's rigorous, cheerless tutorial-marriage recalls Eliot's statement that "Mr. Casaubon was liable to think that others were made for him." What made this state of post-marital pedagogical servitude tolerable were the bride's private pursuits in what she designated as "Offhours of my own time."[24] Sadly, Francis Pattison's "offhours" seem often to have been devoted to spinning feeble mystical tales such as *The Shrine of Death and Other Stories* (1886), *The Shrine of Love and Other Stories* (1891), and, posthumously published, *The Book of the Spiritual Life* (1905). Combining thinly veiled allegories of her hatred for the Rector and Oxford's limiting life, these mawkish, Neo-Arthurian stories might also be parodies of Tennyson, puerile flights into fictional revenge. But Oxford also afforded some fun. Lewis Carroll, reviewing Pattison's performance in an Oxford amateur production, "Ici on parle français" reported that she "acted very fairly."[25] This early flair for the theater proved important both for Francis Pattison's future scholarship (art history depending upon imagination and projection) and her eloquence as a speaker on behalf of working women's education and the need for labor unions.

Bored and frustrated by the provincial manner and hypocrisy of Oxford—"that hole"—the young woman's annoyance and impatience with the stuffy Groves of Academe both contributed to and reflected the failure of her marriage. Then as now a middle-class faculty imitated the manners of its social superiors—the students—tangling with the unpleasant fact that the very professionalism of its knowledge and a risible income excluded the faculty from the aristocratic circle to which many aspired. But though she protested against Oxford's social absurdities, the university prepared Francis for the ways and means of scholarly excellence. Just as Pattison had steered his brilliant wife toward a specialized career with its first focal point in the same area as his current work—sixteenth-century France—so had his dramatic renunciation of orthodox Christianity led her eventually to new, productive forms of ethical expression and concern. Later, Charles Dilke recalled that the Rector's "diatribes on the uselessness of mere monasticism . . .turned his wife from speculative theology to more human forms of devotion."[26]

The paintings of the period, many of them "sermons on canvas," moral messages, reflect the widespread interest in social reform that so often absorbed English art critics. Anna Jameson, John Ruskin, William Morris, and Francis Pattison were all deeply committed to improving the condition of the lives of the only too aptly designated "working class." Such concern, beginning with Jameson's publications on working women in the 1840s and culminating in the socialism of Morris, was intimately allied to a common concept of art as Christian craft and a belief in the sanctity of labor; to a requisite bond between ethics and aesthetics that yielded the truly beautiful and the beautifully true. Artists and writers alike taught at the Workingmen's Colleges—Ford Madox Brown, Dante Gabriel Rossetti, and Val Prinsep all volunteering their services.

Awareness of social injustice was already manifested in Francis Pattison's childhood, and seven years before the emergence of her first major publication, she was prominent in the movement for women's suffrage. Her major cause was the Women's Protective and Provident League, founded in 1874 to advance the appalling position of working women, especially those in the mills, potteries, and match factories. Significantly, many women contributed to the unprecedentedly intricate and abundant decorative arts of the period, a subject of great professional concern to Francis Pattison. With William Morris she advocated a complete system of technical education for women, a cause that had long engaged Ruskin. Anna Jameson, who has been proposed as a possible "role model" of Pattison, championed justice for women workers as early as 1843, writing on this subject for the Dilke-owned *Athenaeum*. That Francis Pattison was active in the women's suffrage movement from the early 1870s is indicated by her recorded presence next to Millicent Fawcett at an 1872 suffrage meeting in Albert Hall.

THE SCHOLARSHIP AND CRITICISM OF FRENCH ART

When Francis Pattison and Charles Dilke renewed their acquaintance in 1875, she was slowly recovering from a form of gout that had made it impossible for her to use her right arm. Ingeniously, she invented a page-turning machine that enabled her to continue research and taught herself to write with her left rather than her crippled right hand so that her scholarly career could continue despite disablement. In our age of insistent psychohistory it is tempting to interpret Francis Pattison's physical inability to write with her spiritual inability to free herself from the Rector, a state recalling Elizabeth Barrett's self-imposed confinement. She maintained a humiliating economic dependency on Mark Pattison that could probably have been relatively easily ended through her remunerative literary career.*

By 1875 Francis Pattison had come to know the Royal Academy's future president, Sir Frederic Leighton. At his request she was entrusted with the preparation of a study of his work as the first chapter of an almost elephant-sized folio-anthology of the leading contemporary masters, *Illustrated Biographies of Modern Artists*, a series of lavishly illustrated biographies prepared under the direction of F. G. Dumas.[27] Like Francis Pattison, Leighton was an unusually cosmopolitan figure, fluent in French, German, and Italian, and a courtly individual of magnificent appearance. He lived in a suitably palatial style in what may have been London's largest closet. Following the death of his platonic beloved, May Sartoris, Francis Pattison was to become Leighton's closest friend. The painter's recent biographers, the Ormonds, suggest that she cultivated Leighton's acquaintance "to manipulate him" for purely professional motives, but this seems less than fair.[28]

*Was this weird dependency maintained as punishment for what would seem to have been a liaison with Dilke?

Many ties bound Leighton to the circle of Sir Charles Dilke. The august academician decorated the opulent house and painted the portrait of one of Dilke's mistresses, Ellen (Mrs. Eustace) Smith, the owner of Leighton's *Venus Disrobing*. It was testimony at the divorce of her daughter Virginia (Mrs. Donald) Crawford, another of Dilke's many lovers, that would lead to his disgrace and the wreckage of his high political hopes.

A collector of Corot, Delacroix, and Rodin, Leighton visited Manet's Parisian studio. His taste represented the same broad artistic sympathies as Francis Pattison's. It was Leighton who brought her to the studio of Jules Dalou, a favorite artist of Dilke's. That she stood to gain by Leighton's friendship is inarguable, but that her sincerity should thereby be impugned does not follow. The Ormonds emphasize Leighton's lifelong efforts to disguise his anxiety and constant, debilitating sense of stress. Pattison cannot be seen as a toady supporting the myth of his serene highness as the imperturbable classical master. This is made clear by a closing judgment from her study of the academician: "Intensely nervous, and of a highly strung organization, the alternate excitements of hope and despair are felt but to be met by sterner self-control, the man is therefore never lost in his work, the work is a part of himself."[29]

Anonymous reviewing, an unfortunate practice finally renounced by England at too long last (1976), has lost the identification of many of Francis' early works. She began writing for the *Saturday Review* in 1863, two years after her marriage, on French literature, contributing, for example, an article on Voltaire and reviewing a work by Tissot, "On the Imagination." She first contributed articles on philosophy to *The Westminster Review* when she was about twenty-five. Founded by followers of Jeremy Bentham, the *Review* had long included works by her friend George Eliot. For many years, Francis Pattison also prepared reviews of foreign political developments for *The Annual Register*; but she wrote increasingly on art, both history and criticism, publishing Salon reviews for *The Portfolio* and *The Academy*, which appointed her art editor in 1873. Beginning in 1876 she became a regular contributor to *The Athenaeum*. Three years later she was made a member of the Radical Club, founded by Charles Dilke's mentor, John Stuart Mill.

Her association with French intellectual currents and the trend among them toward *l'art pour l'art* led Pattison to make a radical break with prevalent English views of an opposite tendency. Reviewing a recent book by Richard St. John Tyrwhitt, she observed: "Work which is not done for its own sake, in which the chief place is claimed by the historical or the moral, in which attention is seized by the subject rather than the rendering of the subject . . .loses its aesthetic character, and cannot possess those poetic elements which fire the fancy and rouse the emotions."[30]

Writing for *The Academy* in 1870, the young critic observed in her review

of Ruskin's *Lectures on Art* and *Catalogue of Examples* that contrary to
that great man's almost holy writ, "Art is neither religious nor irreligious,
moral nor immoral, useful or useless; if she is interpreted in any one of
these senses by the beholder, is she to bear the blame?"[31]

Recalling the days when he knew her as an art student, Ruskin wrote to
Francis Pattison: "I thought you always one of my terriblest, unconquer-
ablest, antagonisticest—Philistine—Delilah powers! I thought you at
Kensington the sauciest of girls—at Oxford the dangerourest of Don-nas.
When you sat studying Renaissance with me in the Bodleian I supposed you
to intend contradicting everything I ever said about Art and History and
Social Science. . . ."[32] Her novel approach is apparent in Pattison's Salon coverage of the 1870s for *The Academy*. Betty Askwith has noted how
open-minded and intelligent her criticism of Courbet and Manet proved to
be, quoting: "We cannot demand from Manet and Courbet expressive
finish which is not in their intention perhaps not in their gift—what we have
to estimate is the value of this terrible effectiveness which is an undoubted
power in their hands. . . ."[33]

During the mid-1870s, when Pattison was preparing her important
volumes on the art of the French Renaissance, a new subject for England
and a work unrivalled to this day for its comprehensiveness, she came
across an album of six hundred drawings in Oxford by the great French
goldsmith of the sixteenth century, Etienne Delaune. Planning a monograph on Delaune as draughtsman and printmaker, she first thought of
collaborating with the distinguished French critic Philippe Burty on this
project. After Burty's death Pattison considered working with Eugène
Müntz, the hugely erudite French art historian and director of the Bibliothèque de l'École des Beaux-Arts. They became lifelong friends. She
bequeathed the bulk of her papers and the Delaune manuscript to the
Bibliothèque in gratitude to Müntz's ever-generous advancement of her
career.

Charles Dilke noted, "It is a curious fact that joint work, proposed to
Mrs. Pattison at various times by Müntz, Burty, Sir Charles Newton, and
others never came to anything; Mrs. Pattison having apparently given
general assent, but not found herself tempted at the last moment to under-
take the difficulties of collaboration."[34] In view of her first unhappy
partnership in marriage, such reluctance for collaboration, no matter how
prestigious and responsible the coauthor, does not, in retrospect, seem quite
so curious as it did to Dilke. An ironic footnote to this pattern of rejected
collaborations is that the publication on Greek and Roman art that Francis
Pattison was to have prepared in 1873 with Sir Charles Newton, Keeper of
Classical Antiquities at the British Museum, was written in the early years
of the twentieth century by another woman who (by marriage) bore the
name Strong. Eugénie Strong's many studies, especially those on Roman

art, were to win her far greater honors than any received by her elder contemporary; she was appointed a Lecturer at the British Museum and awarded a C.B.E.

Perhaps Dilke was right when he wrote that Francis Pattison had "specialized much against her will in the field of French art."[35] One wonders whether she stuck to Gallic studies so resolutely because they proved a popular and remunerative subject, or if she somehow felt bound to them as she had been to Mark Pattison, who launched her in that field with such success.

Her first monograph, *The Renaissance of Art in France*, was issued in 1879 by C. Kegan Paul & Co. It followed two other important publications of the same company, the historian Pasquale Villari's *The Life and Times of Niccolò Machiavelli*, translated by Linda Villari, and the "authorised translation" by S.G.C. Middlemore of Jacob Burckhardt's *The Civilisation of the Period of the Renaissance in Italy*. It is easy to see how a house drawn to such titles would have been attracted to Francis Pattison's documentary approach. Extracts from reviews of both the Italian and Swiss works, taken from *The Academy* and *The Saturday Review* and used by Kegan Paul for promotion, may very well have come from her pen![36] *The Renaissance of Art in France* is sometimes difficult to follow. Utterly without compromise, it is written for the reader with a mastery of the French language and considerable familiarity with the period and with art history in general. The title page's quotation from La Fontaine refers to the writer as well as her reader: "On le peut, je l'essaie, un plus Sçavant le fasse."[37]

Among the finest passages of the *Renaissance* book are those devoted to the classical art of the mid-sixteenth century. Of this epoch Pattison wrote, "The most voluptuous moments are so full of sadness that they never reach directly sensual expression. But if Venus has lost her air of frank expansion, Diana, on the other hand, sits reflecting, 'L'homme trop sobre ne vit pas./ Luy mesme en vivant il s'ennuye.'" She found the expression of such a moment in a sculpture from Anet, probably by Goujon, that represents Diana embracing a stag (Figure 7). It is one of the very few illustrations for this book prepared by the author, who has made the head of the chaste goddess look somewhat more like her own than that of the statue. Pattison's characterization of the marble may apply as much to the writer as to her subject, as evidencing

the struggle of the voluptuous element against a self-imposed restraint, a struggle which seems to be reflected in the very outlines as well as in the general sentiment of the figure. . . . The desire which questions in the eyes and mouth is contradicted by the conscious dignity of the attitude and the general severity of form and line, and this combination yields a type which corresponds precisely to that which we should expect to find enshrining the narrow energy which at once animated and controlled the wishes and conduct of Diane de Poitiers.[38]

DIANE

JEAN GOUJON, SCULPT

Figure 7. *Diane*, from the Château of Anet. Attributed to Jean Goujon. Illustration by Francis Pattison for *The Renaissance of Art in France*, I (London, 1879).

Significantly, *le mythe de Diane* (so effectively explored in the monograph thus titled by Françoise Bardon)[39] was never more popular than in the nineteenth century, when innumerable forgeries, purporting to represent the mistress of Henri II (and supposedly also of his father) flooded the art market. As pious widow, wise mistress to father and son, ever solicitous stepmother, the chaste Diane was seen as a secular realization of the impossible dream of virgin mother and pure yet sexual companion. *The Renaissance of Art in France* also treats the work of such less well-known figures as the engraver Jean Duvet, who had only recently (in 1876) been brought to scholarly attention through a fine monograph of E.J. de la Boullaye. Writing of Duvet's forceful, eccentric art, Pattison observed in connection with his Apocalypse series that "Every touch is impregnate with a weird and fervid pathos."[40]

Most of the all too few (nineteen in all) illustrations provided in the two volumes of *The Renaissance of Art in France* were drawn by the author. Presented by Ernest Renan, a friend of the Pattisons, to the French Academy, the publication immediately established E. F. S. Pattison as a scholar of international reputation.

Her next book appeared in the distinguished *Bibliothèque Internationale de l'Art* series. *Claude Lorrain, sa vie et ses oeuvres* (1884) is written in a far more fluent style, free of the occasional pontification that slowed up *The Renaissance of Art in France*. The French language liberated Francis from the heavy didacticism of the 1879 publication. Claude is presented in a fresh, forthright fashion, with such little-known and stimulating drawings as the *Hollyhocks* (British Museum) used as illustrations. The biographical study included new documents, such as a codicil to the artist's will, which she published in its entirety. Armed with a letter from Müntz, Pattison had persuaded the Roman archivist Bertoletti to search for new biographical data, resulting in the discovery of the will, which brought to light much additional important information. This successful monograph is far more attractive in format than her earlier book, and it is easy to understand why Pattison often regretted that she had not written all her books in French, for Parisian publication.

She now became a frequent contributor to the *Gazette des Beaux-Arts*. Friendship with the Renans, Taine, with Jules Dalou, Alphonse Legros, Léon Bonnat, Henri Bouchot, Gustave Dreyfus, the French Rothschilds and many others also made the language close to her life as well as her scholarship.

THE MIDDLE DECADES

Francis Pattison's staunch advocacy of the women's movement and her generally courageous, outspoken nature, are in curious contrast to her social climbing and maintenance of a union as bitter for her husband as herself, when she could perhaps have become financially independent through writing on subjects as profitable and popular as art. The Pattisons' endless squabbles about money and Francis' failure to make a complete break with her stingy, frustrated spouse are among the sadder aspects of her life. While she had to account for the price of every snippet of ribbon, he assembled Oxford's largest private library: 14,000 volumes in all!

Francis Pattison may have been trapped in a complex social and professional vicious circle. It was expensive to live and dress as the lady she had to be in order to maintain entrée to the collections needed for her work. Moreover, had she officially separated from Pattison, an eminent figure as Rector of Lincoln, it might well have been impossible for her to be received by those who owned what she wrote of, nor might she remarry during his lifetime. Dilke, with his powerful political ambitions, would never have married a divorced woman who could therefore never be received at Court. Francis Pattison's difficulties were perhaps compounded by snobbery, by her somewhat absurd identification with the aristocracy. She viewed middle-class life as "always ugly and unfinished . . .except for the dash of pretension which always accompanies officialdom."[41]

Writing in *Cosmopolis*, Pattison described her feelings as her first marriage advanced:

Why should my days be all duty and those of others all demand? Why should I renounce my own interests and convictions because they were alien to those with whom I dwelt? . . . The self, which I had so long held at bay, now avenged the subjection to which I had been condemned and—in the desperation of the struggle which seemed like one for life—I was unable to place myself in any just relation to my past, and was ready to thrust aside all claims that others might have on me lest my own should be eternally foregone.[42]

This astonishingly frank statement came in 1897, eighteen years after the publication of *The Renaissance of Art in France* (1879). Unsurprisingly, her own final push toward freedom came with that of Mark Pattison, who, at long last, sought love elsewhere in the final years of his life.

It was during those tormented times that Francis completed the extensive research for her important monograph on Claude and prepared the outline for her most speculative and original work, *Art in the Modern State*. That analysis of the role of the French Academy was not published until 1888, four years after Pattison's death. As editor of *The Athenaeum*, Dilke had first suggested that Francis Pattison write on the reform of the Academy for his publication. This study may have led to her trenchant investigation of the role of the Académie Royale in seventeenth-century France, resulting in her new book. She was so disappointed by the poor reception this work received that it was hard to "induce her to write in English, rather than in

French, her four volumes on the Eighteenth Century," Charles Dilke recalled.[43] His may have been very poor advice, as prior French publication could only have enhanced the appeal of an English edition.

Far livelier in style than her presentation of the French Renaissance, *Art in the Modern State* was written as its sequel, despite the very strange title. The study provided an extraordinarily accomplished presentation of the total picture of patronage in all the arts of seventeenth-century France, analyzing their organization in the effort to reinforce and enhance the royal image. The book exhibits the author's total command of French literature as well as of architecture, sculpture, painting and the decorative arts, exploring their interaction and the development from guild to academy. Vivid, three-dimensional, filled with excellent quotations from the period, the text is still unrivalled in its scope, as remains true also for her Renaissance volumes.

Pattison's close study of the competition of guild and academy anticipates that of Nikolaus Pevsner.[44] She used the data that had been dug out by French archivists and freed it from the smell of the wick, recreating the warfare between old and new concepts of art and patronage in an authoritative and lively text. Great artists like Poussin, to whom she had planned to devote a special study, and Claude, already the subject of her monograph of 1884, were of course exempted from her distaste for the propagandistic puffery of *Le Roi soleil*, whose vast bureaucratic art-machine she had so shrewdly analyzed.

Why the book should have been entitled *Art in the Modern State*, however, remains a mystery. The propagandistic utilization and direction of the arts toward imperial goals is as old as classical antiquity. Perhaps Pattison or her publisher felt that emphasis upon the word "modern" would somehow attract readers who otherwise might not consider the book of interest. Whatever the reasons may have been, the results were dismal: the book was a financial failure, to this day not receiving the critical attention it still so richly deserves.

Once again, the author was ill-served by her illustrations or, better said, by their absence. It is hard to know the reader to whom the book is addressed. The range of references is dazzling, the visual documentation almost nonexistent. The *Modern State* had but two "illustrations"—two-page spreads of documents pertaining to the Florentine years of Jacques Callot! Just how a reader not already profoundly acquainted with the period was to follow the author's intent is incomprehensible. Had the book been issued in France, as should have been the case, it would have had an abundance of plates like those customarily found in works of the period by Müntz, Burty, Edouard André, Pierre de Nolhac, and many other scholars who were Pattison's friends and associates. Perhaps the commercial failure of *Art in the Modern State* could in part be ascribed to her dislike of the imperious, pretentious style of seventeenth-century court art in France. Left cold by the pomp and glacial grandeur of *Le Grand siècle*, she may have chosen to deprive it of identification in the title and thus have lost many a reader.

In the fall of 1883, when Mark Pattison's final illness was slowly taking its toll, his wife had a mental and physical collapse. Morphine injections to relieve the pain of "spinal neuralgia" affected her vision and produced partial facial paralysis. The Rector died in 1884. His very substantial estate may provide another reason why they never separated; fifty thousand pounds were left to his widow. Financially independent, she was now free to live and write as she wished.

Having first married a man more than old enough to be her father, Francis Pattison would, within two years, marry one three years her junior and the antithesis of the Rector of Lincoln, Sir Charles Dilke (1843-1911). Motherless at ten, Dilke was brought up by a father he tolerated and by an adored grandfather. A nervous child, Charles, like Mark Pattison, was spared the terrors of the public schools by tuition at home before entering Cambridge. Dilke loved forceful, original, intelligent women somewhat his senior. Katharine Sheil, his first wife, was a gifted amateur singer of striking appearance. Rich, highly independent, with a foul temper and a singular talent for mimicry, she died giving birth to their second child.

Dilke's attraction to powerful women extended to those of the past. One of his first memories was of meeting the Irish writer Lady Sydney Morgan, whose pen was one of his father's most treasured objects. Charles cherished a bust of Margaret of Austria, Governess of the Netherlands, and was noted for his "intense admiration for the governing capacity and the overshadowed life of the woman,"[45] making two pilgrimages to her beautiful burial church at Brou. As a fellow art student of Emily Francis Strong's, Charles "loved to be patronized by her," three years his senior. He was fascinated by her audacity, erudition, and flair at the same time that he was repelled by her religious fanaticism. His own work as a painter had long since been given up for university studies and a lively career in politics and publishing. Dilke's leadership in the radical wing of the Liberal party did not, however, preclude art patronage. In 1873 he commissioned G. F. Watts to paint a superb portrait of his master, John Stuart Mill, and in the same year that artist also painted Dilke and his first wife. (Her likeness so displeased him that he had the canvas destroyed.)

Like Francis Pattison, Sir Charles was deeply interested in the careers of Legros and Dalou. (Legros had lived in England since 1863, and Dalou sought refuge there after the fall of the Commune in 1871.) Dilke's mastery of French and his knowledge and love of many aspects of the country's culture also complemented his future wife's long-standing interest in Gallic art as a reflection of French thought from the fifteenth to the nineteenth centuries.

Long before their marriage, Francis Pattison and Charles Dilke managed individually to combine two often distinctly opposed concerns, those of a sumptuous and aristocratic social life with radical politics on behalf of the labor movement. This duality was made still more involved—in his case, by a sexual life of extraordinary complexity, variety, and adventure, and in hers by the miserable intricacies of the Pattison marriage. Her study of all the visual arts of the eighteenth century, that most comfortable, intelligently intimate, deliciously privileged of all worlds, was combined with work for women's rights and social reform that occupied much of her time. Ethics and aesthetics had to be preserved in meaningful balance for the realization of the first through both protest and prominence, and the second by publication and remuneration.

Both Dilke and Francis Pattison were individuals of special magnetism requiring and receiving "high visibility." He was the personification of Edwardian dash and sensuality while she, a Pre-Raphaelite beauty in her youth, added to her attraction by always dressing with special distinction and elegance. Their close ties to European leaders of state and society provided an extraordinarily catholic range of acquaintance that embraced leaders in the arts, society, and the international labor movement, in a radiant Golden Age of international amity and exchange that was never to return. On their marriage in 1885, Francis Pattison changed her given name as well as her surname to become Emilia Dilke (Figure 8).

World War I destroyed the network of pan-European art-historical erudition laid down by scholars of Lady Dilke's generation and its forebears, Ruskin, Herman Grimm, and Burckhardt. While "Modern Art" was to forge new links between London and Paris and Berlin through Roger Fry and a few of his contemporaries, it was Hitler who reestablished the bond between German and English art-historical scholars by driving so many of his country's leading students and institutes to British refuge.

In her late fifties and early sixties Lady Dilke left the cause of women's suffrage to concentrate upon that of the Labour Party. She opposed A. J. Mundella's Factory Act of 1881, which reduced working hours for women and children as compared with those of men, believing that in the long run the isolation of women's rights could only result in the weakening of their position.

Dilke's main advocacy on behalf of the labor movement was for workers in the dangerous and sweated trades. In part this was due to the influence of his second wife, who had long been associated with the Women's Trade Union League and who attended every Trades Union Congress from 1889 until her death. Most employees in the match-making and white-lead industries were women, and the statistics of industrial disease were appalling, with a 10 percent casualty rate that often resulted in blindness, paralysis, or death. The awful tensions of Francis Pattison's own life may have con-

The Right Hon. Sir Charles and Lady Dilke.

W. & D. DOWNEY
PHOTOGRAPHERS

57 & 61, EBURY STREET
LONDON, S.W.

COPYRIGHT

Figure 8. Sir Charles and Lady Dilke, 1885. Washington, the Library of Congress. (*Courtesy the Library of Congress*)

tributed to her special sympathy for the tragic lives of working-class women, as she herself had often suffered from crippling ailments that probably resulted, at least in part, from conflicts she felt between the contrasting roles of dependent wife and independent working scholar. This conflict was not of Mark Pattison's making but due to her own sense of guilt.

When the art historian Eugène Müntz complained in later years that she was taking on projects that might interfere with her major scholarly works, he may have had either her political or her social concerns in mind. She agreed to some of his objections while noting: "Yet I gain something. Ordinary life widens the horizon for men. Women are walled in behind social conventions. If they climb over, they lose more than they gain. It is therefore necessary to accept the situation as nature and society have made it, and to create for one's self a position from which *on peut dominer ce qu'on ne peut pas franchir.*"[46] But she observed that without the ability to support themselves, women were forced into prostitution, comparing their lamentable fate to that of the survivors of the siege of La Rochelle, who were forced to sell themselves for sustenance.

Curiously, the very books that could have contributed to financial independence during her first marriage were written long after Mark Pattison's death. Her four volumes on the art of the *dix-huitième* were produced when she not only enjoyed Pattison's very substantial estate but that of a rich new husband besides. It is almost as though she were creating a past that should have been, in this conclusive self-realization by self-support. As Francis Strong in 1859, she had horrified pious friends by her enthusiastic studies of anatomy and dissection and by her staunch advocacy of drawing from the nude. Now, with funds made available by Pattison's death, she planned to institute life classes for women at the Royal Academy, but such a "radical" idea proved unacceptable. Her old friend Lord Leighton, initially an advocate of the proposal, opposed it when president of the Academy.[47]

Shortly before marrying Dilke, Emilia (as she now wished to be called) had severe reservations about resuming the marital bond. Enjoying her freedom and ever-increasing income from her own writings, she could face this new tie with requisite confidence only after mutual friends made it clear that she, a highly distinguished individual, was viewed as quite as much a good match for Dilke as he for her. The same independent authority that she showed to Ruskin stood Emilia in good stead when Dilke's career was threatened and he considered leaving politics in the maelstrom of sexual revelations and accusations that descended upon him just before their marriage took place. Only too prophetically, Dilke had recently commissioned a depiction of the fickle goddess Fortuna from Burne-Jones. Although her image was never delivered, Fortuna's inconstancy most certainly was, coming just when Disraeli's prediction of Dilke's prime ministership seemed about to be realized. Writing to her future husband just before their marriage, Emilia noted, "I am sure of my own nerve and sure that I can stand a long pull; all my combative instincts are aroused and I inherit a large supply of them. . . . I am ready to do anything which you think wise to be done. . . ."[48]

Disastrous in its endless qualifications, Sir Charles' convoluted testimony only served to provide him with his own worst witness. Dilke's confused efforts to clear his name in legal actions initiated by him were exacerbated by the dubious if not traitorous behavior of his best friend and political associate, Joseph Chamberlain. Among the motives for Dilke's first ambiguous testimony may have been the desire to avoid a rigorous investigation that would have revealed his long-standing liaison with Francis Pattison, if such had taken place.

To paraphrase Cole Porter, anything went in Dilke's London as long as a discreet silence was maintained. The only real sin lay in breaking this convenient code. Many another lady and gentleman conducted an intricate, inventive private life, but it remained just that. As soon as the abundantly personal fell into the public domain, those concerned were cut dead. Sir Charles may have been "publicized," if not exactly framed, with the help of Lady Rosebery.[49] The former Hannah Rothschild, she had been married to ensure her husband's accession to the prime ministership, and probably nothing could have stopped her "helping" him achieve this goal. Lord Rosebery, a cold, calculating fish, could never have beaten out the charismatic Dilke; but with the latter's all too lively exploits (truly or falsely recounted in the trial) in the tabloids, the coast was clear for the chilly Rosebery's candidacy.

Virginia Crawford, whose divorce brought Dilke's name into the disastrous divorce trial, became a highly successful journalist and Catholic lay leader, converting to the Church after the trials. Like Emilia Dilke, Virginia Crawford (sister of Dilke's brother's widow) was also to be a fearless promoter of the women's movement, associated with St. Joan's Social and Political Alliance. She founded the Catholic Social Guild, and her *The Church and the Worker* sold 50,000 copies. To her passion for social justice she joined an interest in the arts, writing on French literature in 1899 and on Fra Angelico shortly thereafter.[50] What artist could be a more appropriate subject for one unofficially branded as a Fallen Woman, Traitor to her Class and, worst of all, a Papist? Seldom have the consequences of divorce been quite so relentlessly high-minded.

The trials blasted Disraeli's prediction that Dilke would become Prime Minister but did not prevent his repeated reelection to Parliament. His highly successful journalism continued unabated. After Victoria's death the Dilkes were received at Court, Charles having been Edward's chum during the long-drawn-out years of boisterous heir-apparency. Emilia had long ago befriended the prince's youngest brother Leopold at Oxford, and the Dilkes were intimates of the very wealthy, somewhat *parvenu* Francophile circle surrounding the new if middle-aged king. According to Sir Charles' biographer, Roy Jenkins, Emilia Dilke had been "the moving spirit in this somewhat laborious ascent to royal favour. . . . The most important purpose of her later life was to make the world recognize that it had wronged her husband."[51] The huge labor involved in the preparation of her last four books certainly ran a close second.

In 1902, two years before her death, Lady Dilke was invited to help organize the exhibition of early French painting that took place in Paris in 1904. This significant gathering of works of art was to reshape the understanding of Northern European painting of the late medieval period. Another acknowledgment of her mastery in the study of French art came in the form of an invitation to write the introduction to a catalogue of the Wallace Collection, perhaps the most splendid cluster of works of art, many of them French, ever to have been given by a British subject to her nation when they were so bequeathed on the death of Lady Wallace in 1897.

Two aspects of Lady Dilke's approach to art history placed her in the vanguard of scholarship. The first was an appreciation of original research, stressing the context in which the work of art functioned, utilizing all possible documentation as opposed to the esthetic-moralizing *Schwärmerei* so prevalent in the literature of her day. A second goal, realized in her writings, was that of a comprehensive view, in which true perspective could be achieved only by seeing the "major" and the "minor" arts as complementary chords, mutually illuminating the stylistic issues of their epoch. Unfortunately, hers is still an unusual approach, now even more than in the late nineteenth century. Today's scholars are ill at ease with the "decorative arts," which they often feel unworthy of serious attention, as if their own seriousness (or virility as the case may be) would somehow be impugned by a concentrated scrutiny of the "furniture of life." Here Lady Dilke's sex provided an advantage, as *les arts décoratifs* were viewed as an appropriately ladylike extension of women's true place—The Home.[52]

Her four volumes issued between 1899 and 1902 covered almost every aspect of the visual arts in eighteenth-century France, a truly monumental achievement. *French Painters* came out first (1899), followed by *French Architects and Sculptors* (1900), then *French Furniture and Decoration* (1901), and concluding with *French Engravers and Draughtsmen* (1902).

The Goncourt brothers' studies of the same subject, the first sections of which were issued in 1856 (dedicated to the memory of Marie Antoinette and the illustrator Charles Eisen), with the works of Paul Mantz among others, provided an abundantly documented point of departure for Lady Dilke's publications. *Art in the Modern State* established an invaluable platform on which to base the drama of eighteenth-century creativity in all the visual arts, including architecture and sculpture, neither of which much concerned the Goncourts. The brothers' study drew great strength from their intimate association with the many brilliant works of art they owned, from their acute sense for connoisseurship, and inspired recreation of an artistic personality that followed closely upon their gifts as novelists. Lady Dilke had a more deliberately academic approach, placing far less emphasis on "the beauty part." Ever interested in an analysis of how the artist's labors functioned within the economic framework of the times, she was quick to seize the latest of French research and present it in the most accessible fashion to an English audience. Lady Dilke devoted an important chapter to the role of the *marchand-mercier*, Lazare Duvaux. She clarified the complex function of this agent-patron-interior-decorator whose activity was often central to the creation of disarmingly intimate, yet highly elaborate *décors* of the mid-eighteenth century.

Lady Dilke stressed the crucial role of Etienne Falconet's student, nurse, and daughter-in-law, Anna Collot, in the completion of the paralyzed sculptor's statue of Peter the Great at St. Petersburg (1777). Describing the statue, Falconet wrote, "I have entirely remodelled it and finished it in eighteen months. . . . I except the head of the hero, which I have not done; this portrait, bold, colossal, expressive, and marked with character, is by Mademoiselle Collot, my pupil." "For this proceeding and avowal," Lady Dilke wrote, "which he himself characterized as an 'action doublement vertuese,' Falconet was attacked with ridicule, and he had to defend himself not only against the common public but also against a distinguished brother-sculptor."[53] Did she recall the long nursing of Mark Pattison, ending with her nervous collapse, when she wrote, "For eight long years he [Falconet] kept his room, tyrannically insisting on the close attentions of his daughter-in-law, Anna Collot, who had been one of his few pupils. . . . Death delivered her and him on the 24th January, 1791, but Anna Collot never again touched the chisel which she had been forced to abandon"?[54]

One might well expect Lady Dilke to have written a chapter on the Pompadour as patroness of the arts; but this, oddly, is not provided, although generous information about her concern with painters, sculptors, and architects is to be found throughout the volumes. Lady Dilke's criticism of the Goncourts' Fragonard characterization as "too feminine" is entirely correct.

LADY DILKE'S ACHIEVEMENT

Scrutiny of the French Academy's highly erratic policy toward the admission of women is to be found in *French Painters of the XVIIIth Century*, a reflection of the author's lifelong concern with women's rights and of the hazards of separating the rights of women from those of men in professional organizations. Cowed into amateur standing, English women painters of the nineteenth century lost the distinction of such earlier artists as Mary Moser and Angelica Kauffmann, who received academic credentials and professional independence in eighteenth-century London. Lady Dilke had sought after Mark Pattison's death to provide special awards for women at the Royal Academy. Establishment of such honors had been the long-standing wish of her art teacher, William Mulready, but it was rejected by the Academy's directors.

For someone so intimately concerned with social justice, it is curious that the area of ethical issues in art was generally avoided in Lady Dilke's oeuvre. A positivist orientation, keyed toward an objective perspective, devoid of the maundering and prettification of so much nineteenth-century literature doubtless contributed to this view, as did the need to earn money. Reacting against the Ruskinian prescriptions on which her own education was founded, it is as though she decided "to render unto Caesar" the publication of those subjects of enduring, unequivocal appeal to the very rich (and to those who aspired to be)—French art of the sixteenth, seventeenth, and eighteenth centuries. Her *vita contemplativa* was in large part devoted to writing on art for cash while her *vita activa* was directed toward needs and challenges that lay outside her literary career—women's rights and labor organization.

Charles Dilke suggested that his wife may well have felt a certain contempt for the subjects of her publications, strictly keyed to the marketplace as they were. The French Renaissance with its greedy, insistent eclecticism that merged the best of everything from North and South, Gothic and Renaissance, was revived as the omnivorous robber-baron style par excellence in Europe and America of the 1850s, 1860s and 1870s. Nothing was so good that it couldn't be improved by amalgamation with something better still, in the opinion of the period. Later nineteenth-century affluence, bored by the abundant vulgarity of the nouveau riche Second Empire Renaissance, sought something more elegant and expensively restrained. Now the neoclassical chic of Louis XVI replaced the ebullience of *le style François Ier*. In her later writing, Lady Dilke was ready to provide the required detailed analysis of the art with which fashionable wealth then sought association. Her four volumes on painters, sculptors, architects, printmakers, and decorators of the French eighteenth century provided a still more comprehensive view of that period of fin-de-siècle investment and imitation than had her initial two-volume study of *The Renaissance of Art in France.*

Twenty-five years after its original publication, she hoped to prepare a revised edition of the latter study, employing the same abundantly illustrated format that had made her recent works such a success. Late in life she began to write about nineteenth-century France. This impressive project, with her *Art in the Modern State*, would have completed an unprecedentedly profound study of five hundred years of French culture, beyond the scope of any scholar of Gallic art past or present, a gargantuan intellectual feat. That she achieved so much, with the extremely rich lives of society and social consciousness that she also cultivated, verges on the miraculous, only made possible by her ability to work, as Sir Charles had said, with Benedictine fervor.

Lamenting the impossibility of the completion of Lady Dilke's grand historical design, the anonymous author of her lengthy eulogy in the *Quarterly Review* concluded:

we are thankful for what Lady Dilke has given us, and proud that her work was accomplished by an Englishwoman. Considering that it was conceived and executed by one who was never physically robust, who was never secure from prolonged attacks of bodily pain, who had known private sorrows enough to disable a less courageous soul, whose occupations in other lines were sufficient to fill the life of an ordinary man, the result is astounding.[55]

Disapproving of Lady Dilke's labors as "chief mover in the Oxford branch of the Women's Suffrage Society," the same writer nevertheless observed that "the form and delivery of her many speeches were so excellent as almost to banish from the view of an old-fashioned listener the incongruity of the spectacle presented by a refined and personally attractive woman addressing a mixed crowd." This author found a conection between her political interests and Lady Dilke's work as an art historian:

Her historical instinct, developed by a life-long study of politics, enabled her so to utilise her profound technical knowledge of the fine arts that she made herself a unique authority on the influence and position of "Art in the Modern State." . . . It was the philosophy of aesthetics, the history of art, and its connexion with the history of organised and civilised states that she made the object of her studies.

But the writer saw Lady Dilke's commitments to social justice as:

her extraneous work which placed an excessive burden on her physical forces. What wore out her strength was her joining to her life-work an effort to bring about what she might have called a "Social Science Association Arcadia," not with any of Ruskin's fantastic illusions, but simply for the purpose of doing good. The aim was laudable, but life being short and art being long, the result is ever to be lamented.[56]

A friend wrote to Lady Dilke, "Nous autres femmes, nous avons tant besoin de forces pour suffire au double fardeau, de notre tâche, et de celle de notre mari. Vous vous êtes dépensée à cette mission plus qu'aucune autre."[57] Her reluctance to remarry was doubtless based upon the awareness, even before the Dilke scandal, of the "double fardeau" imposed upon those who sought both self-realization and the furthering of their husband's career. Dilke was painfully cognizant of his wife's labors, both on his behalf and for herself. He placed these lines in French, which she had not let him see in her lifetime, on the last page of a penetrating memoir that was his introduction to her posthumously published *The Book of the Spiritual Life* (1905).

Changes in name suggest changes in perspective. From the parental choice of Emily Francis Strong, the scholar, as a girl, preferred E. Francis Strong, a form suggesting the opposite sex and a name close to that of the country whose art was to absorb so much of her life. Her first book came out under the authorship of Mrs. Mark Pattison, with her later articles given the by-line of E.F.S. Pattison, once again allowing for masculine authorship. When Dilke entered the picture she returned to the name of her childhood, restated in matronly Latin fashion as Emilia. Reconciled to her origins, she had come full circle, classicizing her given name, which meant, most aptly, "to better, or improve."

Lady Dilke's interests were largely directed to what lurks beneath the surface of art, a study of the use by power of seduction and display. An almost Conradian fascination seems to lie behind her incisive presentation of the well-ordered veneer of Louis XIV's one-man welfare state. It is as though she sensed the strange heart of darkness glittering in the depths of the Roi Soleil's Versailles. Had this remarkable woman been born in the twentieth century she might have been honored for her own efforts, beginning with a state scholarship to Oxford. There she would have "read" PPE (Politics, Philosophy, and Economy), as the University still, and possibly quite rightly, refuses to recognize Art History as a legitimate undergraduate discipline. With a somewhat different range of choices, she might have become in Ruskin's words, a "Professoressa," a politician or a businesswoman. Art might well have been restricted to "Off-hours of my own time."

From today's perspective, Emilia Dilke is a major member of the second generation of women art historians. Of special interest in this regard but from the viewpoint of women's social history, her scholarship played a larger and more immediate role in a far more profitable women's profession developing rapidly at about the time of World War I—interior decoration. Lady Dilke's authoritative mastery of French architecture, furniture, and the minor arts helped women enter one of the cruelly few new professions deemed genuinely ladylike that was also remunerative—what is now called interior design, previously a male and rather humdrum craft. It is of special importance for the women's movement, as the profession proved the back door to that of architecture, from which women were excluded for a very long time. They could first approach architecture through the garden (landscape design—all flowers are supposedly feminine if not female) and the matching of curtain to wallpaper to carpet. Successful interior decoration requires a knowledge of class, style, and history, together with a lot of "social push coming to shove," and in all these activities Lady Dilke was most definitely a pathfinder.

Rather than regret this powerful, gifted woman's conflicting aspirations, one should see how essentially they balance one another. The concept of influence, that central, overwrought tenet of history, coincided with the animating tension that structured Emilia Dilke's life in work. As Sir Charles observed in his trenchant memoir, "no influence ever ended" in Emilia's life. The contradictory forces and concerns motivating her personal, social, and professional lives were united in vibrant opposition—the classical definition of harmony.

NOTES

The principal published sources for the biography of Lady Dilke are the *Memoir* by Sir Charles Dilke, which appeared in her *The Book of the Spiritual Life* (London, 1905), and *Lady Dilke, A Biography* by Betty Askwith (London, 1969). For a full bibliography of manuscript sources and of published sources to 1969, see Askwith, *Lady Dilke*, pp. 235-36. The author has also consulted the recent monograph, *Lord Leighton*, by Leonée and Richard Ormond (New Haven and London, 1975). For two early accounts, see Anonymous, "The Art-Work of Lady Dilke," *Quarterly Review*, 205 (Oct. 1906), 439-467, and "Lady Dilke," *Dictionary of National Biography*, 23 (Supplement, 1901-1911).

1. Dedicated to Mme. Dyveke Helsted, whose shining career reflects only the happiest aspects of this essay's subject. Although women's contributions to scholarship in the arts have gained in volume, such work is still too often seen as a privilege, to be won again by successive generations. When Mme. Helsted was given the directorship of the Thorvaldsens Museum in Copenhagen, this was conceived more as a custodial than as a curatorial appointment. Her inspired work has revealed two of Denmark's greatest cultural resources, the splendid sculptor's works and those of his radiant rediscoverer.

Many thanks to the editors and also to David Robertson, who called my attention to the works of Lady Callcott and gave me new information about Mary Margaret Heaton. His study of *Sir Charles Eastlake and the Victorian Art World* (Princeton, 1978) has done much to explore and elucidate a rich period.

2. George Eliot, *Middlemarch*, Signet Classic, chapter XIX, p. 185.

For a most informative discussion of the links between the Casaubons and the Pattisons, and of the whole scholarly controversy on the subject, see Betty Askwith, *Lady Dilke, A Biography* (London 1969), Chapter 2, "Dorothea Casaubon." Gordon S. Haight in *George Eliot* (Oxford, 1968) and in *Letters and Journals of George Eliot* (Oxford, 1968) disallows any extensive identification between the Oxford couple and Eliot's characters. For a chilling portrait of the Pattisons in their final years, see "The Don" in Stephen Gwynn, *Saint and Sinners* (London, 1929). Dilke selected Gwynn to be his posthumous biographer. *The Life of Sir Charles Dilke* (2 vols., London, 1917), begun by Gwynn, was completed by Lady Dilke's niece, Gertrude Tuckwell. John Sparrow in *Mark Pattison and the Idea of a University* (Cambridge, 1967, pp. 9-18) is convinced of the identity between the Casaubons and the Pattisons; he also points out some adventitious correspondences between the novel and Francis Pattison's life after publication of *Middlemarch* in 1872.

3. See the *Memoir* appended by Sir Charles Dilke to his late wife's *The Book of the Spiritual Life* (London, 1905, pp. 1-155, p. 3), referred to hereafter as *Memoir*.

4. *Memoir*, pp. 12-13.

5. *Memoir*, p. 9.

6. *Memoir*, p. 15.

7. *Memoir*, pp. 14-16. Lecoq de Boisbaudran's work first appeared in Paris in 1848.

8. Dilke Papers 43932, quoted by Askwith, p. 8.

9. Askwith, p. 8.

10. Quoted in Askwith, p. 29.

11. *Memoir*, p. 120.

12. Quoted in John Sparrow, *Mark Pattison and the Idea of a University*, p. 131.

13. Askwith, p. 16.

14. For Albert's activities as animator and patron of the arts, see Winslow Ames, *Prince Albert and Victorian Taste* (London, 1968).

15. June Wayne, "The Male Artist as Stereotypical Female," *Art Studies for an Editor: 25 Essays in Memory of Milton S. Fox* (New York, 1975), pp. 269-75. Ann Douglas, *The Feminization of American Culture* (New York, 1977).

16. See Käte Laserstein, *Die Gestalt des Bildenden Künstlers in der Dichtung* (Berlin, 1931), p. 19.

17. See Rosamund Brunel Gotch: *Maria, Lady Callcott* (London, 1937); Robertson, *op. cit.*, pp. 208-09, 449-50; and Chapter 1 of this book.

18. *Memoir*, pp. 26-27.

19. *Memoir*, p. 27.

20. *Memoir*, p. 19.

21. *Memoir*, pp. 19-20.

22. Quoted in Askwith, p. 24.

23. Robertson, *op. cit.*, p. 435, cites her *A Concise History of Painting* among the major general works on the old masters published in England between 1820 and 1875.

24. *Memoir*, p. 20.

25. Quoted in Askwith, p. 26.

26. *Memoir*, p. 43.

27. Listed as by Emilia F.S. Pattison.

28. Leonée and Richard Ormond, *Lord Leighton* (New Haven and London, 1975), p. 73.

29. "Sir Frederick Leighton, P.R. A.," in *Illustrated Biographies of Modern Artists* (London, 1882), p. 24.

30. *The Saturday Review*, 23.8.68. Quoted in Askwith, pp. 37-38.

31. Quoted in Askwith, p. 38.

32. Quoted in Askwith, p. 39.

33. Quoted in Askwith, pp. 41-42.

34. *Memoir*, p. 37.

35. *Memoir*, p. 4.

36. Many of her early, anonymous reviews were for these publications.

37. It can be done, I am attempting it, let someone who is more knowledgeable than I do it.

38. *Renaissance of Art in France*, I, p. 203.

39. Paris, 1963.

40. *Renaissance of Art in France*, II, p. 121.

41. Quoted in Askwith, p. 95.

42. Quoted in Askwith, p. 77.

43. *Memoir*, p. 67.

44. Nikolaus Pevsner, *Academies of Art, Past and Present* (Cambridge, 1940).

45. Gwynn and Tuckwell, *Dilke*, II, 237.

46. One can master what one is not able to escape. *Memoir*, p. 55.

47. Ormond, *Leighton*, p. 73.

48. Askwith, p. 131.

49. Roy Jenkins, *Sir Charles Dilke: A Victorian Tragedy* (London, 1958), p. 353.

50. Jenkins, p. 332.

51. Jenkins, p. 406.

52. At the time of Emilia Dilke's death, two American collectors, the Hewitt sisters, were assembling a treasury of European crafts to supplement the technological concerns of their engineer/inventor grandfather, the philanthropist, Abraham Cooper.

53. *French Architects and Sculptors of the Eighteenth Century* (London, 1900), p. 113.

54. Ibid.

55. Anonymous. Article VII: "The Art-Work of Lady Dilke." *Quarterly Review*, 205 (Oct. 1906), 467.

56. Ibid., 441, 443, and 446.

57. We women, we have such need of strength to suffice for the double burden of our own task, and that of our husband. You have extended yourself in this mission more than any other. Quoted by Sir Charles Dilke in *Memoir*, p. 128.

SELECTED BIBLIOGRAPHY OF LADY DILKE*

This bibliography includes only signed individual articles and reviews or those identified in *The Wellesley Index to Victorian Periodicals 1824-1900*, edited by Walter E. Houghton, Esther Rhoads Houghton, et al., 3 vols., Toronto, 1966-1979, or by Sir Charles Dilke in his *Memoir* of Lady Dilke in her *Book of the Spiritual Life*, London, 1905. It has not been possible to attribute the many unsigned articles and reviews by Lady Dilke in such journals as *The Annual Register: A Review of Public Events at Home and Abroad*, *The Athenaeum*, and *The Saturday Review*. In addition, "Art Notes," written while Lady Dilke was art editor of *The Academy* are omitted. For Lady Dilke's notes on contemporary literature and art in *The Westminster Review*, see *The Wellesley Index*, 3, p. 766 for a listing of these items. It should be noted that until 1885, the date of her marriage to Sir Charles Dilke, her writings were almost always signed E. F. S. Pattison. After 1885 they were signed Emilia F. S. Dilke.

Books, First Editions

The Renaissance of Art in France. 2 vols. London, 1879.

Claude Lorrain, sa vie et ses oeuvres. Paris, 1884.

The Shrine of Death, and Other Stories. London, 1886.

Art in the Modern State. London, 1888.

The Shrine of Love and Other Stories. London, 1891.

French Painters of the Eighteenth Century. London, 1899.

French Architects and Sculptors of the Eighteenth Century. London, 1900.

French Furniture and Decoration in the Eighteenth Century. London, 1901.

French Engravers and Draughtsmen of the Eighteenth Century. London, 1902.

The Book of the Spiritual Life, including a *Memoir* of the author by Sir Charles Dilke. London, 1905.

Articles

"Art and Morality." *Westminster Review*, n. s. 35 (Jan. 1869), 148-84.

"Carstens." *Portfolio*, 1 (1870), 76-80.

"Palissy." *Portfolio*, 1 (1870), 189-91.

"Jehan Cousin." *Portfolio*, 2 (1871), 7-9.

"Jehan Goujon." *Portfolio*, 2 (1871), 22-24.

"Germain Pilon." *Portfolio*, 2 (1871), 72-75.

"Eight Miniatures of Jean Cousin." *Academy*, 2 (15 Nov. 1871), 516.

"Nicolas Poussin." *Fortnightly Review*, n. s. 11 (April 1872), 472-77.

"The Exhibition of the Royal Academy of Arts." *Academy*, 3 (15 May 1872), 184-85.

*Compiled by Claire Richter Sherman

"Summer Exhibition of the Society of French Artists." *Academy*, 3 (1 June 1872), 204-05.

"Jean Cousin." *Academy*, 4 (15 Jan. 1873), 26.

"The Use of Looking at Pictures." *Westminster Review*, n. s. 44 (Oct. 1873), 415-23.

"Five Paintings by Frederic Leighton, R. A." *Academy*, 5 (28 March 1874), 351.

"Eighth Exhibition of the Society of French Artists." *Academy*, 5 (2 May 1874), 500.

"The Picture by Piero della Francesca." *Academy*, 6 (22 Aug. 1874), 219-20. [Signed "Editor."]

"The Studios." I, *Academy*, 7 (20 Feb. 1875), 202-03; II (27 Feb. 1875), 228-29; III (6 March 1875), 251; IV (13 March 1875), 277-78; V (20 March 1875), 304-05; VI (27 March 1875), 330-31; VII (3 April 1875), 357-58.

"The Salon of 1876." *Academy*, 9 (13 May 1876), 463-65; (20 May 1876), 494-96; (27 May 1876), 516-17.

"The Collection of M. Gambart at Les Palmiers, Nice." *Athenaeum* (26 Aug. 1876), 276-78.

"Exhibition of the Société des Beaux-Arts, Nice." *Academy*, 11 (14 April 1877), 328-29.

"The Salon of 1877." *Academy*, 11 (12 May 1877), 422-23; (19 May 1877), 445-46; (2 June 1877), 494-95; (9 June 1877), 518-19.

"A Chapter of the French Renaissance." *Contemporary Review*, 30 (Aug. 1877), 466-80.

"French Châteaux of the Renaissance, 1460-1547." *Contemporary Review*, 30 (Oct. 1877), 579-97.

"The International Exhibition: Paris, 1878." *Academy*, 13 (1 June 1878), 493-94; (15 June 1878), 538-40; (22 June 1878), 563-65; *Academy*, 14 (6 July 1878), 20-21; (20 July 1878), 70-72; (3 Aug. 1878), 122-24.

"Fragonard and His Decorative Paintings at Grasse." *Academy*, 14 (10 Aug. 1878), 149-50.

"Notes from Paris." *Athenaeum* (8 May 1879), 641; and (24 May 1879), 671-72.

"The Salon of 1879." *Academy*, 15 (24 May 1879), 463-64; (31 May 1879), 484-85; (7 June 1879), 505-06; (14 June 1879), 528-29; (21 June 1879), 547-49.

"Jean Baptiste Greuze." *Encyclopaedia Brittanica*, 9th ed. (Edinburgh, 1880), 11, pp. 188-89.

"The Salon of 1880." *Academy*, 17 (15 May 1880), 370-71; (22 May 1880), 389-90; (5 June 1880), 427-28.

"Jean Antoine Houdon." *Encyclopaedia Britannica*, 9th ed. (Edinburgh, 1881), 12, p. 314.

"Jean Auguste Dominique Ingres." *Encyclopaedia Brittanica*, 9th ed. (Edinburgh, 1881), 13, pp. 74-76.

"The Salon of 1881." *Academy*, 19 (14 May 1881), 360-61; (28 May 1881), 399-400; (4 June 1881), 418-20; (11 June 1881), 439-40.

"Sir Frederick Leighton, P. R. A." In *Illustrated Biographies of Modern Artists*. Edited by François G. Dumas, pp. 3-24 (Paris, 1882).

"The Salon of 1882." *Academy*, 21 (6 May 1882), 327-28; (13 May 1882), 344-45; (20 May 1882), 365-67; (3 June 1882), 401-03.

"Jean François Millet." *Encyclopaedia Brittanica*, 9th ed. (Edinburgh, 1883), 16, pp. 321-22.

"Edward J. Poynter, R. A." *Magazine of Art*, 6 (April 1883), 245-51.

"The Royal Academy." *Academy*, 23 (12 May 1883), 334-35; (19 May 1883), 353-54; (26 May 1883), 372-74.

"The Glass-Paintings of Jean Cousin at Sens." *Academy*, 24 (22 Dec. 1883), 423.

"The Painter of the Dead (Jean-Paul Laurens)." *Magazine of Art*, 7 (1884), 51-57.

"France Under Richelieu." *Fortnightly Review*, n. s. 38 (Dec. 1885), 752-67.

"France Under Colbert." *Fortnightly Review*, n. s. 39 (Feb. 1886), 209-20.

"The Royal Academy of Painting and Sculpture in France." *Fortnightly Review*, n. s. 40 (Nov. 1886), 605-16.

"The Next Extension of the Suffrage." *Universal Review*, 4 (May-Aug. 1889), 371-79.

"The Great Missionary Success." *Fortnightly Review*, n. s. 45 (May 1889), 677-83.

"Benefit Societies and Trades Unions for Women." *Fortnightly Review*, n. s. 45 (June 1889), 852-56.

"Parables of Life." *Universal Review*, 5 (Sept.-Dec. 1889), 535-50.

"The Triumph of the Cross." *Universal Review* (Sept.-Dec. 1889), 253-67.
"The Coming Elections in France." *Fortnightly Review*, n. s. 46 (Sept. 1889), 334-41.
"The Adventures of Belzebub." *Universal Review*, 6 (Jan.-April 1890), 223-41.
"Trades Unionism for Women." *New Review*, 2 (Jan. 1890), 43-53.
"Art-teaching and Technical Schools." *Fortnightly Review*, n. s. 47 (Feb. 1890), 231-41.
"The Seamy Side of Trades Unionism for Women." *New Review*, 2 (May 1890), 418-22.
"The Hangman's Daughter." *Universal Review*, 8 (Sept.-Dec. 1890), 499-512.
"The Starved Government Department." *New Review*, 4 (Jan. 1891), 75-80.
"Trade Unionism Among Women." With Florence Routledge. *Fortnightly Review*, n. s. 49 (May 1891), 741-50.
"Trades Unions for Women." *North American Review*, 153 (Aug. 1891), 227-39.
"France's Greatest Military Artist (Edouard Detaille)." *Cosmopolitan* 11 (Sept. 1891), 515-24.
"Women and the Royal Commission." *Fortnightly Review*, n. s. 50 (Oct. 1891), 535-38.
"Mulready." *Fortnightly Review*, n. s. 52 (Sept. 1892), 346-51.
"The Industrial Position of Women." *Fortnightly Review*, n. s. 54 (Oct. 1893), 499-508.
"Preface." In A. Amy Bulley and Margaret Whitley, *Women's Work* (London, 1894), pp. v-xiii.
"Christophe (Ernest Louis Aquilas)." *Art Journal*, 46 (1894), 40-45.
"Madame Renan." *Athenaeum* (2 June 1894), 709.
"Randolph Caldecott." *Art Journal*, 47 (1895), 138-42 and 203-08.
"Woman Suffrage in England." *North American Review*, 164 (Feb. 1897), 151-59.
"S. A. R. the Duc d'Aumale." *Athenaeum* (15 May 1897), 650-51.
"The Idealist Movement and Positive Science: An Experience." *Cosmopolis*, 7 (Sept. 1897), 643-56.
"Le Boudoir de la Marquise de Serilly au Musée de South Kensington." *Gazette des Beaux-Arts*, 20 (1 July 1898), 5-16; (1 Aug. 1898), 118-28.
"L'art français au Guildhall de Londres en 1898." *Gazette des Beaux-Arts*, 20 (1 Oct. 1898), 321-36.
"Jean-François de Troy et sa rivalité avec François Le Moine." *Gazette des Beaux-Arts*, 21 (1 April 1899), 280-90.
"Chardin et ses oeuvres à Potsdam et à Stockholm. *Gazette des Beaux-Arts*, 22 (1 Sept. 1899), 177-90; (1 Oct. 1899), 333-42; and (1 Nov. 1899), 390-96.
"Samuel Strong and the Georgia Loyalists." *Annual Transactions of the United Empire Loyalists' Association of Ontario*, 3 (1899-1900), 23-28.
"Ary Renan." *Athenaeum* (11 Aug. 1900), 194.
"Letters of Antoine Watteau." *Athenaeum* (29 Sept. 1900), 418.
"Les Coustou: les chevaux de Marly et le tombeau du Dauphin." *Gazette des Beaux-Arts*, 25 (1 Jan. 1901), 5-14; and (1 March 1901), 203-14.
"Introduction." In London, The Wallace Collection. *Objets d'art at Hertford House*. Text by E. Molinier. London, 1903, pp. i-xi.

Reviews

Richard St. John Tyrwhitt. *A Handbook of Pictorial Art* (Oxford, 1868). *Saturday Review*, 26 (22 Aug. 1868), 261-63.
"Tissot *On the Imagination*." [Claude J. Tissot, *L'Imagination, ses bienfaits, et ses égarements, surtout dans le domaine du merveilleux* (Paris, 1868).] *Saturday Review*, 28 (10 July 1869), 56-58.
John Ruskin, *Lectures on Art* and *Catalogue of Examples* (Oxford, 1870). *Academy*, 1 (10 Sept. 1870), 305-06.
John Charles Robertson, *A Critical Account of the Drawings by Michel Angelo and Raffaello in the University Galleries, Oxford* (Oxford 1870); and Burlington Fine Arts Club Catalogue, *Raphael Sanzio and Michel Angelo Buonarotti* (London, 1870). *Academy*, 2 (22 Oct. 1870), 6-7.

"Herman Riegel, *Cornelius.*" [Herman Riegel, *Cornelius, der Meister der deutschen Malerei* Hanover, 1866).] *Academy*, 2 (15 Feb. 1871), 129-30.

Life and Letters of William Bewick, Artist. Edited by Thomas Landseer, A. R. A. 2 vols. (London, 1871). *Academy*, 2 (15 Oct. 1871), 471.

Johann D. Passavant, *Raphael of Urbino and his Father, Giovanni Santi* (London, 1872). *Academy*, 3 (1 Jan. 1872), 6.

"Grimm's *Select Essays.*" [Herman Grimm, *Zehn ausgewählte Essays zur Einführung in das Studium der modernen Kunst* (Berlin, 1871).] *Academy*, 3 (1 April 1872), 124-25.

Academy, 3 (1 April 1872), 124-25.

"Max Schasler, *History of Aesthetic.*" [Maximilian F. A. Schasler, *Aesthetik als Philosophie des Schönen und der Kunst*, Erster Band (Berlin, 1871-72).] *Academy*, 3 (15 July 1872), 266-67.

"Recent Works on Voltaire." [Gustave Desnoiresterres, *Voltaire et la société française au XVIIIe siècle* (Paris, 1867-76); David F. Strauss, *Voltaire, Sechs Vorträge* (Leipzig, 1870); and John Morley, *Voltaire* (London, 1872).] *Academy*, 3 (15 Aug. 1872), 301-02.

Walter Pater, *The Renaissance; Studies in Art and Poetry* (London, 1873). *Westminster Review*, n. s. 43 (April, 1873), 639-41.

Philip G. Hamerton, *Thoughts About Art* (London, 1873). *Academy*, 5 (24 Jan. 1874), 101.

"Art Books." *Academy*, 7 (1 May 1875), 460-62; 8 (30 Oct. 1875), 460-62; and 8 (20 Nov. 1875), 535. [Signed "Editor."]

Gustave Desnoiresterres, *Voltaire et Genève* (Paris, 1875). [*Voltaire et la société française au XVIIIe siècle*, 7.] *Academy*, 9 (8 Jan. 1876), 25-26.

Three Hundred French Portraits Representing Personages of the Courts of Francis I, Henry II, and Francis II, by Clouet. Autolithographed from the Originals at Castle Howard, Yorkshire by Lord Ronald Gower. 2 vols. (London, 1875). *Academy*, 10 (1 July 1876), 18.

René Ménard, *L'Art en Alsace-Lorraine* (Paris, 1876). *Academy*, 10 (7 Oct. 1876), 365-66.

Frederick Wedmore, *Studies in English Art* (London, 1876). *Academy*, 10 (16 Dec. 1876), 591-92.

"Caldecott's Illustrations to *Bracebridge Hall.*" [Washington Irving, *Bracebridge Hall* (London, 1877). Illustrated by Randolph Caldecott.] *Academy*, 11 (20 Jan. 1877), 58.

Pierre Petroz, *L'Art et la critique en France depuis 1822* (Paris, 1875). *Academy*, 11 (10 March 1877), 213-14.

Inventaire général des richesses d'art de la France; Tome premier, Monumens [sic] religieux (Paris, 1877). *Academy*, 13 (23 March 1878), 265-66.

Edward J. Poynter, *Ten Lectures on Art* (London, 1879). *Academy*, 16 (27 Sept. 1879), 235-36.

[Moritz Thausing], *Die Votiv Kirche in Wien* (Vienna, 1879). *Academy*, 17 (24 Jan. 1880), 71-72.

Summary of *Jahrbuch der königlichen preussischen Kunstsammlungen*, 1 (1879). *Athenaeum* (3 Jan. 1880), 26. [According to Sir Charles Dilke, these summaries appeared annually in this publication until Lady Dilke's death in 1904.]

Salon illustré de 1879 (Paris, 1880?). Publié sous la direction de François G. Dumas. *Academy*, 17 (27 March 1880), 239-40.

Henry Weekes, A. R. A., *Lectures on Art Delivered at the Royal Academy, London* (London, 1880). *Academy*, 17 (12 June 1880), 443.

Lettres de Eugène Delacroix, Recueillies et publiées par Philippe Burty (Paris, 1880). *Academy*, 18 (11 Sept. 1880), 192.

Eugène Müntz, *Raphael: sa vie, son oeuvre, et son temps* (Paris, 1881). *Academy*, 19 (29 Jan. 1881), 85-86.

Louis Gonse, *Eugène Fromentin, peintre et écrivain* (Paris, 1881). *Athenaeum* (23 July 1881), 118-19.

CHAPTER 7

MARIANA GRISWOLD VAN RENSSELAER (1851-1934): AMERICA'S FIRST PROFESSIONAL WOMAN ART CRITIC

Cynthia D. Kinnard

Mariana Griswold Van Rensselaer, the first American woman to become a professional art critic, was born in New York City on 25 February 1851, the second child and first daughter of George Catlin and Lydia Alley Griswold. Born to wealth, social distinction, connection with powerful political figures, and membership in a family that traced its American ancestors back over two hundred years, she was to acquire the culture and sophistication that led to her characterization as late nineteenth-century America's "foremost female art critic"[1] at her death in 1934.

George Griswold was a wealthy merchant, and his daughter was tutored at home in childhood, "taking special interest in art, archaeology, and architecture."[2] At seventeen she went with her family to Dresden, where she finished her education, toured Europe, met and at twenty-two married Schuyler Van Rensselaer, who had augmented his Harvard A.B. with advanced study at the Freiburg Mining Academy from 1868 to 1871. Like Mariana, Schuyler could trace his American family roots back to the early seventeenth century and Kiliaen Van Rensselaer's patroonship along the Hudson River, although his branch of the Van Rensselaers was nowhere near as wealthy as the Griswolds. The young Van Rensselaers returned to the United States in May 1873 and lived for eleven years in New Brunswick, New Jersey, where their only child, George Griswold Van Rensselaer, was born in 1875.

Schuyler and his partner, George W. Maynard, a chemist, had opened an analytical laboratory in New York City in 1872 and specialized in mining and metallurgical engineering, a specialty that in 1876-1877 allowed the young family a combined business and personal trip of over a year in Europe, Mariana visiting with her parents, who were still in Dresden, and Schuyler investigating chemical patents. When they returned, Maynard and

Van Rensselaer was dissolved and Schuyler began working for a railroad as an iron expert, a position he held for five years. Within a year he had his first attack of the lung disease that eventually caused his death six years later, in March of 1884.

Despite such attributes of upper-class gentility as trips to Europe, summers at fashionable resorts, and a comfortable home in a suburban university town, Van Rensselaer had decided very early on a career as a professional writer. Initially she hesitated between poetry and art criticism, publishing in both areas in 1876, only a year after her son's birth and even before the 1876-1877 trip to Europe. Art criticism soon won out, and she began contributing regularly to the new Boston-based weekly journal, *American Architect and Building News*, serving for many years as its New York art correspondent and writing other pieces of occasional criticism— over seventy articles appeared in that journal alone from 1876 to 1887. Her first article for the *American Architect and Building News* was a translation, but the second, "The Portal of the Old Palace Chapel, Dresden," was her own work and clearly came from her recent sojourn in Dresden.[3] For Mariana as for Schuyler, the trip to Europe had combined business and pleasure.

Another piece of art criticism to come from this 1876-1877 trip was a long article in *Lippincott's* on "Some Aspects of Contemporary Art," drawing heavily on her recent visits to European museums and exhibits. This early article is notable, for the fledgling art critic here set out the ideals that would motivate her throughout her career: to foster in her readers an instinct for art and a desire for more beauty in their lives and to provide the knowledge of how best to obtain it. She stressed not theory—she was impatient with what she saw as Ruskin's theorizing bent when he had such an instinctive sense of beauty—but rather technical judgment and sober artistic criticism. She closed with advice for painter, critic, and patron alike: "Let us shun self-analyzation, self-consciousness, morbidness, affectation, attitudinizing. Let us look ahead as little as possible, keeping our eyes on our brushes and on the world of beauty around us." Technique, not "the wind of art-philosophy," the eye, not reason, were to be our guides.[4] Little of Van Rensselaer's work appeared in *Lippincott's* in subsequent years, and then it was on such diverse topics as American fiction, decorative art, Sarah Bernhardt, and a trip to the Alleghenies.[5] As a magazine with a special interest in travel and manners, it was not the sort of publication to find her work lively and anecdotal enough.

From the start, Van Rensselaer struggled to find a suitable audience for her art criticism, publishing here and there before finally finding her niche and often writing on popular rather than scholarly subjects. This was caused in part by her initial lack of clear direction but more significantly by the scarcity of major art journals to which she could address her work. Although the 1850s had witnessed a growing number of art magazines and journals, the Civil War had brought publication of many of these abruptly to an end, and it was not until the Centennial Exposition at Philadelphia in 1876 that public awareness of art was rekindled sufficiently to stimulate new art publications. As she began her career as an art critic, Van Rensselaer's options were limited: she could try to review art shows for the general periodicals of the day like *Scribner's* (later the *Century*), *Harper's*, and *Lippincott's*; or she could try to place articles in European-based art publications like the *American Art Journal* (an American edition of the *London Art Journal*) or the *London Magazine of Art*, which published a New York edition; or she could turn to the few American art journals like the *American Art Review*. In time, as we shall see, she tried all of these possibilities.

Perhaps we can catch a glimpse of the life of an upper-class American woman in the 1870s, a life Van Rensselaer was clearly rejecting, in an article she wrote on "The Plague of Formal Calls," published in the "Home and Society" section of the March 1880 issue of *Scribner's Monthly*. "Is it not time that a protest should be made against the absurdity and unprofitableness of our custom of 'paying calls?'" she asked. The ceremony has become "an intolerable burden . . . Sysyphean" in large cities and almost worse in small towns, "for there one gets but meager compensation in social pleasures of any kind, and though the list is briefer, the names bring more constantly recurring obligations." She remarked to her readers that in Europe women are allowed simply to leave their cards rather than waste time in chatting, and she ended by urging the wisdom of granting a woman "perfect liberty to visit where she wished to go, and to stay away when she felt no contrary impulse" without giving offense to others.[6]

Several brief biographical sketches of Van Rensselaer have described her as turning to writing only after her husband's death in 1884.[7] Nothing could be more mistaken, for she had written and published much before then, and her future topics and themes were already apparent. More than fifty articles appeared in the *American Architect* before Schuyler's death, for example. There were six articles in the *Century* from June of 1882 to February of 1884, and her important nine-part series on recent American architecture, much of which was already written before her husband's death, was published in the *Century* from May 1884 to June 1886.

Considering the fact that Van Rensselaer was nursing her husband for much of the last five years of his life, this remarkable output testifies to her early determination for a career in writing art criticism. At times she was diffident about trying to get her work in print. For instance, there exists in an autograph collection a rather plaintive note handwritten on 30 December 1880 to an unidentifiable publisher: "Gentlemen, Can you make use of the enclosed little paper in any of your publications? Yours respectfuly, M. G. Van Rensselaer."[8] Nevertheless, some were making use of her work, and as time went on, she became more confident.

The assumption that Van Rensselaer sought a career for herself only after Schuyler's death has persisted because it conforms to the common view of nineteenth-century women that no woman, particularly one of Van Rensselaer's class, would have needed or wanted a professional life unless forced into it by economic necessity. However, the example of Van Rensselaer also serves to dispel other stereotypic views of women: she was active, not passive; she purposefully resolved on a career rather than coming to it accidentally or through her father's or husband's tutelage; a devoted wife and mother, as well as daughter and sister, she was not frustrated by her lot but wanted something additional. Schuyler's death allowed her to pursue her career with more freedom, but like Queen Victoria, she wore black for the rest of her life, almost fifty years (see Figure 9).

Yet one looks in vain for evidence that Van Rensselaer was inspired by some of the earlier women art critics like Margaret Fuller or Anna Jameson to determine to seek a career as an art critic herself. She mentioned Ruskin often, usually in negative terms, but she obviously read him carefully. She cited other notable art critics from the nineteenth century and earlier—Winckelmann, Charles Eastlake, Fromentin, and Matthew Arnold, to name just a few. She knew Pugin's work if she did not admire it, Owen Jones's *Grammar of Ornament* (1854), and Christopher Dresser on the art and architecture of Japan; but nowhere does she mention Jameson or Fuller or Lady Eastlake. The education and travel opportunities provided by her wealthy parents seem to have been what opened Van Rensselaer's eyes to the possibility of a career in writing about art. She seems not to have looked to female precedents nor to have thought of herself as anything but an art critic, not a pioneering female art critic.

Within weeks of Schuyler's death Van Rensselaer received word that her father had died in Dresden. With her young son she hastened to join her mother; and they alternately traveled and lived in Dresden for eighteen months, Van Rensselaer gathering material for many articles and for a series on English cathedral churches commissioned by the editor of *Century* before Schuyler's death. Although ill for a time, no doubt suffering from the strain of Schuyler's last illness, her father's unexpected death, and the disruption of traveling to Europe, Van Rensselaer slowly regained her strength; and soon articles came pouring from her pen, some published in *Century*, many in the *American Architect*. Of the more than seventy of her articles appearing in the latter from 1876 to 1887, four multipart articles came from the 1884-1885 European trip.

Even in an essay as brief as this must be, Van Rensselaer's writings for the *American Architect* deserve some attention, for although there were articles

Figure 9. Portrait of Mariana Griswold Van Rensselaer, by William A. Coffin, 1890. New York, Museum of the City of New York. (*Courtesy Museum of the City of New York*)

in other magazines from time to time in her early years as an art critic, she got her start in that journal. The first American art journal devoted to building and architecture, the *American Architect* advertised itself as "an illustrated Journal of Constructive and Decorative Art, devoted to the Interests of Architects, Builders, Decorators, etc.," but emphasis was clearly on building and construction rather than art and architecture. Van Rensselaer was to fill that lack, and early in January 1878 she began her regular reviews of art shows, which continued to appear there almost uninterrupted for the next ten years. This work consists of occasional criticism—that is, criticism written for a particular occasion rather than general criticism—and often loses the twentieth-century reader in a bewildering list of unknown and presumably unimportant artists and works. Still, amid material of a topical nature are interesting appraisals of artists of permanent importance in American art history—Hunt, Chase, Homer, Whistler, Eakins, and Twachtman, among others—as well as fascinating essays on American culture and taste. Certainly everything she wrote is not important, but even her trivia illuminate the period.

A consistent feature of Van Rensselaer's writings in the 1870s was her impatience with American art standards and achievements, perhaps a result of her own sophisticated European education as well as her youth (she was not yet thirty). Writing of a loan exhibition held at the Academy of Design in New York in January of 1878, for instance, she was highly critical of the show, finding it pecuniarily successful but strongly lacking in educational results, which the organizers of the exhibition had promised. This lack she found particularly regrettable in view of the efforts toward art education being made in the city at the time, "earnest though sometimes lamentably undirected."[9] In writing of the fifty-third annual exhibition of the National Academy of Design in April of the same year, she told her readers that she had not visited the Academy since the spring of 1874 and found the work of the artists now advanced; she then betrayed her own standards, however, by finding them all lacking in comparison with Corot, Millet, Daubigny, and other Barbizon painters. One views these French painters, she commented, and then "realiz[es] the deficiencies of our own art."[10]

In holding up the Barbizon painters as her ideal, Van Rensselaer was trying to expand her countrymen's ideas of art beyond their own shores. Most of the gold medals at the Centennial Exposition in Philadelphia (1876) were won by latter-day Hudson River painters rather than those following the more recent Barbizon style. Many American artists had already discovered the Barbizon painters, but most critics still rejected or ignored them. Thus Van Rensselaer belonged to what Peter Bermingham, in a history of American art in the vein of the Barbizon school, has called the "new breed of critics" that emerged just about the time of the Centennial:

"young, well-traveled, thoroughly cosmopolitan, and, for the most part, French-oriented in their views on art matters."[11] Van Rensselaer was the only woman among this group.

Van Rensselaer's views were not always so advanced, however. In reviewing a 1879 water color exhibition, she disparaged Homer's "indistinct crudeness" and also slurred impressionism.[12] Her tongue could be acid, her approbation somewhat negative: "Each successive year we count on the Academy walls fewer pictures that are absolute failures or ludicrous mistakes—fewer attempts at art showing a lack of all artistic knowledge." Of one painter she remarked that he "has talent,—taste seems to be the thing he needs."[13]

Although demanding in her evaluation of American art, Van Rensselaer reserved her most devastating criticism for John Ruskin. By the late 1870s and early 1880s, the influence of Ruskin on American ideas of art was decidedly waning, as Roger Stein has demonstrated,[14] and Van Rensselaer's criticism was central in reducing Ruskin's impact in the United States. She faulted his emphasis on truth to nature and on morality as criteria for judging art. She argued that Ruskin's facts were not art. Rather, we should want "a picture of artistic beauty . . . or aesthetic value and truth in its effect upon our minds . . . a beautiful dream [which] we shall not confuse . . . with reality, shall not even bring them into comparison."[15] As for morality in art, Van Rensselaer believed it was the responsibility of the spectator rather than the artist. She urged the development of "a high artistic culture, a deep and even technical acquaintance with art."[16] Clearly she saw herself as providing this education for her readers. She wanted them to base their perception of art on aesthetic rather than theoretical grounds. Whereas Ruskin had wished to move evaluation of art away from "the well-established European aesthetic traditions of 'taste' to the imaginative insight of the individual observer,"[17] Van Rensselaer wished to return to "standards."

Perhaps the most advanced stand Van Rensselaer took during these early years was in championing the Society of American Artists when it broke away from the more conservative National Academy in 1877. According to Oliver Larkin, "The public stayed away from the Society's early shows, and even in the liberal *Nation* a writer referred to the work of its members in 1878 as 'college exercises' of a 'pulpy vagueness.'"[18] Van Rensselaer was one critic who did not stay away from exhibits by the Society; in fact, she usually found them much more interesting and exciting than those of the National Academy and minced no words in telling her *American Architect* readers the reasons for her preferences, a partiality that continued in every spring review of the exhibitions of the two groups through that of 1887, the last Van Rensselaer wrote for the *American Architect*.

In addition to serving as New York art critic and writing occasional criticism for the *American Architect*, Van Rensselaer regularly reviewed books on art. In 1881 she rejoiced in a republication of Winckelmann's *History of Ancient Art*:

we *must* go to it to learn how to reverence and understand the spirit of antiquity, how to think of and appreciate its works of art. I know of no more useful antidote to the critical habits of to-day than the persual of this book. What a reproach is offered by its sober enthusiasms, its deliberate and judicious and yet sympathetic spirit to the hard and mechanical style of criticism we so often use, and as well to the meaningless "gush," the rhetorical extravagance into which, on the other hand, we are also apt to fall.

She expected every reader to be touched by Winckelmann's "reverent attitude towards beauty" and his "conviction that art is indeed a useful and a vital thing to men."[19] As in other of her writings, often what is important in her book reviews is not so much the books being reviewed as the revelation of her own standards of criticism, her hopes for American art and criticism, and her attempts to inform and mold public taste. To this latter end she often developed her reviews into long, multipart articles—essays on the subject rather than critiques of a book.

Always Van Rensselaer's aim was to educate the public, and when a new book failed in this mission, she was ruthless in her review. In evaluating a new history of art by Julia B. DeForest (1881), she demolished the book, citing errors of omission as well as commission, grievous mistakes and errors of fact, and its lack of any conceptualization. She was particularly annoyed because the book appealed to "our youngest and most ignorant, and therefore most defenceless, band of readers." This was all the more serious because "we are at a point now in our national education when there is a widespread craving for art-instruction. It is more than ever necessary, therefore, that none should be encouraged, especially of an elementary sort, which is not accurate and edifying." The need was there, and "it *is* because that need is so real that the absolute uselessness of the volume is so strongly insisted upon." Van Rensselaer excused the harshness of her review—and it was harsh—by noting that the book was addressed to a wide audience, one she knew to be composed partly of parvenus in matters of art, and that "beginners cannot criticise for themselves."[20]

Always her own approach was towards instruction. She continually addressed herself to "students of art," providing them with lessons. She valued works that were "instructive" or "edifying," standards she tried to emulate in her own writing. She dismissed those that were not. At her worst she sermonized, but at her best she was an excellent teacher.

Prolific as she was in writing for the *American Architect*, it should not be assumed that it was her only outlet in her first decade as a writer on art and architecture. On the contrary, even before Schuyler's death she had begun publishing in two other important periodicals, the short-lived *American Art Review* and *Century* magazine, as well as scattered articles in *Lippincott's*, the *Atlantic Monthly*, and *Scribner's*. The *American Art Review*, devoted to the practice, theory, history, and archaeology of art, was no doubt more to Van Rensselaer's liking than the more tradesmanlike *American Architecture and Building News*, where she often found her tasteful articles sandwiched between discussions of methods of sewage disposal for isolated homes, judging the wholesomeness of drinking water, and preventing fires, as well as articles on the latest methods in plumbing, heating, masonry, and other elements of construction. Published in Boston, the *American Art Review* was large, beautifully printed, and richly illustrated. It was also doomed to an early death, there being as yet insufficient public support to maintain it. Yet in the two years of its publication, Van Rensselaer contributed an ardent two-part plea for art education to train amateurs who would foster great art through intelligent appreciation, short reviews of two books and of a new French fashion journal, as well as articles on the American painters William Merritt Chase and Frederic Arthur Bridgeman, a two-part article on Correggio, and an article on the famous Green Vaults of Dresden. Particularly in the first contribution we have Van Rensselaer's short criticism at its best—a hortatory tone that never condemns present ignorance but rather points the way toward improvement, a belief in education, and no shortness of temper or haste in composition.

When the *American Art Review* folded in 1881, Van Rensselaer was thirty. Already she had five years' experience as a professional art critic. She had the education, she had the verbal ability, she had the sense of mission to be an excellent critic. When given the opportunity or when she took the trouble, when assured of a somewhat sophisticated audience, she *was* an excellent critic. She lost that audience, however, and surely could have had no assurance that her *American Architect* audience was of the level she desired.[21] Her problem in the early 1880s was to find a suitable outlet for her work. I believe that she had realized that she would have to adjust her work to her audience if she was to have any professional life at all and that she was willing if not eager to do this. By 1884, when Schuyler died and her profession became a source of support for herself and her family, she had found an acceptable outlet in *Century Magazine*.

Century had been created out of *Scribner's Monthly* by its new editor Richard Watson Gilder and published its first issue in November 1881. Van Rensselaer began contributing regularly in 1882, and despite the losses she suffered in family deaths and her prolonged stay in Europe in 1884-1885, she published more than thirty articles in *Century* in the 1880s alone. There were essays on wood-engraving, in which Van Rensselaer again championed "our younger men," as she had supported the Society of American Artists[22];

a substantial piece on American etchers (February 1883), which was later issued in pamphlet form by Frederick Keppel (1886); and in 1884 a series on recent architecture in America that was interrupted by her personal tragedies and stretched over nine installments in two years. Whereas she had sometimes been hesitant to address the professional audience that read the *American Architect* on matters architectural, in *Century* she had a more general audience and developed a much surer, more authoritative tone. Now her message always was that Americans are doing good and even original work. In American wood-engraving today, she wrote, we have "the most original development of which American art as yet can boast."[23] Already we have an "American school of etching," which she praised highly.[24] In the first article of the "Recent Architecture in America" series, she told her readers, "There is much good building going on at the present moment in this country. . . ."[25]

In addition to her writings for periodicals, Van Rensselaer provided notes for two exhibitions in 1884, before leaving for Europe. The first was a loan exhibition of over two hundred oil paintings to raise money for the pedestal for Bartholdi's Statue of Liberty. As the exhibition was held in the galleries of the Brooklyn Art Association in January 1884, Van Rensselaer must have been writing it as she was nursing her dying husband. This would have been an extremely difficult task, for she did not receive a complete list of the paintings to be lent to the exhibit in time to prepare her text, so that her references are extremely vague. No doubt she also felt some pressure to say something favorable about the works lent by their owners for charity; we find her insincerely praising works by painters whom she had elsewhere lambasted.

Her catalogue for a memorial exhibition of the works of George Fuller held in Boston in the spring of 1884 was different. As she herself observed, "it is always pleasant to write of a painter whom one admires."[26] Yet once again she was handicapped in writing her text without knowing with certainty what works would be gathered together for the exhibition, and there appears again the vagueness that characterized the Brooklyn loan exhibition. There is also fulsome praise for Fuller, a painter who was extraordinarily popular during the late 1870s and 1880s. Peter Bermingham has attributed the "somewhat exaggerated acclaim accorded Fuller during his final years" to "Eastern America's growing taste for the sweet, sad look of America's tone poets."[27] Here in particular we sense that Van Rensselaer is more a product and reflector of her period and class than a critic of it.

No doubt Van Rensselaer had been sought to write the Fuller catalogue because of an excellent essay on Fuller in *Century* some months earlier. Here she could write professional criticism rather than the appreciative essay called for in the memorial catalogue, evaluating Fuller's achievement rather than merely describing it. The Brooklyn Loan Exhibition catalogue and these two Fuller essays further illustrate Van Rensselaer's difficulty in speaking to a variety of readers in her role of art critic. She preferred to be a tough, businesslike critic, but she occasionally had to soft-pedal her comments to suit the context, which inevitably blunted her discernment.

Upon her return to the United States in the fall of 1886, Van Rensselaer's first project was the introduction for a huge, ambitious volume, *Book of American Figure Painters*, in which she continued to find the "general trend" of American art "unquestionably upward and the general prospect cheering."[28] This is true in many branches of art, she wrote—building, wood-engraving, etching, sculpture—and not the least in figure painting. Van Rensselaer closed her introduction with a reminder to her readers that "we also, and not our artists only, have a duty to perform if we wish the stream of progress to grow wider, deeper, swifter. We must give ourselves more earnestly and intelligently and generously than we have to the happy duty of appreciation."[29]

During this period Van Rensselaer also wrote an appendix to Kenyon Cox's illustrations for Dante Gabriel Rossetti's poem *The Blessed Damozel* (1850). Although Rossetti had not yet created a interpretation of his poem, his other work was well known to Van Rensselaer; and she found it, she wrote in the appendix, unwholesome, morbid, melancholy, and perplexing if original. She believed him a born poet rather than painter (an opinion few would concur in today) and so found it perfectly fitting that Cox illustrate his poem.

Van Rensselaer's appendix is notable not for its opinions of Rossetti, however, but rather for a short discussion of the nude in American art. As nude studies were a basic element in academic training, when American painters began showing more nudes, it was taken by a traditional critic like Van Rensselaer to indicate an elevation of subject and a strengthening of training and seriousness. This is the source of some of her pleasure over the figure painting in *Book of American Figure Painting* of the same year.

In her Cox essay she deplored the prejudice against undraped figures, saying that even though "the true lover of true art" will admit that there are "many examples of an unquestionably pernicious sort," still "no excuses can be found for [such prejudice] either in right artistic theory or in examples drawn from high artistic practice." Cox's nudes were neither too pure, etherealized, or refined to have any reference to living bodies nor, at the other extreme, too baldly realistic, "too suggestive of modern forms deprived for a moment of modern dress," that is to say, naked. Not in all her other writings did Van Rensselaer come closer to a true Victorian spirit of semantic nicety than in her insistence that the right word, the right sentiment, was *nude:* "and all the difference between the right and the wrong, the noble and the ignoble, the desirable and the pernicious use in art of the human forms which God has made, seems to me to explain itself in words like these.''[30]

Van Rensselaer was floundering in the mid-1880s, writing too much, going off in too many directions, and involving herself in projects of questionable value. Then early in 1886, shortly after the premature death of the eminent American architect Henry Hobson Richardson, she was asked by friends and colleagues to write his biography; thus commenced her most fruitful period.

Van Rensselaer worked on the book throughout the rest of 1886 and all of 1887, consulting Richardson's friends and colleagues, visiting buildings, seeking out letters and published materials relating to Richardson's life, and collecting illustrations and photographs. She was especially pleased to be permitted to use a photograph of Richardson for the frontispiece (see Figure 10).

The book was published in June of 1888 and received mixed notice, one critic finding the biography ''rather sisterly than judicial in tone''[31] while another wanted more biographical data and glimpses into Richardson's personal life. By current standards, the book is a careful balance of the personal and the professional man. The first third was devoted to Richardson's early life, education, architectural studies in Paris, setting up professional practice, and personal characteristics, including likely hereditary influences (Joseph Priestley was his great-grandfather). The bulk of the book took up Richardson's works, and here Van Rensselaer was not afraid to make bold assessments. Her judgment that the Marshall Field Wholesale Store was one of his best and most important buildings still holds up today. Van Rensselaer rounded out her study with consideration of Richardson's characteristics as an artist, his method of teaching, and finally his influence upon his profession and the public. In the appendix appeared a valuable list of Richardson's works, a discussion of the methods of instruction at the Ecole des Beaux Arts, where he studied, extracts from his professional writings, and a ''circular for intending clients.'' This was truly a complete picture of the entire professional man, and one cannot help believing that Van Rensselaer was holding Richardson up as the ideal American architect.

The book is important in Van Rensselaer's oeuvre in marking her first attempt at a full-length book. Even more notable, however, is the fact that as *Richardson and His Works* was the first substantial study of an American architect, in writing her monograph Van Rensselaer could look to no American precedents. Although she often despaired of achieving the task she had accepted, her work was to serve not only as the basis of all Richardson scholarship to come but also as the form for monographs on other American architects.

Figure 10. Portrait of Henry Hobson Richardson (1838-1886). From *Henry Hobson Richardson and His Works*, by Mariana Griswold Van Rensselaer, 1888. Reproduced from facsimile edition published in 1967 by the Prairie School Press. (*Courtesy the Prairie School Press*)

Richardson and His Works still stands today as a careful and interesting study of an important architect. Mentioned by Lewis Mumford in *The Brown Decades* (1931), praised by Henry-Russell Hitchcock even as he superseded it with *The Architecture of H. H. Richardson and His Times* (1934) as "the foundation of all study of Richardson,"[32] the book was reprinted in a handsome facsimile edition in 1967 by the Prairie School Press, and in 1969 Dover published a paperback edition, finally making the book available at reasonable cost.

Regrettably, critics chosen to provide an up-to-date introduction to the book have tended to ignore the careful scholarship, misrepresent the amount of biographical material in comparison to the overwhelming preponderance of architectural criticism, and show more curiosity over the supposed mystery of Van Rensselaer's relationship with Richardson than is justified. One finds slighting references to her that ignore her professionalism and the fact that she knew and wrote about many important people in art, architecture, and landscape gardening: John Singer Sargent, Augustus Saint-Gaudens (see the relief portrait Saint-Gaudens did of her in 1888, Figure 11), Kenyon Cox, George Fuller, Richardson, Frederick Law Olmsted, and Charles Sprague Sargent, to name just a few. That her relationship with Richardson was thoroughly professional still seems inconceivable to some who assume that it must have involved a romantic attraction.

Van Rensselaer's time was devoted to the Richardson book for almost two years, and it would be reasonable to expect that she wrote little else, but that would be underestimating her energy. She finally began publishing her English cathedrals series in *Century* in March of 1887, a project commissioned before Schuyler's death in 1884. The number of magazine articles was dropping noticeably during this period as she learned to focus on several rather than many topics at once; or perhaps she was finally finding it possible professionally to be more selective. Yet during this busy time there were notable articles like "Architecture as a Profession" in the *Chautauquan* of May 1887, a new book in late 1889, a collection of essays entitled *Six Portraits: Della Robbia, Correggio, Blake, Corot, George Fuller, and Winslow Homer*. Each of these essays had been printed previously and was reworked for publication, but five are basically unchanged.

In the one on Homer, however, Van Rensselaer showed that she had done some important rethinking since her initial essay written in 1883 and her even earlier notices of Homer in the *American Architect*, and it is a pleasure to watch her critical estimation of Homer grow. Her first estimation had been, as I noted, that Homer was "indistinctly crude." She was frankly repulsed by his work. Not until 1883, when she saw the work that came from his period at Tynemouth, England, facing the North Sea (1881-1882), did she even begin to appreciate not only that work but his earlier attempts, and in an 1883 essay she publicly admitted her earlier bias. Appreciative

Figure 11. Portrait of Mariana Griswold Van Rensselaer, by Augustus Saint-Gaudens, 1888 (bronze plaque). New York, Metropolitan Museum of Art. (*Courtesy the Metropolitan Museum of Art*)

notices of Homer continued in Van Rensselaer's annual reviews of painting
exhibitions, and the essay in *Six Portraits* recapitulated and extended all her
earlier writings as well as sounding the theme for all the essays—an artist
must be an individual, free from conventional thought or method, well
trained but owing allegiance to no school.

Richardson and His Works had turned Van Rensselaer from occasional
criticism and also from writing about painting. There were few articles on
painting after *Six Portraits*; increasingly she devoted her research and
writing to architecture and landscape gardening. "Client and Architect,"
for example, appearing in the *North American Review* in 1890, did much to
improve public consciousness of architectural style and of the need for
professionals in designing buildings.[33]

None of Van Rensselaer's works was longer in production, gave her more
trouble, or was ultimately more disappointing to her than *English Cathedrals*. I have noted her penchant for shifting her focus—from poetry to art
criticism, from architecture to painting and back with the Richardson book,
with side interests in decorative art, etching, engraving, and fiction and
poetry. Nowhere is this intellectual restlessness, this inability to concentrate,
more evident than in the decade that encompassed the writing and the serial
and then book publication of *English Cathedrals*. In fact, this book seems
to have finished Van Rensselaer's involvement in the fine arts.

Gilder first proposed the series in 1883. Van Rensselaer was to write the
text, and Joseph Pennell, brash, rising young illustrator, was to do the drawings. Right from the start there were disagreements with Pennell. She
wanted drawings of things he found "unillustrateable," and he took
enormous latitude in his representations, always preferring the picturesque
view over accuracy. Many circumstances intervened to keep Van Rensselaer
from meeting *Century* deadlines: Schuyler's death, the Richardson book,
Six Portraits, her own increasing interest in landscape gardening, and early
in the 1890s, her son's illness. The series began to appear in March 1887,
with five chapters in that year, three the next, two in 1889 and 1890, and the
last in 1892. Clearly Van Rensselaer had lost interest.

Pleased with the initial popularity of their work, however, Gilder commissioned the pair to produce a French series late in 1888. Circulation of the
magazine reached its highest point in the late 1880s, when it exceeded
200,000.[34] No doubt Gilder attributed this prosperity in no small part to
Van Rensselaer's articles and Pennell's illustrations. Yet in his zeal to ex-
ploit their appeal, Gilder pushed Van Rensselaer too far and ultimately lost
her as a contributor.

Pennell and Van Rensselaer battled for control over the new series, and
finally Pennell won. One can only conjecture what the outcome might have
been had Van Rensselaer been a man. Over a five-year period, marked by
many delays, Van Rensselaer produced a few articles on French churches

but finally quit the series in 1899, after five articles had been published. Pennell's wife, Elizabeth Robins Pennell, also a writer on art and architecture and Pennell's collaborator on many articles and books, took over and furnished the kind of text Pennell and Gilder obviously wanted (and thought the public wanted)—charming, personal travel reminiscences with little historical or architectural interest and little solid research. The articles were entertaining but hardly instructive, as all of Van Rensselaer's were.

The English cathedral series was pulled together and published as a book by Century and Company in time for the Christmas trade in 1892. It was sufficiently successful to warrant a revised edition the next year and several reprints.[35]

Reviews of the book were mixed and illuminate Van Rensselaer's increasing difficulty with her audience. Some, like that in the *Critic*, were uncritically effusive, attempting to outdo Van Rensselaer in well-turned phrases: "Let *technickers*, as the Germans would say, criticize or appraise this work: we revel in its beauty as a book, in its artistic and literary attractions, in its intelligent appreciation of England's glorious architectural achievements."[36] The *Nation*'s reviewer, recalling the origin of the book in magazine form, found it "a book for magazine-readers still" and chided Van Rensselaer for her kindergarten-instructor tone and her many errors of fact.[37] C. H. Moore, noted writer on medieval art, took Van Rensselaer to task for numerous factual errors in his *Atlantic Monthly* review but still found the book valuable enough as a popular introduction to the study of English cathedrals to call for a corrected edition.[38]

And here exactly was Van Rensselaer's dilemma as an art critic. Gilder was constantly urging her to be less scholarly, less technical, to inject more human interest in her writings—in short, to write for a popular audience. When she did, scholars dismissed her work. Moreover, as we have seen, some popular reviewers still found her too pedantic. Probably as an art critic her only audience was in magazines and newspapers; she certainly did not have the comparable opportunity to teach at Harvard, as Charles Moore did. But what magazine and newspaper editors assumed their readers wanted was the sort of picturesque travelog the Pennells turned out, which no self-respecting art critic even took seriously. Van Rensselaer finally could satisfy neither audience, the professionals or the amateurs; and that is why, I am convinced, she once again shifted her focus.

Now she addressed herself to landscape gardening. Interestingly, her last article in the *American Architect* was on that subject. In it she called upon architects to assist the new profession in impressing its value upon clients; and believing that recruits for the profession might come from the ranks of those showing some interest in architecture, in her best Chautauqua manner she described the education and practice of landscape gardeners, rounding out her three-part article with an annotated book list. In all of this work she was strongly influenced by Frederick Law Olmsted, whom she met through Henry Adams, with whom she worked on the Richardson book, and about whom she wrote for *Century*. Theirs was a mutual admiration, and he credited her articles with bringing the profession to the attention of more young men, many of whom turned to him for advice.[39]

Her main outlet for this new interest, however, was *Garden and Forest*, a journal devoted to horticulture, landscape art, and forestry. Started by Charles Sprague Sargent in 1888, the journal was published for ten years before it succumbed to a lack of sufficient interest. Van Rensselaer began appearing in its pages with the first issue and published there until its last volume, contributing over forty articles, many of them in several parts, on such topics as flower and fruit pictures, Japanese gardening, a trip down the Rhône, flowers in town, John Brown's grave, orchids, native plants for ornamental planting, and color in rural buildings, to name just a few. Two of her longer essays on landscape art bear tangentially on her work as a critic of the fine arts—"Landscape Gardening," which appeared in seven parts in 1888, and "The Art of Gardening—An Historical Sketch," whose twenty-one installments appeared during 1889-1890. All of these writings were reworked and augmented by Van Rensselaer to appear in *Art Out-of-Doors: Hints on Good Taste*, published first in 1893, reappearing in a new and enlarged edition in 1925 and reprinted by the National Council of State Garden Clubs in 1959 as a basic reading reference in the National Council's landscape design study courses. With chapters on roads and paths, piazzas, formal flower beds, and the beauty of trees, among more technical or artistic chapters, the book is another step in Van Rensselaer's movement away from the main channels of art criticism and need not be taken up in detail; but the history of her concern with landscape art is indicative of the flow of her mind.

By 1893 Van Rensselaer had put much of her art-critical and art-historical writings behind her. Only forty-two, with half her life yet to live, she had done her major work as an art critic. Her response to the World's Columbian Exposition in Chicago (1893) demonstrates her inability to continue to grow in discernment and respond to the coming growth and excitement in art and architecture. Simply stated, she loved it. The exposition Sullivan thought (with hindsight, it is true) dealt American architecture a mortal blow was to Van Rensselaer "one of the most nobly beautiful and distinctly the most interesting of the existing creations of the hand of man." She believed that "no place of its extent in the modern world has been so impressive, so magnificent, so imperial in its beauty."[40] Although she was still living in New York City when The Eight exhibited in 1908 and the Armory Show was held in 1913, we can be sure she did not respond to these exhibits as she had to the maverick Society of American Artists three decades earlier. The members of the so-called Ash Can School were boldly painting the squalor of lower-class urban life, spurning the more genteel themes of the late nineteenth-century mood painters Van Rensselaer loved, and she would hardly have recognized Duchamp's *Nude* as in the same genre as that of Cox.

What is more, her attention was turning increasingly to writing and publishing volumes of short stories and poetry and travel literature, to public affairs—serving as a public-school inspector and later president of the Public Education Association of New York, teaching at the University Settlement, serving on a committee to put good works of art into public schools, writing and organizing in opposition to the extension of suffrage to women—and to a monumental two-volume history of the city of New York in the seventeenth century, the research and writing of which took more than a decade. She had planned to continue this work up to 1789 and had begun outlining and writing the third and fourth volumes, as indicated by a manuscript in the New York Public Library; perhaps the war intervened, or perhaps she once again lost interest, for the second part of her study never continued past the early stages. Her only son died of tuberculosis in 1894, and this tragedy certainly affected her growing disenchantment with art criticism and pushed her into new spheres.[41] During the war she served as president of the American Fund for the French Wounded. In 1923 she published a volume of poetry for children strongly influenced by R. L. Stevenson, whom she admired greatly.

There were occasional popular essays on art during these years—articles like "'Who Wants Art Nowadays?'" and "The Art Museum and the Public," both in the *North American Review*, or "A Living Picture-book for Artists" in *Century*—articles appearing well into the 1920s. There was also a translation from the German of a book on Netherlandish art by Wilhelm Valentiner which she published in 1914. She wrote a graceful and appreciative essay for a memorial exhibition of the works of John Singer Sargent in 1926. But Van Rensselaer's years as an important art critic were over. She entertained weekly at tea, spent summers at fashionable watering places, and quietly lived the life of an American lady that was hers by birthright. She died early in 1934, just weeks short of her eighty-third birthday, and was lauded in obituaries, letters to the editor, and an editorial in New York newspapers as a distinguished art critic and very notable woman, "a significant figure in the formation of American taste" who "rendered substantial services in smoothing the path of the artist."[42]

As a professional female art critic, Van Rensselaer struggled against many difficulties, some of which she could not overcome. The expected role of a woman of her class made it problematic for her to think of herself as a professional, to develop single-mindedness and concentration; while serious about her art criticism, she was constantly turning to new concerns and seems at times to have been dabbling in writing. Often she presented herself to her editor as impoverished—she was, after all, the sole support of her son and herself and maintained a home also for her mother and sister—apparently as a more acceptable reason for her writing than ambition. Yet one doubts that she was driven to writing because of her husband's death, as she was writing before his death and also because her inheritances from both the Griswold and the Van Rensselaer families would have made a life of leisure and relative luxury within her means.[43]

Like other Americans of her period—Howells, Twain—she also wrote altogether too much: thirteen books, over 230 articles in more than twenty periodicals, several dozen newspaper articles, and three exhibition catalogues—the bulk of this in a twenty-year period. She never seems to have had a clear sense of her audience, and indeed we can see why, for it was constantly changing.

How can one be a lady and an art critic at the same time? Apparently this contradiction bothered some of Van Rensselaer's employers as well as herself and has remained to confound appreciation of her to this day. "She wore her learning lightly as a flower," eulogized a New York editor.[44] In fact, she worked diligently to augment her rather unsystematic education; if her writing and demeanor belied this seriousness and, yes, heaviness, it was because prevailing standards in her world demanded delicacy rather than scholarship of women.

Decidedly not a feminist, Van Rensselaer had definite ideas about the role of woman that also colored her practice of art criticism. Stated simply, Van Rensselaer believed it was woman's role to influence and to educate, and it was this goal she pursued through her art criticism—to elevate public taste, to improve the practice of the arts in America, to persuade, preach, and uplift. Such a role was in perfect harmony with her views of woman's mission. She neither championed nor ignored women artists, although she wrote very little about a recognized giant of her times, Mary Cassatt; but the painter, architect, landscape gardener, and patron were always "he" in her writings.

In searching for American antecedents or contemporaries, we can compare to Van Rensselaer only Clara Clement Waters, whose art handbooks and art histories were mainly for beginners and students; Van Rensselaer addressed a larger and often professional as well as popular audience. Van Rensselaer attempted to write serious art criticism in popular publications, with the result that her main editor, R. W. Gilder, constantly urged her to be less scholarly and more entertaining, a debilitating injunction for any critic. Edith Wharton too chafed from Gilder's "editorial timidity." He found her articles on Italian villas, she remembered, "too dry and technical" and asked her to "introduce . . . a few anecdotes, and a touch of human interest."[45] Fearing to bore his readers, Gilder instead perverted his writers. Wharton continued in her own way and soon turned to fiction; Van Rensselaer, regrettably, was spoiled. Yet she did accomplish a great deal.

The Richardson book alone would be enough to guarantee her a place in the history of art criticism. She was the first American woman who could be described as a professional art critic, Margaret Fuller having had wider interests than just art. She was not finally a scholar as we understand that term, but she was a pioneer, and as such she deserves our respectful attention and appreciation.

NOTES

As there is no major source like a published biography or autobiography for Van Rensselaer's life, biographical data had to be pieced together from a variety of sources. Entries in biographical dictionaries were helpful: *Dictionary of American Biography* (New York, 1936) and *Notable American Women* (Cambridge, Mass., 1971). New York and New Brunswick, New Jersey, city directories allowed me to trace where the Alleys, Griswolds, and Van Rensselaers lived from year to year; and the *New York Social Register* reported their comings and goings and summer vacations. Obituaries and other notices at the time of the deaths of her husband, father, son, mother, and herself in newspapers of New York City, New Brunswick, and Colorado Springs (where her son died) were consulted.

Family and business background was found in the following: Joseph A. Scoville (pseud.), *The Old Merchants of New York City*, by Walter Barrett, Clerk, 3 vols. (New York, 1872); Edward Elbridge Salisbury and Evelyn McCurdy Salisbury, *Family-Histories and Genealogies*, 3 vols. (New Haven, 1892); Walter W. Spooner, ed., *Historic Families of America*, 3 vols. (New York, 1908); Glenn E. Griswold, compiler, *The Griswold Family: England-America* (Rutland, Vt., 1943); Abraham Kingsley Mosley, compiler, *Chart of the Van Rensselaers, Their Patroonship and Family Descent* (privately printed, 1944); Frank N. Bradley, *A Brief History of the Firm of Taylor, Pinkham and Co., Inc., Founded by Saul Alley in 1816* (New York, 1946); Florence Van Rensselaer, *The Van Rensselaers in Holland and America* (New York, 1956). The Harvard College *Class of 1867 Reports* (Cambridge, Mass., 1867-1907) and Harvard College *Class of 1896 Reports* (Cambridge, Mass., 1896-1916) helped trace her husband's and son's educations.

Background for *Century Magazine* came from Richard Watson Gilder's *Letters*, edited by his daughter, Rosamond Gilder (Boston, 1916), and from Robert Underwood Johnson, *Remembered Yesterdays* (Boston, 1923). Information on the Pennells is in Joseph Pennell, *The Adventures of an Illustrator, Mostly in Following His Authors in America and Europe* (Boston, 1925); Elizabeth Robins Pennell, *The Life and Letters of Joseph Pennell*, 2 vols. (Boston, 1929); and Edward Larocque Tinker, *The Pennells* (New York, 1951). Finally, Ida C. Clarke's *American Women and the World War* (New York, 1918) described Van Rensselaer's war activity. For a more complete biography of Van Rensselaer, see my unpublished dissertation, "The Life and Works of Mariana Griswold Van Rensselaer, American Art Critic," Johns Hopkins University, 1977. A second dissertation on Van Rensselaer was written by Lois Dinnerstein, City University of New York, Graduate Center, 1979.

Manuscript sources include the American Fund for the French Wounded Papers, The Alfred W. Anthony Collection, and the Century Collection and the Richard Watson Gilder Collection, both of which contain many letters between Van Rensselaer and Gilder and other members of the *Century* staff. All these are in the New York Public Library. The Frederick Law Olmsted Papers at the Library of Congress were also useful.

1. "Mrs. Van Rensselaer, Art Authority, Dies," *New York Times*, 21 January 1934, p. 29.
2. "Mrs. Van Rensselaer Dies; Descendant of Pioneer New York Family," *New York Herald Tribune*, 21 January 1934, p. 18.
3. "Optical Illusions as Affecting Architecture," *American Architect and Building News*, 1

(27 May 1876), 174-75. This journal will hereafter be abbreviated *AABN*. "The Portal of the Old Palace Chapel, Dresden," *AABN*, 2 (18 August 1877), 263-65.

4. "Some Aspects of Contemporary Art," *Lippincott's*, 22 (December 1878), 717-18.

5. "American Fiction," *Lippincott's*, 23 (June 1879), 753-61. "Decorative Art and Its Dogmas," *Lippincott's*, 25 (February and March 1880), 213-20 and 342-51. "Sarah Bernhardt," *Lippincott's*, 27 (February 1881), 180-87. "In the Heart of the Alleghenies," *Lippincott's*, 30 (July and August 1882), 84-92 and 163-72; this was published in pamphlet form in 1885.

6. "The Plague of Formal Calls," *Scribner's Monthly*, 19 (March 1880), 787-88.

7. This error was begun by Talbot Faulkner Hamlin, in his 1936 sketch, "Mariana Griswold Van Rensselaer," *Dictionary of American Biography*, 10, part 1 (New York, 1936), 208. It was repeated by James D. Van Trump in his introduction to the 1967 Prairie School Press facsimile edition of Van Rensselaer's *Henry Hobson Richardson and His Works* (Park Forest, Ill., 1967). William Morgan continued the misconception in his 1968 introduction to the Dover paperback edition of the Richardson book. Only James Early in his *Notable American Women* sketch accurately dates the beginning of Van Rensselaer's professional writings as 1876, eight years before Schuyler's death. "Mariana Alley Griswold Van Rensselaer," *Notable American Women, 1607-1950* (Cambridge, Mass., 1971), 3, 511.

8. Anthony Collection, New York Public Library.

9. "The 'Loan Exhibition in Aid of the Society of Decorative Art,'" *AABN*, 3 (26 January 1878), 34.

10. "National Academy of Design, New York. Fifty-third Annual Exhibition," *AABN*, 3 (27 April 1878), 150.

11. *American Art in the Barbizon Mood* (Washington, D.C., 1975), pp. 69-70. It is disappointing that Bermingham omits any mention of Van Rensselaer.

12. "Recent Pictures in New York," *AABN*, 5 (22 March 1879), 93-94.

13. "Spring Exhibitions in New York," *AABN*, 5 (10 May 1879), 149.

14. *John Ruskin and Aesthetic Thought in America, 1840-1900* (Cambridge, Mass., 1967), p. 155.

15. "Munkácsy's Picture of Milton," *AABN*, 6 (20 December 1879), 195.

16. "Sir Frederic Leighton on Morality in Art," *AABN*, 11 (25 February 1882), 87-88.

17. Stein, *Ruskin in America*, p. 41.

18. *Art and Life in America* (New York, 1949), p. 265.

19. "Winckelmann's History of Ancient Art," *AABN*, 9 (8 January 1881), 15-16.

20. "A New 'History of Art,'" *AABN*, 10 (15 October 1881), 181.

21. She had for instance prepared an article on Sanford Robinson Gifford for the *American Art Review*, which ceased publication before it could appear. She then recast the Gifford study on a much simpler level than her two published articles on American painters in that journal, and it came out in the *American Architect*.

22. "Wood Engraving and the Century Prizes," *Century*, 2 (June 1882), 236.

23. Ibid., p. 233.

24. "American Etchers," *Century*, 3 (February 1883), 483-99.

25. "Recent Architecture in America, 1: Public Buildings," *Century*, 6 (May 1884), 48.

26. *Memorial Exhibition of the Works of George Fuller*, 24 April to 13 May 1884, Boston Museum of Fine Arts (Boston, 1884), p. 3.

27. *American Art in the Barbizon Mood*, p. 140.

28. *The Book of American Figure Painters* (Philadelphia, 1886), pp. 1-2.

29. Ibid., pp. 4-5.

30. Dante Gabriel Rossetti, *The Blessed Damozel*, with drawings by Kenyon Cox and appendix by Mariana Griswold Van Rensselaer (New York, 1886), p. 8 of unpaginated appendix.

31. "Henry H. Richardson," *The Nation*, 2 August 1888, p. 94.

32. P. xii.

33. "Client and Architect," *North American Review*, 151 (September 1890), 319-28. Reprinted in Lewis Mumford, *Roots of Contemporary American Architecture*, 2nd ed. (New York, 1959). Mumford clearly believes that the climate so receptive to modern architecture in the period after Van Rensselaer's best work owed thanks to her for authoritatively telling the potential client that he needs an artist (architect) for every building he proposes to erect, that he should give the architect free rein, and that he should treat the architect as the professional that he is and trust him.

34. Frank Luther Mott, *A History of American Magazines* (Cambridge, Mass., 1938), 3, 475.

35. The 1914 edition, which I have examined, is called the sixth, and there were others in 1898 and 1902. Actually there were only two editions, 1892 and 1893, those coming later being reprints.

36. *The Critic*, 21 (3 December 1892), 307.

37. *The Nation*, 105 (22 December 1892), 479.

38. "English Cathedrals," *The Atlantic Monthly*, 121 (February 1893), 270-75.

39. Laura Wood Roper, *F. L. O.: A Biography of Frederick Law Olmsted* (Baltimore, 1973), pp. 404-05.

40. "The Artistic Triumph of the Fair-Builders," *The Forum*, 14 (December 1892), 528-29.

41. In a letter to the editor of the *New York Times* commemorating Van Rensselaer, Helen Moore, who had worked with her at the University Settlement, dated her involvement with that settlement to George's death and her attempt to solace her grief through sharing with others. 8 February 1934, p. 18.

42. "Mrs. Van Rensselaer," editorial in *New York Herald Tribune*, 23 January 1934, p. 14.

43. At her death, at the height of the Depression, Van Rensselaer had a net worth of over $200,000. "Woman Art Critic Left $214,958 Net," *New York Times*, 16 August 1934, p. 20.

44. "Mrs. Van Rensselaer," editorial in *New York Herald Tribune*, 23 January 1934, p. 14.

45. *A Backward Glance* (New York, 1934), pp. 138-39.

SELECTED BIBLIOGRAPHY OF MARIANA GRISWOLD VAN RENSSELAER

A complete bibliography can be found in my unpublished dissertation, "The Life and Works of Mariana Griswold Van Rensselaer, American Art Critic," Johns Hopkins University, 1977.

Books. First Editions:

A Catalogue of Oil Paintings Exhibited by the Brooklyn Art Association in Aid of the Bartholdi Pedestal Fund. New York, 1884.
Introduction to *Memorial Exhibition of the Works of George Fuller*. Boston, 1884.
In the Heart of the Alleghenies, Historical and Descriptive. Philadelphia, 1885.
American Etchers. New York, 1886.
Book of American Figure Painters. Philadelphia, 1886.
Appendix to *The Blessed Damozel*, by Dante Gabriel Rossetti, with drawings by Kenyon Cox. New York, 1886.
Henry Hobson Richardson and His Works. Boston, 1888.
Six Portraits: Della Robbia, Correggio, Blake, Corot, George Fuller, and Winslow Homer. Boston, 1889.
English Cathedrals: Canterbury, Peterborough, Durham, Salisbury, Lichfield, Lincoln, Ely, Wells, Winchester, Gloucester, York, London. New York, 1892.

Art Out-of-Doors: Hints on Good Taste in Gardening. New York, 1893.

Should We Ask for the Suffrage? New York, 1894.

One Man Who Was Content and Other Stories. New York, 1897.

Jean-François Millet. New York, 1901.

Niagara: A Description. New York, 1901.

History of the City of New York in the Seventeenth Century. 2 vols. New York, 1909.

Poems. New York, 1910.

Introduction to *Jacob Leisler, A Play of Old New York*, by William Oscar Bates. New York, 1913.

Translation of *Essay on Bibliography and on the Attainments of a Librarian*, by Parent, the Elder. Woodstock, Vt., 1914.

Translation of *The Art of the Low Countries*, by Wilhelm Reinhold Valentiner. Garden City, New York, 1914.

Translation of *Early Textiles in the Cooper Union Collection*, by R. Meyer Riefstahl. New York, 1915.

Many Children (poems). Boston, 1921.

Introduction to *Memorial Exhibition of the Works of John Singer Sargent.* Boston, 1926.

Articles

"Some Aspects of Contemporary Art." *Lippincott's*, 22 (December 1878), 706-18.

"Decorative Art and Its Dogmas." *Lippincott's*, 25 (February and March 1880), 213-20 and 342-51.

"Artist and Amateur." *American Art Review*, 1 (June and July 1880), 62-66 and 105-10.

"William Merritt Chase." *American Art Review*, 2 (January and February, 1881), 91-98 and 135-42.

"Correggio." *American Art Review*, 2 (September and October 1881), 193-97 and 233-38.

"Wood-Engraving and the Century Prizes." *Century*, 2 (June 1882), 230-39.

"American Etchers." *Century*, 3 (February 1883), 483-99.

"Artistic Embroidery.—Work by the 'Associated Artists.' " *AABN*, 14 (15 and 22 September 1883), 127-28 and 140-41.

"An American Artist in England." *Century*, 5 (November 1883), 13-21.

"George Fuller." *Century*, 5 (December 1883), 226-36.

"The Metropolitan Opera-House, New York." *AABN*, 15 (16 and 23 February 1884), 76-77 and 86-89.

"Recent Architecture in America." *Century*, 6 (July 1884) through 10 (July 1886).

"Courbet, the Artist." *Century*, 7 (March 1885), 792-94.

"Architecture as a Profession." *Chautauquan*, 7 (May 1887), 451-54.

"St. Gaudens's Lincoln." *Century*, 13 (November 1887), 37-39.

"Mr. Arnold and American Art." *Century*, 14 (June 1888), 314-16.

"Corot." *Century*, 16 (June 1889), 255-71.

"Client and Architect." *North American Review*, 151 (September 1890), 319-28.

"The Development of American Homes." *The Forum*, 12 (January 1892), 667-76.

"American Artist Series: John S. Sargent." *Century*, 21 (March 1892), 798.

"The Waste of Women's Intellectual Force." *The Forum*, 13 (July 1892), 616-28.

"The Artistic Triumph of the Fair-Builders." *The Forum*, 14 (December 1892), 527-40.

"Picturesque New York." *Century*, 23 (December 1892), 164-75.

"At the Fair." *Century*, 24 (May 1893), 2-13.

"Frederick Law Olmsted." *Century*, 24 (October 1893), 860-67.

"Fifth Avenue." *Century*, 25 (November 1893), 5-18.

"The Madison Square Garden." *Century*, 25 (March 1894), 732-47.

"People in New York." *Century*, 27 (February 1895), 534-48.

"The New Public Library in Boston: Its Artistic Aspects." *Century*, 28 (June 1895), 260-64.
"Places in New York City." *Century*, 31 (February 1897), 501-16.
"New York and Its Historians." *North American Review*, 171 (November and December 1900), 724-33 and 872-83.
" 'Who Wants Art Nowadays?' " *North American Review*, 204 (August 1916), 235-44.
"The Art Museum and the Public." *North American Review*, 205 (January 1917), 81-92.
"Museums of Art." *North American Review*, 216 (September 1922), 393-404.
"American Art and the Public." *Scribner's Magazine*, 74 (November 1923), 637-40.

Reviews

Review of J. J. Winckelmann, *The History of Ancient Art*, trans. G. Henry Lodge (Boston, 1880). *AABN*, 9 (8 January 1881), 15-16.

Review of Julia B. DeForest, *A Short History of Art* (New York, 1881). *AABN*, 10 (15 October 1881), 180-81.

Review of Eugène Fromentin, *Les Maîtres d'autrefois*, trans. Mary C. Robbins (Boston, 1882) *AABN*, 12 (9 December 1882), 279.

Review of Louis Gonse, *Eugène Fromentin, Painter and Writer*, trans. Mary C. Robbins (Boston, 1883). *AABN*, 14 (15 December 1883), 280-81.

Review of Georges Perrot and Charles Chipiez, *A History of Art in Chaldea and Assyria* (London, 1884). *AABN*, 16 (11 and 25 October and 8 and 15 November 1884), 175-76, 197-98, 221-22, and 235-36.

Review of William Dean Howells, *Tuscan Cities* (Boston, 1886). *AABN*, 18 (12 December 1885), 279-80.

Review of René Ménard, *L'Art en Alsace et Lorraine* (Paris, 1886). *AABN*, 20 (18 September and 9 and 16 October 1886), 132-34, 168-69, and 181-82.

Review of Henry Van Brunt, *Greek Lines and Other Architectural Essays* (Boston, 1893). *Atlantic Monthly*, 73 (June 1894), 847-49.

PART III

ART HISTORIANS AND ARCHAEOLOGISTS OF THE LATE-NINETEENTH AND EARLY-TWENTIETH CENTURIES

CHAPTER 8

GEORGIANA GODDARD KING (1871 - 1939): EDUCATOR AND PIONEER IN MEDIEVAL SPANISH ART

Susanna Terrell Saunders[1]

In 1914, Bernard Berenson told the president of Bryn Mawr College that Georgiana Goddard King was "in his opinion, the best equipped student of Italian art in the United States or in England and that the photographs and slides of Bryn Mawr College had been better catalogued and classified [by Miss King] than those of any other collection that he knew of."[2] King had previously turned down Berenson's offer to work with him in Florence. For a woman of only forty-three, such recognition by the famous scholar and connoisseur of Italian Renaissance art was all the more remarkable because her special field was Spanish, not Italian art. She had founded the Bryn Mawr art department only two years earlier.

Georgiana Goddard King headed the Bryn Mawr art history department for the next twenty-five years until her retirement in 1937. The heyday of her career encompassed the 1920s and early 1930s, a period that Erwin Panofsky called the "Golden Age" of art history in the United States.[3] This period marked the emergence of art history in America as a separate academic discipline distinct from both archaeology and art criticism. Exceptional before the first World War, doctorates grew in number during the 1920s as graduate programs in American universities were developed. King belonged to what James Ackerman has called "the second generation" of art historians "distinguished by an extraordinary perseverance and enthusiasm in the search for unknown monuments and documents, especially when they were to be found in inaccessible places (such as the Pyrenees and other unpaved parts of Spain, which attracted Georgiana Goddard King, Kingsley Porter, Chandler Post, Walter Cook, and others during the 1920's.)"[4] Furthermore, King helped open the field to women, and until the mid-1920s, Bryn Mawr was the only independent women's college to offer a

Ph.D. in art history, as distinguished from archaeology.[5] By 1934, Bryn Mawr's graduate department of art history had been ranked beside those of Harvard and Princeton by the American Council of Education.

Georgiana Goddard King's role as a pioneer in medieval Spanish art began in 1913, when she offered the first graduate courses on Spanish art in the United States. By 1914 she received immediate recognition for her annotated edition of *Some Account of Gothic Architecture in Spain*, written by the distinguished nineteenth-century architect and historian George E. Street and first published in 1865. King updated the factual information and inserted new material. *The Way of Saint James, Mudéjar,* and *Pre-Romanesque Churches of Spain* are a few of the dozen or more books and more than forty articles on art and related subjects that she published. One of the earliest members of the College Art Association, King was highly regarded as a scholar and teacher by eminent colleagues like Kingsley Porter and Chandler Post, who also were specialists in Spanish art. Her friends Leo and Gertrude Stein considered her a perceptive literary critic. Her extraordinary range of knowledge and interests was typical of her generation of art scholars. King, moreover, was a sensitive poet and an acknowledged scholar of Oriental philosophy and of early texts written in Greek, Latin, and Arabic. In addition, she sought out and welcomed the newest ideas in modern art and literature. Few fields were closed to her highly disciplined and curious mind.

It is difficult to talk about her achievements without first mentioning her unique and dynamic personality. Her students and colleagues commented on her highly individual character and the tremendous style with which she carried herself. On the campus she made a lasting impression, as she always wore the same billowing, frayed academic gown for practically all her years at Bryn Mawr. It appears that King had rented the gown, which she continued to wear in class long after street dress was permitted. At dinner, which was a rather stiff affair at the college, King dressed as a Spanish *dona* in a severely tailored black suit with a usually white or cream-colored blouse, perhaps a pin or earrings, and a cut-steel comb and black lace for special occasions. She made an imposing sight with her short, solid frame, and her steel-gray hair smoothly tied back in a bun covered with a crocheted net. She always carried herself with unyielding poise and composure (Figure 12).

King cared a great deal about public opinion and was always very proper about manners and etiquette. Although she herself was a constant smoker, she was careful to extinguish her cigarette when smoking was not permitted. She was fanatic about correctness and was very precise about titles and the manner in which one addressed the clergy and other dignitaries. This is not to imply that G.G., as she preferred to be called, was a stiff, quiet person. On the contrary, she was very lively, loved to be considered *l'enfant terrible,*

Figure 12. Georgiana Goddard King, ca. 1934. (*Courtesy the late Dorothea C. Shipley*)

and always had a twinkle in her vivid green eyes. Many people even said she was too enthusiastic, too sentimental, and too emphatic for them to feel comfortable in her presence. G.G. was in fact very opinionated and repeatedly stated that she had no tolerance for two things: mediocrity and people who were dull. She herself was not lacking in egotism and delighted in her position as a legendary campus figure. Even her everyday speech was peculiarly her own, spiced with quaint, antiquated words like "snoods" and "corsets," both of which she wore. She had a quickness and an extraordinary facility with words, and she apparently loved coming out with an unexpected remark and watching people's reaction. All these traits she combined with a lively wit and dry humor.

G.G. craved adventure, the unexpected, and the sense of discovery. In the tradition of eighteenth- and nineteenth-century female travelers, her fascination with exploration is attested to by her love of travel, her extensive readings in geography, and above all, by her preference for excursions to the most remote and inaccessible places. These predilections partially explain her initial attraction for Spanish primitive art, which was a totally unexplored field of scholarship at the time. G.G. also traveled extensively in Europe and North Africa. She described to Gertrude Stein a trip to Africa in 1927, and said she planned to:

see whatever is permitted to Christians and females from Kaironon to Marrakesh. It is certainly my immediate need: Moslem art on Moslem soil. Last week I saw what they have excavated of the palace of the Western Caliphs at Condora—it was immensely picturesque and vivid and the scraps of stone and pottery had . . . exciting implications . . . [more than] Troy or Knossos, Mycenae or . . . I suppose I felt it more.[6]

Travel meant adventure to G.G. Those students who were fortunate enough to accompany her on several trips have countless stories, like the one about the inebriated one-eyed taxi driver who ran his car off the road and had to be dug out and driven back to the nearest town by the Bryn Mawr ladies. Whether King was in a dilapidated Spanish railroad station in Fromista or in an obscure mountain monastery, at precisely five o'clock she would bring out her alcohol stove from her tea basket and make herself comfortable.[7] In 1911, she decided to learn photography, not as an art medium, but as a research tool. She became quite a competent photographer, and it is mainly her own photographs and those of her traveling companion, Edith Lowber, that illustrate her writings and document her travels.

This unique character was actually a very private person. Her students were surprised that they knew almost nothing about her family or the first thirty-five years of her life before she joined the Bryn Mawr faculty. Most people simply said, "She never talked about herself."[8] Only occasionally, in her correspondence to friends like Stein, did she ever refer to her father or to other relatives. For this biography, a casual reference to Agnes De Mille, the noted choreographer, from one of King's former students has led to other sources that have filled most of the gaps in the chronology of G.G.'s early life.[9]

Georgiana Goddard King was born on 5 August 1871 in West Columbia, West Virginia. She was the first of four children, with Ella, Margaret, and John or "Jack," following in that order. Her father, Morris Ketchum King, was born in Massachusetts and worked for various railroads. His work took him tò Norfolk, Virginia, where he spent many years working on the Drummond Canal. Norfolk became home to G.G. and her sisters and brother. G.G.'s mother, whose family name was Goddard, may have come from Ohio, or perhaps originally from Rhode Island.

G.G.'s mother was a very intellectual woman with pronounced literary interests. She was highly respected in Norfolk and was a member of the first literary club founded there after the Civil War. Her cultural pursuits prevented her from fulfilling her domestic duties, and it was her sister, known as Aunt Betty, who moved into the household and raised the children. Unfortunately, Mrs. King died when Georgiana was about thirteen years old. Mr. King remarried shortly thereafter, but G.G. resented the marriage and never grew close to her stepmother. Aunt Betty stayed on and was genuinely loved by the whole family. Georgiana was very proud of her mother and consequently always included her mother's name, Goddard, in her signature.

Mrs. King's interest in literature had a lasting influence on her three daughters. Both G.G. and Margaret began teaching careers in the field of English literature. Ella was also interested in literature and later in her life worked as a reader for the De Mille Studio in Hollywood, California. Ella married John Adams, a New Jersey Supreme Court judge, who was then a widower with five children.[10] One of Judge Adams' daughters, Constance, married Cecil B. De Mille, the Hollywood producer and director. Constance was very fond of Ella, her stepmother, and persuaded her to move to Hollywood. After her retirement from Bryn Mawr in 1937, G.G., already in poor health, joined her sisters in California. She shared an apartment with Margaret, who had previously lived with G.G. in Bryn Mawr. Agnes De Mille, Constance's niece, remembers the King women as well-educated, literary types whose intellects and eccentricities were a welcome addition to the De Mille movie entourage in Hollywood.

G.G.'s early interest in English literature received further encouragement from Irene Leache and Anna Cogswold Wood. In 1872, these two women had founded a girls' school in Norfolk later called the Leache-Wood Seminary. The school was described as a "large day and boarding school of local patronage."[11] It offered excellent instruction, and Georgiana was one of its most exceptional students. Leache and Wood, along with a young woman named Collier, encouraged G.G. to go to Bryn Mawr College. Founded in 1885 by a New Jersey physician and prominent Quaker named Dr. Joseph Taylor, Bryn Mawr was the first college for women that offered both undergraduate instruction and graduate programs for the M.A. and Ph.D. degrees in all departments.[12] Dr. Taylor had been sympathetic to the problem facing his good friend Dr. James Thomas of Baltimore, whose daughters, Carey and Helen, were frustrated by the lack of graduate schools in American universities that accepted women. Bryn Mawr College not only fulfilled this need for graduate study but also established a women's college in the Middle Atlantic states.

King graduated from Bryn Mawr in 1896 as an English major, although she had originally planned to major in Greek. She also took a number of economics and philosophy courses. During her undergraduate years she was remembered because she received the important George W. Child Essayist Award for English literature and also because of her dog named Reggie, to whom she fed almonds. This anecdote shows that G.G. had become a topic of conversation among the other undergraduates, a position she held and treasured throughout her years at Bryn Mawr.

King stayed at Bryn Mawr for graduate study. In 1896/97, she was a "fellow" in philosophy and wrote a paper on the German philosopher Fichte. She received her master's degree in 1897 in philosophy and political science. The following year, she was a "fellow" in English. She left Bryn Mawr in 1898, traveled in Europe, and enrolled for one semester at the Collège de France in Paris. This trip to Europe was the first of many she was to make throughout her lifetime. By the fall of 1899, King returned to New York City to begin her teaching career. From 1899 to 1906, she taught English, philosophy, and art at the Graham School, a private boarding and day school for girls in Manhattan.[13] In 1906, G.G. describes herself to Gertrude Stein as being, "restless and discontented . . . in a cramped little flat . . . with dreadful red brick. . . .I called the town a provincial capital."[14] That fall, King moved to Bryn Mawr and wrote, just a year after she had left New York City, "I felt when I left New York last spring that, though I was going away for twenty years very like, yet it was only an interval, that I should be coming home again presently—but now I feel that I'll never leave Bryn Mawr."[15] She stayed there, in fact, for the next thirty years until her retirement in 1937.

Georgiana Goddard King was hired to teach in the English department by M. Carey Thomas, Bryn Mawr's first dean and second president when she succeeded Dr. James Rhoads in 1893. During almost thirty years, until her retirement in 1922, Thomas' ardent feminist stand and her dominating personality permeated the Bryn Mawr campus.[16] Bertrand Russell and

Woodrow Wilson, who both taught at Bryn Mawr, vividly recalled Thomas' personality and the feminist orientation at Bryn Mawr College.[17] Much of the controversy surrounding President Thomas had subsided when G.G. joined the staff in 1907. King was not one of Carey Thomas' close companions like Mamie Gwinn, Mary Garrett, and Lucy Donnelly, who were all at one time on the staff, but she was heavily influenced by Thomas, especially in the initial stages of her career at Bryn Mawr. For five years G.G. was a reader in the English department and then was promoted to lecturer in comparative literature in 1911. Her devotion to English and writing predated any involvement with art history.

King's first two books, written while she lived in New York, reflect her extensive study of English literature, especially Shakespeare and Browning. *Comedies and Legends for Marionettes: A Theatre for Boys and Girls* was published in 1904. In the introduction King made numerous references to Shakespeare's comedies, especially noting the characters and sets he had used. The book began with lengthy instructions on how to make a marionette theater, puppets, props, and sets. Three comedies, two legends (those of St. Francis and St. Dorothy), and two pantomimes followed. The characters in the comedies had classical names like Pyramus and Thisbe; and the plots, like those of the *commedia dell'arte*, are stories involving the mistaken identity of identical twins, beautiful unmarried daughters and handsome suitors, and the reuniting of fathers and daughters.

Her second book, *The Way of Perfect Love*, published four years later in 1908, shows not only the influence of Browning's poetic dramas but of Elizabethan masques and the pastoral tradition. Its allegorical elements receive an elaborate, if cryptic, summary in the Interpretation that concludes the complex, four-act verse drama. G.G. was only partially correct when she wrote a friend, "When it is done the world will vastly disapprove and no publisher will risk it." More perceptive was her remark written a year later: "I have, I recognize, more taste than talent and take the rejection with a sad mildness."[18]

King's roots were in English literature, with Robert Browning her acknowledged hero. *The Way of Perfect Love* and her other verse illustrated his influence on her writing style early in her career. There was the same complexity of sentence structure and imagery that was typical of the English poet. *The Way of Perfect Love* was her last dramatic work. She did, however, submit poems during the years 1908-1913 like "I Passed an Ancient Way" and "Nocturne," which were both published in *McClure's* in 1913. Ten other poems and essays appeared in *Harper's Weekly*. She also had book reviews and articles published in *North American Review* and again in *Harper's Weekly*. Many years later, when King was a well-known art historian, she brushed off *The Way of Perfect Love* as an "indiscretion of my youth."[19] She made no reference to the poems or to her first book, which leads one to assume that she preferred to dismiss them in the same fashion.

All of G.G.'s students remembered her strict attention to grammar and spelling, but few were aware that she had written a book, published in 1909, called *The Bryn Mawr Spelling Book*. This small book of only 114 pages consists of alphabetized lists of words freqently misspelled by students in college and preparatory school. King added rules of spelling and their exceptions, as well as irregular and confusing forms. In the introduction, she wrote, "English spelling is an affair of memory, not of reason." Her obsession with correctness is exemplified by this publication.

King's first published works and employment in a field other than art history was typical of her generation of art scholars. Charles Rufus Morey, Kingsley Porter, and Paul Sachs also came from other disciplines, like classical philology, theology, literature, and philosophy. At Wellesley, it was the German teacher Elizabeth Denio who, in 1887, gave the first art history lectures there.[20] In general, "history of art courses at Vassar, Smith, and Wellesley developed as an outgrowth of practical art departments with history introduced only as a very general background."[21] Bryn Mawr, however, had a strong archaeology department founded in 1895 by Richard Norton, son of Charles Eliot Norton, who began the study of art history at Harvard. Caroline Ransom (later Williams) directed Bryn Mawr's archaeology department for many years. She was one of the first holders of a doctorate in classical archaeology from the University of Chicago.[22] The only attempt during those years to instruct students at Bryn Mawr in the fine arts was made by Mamie Gwinn, the head of the English department and a leading intellectual force at Bryn Mawr, who hung photographs from Pater's *The Renaissance* in the parlor of Merion, a school dormitory. She referred to these photographs in one of her English courses.[23] After Gwinn left Bryn Mawr in 1904, she and her photographs of Renaissance art were more or less forgotten for several years.[24]

In 1909 or 1910 President Thomas asked G.G. to give elective courses in Gothic and Renaissance art; these at first alternated with her main courses in comparative literature. Art had been an interest of Carey Thomas since her girlhood days in Baltimore. She had traveled widely and was an avid museum visitor.[25] As King realized that her own possiblities of advancement in the English department were limited, she devoted full time to her art courses. In 1913, the history of art became a department separate from the long-established archaeology department, covering all periods of art from the Middle Ages to the present. King was made a full professor in the history of art in 1916.

Georgiana King's decision to teach art courses was a natural one. She had been exposed to art since her student days in Norfolk, when both Leache and Wood had passed on their enthusiasm for art to G.G., and possibly their love of travel as well.[26] She may have received lessons in painting or possibly in art appreciation. More likely, she probably taught herself about the field by visiting museums and by avid reading, especially in the area that seems to have interested her, Gothic architecture. Edith Finch in her book *Carey Thomas of Bryn Mawr* mentions that King "had become interested in art because, she said, of a visit in London to the National Gallery with Lucy Donnelly, who awakened her suddenly to pleasures she had missed."[27] King's colleagues and students, however, do not credit Donnelly with introducing G.G. to the pleasures of art; rather, they support the theory that King was already well read in art before she went to Europe in 1898.[28]

During the early years of art history at Bryn Mawr, King *was* the department. There was an absolute identity of the subject with the faculty, which in the early 1920s consisted of King and George Rowley, recently hired from Princeton. The curriculum consisted of a two-year program, starting with the junior class. King developed a basic course called "Italian Painting of the Renaissance from the Middle of the Thirteenth to the Middle of the Sixteenth Century." This was her chef d'oeuvre. For the senior or second year, she offered medieval art and modern painting from the nineteenth century from William Blake to the present. King's graduate students were offered a semester of Spanish art. George Rowley gave a course on Oriental art and two courses in the second year, Northern European painting and Gothic architecture.

Around 1930, there began an influx of European scholars into American universities that was eventually to transform the discipline of art history.[29] In the late 1920s, King almost persuaded the famous (if controversial) medievalist Professor Strzygowski to come from Vienna, but because he was so near retirement, he sent his most brilliant student, Ernst Diez. Joining Diez and King during the late 1920s and early 1930s were Harold Wethey, Edward King, Edward Warburg, Richard Bernheimer, Joseph Sloane, and Alexander Soper. The latter two men were considered by President Marion Park of Bryn Mawr to be the two best young art historians in the country in 1938. Sloane was chosen to succeed King as head of the department after a search by President Park had failed to find a woman whom she considered to be of equal ability.[30] King had hired continually the most promising students from Princeton's and Harvard's graduate programs. The instructors were hardly older than Bryn Mawr's own graduate students, but G.G. was adventurous, and in each case her judgment proved correct. In a letter to a friend she described the "junior instructors as indistinguishable from graduate students except that they have more sense."[31]

The art department's main shortcomings were its limited course selection and the rapid turnover of the teaching staff. The lack of stability probably reflected the status of the largely young faculty, who were generally expected to move on to other universities after a few years. G.G. was very aware of these problems and encouraged her students in many cases to enroll at Radcliffe or other institutions with more varied courses and faculty. In the 1920s, Bryn Mawr limited itself to approximately 500 undergraduate and a hundred graduate students. Wellesley and Smith had much higher enrollments and could support larger and more varied art programs. Bryn Mawr's slide and photograph collections also could not compare with those of the larger colleges. Its library, however, was quite strong and well used by the students. In 1928, G.G. wrote to President Park, Thomas' successor, "I must be glad that all my students are so well employed—but I wish Radcliffe were not quite so attractive."[32]

King was not discouraged by Bryn Mawr's limited budget during the Depression. When Edward Warburg, nephew of Aby Warburg and a promising Harvard graduate from a wealthy New York family, applied for a job, she told him there was no appropriation in the budget. She was "stormily angry"[33] when he offered to volunteer his services for one semester and replied to him, "What! Do you want to ruin our profession?"[34] G.G.'s solution was to have Warburg write an anonymous check that exactly covered his teaching fee for that semester. The following semester, faced again with the same budget, King sent letters to Edward Warburg's friends like Lessing Rosenwald and Alfred Barr asking for contributions to "save Ed Warburg for Bryn Mawr."[35]

King was equally resourceful and innovative as far as the curriculum was concerned. Unlike the more traditional "mainstream" courses on classical, medieval, and Renaissance art of the West, the study of Far Eastern and Oriental art took longer to develop as a regular offering on the curriculum. At Bryn Mawr, King herself gave the first course on Chinese and Japanese art at the request of a student who had been stimulated by G.G.'s references to the Orient in her Renaissance lectures. This was in 1913,[36] and the student recalled that "G.G. made it very vivid."[37] In 1918, Helen Fernald, who taught aesthetics, offered an elective in Japanese and Oriental art; and the following year George Rowley was hired to teach the course. Although Harvard and Princeton reportedly considered the subject too difficult for undergraduates, G.G. kept it in the curriculum throughout her entire teaching career.

As G.G. did not believe in survey courses, none was given. Neither were syllabi or course outlines furnished. Preferring a spontaneous approach, she rarely lectured from notes and purposely kept the lecture room pitch-black so that students could not easily take notes. There must have been an uncanny mixture of curiosity, amusement, and fear when King began a lecture. Which student was going to be suddenly called upon to "speak to the picture?" Recollections of her more memorable quotations include "hair under the arms was a secondary sexual attribute," and another favorite was "the French Renaissance was the vengeance of God on the French for having invaded the Lombard Plain." In the same category fell her favorite: "never pat a masterpiece on the head."[38] She thought it was great sport to find and create witty epigrams and considered herself the champion. G.G.'s department was certainly not the place for the student who wanted a structured and comprehensive fine arts program.

In teaching, she followed the Socratic method. By skillful and subtle inquiry, she led her students to teach themselves and to experience a sense of discovery. To evoke the social and cultural spirit of the past, students read extensively from G.G.'s list of such diverse "mood-creators" as Boccaccio, Pater, Ruskin, D.H. Lawrence, and Berenson. King stressed the importance of iconography and believed it necessary to examine every document in its original language. Appropriately, G.G. knew Anna Jameson's books on Christian iconography by heart. Above all, she expected students to follow the countless allusions to historical and cultural data that saturated her lectures and writings. One student described her lectures as a "continuous stream of oblique, elliptical, and witty references to everything under the sun about which it was assumed that you knew something, or that if you didn't, you would read up and find out."[39] She was a tough and very demanding teacher who expected and somehow got excellence from her students. G.G.'s students, especially the graduates, worked on their own and were independent and self-reliant.

King was ahead of her time in her appreciation of contemporary avant-garde artists like Picasso, Matisse, Gris, Picabia, and the Italian Futurists. She knew quite well Leo and Gertrude Stein's collection on the Rue de Fleurus in Paris and often spoke to her students about "that wonderful and bewildering room."[40] She also told them anecdotes about Gertrude Stein's seating at dinner each artist strategically opposite his own painting. For her course on modern art, King frequently assigned readings from Stein's books like *Portraits and Prayers* and *The Autobiography of Alice B. Toklas*, which included passages on Matisse, Picasso, and Juan Gris. In 1912, G.G. was discussing Picasso and what she had seen in Kahnweiler's gallery in Paris. Kahnweiler was the shrewd dealer and friend of the avant-garde painters and writers to whom Gertrude Stein had gone on several occasions to talk and purchase paintings. King wrote to Stein, "Is there nowhere I can read about the last manner of Picasso and what it means/for at about 1908 on I get hopelessly lost/tho' I worked hard over the photographs at Kahnweiler's."[41]

King no doubt had seen the famous portrait Picasso had painted of Gertrude Stein in 1906 (Figure 13). This painting is considered to be an important work showing the transition between the Rose Period to *Les Demoiselles d'Avignon* of 1907 and eventually in 1908-1909 to the Cubist

Figure 13. Portrait of Gertrude Stein, by Pablo Picasso, 1906. New York, Metropolitan Museum of Art. (*Courtesy the Metropolitan Museum of Art, Bequest of Gertrude Stein, 1946*)

Period. Not only did the portrait look like Stein, but she was completely satisfied with it. Georgiana Goddard King probably found the portrait easier to understand because it retained the elements of traditional representation; and yet the face, painted in a wholly different manner with a sculptural, almost brutal, treatment of form, pointed to a radical new direction for art. Picasso had begun the portrait in the winter of 1905/06 with a "sketch of startling likeness,"[42] but after eighty or ninety sittings, he painted out the head and abandoned the work. On the day he returned from his summer vacation in the Spanish village of Gosol, he painted a masklike face into the portrait. Much has been written about the similarity to Iberian votive bronzes, the austerity and expressive power of the mask, and the freedom of reconstruction of form in this transitional work. Michael Hoffman in his book *Gertrude Stein* points out a parallel between her and Picasso. "Stein's writings quite often went through the same stages of experimentation as the paintings of her Spanish friend."[43] G.G. also must have sensed this feeling of experimentation when she studied the portrait.

Most Americans were totally unaware of Picasso and certainly were not trying to analyze his strange Cubist creations. The majority of Americans were first exposed to radical currents in modern European art in 1913 at the Armory Show. Although the press and general public reacted to the exhibition as a scandal, it was the first time in American history that modern art achieved national recognition. Although over sixteen hundred paintings, sculptures, drawings, and prints were displayed, only one-fourth were European. Besides works by nineteenth-century masters like Cézanne, Gauguin, and Van Gogh, the most contemporary artists like Matisse, Picasso, Braque, and Duchamp were well represented.[44]

Besides consulting Gertrude Stein, G.G. wrote Alfred Stieglitz, the famous pioneer photographer and promoter of radical modern European art, about a short course on modern art she was proposing for the spring of 1916.[45] She had singled out Picasso, Matisse, and the Futurists and was having a difficult time finding the necessary pictures for the course. Stieglitz, having already reproduced works by these artists in his magazine, *Camera Work*, was King's most likely source for reproductions. Around 1908, Stieglitz was showing revolutionary works in Matisse's "fauve" and Picasso's "negro" periods at "291," his small photography gallery at 291 Fifth Avenue, New York. This gallery became the first important American center for the radical new forms of modern art. King probably visited "291"; she certainly read *Camera Work*, which was similar to periodicals like *The Dial* and *The New Republic*, which were supported by the community. Stieglitz's magazine was the first to regularly present both "modern" art criticism as well as serious examinations of American artistic life and culture.[46] Fascinated by the ideas in the periodical, G.G. would often post in the seminar room photographs of contemporary art taken from it and similar journals.

G.G. encouraged her students to study contemporary art by assigning them term papers on the works shown in galleries. When the newly formed Société Anonyme gave an exhibition of modern sculpture and painting, King had her students go to New York City to see it. The Société Anonyme had been created after 1920 as an outgrowth of Stieglitz's "291." Katherine Dreier, a lecturer and an amateur painter, was the dominating force along with the surrealist artist Marcel Duchamp and the photographer Man Ray.[47] This organization was formed nine years before the founding of the Museum of Modern Art.

Equally revolutionary was an exhibition held at the Pennsylvania Academy of Fine Arts in Philadelphia in April 1923. This particular exhibition was organized by Albert C. Barnes,[48] an early collector of contemporary paintings and sculpture and the inventor of the chemical Argyrol.[49] The seventy-five works displayed at the Pennsylvania Academy consisted of Barnes' newly acquired paintings by Soutine, Modigliani, Pascin, Matisse, Picasso, and other artists, which he had just exhibited in Paris at the Paul Guillaume Gallery. The public's response in the United States to Barnes' collection was so critical that he henceforth refused to exhibit it publicly or to have works from his collection photographed. Even today, that policy banning reproductions is strictly enforced. G.G. was not influenced by the derogatory newspaper reviews and insisted that her students examine works like Matisse's *Joie de Vivre* and Picasso's *The Peasants* from the latter's Rose Period before they were locked behind the doors of the Barnes Foundation. Sometime in the 1920s, however, Bryn Mawr College students were excluded from the Barnes Foundation. The story perpetuated by Albert Barnes was that because while "guiding a group of Bryn Mawr students, the head of the art department [King] made some critical remark about one picture, they were all asked to leave."[50] G.G. insisted that her students wrestle on their own with these revolutionary paintings. As the students always knew that she did not close her eyes to modern artists, they were encouraged to have open and discerning minds.

During the 1930s, King let the younger faculty members teach the modern painting course. They were mainly responsible for inviting as guest lecturers at Bryn Mawr leading architects like Frank Lloyd Wright and Philip Johnson, Alfred Barr, the influential director of the Museum of Modern Art, and Lincoln Kirstein and George Balanchine, leaders in the development of an American ballet. G.G. was also interested in the work of the Dada photographer Man Ray, and wanted to contact him so that her friend Edith Lowber could "sit to him."[51]

Her own portrait, now lost, was painted by a man whose career she tried to encourage, Charles Webster Hawthorne (1872-1930). G.G. may have met

Charles Hawthorne while she was in New York, when he was apparently poor and unrecognized. She persuaded her father to invite him to Norfolk for a long summer visit. Hawthorne painted three portraits of the King family; the first of Mr. King and his wife, G.G.'s stepmother; the second of Ella and Margaret; and the third of G.G.[52] Charles Hawthorne went on to become an important teacher, establishing his own school in Provincetown that specialized in outdoor classes of figure painting. His paintings are in leading museums around the country, including the Metropolitan Museum in New York, the Corcoran Gallery of Art in Washington, D.C., and the Detroit Institute of Arts. Hawthorne's style has been described by critics as a kind of "dark" impressionism expressing the romantic spirit of the artist. His work is grouped with that of artists such as Duvenek, Chase, Henri, and Glackens.[53]

King traveled in the most prestigious academic circles. Among academic art historians her friends included the Hispanic specialists Kingsley Porter, Chandler Post, and Walter Cook, as well as the dean of medieval art-historical studies, Charles Rufus Morey of Princeton. Post was quoted as saying to one of G.G.'s graduates, "Don't you realize young woman that you have had a unique educational experience?"[54] King's course on Italian art was cited by Chandler Post as actually being of graduate caliber and thus far more advanced than the first-year level for which it was designated. Similar respect was generously bestowed on her by Kingsley Porter as well. Although she rarely visited the Berensons in Florence, King remained on friendly terms with them. Bernard Berenson often spoke of her with admiration and affection, while she expressed the highest regard for his writings. Another acquaintance was the English traveler and amateur archaeologist, Gertrude Bell. Georgiana Goddard King must have been fascinated with Bell's travel accounts from Baghdad and other exotic places.

G.G.'s previously mentioned friendship with Gertrude and Leo Stein was a very interesting one. According to an authority on Leo Stein, King was one of the few who remained a friend of both sister and brother.[55] Georgiana knew such members of the Stein circle as Alice B. Toklas, Mabel Dodge, and Mabel Weeks, as well as May Bookstaver and Maybel Haynes, two of the Bryn Mawr women Gertrude knew from her Baltimore days.[56] From 1897 to 1901, while Stein attended the medical school of Johns Hopkins, she and her brother attracted a circle of younger students. This group included emancipated women, mainly from Bryn Mawr and Smith, who met regularly for spirited discussion, especially of moral issues, in the apartment of Maybel Haynes and Grace Lounsbery, two Bryn Mawr graduates of the class of 1898.

As G.G. was in Europe in 1898, she probably did not participate in this Baltimore discussion group. Gertrude Stein moved to New York in 1902,

three years after G.G. Stein lived on Riverside Drive with three former
Johns Hopkins students, Harriet Clark, Estelle Rumboldt, and Mabel
Weeks. King probably met Gertrude Stein in 1902. Many years later, in
1934, on the visit of Stein and Toklas to Bryn Mawr, G.G. recalled that she:

had met Miss Stein first in New York through Mabel Weeks, and Estelle Rumboldt,
the sculptor, who married the architect Robert Kohn. Miss Stein used to visit G.G.
in her roof-top apartment, built chiefly out of packing boxes and tar-paper, on 57th
Street, cram herself out of the window to admire the vista of the river and the
buildings, and finally settle down to talking at length about anything from art to
psychology.[57]

Soon after their meeting Gertrude and Leo moved abroad, and G.G. enjoyed several memorable times with them in Italy one summer, as well as
visits in Paris:

The scene shifts after a lapse of several years to Paris, where the two had taken a
studio. Mr. Stein was selling his fine collection of Japanese prints in order to buy
paintings by the modern French—Renoir, Cézanne, Matisse, and Picasso. [1906]
Miss King did not see Miss Stein again until just before the War, when she enjoyed
for long evenings sitting in the studio staring at a picture and presently moving
around to the other side of the table and staring some more. . . .Today [in 1934]
when Miss King is in Paris, she always goes over to Rue Fleurus, sits and stares at
paintings, and talks with Gertrude Stein.[58]

G.G. was one of Stein's earliest supporters, and she and Mabel Weeks
attempted to get Gertrude's books published. Alice B. Toklas, in *What is
Remembered*, talked about Stein's *Three Lives*, which was written between
1905 and 1906: "The few friends to whom Gertrude had sent copies wrote
warmly. Georgiana Goddard King of Bryn Mawr, an old friend from
Baltimore, not only wrote enthusiastically but from that time introduced
Gertrude's work into her lectures."[59] G.G. frequently reviewed Gertrude
Stein's writings for periodicals like *Harper's*, *International*, and the *Christian Science Monitor*. King discussed the difficult Stein style in one of her
lectures at Bryn Mawr by establishing parallels between Stein's writings and
the successive influences affecting modern French painting:

The first parallel lies in her affinity to impressionism, with its all-over, flat patterns,
its lack of relief and centralization, and its passion for the momentary image. The
Pointillists offer even more of a flat pattern. The work of Cezanne affords a second
parallel. The canvas is a plenum and the composition an adjustment of tensions
which are three-dimensional, and there are no interstices.[60]

G.G. also drew an analogy between the interpenetration of masses characteristic of the work of the Cubists and a similar aspect of Stein's writing

style. Lastly, G.G. cited a similarity to works by the Dadaists and the Surrealists in Stein's spontaneous and whimsical approach.

On many occasions Gertrude sent copies of her books to Georgiana for her library. Her handwritten inscriptions with her cryptic abbreviations show her fondness for G.G. "To my very dear friend Ggiana Goddard King from Gtde Stn." (*Geography and Plays*, Boston, 1922); "my dear Ggiana . . .Gtde" (*Chicago Inscriptions*, 1934); "For my very dear friend Georgiana who always liked what I did and whose liking it has always made me very happy in memory of our lasting friendship always Gertrude" (*Portraits and Prayers*, New York, 1934).[61] This last book contained vignettes of Cézanne, Matisse, Picasso, Apollinaire, Max Jacob, Emile Vollard, and Juan Gris.

G.G. got Gertrude to lecture at Bryn Mawr on 21 November 1934 on the occasion of her first trip back to the United States after about thirty years. But, she was unsuccessful in persuading Leo Stein to give a lecture. In a letter to Gertrude dated 15 February 1916, he wrote, "I have also promised Georgiana King to give a talk on art at Bryn Mawr some time in April."[62] Leo never gave that talk, nor did he give a course at Bryn Mawr in 1919, which she also tried to arrange. He wrote about his shyness in another letter to Gertrude on 14 December 1919:

Georgiana wanted me to give a course at Bryn Mawr, but unfortunately I couldn't risk it, as I didn't know what minute I might shut up like a trap and the course come to an end. I'd like to have found out, though, whether some notions of mine about teaching are practicable or not. . . . I suppose that I shall write about them this winter, but I'd like to have been able to put them to the test.[63]

Furthermore, Leo respected King's evaluation of his sister's writings and, in a letter to Mabel Weeks critical of Gertrude's autobiography, he wrote, "Please let me know what Georgiana King has to say. About that I am curious." He had just received an article King had written on Gertrude Stein and he disputed one of G.G.'s points, but went on to say, "In any case I shall be interested to hear what she has to say to Gertrude's public utterance."[64]

G.G.'s profound knowledge of both Spanish history and literature led to many friendships and associations with cultural activity in that country. King enjoyed friendships with Spanish scholars and poets like Manuel Gómez-Moreno, Vincente Lampérez, Elias Tormo, and Sanchez Canton. They "admired her as this strange, enthusiastic American woman who dashed about Spain."[65] A token of her pride in these Spanish friends was her dedication of two of her important books, *Mudéjar* and *Pre-Romanesque Churches of Spain* to Manuel Gómez-Moreno and Vincente Lampérez (or, as she called him, "my dear Master L") respectively. An active member

of the Hispanic Society of America and a corresponding member of the
Real Academia Gallega, G.G. held the distinction of being the only female
member of two learned societies in Spain. Although early in her career she
had turned down an offer of employment from the founder of the Hispanic
Society of America, Archer M. Huntington, she always maintained close
ties with the Society. The Society supported her work with generous travel
grants and published many of her writings. She was a good friend of Huntington and dedicated her book on *Sardinian Painting* to him, describing
him as a man of "genius and divination."

G.G.'s appreciation of Spanish culture found expression in several literary projects. In the first of these, G.G.'s sensitivity and creativity as a poet,
coupled with her proficiency in Spanish, gave her English translations of the
coplas true literary distinction. The term *copla* refers to old Spanish ballads
native to each region, which were originally composed of couplet stanzas.
Eventually the form evolved into four stanzas of four octosyllabic lines with
rhyme or assonance in the even lines, a form that varied with the number of
syllables and lines.[66] King was able to translate these poems and at the same
time preserve the inherent musical quality of the old romances. One critic
was led to write, "They never seem to have left their native language."[67]

G.G.'s love of literature extended to writing an innovative biography of
José Anunción Silva (1865-1896), the Colombian poet, published in 1921. It
was one of the first studies devoted to the life and work of a Hispano-
American poet. *A Citizen of the Twilight* is a short book dealing with Silva's
tragic life, which ended in his suicide at the age of thirty-one. A preoccupation with death, King demonstrated, pervaded even his approach to nursery
lore. Although the Colombian poet left few works, G.G. believed that
Silva, in his choice of themes and his poignantly haunting evocations,
ranked with Verlaine in his contributions to the Symbolist movement in
poetry.

In addition to her English and Spanish literary studies, Georgiana
Goddard King's art historical scholarship produced an impressive and
varied bibliography. Her early interests in travel and architecture merge in
her first work of a scholarly character, her annotated edition of George
Edmund Street's *Some Account of Gothic Architecture in Spain*. From
1911 to 1914, retracing his steps in Spain, she added not only notes but new
material on Pre-Romanesque buildings and Gothic painting. This book, in
turn, laid the groundwork for her most ambitious and probably best-known
book, *The Way of Saint James*. Originally, the purpose of the book was to
supplement the writings of earlier writers like Lampérez, Dieulafoy,
Bertaux, and Street. In 1917, after about six years of long and laborious
research, the three-volume book was finished. In it, she traced the medieval
pilgrimage routes leading to the shrine of St. James at Santiago de Compostela. The patron saint of Spain, Saint James Major (or Santiago in

Spanish), was one of the twelve Apostles. Two important legends claimed that he had brought Christianity to Spain and that later he miraculously aided in the liberation of Spain during the crucial battle of Clavijo. His shrine at Compostela in northern Spain, the site of many miracles, became the goal of a famous medieval pilgrimage route. The cathedral of Santiago of Compostela was an outstanding achievement of Romanesque architecture in its plan, structure, and sculptural decoration.

King conducted her own pilgrimage, following the ancient roads leading to the historical site. During her travels she proceeded to record and interpret the architecture and the iconographic material along the pilgrimage routes.

The original intention [she wrote] was to examine the claims for the sources of Spanish architecture in the Gothic and Romanesque period. They are various. Was everything invented in Persia? or Syria, or Asia Minor, or Mesopotamia? Was everything borrowed from France? Was nothing learned from outside the Peninsula?[68]

As she traveled each route, she would comment on variations in the Romanesque architecture of each region, emphasizing the contributions channeled by the Templars and other orders from Syria and by the Arabs from the Moslem world. For Spanish buildings in the Gothic style, King stressed the heavy debt to French and English architecture.

G.G.'s pursuit of historical questions about the sources of Spanish architecture led her to explore in an extremely full and sensitive manner the cultural roots of medieval Spanish civilization. With her detailed discussion of individual buildings, she interwove the diverse strands of national and regional legends, history, and religion. She also incorporated literary sources relating to Spain's past. The French *chansons de gestes*, the poem *El·Cid*, and the writings of the Spanish mystics were interpreted with her own understanding of their ritual and symbolism. G.G. lingered at each site, absorbing its every detail, from the historical to the present. Even the food and farm animals were noted in her book. This interweaving of diverse material, first introduced in *The Way of St. James*, became the distinctive characteristic of her writing style in almost every subsequent work.

The Way of St. James, moreover, referred to current art scholarship such as Kingsley Porter's *Lombard Architecture* and Chandler Post's *Medieval Spanish Allegory*. The scholarly value of *The Way of St. James* was enhanced by the index of forty-six pages of older literature, including unfamiliar and valuable periodicals. King also attempted to establish a chronology for the entire range of buildings based on firmly dated structures. Occasionally, she offered her own hypothesis on such controversial matters as the date of the original west front of the cathedral of Santiago at Compostela and its relationship to the beginnings of the cult of Saint James.

More important, however, was the inclusion of material that had never been published. King discussed many churches, like the ones at Torres, Barbadelo, and Puerto Marin, that had not been mentioned by previous writers. *The Way of Saint James* was the most extensive and comprehensive of all her works and firmly established her reputation as an authority on Spain.

The Way of Saint James was the first of King's books supported and published by the Hispanic Society of America and established a pattern of patronage of her scholarly writings on Spain. Her only other book dealing with pilgrimage routes and crusades was *A Brief Account of the Military Orders in Spain*. Here she cited the three orders—Calatrava, Alcantara, and Santiago—and recounted their formation in the twelfth century and their eventual fall. Again, as in so many of her books, G.G. included in her account of the orders legends and literary portraits of outstanding personalities, as well as translations of *coplas* and poems.

During the years 1912-1915, G.G. planned and completed most of the work on another book, *Pre-Romanesque Churches of Spain*. This book was part of her ultimate goal of writing a series of volumes that would cover every period of Spanish architecture. *Pre-Romanesque Churches* provided a survey of Spanish ecclesiastical architecture previous to the periods discussed in *The Way of Saint James*. King divided the seventh to the eleventh centuries covered in *Pre-Romanesque Churches* into three distinct styles: Visigothic, Asturian, and Mozarabic.[69] The historical evolution of Spanish architecture prior to the Romanesque period was directly related to the character of each wave of invaders, who brought their own architectural features and building methods and blended them with the indigenous style. In *Pre-Romanesque Churches*, G.G. examined over thirty buildings, many of which were here first published in English. Delayed by the demands of *The Way of Saint James* and other obligations to the Hispanic Society, *Pre-Romanesque Churches* did not come out until 1924. Despite her insistence on implausible direct influences between the Near East and Spain, King's opening up of this difficult field by examining complex questions made the book an important contribution to scholarship.

As a constant theme of her analysis in *Pre-Romanesque Churches*, King asserted a consistent and logical development of complex architectural forms stimulated by Eastern, mainly Byzantine, contacts beginning in the sixth century during the Visigothic period. When King discussed the third style, the Mozarabic, which was introduced by exiled monks from Cordova into León, she also emphasized its foreign origins. It was in her presentation of the Asturian style, when she points as sources to several Syrian buildings of an earlier epoch, that her Eastern attributions became the most controversial. Few art historians restricted the sources for the enigmatic Asturian period solely to Near Eastern sources from Constantinople and Syria without considering the indigenous traditions and Western, particularly

Carolingian, influences. G.G. admitted her bias in this revealing statement, "Like other things that came out of the East, it is always a little intoxicating."[70]

In Georgiana Goddard King's next book, *Mudéjar*, published in 1927, her references to Near Eastern sources were no longer pure speculation. She wrote this text after years of experience of and interest in Mudéjar art. Mudéjar was the name given to the distinct style of art executed by the Arab workmen living under Christian domination in Spain from the end of the twelfth through the sixteenth century.[71] The use of color, interlaced composition, and the distinct shapes of the curves and angles, King felt, suggested a different and non-European imagination at work. Its sources were exotic places like "Mesopotamia, Egypt, Persia, and the lands that lie back of Iran-Khorassan, Afghanistan, Seistan, and perhaps India."[72] "It is visibly unlike other things, as art-nouveau is, and steel structure. It can hardly be defined more exactly; it is not Semitic, for the latter Moors were all African, and not Islamic, and the workmen were probably baptized; but it can be recognized."[73] The finest example of Mudéjar was the castle of Coco in Castile built by Arab master masons in the fifteenth century. Coco, G.G. declared, was "in its own kind the most beautiful ruin in Spain . . . like a flawed ruby."[74]

In addition to eleven books, King also wrote about forty articles, which were published in the College Art Association's *Art Bulletin* and *Art Studies*, as well as in prestigious architectural and archaeological periodicals like the *Journal of the American Institute of Architects, Arquitectura*, and the *American Journal of Archaeology*. Among the subjects favored were iconographic problems like her early study in 1935 of the Madonna of Humility theme. Many of these articles developed into books. The discussion of the castle ruin of Coco and its Mudéjar style from "Castles in Spain" in the *Journal of the American Institute of Architects*, 1921, became an important part of *Mudéjar* in 1927. The wording was even repeated in some instances. Many of the articles were published as a three-part series like "Towered Cities" and "Castles in Spain." G.G.'s informal commentaries on castles and fortified towns began with their history and then evolved into a discussion of their general character and a comparison in some instances with French and English types. As in her books, King interwove the history, literature, and legends of the various regions. Secular architecture, like castles and fortified towns, was a subject that had not been previously pursued in depth; Street had seen very few of them, and the Spanish author Lampérez restricted his work mainly to religious buildings. Spanish abbeys, cloisters, writers, and manuscripts also were the subjects of many articles. King's lengthy article about a tenth-century illuminated manuscript entitled "Divagations on the *Beatus*" was an important undertaking.[75] Although the manuscript was only a fragment, twenty-four folios in length, G.G.

approached the illuminations as paintings that "constitute the most important body of Spanish painting during nearly half a millennium."[76] She proceeded to discuss the "struggle of the art of representation . . .— symbolic and mystical with pure pattern and color intellectualized."[77]

Not all G.G.'s subjects were Spanish, however. Ten days after his death in 1926, she wrote a short tribute to the French Impressionist painter Claude Monet. "Gertrude Stein and French Painting" was another subject. Equally diverse were her articles on the Roman reliefs in the Budapest Museum and on churches in Greece. G.G.'s only book not specifically on Spain was one that dealt with the art of Sardinia, the island off the coast of Italy that was part of the Spanish empire in the Middle Ages. Her book on *Sardinian Painting* of 1923 was the first comprehensive study of the topic, predating Chandler Post's work on Sardinian art. Confined to the Romanesque and Gothic periods, the sequel on Renaissance and Baroque Painting never appeared.

Among other proposals that she did not execute was a book suggested by Professor Post on Iberian hagiology that would draw on her extensive knowledge of the saints and their legends. A final project that never reached fruition was a book on Portugal, which she started to research in 1935. Her plan divided the book into three parts, the first a survey of the history and the second and third an account of the painting and architecture of Portugal. Tragically, a series of strokes forced her to return to the United States, and the project remained unfinished when she died in 1939.[78]

Although King had finished *Heart of Spain* in 1926, it was published posthumously in 1941 as a tribute both to her and to her beloved Spain. The book was a collection of six essays each in the form of a journey to a particular city or region of central Spain—particularly Castile—and closed with the major literary forms or figures associated with each area. At Burgos, King writes on its hero Ruy Diaz, *El Cid*. In the second chapter, on the towered cities of Daroca, Madrigal, and Cuenca, she translates and discusses one of her favorite Spanish poetic forms, the *copla*. The cathedral of Cuenca is the only building she discusses in any detail. An essay on the ballad (with examples like *Romance Viejo*) accompanies the section on the frontier cities of Segovia, Avila, and Toledo. As part of her essay on the west country, King has a remarkable account of the sixteenth-century poet and mystic Fay Luis de León from the town of Salamanca, whose poetry is included. All in all, the book reads as a eulogy to Spain with its evocation of great moments from the country's history and literary tradition.

Heart of Spain was edited by Agnes Mongan, one of Georgiana Goddard King's most outstanding protegees, and its publication was funded by many of King's devoted friends. Ironically, most people probably were not aware of her deep feelings about the book. In a letter to Gertrude Stein, G.G. wrote, "I am not competent to have an opinion about publishing, having never succeeded in selling the one thing I really cared for to any publisher—Edith's and my *Heart of Spain*. . . . I love Spain with such a hopeless passion."[79] This book was the last work on which she collaborated with Edith Lowber, a Bryn Mawr protegee who was a close friend and constant traveling companion to King for about fifteen years until her death in 1934. During the school year, while G.G. was at Bryn Mawr, Edith Lowber would travel with Carey Thomas, the former president of Bryn Mawr, and stay with her at her villa. Edith Lowber was a competent photographer, and she and King took all the photographs for the latter's books and articles.

G.G.'s "passionate" attachment to Spanish culture, ironically, tended to restrict the effectiveness of her art scholarship. The limitations of her scholarly approach are revealed by the index of *Heart of Spain*. At first glance, it resembles a random syllabus for an encyclopedic course on literature, philosophy, religion, and art. She refers to important thinkers like Nietzsche and Tolstoy and literary and visual artists of different periods, including Giotto and Euripides, in a loose conceptual framework.

King's numerous interests and her incessant reading in almost every art field were almost her undoing. A similar array of culturally and historically separate works of art and artists are a feature in her article "Divagations on the *Beatus*." In this piece, G.G. mentions Chevreul's *The Laws of Contrasts of Color*, Hokusai's prints, Persian miniatures, a Chinese stone buddha, Cézanne, Van Gogh, Picasso, Juan Gris, and finally, the two giants of Spanish art, Velasquez and El Greco. All of these seemingly unrelated names probably led one art historian to call her writing "stream of consciousness" scholarship.[80] A present-day criticism of her writings is that she was too eager to find direct stylistic or thematic influences between things, no matter how implausible and illogical the connections were historically and geographically.

Besides this tendency toward bold hypotheses, G.G.'s profound sensitivity to historical setting made her reluctant to omit any of the details of her treasured research from her writings. This does not imply that she was not analytical, because she certainly was extremely meticulous and perceptive. Her approach to art scholarship, however, was more that of an anthropologist or a sociologist, and characteristic of the generation of art scholars who were primarily polymaths. The richness of texture and sensitivity to works of art in her lectures and writings were also typical of her generation and more than compensated for the lack of other qualities.

Central to her writings was her love of Spain. In an interview she stated, "I am a real Hispanophile—I came there last, and it has not yet become a part of the general scheme of things as Siena, for instance, has."[81] In the latter part of her life, around 1936–1938, she was an ardent supporter of the Spanish Republican cause during the Spanish Civil War. In all of her writings she would digress from her theme to discuss at length the legends of a particular area, as well as its local literary, religious, or military heroes. References to literature commemorating great moments of Spain's past were almost always included in Georgiana Goddard King's writings whether the texts were ancient or contemporary. Hers was the personal knowledge and love of a country and a people, which she had absorbed slowly over many years of travel and reading.

Her preference, she wrote, was to "linger less over the celebrated than the significant, preferring a little the rare and strange."[82] One of her most important contributions to art scholarship, in fact, was her uncovering of many obscure and long-forgotten historical facts before they were permanently lost. She was a romantic. It was her adventuresome spirit, rather than her desire to break away from the provincial European image of art scholarship, that impelled her to devote her life to early Spanish art. G.G.'s first trips to Spain took place in 1911/12, the same year that the University of Chicago added Spanish art to its curriculum. Bryn Mawr and Harvard followed suit in 1913, although Bryn Mawr was the first to offer it as a graduate course. All through the 1920s, there was a great deal of interest in the field; and in 1931 alone, there were fourteen dissertations in the field of Spanish art.[83] Georgiana Goddard King's writings today may seem chatty, and more like a delightful traveler's Bible or an unselective compilation of all the essential historical, literary, and artistic information about a region; but it is generally agreed, however, that King's pioneering efforts and her enthusiasm for Spanish art prepared the way for A. Kingsley Porter's milestone work, the monumental *Romanesque Sculpture of the Pilgrimage Roads*, published in 1928.

To most people, G.G. is remembered more as a teacher whose dedication both to a career and to a standard of excellence was inspirational. Her protegees became the heads of other art history departments as well as scholars at museums. Some of the best known in the museum field are Agnes Mongan, the former director of the Fogg Art Museum at Harvard, and Margaretta Salinger, the former curator of European painting at the Metropolitan Museum of Art. More numerous, however, are the students who chose the teaching profession, like Leila Barber of Vassar College, Marianna Jenkins of Duke University, Katharine Neilson of Wheaton College (d. 1977), and Marion Lawrence of Barnard College (d. 1978). Following a characteristic social pattern for professional women of this period, almost none of her students with advanced degrees ever married.[84] G.G.'s only doctoral student, Delphine Fitz Darby, whom she called her "first chick," was one of the few who combined marriage and a career.[85] It is hard to imagine King herself, however, either tied down by domestic responsibilities or deterred from any experience because she was a woman. Repeatedly she told her students, "I've done everything known to man." Certainly, she led a very active and full life.[86]

After her death, the College Art Association adopted a resolution commemorating her contribution to art history as a scholar, a friend, and especially a teacher. They wrote: "The results of her training were the possession of a method and at the same time the humble recognition that methodical research alone can never completely encompass the significant."[87] Most of her life was spent at Bryn Mawr College as a student and as a teacher. It seemed appropriate, therefore, that Georgiana Goddard King asked for her ashes to be placed in the cloister of the college library where the history of art library and offices are located. She gave to the college over a thousand books from her own library, as well as notes, photographs, and her unpublished manuscript on Portuguese art. Above all, she left a younger generation of art scholars who had the rare opportunity to begin their careers under the guidance of this exceptional woman.

NOTES

Almost all the sparse published material on Georgiana Goddard King appeared in 1939 directly after her death. The most extensive article is by Harold Wethey, "American Pioneer in Hispanic Studies: Georgiana Goddard King," *Parnassus* 11 (November 1939), pp. 33-35. Most important, however, is the thorough bibliography prepared by Dorothea Shipley that follows the Wethey article. Other articles are: Agnes Mongan, "Tribute," *Bryn Mawr Alumnae Bulletin* (July 1937); in the Bryn Mawr newspaper, *"The College News"* (7 November 1934), pp. 1 and 4; (10 May 1939), p. 3; Rhys Carpenter, "Faculty Tribute," *Bryn Mawr Alumnae Bulletin* (June 1939); Katharine Neilson, "In Memoriam," *Bryn Mawr Alumnae Bulletin* (June 1939), p. 14; Dorothea Shipley, "Gift of Books to the College," *Bryn Mawr Alumnae Bulletin* (January 1940), p. 5; and Charles Mitchell, "Mr. Cooper and Miss King," *Bryn Mawr Alumnae Bulletin* (Spring 1961), pp. 5-7.

Unpublished material on King was found in the following locations: the Gertrude Stein and Alfred Stieglitz Collections, both preserved in the Beinecke Rare Book and Manuscript Library of Yale University; the M. Carey Thomas Collection and college archives, both in the Canaday Library of Bryn Mawr College; the Presidents' File of Bryn Mawr College; the Alumnae Office files of Bryn Mawr College; the Hispanic Society of America correspondence file in New York; the Archer Milton Huntington Collection at the George Arents Research Library at Syracuse University; and in the minutes of the College Art Association. Most of the biographical information was derived from interviews with friends, students, colleagues, and family of Georgiana Goddard King conducted between 1975-77. All letters and tapes are in the author's possession unless otherwise specified in the footnotes.

1. I want to express my sincere gratitude to all of King's students and colleagues who shared their recollections with me and patiently tried to answer my numerous questions. Especially helpful were Delphine Fitz Darby, Dorothea Shipley (deceased in 1976), Marion Lawrence (deceased in 1978), Leila Barber, Margaretta Salinger, Eleanor P. Stewart, Agnes Mongan, and Harold Wethey. Eleanor L. King, one of King's few surviving relatives, supplied valuable information on family history.

2. Extract from faculty meeting minutes at Bryn Mawr College, 21 June 1916, p. 1. Canaday Library of Bryn Mawr College.

3. Erwin Panofsky, "Three Decades of Art History in the United States," in Franz L. Neumann et al., *The Cultural Migration: The European Scholar in America* (Philadelphia,

1953), pp. 82-111; reprinted in Panofsky, *Meaning in the Visual Arts* (Garden City, N.Y., 1955), p. 326.

4. James S. Ackerman and Rhys Carpenter, *Art and Archaeology* (Englewood Cliffs, N.J., 1963), p. 191.

5. Radcliffe awarded the first doctorates to women in art history (as distinguished from archaeology) in the 1920s. Radcliffe continued to administer all advanced degrees given to women by Harvard in the Faculty of Arts and Sciences until 1963.

6. King to Gertrude Stein, 20 November 1927. The Gertrude Stein Collection in the Beinecke Rare Book and Manuscript Library of Yale University.

7. Dorothea Shipley to author, 5 August 1975; also Delphine F. Darby to author, 17 November 1975.

8. Most of the descriptions of King's appearance, adventures, and teaching methods derive from the recollections of her former students contained in interviews and letters to the author dating from 1975 to 1977.

9. Agnes De Mille to author, August 1976, telephone conversation. Miss De Mille's cousin referred the author to Eleanor L. King. Eleanor L. King to author, 15 September 1976.

10. John Adams' first wife had been named Ella King. G.G.'s sister, Ella, was not only Judge Adams' niece but also his former wife's namesake.

11. Porter E. Sargent, *The Best Private Schools of the United States and Canada* (Boston, 1915), p. 147.

12. *Bryn Mawr College Undergraduate Catalogue, 1975-76*, pp. 22-23.

13. Sargent, *Best Private Schools*, p. 123. The Graham School, established in 1816, was the oldest private girls' school in New York.

14. King to Stein, 10 December 1906. Yale University.

15. Ibid.

16. Edith Finch, *Carey Thomas of Bryn Mawr* (New York, 1947), and the M. Carey Thomas Collection in the Canaday Library of Bryn Mawr College.

17. Bertrand Russell, *The Autobiography of Bertrand Russell: 1872-1914* (Boston, 1967), Vol. 1, p. 195; and Elaine Kendall, *Peculiar Institutions* (New York, 1975), p. 134.

18. King to Stein, n.d. Yale University.

19. Harold Wethey, "American Pioneer in Hispanic Studies: Georgiana Goddard King," *Parnassus*, 11 (November 1939), p. 33.

20. Priscilla F. Hiss and Roberta Fansler, *Research in Fine Arts in the Colleges and Universities of the United States* (New York, 1934), p. 27. In 1867, Vassar offered instruction in drawing and lectures on theories of art history. See ibid., p. 18.

21. Ibid., p. 27.

22. Ibid., p. 69. This brief account of the art department at Bryn Mawr points out that courses in Greek and Italian art were given by the archaeology department during Bryn Mawr's early years.

23. *Bryn Mawr College News*, 7 November 1934, pp. 1 and 4.

24. Carey Thomas' close friendship with Mamie Gwinn began when they grew up together in Baltimore. After six years of gossip, Gwinn received a certain notoriety when she left Thomas to elope with Alfred Hodder, a married man and brilliant philosophy professor at Bryn Mawr. The enigmatic Gwinn and her lover were married in 1904. They moved to Switzerland, where he died the following year. This episode, mentioned by Bertrand Russell in his autobiography, became the subject of Gertrude Stein's first novel, *Fernhurst*. Because of the sensitivity of the material, the book was published only posthumously in 1971 together with an early story based on Stein's involvement with several Bryn Mawr women, *Q. E. D.*. For *Q. E. D.*, see note 56. Russell, *Autobiography*, p. 194; Gertrude Stein, *Fernhurst, Q. E. D., and Other Early Writings*, (New York, 1971), introduction by Leon Katz; and Kendall, *Peculiar Institutions*, pp. 134-37.

25. For Carey Thomas' interest in art, see Finch, *Carey Thomas*, pp. 109-14. In later years,

President Thomas' interest in art was probably further encouraged by her friendship with Mary Garrett, a Baltimore philanthropist active in women's education and suffrage causes. See ibid., pp. 236-41, and Hugh Hawkins, "Mary Garrett," in *Notable American Women*, ed. Edward T. James, Janet W. James, and Paul S. Boyer, 2 (Cambridge, Mass., 1971), pp. 21-22.

26. After Leache and Wood sold their school in 1892, they spent their retirement in Europe.

27. Finch, *Carey Thomas*, pp. 269-70.

28. Eleanor King to author, 15 September 1976; and Agnes Mongan to author, 8 July 1976.

29. Colin Eisler, "*Kunstgeschichte* American Style," in *The Intellectual Migration*, ed. by Donald H. Fleming and Bernard Bailyn, Cambridge, Mass., 1969, pp. 544-629.

30. Park to King in California, 24 July 1938; the Presidents' file at Bryn Mawr College.

31. King to Stein, n.d. Yale University.

32. King to Marion D. Park, 1928; the Presidents' file at Bryn Mawr College.

33. Edward Warburg to author, 5 August 1976, tape.

34. Ibid.

35. Ibid. Mr. Warburg later became the publicity director and manager of the New York City Ballet Company.

36. *Bryn Mawr College News*, 10 May 1939, p. 3.

37. Helen Whitcomb Barss to author, 3 December 1975.

38. King's students to author, 1975-76. See note 8.

39. Leila Barber to author, 2 September 1975.

40. King to Stein, n.d. Yale University.

41. King to Stein, n.d. Yale University.

42. Pierre Daix and Georges Boudaille, *Picasso: The Blue and Rose Periods* (Greenwich, Conn., 1966), p. 99. Gertrude Stein left her art collection to Alice Toklas, with the exception of this portrait, which was her bequest to the Metropolitan Museum of Art, New York.

43. Michael J. Hoffman, *Gertrude Stein* (London, 1976), p. 132.

44. This exhibition, which opened at the Armory of the New York National Guard's 69th Regiment on 17 February 1913, traveled to Chicago and Boston. It achieved a record breaking attendance figure of half a million people for an art exhibition in America. Sam Hunter, *American Art of the Twentieth Century* (New York, 1972), pp. 78-81.

45. King to Stieglitz, 30 December 1915, Beinecke Rare Book and Manuscript Library of Yale University. There is no further reference to G.G.'s proposed course. If she was able, in fact, to give it in 1916, the course apparently was not continued afterward. Hiss and Fansler, *Research in Fine Arts*, p. 42, do not cite Bryn Mawr's course, but mention Schapiro's course at N.Y.U. for graduate students on modern painting in 1933-34, and the one given by Post in 1932-33 at Harvard emphasizing American sculpture. King referred to modern artists in her courses, but Bryn Mawr did not offer a course on modern art per se that predated those of N.Y.U., Harvard, and Wellesley. The Wellesley course, dating from 1927, was apparently first. For more details, see Chapters 2 and 3 of this volume.

46. Hunter, *American Art*, p. 84.

47. Most of the collection of the Société Anonyme was given to the Yale University Art Gallery in 1941.

48. Prior to 1912, Barnes had been collecting the work of traditional nineteenth-century, primarily American artists. His friend, the Ash Can School painter William Glackens, persuaded him to let him go to Paris with twenty thousand dollars to buy contemporary European art. Barnes had the option to return the paintings after six months if he did not like them. Although initially unappreciative, in less than six months Albert Barnes was buying on a large scale works by radically new European artists.

49. Barnes and Herman Hille invented in 1902 a silver nitrate compound, known commercially as Argyrol.

50. William Schack, *Art and Argyrol* (New York, 1963), p. 188.

51. King to Stein, n.d., Yale University.

52. Eleanor King to author, 15 September 1976.

53. John I. H. Baur, "The Tradition: Impressionism and Romantic Realism" in: John I. H. Baur, *Revolution and Tradition in Modern American Art* (New York, 1967), pp. 80-96. Thirty-some years after his death, the critic Hilton Kramer wrote an article, "Charles Hawthorne, Gifted but Minor," that appeared in *The New York Times*, 7 December 1968. In discussing Hawthorne's portraits, Kramer pointed out, "On the whole, women were his best subjects, and young women best of all—he had a facility for depicting their moods, with an affectionate sensitivity."

54. Marianna Jenkins to author, 21 June 1976.

55. Irene Gordon to author, 24 October 1975, telephone conversation.

56. Gertrude's involvement with May Booksaver and Mabel Haynes became the subject of her first fictional work, entitled *Q. E. D.* and finished in October 1903. This story and *Fernhurst* were published posthumously (see note 24).

57. "Gertrude Stein and French Painting," *Bryn Mawr Alumnae Bulletin* (May 1934), p. 2.

58. Ibid., p. 2.

59. Alice B. Toklas, *What is Remembered* (Boston, 1963), p. 53. Toklas may have confused King in this instance, as G.G. stated that she met Gertrude Stein in New York.

60. "Gertrude Stein and French Painting," pp. 3-4.

61. The inscriptions are in the books by Gertrude Stein that were given by King to the Canaday Library of Bryn Mawr College. Many of these inscriptions were found by Charles Mitchell. See Charles Mitchell, "Mr. Cooper and Miss King," *Bryn Mawr Alumnae Bulletin* (Spring 1961), p. 5.

62. Leo Stein, *Journey into the Self* (New York, 1950), p. 71.

63. Ibid., p. 78.

64. Ibid., p. 152.

65. Harold Wethey to Claire Sherman, 22 May 1976.

66. The number of syllables may vary from eleven to twelve.

67. Elizabeth Dodge, Review of *Heart of Spain*, *Magazine of Art*, 34 (October 1941), 440.

68. *The Way of Saint James* (New York, 1920), 1, p. 3.

69. The Visigoths, a Germanic people, held northern and central Spain from 414-717. The Asturian kings from the area north of Orieda began the Reconquest of Spain from the Moslems in the ninth century. The second stage of the Reconquest was called the Mozarabic period and lasted from the end of the ninth to the mid-eleventh centuries.

70. "Castles in Spain," *The Journal of the American Institute of Architects* (1921), p. 298. See bibliography for complete reference.

71. Mudéjar art is distinguished by the constant use of cusping and by brickwork ranging in color from deep rose to purplish brown. Other features of the Mudéjar style are horseshoe arches, interlaced polygons, and arcading.

72. *Mudéjar*, p. 190.

73. *Mudéjar*, p. viii. The same quotation appears in "Castles in Spain," p. 298. See bibliography for complete reference.

74. "Castles in Spain," p. 298.

75. Beatus' *Commentary on the Apocalypse* was a selection of passages from the Church Fathers interpreting the Vision of St. John. Beatus of Liébana was an eighth-century monk of the monastery of San Martin.

76. "Divagations on the *Beatus*," p. 50. See bibliography for complete reference.

77. Ibid., p. 50.

78. The manuscript of the Portuguese project survives in a fragmented state and is located in the Canaday Library of Bryn Mawr College.

79. King to Stein, 13 March. Yale University.

80. John Williams to author, 13 May 1976. Many of his observations are included in this evaluation.

81. She was probably referring to the overwhelming importance placed on the early Italian "primitives" by art historians, especially those of the Bernard Berenson circle.

82. *Heart of Spain*, author's preface.

83. Hiss and Fansler, *Research in Fine Arts*, p. 48.

84. Roberta Wein, "Women's Colleges and Domesticity, 1875-1918," *History of Education Quarterly*, 14 (Spring 1974), pp. 31-47.

85. Darby wrote articles on Ribalta, her doctoral subject, and Ribera, as well as a small book on Zariñena that was published in Spain.

86. A verse which some "wicked" students devised was probably prompted by G.G.'s brash statement and flamboyant style:

> Hark the herald angels sing,
> Here's to Georgiana Goddard King,
> Who is this who knows each thing,
> Yet she wears no wedding ring?
> Peace on Earth and mercy mild
> Has she ever had a child?

87. Unpublished resolution in the College Art Association minutes, n.d., provided by the late Marion Lawrence to author.

SELECTED BIBLIOGRAPHY OF GEORGIANA GODDARD KING

Books

Street, George Edmund, *Some Account of Gothic Architecture in Spain*, London, J.M. Dent & Sons Ltd., 1914, edited by Georgiana Goddard King; Spanish edition, Madrid, 1926. First published 1865.

Street, George Edmund, *Unpublished Notes and Reprinted Papers*, with an essay by Georgiana Goddard King, New York, The Hispanic Society of America, 1916.

The Way of Saint James, 3 vols., New York, G. P. Putnam's Sons, 1920 (Hispanic Notes and Monographs).

A Brief Account of the Military Orders in Spain, New York, The Hispanic Society of America, 1921 (Hispanic Notes and Monographs).

The Play of the Sibyl Cassandra, New York, Longmans, Green and Co., 1921 (Bryn Mawr Notes and Monographs, 2).

A Citizen of the Twilight: José Asunción Silva, New York, Longmans, Green and Co., 1921 (Bryn Mawr Notes and Monographs, 4).

Sardinian Painting, New York, Longmans, Green and Co., 1923 (Bryn Mawr Notes and Mongraphs, 5).

Pre-Romanesque Churches of Spain, New York, Longmans, Green and Co., 1924 (Bryn Mawr Notes and Monographs, 7).

Mudéjar, New York, Longmans, Green and Co., 1927 (Bryn Mawr Notes and Monographs, 8).

Little Romanesque Churches in Portugal, Cambridge, Mass., Harvard University Press, 1939 (Reprint from *Medieval Studies in Memory of A. Kingsley Porter*).

Heart of Spain, Cambridge, Mass., Harvard University Press, 1941, edited by Agnes Mongan (published posthumously).

Periodicals

"French Figure Sculpture on Some Early Spanish Churches," *American Journal of Archaeology*, 19 (1915), 250-67.

"A Note on the So-Called Horse-Shoe Architecture of Spain," *American Journal of Archaeology*, 20 (1916), 407-16.

"Three Notes on Capitals," *American Journal of Archaeology*, 20 (1916), 417-25.

"Some Famous Paintings in Barcelona," *Art and Archaeology*, 4 (July 1916), 55-56.

"A Change in León Cathedral, Spain," *Art and Archaeology*, 4 (Oct. 1916), 243.

"Saint Mary of Melón," *American Journal of Archaeology*, 21 (1917), 387-96.

"Early Churches of Spain," *Journal of the American Institute of Architects*, 6 (1916), 395-402; 435-42; 559-66.

"Fiona Macleod," *Modern Language Notes*, 33 (1918), 352-56.

"Three Unknown Churches in Spain." *American Journal of Archaeology*, 22 (1918), 154-65.

"Notes on the Portals of Santiago de Compostella," *American Journal of Archaeology*, 23 (1919), 73.

"The Vision of Thurkill and Saint James of Compostella," *The Romanic Review*, 10 (1919), 38-47.

"Granada of the Moors," *Journal of the American Institute of Architects*, 7 (1919), 71-77.

"Soria, Osma and Cuenca," *Journal of the American Institute of Architects*, 7 (1919), 103-11.

"Spanish Abbeys," *Journal of the American Institute of Architects*, 7 (1919), 399-405.

"Spanish Cloisters," *Journal of the American Institute of Architects*, 7 (1919), 481-88.

"Bryn Mawr Notes and Monographs," *Bryn Mawr Alumnae Bulletin* (April 1921), 13-14.

"The Shepherds and the Kings," *Art and Archaeology*, 12 (Dec. 1921), 265-72.

"The Importance of Sometimes Looking at Things, as Exemplified in the Cardona Tomb at Bellpuig and the Retables of Barbastro and S. Domingo de la Calzada," *American Journal of Archaeology*, 35 (1921), 81.

"Castles in Spain," *Journal of the American Institute of Architects*, "Part 1," 9 (1921), 271-4; "Part 2," ibid., 294-301; 10 (1922), 377-82.

"Towered Cities," *Journal of the American Institute of Architects*, "Part I," 9 (1921), 349-58; "Part 2," ibid., 10 (1922), 346-52; "Part 3," ibid., 12 (1924), 103-9.

"The Rider on the White Horse," *The Art Bulletin*, 5 (1922), 3-9.

"Prettiness and Discomfort, with some Sociological Implications," *Journal of the American Institute of Architects*, 10 (1922), 43-44.

"Some Oriental Elements in Medieval Spanish Architecture," *American Journal of Archaeology*, 26 (1922), 79-80.

"Algunos elementos ingleses en las fundaciones de Alfonso VIII," *Arquitectura*, 4 (1922), 453-58.

"Some Churches in Galicia," *Art Studies*, 1 (1923), 55-64.

"Algunos rasgos de influjo oriental en la arquitectura española de la edad media," *Arquitectura*, 5 (1923), 85-193.

"Little Churches in Greece," *Journal of the American Institute of Architects*, "Part 1," 12 (1924), 13-16, 23-24; "Part 2," ibid., 14 (1926), 434-41.

"The Problem of the Duero," *Art Studies*, 3 (1925), 3-11.

"Fact and Inference in the Matter of Jamb Sculpture," *Art Studies*, 4 (1926), 113-46.

"Claude Monet," *Bryn Mawr Alumnae Bulletin* (Feb. 1927), 20-21.

"The Triumph of the Cross," *The Art Bulletin* 11 (1929), 316-26.

"Divagations on the *Beatus*," *Art Studies*, 8 (1930), 1-58.

"Some Reliefs at Budapest," *American Journal of Archaeology*, 37 (Jan. 1933), 64-76.

"Gertrude Stein and French Painting," *Bryn Mawr Alumnae Bulletin* (May 1934), 2-5.

"Iconographical Notes on the Passion," *The Art Bulletin*, 16 (1934), 291-303.

"The Journey of Ferrer Bassa," *The Art Bulletin*, 16 (June 1934), 116-22.

"The Virgin of Humility," *The Art Bulletin*, 17 (Dec. 1935), 474-91.

"Mattia Preti," *The Art Bulletin*, 18 (Sept. 1936), 371-86.

CHAPTER 9

MARGARETE BIEBER (1879-1978): AN ARCHAEOLOGIST IN TWO WORLDS

Larissa Bonfante[1]

INTRODUCTION

Twenty-two years ago Otto Brendel, my dissertation adviser, introduced me to Margarete Bieber—Dr. Bieber, as she liked to be called. I was
one of many graduate students she helped long after she had officially
retired from Columbia University's Department of Art History and Archaeology in 1948. Professor Brendel and I were invited to tea in her warm, old-
fashioned apartment at 605 West 113th Street, near Columbia University.
Tea was served by her companion and housekeeper, Fräulein Katharina
Freytag, with porcelain cups and silver spoons and good cakes, as at the
houses of aunts and grandmothers I had been brought to visit as a child in
Italy. Young, newly divorced, uncertain of my bearings, I felt at home
again. She took me under her wing, as she had so many others in her life,
and invited me back to discuss my work with her. I came to help her show a
visitor how Christ's dress had been draped. Patiently she read draft after
draft and chapter after chapter of my dissertation on Etruscan dress,
suggesting organization, references, ideas, and information. We became
friends and talked of America, travel, friendship, life, our families, the
books we were reading, our news. She gave useful advice: "Hope for the
best, and expect the worst"; "Sweets are good for the nerves." She was
fun-loving, with a mischievous smile I have never seen on any photograph.

For her ninetieth birthday, Professor Brendel helped me and a young
scholar from Giessen, Rolf Winkes, publish her bibliography: there were
over 300 items. Some time later, she gave me a copy of her unpublished
memoirs, "The Autobiography of a Female Scholar," written when she was
eighty years old. Most of the following essay is based on this account of her
life before I knew her. Typically, though planned to end with her eighty-

first year, it starts over again, with a "Last Chapter," in 1961. For Dr. Bieber there was always another chapter.

EARLY LIFE (1879-1914)

She was born 31 July 1879, in Schoenau, Kreis Schwetz, West Prussia (now Przechowo, Kreis Swiece, Poland). Her father, Jacob Heinrich Bieber, and mother, Valli Bukofzer, were well-off, and long able to give her the economic security she needed to prepare for a career. Her earliest memories were of a spacious villa, its barns, stables, and gardens, where the four children played; because of its tower, it was called "the castle," or *Schloss*, by the villagers of Schoenau (pop. 1,000) and the townspeople of nearby Schwetz. She spoke proudly of her father, an industrialist who had built new flour mills, mechanized for the first time in Germany, and was loved and respected by local Germans and Poles alike. Margarete and her two sisters, she recalls, were called the Princesses of Schoenau. But while the son and heir was spoiled and carefully educated, the girls saw little of their parents and received perfunctory instruction at the hands of a governess:"reading, writing, stories from the New Testament, and very little else." Yet her mother had an excellent education for a woman of her time, including languages, literature, and music. Dr. Bieber, who enjoyed robust health—then and always—remembers that she was expected to nurse her asthmatic older sister as well as her mother, sick with "nervous depression." Passionately mothering her little sister, Anna, she vowed that she would spare her her own unhappy childhood. At this time she developed her earliest ambition, to become a doctor, a pediatrician, in order to treat children.

A doctor who took women's illnesses seriously, she felt, would have been able to cure her mother's nervous sickness. Though she did not pursue this career, the desire never quite left: long after, she hoped her daughter would study medicine at the University of Giessen.

For six years Dr. Bieber happily attended the Töchterschule, a girls' school in Schwetz near her home town of Schoenau. When the principal was too drunk to teach, she took over the class: the girls played games or performed short plays which she wrote. She wrote a poem a day. Homework was easy, except for the math problems, which her favorite young uncle Paul did for her. (Later she often protested, raising her hands in mock horror, "don't ask me about numbers!") After school she roamed in park and garden. (In her New York apartment, flowers crowded the tables and plants grew all around the bright window; and in Connecticut, during the final months, she carefully traced the shifting colors of the leaves in the fall and the flowers of spring and summer.)

She had thus discovered the joy of independent thinking and learning when fate, in the form of her sister's illness, sent the girls to the warmer climate of Dresden and the pension of Frl. Hessling, an excellent international finishing school. Here they had proper dresses and attended the opera, which Margarete loved ever after. She studied literature, history, and music, and learned to speak English. She made lifelong friendships: Marie Vogel of Rotterdam accompanied her through Holland when she left Germany in 1933.

When she returned home at the age of sixteen, her education was considered to have ended. The family opposed her idea of becoming a doctor, her mother reluctant to lose housekeeper and nurse, while aunts prophesied mental breakdown, doom, and disaster. The current wave of feminism came to her aid at this point. Two "suffragettes," as she called them, Anita Augsburg and Mrs. de Witt, persuaded her mother; and her father, who thought girls did not need to learn but adored his wife, gave permission, provided she study to become not a doctor but a schoolteacher.

After some private instruction and further delays, she finally went off to Berlin. It was 1899; she was almost twenty. In the pension where she lived she again made lifelong friendships. For a year she attended the *Gymnasialkurse*, a private school for girls founded by feminist educator Helene Lange. Finding it too slow, she prepared privately for the *Abiturium*, the high school certificate or qualifying examination that would allow her to attend the university. She had excellent teachers. Professor Kurt Busse awakened in her a love for classical antiquity.[2] Her German tutor, Hildegard Wegscheider-Ziegler, the first woman ever to pass the difficult German state and doctor's exams, set her to reading and discussing Kant and Plato. In 1901 Dr. Bieber passed the *Maturitätsprüfung* exam in Thorn, the first woman of her home province of West Prussia to do so.

She registered at the University of Berlin. As a woman she needed the professors' permission in order to attend courses. The professors in the relatively liberal Department of Classics accepted her, and she was able to study with outstanding scholars of the beginning of this century, Hermann Diels, the authority on pre-Socratic philosophy, and Eduard Meyer, professor of ancient history. For Ulrich von Wilamowitz-Moellendorf she wrote a paper, in Latin, as was usual, on the Greek sources of Catullus.[3] She wrote poems in Greek.

Her interest in philosophy declined. The learned Diels was dry in class. After listening to him debate for an hour on whether *batrachos* or *bartrachos* was the right form for "frog" in the manuscripts, she gave up. Attracted by the collection of ancient art in the Alte Museum in Berlin, she registered for a course in Greek sculpture with the director, Reinhard Kekulé von Stradonitz, but she found this excellent scholar's lectures boring. She then went to Bonn, in accordance with the German system of students moving from one university to another to find the teacher with whom one wants to work. She had heard that Georg Loeschcke, in Bonn, was the most inspiring teacher of ancient art, and she was not disappointed.[4] After a short-lived attempt to go back to Berlin and her first love, medicine—she felt that the professor of anatomy treated her as a female, rather than as a student—she settled down in Bonn in 1904. Here she studied the subjects she loved, again with famous scholars: Greek art with Georg Loeschcke, history of art with Paul Clemen, and Latin with Franz Buecheler, who introduced her to Plautus and to the ancient theater. Loeschcke above all became her inspiration and model. His portrait used to hang in her apartment in New York opposite her chair, from which she would point it out to first-time archaeological visitors, asking them, as a friendly exam, to identify the works of art hidden in the picture. (Answer: the green curtain in the background was really the drapery of the charioteer of Delphi; the white column was the *kouros* of Tenea.) For his seminar, she gave a report on a relief in Dresden depicting an actor, which then became the subject of her doctoral dissertation.[5] With characteristic efficiency, she finished it during the summer vacation of 1906. By Christmas of that year, she had passed her doctoral examination. In 1907, with the publication of her dissertation, she was officially awarded the doctorate and became Dr. Bieber (Figure 14). This was the title she used for the rest of her life.

Now, to finish her archaeological education, she had to travel in Greece and Italy, not an easy goal for a woman to accomplish at that time. Her family had never stopped making demands upon her and still expected her to serve as nurse.[6] Loeschcke came to the rescue. He explained to her parents that her studies were not a frivolous pastime and that she still needed some years abroad, the German *Wanderjahre*, to become a good scholar. Finally, in 1907, she set off for Rome, financed by her father. The next seven years (1907-1914) she spent in classical lands, returning in the summer to see her family and Loeschcke.

In Rome she spent the happiest and most interesting days of her life. She lived in a small Italian *pensione* within the ruins of the Capitoline Hill, with a splendid view of the Roman Forum and the Palatine. Happily she roamed over Forum and Palatine, studied the Colosseum, dreamed in the Pantheon. She visited museums, made notes for later papers, and again made lifelong friends. Walther Amelung, the author of the Vatican catalog of ancient sculpture, taught her how to look at statues. He took her and others to museums and to dealers. The Villa Albani she visited disguised as a lady of the court of a Bavarian prince, as Count Torlonia did not want scholars in his collections, though kings and aristocrats were welcome. She met Amelung's friends, Professor Friedrich Spiro, editor of the text of Pausanias' *Description of Greece*, and his Russian-born wife, Assia, a

Figure 14. Margarete Bieber in 1906. (Collection of the late Margarete Bieber)

violinist; attended musical evenings in the beautiful Villino Assia; and met Ottorino Respighi, Ettore Romagnoli, and other Italian and international artists, musicians, and archaeologists. Sundays were spent with Amelung, the Spiros, Ernst Noether, a portrait painter, and his wife, a pianist, in the Villino Antonia of Amelung or in the Noethers' old-fashioned apartment, both full of precious works of art. The six of them went to movies, restaurants, and excursions to the Alban Hills, Tivoli, and Hadrian's Villa. They talked endlessly.

In 1909 came a new triumph: she was the first woman to receive the German travel fellowship awarded yearly to four promising young archaeologists.[7] But her encounters with prejudice were not over. She was ostracized by the other fellows.[8] At Pergamon, where she was received kindly by the great Wilhelm Dörpfeld, she turned the tables on her colleagues, walking ahead with Dörpfeld and climbing with ease Pergamon's many terraces. This great archaeologist, then also the director of the German Archaeological Institute, had excavated with Schliemann in Troy and Mycenae, and later in Olympia, on the Acropolis of Athens, and in the theater of Epidauros. All of these sites Dr. Bieber later visited with him. Adventuresome trips took her to all the important sites, which she visited with the excavators: to Didyma with Theodor Wiegand, to Miletus with Hubert Knackfuss and Erich Pernice, and to Smyrna, Priene, and others. Later, in Crete, Sir Arthur Evans entertained them at the Villa Ariadne.

At the German Institute at Athens, she was welcomed by Georg Karo,[9] who was soon to become director, and spent the next few years quite happily, after the youngest of her colleagues, the gifted Gerhart Rodenwaldt, broke the ice. Dr. Bieber, on her rented piano, would accompany Rodenwaldt, who sang German *Lieder*. Soon everyone was taking part in these musical evenings, and the thirty-year-old Dr. Bieber had "adopted" these young men, far from home. They thought of themselves as a "family," ate together, and traveled all over Greece. She kept their buttons sewn on and their coats mended, helped choose presents for wives and families, and took pride in their accomplishments and careers when they became well-known scholars. Gerhart Rodenwaldt became a professor in Giessen and Berlin and director of the German Institute.[10] Georg Lippold became editor of important publications of ancient sculptures[11] and a professor in Erlangen. Eduard Schmidt was the author of important works of archaic art and became a professor at the University of Kiel, as did Hugo Prinz, who wrote on astronomical symbols.[12] Later a fifth "son," Hans Nachod, joined these scholars.[13] A photograph in Dr. Bieber's collection (Figure 15) shows some of these young archaeologists striking classical poses in the National Museum in Athens, ca. 1910. They are dressed as famous Greek archaic statues, displayed on their bases: Georg Lippold as a *kouros*, Eduard Schmidt as the

Figure 15. (*Left to right*) Georg Lippold, Eduard Schmidt, Camillo Praschniker, and Otto Walter in the National Museum, Athens, ca. 1910. (Collection of the late Margarete Bieber)

winged sphinx from Naxos, and Camillo Praschniker as another statue.
Otto Walter acts as the museum guard.

In Athens, the German Institute was the intellectual center for scholars
from the whole world, as well as for personages such as the Crown Prince of
Greece and the Princess Sophie, sister of the last German emperor. The
latter, we are told, praised Dr. Bieber's domestic virtues, not realizing she
was a scholar, too!

Probably at this time she received the nickname, *die Bieberin* ("female
beaver"). She worked indefatigably, and in the years 1910-1913 published
many articles in the German Institute's publications. Together with Rodenwaldt, she wrote on the mosaics of Dioskourides representing scenes from
the theater.[14] She wrote on satyr play vases[15] and on the medallions of the
arch of Constantine, which she correctly dated to the Hadrianic period,[16] a
work she first wrote for Franz Studniczka in a seminar at the Institute and
which contributed to her election as a fellow of the German Archaeological
Institute in 1912.[17] One of the greatest honors to which a German archaeologist could aspire, it brought with it very real advantages. For the next
two years (1912-1913), she could live at the German Institute in Rome, on
the Capitoline Hill.

The summers of 1915 and 1916 she spent in Kassel, having been commissioned to write a catalogue of the museum's small but choice collection of
ancient sculptures. She took full advantage of this opportunity. Persuading the museum's director, Professor Johannes Boehlau, to let her take the
statues apart, she set about removing eighteenth- and nineteenth-century
restorations, with the assistance of the sculptor Nüsslein. This project,
which involved restoring missing pieces with casts of better preserved copies
and setting heads and limbs at proper angles, showed her courage and
imagination and also gave her an intimate and practical knowledge of
sculpture, copy and original, and drapery and portrait, central to all her
work. The account she gives in her autobiography shows how risky the
work was. The celebrated Kassel Apollo was taken apart, its upper part
hung in chains in order to restore its legs properly. "I suffered agony during
these proceedings, particularly as the marble was brittle and the artist
always a little drunk in the afternoon. I therefore omitted all work after his
drinking hour." The results were gratifying. The Kassel collection almost
doubled with the copy of a head by Polycleitus now exhibited beside the
copy of a torso by Praxiteles to which the restorer had once joined it. The
project was of great interest to museum directors[18]; and her method was
later used in Dresden, Berlin, and the Metropolitan Museum.

Back home in Rome, she worked hard too. She did research in the
German Institute, which boasted the best archaeological library in the
world. She combed the museums for parallels to the statues from Kassel
she was working on and discussed problems with Amelung. The director's

amiable wife, Frau Delbrueck, was, like most German scholars' wives, not much interested in anyone other than her husband, so Dr. Bieber once more "mothered" the resident scholars and invited them all for Christmas Eve celebrations.

The catalogue of ancient sculptures in the Kassel museum was finished in 1914 and appeared in 1915.[19] Meanwhile, she had started working on theater masks, a new project she hoped to finish at the Villa Falconieri in Frascati, a home for artists and scholars given to the German emperor by the Jewish banker Mendelssohn. There were initial difficulties. "As usual I was at first not welcome being a woman; a single woman, for of course the men brought their wives." Then her old friend Wilhelm Dörpfeld used his influence with the emperor to have her invited, and soon all the inhabitants were friends. "Life in this earthly paradise was enchanting. But when I had just celebrated my thirty-fifth birthday, World War I broke out and destroyed, like a bomb, our enchanted life."

CAREER IN GERMANY (1914-1933)

"When the successor to the throne of Austria was murdered, we were excited but not fearful. But when war was declared by England on 1st August, we became alarmed. . . ." West Prussia had been taken by the Russians; and she feared that her brother, who was of military age, might be in the fighting. She returned to Germany, stopping off for a few days only in Munich to confer with Paul Arndt about some texts she was writing for his photographic survey of ancient sculpture, on the statues of the Vestal Virgins in the Roman Forum.[20] From her family came good news and money. Hindenburg had turned back the Russian attack, the frightened peasants had returned home, and a weak heart had kept her brother at home. Back at Schoenau she and her sister Anna organized a branch of the Red Cross, visiting wounded soldiers, bringing city children to the country, and setting up women's groups to make warm underwear for the soldiers. This work earned her a Red Cross medal and a permanently weak right wrist, resulting from an improperly treated sprain.

At Easter in 1915 she went to Berlin to work for the Red Cross, as well as to continue some of her own research on the ancient theater. She had come at a providential moment for Loeschcke, who, now a Professor at Berlin University, had suffered a stroke. His memory had begun to fade. His assistants, Rodenwaldt and Valentin Müller,[21] had been called into the army, and he received Dr. Bieber with open arms. She prepared his classes, which she knew so well, and allowed Valentin Müller, who had to provide for a mother, to keep the salary. With her father's financial support and encouragement, she moved into her own four-room apartment in the *Familienheim*, a residence for single ladies in the Marchstrasse, near the

former house of the historian Mommsen. Now, for the first time, she had
her own home. She hired a young housekeeper. She chose furniture designed by a young man, Bruno Paul,[22] suiting it to her own taste and needs,
replacing his sculptured friezes with Greek embroideries under glass and
adding deep shelves for large photographs. (Much of this handsome furniture, and some Biedermeier pieces, still surrounded her in her New York
apartment, though heavy chairs and sofa, antique rugs, and grand piano
had had to be left behind). World War I brought her the opportunity to
teach at last, when Loeschcke had a second stroke. She took over the
beginners' seminar and faced students for the first time. "By and by their
astonishment and my fear disappeared." When Loeschcke died that winter,
her former teachers Wilamovitz, Diels, and Eduard Meyer wanted her to
continue to teach the seminar. She had by this time organized a smoothly
running Archaeological Institute, free of debts, and a well-educated student
body. Yet she could not, as a woman, under the Empire, officially become
an instructor or "Privatdozent." When Loeschcke's successor, Ferdinand
Noack, was appointed, she left.

The students, however, asked her to teach them privately. In her home,
during those war years, 1916-1918, she met with an outstanding group.
Some of these she was to see many years later, in the United States: Erwin
Panofsky, later professor at the Institute for Advanced Study at Princeton;
his wife, then Dora Mosse; and Elizabeth Jastrow, who later taught in
Greensboro, North Carolina.[23] She introduced her young friend Jane van
Heuckelum to Gerhart Rodenwaldt: within two weeks they were engaged.
"They lived happily until they died hand in hand, in 1945, when the Rus-
sians broke into their house, attacking every woman between six and sixty.
But in between they had a happy and rich life."[24] Discussions with this elite
were a joy. Though her own scholarly work was pushed into the back-
ground, some of her most important contributions date from this period.
She published on theater masks, on the portraits of Socrates and Aristophanes, on the origin of the costume of tragedy, and on the chiton of the
statues of the Amazons attributed to Polycleitus, Phidias, and Kresilas.[25]
All of these subjects she was to pursue more deeply in the following years.
She attended meetings of the Archaeological Institute and of the Archaeological Society, whose director was Theodor Wiegand and whose secretary
was her friend and colleague Anton Neugebauer.

Her home in the Marchstrasse was a lively place. Old friends like Amelung and the Spiros came to visit, and new "sons" like Bernhard Schweitzer,[26] who played on her grand piano, accompanying singers and violinists
at her musical evenings. Replacing her flighty young housekeeper, there
now came into her life Katharina Freytag, her loyal companion.[27] For Dr.
Bieber had a plan: Fräulein Freytag, an experienced governess, would help
her educate the child she hoped to adopt.

Meanwhile, history brought her the opportunity she longed for; the liberal Weimar Republic opened university teaching professions to women. Her dream, to become a lecturer at a German university, could now come true. Rodenwaldt wrote her from Giessen at once, and she sent off her application, as well as the manuscript of her book on the ancient theater as the prescribed *Habilitationsschrift* and a list of her publications. When she had passed the trial lecture and the qualifying exam or *Kolloquium*, she became, as a *Privatdozentin*, a member of the faculty of the University of Giessen.[28] These years at Giessen saw the high point of her career. She set up housekeeping in Wilhelmstrasse 41/III, where she stayed until her dismissal in 1933. She lectured on ancient cities, Greek and Roman art and private life, and Greek mythology and taught courses on numismatics with the economic historian, Fritz Moritz Heichelcheim, using casts of coins from the university collection. She gave talks at the seminar of the faculty. She took part in the lively social life of the university, led by Geheimrat Poppert, professor of surgical medicine, and Richard A. Laqueur, the ancient historian, and their wives. Otto Behaghel, the celebrated Germanist—"the Nestor of the Faculty of Philosophy"—and Karl Kalbfleisch, papyrologist, became her close friends. The distinguished philologist Rudolf Herzog, the excavator of Kos, asked her to work on the sculpture from Kos, a project that enlarged her knowledge of late Classical and Hellenistic sculpture. Characteristically, her part was finished long before the others were ready; but although she wrote articles on a few pieces (1923-1928),[29] the manuscript was never published. She developed a new interest in Roman provincial art and organized field trips in which students and colleagues participated: in 1928 to Trier, with Wilhelm Gundel, Siegfried Loeschcke, Herzog, Kalbfleisch and others; in 1929 to the Wiesbaden Museum and sites of the Roman *limes*, or ancient army posts.[30] She published articles showing the change from Greek to Roman to medieval forms on tomb reliefs; on Greek sculpture; on the university's pottery collection, which she rearranged; and on the Villa of the Mysteries. The last article was the basis of all later work, including Maiuri's monumental publication.[31] She wrote her most important book of this period on Greek dress (1928). The contribution she wrote for Amelung's *Festschrift* appeared in 1928—as often, too late, for he died in 1927.[32]

Yet for all this activity, she received no salary. Only scholars with independent means could become lecturers at the university. By 1926, however, her family could no longer support her. When her birthplace was handed over to Poland by the Treaty of Versailles, her father was forced to sell the flour mills and move to Germany. The family's fortune was badly invested, and the rising inflation ate the rest. Fortunately, the Hessian state now begun to pay its instructors, most of whom had, like Dr. Bieber, lost their money in the terrible inflation.[33]

In 1922 Rodenwaldt left Giessen to become a professor in Berlin and was in 1923 succeeded by Richard Delbrueck, author of important works on late Roman art. At Delbrueck's suggestion, Dr. Bieber was made Professor Extraordinarius, the equivalent of assistant or associate professor and an honor after only two years. She thus became the second woman professor in Germany, the first being Emma Noether in Göttingen.[34] In 1927 Delbrueck left Giessen to become a professor in Bonn. Dr. Bieber was now in charge of the Archaeological Institute of the University of Giessen. In 1931 she was promoted to Planmässige Professor, not yet a full professor, but on a regular budget line.[35]

When she finally succeeded, it was all she had hoped for and more. She had gifted students.[36] The Institute was flourishing. Cooperating with the departments of classical philology and ancient history, it had more students than the larger neighboring universities of Frankfurt and Marburg. Under her care, students and professors went on archaeological excursions and became a close-knit group. On her fiftieth birthday, the students serenaded her under her window. An International Fellowship of the AAUW, the American Association of University Women, allowed her, in 1931-1932, to travel in London, Paris, and Rome—where she met Ludwig Curtius, the successor to Amelung, in the new building of the German Archaeological Institute in Via Sardegna 79—and to finish her book on the historical development of Greek dress.[37]

In 1932 she was named full professor for the following year, with a salary guaranteed for life, as is the rule in German universities. Secure at last in position and finances, she adopted little Ingeborg, with her dark, wistful eyes and blond hair. Dr. Bieber joyfully planned for Inge to go to Giessen's excellent medical school and felt her life at last had its final form. "Nobody could be more wrong, for in the Spring of 1933 Hitler came to power and catastrophe engulfed me like so many others."

FLIGHT AND NEW LIFE (1933-1948)

Dr. Bieber was apolitical, but history and politics shaped the pattern of her life. The Weimar Republic made her career possible; Hitler destroyed it. Yet this was not clear at once. Engrossed in her teaching, her research, and the education of her darling Inge, she was not at first overly concerned by the ascendance of Hitler as leader of the German Reich. She was shocked when the Jewish members of the faculty were dismissed; it had never occurred to her it could happen to her.

On 29 June, an order came dismissing her, because of her Jewish ancestry, by 1 July. The economist Momber, the physicist Georg Jaffe, and the Orientalist Julius Lewy, who were also dismissed, had their Judaism to give them strength.[38] For Dr. Bieber, the blow was totally unexpected. Her first thought was suicide. She recovered her courage, helped not only by the thought that Nazism would blow over quickly but by the reaction of colleagues and students to her dismissal. Horneffer, the Anglicist Fischer, Herzog, and Kalbfleisch stood by her. So did her students: she always treasured a letter they wrote expressing their devotion and admiration. Her own first thought was for her students. During the whole of 29 and 30 June she gave the state's and doctoral exams to all those who were ready, with Herzog and Kalbfleisch alternating as supervisors in order to maintain the legality of the proceedings.[39]

She now considered the alternatives open to her. She could stay in Germany. In Berlin or Bonn she had friends and family. She could go to Heidelberg, where Arnold von Salis was Professor of Archaeology, though she might damage his position.[40] By September, she had received two offers, from Sofia and from Oxford. In Sofia, a Swiss fellowship would allow her to work for one year in that city's museum; the offer was tempting, for her sister's family was there, but the money was not sufficient. Oxford at least promised lodgings for the three of them. In November 1933, she sold the grand piano and the fine arts—but not the archaeological—books to Frau Gemeinrat Merck of the Merck Farben-Fabrik, a German company, left the remaining books and furniture in care of a friend, and set off with her little family to England.

At Oxford there were disappointments. The family was separated. In spite of bronchitis she had picked up on the way, she went daily to the warm study assigned her and read proofs for her *Entwicklungsgeschichte*, the book on the history of Greek dress. She was an honorary fellow of Somerville College, but there was already a Reader in Archaeology, Helen L. Lorimer. Dr. Bieber could not lecture and therefore received no salary. Fortunately, the Dean of St. Hilda's College asked her to tutor the students; and Professor J.D. Beazley, the foremost English archaeologist, whose legendary eye and understanding revolutionized the study of Greek vases, arranged for her to lecture at the Ashmolean museum. In order to put Inge in boarding school, Fräulein Freytag worked as a cook in a boardinghouse. It was hard to be refugees. At Christmas, Inge received many toys, but only one practical gift, warm slippers from Mrs. Beazley. On Christmas Eve, it was Dr. Bieber who entertained two lonely colleagues, Fritz M. Heichelheim from Giessen and Melitta Gerhard, who later taught in the United States.[41] Two Oxford colleagues received her kindly: Sir Arthur Evans, whom she had met in Crete, who showed her through his property and collection of antiquities, containing gems and other objects, and Professor Gilbert Murray, whose translations of Greek plays she later used at Columbia University.

But the family situation was painful. Fräulein Freytag had a nervous breakdown; Inge got sick. Her sister Gertrud died in Sofia, her mother in

Germany. She had hoped to return to Germany, but Hitlerism became worse and worse. She hoped to remain in Oxford with a research fellowship, but it went to Lorimer. Then she was invited to come for a year as visiting lecturer to Barnard College, whose Dean, Virginia Gildersleeve, a former president of the AAUW, knew Dr. Bieber as the recipient of an award ten years earlier. Three American colleagues also recommended her: Gisela Richter of the Metropolitan Museum, who had met her in London; Mary Swindler of Bryn Mawr, author of *Ancient Painting*; and Hetty Goldman, the eminent excavator of Tarsus, who was generously to help her in later difficulties. Inge and Fräulein Freytag must wait in Dresden with friends, however, as they were in no condition to travel. First, she went to see her ninety-year-old father in Berlin, as well as her surviving family. At this time she managed to be part of the 5 percent who voted against Hitler, by voting in her father's place. When, in September, she embarked for the United States, she took with her *Mein Kampf*, to try to understand what kind of man Hitler was. Repulsed by content and style, as she said, she wondered "how a clever people with an intelligent culture could ever have fallen for Hitler and his ideas."

She landed in New York on 21 September 1934 and was enchanted by the ride along Riverside Drive. In Barnard College she had a suite of her own. The temperature, Fahrenheit and emotional, was far warmer than in England. She liked the friendly informality of social life, so different from cold English politeness. In contrast to the Americans, she pointed out, the British kept with them fewer foreign scholars.[42]

Gisela Richter and Marion Lawrence of the Fine Arts Department welcomed her to New York. She collaborated with Gisela Richter in teaching courses and on the exhibition of sculpture at the Metropolitan Museum, where she was treated like a member of the staff: labels were changed at her suggestion, and methods of reconstruction used in Kassel applied to statues in the Museum's collection.[43]

Yet there were initial difficulties, personal and professional. After a year at Barnard, she joined the Department of Fine Arts and Archaeology (later Art History and Archaeology), under the chairmanship of William B. Dinsmoor, first as Visiting Professor, then as Assistant and Associate Professor (1935-1948). Her colleagues were Emerson Swift, Millard Meiss, Meyer Schapiro, and her friend Marion Lawrence.

She was invited to join the Archaeological Club,[44] a private, very select group of some twenty members, where she met with the outstanding scholars in her field: Leslie Shear, the excavator of the Athenian Agora, and his wife Josephine; Benjamin Meritt, the epigraphist; Hetty Goldman, Gisela Richter, William Dinsmoor, and Edith Hall Dohan; and archaeological couples such as George and Kate Elderkin, Richard Stillwell and his wife Agnes, and later Toni and Isabel Raubitschek. The Raubitschek children soon called her Grandma Bieber, as generations of children were to do. The club met at the house of members or at the Numismatic Society, whose director was Professor Newell, the numismatist and collector. Albert Gallatin invited the members to a sumptuous feast.

This first academic year in New York, 1934/35, was a busy one. She lectured in English, an unfamiliar language, on Greek sculpture, ancient painting, and the Greek and Roman theater. The latter she put into historical perspective, as she had done for Greek dress, in her book *The History of the Greek and Roman Theater*, published by the Princeton University Press in 1939. She attended official and unofficial events at Barnard College. For twenty years she helped plan the costumes for the yearly Greek Games, a competition between the Barnard freshmen and sophomore classes, pleased to see the garments and the statues she had studied come to life. In the spring of 1935, encouraged by Edith Hall Dohan and other friends, she decided to stay in America.

She had planned to bring Inge over herself until she learned that she ran the risk of losing her passport and being forbidden to take Inge, who was "pure Aryan," out of Germany. So the faithful Fräulein Freytag would bring Inge and, if possible, the library and some furniture. No money, for that would involve negotiations with the government and the danger of losing Inge. Money, however, was going to be a problem. Barnard's invitation for the following year had been renewed at the same salary of $2,000, so she earned extra money by lecturing. A fee of fifty dollars seemed stupendous.[45] After difficulties and delays, Inge and Fräulein Freytag arrived on the *Europa*,[46] bringing with them thirty boxes of books and furniture, which went into the apartment at 605 West 113th Street.[47] There was bad news from home: she learned of the deaths of her brother and her little sister Anna. In 1937 her father died.

The end of one world coincided with the beginning of a new one. Inge was registered in the Horace Mann School of Columbia. Her new life was not easy. She was shy, after difficult years and five different schools in two years. Her Oxford English was forgotten, and there was no one who knew German to help her. All of us who grew up in those years as refugees remember the shame of our funny dresses, our accents, our ignorance of the most elementary facts of social life, such as Halloween, our wrong friendships.[48]

Dr. Bieber's loyalties were now directed toward Columbia University's Department of Fine Arts and Archaeology even though the absent-minded or single-minded chairman William Dinsmoor forgot to raise her salary and promoted her only in answer to a rival offer, when Professor Westermann, the eminent papyrologist, suggested that she teach archaeology in the Department of Greek and Latin.[49]

Columbia University's international reputation in those days was largely due to the European contacts of its president, Nicholas Murray Butler. When he received her and other foreign scholars in his residence on Morningside Drive, she was moved to see hanging on the wall the picture of his friend Gustav Stresemann. Dr. Bieber had long admired Stresemann as apostle of peace and founder of the liberal *Deutsche Volkspartei* in Germany, to which she had belonged.[50]

The work was strenuous and rewarding. As the department stressed independent research and publication over teaching, the students were often given short shrift; and they welcomed her energetic efforts and interest. She founded a new course, "Reading German for Art Historians." She collaborated with Professor Emerson Swift in the teaching of Roman Art in the department. Once, when she took over the class during his illness, she upset the students by giving them dates that conflicted with their textbook and Bible, the 1907 edition of Eugénie Strong's *Roman Sculpture*.[51] She took her students to the Metropolitan Museum to study the original monuments, teaching several courses in sculpture and painting there together with Gisela Richter.[52]

Her list of publications during these years is impressive: she prepared a special set of texts on the history of archaeology, *German Readings in the History and Theory of Fine Arts* (New York, 1946); her friend Alice Muehsam added *German Readings II*, for medieval through modern art. She continued to write for German publications.[53] From 1936 on, her reviews and articles also appeared more and more frequently in American scholarly journals. She felt she had to work twice as hard to make up for having to start all over again. Not being committed, like Americans and Englishmen, to taking weekends and vacations off, she devoted her time to research work, friends, and students. The latter often became her friends, and she derived much satisfaction from their successes.[54]

Yet she still felt bound to Giessen and was glad to hear from former students there.[55] After the war, she was made Senator for life of the University of Giessen. Her bibliography bears the seals of Giessen and Columbia, the two universities that received so much of her knowledge and affection.[56]

German colleagues who came to New York visited her, though she was not equally eager to see them all. She welcomed Robert Zahn, in 1938, and Hans Dragendorff, the great authority on Roman relief ware or *terra sigillata*. Her "Venus Genetrix des Arkesilaos,"[57] of 1933 had prompted an appreciative letter from Otto Brendel, then the assistant of Ludwig Curtius, director of the German Archaeological Institute in Rome. She and Brendel were destined to be in close contact when he came to Columbia University as Professor of Archaeology in 1956, inaugurating, with Rudolf Wittkower, a new and brilliant period for the department.

World War II (1939-1945) saw a transformation take place. During her early years in New York, she had felt "like a split person, with one leg still

in Germany across the ocean.'' In 1939 she applied for American citizen-
ship.[58] She worked hard for the examination, studied American history
along with Inge, and became enthusiastic about the Constitution and
democratic government, with its roots in the Athenian democracy of the
fifth century B.C. Thus she drew, in her words, her second leg energetically
over the ocean to America. She found she could help family and friends.
Her nephew Kurt joined her in the United States. Most of her family
emigrated, several, like Dr. Bieber, faring better in the United States and
Canada than in England. After the war, news of calamities came in a steady
stream. She learned of the Rodenwaldts' suicide and of the death of their
only son. Karl Anton Neugebauer died soon after his return from Russia.
Karl Kalbfleisch and his wife fled from a burning Giessen, and he died in
1946. One hundred and fifty German cities were destroyed by Allied
bombers.

The survivors needed help. During all of 1946 and 1947, Dr. Bieber and
Fräulein Freytag sent hundreds of parcels to former students, colleagues,
and old friends. She was asked for ''cleansing papers'' on behalf of many
Germans accused of war crimes who, threatened with losing their jobs, tried
to find Nazi victims who would testify in their favor. She was now placed
in a curious position of power when people wrote from whom she had not
heard since she emigrated.[59]

Her published work in this period, which was still considerable in spite of
all this activity, reflects her new interests and her influence on American
archaeology. There was *The History of the Greek and Roman Theater*
(1939), still used in theater courses throughout the country.[60] As usual, her
interdisciplinary approach opened her work to scholarly criticism,[61] at the
same time that it earned her the gratitude of a wider public to which specialized knowledge became available for the first time.[62] Her pragmatic approach fitted in with the down-to-earth character of archaeology in America, as can be seen in the numerous articles she published on works of art,
particularly sculpture, in this country: once isolated statues in Boston,
Toledo, Buffalo, Cleveland, and Chicago were put into a historical context.
A paper she read at the annual meetings of the Archaeological Institute of
America in 1941 was appropriately entitled ''Excavations in American
Museums.''[63]

She also contributed to the influx of German art-historical scholarship
that enriched American archaeology and classical studies in this period[64] by
her reviews of German books and by the necrologies she wrote for the
American Journal of Archaeology and the *American Journal of Philology*
on German scholars.[65] Two small books reflect her contact with graduate
students and her concern for their training. *Laocoon: The Influence of the
Group Since its Rediscovery*,[66] illustrated with new detailed photographs
obtained from Ernest Nash in Rome, as well as charming reproductions

of etchings and engravings, was, as she wrote in the preface, the result of the convergence of different studies, on the character of late Hellenistic art, on the views of ancient art of three great German "classical" authors, Winckelmann, Lessing, and Goethe, and on the best way of illustrating lectures on ancient art. As usual Dr. Bieber saw the subject from several points of view. Her old friend, Erwin Panofsky, suggested adding the section on the effect of the Laocoon on the artists of the sixteenth and seventeenth centuries. The passages from the German authors were included because Dr. Bieber, who instituted a course in "art-historical" German in the department, felt graduate students should become acquainted with important works of art criticism as well as with the works of art themselves. Her anthology of *German Readings in the History and Theory of Fine Arts* (1946), still in print and used by new generations of graduate students, was also the result of this concern.[67]

Her teaching and her writing made intelligible the more theoretical ideas of other scholars, for example in her review of Guido Kaschnitz von Weinberg's selected works, the *Ausgewählte Schriften*.[68] She had the ability to simplify an apparently bewildering variety, both in material and in ideas, and bring it into some kind of order. In her publications, too, she was teaching, making material available for others to work on. She had the courage to deal in larger areas, moving outside safe compartments of specialization—a courage some might call masculine.[69] The fear of making mistakes never held her back, but neither did the wish to appear "brilliant" mislead her to express audaciously controversial theories.[70]

Eminently practical and positive, she collected, remembered, and organized. But one must not confuse her interest in facts with lack of imagination. When she first started to work on her last book, *Ancient Copies: Contributions to the History of Greek and Roman Art* (1977), some fifty years ago, scholars were studying Roman copies almost exclusively as reflections of the more "sublime" Greek art. Only recently has her view that Roman copies were first of all Roman art become acceptable among art historians. The nineteenth-century taste for *realia*, the study of ancient life and society, which she never lost, is also returning, after the heady philosophy of the 1930s. We are grateful to her for preserving for us as a precious gift that solidity which she brought over with her from the nineteenth century. She was not afraid of her subconscious, nor of seeing the obvious. In the words of the citation which acompanied, in 1974, the award of the Archaeological Institute of America's gold medal for distinguished archaeological achievement, "A vivid sense of reality, especially human reality, kept her work always free from the mystifying abstractions of the European tradition as well as from the dry factuality of the American."[71]

Her practical sense, her feeling for the reality of an object, a person, or a work of art allowed her to feel at home in America. At the same time, the

German scholarly world in which she had grown up was, in fact, transplanted to America. Thus it was that, as a student of Otto Brendel and
Margarete Bieber, I was later, in turn, to feel surprisingly at home on
occasional visits to museums and universities in Germany.

"RETIREMENT"—ANOTHER NEW LIFE (1948-1978)

When Dr. Bieber was forced to retire from Columbia in 1948, the blow
was nearly as cruel as her dismissal in 1933. She had hoped to stay on until
she was seventy, with a sabbatical leave, like Professor Dinsmoor. She was
working with graduate students on their master's and doctor's theses and
had plans for research that involved expenses for photographs, secretarial
help, and travel. Inge was still in high school and would need money for
college. Unfortunately, President Butler, who had himself stayed on long
past the normal retirement age, was no longer there to back her up.

Once more, time marked a new beginning. The remarkable productivity
of these last thirty years makes one wonder whether the word "retirement"
is appropriate; it also brings up the question of the wisdom of enforced
retirement. As she says in the preface to her indispensable book, *The
Sculpture of the Hellenistic Age*, "the rules of Columbia University enforced my retirement, while I felt that I might do better work than ever
before."[72] Bollingen gave her a new lease on life by a grant that enabled
her to write this book and have it adequately illustrated. But she never
liked doing only research, and there was also the question of money.[73] In
spite of her many contributions to the Department of Fine Arts at Columbia, its chairman, William Dinsmoor, had never promoted her to full
professor. Not being an "Emerita," she could not continue to teach her
courses. She wanted to go on teaching, both because of the money and
because it was a central part of her life; in fact, the next few years were
busier than ever. For two years she taught a strenuous schedule of more
than twelve hours a week. During the six-week summer session at Columbia, where she had been teaching since 1940, she held classes all day. She
also taught at the New School Social Research, whose founder, Alvin
Johnson,[74] had set a precedent of hiring scholars persecuted by Hitler
(1948-1950); at Barnard College; and at the newly founded School of
General Studies at Columbia (1948-1956).

Then, in 1949, to her great surprise and delight, she was invited to be
visiting lecturer in Princeton, where, she said, no women, except some
language teachers, had ever taught. Professor Eric Sjövquist, on leave in
Rome as head of the International Institute (the old German Archaeological
Institute), was staying on there for another year at the request of the Crown
Prince of Sweden. The only person Princeton could find to take this one-
year vacancy at the last minute was Dr. Bieber. Her schedule now included

commuting two days a week to Princeton, where she taught during the day and saw old friends now at the Institute for Advanced Study, Hetty Goldman and the Panofskys. She also enjoyed the contact with her colleagues: Professor Albert M. Friend, the head of the Art Department, "whose name was true to his character"; Richard Stillwell and his wife, Agnes; Kurt Weitzmann, with whom she discussed problems of late Roman art; and Frances Jones and Ernest T. DeWald, both of the Princeton University Art Museum. At the end of the second year, the old king died, Sjövquist came back, and she had to leave, her fate depending, as she ruefully noted, on the life and death of the Swedish ruler.

Though she rejoiced in the variety of students she had in New York after her "retirement," the students at Princeton gave her the greatest satisfaction. Her life and her house were as always full of young people—including Inge's boyfriend—whose lives and careers concerned her closely. She liked to tell you about the dentist who took her course in Greek art at the New School and wrote a term paper on "The Smile through the Ages," or the delicate-looking girl she interviewed for an American Association of University Women grant, whose subject was "Despair in English Literature."

Her contacts with Europe were still close. On her seventieth birthday, 31 July 1949, she received as a *Festschrift* a box with books, articles, papers, photographs, and poems from former colleagues and students, a *Who's Who* of German archaeologists and intellectuals, as well as such European greats as Beazley. And then, in 1951/52, she went to Italy for the last time.

During those busy years of teaching she had decided to clear her desk, giving away several collections of material. Photographs and notes for a book on ancient portraits[75] she now gave to Gisela Richter, who used it in her book on Greek portraiture.[76] Two other projects still remain unpublished. To Mrs. Semne Karouzou in Athens went material for an article on some torsos from the storerooms in Athens, similar to some excavated in the Athenian Agora. The manuscript of the finds from Kos—finished in 1927 and never published—was sent to Carl Weickert at the German Archaeological Institute, in hopes that a young archaeologist would update and publish this material.

Some projects, however, she could not hand over to anyone else. Thirty years before, in Germany, she had started working on Roman copies of Greek draped statues.[77] In order to finish this project she asked for and received a small travel grant from the American Philosophical Society, which she supplemented with savings and the proceeds from the sale of part of her library.[78] On 25 September 1951, she sailed on the *Liberté*, the same ship that had brought Inge and Fräulein Freytag to America.

There were changes, but many old friends and old memories. In Paris she ran into her old friend Hans Möbius in the Bibliothèque Nationale. She came to Rome, the Mecca of archaeologists, in October. (Later, when I called on her to say goodbye before leaving for Rome in the summer, I would tell her I would miss her. She always answered firmly, "No, you won't. I never missed *anyone* when I was in Rome!")

The German Archaeological Institute was under the trusteeship of the United Nations. The library was still there, thanks to Friedrich Deichmann, who had saved it from the Nazis, and Charles Rufus Morey, who had saved it from the Allies, but it could not be used. During the week she worked in museums; on Sundays she roamed around, once again visited the Pantheon, munched roasted chestnuts for lunch. In the Museo Nazionale Romano she saw Salvatore Aurigemma, Enrico Paribeni, and Bianca Maria Felletti Maj, meeting the new generation of archaeologists.[79] In the Photographic Archives of the German Institute, she saw Raissa Calza, former wife of the painter de Chirico and widow of the excavator of Ostia Antica, which the Calzas had made a secret haven for hundreds sought by the Nazis during the German occupation.[80] With Hermine Speier, curator of the Vatican collection and editor of the new edition of Helbig's catalogue of Rome's museums,[81] she became close friends despite, as she says, the difference in their religions, for Hermine Speier had converted to Catholicism. She saw once more Ludwig Curtius, former director of the German Institute, and Guido Kaschnitz von Weinberg, its director when it reopened in 1954.[82] At the American Academy she was welcomed by the director, Frank Brown, and the librarian, Inez Longobardi. She saw her German colleagues, Reinhard Herbig and Georg Lippold, who had changed so little, "with his boyish expression and blue eyes, only his red hair was now white," and her American colleague Kurt Weitzmann. She met Luisa Banti, Etruscologist and Minoan scholar, who excavated with Luigi Pernier in Crete and who came to Barnard next year as a visiting professor;[83] and Paola Zancani Montuoro, who excavated the astonishing archaic temples at the mouth of the river Sele in southern Italy.[84]

In Florence she saw her old friend Else Milhaupt. Then down to Naples, to see Amedeo Maiuri, and the mosaics in the museum, to Pompeii and the Villa of the Mysteries, about which she had written important articles.[85] Naples was changed, the Aquarium neglected, the animals starved. Yet her eyes still caught the old Naples and the South Italy of antiquity: "the street life was still amusing, with singers and little scenes improvised as in ancient times."

And so, on board the *Constitution* and home again, back to New York and her busy life. She continued to teach in Columbia's School of General Studies until 1955 and in its Summer Session until 1956. Putting her books through the press took much time and energy. *The Sculpture of the Hellenistic Age* was chosen as one of twelve books to be printed in the Columbia University Bicentennial Editions and Studies as examples of current scholarship. The honor, as she said, seemed to her ironic: first they prevented her from teaching graduate courses and then they chose her to represent Columbia's scholarship! Soon after this honor came another. At the Bicentennial Convocation, on 31 October 1954, she was awarded the title of Doctor of Literature Honoris Causa. She describes the occasion in her memoirs. On the dais with President Grayson Kirk were forty other honorary degree candidates, including Queen Mother Elizabeth of England and Adlai Stevenson, for whom she had voted in the presidential election. At first she was frightened, but she felt more at home after meeting the noted classicist Lily Ross Taylor, who also received an honorary degree. There were only two other women, the Queen Mother and a Mexican poet. Losing her shyness, she talked to her neighbor, the German Foreign minister Heinrich von Brentano, representing Chancellor Adenauer, who turned out to have studied art history at Munich. She charmed everyone; later, she proudly reported, the applause that greeted every candidate was the third loudest for her—after the Queen Mother and Adlai Stevenson!

"Old Age" is the title of the chapter referring to the years 1956-1960, in the "Autobiography of a Female Scholar," which she wrote in her eightieth year. Old age did not arrive then, as she thought it would. Her retirement from Columbia and the loss of her office still seemed hard to her. She was deeply disappointed at not having been named Professor Emeritus, but she still felt very much a part of the University. As member of the Seminar on Classical Civilization—which she attended as long as she was able to leave the house and with which she always kept in touch—she figured officially in the Columbia University address book. Unofficially, she never stopped working with students. As always in her life, her house was full of young people and music. When you visited Dr. Bieber in the 1970s in her warm West Side apartment on West 113th Street near Broadway, you heard, coming from the room of the Chinese music student who lived with her, the sound of piano music. Emerging from the long book-filled corridor into a bright sunny room, recently painted despite her protest (she refused to believe that a rafter hanging Damocles-like above her head presented a real danger and must be removed), you faced her expectant smile. There she sat, in the armchair she ruefully called her "Old People's Home," fully in control of all the activity taking place around her. In the room next door, her young secretary-typist, Susan Schumer, was setting up the index to her forthcoming book on Roman copies of Greek draped statues ("I'm not interested in nude statues," Dr. Bieber used to say, smiling). Another young assistant worked on the catalogue of her coin collection, or made tea in the kitchen.

After her "archaeological accident," when she fell against an Ionic column in front of her house, she went out rarely, though she was active enough within the apartment and regularly made her own breakfast after

Fräulein Freytag's death in 1968. Her assistants, graduate students at Columbia in the Department of Art History and Archaeology, whom she had "adopted" like others before them, brought her the books she needed from the Columbia libraries. One assistant once brought to her house, on a field trip, the students with whom he was reading in Latin Cicero's treatise on old age, *De Senectute*. She was delighted and, turning the tables on them, interviewed them all closely, giving me a detailed report the next day about each one's projects and ambitions.

She received from the National Endowment for the Humanities a research grant for 1976 to work on her next book, on Greek, Etruscan, and Roman dress.[86] More involved, as usual, in new projects than in old ones, during the last few years, she surrounded herself with numismatic books and catalogues, as she worked on articles on portraits on coins.[87]

Her house in New York was a salon where one could meet scholars from all over the world. Her books—on the ancient theater, on Alexander the Great (1964),[88] and others—made available material in a form comprehensible to a wider public, and one always felt welcome in her house, whose openness must have reflected that of her homes in Athens, Rome, and Giessen. Among her visitors were also non-scholars, journalists like Joseph Alsop, and poets and artists like Ruth Vollmer and Vera Lachmann. The discussion might or might not be archaeological; all kinds of small, but not unimportant, things interested her. Anything but a "little old lady," for all her white hair and pretty smile, she was hardheaded but kind, gentle yet firm, and unafraid of the new or untried, for she knew that really important things never change. She accepted divorce and different lifestyles as a matter of course: her opinions were as realistic as her life, which she had so independently arranged. She was a shrewd judge of people. A younger colleague she once characterized as "a many-sided scholar; and some of these are right." Of another, she remarked that, though his work was first-rate, his character was not. Such critical moments were rare, in both her private life and her published work. The latter never exhibited that European tendency to demolish the work of previous scholars before getting to the point. As Salomon Reinach long ago noted in a review,[89] when she disagreed with another scholar's interpretation she simply ignored it, thus saving the reader time and patience. That was surely one reason that she produced so much, dealing so efficiently with such remarkable collections of material as those on the ancient theater, or Hellenistic sculpture, or Greek dress, or now her recent *Copies*, each one of which might justify a single scholar's life's work.

This realistic attitude she also exhibited in her scholarly work. When she was awarded the Archaeological Institute of America's gold medal for archaeological achievement at the society's Christmas meetings in 1974, the citation noted that "this sense of reality is perhaps her most precious gift to archaeology. Classical drapery, in her works, is still clothing, even when it reaches the heights of formal beauty and expressive power. Classical drama is a union of the several arts which went into its presentation and is never wholly cut off from its early simple roots.'' In her acceptance speech to this award, which meant more to her than any other, Dr. Bieber modestly replied that she was delighted to accept this honor and would do her best to deserve it.[90] That was in her ninety-fifth year; and she was true to her word.

In 1959 the University of Giessen named her honorary senator. In 1970 she was elected a member of the American Academy of Arts and Sciences. In fact, after she reached the age of ninety, honors, awards, and some degree of notoriety came to her as they never had before (Figure 16). She took many with a grain of salt, but conscientiously filled out questionnaires and submitted to interviews. Her example was an inspiration to many; an article in the *New York Times* gave new hope to many old people who read it, as they wrote to tell her.[91] On 31 July she celebrated her birthday quietly, happily receiving visits and good wishes from her family—her daughter, son-in-law, and grandchildren—and many friends, old and new. In October 1976, in her ninety-eighth year, she retired at last to her daughter and son-in-law's house in New Canaan, Connecticut. Here she kept up with her correspondence, spoke German once more with her daughter, enjoyed the company of her three grandchildren, and watched the changing colors of garden and country. In May 1977, she received the first copies of her latest book, *Ancient Copies*. When I went to see her she was reading Kleist, and Shaw's *Man and Superman*. She died in her sleep on 25 February 1978.

CONCLUSION

Working with people was always important to Dr. Bieber. In childhood she fiercely protected her little sister; later, and throughout her life within the stability and security of the scholarly world, she created "families" of bright young archaeologists at the German Institutes in Rome and Athens, of her students at Giessen, Columbia, and elsewhere, of assistants and younger colleagues in New York. This "family" feeling was characteristic of both her life and work, and in fact bound the two together. As soon as she had attained independence and a stable position, she adopted her daughter: her life was not complete without a family of her own. Teaching allowed her to educate the young, to take care of them, to follow their progress and enjoy their successes. Perhaps if she had been a little more aloof, more professionally calculating, she might have received recognition earlier, when it would have made her life easier. It might not have been so happy.

In the face of enormous difficulties—starting with being a woman to whom educational and professional opportunities were closed and through

Figure 16. Margarete Bieber in 1971, by Eric Magnuson. (*Courtesy Eric Magnuson*)

politics, poverty, war, and exile—her accomplishments, as a person and as a scholar, were remarkable. Difficulties seemed to make her stronger. Never resigned or bitter, she did not envy those who had gained more success, money, or recognition. She remained independent, spiritually and economically, working in her field and earning enough money from her profession to maintain herself and her family with dignity.

Her autobiography ends with a question: What would her life have been if Hitler had not forced her to emigrate? She would have travelled in classical lands, risen to the top of her career in Rome or in Berlin. She would have been a full professor, her handsome salary allowing her to pursue her research without financial worries. Her daughter Inge might have studied medicine, as she had dreamed, and married one of her former students. One the other hand, she muses, they might have been killed or crippled during World War II; and she would not have had the experience of living in the United States and meeting so many friends and colleagues. On the whole, it was an interesting life. If she never quite reached the top, she says, with characteristic pride, it was not because of external circumstances: it was because she did not fight hard enough.

In fact, she did fight hard, for others as well as for herself. She pioneered in many areas: in education, and a fuller life for women, combining career with motherhood; in interdisciplinary study, which she encouraged in her teaching and embodied in her books; in communicating knowledge to a wider public while maintaining high standards of scholarship; in the study and restoration of ancient statues; in making people aware of the contributions of people over seventy. Tenacious but not hard, flexible but not soft, she strengthened us by her example and enriched us with her work.

NOTES

The major source of Margarete Bieber's biography is her unpublished autobiography, "Memoirs of a Female Scholar," written in 1959, with a last chapter added in 1960. An account published in the *Korrespondenz Frauenpresse* 52 of 1 July 1929 summarizes her German career to 1933; an English translation appears in the necrology by Evelyn Harrison in *American Journal of Archaeology* 82 (1978), pp. 573-75. Two newspaper interviews featured Dr. Bieber's expertise in the field of classical sculpture: Peter Kihss, "Women in Science: She Finds Out What Makes Statues Tick," *New York World-Telegram*, 24 January 1942; and George McCue, "Is City's $56,000 'Diana' a Fake?," *St. Louis Post-Dispatch, The Everyday Magazine*, 20 July 1958. For Dr. Bieber's career at Columbia University, see William Bell Dinsmoor, "The Department of Fine Arts and Archaeology," in *A History of the Faculty of Philosophy, Columbia University* (New York, 1957), pp. 252-69, especially pp. 262-63. On the occasion of Dr. Bieber's ninetieth birthday, several articles and interviews appeared. Among them, E.R., "Griechische Tracht. Margarete Bieber wurde 90," *Frankfurter Allgemeine Zeitung*, 8 February 1969; a letter to her friends is included with her article in "Women and Ideas: Roman Copies as Roman Art," *Columbia Forum* 13 (1970), pp. 36-39. There followed interviews with Dr. Bieber regarding her views on old age: Rita Rief, "At 91, A Historian Relates the Story of Her Own Life," *New York Times*, 22 May 1971; and Larissa Bonfante

Warren, *"De Senectute*—On Old Age," *Cold Duck* (New York University Student Magazine) 8, 16 October 1972, pp. 10-15. For Dr. Bieber's continued creative activity as a scholar, see "NEH Grant Profiles: The Seniorest Fellow," *National Endowment for the Humanities* II, 2 (March 1972), p. 3; the citation read on the occasion of the award of the gold medal of the Archaeological Institute of America, and Dr. Bieber's response, in the *American Journal of Archaeology* 79 (1975), pp. 146-47; and *Archaeology* 28 (1975), pp. 74-75. See also Rolf Winkes, "Margarete Bieber zum 95. Geburtstag," *Giessener Universitätsblätter* 7 (June 1974), pp. 68-75, and a newspaper article, W. Nippert, "Modellkleider für die Griechinnen," *Giessener Allgemeine Zeitung* 289 (13 December 1974), p. 7. For her place in the history of women in German universities, see Elisabeth Boedeker and Maria Meyer-Plath, *50 Jahre Habilitation von Frauen in Deutschland: 1920-1970* (Hanover, 1974), No. 1, pp. 15-16. For her role in the history of the German Archaeological Institute, see Lothar Wickert, *Das Deutsches Archäologisches Institut Geschichte und Dokumente* II: *Beiträge zur Geschichte des Deutschen Archäologischen Instituts von 1879 bis 1929* (Mainz, 1979), pp. 15, 17. Among the many accounts of Dr. Bieber's life in biographical dictionaries, the most recent was that in the *International Who's Who* (42nd ed., 1978-79). For obituaries, see the *New York Times*, 28 February 1978; Evelyn B. Harrison, *American Journal of Archaeology* 82 (1978), pp. 573-75; and Larissa Bonfante, *Gnomon* 51 (1979), pp. 621-24. Unpublished papers and correspondence are in the possession of DR. Bieber's daughter and, along with her books, in the Tulane University Library, New Orleans, Louisiana. The author's correspondence and conversations with Dr. Bieber from 1958 to 1978 also furnished information.

1. I wish to thank Dr. Bieber's daughter Inge Sachs (Mrs. William S. Sachs) for her help and for allowing me to quote from her mother's unpublished autobiography and other papers.

2. Later director of the Askanische Gymnasium in Berlin.

3. Even classicists were often reluctant to teach women. For Wilamovitz on teaching women see William M. Calder III, *Harvard Studies in Classical Philology* 81 (1977), 277, n. 13. See, however, the list of Loeschcke's students (note 4 following).

4. Georg Loeschcke (1852-1915), editor, with Adolf Furtwängler, of *Mykenische Vasen* (1886), author of works on ancient Greek and provincial Roman art. Of his influence Margarete Bieber said (*American Journal of Archaeology* 79 [1975], 147): "The method of teaching which I learned from my teacher in Bonn, the eminent Professor Georg Loeschcke, I have transferred to my students here. This method consists of studying the character, intelligence, and inclinations of the individual students and then giving them work in a field consistent with their special qualities." See Paul Friedländer, "Erinnerung an Georg Loeschcke," *Bonner Jahrbücher* 152 (1952), 13-16; and Franz Oelmann, "Zum hundertsten Geburtstag Georg Loeschckes," *Bonner Jahrbücher* 152 (1952), 1-12. Franz Oelmann includes a list of Loeschcke's students (11), a photograph of his portrait, and a useful bibliography (12). Friedländer (15) remembers Loeschcke's remark to him, "I'm not a scholar, I'm a teacher" ("Ich bin ja kein Gelehrter, ich bin ein Lehrer!"). Of course he was a great scholar; but much of his warmth and energy went into teaching, with evident success.

Reinhard Kékulé von Stradonitz (1839-1911) edited *Die antiken Terrakotten* (Berlin and Stuttgart, 1880-1911).

5. *Das Dresdner Schauspielerrelief. Ein Beitrag zur Geschichte des tragischen Kostüms und der griechischen Kunst*, published in 1907.

6. She was a good one. Once she recognized the symptoms of typhoid fever, misdiagnosed by the drunken family doctor. Her knowledge of Latin saved her sister Gertrud's child during a difficult delivery, when she opposed a doctor's order, given in Latin, to crush the baby's head; mother and child survived.

7. According to her "Memoirs," when she had applied before, Professor Ernst Fabricius had been against having any woman receive that fellowship while he was director of the German Archaeological Institute: now that he had been overridden, she had the pleasure of reading his signature on the form letter, "I am happy to inform you. . . ."

8. Was she ostracized as a woman, as she claims in her "Memoirs," or as a Jew, as has been suggested?

9. Also a Jew.

10. He went to Berlin in 1922. In 1945 he committed suicide: see text.

11. Georg Lippold edited Paul Arndt, Friedrich Bruckmann, *Griechische und römische Porträts* (Munich, 1891-1942); and Paul Arndt, Walther Amelung, Georg Lippold, *Photographische Einzelaufnahmen antiker Skulpturen* (Munich, 1893-1941).

12. Eduard Schmidt, *Archaistische Kunst in Griechenland und Rom* (Munich, 1922). Hugo Prinz (1883-1934), *Funde aus Naukratis* (Leipzig, 1908).

13. Hans Nachod (1885-1958), *Der Rennwagen bei den Italikern und ihren Nachbarn* (Diss. Leipzig, 1909).

14. "Die Mosaiken des Dioskurides von Samos," *Jahrbuch des deutschen archäologischen Instituts* 26 (1911), 1-22.

15. "Wiederholungen einer Satyrspielvase in Athen und Bonn," *Mitteilungen des deutschen archäologischen Instituts, Abteilung Athen*, 36 (1911), 269-77.

16. "Die Medaillons am Konstantinsbogen," *Mitteilungen des deutschen archäologischen Instituts, Abteilung Rom* 26 (1911), 214-37.

17. She was elected "corresponding member" in 1912; regular member in 1922. Studniczka had been substituting for the director of the German Institute after C. Hülsen, before Richard Delbrueck became director.

18. "Bericht über Arbeiten im Museum von Kassel," *Archäologischer Anzeiger* 29 (1914), 1-32.

19. *Die antiken Skulpturen und Bronzen des Kgl. Museum Fridericianum in Cassel* (Marburg, 1915). Even today, each piece is neatly labeled with a "Bieber Nr."

20. "Vestalin im Thermenmuseum in Rom," and "Vestalinnen im Atrium der Vesta auf dem Forum in Rom," in *Photographische Einzelaufnahmen antiker Skulpturen* (1929), Nos. 3217-30.

21. Valentin Müller was later to teach at Bryn Mawr College (1930-1947).

22. Bruno Paul became a famous interior decorator.

23. For Erwin Panofsky's account of his career in Germany and the United States, see "Epilogue. Three Decades of Art History in the U.S.: Impressions of a Transplanted European," *Meaning in the Visual Arts* (New York, 1955), 321-46. Elizabeth Jastrow later taught in Greensboro, North Carolina (1941-61).

24. From Dr. Bieber's "Memoirs."

25. "Ikonographische Miszellen. 1. Das Porträt des Sokrates. 2. Aristophanes. 3. Das Relief aus dem attischen Ölwald," *Jahrbuch des deutschen archäologischen Instituts, Abteilung Rom*, 32 (1917), 117-46. "Die Herkunft des tragischen Kostüms," *Jahrbuch des deutschen archäologischen Instituts* 32 (1917), 15-104. "Der Chiton der ephesischen Amazonen," *Jahrbuch . . .* 33 (1918), 49-75.

26. Later Professor of Archaeology at Tübingen.

27. She came in 1917 and stayed with Dr. Bieber until her death in New York in 1968, at the age of 84.

28. *Die Denkmäler zum Theaterwesen im Altertum* (Berlin and Leipzig, 1920). The *Habilitationsschrift* was a publishable scholarly work qualifying the candidate for university teaching *(Habilitation)*. When she was "habilitated," she obtained the *venia legendi* (permission to lecture) as a *Privatdozentin*, an instructor receiving no salary, but dependent on "contributions" by her students (Hörgeld). (See Panofsky, "Three Decades of Art History," nn. 4, 6.)

29. "Späthellenistische Frauenstatuen aus Kos," *Antike Plastik. Walther Amelung zum 60. Geburtstag* (Berlin and Leipzig, 1928), 16-24. "Die koische Aphrodite des Praxiteles," *Zeitschrift für Numismatik* 34 (1923), 315-20.

30. Her publications reflect this new interest: "Die ältesten Darstellungen der Hessen," *Heimat im Bilde* (Giessen, 1928). In this respect also she was probably influenced by Loeschcke.

Wilhelm Gundel, well-known historian of science, was her colleague at Giessen. Siegfried Loeschcke was the son of her former professor, and also an archaeologist; Dr. Bieber later wrote his necrology, in *American Journal of Archaeology* 62 (1958), 105.

31. "Die Form der mittelalterlichen Grabtumben," *Hessen Kunstkalender* (1924), 39ff. "Der Mysteriensaal der Villa Item," *Jahrbuch* (see note 85) 43 (1928), 298-330. See also Warren-Winkes, *Bibliography*.

32. *Griechische Kleidung* (Berlin and Leipzig, 1928). For Amelung's *Festschrift*, see note 29. Their scholarly interests were close. He wrote an important, original study of ancient dress: W. Amelung, *Die Gewandung der alten Griechen und Römer* (1903). As Dr. Bieber had been the last to discuss his projects with him, his widow asked her to publish some of his papers, for example, an unfinished manuscript on the reconstruction of the head of an athlete by the Greek sculptor Myron: "Wiederherstellung einer myronischen Athletenstatue durch Walther Amelung," *Jahrbuch des deutschen archäologischen Instituts* 42 (1927), 152-57. By some strange chance, the offprints of this article were found in a cellar in Berlin fifty years later and sent to her in New York in 1975.

33. Cf. Erwin Panofsky, "Three Decades of Art History," 336: "when, by 1923, my private fortune had been consumed by the inflation, I was made a paid assistant of the very seminar of which I was the unpaid director . . . [an] interesting post of assistant to myself, created by a benevolent State. . . ."

34. I am grateful to Elizabeth Boedeker for confirming this information.

35. The new dean, Karl Viëtor, later appointed a professor at Harvard, died in 1953.

36. Many, unfortunately, died later in the war. Closest to her were three students who wrote their doctoral dissertations with her: Ernst Rink, her assistant, who wrote on the representation of the personification of the Roman Genius, *Die bildlichen Darstellungen des römischen Genius* (1933). Karl Bettermann, who wrote on Roman ceramics in Germany, *Die bemalte Keramik der frühen römischen Kaiserzeit im rheinischen Germanien* (1932), died in World War II. Julius Froeber wrote an important work on Greek metopes: *Die Komposition der archaischen und frühklassischen griechischen Metopenbilder* (1933). Another dear student, Hermann Klöter, wrote on the Greek sculptor Myron; while Alfons Beck, who started work with her but finished under another professor, wrote on the Christian angels and their pagan prototypes: *Die Typen der christlichen Engel und ihre heidnischen Vorbilder* (1936). Many of her students from Giessen, like Hans Gundel, son of the famous historian of science and himself also a professor at Giessen, long kept in touch with her.

37. *Entwicklungsgeschichte der griechischen Tracht* (published in 1934). In 1925 a fellowship from the Notgemeinschaft der Deutschen Wissenschaften and Deutsches Archäologisches Institut had allowed her to travel to Athens, Rome, and Constantinople, to study Greek dress and the sculpture from Kos and to prepare *Griechische Kleidung* for the press.

38. Georg Jaffé and Julius Lewy went to the United States: Jaffé to become a professor at Baton Rouge, Louisiana, and then to retire to Berkeley, Lewy to Hebrew Union College, Cincinnati. Dr. Bieber was not Jewish in religion. Her religious training as a child had been minimal; later, as a young adult, when she was attending the University in Bonn, she had joined the *Altkatholiken*, the "Old Catholic religion," a group which broke with Rome over the issue of papal infallibility in 1870. She enjoyed reading the Bible and discussing theological questions, intellectually rather than passionately, and had a distaste for the Catholic religion.

39. On the Ph.D. exams of students ousted by the laws of spring 1933, still possible in the initial stages of the Nazi regime, see Panofsky, "Three Decades of Art History," 321-22.

40. In fact von Salis, a *Privatdozent* when she studied in Bonn, later left Heidelberg for a lesser position in Zürich, away from Nazism.

41. Fritz M. Heichelheim later became professor of ancient history at Toronto and published a very successful text book: Fritz Heichelheim and Cedric A. Yeo, *A History of the Roman People* (Englewood Cliffs, New Jersey, 1962).

42. Two were in Oxford: Eduard Fränkel, Corpus Christi Professor of Latin, and Paul

Jacobsthal, who published with Beazley monographs on Greek vases, *Early Celtic Art* (Oxford, 1944), and, shortly before his death, *Greek Pins and Their Connections with Europe and Asia* (Oxford, 1956).

43. For example a Hellenistic Muse, the head of a Hellenistic ruler, a replica of the Apollo Lykaios of Praxiteles, a replica of the Hermes of Alkamenes, etc. ("Memoirs").

44. The Archaeological Club was founded in 1921: Gisela M. A. Richter, *My Memoirs: Recollections of an Archaeologist's Life* (Rome, 1972), 34-35. See Chapter 10 of this volume.

45. Some of the lectures on the Laocoon controversy she later published in a little book, *Laocoon: The Influence of the Group Since Its Rediscovery* (New York, 1942).

46. Later called the *Liberté*. Dr. Bieber described the ship, redecorated by the French, as "combining German solidity and French grace, just as in Inge French and German qualities are united."

47. The library, one of the few scholarly collections of this period to have come to America, was bought in 1975 by Tulane University, New Orleans, Louisiana.

48. Inge eventually finished high school at Riverdale Country School, went on to college, married Dr. William S. Sachs, a professor of economics, and became the mother of Dr. Bieber's three adored grandchildren.

49. As she was never, in fact, promoted to full professor, her title remained what it had been in Germany when she left. What really hurt her was that, since she was not a full professor at the time of her retirement in 1948, she could not become "Emerita" and go on lecturing in the department. I thank Evelyn Harrison for the explanation of the situation.

50. Gustav Stresemann, 1878-1929, German Minister of Foreign Affairs, 1923-1929. Butler, Dean of the Faculty of Philosophy, 1890-1901, and President of the University, 1901-1945, tells of his friendship with Stresemann in his memoirs, *Recollections and Reflections: Across the Busy Years* (New York and London, 1940), 144, 303-04. The picture Dr. Bieber saw is probably the photograph, signed by Stresemann, reproduced facing page 144.

51. Eugénie Sellers Strong, *Roman Sculpture* (London, 1907; 1911); *La scultura romana*, a revision of this book (Florence, 1923-1926). She showed Professor Swift a letter from the great scholar Eugénie Strong herself, written in 1932, asking his advice on the revision of this book, and provided him and his class with literature he had missed when his interest had shifted to early Christian art, in preparation for his book, *Roman Sources of Christian Art* (1951).

52. Dinsmoor, "Department of Fine Arts and Archaeology," 262.

53. For example the dictionary of ancient artists, *Allgemeines Lexikon der bildenden Künstler von der Antike bis zur Gegenwart*, edited by Ulrich Thieme and Felix Becker, writing all the articles on Greek sculptors from *K* to *Z* after Walther Amelung had given up doing them; and the *Photographische Einzelaufnahmen antiker Skulpturen*, edited by her friend Georg Lippold after the illness and death of Paul Arndt. See bibliography, 1929, 1931, 1933, 1937, 1947 (Thieme-Becker), cf. *Colliers Encyclopedia* 1956; 1938, 1940, 1943, 1947 *(Einzelaufnahmen)*.

54. She was proudest of Evelyn Harrison, her student and, in the German tradition, as it were, her successor at Columbia before going on to Princeton and the Institute of Fine Arts. (See her answer to the presentation of the Archaeological Institute of America's Gold Medal, in preceding note 4). She wrote at length in her memoirs of other students, many of whom kept in touch: Sidney Markman, who wrote his dissertation on *The Horse in Greek Art* (Baltimore, 1943); Penelope Dimitrov and her unpublished dissertation on "Color in Greek Sculpture"; Thalia Phillies Howe, Alfred Russell, Cecil Golann, Cecilia Sieu-Ling Zung, the first of many Chinese in her life, and others.

55. See note 36.

56. Larissa Bonfante Warren, Rolf Winkes, *Bibliography of the Works of Margarete Bieber. For her 90th Birthday July 31, 1969* (New York, 1969). Rolf Winkes received his Ph.D. from the University of Giessen, Larissa Bonfante [Warren] from Columbia University.

57. "Die Venus Genetrix des Arkesilaos," *Mitteilungen des deutschen archäologischen Instituts, Abteilung Rom* 48 (1933), 261-76.

58. She became a United States citizen 26 September 1940.

59. Her former colleague Fritz Moritz Heichelheim, who later went to Toronto, refused to write in favor of Rudolf Herzog, their dean at Giessen. Dr. Bieber wrote a sympathetic defense. There were problems of conscience, and it was a shock for her to learn that Martin Schede, who had succeeded Theodor Wiegand as Director of the German Archaeological Institute under the Nazi regime, had died of starvation in a Russian concentration camp.

60. *The History of the Greek and Roman Theater* (Princeton, 1939; rev. ed. 1961).

61. See Warren-Winkes, *Bieber Bibliography* for reviews. In general, archaeologists had reservations about the archaeological material but praised the philological sections, while philologists found the archaeological sections excellent.

62. See Panofsky, "Three Decades of Art History," 330, on the reaction of German art historians of his generation to the different atmosphere in the United States: "we suddenly found the courage to write books on whole periods instead of—or besides—writing a dozen specialized articles. . . ." Dr. Bieber had already had the courage, before leaving Germany, to write the definitive book on Greek dress in its historical context: *Entwicklungsgeschichte der griechischen Tracht* (Berlin, 1934). See note 69.

63. "Excavations in American Museums," *American Journal of Archaeology* 46 (1942), 125; "An Attic Tombstone in the Art Institute of Chicago," *Art in America* 30 (1942), 104-9; and others. More than twenty-five years later, she was publishing "The Statue of Cybele in the J. Paul Getty Museum," *J. Paul Getty Publication* No. 3 (Malibu, California, 1968). On "Anglo-Saxon positivism which is, in principle, distrustful of abstract speculation," see Panofsky, "Three Decades of Art History," 329.

64. Panofsky, "Three Decades of Art History," 321-46.

65. She wrote necrologies in the *American Journal of Archaeology* and the *American Journal of Philology* for Ernst Pfuhl (1941), Johannes Boehlau (1942), Gerhart Rodenwaldt, Heinrich Bulle, Karl Anton Neugebauer (1946), Hans Schrader, Ernst Fiechter (1949), Camillo Praschniker, Carl Watzinger (1950), Wilhelm Dörpfeld (1953), Ludwig Curtius, Georg Lippold (1955), Siegfried Loeschcke, Arnold von Salis (1958), and Franz Oelmann (1964); for Alice Muehsam in the *Art Journal* (1968). Her last publication was "Otto Brendel: A Memorial Notice," in *Archaeological News* 5 (1976), 3-4.

66. *Laocoon: The Influence of the Group Since its Rediscovery* (New York, 1942). See note 45.

67. *German Readings in the History and Theory of Fine Arts. I. Greek and Roman Art* (New York, 1946); *German Readings: A Short Survey of Greek and Roman Art for Students of German and Fine Arts* (New York, second revised edition 1950); *German Readings I: A Short Survey of Greek and Roman Art for Students of German and Fine Arts* (Philadelphia, third edition 1958; reprint New York, 1968). When taking the course on reading art-historical German in 1958—it was taught, after Dr. Bieber's retirement, by her friend Alice Muehsam—I enthusiastically resolved to translate into English Alois Riegl's *Stilfragen* (Berlin, 1893), or his *Spätrömische Kunstindustrie* (Vienna, 1901): Professor Meyer Schapiro even recommended the idea to a publisher. I mention this incident as an example of the excitement caused by German works and by the scholars who taught us to see the hidden riches beneath the surface of what we thought we knew.

68. "A Monument for Guido Kaschnitz von Weinberg: a review article of selected writings of Guido Kaschnitz von Weinberg, the *Ausgewählte Schriften* (Berlin 1965)," in *American Journal of Archaeology* 71 (1967), 361-86. "Kaschnitz shares Riegl's [Alois Riegl's *Spätrömische Kunstindustrie*, 1901] violent reaction against the materialistic conception of art held by . . . art historians of the nineteenth century, and against reconstructing the history of art only from literary sources . . . ," 362.

The conclusion illustrated her method, style, and judgment. "One may contrast this gigantic work with a modest volume . . . , Karl Schefold, *Römische Kunst als religiöses Phänomen* . . . . One may call his style transparent, while that of Kaschnitz is transcendent. The new edition of *Die Antike*, in the *Propyläenkunstgeschichte* by Rodenwaldt, entrusted to Schefold, may attain the ideal of transparency, transmitting ways of light without diffusion so that bodies behind may be clearly seen. . . . Kaschnitz has really penetrated into fundamental principles and has grasped precise ideas behind the phenomena, the objects of direct perception, of Greek and Roman art. The study of this work, therefore, is difficult but rewarding. . . ," 386.

69. See note 62. As my colleague Kenan Erim points out, most of the standard works in archaeology were written by women scholars: Marion E. Blake, *Ancient Roman Construction in Italy from the Prehistoric Period to Augustus*—a chronological study based in part upon the material accumulated by Esther Boise von Deman (Washington, 1947); *Roman Construction in Italy from Nerva through the Antonines*, edited and completed by Doris Taylor Bishop (Philadelphia, 1973). Mary Swindler, *Ancient Painting* (Oxford, 1929); Eugénie Strong, *Roman Sculpture from Augustus to Constantine* (London, 1907); Gisela Richter, *Korai* (London, 1968), *Kouroi* (London, 1942), *Handbook of Greek Art* (London, 1959), *Greek Portraits* (Brussels, 1955-1962). See Chapter 2 of this volume for further information on these women archaeologists; and for Gisela Richter, Chapter 10.

70. Thus one can understand apparently contradictory criticism such as the following: "Controversy lurks on almost every page. . . . In general, Miss Bieber's positions are marked by conservatism and caution." Roy C. Flickinger, review of *The History of the Greek and Roman Theater* (1939), *Classical Weekly* 35 (1940), 71.

71. *American Journal of Archaeology* 79 (1975), 146.

72. *The Sculpture of the Hellenistic Age* (New York, 1955), vii.

73. Her pension, she once told me, was the same as that of a cleaning lady. Whether true or not, the statement reflects her feelings.

74. On the role of the New School for Social Research and its director, Alvin Johnson, in helping refugee scholars carry on their academic careers, see Maurice R. Davie, *Refugees in America* (New York and London, 1947), 303, 317.

75. Her proposed collaboration with the numismatist Agnes Baldwin Brett (Mrs. George M. Brett) had not worked out.

76. Gisela M. A. Richter, *The Portraits of the Greeks* (London, 1965).

77. *Ancient Copies: Contributions to the History of Greek and Roman Art* (New York, 1977), Preface, v: "I had already written some chapters in German when I had to leave Germany and emigrated to the United States. Bruno Schröder [the scholar and artist with whom she had been collaborating] took his life when he was persecuted by the Nazis for his anti-Hitler attitude."

78. *Antike Denkmäler* went to Havana, purchased by the Count de Lagunies, a collector, then Minister of Education in Cuba.

79. Bianca Maria Felletti Maj (1908-1979). *La tradizione italica nell'arte romana* (Rome, 1977), attempts to characterize the "Romanness" of Roman art, at the same time collecting the evidence on which such attempts have been based; it may be added to the list in n. 69. See Larissa Bonfante, *American Journal of Archaeology* 83 (1979), 242-44.

80. Raissa Calza, *Ostia* (Florence, 1959); *Scavi di Ostia: I ritratti* (Rome, 1964-1977); *Iconografia romana imperiale* (Rome, 1972), etc.

81. Wolfgang Helbig, *Führer durch die öffentlichen Sammlungen klassischer Altertümer in Rom* (4th edition, edited by Hermine Speier, Tübingen, 1963-72).

82. See note 68.

83. Luisa Banti (1894-1978) taught at Columbia as visiting professor 1953-54. She died 17 February 1978, a week before Margarete Bieber, at her home in Florence, after having finished her book on the excavations of Haghia Triada.

84. Paola Zancani Montuoro, Umberto Zanotti-Bianco, *L'Heraion alla foce del Sele* (Rome, 1951-1954).

85. "Der Mysteriensaal der Villa Item," *Jahrbuch des deutschen archäologischen Instituts* 43 (1928), 298-330. "The Mystery Frescoes in the Mystery Villa of Pompeii," *Review of Religion* 2 (1937), 3-11.

86. National Endowment for the Humanities; renewed for 1977. The book will be completed by the author of this essay, together with Dr. Bieber's former assistant on this project, Eva Jaunzems.

87. The first appeared in 1973: "The Development of Portraiture on Roman Republican Coins," *Aufstieg und Niedergang der römischen Welt*, ed. Hildegard Temporini, I.4 (Berlin, 1973), 871-98. The other two, on coins of the Principate and of the later Empire, she would have finished had her numismatic assistant not left.

88. *The History of the Greek and Roman Theater* (Princeton, 1939, 1961); *Alexander the Great in Greek and Roman Art* (Chicago, 1964).

89. Salomon Reinach, review of *Griechische Kleidung* (Berlin and Leipzig, 1928), *Revue archéologique* 28 (1928), 164. Dr. Bieber told me of a meeting with Salomon Reinach in Paris, after World War I. She was afraid to find the French scholars hostile to her as a German: but Salomon Reinach, who came to meet her at the train station, allayed her fears at once, saying, "Madame, tous les savants vous attendent avec impatience."

90. *American Journal of Archaeology* 79 (1975), 147.

91. Rita Rief, "At 91, A Historian Relates the Story of Her Own Life," *New York Times*, 22 May 1971.

SELECTED BIBLIOGRAPHY OF MARGARETE BIEBER

A list of published works to 1969—327 items—may be found in Larissa Bonfante Warren and Rolf Winkes, *Bibliography of the Works of Margarete Bieber. For her 90th Birthday* (Privately printed for Columbia University, New York, 1969). Addenda, 1969-1974, were published in the *American Journal of Archaeology* 79 (1975), pp. 147-48; and *Giessener Universitätsblätter* 1 (1974), pp. 74-75. The following bibliography, based on these publications, contains a second section, Miscellaneous Additions to the Bibliography of Margarete Bieber.

Books

Das Dresdner Schauspielerrelief. Ein Beitrag zur Geschichte des tragischen Kostüms und der griechischen Kunst (Bonn, 1907).
Die antiken Skulpturen und Bronzen des Kgl. Museum Fridericianum in Cassel (Marburg, 1915).
Die Denkmäler zum Theaterwesen im Altertum (Berlin and Leipzig, 1920).
Griechische Kleidung (Berlin and Leipzig, 1928).
Entwicklungsgeschichte der griechischen Tracht von der vorgriechischen Zeit bis zur römischen Kaiserzeit (Berlin, 1934; second edition, revised by Felix Eckstein, 1967).
The History of the Greek and Roman Theater (Princeton, 1939; second revised edition 1961).
German Readings in the History and Theory of Fine Arts, I. Greek and Roman Art (New York, 1946; second revised edition 1950; reprint 1968).
Laocoon: The Influence of the Group Since Its Rediscovery (New York, 1942; second revised edition, Detroit, 1967).
The Sculpture of the Hellenistic Age (New York, 1955; second revised edition 1961).
Alexander the Great in Greek and Roman Art (Chicago, 1964).
Ancient Copies: Contributions to the History of Greek and Roman Art (New York, 1977).

Articles

With Gerhart Rodenwaldt, "Die Mosaiken des Dioskurides von Samos," *Jahrbuch des deutschen archäologischen Instituts* 26 (1911), pp. 1-22.

"Bericht über Arbeiten im Museum von Kassel," *Archäologischer Anzeiger* 29 (1914), pp. 1-32.

Articles on Greek sculptors for Ulrich Thieme and Felix Becker, eds., *Allgemeines Lexikon der bildenden Künstler von der Antike bis zur Gegenwart* (1929-1947).

Articles on Greek sculpture for Georg Lippold, ed., *Einzelaufnahmen antiker Skulpturen* (1938-1947).

"Der Mysteriensaal der Villa Item," *Jahrbuch des deutschen archäologischen Instituts* 43 (1928), pp. 298-330.

"Die Venus Genetrix des Arkesilaos," *Mitteilungen des deutschen archäologischen Instituts, Abteilung Rom* 48 (1933), pp. 261-76.

"The Mystery Frescoes in the Mystery Villa of Pompeii," *Review of Religion* 2 (1937), pp. 3-11.

"Excavations in American Museums," *American Journal of Archaeology* 46 (1942), p. 125.

"Greek Sculpture in the Cleveland Museum of Art," *Art in America* 31 (1943), pp. 113-26.

"Roman Sculpture in the Cleveland Museum of Art," *Art in America* 32 (1944), pp. 65-83.

"Archaeological Contributions to the Roman Religion (Two Graeco-Roman Statues in Buffalo, Albright Art Gallery)," *Hesperia* 14 (1945), pp. 270-77.

"The Normative Approach of Scholarship in the Classics, Answer to Prof. Grube," Princeton, 7 September 1949 (unpublished typescript).

Sir Arthur Wallace Pickard-Cambridge, Necrology, *American Journal of Archaeology* 57 (1953), pp. 113-14.

With Dietrich von Bothmer, "Archaeological Notes: Notes on the Mural Paintings from Boscoreale," *American Journal of Archaeology* 60 (1956), pp. 171-72.

"Costume teatrale," "Romano teatro," "Scenografia," "Scenotecnica," etc., *Enciclopedia dello Spettacolo* (1956-1962).

"The Aqua Marcia on Coins and in Ruins," *Archaeology* 20 (1967), pp. 194-96.

"The Statue of Cybele in the J. Paul Getty Museum," *J. Paul Getty Museum Publication* No. 3 (Malibu, California, 1968), 27 pp.

Reviews

Louis Séchan, *Études sur la tragédie grecque dans ses rapports avec la céramique* (1926), *Gnomon* 7 (1931), pp. 241-45.

Arnold von Salis, *Theseus und Ariadne* (1930), *Gnomon* 11 (1935), pp. 254-58.

Ludwig Curtius, *Die klassische Kunst Griechenlands* (1938), *American Journal of Archaeology* 43 (1939), pp. 528-29.

Lillian M. Wilson, *The Clothing of the Ancient Romans* (1938), *American Journal of Archaeology* 43 (1939), pp. 171-73.

Hans Peter L'Orange-Arnim von Gerkan, *Der spätantike Bildschmuck des Konstantinsbogens* (1939), *American Journal of Archaeology* 44 (1940), pp. 410-14.

Arnold von Salis, *Antike und Renaissance. Über Nachleben und Weiterwirken der alten in der neueren Kunst* (1947), *American Journal of Philology* 70 (1949), pp. 320-25.

Reinhard Herbig, *Die Terracottagruppe einer Diana mit dem Hirschkalb* (1956), *American Journal of Archaeology* 62 (1958), pp. 341-43. Discusses controversial "St. Louis Diana."

A Review. Rhys Carpenter, *Greek Sculpture, A Critical Review* (1960), *American Journal of Archaeology* 66, *In Honor of Gisela M.A. Richter* (1962), pp. 237-44. Defends view of "female scholars," Bieber and Richter, and discusses golden section.

A Monument for Guido Kaschnitz von Weinberg, Review article of *Ausgewählte Schriften* (1965), *American Journal of Archaeology* 71 (1967), pp. 361-86.

Miscellaneous Additions to the Bibliography of Margarete Bieber

Athen. Aus Welt und Winkel, Beiblatt *"Frankfurter Nachrichten"* (18 August 1925), p. 5.

Ein Meisterwerk frühgriechischer Kunst, *Unterhaltungsbeilage der Schlesischen Zeitung* 83 (Breslau, 18 October 1925).

Review of Margarete Bieber, *Griechische Kleidung* (1928), by Salomon Reinach, *Revue archéologique* 28 (1928), p. 164.

Report on Grants No. 1286 (1950) and No. 1406 (1952). Research on copies of Greek draped statues and of Greek portraits made in the Roman period, *Year Book of The American Philosophical Society* (1952), pp. 283-85.

Report on Grant No. 3411 (1963). History of copying in the Roman period, *Year Book of The American Philosophical Society* (1964), pp. 449-50.

The Images of Cybele in Roman Coins and Sculpture, *Hommages à Marcel Renard*, Coll. Latomus 102 (Brussels, 1969), pp. 29-40, pls. 16-17.

Comments on the Statue of Aphrodite-Venus, *The Dayton Art Institute Bulletin* 28 (1969), pp. 2-3.

Review of Daria de Bernardi Ferrero, *Teatri classici in Asia Minore. I. Cybera, Selge, Hierapolis* (1966), *Gnomon* 41 (1969), pp. 521-23.

A Critical Review of Walter-Herwig Schuchhardt, ed., *Antike Plastik*, Lieferung VI-VIII (1967), *American Journal of Archaeology* 74 (1970), pp. 79-95.

Bronzestatuette des Asklepios in Cincinnati, *Antike Plastik* 10 (1970), pp. 55-56, pls. 46-50.

Roman Copies as Roman Art, *Columbia Forum* 13 (1970), pp. 36-39.

Review of Dorothea Arnold, Die Polykletnachfolge, *Jahrbuch des deutschen archäologischen Instituts, Ergänzungsheft* 25 (1969), *American Journal of Archaeology* 74 (1970), pp. 306-9.

Die Wichtigkeit der römischen spätrepublikanischen Münzen für die Geschichte der Kunst, *Antike Kunst* 14 (1971), pp. 107-22.

Review of Jean Marcadé, *Au Musée de Delos* (1969), *American Journal of Archaeology* 75 (1971), pp. 344-46.

Review of Daria de Bernardi Ferrero, *Teatri classici in Asia Minore* II (1969), *Gnomon* 44 (1972), pp. 377-85.

Review of Hans Lauter, *Zur Chronologie römischer Kopien nach Originalen des V. Jahrhunderts* (1970), *American Journal of Archaeology* 76 (1972), pp. 96-98.

Review of *Antiken aus dem Akademischen Kunstmuseum Bonn* (1969), *Erasmus* 24 (1972), pp. 303-9.

Review of Tonio Hölscher, *Ideal und Wirklichkeit in den Bildnissen Alexanders des Grossen* (1971), *American Journal of Archaeology* 76 (1972), pp. 340-42.

Review of Alan Little, *Roman Perspective Painting and the Ancient Stage* (1971), *American Journal of Archaeology* 76 (1972), pp. 454-56.

The Development of Portraiture on Roman Republican Coins, *Aufstieg und Niedergang der römischen Welt*, ed. Hildegard Temporini, I. 4 (Berlin 1973), pp. 871-98.

Charakter und Unterschiede der griechischen und römischen Kleidung, *Archäologischer Anzeiger* (1973), pp. 425-47.

Review of Alan Little, *Roman Bridal Drama at the Villa of the Mysteries* (1972), *American Journal of Archaeology* 77 (1973), pp. 453-56.

Three Coins of Gordian III, *In Memoriam Otto J. Brendel. Essays in Archaeology and the Humanities*, eds., Larissa Bonfante and Helga von Heintze, von Zabern, Mainz, 1976, pp. 179-184.

Otto Brendel: A Memorial Notice, *Archaeological News* 5 (1976), pp. 3-4.

Ancient Copies. Contributions to the History of Greek and Roman Art. New York University Press, New York, 1977.

Reviewed by:
Anon., *Gazette des Beaux-Arts* 90 (1977), p. 23.
Gloria K. Rensch, *Library Journal*, September 1977.
Christina Huemer, *Art Libraries Association of North America*, October 1977.
Anon., *Choice* (October 1977), p. 84.
Anon., *American Artist* (1977).
Ruth Michael Gais, *Classical Outlook* 56 (Sept.-Oct. 1978), pp. 13-14.
William R. Biers, *Classical World* 72/3 (1978), p. 176.
Carol C. Mattusch, *American Journal of Archaeology* 83 (1979), pp. 115-16.
Jenny Vafopoulos Richardson, *Classical Review* 29 (1979), pp. 291-94.
E. Schmidt, *Gnomon* 51 (1979), pp. 582-86.

CHAPTER 10
GISELA MARIE AUGUSTA RICHTER (1882-1972): SCHOLAR OF CLASSICAL ART AND MUSEUM ARCHAEOLOGIST

Ingrid E. M. Edlund,
Anna Marguerite McCann, and
Claire Richter Sherman[1]

Gisela Marie Augusta Richter, in a career of over sixty years as a scholar and museum archaeologist, helped open up a new era for classical art in America. Through her galaxy of publications, which span the classical fields, and her achievements as a pioneering woman curator at the Metropolitan Museum of Art, she also helped greatly to lay the foundations for our present knowledge of Hellenic art and in particular our appreciation of Greek sculpture. As few other scholars have done, she succeeded in reaching a worldwide community of both scholars and laymen. Motivated by a love of and total commitment to her chosen field of research and a deep humanity, which found expression in her devotion to her family and to her many friends, Gisela Richter moved ahead into the new era of the professional, independent woman, even though she never identified herself with feminist causes. Her long life provides a unique example of what women with focus, ability, and vigorous enthusiasm can achieve in the museum and scholarly worlds.

Our chief guide in tracing the course of her career is Gisela Richter's own account of her life, *My Memoirs: Recollections of an Archaeologist's Life*, published in Rome shortly before her death in 1972. Although it is brief, reserved, and modest, the generously illustrated booklet does convey clearly the major interests of her life: family, work, and friends. Of these, her family was decisive in focusing on the visual arts and encouraging her personal development. Gisela Richter was born in London on 14 August 1882, the third child of the former Louise Schwab (1852-1938) and Jean Paul Richter (1847-1937). The family was cosmopolitan in origin and outlook and very much engaged in a wide variety of literary and artistic activities that involved both parents and later their children.

Although little known in comparison to her husband, Louise (Luise) Schwab Richter had an identifiably independent literary career.[2] Except for her exotic birthplace, details of her early life are meager. Her mother and father, Heinrich Schwab (also spelled Schwaab), were German. Mr. Schwab is variously described as the man who introduced the manufacture of silk to Broussa (now Bursa) and as the Austrian and American consul in that city, located near the Sea of Marmara in Turkey. Louise Schwab studied from 1863 to 1866 at the Diakonessenschule (Deaconess School) in Smyrna. When her father died in the late 1860s, she and her mother returned to Germany. She received her later education in that country and also in England, where she went in 1871. Her bilingual literary activity shows her excellent grounding in both German and English. Before turning to writing, Louise Schwab first desired a career as a singer; maternal opposition apparently thwarted these ambitions.

Where Louise Schwab met Jean Paul Richter is not clear. They were married in 1878. The next decade saw her debut as a published writer. The first of two novels, *Melita: A Turkish Love Story*, drew on the background of her youth. Published in 1886, it was later translated into German by a Professor Brandl in Berlin and serialized in the *Mainzer Tageblatt*. A second and later novel, *Naïda*, was originally written in German and later translated into English. After her marriage, her interest naturally turned to artistic subjects, although later she envisioned a book on the "Woman Question," based on her observations of women's status in the various countries in which she had lived. The next area of her literary activity, that of a translator, was the way in which she began to write on art. In 1883 Louise Richter published the English version of Giovanni Morelli's controversial work, *Italian Masters in German Galleries*.[3] Two later books of travel literature written by Louise Richter belong to another genre much favored by nineteenth-century women writers on art. She benefited from the family's long stays in Italy for her study of the history and monuments of Siena, published first in 1901 in a series on famous art cities.[4] In her foreword, Louise Richter discussed the need for interpreting the less familiar artistic heritage of Siena in terms of its distinctive political, social, and religious institutions. By consulting archival documents, as well as the work of earlier scholars, she provided a very thorough guide to Sienese history and monuments. Also impressive is her book on *Chantilly in History and Art*, the first work in English intended for a general audience to discuss the superb collections of the Musée Condé.[5] Inspired by the great exhibition of French primitives held in Paris in 1904, she tackled many difficult problems in her full descriptions of the late medieval manuscripts and Renaissance drawings in the Chantilly collections. Her enthusiasm for the architecture and landscape of Chantilly is successfully communicated to her readers. After World War I, Louise Richter continued to contribute various articles to art periodicals.[6] For her daughter Gisela, her mother's successful career as a writer on art must have provided an important model.

Beside her mother's example, Gisela Richter had the lifelong devotion and support of her sister. In *My Memoirs*, Irma Richter is mentioned as her sister's companion during museum visits and lectures that deeply impressed the teenage girls. Irma became a gifted artist and writer on the arts. Her book on *Rhythmic Form in Art* draws upon her interests as a painter in the general principles of composition; she persuasively relates aesthetic theories of geometric organization developed in individual historic periods to specific works of art.[7] Irma Richter is listed with her father as co-editor of the second edition of the *Literary Works of Leonardo da Vinci* (1939). As the result of her work on that project, her translation of Leonardo's *Paragone* ("Comparison of the Arts") was published separately in 1949.[8] After her parents' deaths in 1937 and 1938, Irma Richter joined her sister in New York. Irma is credited with coauthorship of Gisela Richter's important book on Greek male archaic nude statues, *Kouroi* (1942). The two moved together to Rome in 1952 after Gisela Richter's retirement. At the time of Irma's death in 1956, the sisters had undertaken the publication of their father's correspondence with Giovanni Morelli, Irma Richter's godfather.[9]

The publication of the Richter-Morelli letters indicates the decisive role the Italian critic and connoisseur played in the life of Jean Paul Richter. Richter was born in Dresden in 1847. His mother, the former Frédérique Mock, was French; his father, Charles Richter—of French Huguenot and German descent—was an official of the Evangelical church. After completing his studies in theology at the University of Dresden, Jean Paul Richter served from 1871 to 1873 as tutor to the Landgrave Alexander Friedrich of Hesse. In the next three years his travels to Italy and the Near East caused him to leave theology for the study of Italian Renaissance art. His meeting of 1876 with Morelli greatly encouraged him in this objective.[10]

Jean Paul Richter's theological interests may have prompted his earliest publications on early Christian art and architecture. For a period of thirty years he continued to publish monumental studies like his books on the sources of Byzantine art in Constantinople, *Quellen der byzantinischen Kunstgeschichte* (Vienna, 1897) and *The Golden Age of Classic Christian Art* (London, 1904).

Towards the end of the 1870s, in a series of monographs on individual artists, Jean Paul Richter began to write on Italian Renaissance subjects. Perhaps his most lasting work of scholarship in that field dates from 1883, when the *Literary Works of Leonardo da Vinci* was published in London.[11] This massive two-volume work represented the first attempt to publish the scattered and internally disorganized manuscripts written by Leonardo in his celebrated "mirror" script. Working in various European libraries and collections, Dr. Richter deciphered Leonardo's notoriously difficult hand (written from right to left), and he also established a chronology for the literary fragments and arranged the five thousand loose pages in coherent order. Providing an overview of all aspects of Leonardo's thought—artistic, scientific, and philosophic—the *Literary Works* became the basis of subsequent scholarship on the great Renaissance genius. Dr. Richter's devotion to the project extended to putting out fifty years later a second edition of the work to incorporate the tremendous expansion of Leonardo scholarship. Very much a family enterprise, this second edition was largely completed before his death in 1937. Not only did Irma Richter serve as co-editor, but the book is dedicated to Gisela, who along with Robert Mond, provided the necessary financial support for the publication.

The 1880s also saw the beginning of another family undertaking, the Richters' involvement in disseminating the ideas of Giovanni Morelli. At the time, Morelli's revolutionary doctrines setting forth a scientific method of connoisseurship were encountering fierce opposition from Wilhelm von Bode, director of the Kaiser Friedrich Museum in Berlin, and from the partisans of subjective art criticism. The flavor of the controversies is preserved in the correspondence between Jean Paul Richter and Giovanni Morelli published almost eighty years later by Richter's daughters. Louise Richter's 1883 translation of Morelli's *Italian Masters in German Galleries* also expresses the fervor of the debate. In the preface Morelli compares his method of attaining a real "science of art" to a crusade against "dreary dilettantism" and urges his followers to "take up the cross and follow me."[12]

In addition to the written dissemination of Morelli's ideas, Ernest Samuels' recent biography of Bernard Berenson brings out Jean Paul Richter's personal role in "spreading the word." In the first note of *My Memoirs*, Gisela Richter mentions that her father introduced Berenson to Morelli (in 1890). In fact, Samuels states that Berenson's meeting with Jean Paul Richter in Florence in 1889 marked the beginnings of Berenson's "real apprenticeship to the profession of art critic and connoisseur."[13] By taking Berenson under his wing, Dr. Richter found a highly influential convert to the Morellian cause in the man who became the most famous connoisseur of modern times.

Jean Paul Richter also applied the principles of connoisseurship in a practical manner. Beginning in the 1880s, his preparation of a series of catalogues of various English private collections shows one side of his growing reputation as an expert on art.[14] Like so many other contemporary art scholars, he was also active on the art market. Dr. Richter formed a collection of his own. Using his connections with Berenson, he tried to sell it in the booming art market of the 1890s. Among the American collections to which Richter's Italian Renaissance pictures were sold in this period were those of Theodore Davis, Isabella Stewart Gardner, and Henry White Cannon. Indeed, in the last year of his life, Jean Paul Richter wrote the catalogue for the Cannon collection, given to Princeton University in 1935 by his son.[15] Some of Richter's paintings found their way into a collection, now in the National Gallery, London, which he was asked to form in 1884 by the noted scientist, Ludwig Mond. Richter's two-volume catalogue, *The Mond Collection: An Appreciation* (London, 1910) contains a great deal of fascinating information on his philosophy of collecting and connoisseurship—including tributes to the "Morellian method"—and on the formation of nineteenth-century European and English museums. The Mond catalogue offers also ample evidence of Richter's broad knowledge of Italian painting and a testimony to his family's long friendship with the Mond family.[16]

Gisela Richter does not discuss her father's activity as a connoisseur as an influence on her future profession. But family connections and familiarity with the world of European private collections were undoubtedly assets in her career as a museum curator. Certainly the family's long residence in Italy and other countries provided her with the opportunity to learn languages and to visit museums and other art collections. Indeed, in *My Memoirs* she mentions a visit to the National Gallery in London with her sister that became an essential step in their art education. Their father "made us see the difference between a real Botticelli and a questionable one. First we were made to look at the former with great attention, taking in all the details of the drawing and then at the hypothetical one. The contrast was obvious to us in spite of our youth." In the following sentence she brings out the importance of this Morellian exercise in her subsequent studies of art: "I later found this method the best possible one also in evaluating Greek and pseudo-Greek Sculpture."[17] In her preface to the Morelli-Richter correspondence she says of Morelli's method: "It has become the basis of connoisseurship not only in Renaissance paintings, but in all art, including Greek vase-painting."[18]

Another turning point in Gisela Richter's life came when she was about fourteen as the result of visiting museums in Rome and attending the lectures of Professor Emmanuel Loewy at the University of Rome: "I became enamoured of Greek and Roman art and decided to become an archaeologist."[19] Her early fascination with defining the essence of Greek style and the conflicting strains evident in its chronological development dominated Gisela Richter's later thinking and writing.

When in 1892 the Richter family returned from Italy to live in England, Gisela's education there gave her the opportunity for independent development and for acquiring the foundation of classical studies. Although she does not say so, her education first at Maida Vale High School and Girton College, Cambridge, grew out of the tremendous struggle in the second half of the nineteenth century to secure adequate higher education for women. Maida Vale High School, founded in 1878, belonged to the institutions formed by the Girls' Public Day School Company (later Trust). These nondenominational schools charged only modest fees and were open to all classes. Their aim was to give girls the same academic preparation as boys for the local university examinations.[20] Girton College, first known as Hitchin, was founded in 1869 by Emily Davies (1830-1921) in the face of fierce opposition from Cambridge University. The period of Davies's active leadership at Girton, which saw women admitted to the Tripos (honors qualifying) examination—but not to any form of Cambridge degree—ended in 1904, about the time Gisela Richter finished her studies there.[21] Gisela Richter's don at Girton in Greek and Latin literature and ancient history during her three year stay (1900-1903) was Katharine Jex-Blake (1860-1951), later appointed Vice-Mistress (1903-1916) and then Mistress (1916-1922) of the college. It was during her tenure that Girton first acquired a thoroughly qualified scholar as an administrator. She was one of the early group of women who as a student at Girton had taken the Tripos examination at Cambridge. In 1896 Katharine Jex-Blake collaborated with her Girton classmate Eugénie Sellers (later Strong) on the translation of *The Elder Pliny's Chapters on the History of Art.*[22] Katharine Jex-Blake was the niece of Dr. Sophia Jex-Blake, a determined leader of the bitterly contested fight to open British medical schools to women. A distinguished teacher and forceful personality, Katharine Jex-Blake's students went on to classical lectureships at Newnham (the other early woman's college at Cambridge), at Somerville College and Lady Margaret Hall (Oxford), and at Bedford and Royal Holloway Colleges of London University. During her residence at Girton for over forty years, Katharine Jex-Blake knew all the students personally.[23] Her example must have been especially important to Gisela Richter when she began serious studies in classics. Although Gisela Richter's consuming interest in her field of study seemed to remove her from identification with feminist issues, the account of her experiences at Girton in *My Memoirs* indicates that she was affected by the spirit of adventure in this pioneering school for women.

Gisela Richter's enormous capacity for friendship also flowered at Girton. In *My Memoirs* she writes especially warmly of her friends there. During her vacations she remembers her visits with one of her classmates, Lady Dorothy Howard, daughter of the Earl of Carlisle, at Castle Howard and Castle Naworth. She must have enjoyed the famous classical collections of the Earls of Carlisle as well as contact with the classical scholar Gilbert Murray, married to the elder sister of her friend Dorothy. These early friendships, Gisela Richter remarks, lasted all their lives for "the fact of having been young together is a very special tie."[24] Throughout her long life, love for and joy in her friends with loyalty and concern for them and, a genuine rapport with scholars of all ages with whom she helpfully shared her knowledge and experience, were qualities that touched with extraordinary depth all who knew her. The devotion was mutual, and Gisela Richter's friendships spanned the oceans and years.

Her pursuit of learning in her chosen field began early and never ceased. After Girton College she went to Athens in 1904 to spend the year at the British School of Archaeology. Her situation was an unusual one; because she was the only woman at the British School she could not "live in" but had to take up quarters at the Pension Merlin instead. The "open" college housing system commonly accepted today was inconceivable then. At this same pension were other women scholars studying at the American School of Classical Studies, and strong bonds of friendships were formed with Edith Hall (later Dohan), Rachel Berenson (later Perry), and Nora Jenkins (later Shear). When it came to their classical training at these graduate schools, however, there appears to have been no distinction between Gisela Richter and her friends and their male colleagues. Here she first learned to "ferret out things by myself," an experience she valued for her future life.[25] The director of the British School, Charles Bosanquet, guided and helped her with her first published study: "The Distribution of Attic Vases: A Study of the Home Market," *Annual of the British School at Athens*, 11 (1904-1905), 224-42. During this time, traveling to see classical sites of Greece and Asia Minor, Gisela Richter also learned to ride horseback, an interest she continued later in Central Park in New York.

A visit to Crete in 1905 proved decisive for Gisela Richter's future career. She thought nothing of traveling by herself from Athens to Crete by ship, although in a rare and brief allusion to social constraints on women, she admits that a young girl traveling alone in those days was a "surprising sight" and "aroused considerable interest."[26] Upon her arrival she stayed with the famous American archaeologist and discoverer of Gournia, Harriet Ann Boyd, later Hawes (1871-1945), who became a lifelong friend. Harriet Boyd, an early graduate of Smith College (class of 1892), began graduate work at the American School of Classical Studies in Athens in 1896. Although discouraged by the administration at the American School from active archaeological excavation, she used part of her Agnes Hoppin Memorial Fellowship to begin excavating at Kavousi in eastern Crete, encouraged by Sir Arthur Evans, the discoverer of Knossos. Her discovery of Iron Age sites there provided the material for her master's thesis from Smith College. In 1901 she began her excavations at Gournia, which continued under the sponsorship of the American Exploration Society of Philadelphia in 1903 and 1904. Gournia was a Bronze Age town, the only one of that period yet discovered in Crete. When these finds were first published in 1904, Harriet Boyd became famous not only as the first American to have excavated in Crete but also as the first woman of any nationality to have been responsible for the direction and publication of an excavation.[27]

Harriet Boyd was a woman of an unusual and engaging character by the standards of any period; her independence and achievements were particularly remarkable when ideals of women's conduct were so circumscribed. Before she met Gisela Richter, she had astounded the residents of Athens by riding around the city on a bicycle. Always involved in social problems, Harriet Boyd served as a volunteer nurse in the Greco-Turkish war of 1897, receiving for her services the decoration of the Red Cross from Queen Olga of Greece.

All these experiences were behind Harriet Boyd when Gisela Richter visited her in Crete. Unfortunately, Richter was taken ill soon after her arrival and was not able to see as much of the island as she had hoped. Instead, the two archaeologists took off for Brittany, where Richter's parents were spending the summer. She reports that "my parents and Harriet liked each other. Indeed there were few people who could resist the charm and kindness of Harriet Boyd." At the end of the summer, Boyd was returning to the United States, and she invited her friend to join her to see the "New World" after having seen the old one. Gisela Richter mentions that she needed to make a living, and Boyd thought that in the United States "you are sure to be able to pick up some lectures that will at least pay for your expenses."[28] Thus, almost by chance, a scholar who would so profoundly influence classical studies in America came to the United States.

After the two young women landed in Boston, Harriet Boyd looked for ways in which Gisela Richter could justify her trip. Together they explored the possibilities at the Boston Museum of Fine Arts and also at Smith College, where Boyd was teaching. To Gisela Richter's disappointment, neither offered any work. But in New York, Edward Robinson, former director of the Boston Museum and at the time vice-director of the Metropolitan Museum of Art and a friend of Harriet Boyd, asked Richter to catalogue a newly purchased collection of Greek vases. She accepted the opportunity at the salary of five dollars a day, and the vases were put on exhibition. After the successful completion of this project, Robinson asked if she wished to prepare labels for a collection of electrotype reproductions of jewelry. At the end of this memorable year, Richter returned to England with an offer to come back to the museum, this time as a permanent member of the staff. As the result of a family council, she asked for three months vacation a year in order to return to Europe. With the utmost simplicity and apparent acceptance of her new country, Gisela Richter describes these first disappointments and her final success in finding work in New York, concluding "that a series of failures may culminate in the best possible result."[29]

Gisela Richter was among the earliest women on the staff of the Metropolitan; Frances Morris had worked there part-time from 1897. At the beginning of their employment, Morris and other "women assistants" ate lunch in Morris's office in the attic of the museum to stay out of the sight of General Cesnola, who had an "aversion" to them. Winifred Howe mentions that Gisela Richter was one of the group of six women who used Frances Morris's office as a lunchroom, and where "slight preparations were made for a common luncheon, which cost the participants less than ten cents a day.''[30] As this arrangement was unsatisfactory, the then assistant secretary of the museum Henry Watson Kent and Morris found a site in the basement, originally destined for the engineer, consisting of space for a dining room, kitchen, and sitting room. This served as the permanent location of what became the Ladies' Lunch Club. In 1910 the club numbered ten members, each of whom had to take an active part on a weekly basis in planning, shopping for, and serving the food. Eventually, when the membership rose to forty, Mrs. Elizabeth Budds, a former museum "matron" known as Mother Budds, took full responsibility for planning and serving the meals, aided by one club member serving as menu consultant and another as treasurer. At its peak, the membership numbered forty people; the Guest Book records many festive occasions on which members and guests (including illustrious men and women of varied backgrounds) gathered before the club was disbanded in 1932. It was not until sometime in the 1940s shortly before Gisela Richter's retirement that women staff members were admitted to the director's dining room during the tenure of Francis Taylor.[31]

The year 1905 in which Gisela Richter joined the Metropolitan coincided with a new era of administrative and professional organization of the museum. At the time, the museum had no information desk and only one telephone, situated in the library. There was no formal training of professional staff, and the recording of museum objects, planned educational programs, and a sustained publication program were lacking. In 1905, Sir Gaspar Purdon Clarke left the directorship of the South Kensington Museum to assume the same post at the Metropolitan, succeeding the first director, General Louis Palma di Cesnola. Edward Robinson became vice-director and, in 1910, third director. Robinson reorganized the museum, including the formation of various departments on art historical lines, generally following the system adapted from the British Museum. Robinson was greatly aided by the work of Henry Watson Kent, who became secretary of the museum. Trained as a librarian in the first course ever given on "library economy" by Melvil Dewey at Columbia, Kent applied the methods of library science to museum administration. He used Dewey's system to record accessions and set up a card catalogue of every object in the museum. Kent also hired a photographer to equip a studio to take photos of individual works in the collections and slides for lectures. Consistent with his belief as a librarian in the duty of museums to teach and serve the public, he set up the first educational program and a coherent system of publication.[32]

In addition to these administrative reforms at the Metropolitan, the years 1906-1928 were of great importance within the department of Greek and Roman art. Again, Edward Robinson, who served as curator of the department in addition to his other posts, was the crucial figure in a period of tremendous expansion. He had been professionally trained as a classical archaeologist. In 1906 what became the department of classical art (later Greek and Roman art) "consisted only of the Cesnola Collection of Cypriot antiquities (still the most important of its kind outside Cyprus), and a few outstanding objects such as the frescoes from Boscoreale and the Etruscan chariot from Monteleone." Robinson desired to expand the collections "along systematic lines, strengthening it where it was weak, rounding it out as a whole, and maintaining a high standard of artistic excellence."[33] Not only were substantial purchase funds available, but Robinson was able to call on the talents of John Marshall, an Englishman who had aided him in a series of superb acquisitions of classical art for the Boston Museum of Fine Arts. The Metropolitan was able to garner for its collections a series of major acquisitions made available by the dispersion of European private collections, a process advanced by the events of World War I.

At first, as an assistant, Gisela Richter took no part in the actual buying of objects. She cared for the objects as they arrived and later identified and published them. During her annual three-month trips to Europe, she was able to continue to study the museum collections there. With time, her responsibilities in the department increased. She had been promoted from assistant to assistant curator and associate curator in 1910 and 1922 respectively, and in 1925 she was appointed full curator—the first woman to hold such a prominent position in a major American museum. After the deaths of Marshall in 1928 and of Robinson in the following year, Richter assumed full responsibility for running the department. She continued as curator until her retirement in 1948. Until 1952, she remained as Honorary Curator. In that year, when she moved to Rome, she was named Curator Emeritus.

Gisela Richter's long employment at the Metropolitan resulted in an impressive array of publications that included twenty books and over 142 articles. She described herself as a "museum archaeologist"[34] whose main task was to assess objects already in the museum's collections or those offered for sale. Her eye was trained through many years of looking at art to estimate the artistic value of each object and to place it within its proper context and chronological sequence. Through continual direct study of the objects, which gave her special pleasure, she became accustomed to exactness in description and analysis. She likewise responded to the combined need for the museum curator to make these objects known both to other scholars and to the general public.[35]

Outside the museum, she gave lectures at several major American universities, including Yale, Bryn Mawr, and Oberlin, but her main concern was never classroom teaching. Instead, Gisela Richter focused through her writing upon clarifying the essence of Greek art by careful stylistic analysis of the different media. This opening up of the whole realm of Greek art was a unique contribution of creative magnitude. She viewed artifacts in categories and was concerned with placing each piece stylistically and chronologically. Individual objects were published in the *Bulletin of the Metropolitan Museum*; collections or groups of material were presented in handbook form as guides for visitors to the Museum. There Richter described and outlined in her inimitably clear and concise way the different collections of the Museum arranged by material or type. Handbooks of the Classical collections (1917, 1927, 1930), the Etruscan collection (1940), and the Greek collections (1953) were thus published.

A catalogue was much more than a list of objects for Richter. It always reflected a chronological development and her introductions contain the essence of a period or subject. In this way her catalogues have also become standard texts on a subject. Through them she made at least the rich Greek collections of the Museum accessible to all. She began with the collection of ancient glass in 1911,[36] followed by the Greek, Etruscan and Roman bronzes in 1915 and the classical gems in 1920 (revised in 1942 and 1956). The catalogue of Greek sculpture was published after her retirement in 1954. Separate studies were also made of ancient furniture (1926 and 1966) and the Roman portraits in the collection (1941 and 1948). The Attic red-figured pottery she published in two large volumes in 1936, followed by her useful survey book on the subject in 1946 with a second edition in 1958. The Attic black-figured *kylikes* (drinking cups) in the museum appeared in the *Corpus Vasorum Antiquorum* (United States of America, fasc. 11; The Metropolitan Museum of Art, New York, fasc. 2) in 1953.[37] For her study of pottery, Gisela Richter took up the craft of making pottery herself and became firm friends with Maude Robinson, a professional potter. Together they delighted in solving technical problems, the results of which appear in Richter's scholarly writing. In this same inquisitive way, she later learned the techniques of marble carving and bronze casting, encouraged by her artist sister Irma. For her study of ancient furniture she had full-scale reproductions made by a firm in Athens in order to get a better sense of proportions and harmony of lines. Before her time in her recognition of the value of technical research, she added yet another dimension to our understanding of the Greek artistic achievement. In her own words, she advised the universities to also teach "the practical side." Through it one can also experience the human side "for one is brought nearer to the ancient artists by trying to do similar work."[38]

That Gisela Richter was acutely aware of the difficulties and criticisms involved in her job as a museum curator is clear from her 1970 article in the *Metropolitan Museum Journal* dealing with the general history and growth of the department of Greek and Roman art. The character of the text is clear from the subtitle, "Triumphs and Tribulations." The triumphs were many as she watched the collections grow in all areas under her carefully trained eye and particular taste for Greek sculpture and Greek pottery.

Through her many European contacts, she was able to discuss and compare notes with other specialists in her field, an opportunity which gave her the greatest of pleasure. Many of these colleagues remained her lifelong friends.

As a curator and museum archaeologist Gisela Richter was concerned with improving the collection by making new purchases. Most items were acquired separately, but the museum also bought complete collections or parts of collections. Other objects were donated as gifts or bequests. Furthermore, objects could change in appearance at any time. The hope of completing a fragmentary statue or vase is always slim, especially if the piece was discovered long before it came into the museum's collection. But occasionally this happens, and it was with obvious pleasure and enthusiasm that Richter records successful "treasure hunts" to complete pieces in the Museum's collections. One of these "triumphs" added fragments to the important archaic Attic gravestone, the so-called Megakles stele, purchased in 1911. To the gravestone, Richter was able to add the crowning sphinx found in an English collection. Her work was continued by others in 1966 and 1967, when further pieces were identified in the National Museum in Athens,[39] plaster casts of which have been added to the stele on exhibition in New York. Perhaps one day the remaining pieces of the stele will be joined in one museum.

But as a museum curator, Gisela Richter also had to face difficulties. These seem to have been surprisingly few, but, as so often happens, the ones that occurred were publicized and caused more excitement than the many problem-free acquisitions of precious and outstanding artifacts. In addition to the worries of acquiring new pieces, a curator always has to face the possibility that purchases may turn out to be fakes. Richter accepted this challenge with both concern and grace. Sometimes as a representative of the museum she was vindicated. At other times she accepted adverse developments. In all situations, however, she remained self-possessed and civil, even under severe provocation. After a particularly insulting affront, she quietly remarked to a friend, "In some situations, to be polite—is enough." She also practiced courtesy in her written scholarly work for "one increasingly realizes that we archaeologists—a relatively small group—are all attempting, as best we can, to understand and put in order sometimes difficult and seemingly contradictory evidence. A friendly appraisal of a colleague's findings, therefore, seems preferable to harsh criticism."[40]

The so-called New York *kouros* (Figure 17) may serve to illustrate some of the trials Gisela Richter sometimes had to endure before a piece became accepted by her colleagues in the field of ancient sculpture. The *kouros* was purchased by the museum in 1932 and was received with both admiration and criticism. As there was no exact provenance for the *kouros*, only stylistic criteria could be used to establish its authenticity. Humfry Payne, the eminent English specialist on Greek sculpture, was one of many who

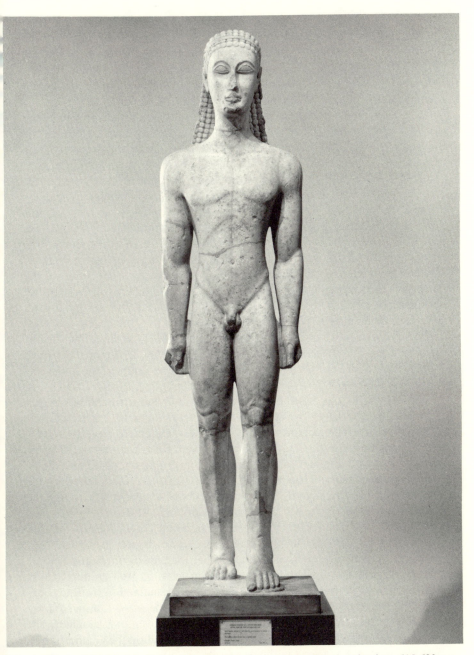

Figure 17. Archaic Marble Statue of a Youth of the Apollo Type, Athenian, 615-600 B.C. New York, Metropolitan Museum of Art. (*Courtesy the Metropolitan Museum of Art; Fletcher Fund, 1932*)

thought the statue was a forgery. What delight Richter must have felt when he actually saw the statue in the museum with her and immediately changed his mind.[41] It is characteristic that Richter made a detailed study of the one statue that formed the beginning of her large corpus of similar statues, *Kouroi* (1942, rev. ed., 1960, 1970), followed by the companion volume on female archaic statues, *Korai* (1968).

The New York *kouros* has now become firmly established as one of the earliest masterpieces of archaic Greek art. Another masterpiece in the museum's Greek collection was brought under scrutiny only recently—the lovely late archaic bronze horse purchased in 1923. It had always been considered genuine until 1967, when the question of its authenticity was raised. Richter's statement at this time was both cautious and laconic: "The question is still open, and we await further findings."[42] The issue here was not one of style but of technique. Those doubting its authenticity argued that the little horse had been cast in a sand mold rather than in the Greek lost-wax process. As the question came up so many years after her retirement, Richter diplomatically did not take sides but chose to await the results of the extensive technical analysis, which she did not live to see finished. In her obituary, Cornelius Vermeule, Curator of Classical Art at the Boston Museum of Fine Arts, points out the coincidence that the article was published by the *New York Times* on 24 December 1972, the day of her death, in which the horse was declared genuine again. But, as Vermeule writes, "Miss Richter did not need to be told, for she never doubted the horse was ancient and Greek."[43]

Equally publicized was the discovery that the huge Etruscan terra-cotta warriors, purchased by the museum between 1915 and 1921 before Gisela Richter became chief curator, were forgeries—extremely cleverly done.[44] The recognition that the handsome figures were fakes was certainly a great disappointment, but inevitable problems concerning acquisitions fade in comparison with Gisela Richter's building up of the classical collections for the museum. In this regard, her achievements as a curator are among the most distinguished in the history of the Metropolitan Museum.

In 1952, after her retirement from the museum Gisela Richter and her sister Irma moved to Rome. Here began a second chapter in the scholarly life of this creative woman. She added to her long list of publications some twenty more books and about forty-four articles, as well as many book reviews. During this period of twenty years, she remained in constant contact with the American Academy in Rome where she was a familiar figure. Wearing a hat with her Greek tourist bag slung over one shoulder, she arrived by the garden gate from her nearby apartment on the Gianicolo hill. She usually could be found in the Academy's library in the cool of the afternoon, and many of her friends regularly sought her out there in her customary chair in the main reading room. Younger scholars particularly came to share an idea, to ask advice, or simply to find encouragement. To one, troubled over a critical review of her first published scholarly effort, Richter responded in her characteristically positive and encouraging manner, "But, my dear, I have always learned from criticism," and proceeded to share her own experience of revising her second volume on ancient gems after a critical review of her first. This objectivity was also characteristic of her written word. "From all of them I have learned much, whether I agreed with the particular theory propounded or disagreed—perhaps especially in the latter case, for it then showed me that another opinion was possible and so had to be countered."[45] In her own many book reviews of other scholars' work, Gisela Richter is always polite while making her own evaluation of the material clear to the reader.

Gisela Richter's choice of Rome as her place of retirement may seem a strange one for a scholar of Greek art. She remarked that she had expressly chosen Rome rather than Athens because she wished to live in a more cosmopolitan city that also afforded privacy and where her friends traveling in Europe could most easily visit her. She herself visited Greece from Rome frequently and held the Annual Professorship at the American School of Classical Studies at Athens in the spring of 1961. Besides her contact with the American Academy in Rome, she was also widely loved by the Italian archaeological community. She especially enjoyed their monthly gatherings at the Sodalizio fra Studiosi d'Archeologia e Storia d'Arte, an Italian equivalent of the Archaeological Club she had organized in the United States in 1921. Members of the other foreign academies were also included in her wide circle of friends. Among these, the former director of the Norwegian Academy, H. P. L'Orange, was a special friend until her death. They shared a love of George Simenon's Maigret detective stories.

When once asked whether she had found the adjustment to retirement difficult after so many years as an active museum curator, Richter confessed that at first she had missed her busy life in the museum very much. "But, then," she smilingly responded, "I woke up one morning and said to myself, 'Gisela—you are free,' and after that moment I have been very happy in Rome." She could now devote her time to writing. She speaks of the value of retirement for "uninterrupted work" and especially for "uninterrupted thinking."[46] Along with her writing, until her last years, she continued to travel to England, especially to confer with her colleagues in the British Museum and to visit friends at Somerville College, Oxford, where she retained close ties.

In Gisela Richter's inviting apartment in Rome, overlooking the green park of the Villa Sciarra, archaeologists of all nationalities and all ages were invited to gather for large parties. In her later years Gisela Richter remained a handsome woman (Figure 18). Her contagiously warm smile illuminated her finely carved features, and her eyes twinkled when she began to talk about her favorite subject, Greek art. In her last years, she contented herself with smaller gatherings of just a few friends. Among the most frequent visitors of the younger Italian scholars were Giovanni Scichilone and the Conticello and Panciera families. At these intimate parties, the young children were invited as well and given milk to drink at a separate table where drawing pencils and paper were also spread out. It was part of her warm humanity that she loved children. In fact, in her last study on perspective, she uses drawings made by the Conticello children to illustrate a naturally "primitive" style of perspective.[47] Her friends and her work remained her focus throughout her life. For one who knew her, it would be hard to say which was the more important. The two elements were intertwined and accommodated in her life, as she remarked to a friend when she gave up "a precious morning of work" to attend the baptism of one of the Conticello children of whom she was so fond.

In these later years in Rome, Gisela Richter's scholarly productivity continued to flourish. To the editors of the Phaidon Press in London, she credits the suggestion to write her *Handbook of Greek Art: A Survey of the Visual Art of Ancient Greece* (1959, 7th ed., 1974).[48] This was the beginning of her long and fruitful association with the Phaidon Press, who published with handsome photographs her monographs on major topics previously only covered in articles and catalogues. During these twenty years she also revised and expanded some of her earlier books.[49] With the exception of the Jerome Lectures on *Ancient Italy*, published by the University of Michigan in 1955, and her books on ancient furniture (*The Furniture of the Greeks, Etruscans, and Romans*, 1966), her studies continued to focus on different aspects of Greek art, sculpture, and vase painting. *The Sculpture and Sculptors of the Greeks*, first published in 1929, came out in a fourth edition in 1970. Her two books on *Kouroi* and *Korai* mentioned previously are fundamental studies for archaic Greek art. She speaks of her special pleasure in doing these particular books and her association with the skilled photographer of the Athenian Agora, Alison Frantz.[50] In an amusing incident told to a friend, she enlisted her affection for these archaic Greek "youths" and "maidens" in her successful attempt to bridge the "generation gap." One day she decided to approach the long-haired Roman youths who gathered on their motor scooters along the Aurelian walls which she followed on her daily path to the American Academy library. She asked them why they gathered there doing nothing when they could be reading good books and learning something worthwhile. The youths remained polite but noncommittal. Later, Gisela Richter confessed that at first the "hippy" appearance of the young men had been distasteful to her until she remembered that her precious *kouroi* had had long locks too and that one

Figure 18. Gisela M. A. Richter, by J. Felbermeyer. (*Courtesy J. Felbermeyer, American Academy in Rome*)

should not judge the Roman "capelloni" too harshly. After all, she said, it was really just a matter of taste and custom.

For her studies of *Greek Portraits* and *The Archaic Gravestones of Attica* (a revised version of the Martin Classical Lectures of 1944), Richter used the same format featured in her previous studies. Each book is a catalogue in which the pieces are described individually and then placed in their respective stylistic and chronological framework. She based her relative and absolute chronology on the theory of a gradual development from a stylized and conventional rendering of the human body to a more naturalistic one. Her approach has been criticized by some as too formalist,[51] and also for not allowing for regional variations in style; but who else has contributed such a vast number of research tools so continually used by both scholar and layman alike?

Perhaps the most used of all her many books are her *Sculpture and Sculptors of the Greeks* and her *Handbook of Greek Art*. In the former, she brought together the ancient literary sources and the archaeological evidence with stylistic analysis in the attribution of works of art to leading masters. This method of connoisseurship had already developed, but Richter's publication in 1929 was one of the first in the English language to use it extensively for the ancient field. Her *Handbook of Greek Art* remains a standard text for many courses on this subject all over the world. Her ability as a scholar to communicate with both the specialist and the general reader gives her books a universality no other scholar in this field has achieved. She laid the foundations for the scholars' knowledge of the stylistic evolution of Hellenic art but she also opened wide its doors to the general public seeking an appreciation of this rich field.

Gisela and her sister continued to live together in Rome until Irma's death in 1956. The loss so soon after moving to Rome of her beloved sister she faced with courage. In her memoirs she speaks of the void caused by the loss of relatives and friends but recommends "the concentration on interesting problems . . . as a prevention from brooding on the upsetting things which inevitably happen."[52] That Gisela Richter remained active, in good health, always interested in her work and many friends up until her death at ninety years of age is a remarkable achievement in itself. The last meeting with her for many of her friends was her ninetieth birthday party in the gracious garden of the Villa Richardson at the American Academy, then the residence of Frank and Jackie Brown. Still distinguished and aristocratic in her bearing, she received all the guests with her warm, vivacious smile. Indeed, she had been the catalyst for many of the friendships among the varied group of people gathered among the cool pines of the Gianicolo on a warm August afternoon. Afterwards, she remarked that it had given her the greatest happiness to see so many of her closest friends for one last time. She seemed to sense, with her characteristic courage and objectivity, that the end of her remarkable life was drawing to a close.

For all who had the good fortune to know Gisela Richter, her warm presence will remain undimmed amid the classical collections of the Metropolitan Museum of Art and the pines of Rome. Her many books now fill the shelves of libraries over the world. Although a specialist in Greek art, her scholarship spanned the fields of Etruscan and Roman art and classical and Persian gems and bronzes. She was a distinguished woman scholar but above all a warm human being who delighted in learning and sharing her knowledge with others until the last days of her long and productive life. Her modesty in assessing her own monumental accomplishments is apparent in her acceptance of the award of the Archaeological Institute of America for distinguished archaeological achievement in 1968, the highest honor given in America in this field of study.

In response I should like to say a word or two about archaeology—my particular type of archaeology, that is, the trying to understand the achievements of the Greeks and Romans in the field of art. In my experience it is one of the happiest of pursuits and I can highly recommend it. It never ends, for new factors are continually being added to the old. It requires the exercise of whatever faculties you may happen to have. You are obliged to travel hither and yon to see sites and objects. And it never leaves you, remaining a precious companion throughout your life. Moreover, it is a bond with the people who have the same interests: age, nationality, politics, all sink into insignificance compared with the great common interest. And finally, for having done all one's life what one likes best, one gets a medal.[53]

Gisela Richter died on Christmas Eve of 1972 and is buried beside her sister in the Protestant Cemetery in Rome. She left behind a rich heritage for all who continue with the study of classical archaeology. Her special type of archaeology combined meticulous and imaginative scholarship with a breadth of human understanding that bridged the gap between scholar and layman, young and old, American and European.[54] Her unique qualities as a person and the humanistic values underlying her work give her scholarship and life a distinctive resonance.

NOTES

The best source is Gisela Richter's brief autobiography, *My Memoirs: Recollections of an Archaeologist's Life* (Rome, 1972). A shorter account connected with her retirement from the Metropolitan Museum appears in the *Bulletin of the Metropolitan Museum of Art* (April 1948), n.p., while a notice in *Archaeology*, 5 (June 1952), pp. 122-23, was published on the occasion of Richter's award of an honorary doctorate from Oxford University. Richter reviewed her career in "The Department of Greek and Roman Art: Triumphs and Tribulations," *Metropolitan Museum Journal*, 3 (1970), pp. 73-95. See also Calvin Tomkins, *Merchants and Masterpieces: The Story of the Metropolitan Museum of Art* (New York, 1970). Brief notices in biographical dictionaries include those in *Who's Who in American Art* (1970); *Who's Who in the World* (1971-72), and *Contemporary Authors*, 1st ed. rev. (Detroit, 1969). Among the obituaries and tributes, see the *New York Times Biographical Edition* (Nov./Dec. 1972) for the notice of 26 December 1972, pp. 2245-46; Frank E. Brown, "Gisela

Marie Augusta Richter,'' *Studi Etruschi*, 41 (1973), pp. 597-600; and Cornelius Vermeule, "Gisela M. A. Richter," *Burlington Magazine*, 115 (1973), p. 329. An article by Evelyn Harrison will appear in the Supplement to *Notable American Women,* eds. Barbara Sicherman and Carol Hurd Green (Cambridge, Mass., 1980). Documents concerning her work at the Metropolitan Museum are preserved in the files of the department of Greek and Roman art. Her papers are on deposit in the library of the American Academy in Rome. Conversations with friends and colleagues were conducted in 1975-1976.

1. In the preparation of this article, the main research on the biographical and bibliographical material has been contributed by Ingrid Edlund. The personal reminiscences have been contributed by Anna Marguerite McCann from her friendship with Gisela Richter during her years in Rome. Claire Sherman added the material on the Richter family and the early history of the Metropolitan Museum.

Ingrid Edlund would like to thank the following friends and colleagues of Gisela Richter who kindly shared information as well as their recollections: the late Dr. Margarete Bieber, Dr. Dietrich von Bothmer, Professor Frank E. Brown, Dr. Baldassare Conticello, and Mrs. Inez Longobardi. Professor Larissa Bonfante discussed the format of the essay in a most fruitful way. Professor Malcolm and Mrs. Ruth Bell read a draft of the essay and made helpful comments. Dr. Lucy Shoe Meritt generously provided bibliographical advice. Barbara Nagel and Mary Lou Ross assisted by patiently compiling material for the bibliography.

2. Biographical dictionaries are the main sources for Louise Richter's life; for a complete list see the last section of the bibliography at the end of this volume. Especially helpful were *Who Was Who, 1929-1940,* and *Lexikon deutscher Frauen der Feder*, ed. Sophie Pataky (Berlin, 1898; reprint ed. Berne, 1971). The later contained valuable information supplied by Louise Richter.

3. Giovanni Morelli, *Italian Masters in German Galleries; A Critical Essay on the Italian Pictures in the Galleries of Munich, Dresden, Berlin* (London, 1883). A second translation by Louise Richter is: Hermann Knackfuss, *Rubens* (Bielefeld and Leipzig, 1904).

4. *Siena, Berühmte Kunststätten no. 9* (Leipzig and Berlin, 1901); 2d ed. 1915).

5. The book was published first in London in 1913, and an American edition came out in New York the following year.

6. Louise Richter later published a short thirteen-page booklet, *Algeria and Its Centenary* (London, 1930).

7. *Rhythmic Form in Art: An Investigation of the Principles of Composition in the Works of the Great Masters* (London, 1932).

8. Leonardo da Vinci, *Paragone: A Comparison of the Arts*, introd. and tr. Irma A. Richter (London and New York, 1949).

9. *Italienische Malerei der Renaissance im Briefwechsel von Giovanni Morelli und Jean Paul Richter, 1876-1891,* eds. Irma and Gisela Richter (Baden-Baden, 1960). A portrait of her father by Irma Richter is included.

10. For a biographical account see Giorgio Nicodemi, "Necrologia del Dottore Giovanni Paolo Richter," *Raccolta Vinciana,* 16 (1939), ix-xi. See also *My Memoirs,* 7; and for the information in biographical dictionaries, see note 2. For an account of the Richters' arrival in England, see John Michael Cohen, *The Life of Ludwig Mond* (London, 1956), p. 171.

11. The translations from the Italian were furnished by Mrs. R. C. Bell. For an evaluation of Richter's contribution to Leonardo scholarship, see George Sarton's review of the second edition of *The Literary Works of Leonardo da Vinci* in *Isis*, 35, pt. 2 (1944), 184-87.

12. Morelli, *Italian Masters*, vii. For further discussion of Morelli's importance, see Chapter 1 of this book.

13. Ernest Samuels, *Bernard Berenson: The Making of a Connoisseur* (Cambridge, Mass., 1979), p. 94.

14. Among these catalogues were: *Catalogue of the Pictures in the Dulwich College Gallery*, with John C. L. Sparkes (London, 1880, 2d ed.); and *Catalogue of the Collection of Paintings Lent for Exhibition by the Marquess of Bute* (Glasgow, 1884).

15. For the sale of Richter's collection to the three Americans, see Samuels, *Berenson*, 182, 219, 309, 337, and 378. See also Jean Paul Richter, *The Cannon Collection of Italian Paintings of the Renaissance, Mostly of the Veronese School*, Princeton Monographs in Art and Archaeology, 20 (Princeton, 1936). For the earlier catalogues of this collection by Dr. Richter, see pp. v-vi of the Preface to this volume by Frank J. Mather, Jr.

16. For the Richters' connection with the Monds, see Cohen, *Mond*, 171-74, 246-47, and 254-55. For an evaluation of Richter's catalogue of the Mond collection, see Frank Herrmann, *The English as Collectors, A Documentary Chrestomathy* (London, 1972), p. 430. Earlier Louise Richter had written two articles "The Collection of Dr. Ludwig Mond," *The Connoisseur* 4 (Oct. and Nov. 1902), 75-83 and 229-36. After Dr. Mond's death in 1909, she wrote a privately printed tribute, *Recollections of Dr. Ludwig Mond* (London, [1910]); her book on Chantilly was dedicated to Mrs. Mond. See also the Preface by Robert Mond to Jean Paul Richter, *La Collezione Hertz e gli affreschi di Giulio Romano nel Palazzo Zuccari*, Römische Forschungen der Bibliotheca Hertziana, 5 (Leipzig, 1928).

17. *My Memoirs*, 8.

18. Preface to Morelli-Richter, *Briefwechsel*, ix.

19. *My Memoirs*, 8. For the importance of Loewy's ideas, see Meyer Schapiro, "Style," in *Aesthetics Today*, ed. Morris Philipson (Cleveland, 1961), pp. 99-101.

20. Josephine Kamm, *Hope Deferred* (London, 1965), pp. 214-16; see also idem, *Indicative Past: A Hundred Years of the Girls' Public Day School Trust* (London, 1971), pp. 63 and 73.

21. See Barbara Stephen, *Emily Davies and Girton College* (London, 1927; reprint ed. Westport, Conn., 1976); and Rita McWilliams-Tullberg, "Women and Degrees at Cambridge University, 1862-97," in *A Widening Sphere: Changing Roles of Victorian Women*, ed. Martha Vicinus (Bloomington and London, 1977), pp. 117-45.

22. See Gladys S. Thompson, *Mrs. Arthur Strong, A Memoir* (London, 1949), pp. 13, 18-19, and 32-33. Eugénie Sellers Strong provided the introduction and the commentary to the Jex-Blake translation of Pliny. For further information on Strong (the first Girton Research Fellow), who became a distinguished scholar of Roman art, see Chapter 2 and the bibliography at the end of this volume.

23. For Katharine Jex-Blake's career and influence, see Barbara Stephen, *Girton College, 1869-1932* (Cambridge, 1933), pp. 100-01; and Muriel C. Bradbrook, *'That Infidel Place': A Short History of Girton College 1869-1969* (London, 1969), pp. 66-67.

24. *My Memoirs*, 10; for Richter's Girton friends, see Figures 6-8.

25. Ibid., 10.

26. Ibid., 11.

27. For further information about Harriet Boyd Hawes, see Chapter 2 and the bibliography at the end of this volume.

28. *My Memoirs*, 12.

29. Ibid., 13-14.

30. Winifred E. Howe, unpublished account, "The Ladies' Lunch Club," n.p., preserved with the Guest Book of the Club in the Metropolitan Museum Library. Mrs. Elizabeth R. Usher, former Chief Librarian of the Metropolitan, was kind enough to make these records available to us. See also Winifred E. Howe, *A History of the Metropolitan Museum 1905-41* (New York, 1946), II, pp. 201-02.

31. Calvin Tompkins, *Merchants and Masterpieces: The Story of the Metropolitan Museum of Art* (New York, 1970), p. 278.

32. This account of the administrative and other reforms comes from ibid., 112-19. For a description of the museum in 1905, see Howe, *Metropolitan Museum*, II, 1-5.

33. *My Memoirs*, 15. For Richter's own account, see "The Department of Greek and Roman Art: Triumphs and Tribulations," *Metropolitan Museum Journal*, 3 (1970), 73-95. See also Tompkins, *Merchants and Masterpieces*, 121-25, for the growth of the department.

34. *My Memoirs*, 15.

35. "Triumphs and Tribulations," 80.

36. "The Room of Ancient Glass," *Metropolitan Museum of Art Bulletin*, 6 (1911), 45-58.

37. The full references to these titles can be found in the bibliography following this essay.

38. *My Memoirs*, 28.

39. "Triumphs and Tribulations," 90; see Figure 4.

40. *My Memoirs*, 37.

41. "Triumphs and Tribulations," 88, and Figure 17.

42. Ibid., 93-94, with the bibliography of the controversy; see also Figures 38-39.

43. "Gisela M. A. Richter (1881-1972)," *Burlington Magazine*, 115 (1973), 329.

44. See Gisela M. A. Richter, *Etruscan Terracotta Warriors in the Metropolitan Museum of Art*, Metropolitan Museum of Art, Papers, no. 6 (New York, 1937); for the final report of the forgery see Dietrich von Bothmer and Joseph V. Noble, *An Inquiry into the Forgery of the Etruscan Terracotta Warriors in the Metropolitan Museum of Art*, Papers, no. 11 (New York, 1961).

45. *Perspective in Greek and Roman Art* (London and New York, 1970), p. vii.

46. *My Memoirs*, 30.

47. See note 45.

48. *My Memoirs*, 31.

49. See the bibliography following this essay for further information.

50. *My Memoirs*, 38.

51. See for examples, reviews of her book *Kouroi*, by Herbert Hoffman in *American Journal of Archaeology*, 65 (1961), 320-21; see also the review of her *Korai*, by John G. Pedley in *American Journal of Archaeology*, 73 (1969), 383-84; and by Brunilde S. Ridgway in *Art Bulletin*, 52 (1970), 195-97. For critical reviews of her *Handbook of Greek Art*, see J. M. Cook in *Classical Review*, 10 (1960), 177; L. Guerrini in *Archeologia classica*, 12 (1960), 234-37; and J. H. Young in *American Journal of Archaeology*, 64 (1960), 293.

52. *My Memoirs*, 37.

53. *Archaeology*, 22 (1969), 84.

54. For Richter's view of scholarship and the scholar's role in modern society see her article, "Scholars Past and Present. Popular Education and the Question Mark," *Journal of the American Association of University Women*, 35 (1941), 21-26.

SELECTED BIBLIOGRAPHY OF GISELA RICHTER

After Gisela Richter's death, it was proposed at the Seventy-Fourth General Meeting of the Archaeological Institute of America in Philadelphia, 28-30 December 1972, that a complete bibliography of her works be compiled and printed in the *American Journal of Archaeology*. The only bibliography available so far is that published by Baldassare Conticello, "Gisela M. A. Richter (1882-1972)," *Colloqui Del Sodalizio. Sodalizio fra Studiosi dell'arte*, seconda serie, 4 (1973-74), 21-31. It lists books and articles, but not book reviews.

Books (other than museum catalogues)

The Craft of Athenian Pottery: An Investigation of the Technique of Black-Figured and Red-Figured Athenian Vases. New Haven, 1923.
Shapes of Greek Vases. New York, 1924.

Ancient Furniture: A History of Greek, Etruscan and Roman Furniture. Oxford, 1926.
The Sculpture and Sculptors of the Greeks. Hew Haven and London, 1929. 2d ed., 1930; 3d ed., 1950; 4th ed., 1970.
Animals in Greek Sculpture. New York and London, 1930.
Shapes and Names of Athenian Vases. New York, 1935. In collaboration with Marjorie J. Milne.
Etruscan Terracotta Warriors in the Metropolitan Museum of Art. Metropolitan Museum of Art, Papers, no. 6, New York, 1937.
Kouroi: A Study of the Greek Kouros from the Late Seventh to the Early Fifth Century B.C. New York, 1942. In collaboration with Irma A. Richter. 2d ed., 1960; 3d ed., 1970.
Archaic Attic Gravestones. Cambridge, Mass., 1944.
Attic Red-Figured Vases: A Survey. New Haven, 1946. 2d ed., 1958.
Archaic Greek Art against Its Historical Background: A Survey. New York, 1949.
Three Critical Periods in Greek Sculpture. Oxford, 1951.
Ancient Italy: A Study of the Interrelations of Its Peoples as Shown in Their Arts. Ann Arbor, Michigan, 1955.
Greek Portraits. 4 vols. Berchem-Bruxelles, 1955-62. [*Greek Portraits: A Study of Their Development*, Collection Latomus 20, Bruxelles, 1955; *Greek Portraits II: To What Extent Were They Faithful Likenesses?* Collection Latomus 36, Bruxelles, 1959; *Greek Portraits III: How Were Likenesses Transmitted in Ancient Times?* Collection Latomus 48, Bruxelles, 1960; *Greek Portraits IV: Iconographical Studies: A Few Suggestions*, Collection Latomus 54, Bruxelles, 1962.]
A Handbook of Greek Art: A Survey of the Visual Art of Ancient Greece. London and New York, 1959. 2d ed., 1960; 3d ed., 1963; 4th ed., 1965; 5th ed., 1967; 6th ed., 1969; 7th ed., 1974; Translations: *Handboek voor de Griekse kunst.* Zeist and Rotterdam, 1964. *Handbuch der griechischen Kunst.* Köln, 1966. *L'arte greca.* Torino, 1969.
The Archaic Gravestones of Attica. London and New York, 1961.
The Portraits of the Greeks. 3 vols. and supplement. London and New York, 1965-72.
The Furniture of the Greeks, Etruscans and Romans. London and New York, 1966.
Korai: Archaic Greek Maidens. London and New York, 1968.
The Engraved Gems of the Greeks, Etruscans and Romans. 2 vols. London and New York, 1968-71.
Perspective in Greek and Roman Art. London and New York, 1970.
My Memoirs: Recollections of an Archaeologist's Life. Rome, 1972.

Museum Catalogues

New York, Metropolitan Museum of Art:
Oriental and Greek and Roman Sections in *Catalogue of the Collection of Casts.* New York, 1908. 2d ed., 1910.
Greek, Etruscan and Roman Bronzes. New York, 1915.
Catalogue of Engraved Gems of the Classical Style. New York, 1920.
Handbook of the Classical Collection. New York, 1917. 3d ed., 1920; corrected ed., 1922; 5th ed., 1927; enlarged ed., 1930.
Red-Figured Athenian Vases in the Metropolitan Museum of Art. 2 vols. New Haven and London, 1936.
Augustan Art: An Exhibition Commemorating the Bimillennium of the Birth of Augustus, New York, January 4, 1939, through February 19. New York, 1938.
Handbook of the Etruscan Collection. New York, 1940.
Roman Portraits. New York, 1941; rev. ed., 1948.
Ancient Gems, From the Evans and Beatty Collections. New York, 1942.

Greek Painting: The Development of Pictorial Representation from Archaic to Graeco-Roman Times. New York, 1944. Rev. ed., 1949; 4th ed., 1952.

A Brief Guide to the Greek Collection. New York, 1945.

Corpus Vasorum Antiquorum. United States of America, fasc. 11. The Metropolitan Museum of Art, New York, fasc. 2, Attic Black-Figured Kylikes, Cambridge, Mass., 1953.

Handbook of the Greek Collection. Cambridge, Mass., 1953.

Catalogue of Greek Sculptures. Cambridge, Mass., 1954.

Catalogue of Engraved Gems, Greek, Etruscan and Roman. Rome, 1956.

Harvard University. Dumbarton Oaks Research Library and Collection, Washington, D.C.: *Catalogue of Greek and Roman Antiquities in the Dumbarton Oaks Collection.* Cambridge, Mass., 1956.

Articles

"The Distribution of Attic Vases: A Study of the Home Market." *Annual of the Brittish School at Athens,* 11 (1904-05), 224-42.

"The Room of Ancient Glass." *Bulletin of the Metropolitan Museum of Art* (June 1911), 45-58.

"The Subject of the Ludovisi and Boston Reliefs." *Journal of Hellenic Studies,* 40 (1920), 113-23.

"The Right Arm of Harmodios." *American Journal of Archaeology,* 32 (1928), 1-8.

"The Hermes of Praxiteles." *American Journal of Archaeology,* 35(1931), 227-90.

"Lydos." *Metropolitan Museum Studies,* 4 (1933), 168-78.

"The Greek Kouros in the Metropolitan Museum of Art." *Journal of Hellenic Studies,* 53 (1933), 51-53.

"The Archaic Apollo in the Metropolitan Museum." *Metropolitan Museum Studies* 5 (1934), 20-56.

"The Menon Painter = Psiax." *American Journal of Archaeology,* 38 (1934), 547-54.

"Another Copy of the Diadoumenos by Polykleitos." *American Journal of Archaeology,* 39 (1935), 46-52.

"The Technique of Bucchero Ware." *Studi Etruschi,* 10 (1936), 61-65.

"Perspective, ancient, medieval and Renaissance." *Scritti in onore di B. Nogara* (1937), 381-88.

"Greek Bronzes Recently Acquired by the Metropolitan Museum of Art." *American Journal of Archaeology,* 43 (1939), 189-201.

"Fittings from an Etruscan Chariot." *Studi Etruschi,* 13 (1939), 433-35.

"An Italic Bronze Hut Urn." *Bulletin of the Metropolitan Museum of Art* (March 1939), 66-68.

"Scholars Past and Present." *Journal of the American Association of University Women* (October 1941), 21-26.

"A Greek Silver Phiale in the Metropolitan Museum." *American Journal of Archaeology,* 45 (1941), 363-89.

"Polychromy in Greek Sculpture." *Bulletin of the Metropolitan Museum of Art* (April 1944), 233-40.

"A Bronze Eros." *American Journal of Archaeology,* 47 (1943), 365-78.

"Polychromy in Greek Sculpture with Special Reference to the Archaic Attic Gravestones in the Metropolitan Museum of Art." *American Journal of Archaeology,* 48 (1944), 321-33.

"Greeks in Persia." *American Journal of Archaeology,* 50 (1946), 15-30.

"The Late Achaemenian or Graeco-Persian Gems." *Hesperia,* suppl. 8 (Studies Shear) (1950), 291-98.

"Who Made the Roman Portrait Statues, Greeks or Romans?" *Proceedings of the American Philosophical Society,* 95 (1951), 184-208.

"A Glass Bowl with the 'Judgment of Paris.' " *Burlington Magazine*, 95 (1953), 180-87.

"The Origin of Verism in Roman Portraits." *Journal of Roman Studies*, 45 (1955), 39-46.

"Was There a Vertical Support under the Nike of the Athena Parthenos?" *Studi in onore di Aristide Calderini e Roberto Paribeni* (1956), 147-53.

"Unpublished Gems in Various Collections." *American Journal of Archaeology*, 61 (1957), 263-68.

"La date de la tête ex-cnidienne de Delphes." *Bulletin de Correspondance Hellénique*, 82 (1958), 92-106.

"Was Roman Art of the First Centuries B.C. and A.D. Classicizing?" *Journal of Roman Studies*, 48 (1958), 10-15.

"Pliny's Five Amazons." *Archaeology*, 12 (1959), 111-15.

"How Were the Roman Copies of Greek Portraits Made?" *Mitteilungen des deutschen archäologischen Instituts, römische Abteilung*, 69 (1962), 52-58.

"The Origin of the Bust Form for Portraits." *Charisterion A. K. Orlandos* (1964), 59-62.

"The Furnishings of Ancient Greek Houses." *Archaeology*, 18 (1965), 26-33.

"Newcomers." *American Journal of Archaeology*, 74 (1970), 331-34.

"The Department of Greek and Roman Art: Triumphs and Tribulations." *Metropolitan Museum Journal*, 3 (1970), 73-95.

"New Signatures of Greek Sculptors." *American Journal of Archaeology*, 75 (1971), 434-35.

"Kouroi und Korai." *Altertum*, 17 (1971), 11-24.

"Der Zusammenhang zwischen ägyptischer und griechischer Kunst." *Altertum*, 19 (1973), 74-88.

"Lysippos: The Initiator of Hellenistic Art." *In Memoriam Otto J. Brendel* (1976), 85-86.

Book Reviews:

Carl Blümel, *Griechische Bildhauerarbeit* (Berlin and Leipzig, 1927). *American Journal of Archaeology*, 33 (1929), 334-37.

J.D. Beazley, *Der Pan Maler* (Berlin, 1931). *American Journal of Archaeology*, 36 (1932), 376-77.

Charles Picard, *Manuel d'Archéologie grecque. La Sculpture I. Période archaïque.* (Paris, 1935). *American Journal of Archaeology*, 40 (1936), 559-60.

R. J. H. Jenkins, *Dedalica: A Study of Dorian Plastic Art in the Seventh Century B.C.* (Cambridge and New York, 1936). *American Journal of Archaeology*, 41 (1937), 341-42.

Pierre Wuilleumier, *Tarente, des origines à la conquête romaine* (Paris, 1939). *American Journal of Archaeology*, 49 (1945), 616-18.

Karl Schefold, *Griechische Plastik I. Die grossen Bildhauer des archaischen Athen* (Basel, 1949). *American Journal of Archaeology*, 54 (1950), 439.

Gerhart Rodenwaldt, *Köpfe von den Südmetopen des Parthenon* (Berlin, 1948). *Gnomon*, 22 (1950), 182-83.

Ernst Buschor, *Frühgriechische Jünglinge* (München,1950). *Gnomon*, 23 (1951), 393-94.

J. M. C. Toynbee, *Some Notes on Artists in the Roman World* (Brussels, 1951). *American Journal of Archaeology*, 56 (1952), 186-87.

Bernhard Schweitzer, *Vom Sinn der Perspektive* (Tübingen, 1953). *Gnomon*, 26 (1954), 194-95.

Andreas Rumpf, *Malerei und Zeichnung* (München, 1953). *Journal of Hellenic Studies*, 74 (1954), 228.

J. Marcadé, *Recueil des signatures de sculpteurs grecs I* (Paris, 1953). *Journal of Hellenic Studies*, 75 (1955), 179-80.

E. B. Harrison, *The Athenian Agora. Results of Excavations Conducted by the American School of Classical Studies at Athens. Vol. I, Portrait Sculpture* (Princeton, N.J., 1953). *Journal of Hellenic Studies*, 75 (1955), 178-79.

W.-H. Schuchhardt, *Die Epochen der griechischen Plastik* (Baden-Baden, 1959). *American Journal of Archaeology,* 64 (1960), 202-3.

Patrik Reuterswärd, *Studien zur Polychromie der Plastik, Griechenland und Rom* (Stockholm, 1960). *American Journal of Archaeology*, 65 (1961), 209-10.

A. Hekler, *Bildnisse berühmter Griechen* (Mainz, 1962). *Journal of Hellenic Studies*, 84 (1964), 232-22.

Dorothy Burr Thompson, *Troy: The Terracotta Figurines of the Hellenistic Period* (Princeton, N.J., 1963). *American Journal of Archaeology*, 68 (1964), 81-82.

Roland Hampe and Adam Winter, *Bei Töpfern und Zieglern in Süditalien und Griechenland* (Mainz, 1965). *American Journal of Archaeology*, 71 (1967), 102-3.

Sheila Adam, *The Technique of Greek Sculpture in the Archaic and Classical Periods* (London, 1966). *American Journal of Archaeology*, 72 (1968), 393-94.

E. Homann-Wedeking, *The Art of Ancient Greece* (New York, 1968). *Art Bulletin*, 52 (1970), 115.

H. Prückner, *Die lokrischen Tonreliefs: Beitrag zur Kultgeschichte von Lokri Epizephyrioi* (Mainz, 1968). *Journal of Hellenic Studies*, 91 (1971), 200-201.

Christine Mitchell Havelock, *Hellenistic Art, The Art of the Classical World from the Death of Alexander to the Battle of Actium* (Greenwich, Conn., 1971). *American Journal of Archaeology*, 76 (1972), 101-2.

J. D. Beazley, *Paralipomena* (Oxford, 1971). *American Journal of Archaeology*, 76 (1972), 235-36.

Ann H. Ashmead and Kyle M. Phillips, *Corpus Vasorum Antiquorum*. United States of America, fasc. 13, The Ella Riegel Memorial Museum, Bryn Mawr College, fasc. 1, Attic Red-Figured Vases (Princeton, N.J., 1971). *American Journal of Archaeology*, 76 (1972), 338-39.

CHAPTER 11

ERICA TIETZE-CONRAT (1883-1958): PRODUCTIVE SCHOLAR IN RENAISSANCE AND BAROQUE ART

Madlyn Millner Kahr[1]

More than two hundred scholarly articles, almost forty book reviews, three major books, and a dozen or so smaller ones—these are the contributions to art history that Erica Tietze-Conrat published as sole author between 1905 and 1958. In addition she was coauthor with her husband, Hans Tietze, of a series of volumes dealing chronologically with the works in all media of Albrecht Dürer,[2] of the fundamental corpus of *The Drawings of the Venetian Painters in the 15th and 16th Centuries*,[3] and of a considerable number of articles.[4] An extraordinary endowment of ability, self-confidence, industry, and determination made her achievement possible. Certainly also fostering her productive professional career was her remarkable marriage. "There are few happier instances of the successful teamwork of two independent scholars."[5]

Erica Tietze-Conrat's writings give evidence of the broad range of her interests. In 1905, at the age of twenty-two, she identified previously unrecognized works by Georg Raphael Donner, the late-seventeenth-century Austrian sculptor who was the subject of her doctoral dissertation.[6] The eye of the connoisseur was already making discerning judgments. Alongside her early work on Austrian Baroque sculpture,[7] she produced important studies of German art, particularly the work of Dürer; of contemporary art, an area of which many specialists in earlier art take at best a dim view; and of Venetian drawings and paintings, in which she became one of the world's leading experts. Among other subjects, she wrote on seventeenth-century Dutch painters, on French Renaissance engravings, and on iconographic problems that called for far-reaching erudition.

An exceptional visual memory made feats of connoisseurship possible for her; she felt that her "photographic memory" was her greatest asset as an art historian. Her published works show, however, that her skill at remembering and relating images was only the beginning of her art-historical enterprise. She interpreted her observations with ingenuity, arriving at numerous original conclusions toward which her sensitive understanding of the relations among works of art and between works of art and documents provided the stepping stones. In addition, she was among those rare connoisseurs who fully appreciate the value of iconographic studies, and she investigated meaning as well as formal values. Social and economic factors that affected the making of art, as well as general cultural history, also contributed to the depth and breadth of her research.

According to her fragmentary, unpublished autobiography, cited throughout this essay, Erica Conrat was born on 20 June 1883, in the same flat in the Innere Stadt, Walfischgasse 12, fourth floor, in which her mother was to die fifty-five years later. She was the youngest of the three daughters of a family that was well-to-do, sociable, and active in the musical culture then flourishing in Vienna. They were of Jewish origin, converted to Christianity, as was the case with many assimilated Jews in anti-Semitic Vienna at this period. (The background of Hans Tietze, who was born in Prague on 1 March 1880 and brought to Vienna before he was ten years old, was similar.) It was when she was about ten years old, according to her later recollection, that a schoolmate asked her, "Are you a Jew?" "No, I am a Protestant," she replied, whereupon another girl said, "But your grandfather is a Jew." She reports no emotional reaction to this challenge, but mentions that around this time she had noticed for the first time that her father had a different name from his brothers, whose name was Cohn, and that her mother's brother's name differed from that of his parents.

Erica's father, Hugo Conrat, was employed in his father-in-law's business, but his sole interest was music. Johannes Brahms and members of his circle were regular guests at the family table during Erica's early years. Her Hungarian nursemaid, Vicki (Victoria von Szalay), who could not read or write, had told folktales of her native land, and the governess of the two elder daughters, Fräulein Witzel, had written them down. Versions of them in verse by Hugo Conrat, set to music by Brahms, became the famous *Zigeunerlieder* (Gypsy Songs). Her father played only a minor part in Dr. Tietze-Conrat's later recollections. He was a failure in business, underwent bankruptcy, left the family, and departed from Vienna during her final year in the *Gymnasium*, when she was not yet eighteen years old. "I never missed him," she later wrote.

As a child she dreamed of becoming a ballet dancer. Her mother's response was to offer her the choice of studying ballet and never learning to read and write or going to school. Erica "hypocritically gave the expected answer: school." The Institut Hanausek, which she attended from her seventh to her twelfth year of age, was Hell. There was hardly a day on which I did not experience every degree of anxiety there, and scarcely a day on which I did not learn to sail around suddenly threatening reefs. So it was in the end a good school, which I got through. . . . Mama went to the same school, and, just as I did, she had learned to know the terror of this Hell; why didn't she spare me this?

Erica Conrat was allowed to skip the eighth grade and go instead to the *Mädchengymnasium*, which had been established four years earlier by the Society for the Broadened Education of Women.

I quickly showed the kind of gifts I had; I was above average in all the humanistic areas and below average in the others. It was not that I lacked interest; no, my head simply didn't take it in. That I was nevertheless every year a 'superior' student, I ascribed not to my diligence but to the naïveté of my teachers [all male], who were seduced by my intelligent face.

In her six years in the *Gymnasium*, she reports, she was a conscientious student, developed intellectually but not emotionally, and took advantage of the privilege of being the youngest.

Her life-long "bent for 'theatre' was acknowledged and cultivated as a talent for the last time" when she was about sixteen, when an elocution teacher was provided. (She was also taking piano lessons again at this time, with a famous teacher, Professor Fuchs.) Two weeks before her school-leaving examination, her sister Ilse, who had become a sculptor and was the person who had the most belief in her talent as an actress, took her to the Vienna Conservatory for an audition. The actor who tested her asked whether she was a successful student at the *Gymnasium*. When she replied that she was, he advised her that she would do better to embark on a university career. About this rejection she wrote: "I was oddly happy about this, for [the elocution teacher] had pretty much ruined my pleasure in the stage."

Fortunately for a girl intent on proving herself intellectually, higher education for women in Vienna had become—only recently—a possibility, though with severe limitations. A few had been admitted to study medicine, but the faculties of law and government of the university were not open to women until after World War I.[8] The Doctor of Philosophy degree was first awarded to a woman by the University of Vienna on 3 May 1900, in classical philology.[9] "Female students before the second World War had to battle many prejudices and endure many injuries."[10] In the academic year 1900/01, women numbered only 2.3 percent of the student body. Erica Conrat was among the pioneers. By 1922/23 the proportion of women had risen to 18 percent, and by 1965 to approximately one-third.[11] It was only after long negotiations to overcome the prejudices of the administration that in 1907 a woman was first appointed *Privatdozentin* (Lecturer).[12] From 1907 to 1928 only six women became *Privatdozentinnen* in the Faculty of

Philosophy of the University of Vienna.[13] There was no woman *Ordinarius* (Full Professor) until after World War II.[14] When Erica Conrat received her degree on 20 December 1905, an academic career would not have been a reasonable aspiration.

As she told the story later, when Erica Conrat went to register at the university she had not decided on a field of study. She thought first of medicine, which would have been a surprising choice, given her acknowledged inadequacy in the study of science. She described her selection of art history as capricious. We know from the typescript of her autobiography, however, that she had already met a student in that department, Hans Tietze. He was among the "interesting people" with whom she had become acquainted at the studio of her sister Ilse. While a student he was active in a progressive theater group, and he had commissioned Ilse to make an Ibsen plaquette to commemorate the first production of *Peer Gynt*. Hans Tietze was the first man to play a part in Erica's life. They were both students of Franz Wickhoff, whose assistant Hans Tietze became. Erica was the only woman to be graduated in art history in Wickhoff's time.[15]

Erica was married to Hans Tietze on 16 December 1905. In 1906 Hans Tietze received his first appointment, as executive secretary in the Commission for the Preservation of Austrian Monuments of Art. He travelled to make inventories of all buildings and works of art over one hundred years old in various localities, and his wife travelled with him. Undoubtedly she participated in the work, though her name never appeared on the publications that resulted, altogether thirteen large volumes of inventories. The kind of upper-level civil service position that her husband held would have been no more attainable at that time by a woman than would a high academic appointment. Erica Tietze's energy and ambition found their outlet in research and writing. For fifty-five years, from 1905 to 1959, there was not a year—with the exception of 1942—in which some contribution to art history signed E. Tietze-Conrat was not published. In most of those years her publications were numerous. To these, for which she alone took responsibility, must be added the significant body of work of which she was joint author with her husband. Without encouragement from society, she was nevertheless a professional.

The Tietzes' eldest child, Christopher, was born in 1908; a second son, Andreas, in 1914; a daughter, Walburg, in 1915; and, in 1918, a daughter, Veronika, who died in 1927 of meningitis. Hans Tietze was in the Austrian army from the time of the mobilization in 1914. As an officer concerned with the protection of monuments, he was stationed in northern Italy. Erica was able to join him in this relatively safe location for a time in 1917.

As was not uncommon in the society in which they lived, the children were cared for by a surrogate mother, Theresa, who came to them when the first child was twenty months old and remained until her death at the age of almost ninety. She stayed in the Tietze house in Vienna even during the Hitler years, when the family had left the country. The children grew up knowing that their mother was not to be disturbed when she was working at home. Not only did she have little time for them when she was at home, but her work frequently took her away for extended periods, for close study of works of art was the essence of her research. Her scholarly pursuits evidently took precedence over any of the other demands of life. When a friend asked her: "How can you do all this work as an art historian and at the same time have the responsibilities of a wife and the mother of four children?," she replied: "It's easy. I just go away."

The Tietzes' commitment to art was warmly extended to the art of their own time. The double portrait by Kokoschka that hung in their dining room in Vienna (Figure 19) stands as a monument not only to their marriage and their working partnership but also to their devotion to the advanced art of the early twentieth century in Vienna. The arts and intellectual life flourished with rarely equaled splendor in Vienna both before and after World War I. Revolutionary developments in the visual arts contributed to the brilliance of the sunset of the Hapsburg Empire. Like the other great pathbreakers of the time—Freud, Wittgenstein, Mahler, Schönberg—the innovative artists were generally rejected by the society in which they lived.[16] Neither official Vienna nor the public at large was at all prepared to accept the drastic changes in the arts. The great art historians of the Vienna school set a standard of support for the new art that was having difficulty in finding its audience. Wickhoff was a partisan of Impressionist painting and the paintings of Gustav Klimt, as well as of the technology of engineering as the basis for modern architecture. Wickhoff's successor, Max Dvořák (1874-1921), had a special affinity for the work of Oskar Kokoschka; he devoted his last writing, published in the year of his death, to Kokoschka's graphic work. Erica and Hans Tietze, in their turn, placed themselves in the forefront of the champions of the new developments in art. This was a dangerously exposed position for a man who made his career in government posts, for the modern art of the time aroused strong hostility. Hans Tietze wrote in 1919, "The Hagenbund exhibition of 1911, in which a small group of Austrian artists made their first appearance, has remained one of the strongest artistic impressions and recollections of many a member of my generation."[17] "Through this exhibition I became a writer on modern art."[18] In fact, he became a leading critic of contemporary art. It was likewise in 1911 that Erica Tietze-Conrat published a review of an exhibition of works by women artists.[19]

Besides journalistic efforts to spread the understanding and acceptance of the new trends, both Hans and Erica Tietze wrote prefaces to exhibition catalogues and gave lectures.[20] Their practical as well as moral support for artists was particularly important after the collapse of Austria in 1918,

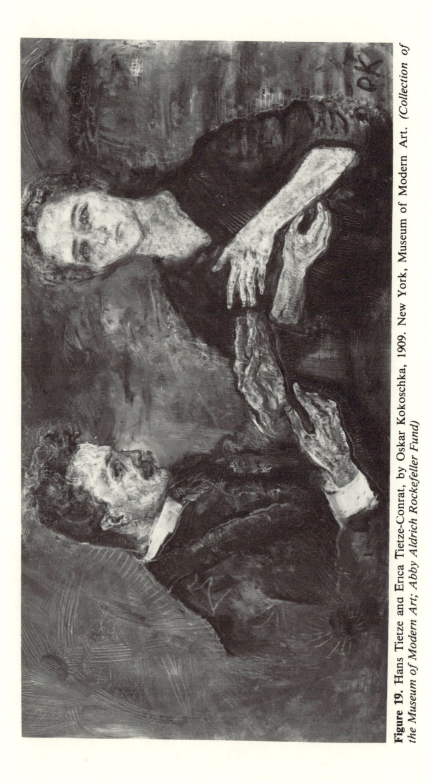

Figure 19. Hans Tietze and Erica Tietze-Conrat, by Oskar Kokoschka, 1909. New York, Museum of Modern Art. *(Collection of the Museum of Modern Art; Abby Aldrich Rockefeller Fund)*

when potential collectors were impoverished along with the artists. As some of the artists of the period look back on it, by cheering them on to look to the future and by devising and energetically fostering means to keep them going in the difficult present, the Tietzes played a significant part in the resurgence after World War I that made Vienna a high point in the history of European culture. They organized the Society for the Advancement of Contemporary Art in Vienna, with Hans Tietze as the first president. To provide patronage for artists in the new economic situation, they arranged for groups of friends to make regular financial contributions. When sufficient money had been collected, each contributor could select a painting by one of the ten participating artists and buy it at half price.

In later hard times, too, after many of the artists had emigrated, the Tietzes continued to find ways to aid them and to make their work known. Among the artists whose works they admired and who, in some cases, became their close friends and maintained this cherished relationship through the years of exile, were Joseph Floch, who died in New York in 1977; the sculptor Georg Ehrlich, who died in 1966, having spent the war and postwar years in London, whose etchings illustrated Erica Tietze-Conrat's book of poetry, *Abschied* ("Farewell"), published in 1926, and who made a bronze head as well as portrait drawings, etchings, and a lithograph of her; Georg Merkel, who returned to Vienna after a period of exile in France; and Viktor Tischler, who died in the south of France in 1951. Schiele, Klimt, and Kokoschka had also been in their circle.

In their home in Vienna, Erica and Hans Tietze worked at two large desks placed back to back, so that they faced each other, with a double-faced clock between them—a fitting symbol of their shared enterprise and the order of their industrious lives. It is perhaps a token of their essential unity that their handwritings were almost indistinguishable one from the other. They appear to have been in complete agreement about everything fundamental, and both of them were fearless and uncompromising in support of what they believed in. The preface to their important book on *The Drawings of the Venetian Painters* provides an intimate picture of the way in which they worked together.

The last word of this preface should be devoted to ourselves, since our way of collaboration, now continued through many years and on various subjects, is indeed rather unusual. A friend in England, after the publication of our Dürer asked us: How is it possible that for thousands of separate questions in such a critical catalogue two authors always agree? Our answer was, and is, that, on the contrary, we very often do not agree, but that many statements we make are the result of long and hard fights in which at the end one opinion wins. These dissensions within a team, however, are no different from those within the mind of one individual author who too at different times looks differently at the same problem. Our conflicts are only more articulate and, consequently, more thoroughly thrashed out. Otherwise we feel solidly united. In many cases we ourselves do not know after a while which of us is to be given credit for this or that idea, objection, discovery. We also honestly do not know who conceived or wrote specific passages, paragraphs, and even chapters. We wonder whether there is a merit to be shared in this book, but we are certainly ready to share the responsibility up to the last word.[21]

A rare renunciation of all individual pride, self-seeking, and competitiveness in relation to the partner made possible the extraordinarily productive joint efforts of this couple. The wife took deliberate measures to foster the collaboration by cultivating the skills that would supplement those of her husband. As he was mainly interested in theoretical questions, she developed to the full her remarkable visual memory and her knowledge of iconography. They both continued to publish independently. Throughout their lives, far more publications appeared under each individual name than under their names as joint authors. Yet much of the time they worked together.

Hans Tietze came to the United States in 1932 and again in 1935 to make lecture tours. In 1935 his wife joined him here, and they returned to Europe together, working in their stateroom on the return voyage on the first (German) edition of *European Paintings in America*, for which Hans Tietze had collected material on his travels and which was published in the same year, under his name alone.

The research that culminated in the monumental book on Venetian Renaissance drawings had its origin in Tietze-Conrat's discoveries in the early 1930s. As she explained it in an unpublished memoir written some two decades later:

While H.T. was preparing his Titian monograph, I, travelling with him, concentrated on the drawings. I had published some smaller papers on Venetian drawings, correcting some attributions in the Albertina catalogue. When I encountered the enormous material in the Uffizi and was able to identify some drawings that were anonymous or superficially listed under collective names, I suggested to H.T. that we make something like a corpus of the Venetian Renaissance drawings. We therefore from 1935 on travelled through Europe with this purpose in mind.

In the course of their travels to study Venetian drawings, the Tietzes had left Vienna in the middle of January 1938. They were in London in early March of 1938, when Schuschnigg had his fateful interview with Hitler which, as was generally recognized, was to lead to the swallowing-up of Austria by Nazi Germany. Hans Tietze decided to return to Vienna, where their elder son and their daughter were, to make the financial arrangements that would be necessary if they or their children were to emigrate. Erica, in a characteristic display of her remarkable single-mindedness, chose not to accompany him but to go instead to Italy, where she would study the drawings in Turin and Genoa and then meet him in Rome. Still more amazingly, she did not even read the newspapers during this crucial period. The *Anschluss* (annexation of Austria by Germany) came as a surprise to her. Her husband managed to escape from Austria and meet her in Rome. They studied the drawings in the Corsini, wrote their notes, took photographs. After a week they heard from their two children, who had succeeded in leaving Austria and had safely arrived in Switzerland. Their second son, a Turkologist, was in Istanbul. (It is noteworthy that by then all three of their children had found independent ways of life. All of them have had outstandingly productive careers. The eldest, Christopher, became a physician. Not interested in practice, he did research on the epidemiology of mental illness and later became a demographer, concerned with population control. Andreas became a professor at the Oriental Institute of the University of Vienna. Walburg was the first girl to be trained at the printing school in Vienna. After spending the war years in England as a munitions worker, she became chief accountant in a large printing firm in Vienna.)

The parents continued their pursuit of Venetian drawings, remaining in Italy for several months despite alarming political tensions. They interrupted a long stay in Florence by going to Switzerland for a few days when Hitler was expected in Florence, and when Hitler had moved on to Rome, they returned to Florence. Afterward they travelled to Holland and made the rounds also of the provincial museums of France, finally settling in Paris for the last three months of 1938. Sometime later in her unpublished memoir Tietze-Conrat wrote about this period:

Our first Christmas in exile. We bought two detective stories and a bottle of excellent wine. . . . We were happy; I felt new-born. . . . We had our visa—extra quota—for U.S.A. A new life in the offing, what a wonderful challenge! . . . Yes, I felt happy.

They moved to the United States at the end of April 1939. Erica Tietze-Conrat was fifty-five years old when she entered with such youthful enthusiasm upon her new life in America.

Hans Tietze had been appointed to a one-year Carnegie Professorship at the Museum of Art in Toledo, Ohio. By all reports the Tietzes made good friends in Toledo and would have been glad to remain there, but the appointment was limited to a single year, after which they settled in New York. They adapted well to the changed circumstances they faced in their life in New York. The sale of their Kokoschka double-portrait to the Museum of Modern Art in New York had contributed to a modest bank account. Though living with limited resources, they managed to maintain their professional and social activities. Erica Tietze learned to cook, a skill she had never been called upon to develop in Europe, and she took pleasure in presenting meals to guests. Dressed in a long gown to add to the festivity of such occasions, she is remembered as a delightful hostess and a brilliant conversationalist. They had close friends among European artists and art historians who were refugees in this country, as well as devoted American friends. Keen to learn about the United States, in 1940 the Tietzes bought a car, and in 1941 they travelled in it all the way from New York to the West coast (though Erica Tietze never learned to drive). They became American citizens on 22 June 1944.

Despite his renown as a scholar and his exceptional experience in museum work,[22] Hans Tietze's only additional paid work for institutions in this country consisted of modest assignments for the Metropolitan Museum of Art and the National Gallery in Washington, with a single exception. On 4 January 1954, a few months before his death from cancer, he was invited to teach a course on Venetian painting at Columbia University. When his deteriorating health prevented him from completing this assignment, his wife was asked to finish the course for him. In 1955 and 1956 she again gave a course at Columbia. This was her only academic appointment in her whole long career. Both in Vienna and in New York she sometimes taught privately in wealthy homes. In addition to her scholarly work, she also wrote plays, poetry, fiction, memoirs, and even an opera libretto. Aside from the poems published privately in an edition of only sixty copies in Vienna in 1926, none of these works was ever published or produced, though she had unsuccessfully submitted some short stories for publication.

Scholarly publications constitute the chief biographical facts of Erica Tietze-Conrat's maturity. Her monograph on *Mantegna* was published in 1955, her book on *Dwarfs and Jesters in Art* in 1957. Her late works represent a triumph over personal tragedies. Through her husband's illness, she nursed him patiently. After his death on 13 April 1954, she lived alone, with help from friends, fellow emigrés, who lived in the same apartment house. Bearing her own painful illness with bravery and stoicism, she never stopped working. When she died on 12 December 1958, at the age of seventy-five, this indefatigable writer left an unpublished manuscript on "Patterns of Suicide in Literature and Art," written during her final illness.[23]

In Erica Tietze-Conrat's time, Vienna boasted one of the leading schools in the still rather new academic discipline of art history. It attracted venturesome thinkers. Famous and stimulating teachers and gifted fellow-students (among the latter, Hans Tietze), besides her already well-established interest in the arts, surely must have drawn her to this field when she was ready to study at the university, though much later she thought of her choice as having been capricious.

The chair of art history at the University of Vienna had been established in 1851.[24] The first *Ordinarius* was Rudolf von Eitelberger (1817-1885), who fostered the unity of museum work and historical research. His successor, Franz Wickhoff (1853-1909) maintained the tradition of constant contact with objects in the museum. He taught the method of connoisseurship through close comparison of details that had been introduced by Giovanni Morelli, whose studies at the Albertina had brought him into association with members of the Vienna school of art historians. Wickhoff employed Morellian techniques in his studies of diverse fields of art and encouraged his students to do likewise.

Wickhoff's brilliant contemporary, Alois Riegl (1858-1905) presented his challenging ideas as early as 1893 in his book, *Stilfragen* ("Questions of Style"), in which he assigned to mental dynamics the central role in the creation and the contemplation of art, in opposition to Semper's more materialistic view of the art work as the product of function, raw material, and technique. Riegl's concept of *Kunstwollen*, a super-individual intellectual factor that determines the style of any period, was the basis for the "scientific" art history he aimed to create. His ideas revolutionized art-historical thinking by rejecting the long-accepted pattern of cycles of rise and decline in art. According to Riegl, art of periods that had been considered decadent should be understood as responding to different artistic intentions, and the styles of various periods cannot usefully be compared on a scale of value.

Wickhoff, in keeping with Riegl's approach, turned the attention of his students toward previously neglected areas of art. Thus Erica Conrat's dissertation was devoted to the late-seventeenth-century sculptor Georg Raphael Donner. Her first published article, which appeared in 1905, brought to light hitherto unidentified works by Donner.[25] Fifteen years later, in her book on Austrian Baroque sculpture,[26] she succinctly surveyed the field and described a characteristically Austrian note, evident in earlier folk art, which Donner carried to its highest point. In 1970, some years after her death, her pioneering work on this aspect of Austrian art was officially recognized with the naming of a room in her honor in the Österreichisches Barockmuseum in the Lower Belvedere in Vienna.

As early as 1916, Erica Tietze-Conrat published an article on three important engravings by Dürer,[27] signaling a profound interest and a major project that was to occupy her and her husband during the following decades. Together they produced a three-volume critical catalogue of Dürer's works in all media, chronologically arranged.[28] The first volume, on the young Dürer, which included his works up to the Venetian trip of 1505, was published in 1928. The catalogue comprises lists of autograph works, shop works, and some of the works that have been seriously attributed to Dürer that the authors reject. With few exceptions, all the works discussed are illustrated. Following the catalogue and illustrations, there is a general explanation of their purposes and methods and nine additional appendices dealing with specific Dürer problems. In Book II, on the mature Dürer, which is divided into two volumes, all the discussion is incorporated into the critical catalogue. The first part covers the works from the period between the Italian trip of 1505 and the visit to the Netherlands in 1520, and also some addenda from the period between 1492 and 1505. This was published in 1937. The second part appeared in the following year, dealing with the works from the final eight years of Dürer's life.

This monumental achievement remains a basic resource on the greatest of German masters, that flexible link between the Italian Renaissance and the art of the North. Dürer is in many ways central to the concerns of the Tietzes: as a great draughtsman; a printmaker of endless influence; a mediator between Renaissance classicism and the Gothic-bound cultures North of the Alps; a modern, scientific artist, contributing to the understanding of perspective, human proportions, the broadening effects of foreign travel, and the incorporation of complex ideas in the visual arts. Tietze-Conrat continued to work on Dürer problems after the third volume of the *Kritisches Verzeichnis* ("Critical Catalogue") was published, as her bibliography attests, but her attention was directed more and more to the Venetians.

The project of compiling a corpus of Venetian drawings, which Erica Tietze-Conrat proposed to her husband in about 1935, would have daunted less assured or less ambitious persons. They "aimed to provide a companion-piece to Bernard Berenson's book on the drawings of the Florentine painters."[29] In contrast with Florentine drawings, however, the area of Venetian Renaissance drawings was relatively unexplored territory at the time. Aside from Hadeln's studies of the 1920s, which were on a limited scale, little had been done to sort out this large body of material. Venetian drawings had never gone through the process of the refinement of attributions by successive generations of connoisseurs like that which had laid a groundwork for scholarly agreement regarding some other types of art—including Florentine drawings—because until recent times they had not been treated as works of art.

As the Tietzes demonstrated, drawings had been handed down in Venetian workshops along with other tools of the trade. That the particular author of the drawings was not a matter of great concern is indicated by the fact that the wills in which drawings were mentioned as legacies to the prospective heads of traditional workshops did not name the artist who had made the drawings. The workshop, the Tietzes stress, was a place not only for the production of art but also for the instruction of young artists; and drawings were used in both of these functions. Apprentices copied them as part of their training in learning the master's style. Later hands altered them whenever this seemed useful. Some drawings had been made and kept to serve as patterns in composing paintings. Only much later did they come into the hands of collectors and under the eyes of scholars. Even then, the discrimination between different hands was not a compelling issue.

Erica and Hans Tietze set themselves the task of grappling with the problems of specific attribution that had previously been given little attention. They succeeded in establishing a framework of order on which other scholars could continue to build. In the years before their material was assembled for the book, they published some of their findings in scholarly journals. They set forth their criteria with admirable clarity in an article published in Italian translation in 1937, in which they demonstrated by examples the application of their method.

The reconstruction of a new body of drawings [by Veronese] must absolutely start from the sheets that have been securely attributed. Sheets of this kind are, in the first place, 'modelli' which are authenticated by their inclusion in contracts; their conformity to the work executed does not constitute certification.[30]

They pointed out—in relation to Titian—that copies of drawings that serve for graphic reproductions must be borne in mind when one considers prints as a basis for the attribution of drawings. Among other possible pitfalls, they called attention to the fact that the wishes of patrons may alter the style of an artist in *modelli* and in drawings for portraits, "in which the constricting demand for likeness has a paralyzing effect on the personality of the artist."[31] "A methodical study of drawing can come about," they concluded, "only when it is possible to put drawings in relation to assured works, as we have attempted to do in the main part of this essay."[32] As they recognized that drawings embodying the first idea of a certain work and definitely connected with the work executed provide the essential basis for the reconstruction of a master's oeuvre, and since very few such sketches by Venetian masters of the first half of the sixteenth century exist, the Tietzes' task was enormously difficult.

Many of their attributions involve the contradiction of the opinions of other scholars. In their turn, the views of Erica and Hans Tietze have been and will continue to be subjected to criticism and, in some cases, revision. Their daring reconstruction of Caravaggio as a draughtsman on the basis of a Giorgionesque pen drawing of a group of men at a table (Uffizi), which they relate to Caravaggio's "Calling of St. Matthew," is one of their more adventuresome efforts in the 1937 article cited.[33] It has not found acceptance.

The book on *The Drawings of the Venetian-Painters in the 15th and 16th Centuries* was published in New York in 1944 in an edition of only six hundred and sixty copies. Rare copies that appeared on the market in later decades sold at very high prices. It was reprinted in 1969 and again in 1979.

The authors by no means claimed to have solved all the problems.

Throughout the work a tone of modesty prevails. In the Preface they gave Franz Wickhoff credit for communicating his enthusiasm for Venetian art while they were his students, and they paid tribute to his *Catalogue of the Italian Drawings in the Albertina* (*Jahrbuch K.H.S.* 1891/92) as "the first attempt at a scientific catalogue of an outstanding collection of drawings."[34] The Preface clearly explains the methods of their study and their criteria for the inclusion and exclusion of artists and of individual drawings. Brief biographies of all the artists represented precede their entries in the catalogue raisonné, which covers 2,267 items. The careful and detailed catalogue includes all the documentary evidence available to the authors and all substantial published opinions on the individual drawings. The judgments made are generally cautious and reserved. Erica and Hans Tietze avoided the trap of over-decisiveness. They proposed ascriptions on a scale ranging from perplexity, on the one hand, to complete conviction, on the other. In arguable cases they scrupulously explained the reasoning behind their judgments. The lucidity with which they defined the problems is as admirable as their tireless efforts to solve them. Their expressed purpose, to move in the direction of truth, was certainly achieved.

In the Introduction to *The Drawings of the Venetian Painters*, the authors discuss the concept of originality in drawings, which had changed in the course of time. Next they draw the boundaries of the Venetian School, which include, for instance, the young El Greco and exclude Mantegna. Pointing out that "art production was a much more collective task in Venice than in Florence," they relate this fact to the total organization of life in Venice, where the family workshop prevailed throughout the whole history of art. Noting that "drawings either derive from or prepare for another work of art" in the period under consideration, they elucidate the varied uses to which drawings were put in workshop practice of the time, with emphasis on their function in developing and maintaining the common style of the shop. As to when Venetian drawings began to be valued for their own sake, the Tietzes state that "a group of very carefully finished drawings by Paolo Veronese stands precisely on the borderline between" the drawing as a step in a working process and the drawing as a work of art in its own right, made with the collector in mind.

Recognizing that "within a school of art drawing does not evolve independently but, while following its intrinsic trends, it also reflects more general currents," the Tietzes provide in their Introduction a capsule history of the stylistic developments in Venetian Renaissance painting, from Jacopo Bellini to Palma Giovane, whose eclecticism marks the end of the classical school of Venetian painting.

While later consensus has led to the correction of some of the Tietzes' findings, all students of Venetian painting and drawing regard their work as indispensable. The Tietzes' belief that the famous "Sketchbooks of Jacopo

Bellini'' were the product not of a single artist but of various hands in the family shop over a period of several decades, for example, is now generally rejected. Their elucidation of workshop practices and of patronage in Renaissance Venice, their grasp of Venetian culture, and their methodology are universally respected, and their attributions must be taken into account by anyone seriously interested in the field.[35]

Hans Tietze's Phaidon Press monographs on Titian (1936) and Tintoretto (1938) were later joined by E. Tietze-Conrat's *Mantegna: Paintings, Drawings, Engravings, Complete Edition*, London, 1955, which also appeared in German and Italian editions. In 1923 she had published a small book on Mantegna, in the series Bibliothek der Kunstgeschichte ("Library of Art History"), edited by her husband, one of a number of books she wrote for this and similar series in the 1920s. She noted in the Foreword of the 1955 book ("written in the main during the year 1947") that Mantegna had always been one of her favorite artists. He was indeed an artist capable of evoking her scholarly, aesthetic, and imaginative faculties at their best. Hers was the first book in English to reproduce and catalogue all of his works in all media that the author regarded as autograph, as well as a number of questionable items that she considered worthy of discussion.

She took a fresh look at Mantegna's works and at the documentation, examined opinions that were already on record, and arrived at her own conclusions as to attributions and dating. Most of these gave rise to no opposition when they were first published, and they have stood up well under years of scrutiny. Only a few of her exclusions and two or three of her attributions are questioned by many scholars today. Quite possibly all reject her identification of the *Dead Christ* then at the Heimann Gallery in New York as a work from the hand of Mantegna. She argued that it was the original *modello* "subsequently used for variants enriched with added figures."[36]

In keeping with the standard Phaidon monograph format, the illustrations and catalogue are preceded by a thirty-page introduction. Here Tietze-Conrat deals perceptively with the artistic traditions that lay behind Mantegna's development, appraising the situation in Padua, a notable city from ancient Roman times, whose great university had made it a center of Italian humanism since the thirteenth century. She considers the role of the elusive Paduan Squarcione, who from the time Mantegna was ten years old was his teacher and adoptive father for six years and with whom he spent several months in Venice in 1446. She also discusses in detail the Florentine contributions to his style, with special reference to Donatello and Castagno; his Venetian connections, reinforced through his marriage in 1454 to the daughter of Jacopo Bellini; and the effect on his style of the conditions of his life as court artist in Mantua from 1459 until his death in 1506.

With her characteristic candor, Tietze-Conrat was careful to make distinctions between hypotheses and facts. For instance, regarding Mantegna's lost work in the Palace Chapel in Mantua, she states: "I put the case before the reader without concealing the uncertainty of the evidence on which my reconstruction of a lost major work by Mantegna rests."[37]

The catalogue, organized topographically, gives full information, including the opinions of other scholars and Tietze-Conrat's reasons for her own conclusions. That this book continues to serve as a major source is shown by the fact that not only specialists but also the authors of currently used survey books on art history cite it—often as the only reference on the subject of the greatest North Italian painter of the fifteenth century.

Dwarfs and Jesters in Art, published by Phaidon in London in 1957, was E. Tietze-Conrat's last published book. It is a kind of scholarly *scherzo*, setting before us a spicy dish of information from many sources, appropriate to the inexhaustible vitality of its zestful author. The eighty-eight works illustrated and discussed range from ancient Egyptian sculptures of the dwarf-god Bes to eighteenth-century porcelains. Not as evenly researched or as strongly organized as her earlier writings, this book presents Erica Tietze-Conrat as the sparkling conversationalist, sharing infectious enthusiasm along with a vast fund of knowledge.

A later work was to come from her pen, a long review of Bernard Berenson's book, *Italian Pictures of the Renaissance: A List of the Principal Artists and Their Works: Venetian School*, London (Phaidon), 1957.[38] This book review was written while she was, and knew she was, suffering her mortal illness. She thought it was important to criticize Berenson's book and correct his errors, and not even severe suffering could prevent her from doing this. About the book as a whole she had two major strictures. The first was that Berenson—unlike the Tietzes in their book on Venetian drawings—had listed only the major artists, avoiding the difficult and necessary task of discriminating between the works of the master of a studio and those of his students, followers, and copyists. "To go through Berenson's Lists," she wrote, "is like taking a guided tour through a gallery and looking at the starred pictures only." Her second general criticism excoriated Berenson's lack of interest in iconography. She responded wrathfully also to Berenson's remark in his Preface: "Nothing of permanent interest in Venetian studies has appeared in the last thirty years." To prove the inaccuracy of this statement, she cited a number of research findings that Berenson had ignored.

A young woman who received a Ph.D. in 1905 at the University of Vienna was obviously no ordinary person. Our curiosity as to the source of the unusual drive and ambition of this woman is further piqued when we consider the course of her life after the university. For over fifty years nothing could stop the flow of her assidous research and writing. The claims of a busy household and four children, the disruptions of political upheaval, the difficulties of starting life anew as a refugee in a time of economic depression—it seems that neither public nor private problems could blunt the indomitable thrust of Erica Tietze-Conrat's determination. How was this will of steel forged? A fragmentary (unpublished) autobiography that she wrote in German in about 1950, which tells of her life up to the time when she entered the university, provides clues to some probable sources of the ambition and the contagious self-esteem without which her remarkable career would not have been possible.

Erica Conrat was the youngest of three sisters. Ilse was three and one-half years older than she, and Lili was exactly between. "In all fairy tales the youngest was always the most beautiful, and though the most dangers threatened her, she was always happy in the end. I was never conceited as a child because I was the youngest and no other came after me, but I was proud of it," she recalled when she was almost seventy.

Her earliest attachment was to her nursemaid, a Hungarian woman called Vicki (Victoria von Szalay) whose sole charge she was, as the two bigger sisters had been taken over by a governess. As she looked back on this, Tietze-Conrat saw this situation as decisive for her later development. Her feeling of being "special," "one against two," "independent because separated," and—particularly—"the youngest" never left her. Ilse and Lili were dressed alike, Erica differently. Erica was brown-haired, her sisters blonde. These distinctions, which presumably could have given a child an unhappy feeling of not belonging, instead had the opposite effect. She understood herself to be the youngest princess, to whom fate would be kind.

The happy life under Vicki's tender protection ended soon and all too abruptly. One day, when she was three or four years old, Erica came home from a visit to her grandparents and "searched for Vicki everywhere, through the whole house, in every room, but she was not there. I have never forgotten it." Erica's mother had discharged Vicki for drinking and sent her away secretly in the child's absence. What must have appeared a desertion to the young child nevertheless did not, at least in her later recollection, deprive her of the positive feelings that Vicki represented to her. "I still remember her in every detail, sixty years later; her fragrance in memory removes all my cares." The security she derived from Vicki's undivided affection may, indeed, have played a part in her lifelong assurance of a special place in the world, a place reserved for the most beloved child.

In her memoir, Tietze-Conrat devoted considerable space to detailed descriptions of herself as a child, as she saw herself after sixty or more years, and of portraits made of her at various times in her life. A note of self-satisfaction repeatedly reveals itself. "I always knew that I was the beauty of us three," she wrote. "My description of myself sounds self-enamoured, but I was not." All her classmates, including her best friend, Hilda Gerhart, who helped her especially with science, were three years older than she, which further strengthened her consciousness of the advantages of being the youngest, as she had been in the family.

"If I were to analyze myself," she concludes, "it would perhaps be as follows: I was the youngest. I always undertook contests with older people —sisters and schoolmates—where I could count on success, namely in the field of the intellect. I sublimated all other abilities in this one direction." Here we see evidence of the feeling of need—understandably common in children who are the youngest in a family or class—not only to catch up with but to surpass the siblings or sibling-equivalents who have the benefit of greater size and skills. While the advantages that Erica Conrat felt in her position as "the youngest," enjoying the exclusive love of a mother-surrogate, fed her self-esteem, the (unacknowledged) disadvantages inherent in her position in the family was a source of fierce competitiveness and tireless drive. The confidence in her own intellectual superiority that buoyed her from her early years, enhanced later by her faith in her "photographic memory," gave her courage for the "contests" of her productive professional career.

Oskar Kokoschka painted his famous *Portrait of Hans Tietze and Erica Tietze-Conrat* (see Figure 19) in 1909, four years after their marriage. This striking early work by a leading Expressionist painter has already taken its place in art history among the memorable portraits of married couples.[39] Hans Tietze was in fact slightly taller than his wife; he was five feet five inches, she five feet three inches in height. In the double portrait, however, Erica, who is shown full-face, dominates. Her husband is seen in profile with his head somewhat bent, his expression introspective. His huge, knobby hands contrast strangely with his delicate facial features. Traditionally the marriage bond has been represented in art through clasped right hands.[40] Here the hands do not meet, but the painting gives the impression that a force like an electrical charge bridges the gap between the two left hands.

It is clear that Kokoschka's perception that the wife was the more dominant personality was well founded in terms of their social behavior. Erica was known for her confidence, candor, and biting wit. Hans, though by no means a retiring or isolated person, as Kokoschka's portrait of him seems to imply, was not so overbearing as his wife. He was a successful, enterprising administrator and at the same time enormously productive in his scholarly activity. Late in her life, his wife not only indicated her deference to his strength, but also commented that it was well that he had been a few years her senior in art history, as the man should be the leader (Figure 20). Still, she never undervalued her status as an independent scholar.

The forceful assurance that from the start promoted Erica Tietze-Conrat's professional activities also characterized her personal relations. Along with abundant energy, candor was one of her most memorable traits. She shot

Figure 20. Erica Tietze-Conrat and Hans Tietze at New Boston, Mass., by Willard Golovin, 1954. (*Courtesy Dr. and Mrs. Christopher Tietze*)

forth arrows of truth that struck their targets all the more woundingly because they were sharpened into wit. For this she was appreciated as well as feared. "She saw nothing wrong with telling the truth," said an old friend who had not been immune to her sarcasm. "At least she was one person with whom you always knew exactly how you stood." She was often imperious and demanding even toward people who were her friends and willing helpers. This seems to have worked well on both sides because they shared with her the conviction that she deserved to be treated as someone special.

Behind this assurance, it appears, there lay a self-confidence that exerted magnetic force. Many of those who came within her orbit felt that it was exciting, fun, and an honor to be her friend, even though they have stories to tell of her unrestrained abrasiveness. They recognized her as a presence. "Only the most insensitive people would have been unaware that they were in the company of someone important, someone who had real weight," says a long-time associate. She was capable of being as objective about herself as she was in her judgments of others. She freely acknowledged her own errors, even in print, and generously credited the views of other scholars, once she was convinced that they were correct, even when they contradicted stated positions of her own.

More than twenty years after her death, Erica Tietze-Conrat is affectionately remembered for her human warmth, her dynamic personality, her sharp mind, and even her sharp tongue. Art historians continue to respect and consult her published works. Her extraordinary visual memory enabled her to make numerous contributions to our knowledge of the transmission of motifs and also to recognize the stylistic features that identify specific artists. With her gift for turning all kinds of experiences to advantage, she transformed her observations into insights enriched by a broad spectrum of humane interests. The sense of her own "specialness" that she carried with her from her earliest years was confirmed by her achievements.

NOTES

E. H. Gombrich's obituary of Erica Tietze-Conrat (*Burlington Magazine*, 101 (1959), p. 149) provides some biographical data. My chief source of information about her early years is a fragmentary autobiography of thirty-five typed pages that Dr. Tietze-Conrat wrote in German in about 1950, telling of her life up to her admission to the University. The quoted passages are my translations from the German in that typescript. She also provided information on the events immediately preceding her emigration to the United States in a memoir of eleven pages handwritten in English. These documents are in the possession of Dr. Christopher Tietze in New York and are cited with his permission. Interviews conducted in 1976 with members of her family and friends and correspondence with other relatives added generously to my understanding of her life and personality.

1. The pleasure I derived from my research on Erica Tietze-Conrat was greatly augmented by the people who helped me with this project. For friendly cooperation, information, and the loan of documents, I am particularly indebted to Dr. Hans Aurenhammer, Mr. and Mrs. Joseph Floch, Mr. and Mrs. Alfred Fraenkl, Mr. Willard Golovin, Professor Julius S. Held, Mrs. Annie Knize, Dr. and Mrs. Franz Reichsman, Professor Andreas Tietze, and Dr. and Mrs. Christopher Tietze. Dr. Andrew S. Kahr gave me the benefit of his invaluable advice. I would also like to express my gratitude to Dr. Adele M. Holcomb and Dr. Claire R. Sherman for their unfailing patience and helpful suggestions.

2. Hans Tietze and E. Tietze-Conrat, *Kritisches Verzeichnis der Werke Albrecht Dürers*, Band I: *Der junge Dürer*, Verzeichnis der Werke bis zur venezianischen Reise im Jahre 1505 (Augsburg, 1928). Band II, *Der reife Dürer, 1. Halbband*. Von der venezianischen Reise im Jahre 1505 bis zur niederländischen Reise im Jahre 1520, nebst Nachträgen aus den Jahren 1492-1505 (Basel and Leipzig, 1937). Band II, *Der Reife Dürer, 2. Halbband*. Von der niederländischen Reise im Jahre 1520 bis zum Tode des Meisters 1528 (Basel and Leipzig, 1938).

3. Hans Tietze and E. Tietze-Conrat, *The Drawings of the Venetian Painters in the 15th and 16th Centuries* (New York, 1944).

4. See "A Bibliography of the Writings of Hans Tietze and Erica Tietze-Conrat," by Otto and Hilde Kurz, in Ernst H. Gombrich, Julius S. Held, and Otto Kurz, eds., *Essays in Honor of Hans Tietze 1880-1954* (Paris, 1958), pp. 439-59. The works Erica Tietze-Conrat published as sole author are listed in chronological order on pp. 454-59. Those of which she was coauthor with her husband are listed only in *his* bibliography, pp. 439-53; they began in 1926 with the only book review credited to them as coauthors.

5. Gombrich, Held, and Kurz, eds., *Essays*, Foreword, p. vii.

6. "Unbekannte Werke von Georg Raphael Donner," in *Kunstgeschichtliches Jahrbuch der k. k. Zentral-Kommission*, N.F. 3, 2. Teil (1905), pp. 195-268.

7. *Österreichische Barockplastik* (Vienna, 1920).

8. Berta List-Ganser, "Das akademische Frauenstudium," in *Frauenbewegung, Frauenbildung und Frauenarbeit in Österreich*, Martha Stephanie Braun, Ernestine Fürth, etc., eds. (Vienna, 1930), p. 194. For this and the following material cited on the Vienna school of art history and higher education for women in Vienna, I am indebted to Dr. Claire R. Sherman.

9. Ibid.

10. Franz Gall, *Alma Mater Rudolphina 1365-1965: Die wiener Universität und ihre Studenten* (Vienna, 1965), p. 113.

11. Ibid., p. 114.

12. List-Ganser, p. 194.

13. Edmé Charrier, *L'Évolution intellectualle féminine; Le développement intellectuel de la femme dans les professions intellectuelles* (Paris, 1937), p. 433.

14. Gall, p. 114.

15. E. H. Gombrich, obituary of Erica Tietze-Conrat, *Burlington Magazine*, 101 (1959), p. 149.

16. On Viennese culture of this period, see Allan Janik and Stephen Toulmin, *Wittgenstein's Vienna* (New York, 1973). See also Carl E. Schorske, *Fin-de-Siècle Vienna: Politics and Culture* (New York, 1980).

17. On the history of the Hagenbund and its members, see Exhibition Catalogue *Der Hagenbund* (Vienna, 1975), Sonderausstellung der Historischen Museums der Stadt Wien, 18 Sept.-30 Nov. 1975, p. 40. Also R. Waissenberger, "Hagenbund 1900-1938: Geschichte der Wiener Kunstlervereinigung," in *Mitteilungen der österreichischen Galerie* (1972), pp. 54-130.

18. Quoted by Edith Hoffmann, *Kokoschka, Life and Work* (London, 1947), p. 102.

19. "Die Kunst der Frau. Ein Nachwort zur Ausstellung in der Wiener Sezession," *Zeitschrift für bildende Kunst*, N.F. 22 (1911), 146-48.

20. Articles by both Hans Tietze and Erica Tietze-Conrat are quoted, for instance, in the Exhibition Catalogue, Vienna 1972, *Joseph Floch, Gemälde und Graphiken,* Österreichische Galerie im Oberen Belvedere, 21 March-22 May 1972, pp. 13-15 and 21-22. See also the book *Georg Ehrlich* (whose author's name appears in the exceptional form "Erica Tietze-Conrat"), London, 1956, for an example of her continued support for the contemporary artists whose work she appreciated.

21. *The Drawings of the Venetian Painters,* Preface, p. x.

22. On the career of Hans Tietze, see Ludwig Münz, obituary of Hans Tietze, in *Alte und neue Kunst,* 3 (1954), 60-64, in which is reprinted the tribute written by Karl M. Swoboda on the occasion of the celebration of the golden anniversary of Hans Tietze's doctorate in 1953 by the University of Vienna. Also Ernst H. Buschbeck, "Hans Tietze and his Reorganisation of the Vienna Museums," in Gombrich, Held, and Kurz, eds., *Essays in Honor of Hans Tietze,* pp. 373-75. Further, Julius S. Held, obituary of Hans Tietze, *Art Journal,* 14 (1954), 67-69.

23. The manuscript is now in the library of the Warburg Institute, London.

24. Udo Kultermann, *Geschichte der Kunstgeschichte. Der Weg einer Wissenschaft* (Vienna and Düsseldorf, 1966), Chap. XV, pp. 278-302, on the Vienna school of art history. Vienna's was the third art history chair to be established, preceded only by the ones at the University of Göttingen, occupied by Johann Dominic Fiorillo in 1813, and that at the University of Berlin to which Dr. Waagen was appointed in 1844.

25. See note 6.

26. See note 7.

27. "Dürerstudien. I. Das 'Meerwunder'. II. Die Kupferstiche B. ùnd ?," *Zeitschrift für bildende Kunst,* 51, N.F. 27 (1916), 263-270.

28. See note 2.

29. Hans Tietze and E. Tietze-Conrat, *The Drawings of the Venetian Painters,* Intro., p. 1. My discussion in this paragraph and the following one is based on this Introduction and on the article by Hans Tietze and E. Tietze-Conrat, "Contributi critici allo studio organico dei disegni veneziani dell '500," *La Critica d'Arte,* 2 (1937), 77-88.

30. "Contributi critici . . .," *La Critica d'Arte,* 2 (1937), 79. My translation from the Italian.

31. Ibid.

32. Ibid., p. 88.

33. Ibid., pp. 82-83.

34. *Drawings of the Venetian Painters,* Intro., p. 1. The full reference is *Jahrbuch der Kunsthistorischen Sammlungen des allerhöchsten Kaiserhauses,* 12, 1891, 205-314 and 13, 1892, 175-283.

35. *The Drawings of the Venetian Painters,* like all the other works for which they shared credit, identified the authors as "Hans Tietze and E. Tietze-Conrat." The non-gender-specific "E. Tietze-Conrat" was likewise the style followed in almost all of her individual art-historical writings. The name "Erica Tietze," however, identifies the author of the book of poetry titled *Abschied,* which was privately published in a very small edition in Vienna in 1926. Perhaps she felt that this work represented a different aspect of her persona. For a judicious evaluation of *The Drawings,* see David Rosand's Foreword to the 1969 edition.

36. E. Tietze-Conrat, *Mantegna: Paintings, Drawings, Engravings. Complete Edition* (London, 1955), p. 192. Hans Tietze had published this painting as an autograph work by Mantegna; he believed it was the version left in Mantegna's studio and acquired by Cardinal Sigismundo Gonzaga (*Art in America,* 29 [1941], 51-56).

37. *Mantegna,* p. 13.

38. *Art Bulletin,* 40 (1958), 347-54. Another article, less than a page in length, by Dr. Tietze-Conrat, was published still later: "The Seven-Year-Old Theseus," *Journal of the Warburg and Courtauld Institutes,* 22 (1959), 362.

39. The Tietzes never lent the portrait for public exhibition. Soon after moving to the United States in 1939, they sold it to the Museum of Modern Art.

40. *Andreae Alciati Emblematum libellus* . . ., Paris (1542) 138, Emblem LXI: *In fidem uxoriam* (Ed. prin., Augsburg, 1531).

SELECTED BIBLIOGRAPHY OF ERICA TIETZE-CONRAT

A complete bibliography of the published works of Erica Tietze-Conrat through 1957 can be found in "A Bibliography of the Writings of Hans Tietze and Erica Tietze-Conrat," by Otto and Hilde Kurz, in Ernst Gombrich, Julius S. Held, and Otto Kurz, editors, *Essays in Honor of Hans Tietze 1880-1954* (Paris, 1958), pp. 439-59. The works Erica Tietze-Conrat published as sole author are listed in chronological order on pp. 453-59. Those of which she was coauthor with her husband are listed only in *his* bibliography, pp. 439-53; they began in 1926 with the only book review credited to them as coauthors.

Books

Österreichische Barockplastik. Vienna, 1920.
Der Utrecht-Psalter (Kunst in Holland, vol. 3). Vienna, 1920. Published also in Dutch: *Het Utrechtsch Psalterium*.
Erasmus von Rotterdam im Bilde (Kunst in Holland, vol. 8). Vienna, 1920. Published also in Dutch: *Erasmus van Rotterdam in de beeldende kunst*.
Gerard Dou, Selbstbildnis (Meisterwerke der Kunst in Holland). Vienna, 1920.
Pieter de Hooch, An der Kellertür (Meisterwerke der Kunst in Holland). Vienna, 1920.
Aert de Gelder, Abraham die Engel bewirtend (Meisterwerke der Kunst in Holland). Vienna, 1920.
Nederlandsch Museum Amsterdam. Drei Genrereliefs des 17. Jahrhunderts (Meisterwerke der Kunst in Holland). Vienna, 1920.
Die Pestsäule am Graben in Wien (Österreichische Kunstbücher, vol. 17). Vienna, 1921.
Oskar Laske. Vienna, 1921.
Die Delfter Malerschule, Carel Fabritius, Pieter de Hooch, Jan Vermeer (Bibliothek der Kunstgeschichte, vol. 27). Leipzig, 1922.
Die Kapuzinergruft (Österreichische Kunstbücher, vol. 30). Vienna, 1922.
Andrea Mantegna (Bibliothek der Kunstgeschichte, vol. 51). Leipzig, 1923.
Der französische Kupferstich der Renaissance. Munich, 1925.
Abschied [Poems], *Radierungen von Georg Ehrlich*. Vienna, 1926.
[With Hans Tietze]. *Kritisches Verzeichnis der Werke Albrecht Dürers*, Vol. I, Augsburg, 1929; Vol. II, Basel and Leipzig, 1937 and 1938.
[With Hans Tietze]. *The Drawings of the Venetian Painters in the 15th and 16th Centuries*. New York, 1944.
Mantegna: Paintings, Drawings, Engravings. Complete edition. London, 1955.
Georg Ehrlich. London, 1956.
Dwarfs and Jesters in Art. London, 1957.

Articles

"Unbekannte Werke von Georg Raphael Donner." *Kunstgeschichtliches Jahrbuch der königlich kaiserlich Zentral-Kommission für Erforschung und Erhaltung der Kunst- und Historischen Denkmale, Wien*, 3,2, 1905, pp. 195-268.
"Des Bildhauergesellen Franz Ferdinand Ertinger Reisebeschreibung durch Oesterreich und

Deutschland." Nach der Handschrift Cgm. 3312 der Kgl. Hof- und- Staatsbibliothek München herausgegeben, Wien and Leipzig *(Quellenschriften für Kunstgeschichte und Kunsttechnik*, 14, 1907.)

"Johann Georg Dorfmeister, Ein Kapitel zur Geschichte der österreichischen Barockskulptur." *Kunstgeschichtliches Jahrbuch der k.k. Zentral-Kommission für Erforschung und Erhaltung der Kunst- und historischen Denkmale*, 4, 1910, pp. 228-44.

"Johann Martin Fischers Brunnen am Graben und am Hof in Wien." *Archivalische Beiträge, Kunstgeschichtliches Jahrbuch der k.k. Zentral-Kommission für Erforschung und Erhaltung der Kunst- und historischen Denkmale*, 4, 1910, Beiblatt, pp. 63-90.

"Giovanni Bologna." Thieme-Becker, 4, 1910, pp. 247-52.

"Die Kunst der Frau. Ein Nachwort zur Ausstellung in der Wiener Sezession." *Zeitschrift für bildende Kunst*, N.F. 22, 1911, pp. 146-48.

"Der Böckchen tragende Satyr. Ein Beitrag zur Frage der skulpturalen Kopie und zum Oeuvre Georg Raphael Donners." *Jahrbuch des kunsthistorischen Institutes der k.k. Zentral-Kommission für Denkmalpflege*, 6, 1912, pp. 61-82.

"Permoser-Studien." *Jahrbuch des kunsthistorischen Institutes der k.k. Zentral Kommission für Denkmalpflege*, 8, 1914, pp. 1-10.

"Die Linearkomposition bei Tizian." *Kunstgeschichtliche Anzeigen*, 1913 (published 1915), pp. 84-125. Also published separately, Innsbruck, 1915.

"Dürerstudien. I. Das 'Meerwunder'. II. Die Kupferstiche B.66 und 67." *Zeitschrift für bildende Kunst*, 51, N.F. 27, 1916, pp. 263-70.

"Correggio-Studien." *Jahrbuch des kunsthistorischen Institutes der k.k. Zentral-Kommission für Denkmalpflege*, 10, 1916, pp. 174-79.

"Kupferstiche als Deutungsbehelfe für Skulpturen, I. L'anima beata, l'anima damnata—der Neid. II. Die Frau auf dem Igel." *Mitteilungen der Gesellschaft für vervielfältigende Kunst*, 1916, pp. 65-68.

"Zur höfischen Allegorie der Renaissance." *Jahrbuch der kunsthistorischen Sammlungen des allerhöchsten Kaiserhauses*, 34, 1917, pp. 25-32.

"Die Bronzen der fürstlich Leichtensteinschen Kunstkammer." *Jahrbuch des kunsthistorischen Institutes der k.k. Zentral-Kommission für Denkmalpflege*, 11, 1917, pp. 16-108.

"Beiträge zur Geschichte der italienischen Spätrenaissance- und Barockskulptur." *Jahrbuch des kunsthistorischen Institutes*, 12, 1918, pp. 44-75.

"Künstlers Erdenwallen im Spiegel der österreischischen Barockkunst." *Die bildenden künste* 2, 1919, pp. 81-88.

"Illustrierte Bücher von heute." *Die bildenden Künste*, 2, 1919, pp. 216-24.

"Simultane und sukzessive Kuenste." *Kunstchronik und Kunstmarkt*, 54, N.F. 30, 1919, pp. 283-85.

"Der Film im kunstwissenschaftlichen Unterricht." *Kunstchronik und Kunstmark*, 55, N.F. 31, 1919, pp. 264-66.

"Die Erfindung im Relief, ein Beitrag zur Geschichte der Kleinkunst." *Jahrbuch der kunsthistorischen Sammlungen in Wien*, 35, 1920, pp. 99-176.

"Korrekturen zu dem von E. Tietze-Conrat zusammengestellten Oeuvre des G.R. Donner." *Kunstchronik und Kunstmarkt*, 56, N.F. 32, 1920, pp. 195-97.

"Atalante und Hippomenes." *Kunstchronik und Kunstmarkt*, 55, N.F. 31, 1920, pp. 361-66.

"Wiener Ausstellungen." *Kunstchronik und Kunstmarkt*, 55, N.F. 31, 1920. pp. 333-35.

"Herbstausstellung im Hagenbund, Wien." *Kunstchronik und Kunstmarkt*, 57, N.F. 33, 1921, p. 44.

"Zur Datierung des hl. Sebastian von Mantegna in der Wiener Galerie." *Kunstchronik und Kunstmarkt*, 58, N.F. 34, 1923, pp. 339-45.

"Das Oesterreichische Barockmuseum in Wien." *Belvedere*, 3, 1923, pp. 166-71.

"Edward Munch." *Die Graphischen Künste*, 47, 1924, pp. 75-88.

"Botticelli and the Antique." *The Burlington Magazine*, 47, 1925, pp. 124-29.

"L'allégorie dans la peinture classique hollandaise." *Gazette des Beaux-Arts*, 70, 1928/I, pp. 1-12.

"Die Vorbilder von Daniel Hopfers figuralem Werk." *Jahrbuch der kunsthistorischen Sammlungen in Wien*, N.F. 9, 1935, pp. 97-110.

"Echte und unechte Tintoretto-Zeichnungen, Plastisches Modell und Kompositionsbehelf, Spiegelverkehrung, Rythmische Wiederholung." *Die Graphischen Künste*, N.F. 1, 1936, pp. 88-100.

"A Lost Michelangelo Reconstructed." *The Burlington Magazine*, 68, 1936, pp. 163-70.

"Decorative Paintings of the Venetian Renaissance Reconstructed from Drawings." *The Art Quarterly*, 3, 1940, pp. 15-39.

"When Was the First Etching Made?" *The Print Collector's Quarterly*, 27, 1940, pp. 166-77.

"A Rediscovered Early Masterpiece by Titian [*The Flight into Egypt*, Hermitage]." *Art in America*, 29, 1941, pp. 144-51.

"Neglected Contemporary Sources Relating to Michelangelo and Titian, I. Michelangelo, Pietro Aretino and the Last Judgment; II. Titian and the Versalius Illustrations." *The Art Bulletin*, 25, 1943, pp. 154-59.

"Was Mantegna an Engraver?" *Gazette des Beaux-Arts*, 6, 24, 1943, pp. 375-81.

"Titian as a Letter Writer." *The Art Bulletin*, 26, 1944, pp. 117-23.

"Dürer's Shop, Three Studies. I. Glass Paintings in San Nazaro in Milan, II. Panels of a Dispersed Altarpiece, III. The Cherub Heads." *Art in America*, 33, 1945, pp. 13-26, 168.

"Titian's 'Battle of Cadore.'" *The Art Bulletin*, 27, 1945, pp. 205-8.

"Titian's Portrait of Paul III." *Gazette des Beaux-Arts*, 6, 29, 1946, pp. 73-84.

"Titian's Workshop in His Late Years." *The Art Bulletin*, 28, 1946, pp. 76-88.

"An Unpublished Madonna by Giovanni Bellini and the Problem of Replicas in his Shop." *Gazette des Beaux-Arts*, 6, 33, 1948, pp. 379-82.

"Two Dosso Puzzles in Washington and in New York." *Gazette des Beaux-Arts*, 6, 33, 1948, pp. 129-36.

"Mantegna's Parnassus: A Discussion of a Recent Interpretation [E. Wind, *Bellini's 'Feast of the Gods,' a Study in Venetian Humanism*]." *The Art Bulletin*, 31, 1949, pp. 126-30.

"Das 'Skizzenbuch' des Van Dyck als Quelle für die Tizianforschung." *Critica d'Arte*, 3, 8, 1950, pp. 425-42.

"Titian's Allegory of 'Religion.'" *Journal of the Warburg and Courtauld Institutes*, 14, 1951, pp. 127-32.

"The Pesaro Madonna: A Footnote on Titian." *Gazette des Beaux-Arts*, 6, 42, 1953, pp. 117-82.

"The Church Program of Michelangelo's Medici Chapel." *The Art Bulletin*, 36, 1954, pp. 222-24.

"Un soffitto di Tiziano a Brescia conservato in un disegno del Rubens." *Arte Veneta*, 8, 1954, pp. 209-10.

"Titian as a Landscape Painter." *Gazette des Beaux-Arts*, 6, 45, 1955, pp. 11-20.

"'Archeologia tizianesca.'" *Arte Veneta*, 10, 1956, pp. 82-89.

Reviews

Review of Berthold Haendke, *Kunstanalysen aus neunzehn Jahrhunderten*, Brunswick [1907?], in *Kunstgeschichtliche Anzeigen*, 1909, pp. 42-43.

Review of Fritz Goldschmidt, *Pontormo, Rosso und Bronzino*, Leipzig, 1911, in *Kunstgeschichtliche Anzeigen*, 1912, pp. 15-18.

Review of Ernst Kris, *Meister und Meisterwerke der Steinschneidekunst in der italienischen*

Renaissance, 2 vols., Vienna, 1929, in *Zeitschrift für bildende Kunst*, 63, 1929, *Kunst-chronik und Kunstliteratur*, pp. 132-133.

Review of Katharine Ada Esdaile, *The Life and Work of Louis François Roubiliac*, London, 1928, in *Zeitschrift für bildende Kunst*, 63, 1929, *Kunstchronik und Kunstliteratur*, pp. 132-33.

Review of Theodor Hetzer, *Das deutsche Element in der italienischen Malerei des 16. Jahrhunderts*, Berlin, 1929, in *Mitteilungen der Gesellschaft für vervielfältigende Kunst*, 1929, pp. 80-81.

Review of M.D. Henkel, *Le dessin hollandais des origines au XVIIe siècle*, Paris, 1931, in *Mitteilungen der Gesellschaft für vervielfältigende Kunst*, 1931, pp. 59-60.

Review of Rodolfo Pallucchini, *I dipinti della Galleria Estense a Modena*, Rome, 1945, in *Gazette des Beaux-Arts*, ser. 6, vol. 29, 1946, p. 64.

Review of Bernard Berenson, *Italian Pictures of the Renaissance, Venetian School* [London, c. 1957], in *The Art Bulletin*, 40, 1958, pp. 347-54.

PART IV

SCHOLARS ACTIVE FROM THE EARLY-TWENTIETH CENTURY TO 1979

SIRARPIE DER NERSESSIAN (b. 1896): EDUCATOR AND SCHOLAR IN BYZANTINE AND ARMENIAN ART

Jelisaveta Stanojevich Allen[1]

Professor Sirarpie Der Nersessian in her long career as educator and scholar has been honored in a number of countries by a number of institutions of higher learning and learned societies, but despite the variety of tributes she has received, no full account of her biography and scholarly contributions has yet been attempted.

Perhaps her personal modesty has discouraged any investigation of her life, while her achievements eloquently speak for themselves. Hers is, however, an unusual life strongly influenced by the major international crises of the twentieth century. World War I transformed young Sirarpie Der Nersessian, the child of a well-to-do family, into a refugee who had to escape her native Constantinople and finally settle in France. Although World War II found her established as a professor in the United States, the long war years severed all her ties with France, her sister, and numerous friends. The life story of Sirarpie Der Nersessian is intertwined with and deeply rooted in the history of the Armenian people. Her life's task was to communicate to the rest of the world Armenian history and civilization, as well as the role played by Armenian culture in East-West relations. Thus she "extended the borders of learning"[2] and expanded the scope of Western scholarship in general.

Sirarpie Der Nersessian was born in Constantinople on 5 September 1896. Her family had long been distinguished in intellectual and ecclesiastical circles. Her father Mihran Der Nersessian was born at Erzerum in northeastern Turkey and later came to Constantinople. By the time he married Akabi Ormanian, he was an established businessman. The young couple lived with her parents. The Der Nersessians had three children; a son, Boghos, born in 1892; a daughter, Arax, born in 1894, and the youngest,

Sirarpie. With the family lived also Akabi's brother, Monsignor Maghak'ia Ormanian, a well-known historian and theologian of the Armenian church. Mgr. Ormanian founded the Armenian seminary of Armash, which he directed until 1896, when he was elected Armenian Patriarch of Constantinople, the highest office of the church. The Patriarch, who received his investiture also from the Porte, the Turkish Government, was at the same time the lawful head of the Armenian nation.[3] Given the precarious situation of the Armenians in the Ottoman Empire, his position was very difficult. For many years the Armenians suffered persecution of varying degrees of brutality. New harassments and atrocities erupted in unpredictable outbreaks of violence. Patriarch Ormanian, an erudite scholar and a distinguished diplomat, succeeded in securing a period of relative peace for the Armenians during his twelve years at the helm of the Armenian church and nation. However, Patriarch Ormanian resigned from his high office in 1908, after the revolt of the "Young Turks," the nationalist movement that sought reform in the Ottoman Empire,[4] when the young Armenian revolutionaries accused him of moderation. At that time, he turned to historical studies and research. In 1910 he published in French *L'église arménienne*, translated into English in 1912. Later printed in Armenian and Russian, this authoritative history is still the most dependable study of the Armenian church.[5]

Such was the background of Sirarpie Der Nersessian's family, the environment in which she grew up. Her deep devotion to her uncle is proved by the dedication of her very first book, published in 1936, modestly stating that his life and work were a source of inspiration and an unforgettable example for her.[6] The image of her distinguished uncle was to serve as a guiding light throughout her life.

Sirarpie Der Nersessian received her primary and secondary education in Constantinople, first at the Armenian grade school and then at the English High School for Girls, from which she graduated shortly before World War I with a first-class honors certificate awarded by the London examiners. Study and research were an established lifestyle of this literate household, and young Sirarpie absorbed learning as a normal principle of life. As subjects not taught at school were supplied by instruction at home, the Der Nersessian children learned French and English equally well, along with their native Armenian. From early childhood, they had to use two different alphabets and communicate in several languages. The children also studied music at home, and their understanding of this art form was exceptional. Arax, a gifted artist, also studied painting. The little girls very much enjoyed driving in their uncle's carriage and peeking from behind the drawn curtains to observe the colorful street scenes of Constantinople. Their mother died when Sirarpie was nine years old, and their father died in 1914, when she was barely eighteen. After their mother's death, an unmarried aunt, Evkiné Ormanian, took care of the children.

The year 1915 brought upon the Armenian people in Turkey new waves of persecutions, which completely changed the course of the life of the Der Nersessian family. The Ottoman pogroms of World War I proved more vicious than ever before, and they spared hardly anyone. When deportations of the Armenians began, Mgr. Ormanian was in Jerusalem on a special mission to the Armenian Patriarchate there. As the Allied troops in 1917 advanced from the south, the Ottomans deported him to Damascus, and upon his return to Constantinople in 1918 he died of exhaustion. At the start of the raids in 1915 the two Der Nersessian girls and their aunt were alone in Constantinople. Friends and relatives urged them to leave the city. The only possible way out was through Bulgaria. Their odyssey took them first to Sofia, where they remained for eight months. They had thought that their stay there would be a short one, but as the war continued they decided to go to Switzerland, where they could continue their studies. The trip through war-ridden Europe took over a month before they reached the Swiss border. They had procured visas for Switzerland, unaware that the Swiss regulations required a three-week quarantine in Austria for anyone crossing the border. At the Swiss border they were turned back to Austria. They got off the train at Telfs-Paffenhofen, in the Tyrol, not knowing a soul in that mountain village. The population of the place grew very suspicious of these foreign women, who did not speak any German, but only French and English—the languages of the enemies. The girls and their aunt were walking desperately toward the end of the village looking for a shelter, when finally at the very last house on the road a motherly looking, very kind elderly woman met them, took them in, and kept them until they were able to enter Switzerland. The warm feeling the Der Nersessian sisters have for Austria dates from this wartime episode.

Once in Switzerland, the Der Nersessian sisters settled in Geneva, where Sirarpie entered the Collège de Genève and Arax enrolled at the Ecole des Beaux Arts, as well as at the Conservatoire de Musique. A year after their arrival, in 1917, their beloved aunt died in Geneva. The same year Sirarpie secured the Swiss Certificat de Maturité (high school diploma) and enrolled at the University of Geneva, where she followed courses at the Faculté des Lettres until 1919. The reversal of the family's fortune in Turkey made it necessary for Sirarpie Der Nersessian to support herself throughout her student years. Though putting oneself through school is an established pattern today, at that time it was rather unusual for a girl of her social stratum to do so.

In 1919, after the war had ended, the sisters moved to Paris. At this time a happy event occurred in their lives. Arax married a distant cousin, the architect Zareh Der Nersessian, to whom she had been engaged before the war and with whom she was reunited. From then on the sisters were respectively distinguished as Mademoiselle Der Nersessian and Madame Der Nersessian.

Sirarpie Der Nersessian continued her studies at the Sorbonne and found there a most congenial intellectual atmosphere. To these Paris student years date some of her lifelong friendships, such as those with the Byzantine historian Father Francis Dvornik and the Byzantine art historian Professor André Grabar and his family. In 1920 she obtained her License ès Lettres and in 1921 the Diplome d'Etudes Supérieures d'histoire et de géographie, equivalent of the bachelor's and master's degrees.

At the Sorbonne her extraordinary intellectual abilities soon commanded the attention of her professors, the foremost Byzantine scholars of the period, the historian Charles Diehl and the art historian Gabriel Millet. To them she owes her scholarly development as a Byzantinist. Charles Diehl guided her in the study of history and later wrote the preface to her published thesis,[7] while Gabriel Millet introduced her to the study of Byzantine art history and gave her unlimited support in her study and work. Another prominent art historian and scholar instrumental in her scholarly formation and development was Henri Focillon. She expressed eloquently her sincere and profound gratitude to her *Maîtres* in the prefaces of her early publications. Originally Sirarpie intended to pursue history as her principal scholarly discipline, while she wished to study the history of art as just one aspect of cultural expression. However, Gabriel Millet's field work and research in Byzantine art opened new horizons to her, and her interest in the history of art became the eventual focus of her life's work. Her basic formation as an historian strongly marks her scholarly approach to research and the methodology she adopted and followed. By 1922 she had become an assistant to Millet at the Ecole pratique des Hautes Etudes of the University of Paris, where she took an active part in organizing the photographic collection of Byzantine monuments. At that time this center was the most important international resource for scholars of Byzantine art. It was in this connection that she came to know prominent American medievalists, like the art historians Professors Charles Rufus Morey and Albert M. Friend, both from Princeton, and Walter Cook from New York University. At the "Ecole pratique" she also took on the project of cataloguing and describing the miniatures of Byzantine illuminated psalters, the Old Testament hymnal books. This task took her to Rome and London, where she worked at the Vatican Library and at the British Museum. Her study of the illuminated manuscripts to which she eventually devoted a major part of her scholarly research originate in this period, the era when Byzantine manuscript illumination was launched as an important area of study.

After she obtained the Diplome des Hautes Etudes in 1925, she began work on her two theses. At the time in France for the Doctorat ès Lettres a candidate had to submit to the jury two theses, already published in book form. In turn these theses had to be defended at the *soutenance*, a solemn session usually lasting four to five hours in the presence of the jury, prominent scholars from other universities, and the public. Der Nersessian's choice of subjects was the illustration of the medieval romance of Barlaam and Joasaph for the major thesis. The supplementary one was a study of the Armenian illuminated manuscripts from the twelfth to the fourteenth centuries in the library of the Mekhitarist monastery at San Lazzaro in Venice. An ideal place to study Armenian manuscripts, the collection was the richest in Europe, second only to those of Etchmiadzin (now at the Matenadaran in Erevan) and the library of the Armenian Patriarchate in Jerusalem. So Der Nersessian went to Venice in 1927. The Mekhitarist fathers left the resources of the library at her disposition. From then on she often spent her summer months in Venice, continuing her study of the manuscripts, which the monks had kindly allowed her to publish. The result of this work eventually became one of her two doctoral theses and was published in 1936/37 in two volumes. This book was the first comprehensive publication on Armenian manuscripts ever attempted, for which Der Nersessian won an award from the Association des Etudes Grecques.

From 1927 to 1929 while working on these research projects, Der Nersessian was "Chargée de conférence temporaire" at the Ecole des Hautes Etudes. A joint study by Der Nersessian and Millet, "Le psautier arménien illustré," was published in 1929 in the *Revue des études arméniennes*.[8] The article discusses the result of an examination of an Armenian psalter (then in the collection of E. Ségrédakis, now in the Freer Gallery, cod. 37.13) and its relation to Byzantine psalters. The synthesis in this important work established the relation of Armenian art to the art of Byzantium.

Just at the time when Sirarpie Der Nersessian was finishing her formal studies in France, the art department of Wellesley College, chaired by Professor Myrtilla Avery, envisioned broadening the curriculum by introducing courses on Byzantine art. Maintaining the high standards of the Wellesley tradition, Avery was searching for an established, or highly promising, scholar in this area. As at the time no person with these qualifications was to be found in the United States, her close friends and colleagues Charles R. Morey, Albert Friend, and Walter Cook recommended to her Sirarpie Der Nersessian. Avery expressed her enthusiasm for this idea and met Der Nersessian in Paris. The meeting was very pleasant, though Der Nersessian was not aware that she was being interviewed for a teaching position in the United States. The subsequent offer took her by surprise, and as she wished to complete her two theses, an arrangement was made according to which she would teach at Wellesley only during the second semester so that she could spend the remaining part of the year in Europe. Thus Der Nersessian came to Wellesley as a lecturer in 1930/31 to give the first courses in Byzantine art ever offered in a woman's college.[9] Over the years she taught sections of the survey courses, senior courses on ancient and medieval art, while her seminars were devoted to Byzantine art.[10]

At first she lived on the campus in a small house for the faculty, where she had one room. Later on she moved to a dormitory where her apartment consisted of a living room, a bedroom, and a bath. She ate in the dining room with the students. Der Nersessian was a rather modest, unassuming person; all that students knew of her life was that she was an Armenian and that she came from Paris and the Sorbonne. Pretty and charming, with a strong sense of humor, she was friendly to the students and very popular with them: they remember her as a vivacious, warm person always ready to help. But a "character" she was not, and there were no anecdotes about her. While not a disciplinarian, academically she was very demanding. Instead of taking comprehensive examinations, graduate students with a B+ average could take a topic for their thesis that in turn they would have to present to the department and defend. In such cases the tutorial assistance of a professor was available. "Miss Der Ner," as the students called her familiarly, expected work to be done to perfection. She would go over the material with the student in great detail, insisting that all points should be clear. She did not spare any time or effort in assisting the students with all the scholarly apparatus available. At this early stage of her career, she had not yet achieved her later reputation as an outstanding scholar. Her standing with the students rested on her considerable talents as a teacher.

Der Nersessian became involved with all aspects of college life, and she also was a close collaborator of Professor Myrtilla Avery. She gained a firsthand knowledge of the problems as well as the ideals and principles of the department.[11] Beginning in 1934, Der Nersessian taught at Wellesley full time. Her summers were always spent in Europe, where she continued her own investigations. The two American centers for Der Nersessian's research were the Pierpont Morgan Library in New York and the Walters Art Gallery in Baltimore. In 1936 as a visiting lecturer at New York University she gave a course on Armenian manuscripts. The lectures took place at the Pierpont Morgan Library, where original manuscripts were available for examination. One of the participants in this course was Dorothy Miner, keeper of manuscripts at the Walters. From this exchange began a friendship that lasted over forty years. Sirarpie Der Nersessian also greatly valued her friendship with Belle da Costa Greene, director of the Morgan Library, who gave her full access to the library's rich resources.

The work on her two theses was completed, one "L'illustration du Roman de Barlaam et Joasaph" and the other "Manuscrits arméniens illustrés des XIIe, XIIIe, et XIVe siècles de la Bibliothèque des Pères Mekhitaristes de Venise," and in 1936 she presented them at the Sorbonne for the degree of Docteur ès Lettres. After she performed brilliantly during the examination, the degree was bestowed on her with the highest possible commendation, "Mention très honorable," handed down by her jury. The two theses were published in 1936/37, each in two volumes, and each won an award.[12]

In those years her other contributions to international Byzantine scholarship was a paper "La Légende d'Abgar d'après un rouleau illustré de la Bibliothèque Pierpont Morgan à New York" which she read at the Fourth International Congress of Byzantine Studies held in Sofia in 1934,[13] and the article "Une nouvelle réplique slavonne du Paris Gr. 74, et les manuscrits d'Anastase Crimovici," which she wrote for the *Mélanges Nicolas Jorga*,[14] to honor the much respected Rumanian scholar and statesman. At that time she also wrote a number of articles published in the United States.

When, in 1937, Professor Avery planned to retire, her personal choice for her successor was Sirarpie Der Nersessian, by then a full professor. After observing the latter's work on the faculty for seven years, Avery realized that Der Nersessian had the qualities of leadership needed to administer a well-known and established department. She also knew that the department of art as organized by Professor Alice Van Vechten Brown in 1897 needed a capable, established scholar of Der Nersessian's reputation to continue the tradition of its "place of distinction in the forefront among colleges and universities, for men as well as for women."[15] Professor Brown in her tenure at Wellesley of some thirty-three years had raised the art department to this high level. Professor Avery had continued to follow in her footsteps and had considerably expanded the curriculum. Consequently she expected her successor to live up to these standards. For Professor Sirarpie Der Nersessian it was not an easy decision to make. A conscientious scholar and educator, she never thought of a career as an administrator. To assume new duties and more responsibilities would mean even less free time, time much needed for research. "She long resisted Miss Avery's persuasive powers, yielding at last only in response to a strong personal appeal which played on her sense of obligation to serve where her usefulness could be so great and where she was so unanimously wanted."[16] So in July 1937 Professor Der Nersessian became the head of the art department and director of the Farnsworth Museum. Her new position resulted from her high standards of scholarship, clarity of judgment, cooperation with the faculty, painstaking work, and devotion to the college. By this time the faculty had increased by three more members.[17] The war years proved to be more difficult for the department and more demanding of the faculty, as several of its members were called to active duty.

The teaching policy of the department was faithfully continued, and the importance of the study of languages was stressed. Both French and German were required of students who were planning to do graduate work in art; and for those majoring in classical archaeology, one college course in Greek and Latin, as well as courses in ancient history, were recommended. Professor Der Nersessian continued to teach some of the courses, especially those for seniors. She made a special effort to enlarge the slide and photo collection, as well as the art library. She also gave guidance to younger teachers to assure well-integrated courses. In order to know how well her faculty members were discharging their duties, she would occasionally come and sit in on classes. Afterwards in her warm, easy, pleasant way she would privately discuss particular details, and point out what should be said and emphasized. Her clear mind saw and presented every question in perspective. Her advice greatly helped young faculty members with limited teaching experience. She did not exert pressure or make unreasonable demands on the faculty. The "publish or perish" trauma was not yet known in the academic world and she didn't expect the faculty to write and publish while teaching, as publications were normally the result of many years of hard work and research. On the other hand, she encouraged faculty members invited by another institution to give a course in the history of art.

The students of those years (1937-1946) remember Professor Der Nersessian with great devotion and realize what she meant in their over-all intellectual formation. By then they were aware that their professor was an outstanding scholar, and for them she was *the Department*. She had an apartment in Davis Hall, and her quick, trot-like little step in the Hall is vividly remembered. She was popular among the students. They admired and stood in awe of her from a distance as she also inspired great respect. In the classroom Professor Der Nersessian opened her students' eyes to the world of art, and when after the war they could travel abroad they knew where, at what, and how to look. The survey courses she gave were the basis of their study of art history. She personally read all the papers written by her students, on which she wrote extensive notes and memorable comments. She did not, however, pressure the students; rather, she fostered their desire to meet her very high standards. The following letter quoted here is from a former art major, and it illustrates what students absorbed for life from Sirarpie Der Nersessian.

I remember Miss Der Nersessian vividly, but no anecdotes! She was, in my mind, not a person about whom anecdotes occurred. She didn't do forgetful or absent-minded [things] or have a rapier-like tongue which devastated people—she was simply a profoundly intelligent woman with care and enthusiasm for her profession. I suspect she taught by osmosis—she was not by any means the most enthusiastic or best lecturer I ever heard (John McAndrew would qualify for the first, Phyllis Lehmann for the second). So what did she have that totally enchanted and fascinated me?

I suspect it was clarity, clarity in the way she spoke, in the way she taught art history. Her handling of Gothic architecture was superb, and I remember it to this day. She was somehow, dimly perceived in those days, a crystalline intellect. . . . And it committed me to a way of looking at the world, which is still the basis of my work in nature writing. . . .

I remember with greatest affection the Byzantine art course that she taught, my senior year, I think. Again it was that absolute clarity of expression, the gleaming intellect.

I remember that somewhere about that time she had word that her sister was alive in Paris, having heard nothing for the years of the war. There was an extra lightness in her face, but otherwise she was a very private person.

And so again I look back and try to define why she was such a fantastic teacher, and why, in this day of "contact" and "one-to-one" concepts, where everyone has to be "warm" and "communicate," how did she do it? For there are just none of those professorial stories about putting the cat in the refrigerator and the milk out. Perhaps it was that she was a pure scholar, so dedicated to her work and interpretation of it to others, that she needed none of those sops that we seem to think we need today. She communicated, not the charm of herself, but the greatness of the history of art, in which she believed and conveyed with absolute perfection. I know without a doubt that what she delivered in that lecture room was the pure stuff, undiluted, and I still draw on it.[18]

Her former students do not remember any anecdotes, her colleagues remember only some in which they were involved, but Professor Der Nersessian recalls and jokingly relates an anecdote of those years. When at a social gathering of academics in the Boston area somebody asked her "Where is your husband, Professor Der Nersessian?" she replied, "I am the husband."

Sirarpie Der Nersessian played a less active role as director of the Farnsworth Museum (presently the Wellesley College Museum) than as the head of the department. As special funds were not available, she could not make major acquisitions. The museum was extensively used for practical exercises with the students, who were also encouraged to visit regularly the great museums of the Boston area. She reorganized the Art Building, improved the displays, and organized several exhibitions. Among them, an innovative display of American Indian artifacts was an imaginative, ethnically oriented presentation.[19] Most remarkable was the exhibition of Chinese Ritual Bronzes and Paintings, held in May 1943, under the auspices of the Mayling Soong Foundation. This foundation "was established in June 1942 in honor of Madame Chiang Kai-Shek for the cultivation at Wellesley College of interest in China and the East."[20] The exhibition was the final feature of the year's activities, as special courses, discussion groups, and public lectures focused on various aspects of Far Eastern culture. A visiting lecturer, Professor George Rowley, a well-known authority in the field, gave a course on Art of the Far East, including India, Japan, and China, with particular emphasis on the latter. With his collaboration the exhibition was organized and the catalogue published. The objects for the exhibition were borrowed from a number of museums such as the Fogg Museum of Art, the Metropolitan Museum, the Museum of Fine Arts in Boston, the Philadelphia Museum of Art, the Princeton Museum of Historic Art, and the Worcester Art Museum. A number of private collections were also represented. Viewers remember it as a magnificent exhibition.

Communication between departments at Wellesley was very lively, with regular biweekly meetings of the larger faculty to discuss various topics. The art department was a closely knit friendly group where, aside from professional contacts, personal friendships were established. Agnes Abbot wrote:

Whatever the particular activity in which she was engaged, Miss Der Nersessian's happy faculty for working sympathetically with all sorts of people, her charm, her warm interest in the personal problems of faculty and staff, and her lively sense of humor made her years at Wellesley a delightful experience for all of us. These same qualities, combined with a wide variety of interests outside her field, in music, in languages and literature, philosophy and science, made her constantly sought after outside the department, and she served on all the important regular committees of the college, as well as on such special ones as that of the Mayling Soong Foundation.[21]

Educational and other organizations outside the college were not slow to recognize her outstanding abilities, and she soon took an active part in the work of many committees, especially those of the American Association of University Women and the College Art Association. She also gave generously of her interest and attention to various Armenian societies and local groups. She found time, moreover, to deliver not only individual lectures in a variety of places but several series of lectures such as those at New York University and at the Ecole Libre des Hautes Etudes in New York. This impressive body of accomplishment was achieved only by an extraordinary capacity to make the most of every spare moment, night or day, including vacations. One may well wonder how she still found time for the many friends who enjoyed her stimulating companionship and who have always been able to count upon her understanding and support.

Although Professor Der Nersessian left Wellesley College in 1946, she continued her ties with it in a special way, most notably by her election in 1949 as "faculty trustee" of the college, a position in which she served another twelve years to the mutual satisfaction of faculty and trustees.[22]

Among the individual lectures Der Nersessian delivered outside Wellesley was one given on 10 March 1939 on "Some Aspects of Byzantine Sculpture" at Dumbarton Oaks, in Washington, D.C. This event took place a year and a half before Mildred and Robert Woods Bliss bequeathed their collections, library, and estate to Harvard University. Sirarpie Der Nersessian probably had no premonition at this time that she would eventually spend seventeen years of her life in that beautiful place.

The migration of many great European scholars to the United States during World War II also benefited medieval and Byzantine studies. Professor Henri Focillon escaped from France, and Professor Henri Grégoire from Belgium. While Professor Focillon was teaching at Yale, Professor Grégoire energetically continued his journal *Byzantion*, of which three volumes were published in Boston by the Byzantine Institute and the Mediaeval Academy of America.[23] Sirarpie Der Nersessian contributed an article to each issue. In his capacity as vice-president of the Institut de Philologie et d'Histoire Orientales et Slaves, affiliated with the Ecole Libre des Hautes Etudes, Grégoire organized lectures and conferences on the civilization of the Byzantine world. Professor Der Nersessian was invited to deliver a set of five lectures on Armenian art and civilization. She gave them in French in April and May of 1942 at the Pierpont Morgan Library.

The first two of the five lectures were devoted to a general survey of Armenian history and an account of religious controversies; the remaining three to the architecture, sculpture, and painting of Armenia. Favorable response to the lectures led to their publication in 1945 by the Harvard University Press as *Armenia and the Byzantine Empire: A Brief Study of Armenian Art and Civilization*, with a five-page French *Préface* elegantly written by Professor Grégoire. The dedication of her third book alludes to Der Nersessian's concern for Arax, whose unknown fate in occupied France remained a subject of intense anxiety: "To My Sister." Der Nersessian shed light in this work on a previously little known subject, the history and civilization of medieval Armenia. She combined her great erudition as both historian and an art historian in her comprehensive account of the political, religious, cultural, and artistic history of Armenia and its relations with neighboring Byzantium.

Before World War II, Early Christian and Byzantine scholarship and research in the United States had a short and yet distinguished background.[24] The art department of Princeton University had become the principal American research center for the study of Early Christian and Byzantine art, under the guidance of Professors Charles Rufus Morey and Albert M. Friend. In 1935 another established Byzantinist, Kurt Weitzmann, joined the faculty. At Yale University Mikhail I. Rostovtsev pioneered important archaeological projects, while New York University had been offering graduate courses in Byzantine art since 1926. At the University of Wisconsin, Alexander A. Vasiliev, an internationally renowned scholar, held the chair of Byzantine history. Scholars could draw on extensive American collections of art objects and manuscripts of the Early Christian, Byzantine, and medieval periods. Originally private, such collections as the Pierpont Morgan Library in New York, the Freer Gallery of Art in Washington, and the Walters Art Gallery in Baltimore had become public institutions in the 1920s and 1930s. Accompanying and related to those scholarly and collecting activities was a series of pioneer exhibitions on Early Christian and Byzantine art like those of *Pagan and Christian Art in the Latin West and Byzantine East* held at the Art Museum at Worcester, in 1937, at which Antioch floor mosaics, sculpture from Dura-Europos, and the copies of the mosaics uncovered in the church of St. Sophia in Constantinople were exhibited for the first time. In 1941 an exhibition of Coptic art, the art of the early Christians of Egypt, took place at the Brooklyn Museum.

A new era in the development of Byzantine studies began on 29 November 1940. When Mildred and Robert Woods Bliss formally conveyed to Harvard University their Georgetown estate, Dumbarton Oaks, with their remarkable collection of Byzantine art, the Research Library (including two important research tools, a copy of the Princeton Index of Christian Art and the Census of Early Christian and Byzantine Art in America), an important center of Byzantine studies was created in Washington. The intention of the donors, well stated in the dedication, read: "The Dumbarton Oaks Research Library and Collection has been assembled and conveyed to Harvard University by Mildred and Robert Woods Bliss that the continuity of scholarship in the Byzantine and Mediaeval humanities may remain unbroken to clarify an ever changing present and to inform the future with wisdom. MCMXL."

The hope that Dumbarton Oaks would become an institution of national importance was evident from the appointments for the first academic year. Such scholars as the art historians Henri Focillon and Charles R. Morey, historian Henri Grégoire, archaeologist Doro Levi, and theologian Dom Anselm Strittmatter were in residence or lectured at the Center the first year. Distinguished appointments continued when in 1944/45 Professor Sirarpie Der Nersessian was named a Senior Fellow, together with Professor Vasiliev and medievalist Edward K. Rand. The Senior Scholar at the Center was Professor Friend of Princeton University, and Dr. John S. Thacher was appointed acting director of Dumbarton Oaks for a period of one year; eventually Thacher became director of Dumbarton Oaks until his retirement in 1969.

On 7 April 1946, the Sunday issue of the *Washington Post* carried Professor Der Nersessian's picture under the heading: "Harvard appoints 8 renowned scholars to Dumbarton Oaks Research Institute staff. Wellesley Professor given post for life." (Figure 21) The other scholars appointed on the same occasion were theologian and biblical archaeologist Professor Carl H. Kraeling of Yale University, historian Professor Alexander A. Vasiliev, church and intellectual historian Milton V. Anastos, philologist Glanville Downey, art historian Ernst Kitzinger, and architectural historian Paul A. Underwood. Professor Friend was invited to chair the board of scholars and the publications committee.

With the appointment of a permanent faculty both the organizational structure and the scope of study and research at Dumbarton Oaks were changed. In addition to the investigations pursued thus far in the field of art and archaeology and also literary sources,[25] two more scholarly disciplines were included in the core of study, namely, history and theology. A couple of years later a new dimension was added to the general activities of the institution, when after the death of Thomas Whittemore, Director of the Byzantine Institute of America, his field work in Constantinople was continued by Professor Paul A. Underwood. Eventually the Byzantine Institute was merged with Dumbarton Oaks.

Figure 21. Sirarpie Der Nersessian, ca. 1946. (*Courtesy Sirarpie Der Nersessian*)

The annual symposia inaugurated in 1944 were planned around a specific topic and were the result of a well-organized and coordinated theme. The participants invited to deliver lectures were always outstanding scholars in their respective fields, and most of the papers read at the symposia were published in the *Dumbarton Oaks Papers*. Catalogues of the collection were begun and the monograph series *Dumbarton Oaks Studies* was established in 1950 to publish results of individual investigations by faculty members. Over the years, the scope of these scholarly activities, the soundness of the research, and the authority of the scholars connected with the projects gained for Dumbarton Oaks an international reputation as the leading center of Byzantine studies.

The annual symposium held in the spring of 1947 had an especially memorable character. In recognition of Princeton University's Bicentennial Celebration,[26] a joint program was organized by Princeton, the Walters Art Gallery, and Dumbarton Oaks, which can indeed be termed a movable intellectual feast. The program began on 22 and 23 April with a series of lectures held at Princeton. The second phase was marked by an exhibition *Early Christian and Byzantine Art* that opened in Baltimore on 24 April. This was the first exhibition held in the United States that showed American holdings in the field. The concluding ceremony took place at Dumbarton Oaks on 25 and 26 April. To complement the splendor of the celebration an evening concert of chamber music was held on the 25th, under the direction of Igor Stravinsky. The entire sequence of events showed both acknowledgement of Princeton's role in developing Byzantine and medieval studies and the progress made in the field generally and at Dumbarton Oaks in particular.

Such was the ambience in which Sirarpie Der Nersessian lived and worked for the next sixteen years. Her duties at Dumbarton Oaks were numerous. As a member of the Board of Scholars she served on the publications and the library committees. During the illness of Professor Friend, she was appointed deputy director for 1953/54 and acting director of studies for the following academic year, 1954/55. The latter duty she performed again during the winter term of 1961/62, when Professor Ernst Kitzinger, then director of studies, was teaching at Harvard. In 1953 she became Henri Focillon Professor of Art and Archaeology of the Faculty of Arts and Sciences of Harvard University. It was a particularly gratifying turn of events for her to hold the chair named for her distinguished professor. Der Nersessian's administrative experience, gained at Wellesley, proved to be an invaluable asset to Dumbarton Oaks. Her special contribution was her logical system of organization. Her sense of duty was deep, and she was totally devoted to her obligations. Objective and frank, she freely discussed problems and gave her opinions but managed to avoid personal comments and gossip. Her strict standards greatly helped the achievement at Dumbarton Oaks of a reputation for distinguished scholarship.

As a person Der Nersessian was, as always, modest and unassuming. Her demands were never unreasonable, nor did she ever "blow her own horn," though she did insist on what she felt were her rights. Greatly experienced in teaching and advising students, she maintained at Dumbarton Oaks close contact with the younger members. To the junior fellows, she was available for consultation at any time. She would never refuse to talk to one of them no matter how tired she might be. The mention of her name evokes the memory of a charming personality, high standards of scholarship, human warmth, and her extraordinary eyes.

The life of the Dumbarton Oaks community was that of an extended family, and, as in all families, despite problems, there was an over-all sense of solidarity and belonging. Professor Der Nersessian maintained even-tempered relationships with her colleagues. The closeness of the "family" was keenly felt on various occasions, especially on the sad ones. The deaths of Professor Vasiliev on 29 May 1953 and of Professor Friend on 23 March 1956 were felt as a personal loss for everybody, and the whole community was deeply affected.[27]

Professor Der Nersessian lived in a house on the grounds of Dumbarton Oaks with her sister, who joined her in 1947 following the death of her husband, and since then they have never been separated. To this day the house is known as "the Der Nersessians'." Professor Der Nersessian took an active part in the life of the institution not only in an official capacity but also in an informal, cordial, and friendly way. The hospitable home of the Der Nersessian sisters contributed all the warmth and charm that two gracious ladies, with international backgrounds, could offer. Their house was "home" for visiting scholars from abroad. Their dinners are much remembered not only for the exquisite food but also for the stimulating company, where young people were invited to share the evening with notable scholars in a relaxed atmosphere. What a delightful social and intellectual entertainment it was to listen to two distinguished historians, Professor Kantorowicz and Father Dvornik, discuss and analyze in a serious manner the best vineyards of the Mosel and Rhine valleys! Indeed, their guests treasured the warmth and stimulation of the gatherings at the Der Nersessians'.

At the Fellows Building, only a few steps away, where lunch was served every day, Professor Der Nersessian took her meals. There, in the dining room, she sat at the head of the table, and after lunch she poured the coffee in the living room. This detail of daily life was for many years an uninterrupted feature of the Dumbarton Oaks family ritual. Every day at five o'clock, tea was served in the main building in a very elegant manner. Mrs.

Bliss, for whom Dumbarton Oaks remained "home," where she had her "Founders'" room and her own staff, came every day to tea. Professor Der Nersessian and Mrs. Bliss enjoyed each other's company. Mrs. Bliss was genuinely impressed with Miss Der Nersessian; in return, the latter recognized Mrs. Bliss's culture, refinement, and wisdom.

The principal work of Professor Sirarpie Der Nersessian at Dumbarton Oaks was scholarly research. She directed two annual symposia and took part in five others.[28] The subject of the first one, which she directed in 1948, was the church of the Holy Apostles in Constantinople. The symposium was the product of cooperative research inaugurated at Dumbarton Oaks and was conducted entirely by members of the faculty. The interplay between the disciplines—art and archaeology, history, literary sources, and theology—recreated the image of the once important church in Constantinople built by Constantine the Great. One of the participants in that symposium was Professor Father Francis Dvornik, Der Nersessian's good friend from student days at the Sorbonne. He, appointed for the spring term of 1948, began a fruitful residence of twenty-seven uninterrupted years that continued until his death in November 1975. The second symposium directed by Professor Der Nersessian, "The Dumbarton Oaks Collection: Studies in Byzantine Art," held in 1958, honored the golden wedding of the founders, the Honorable and Mrs. Robert Woods Bliss (Figure 22). Der Nersessian's last public lecture at Dumbarton Oaks, on "Scholarship in Byzantine Art and Archaeology 1940-1965," was given on 31 October 1965. Already retired, she came from France for the celebration of the twenty-fifth anniversary of Dumbarton Oaks as a scholarly institution. This occasion marked her last visit to the United States, including a return to her beloved Wellesley.[29]

In her almost twenty years of association with Dumbarton Oaks, the principal subject of research that Professor Der Nersessian pursued as a member of the faculty was the area of Byzantine and Armenian illuminated manuscripts. In these years she produced the greatest number of her publications, monographs as well as articles. In addition, certain works published after she left Dumbarton Oaks were prepared during her tenure there. Her major research, which she carried on for many years, concerned Cilician illuminated manuscripts of the twelfth to the fourteenth centuries.[30] She spent her summers in Dublin, London, Paris, Venice, and Vienna, working in the libraries with collections of original manuscripts in this area of research. After a short vacation in the mountains of France, Switzerland, Italy, or Austria, she would resume her work. For her sabbatical year, 1951/52, she organized an expedition to Jerusalem. There, at the library of the Armenian Patriarchate, she spent six months studying unpublished manuscripts. Mrs. Arax Der Nersessian took part in that expedition, photographing the manuscripts and making an inventory of some 2,500

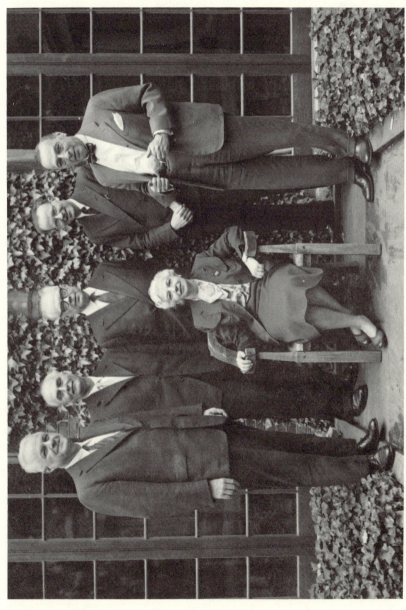

Figure 22. Sirarpie Der Nersessian (*center*) and Group of Lecturers at a Symposium at Dumbarton Oaks, 1958. (*Left to right*) Marvin C. Ross, Otto Demus, André Grabar, Ernst Kitzinger, and Ernst Kantorowicz. (*Courtesy Dumbarton Oaks Center for Byzantine Studies, Washington, D.C.*)

photographs which she had made. Every day from eight in the morning till seven in the evening, with only a short break for lunch, Professor Der Nersessian not only worked on the Cilician manuscripts, which were her major concern, but also was able to study almost all the other illuminated manuscripts in the library. This period of research gave her a complete view of the range of Armenian art and its impact on Byzantine and Western medieval art.

This sabbatical year provided the opportunity for Professor Der Nersessian to study Christian monuments in Egypt, Palestine, Syria, and Lebanon and to examine the important holdings of the Armenian churches in Aleppo and Antilias near Beirut. She and her sister went on to Constantinople, their first return trip to the place of their birth. It was also a reunion, after many years, with their brother, who still lived there.

Despite the thoroughness of Professor Der Nersessian's investigations, she had never had the opportunity to study one of the richest and most important libraries of Armenian manuscripts—the collection at Erevan, formerly at Etchmiadzin. The occasion arose in the summer of 1960 when, after attending the International Congress of Orientalists in Moscow, she traveled on excursions to Georgia and Armenia arranged for congress participants. During that visit to Armenia, the Armenian Academy of Sciences extended an invitation to Professor Der Nersessian to spend a whole month there as a guest of the Academy. The trip to Erevan was a gratifying experience in many ways. For one thing, her work at the Matenadaran (the national library) and visits to monuments throughout Armenia greatly benefited her work. Personally, she found it very satisfying to see firsthand that the Armenian heritage was still alive in terms of language and national identity. The traditional Armenian excellence in art, sciences, and poetry was embodied in the cultural institutions of Erevan: the opera house, symphony orchestra and ballet, museums and art galleries that equal those in some other capital cities. Also outstanding were the university, the Academy of Sciences, and the famous Matenadaran, built in 1958, to house thousands of manuscripts, including the most famous one, the Etchmiadzin Gospel. In that well-organized scholarly center, modern technology has been applied by the capable staff to secure proper preservation, as well as presentation, of the priceless collection. There, among the Armenian manuscripts to which she had devoted most of her life, Professor Der Nersessian felt at home. While there she delivered two lectures. At the Matenadaran she spoke on the Khizan group of manuscripts dating from the fourteenth to the sixteenth centuries, and at the Academy on Cilician manuscripts of the thirteenth century.

Highly gratifying to Professor Der Nersessian was her visit to Etchmiadzin, the seat of the Catholicos of All Armenians. Also memorable were visits to the sixth-century churches of St. Ripsime and St. Gaiane. At the

Armenian theological seminary, she gave a general talk on Armenian manuscripts for members of the congregation and students. A few years later,
speaking to a friend of Professor Der Nersessian, His Holiness the Catholicos, said that he ranked her among the most outstanding Armenians
because of her scholarly contributions to the field of Armenian history and
culture. His Holiness Vasken I, Supreme Patriarch-Catholicos of All
Armenians, previously had formally expressed that sentiment when in the
spring of 1960 on his visit to the United States he had decorated her with the
Medal of the Order of Saint Gregory the Illuminator, first class. In the long
history of the Armenian people, Sirarpie Der Nersessian is the first woman
to be so honored. The Academy of Sciences also acknowledged her achievements in Armenian scholarship by electing her a member of the Academy
(non-resident) in 1966. Thus both the Church and the Academy conferred
upon her their highest distinctions, and today in Armenia her name opens
every door.

During her residence at Dumbarton Oaks in the early 1950s, Sir A. Chester Beatty invited her to publish a catalogue of the illuminated Armenian
manuscripts he had collected. This became the first in a series of systematic
studies of collections and the publication of their catalogues. The Chester
Beatty Library with sixty-seven Armenian manuscripts is the richest among
the private collections in Europe. It contains representative examples of
Armenian illuminations from the twelfth to the end of the seventeenth
century. The richness and diversity of the collection presented Professor
Der Nersessian with the opportunity of writing a survey of Armenian art in
Greater Armenia, Cilicia, and other Armenian centers.[31] This survey she
gave in the introduction to the catalogue. Both the catalogue and the introduction were completed in the summer of 1951, but after her visit to Jerusalem she was able to revise them and incorporate new information in the
supplement section of the catalogue. Thus, the Chester Beatty Catalogue
published in 1958 is a milestone in the study of Armenian miniature painting and also represents the first scholarly survey of Armenian art.

The second catalogue of Armenian manuscripts published by Der Nersessian is that of the Freer Gallery of Art. In 1955, during the directorship
of John Alexander Pope, Professor Der Nersessian started that project. It
was convenient for her to study the seven Armenian manuscripts at the
Freer Gallery in Washington, but equally important for her research were
the new insights afforded by her work at the Matenadaran in 1960.

The third, and the most recent, catalogue is that of the Walters Art Gallery. Sirarpie Der Nersessian's connection with the manuscripts of that
institution dates to the spring of 1934, when she was asked to prepare data
on illuminated manuscripts, both Greek and Armenian, for the gallery's
permanent catalogue.[32] The idea of a separate catalogue of the eleven
Armenian manuscripts was Dorothy Miner's, and she considered Professor

Der Nersessian the most qualified person to carry out such a publication. The Walters' Armenian manuscripts date from the tenth to the seventeenth centuries and contain some 452 miniatures and 104 ornamental pages. Although the project began in 1965,[33] it was not completed until 1973, several months after Dorthy Miner's untimely death prevented her from seeing the publication. Der Nersessian's dedication, "To Dorothy Miner, *In Memoriam*" is an appropriate tribute.

Another major work written by Sirarpie der Nersessian at Dumbarton Oaks is *Aght'amar: Church of the Holy Cross*. The background of this study is rather unusual. In 1956 four young architects on their way to Iran passed by the region of Lake Van. They were interested in Aght'amar, the church on an island built and fortified in 915 and 921 by King Gagik as his refuge. In the year 1113 when Aght'amar became the seat of the Catholicos, it developed as a major religious and cultural center. The young architects systematically photographed the church, reduced today to only a vestige of its former magnificence. All the sculptural details as well as the important fresco cycles of the interior, also dating from the tenth century, were recorded. The work had to be done in twenty-four hours, the extent of the time permitted for the visit. Upon their return this complete photographic coverage was handed over to Professor Der Nersessian. Her monograph is the result of this joint effort.

During the academic year 1958/59, as a member of the Faculty of Arts and Sciences, Professor Der Nersessian spent the spring term at Harvard, where she gave a lecture course and a seminar in Byzantine illuminated manuscripts. In June of the same year (1959) she delivered a series of lectures on Armenia and the Crusades at the Collège de France, where she was the first woman ever invited to lecture at that distinguished institution.

Over the years Sirarpie Der Nersessian attended many international congresses, lectured throughout the United States and Europe, wrote a great number of articles, and contributed papers to thirteen *Festschrifts* honoring her friends and colleagues.

In addition Sirarpie Der Nersessian remained loyal to the Armenian ethnic groups in the United States, as well as elsewhere. Her lectures on Armenian art history and civilization were of great interest to the Armenian communities in New York, Cambridge, and Washington, where she lectured at their organizations. Some of her articles were published in eleven Armenian journals from New York to Jerusalem and Erevan.[34]

Professor Sirarpie Der Nersessian's Harvard University appointment stipulated "without limit of time." The "limit of time" at Dumbarton Oaks for her, however, was her retirement in 1963, when she became an Emerita and, since 1965, an Honorary Associate of the Board of Scholars at Dumbarton Oaks. Thus, as a fitting climax to her career in the United States, Professor Sirarpie Der Nersessian was the only woman ever to gain at Dumbarton Oaks a full professorship at Harvard University. In 1963, she gave the last public lecture of that academic year at Dumbarton Oaks, her final one as a member of the faculty. Her topic was "Armenian Miniature Painting of the Thirteenth Century."[35] To honor the Der Nersessian sisters, a dinner was held in the Orangerie at Dumbarton Oaks, at which Professor Kitzinger gave a moving speech in which he expressed the feelings of all those who long had been associated with both women. It was hard to imagine Dumbarton Oaks without them.[36] They sailed back to France, whose loyal citizens they still remain. Living in Paris, they welcome many of their American friends who come to visit them at their comfortable apartment on the Avenue de Versailles.

Nevertheless, for Professor Der Nersessian, retirement does not mean any diminution of activity. "Twelve months are not long enough as you say —and certainly twenty-four hours per day is too short even when one is so-called 'retired,'" she wrote from Paris to her friend Dorothy Miner.[37] An important portion of her activities were the courses she gave at the Ecole pratique des Hautes Etudes, as well as lectures at various European universities. Her travels continue to be extensive. Sirarpie Der Nersessian's second trip to Armenia took place in 1969 when the Colloque Franco-Soviétique took place at Erevan. On that occasion, she read a paper "Byzance et l'Arménie; problèmes et état des recherches." The Armenian Academy of Sciences, which elected her to membership, invited her to stay longer as their guest. Once again, this visit gave her the opportunity to examine additional manuscripts at the Matenadaran.

Equally remarkable is her record of publications since her return to France. Although a major part of the research for those works published since 1963 was carried out during her tenure at Dumbarton Oaks, nevertheless the five monographs and numerous articles and book reviews constitute an amazing achievement. During these years, new projects were begun and brought to completion. Although plans for a reprint of her book *Armenia and the Byzantine Empire*, begun in 1968,[38] were never realized, Professor Der Nersessian wrote instead another book of a similar character, *The Armenians*, in the series entitled Ancient Peoples and Places, intended for a general readership. As Peter Charanis remarked, however, many a scholar will be included in this audience. He explains that even a "general" work by Sirarpie Der Nersessian is always based on good scholarship and is never superficial.[39] Next there followed in 1970 a monograph devoted to a Byzantine manuscript in the British Library. Der Nersessian's letters indicate that she had made several research trips to London to work on the manuscript.[40] The resulting study, finished in 1968, was published two years later in the series Bibliothèque des Cahiers archéologiques with the title *L'illustration des psautiers grecs du Moyen Age. II. London Add. 19.352*. The book is an investigation of the Studios Psalter of 1066, known also as the Theodore

Psalter, copied in 1066 at the Monastery of St. John Studios in Constantinople by the scribe and illuminator Theodore of Caesarea. The manuscript consists of 208 parchment folios decorated with 435 miniatures. It is the most richly decorated example of the monastic type of psalters with marginal illustrations. As already mentioned, Professor Der Nersessian's interest in the illustrated psalters goes back to 1922/23, when she recorded the Barberini Psalter in Rome (Vatican. Cod. gr. 372) and the Bristol Psalter in London (British Library Cod. Add. 40731) for the photo collection of the Ecole des Hautes Etudes. To relate the Theodore Psalter to other psalters with marginal illustrations as well as to establish its modifications and additions, she compared the historical, iconographic, and codicological aspects of the psalters belonging to the same group and presented her findings in this monograph.

Sirarpie Der Nersessian's connection with the *Revue des études arméniennes* has been a long one, and for many years she has been a faithful contributor. Appropriately enough, the idea of gathering together her articles, which were dispersed in a number of periodicals, in a volume of collected works came from Haïg Berberian, the editor of the *Revue*.[41] Thus the important book entitled *Études Byzantines et Arméniennes—Byzantine and Armenian Studies* was issued in 1973 by the Gulbenkian Foundation. Over seventy articles that had previously appeared in twenty-seven journals and six books came out in two volumes. Articles originally written in Armenian were translated into French by Arax Der Nersessian, her ever helpful sister-assistant.

The most recent book by Sirarpie Der Nersessian, *L'art arménien*, came off the press at the end of 1977 in the series *Orient et Occident*.[42] A synthesis of her research of over half a century is achieved in this monumental folio volume of 270 pages with 185 illustrations. The cultural monuments, witnesses of the long span of Armenian civilization, are examined in six chapters, each of which portrays a major period in the history of Armenia, from antiquity to the eighteenth century. The beautiful pictorial documentation, mostly in color, illustrates the rich Armenian heritage in sculpture, painting, and the minor arts—and above all, in architecture and illuminated manuscripts. Presently Professor Der Nersessian is bringing to completion her long pursued work on the great period of illuminated manuscripts in Cilicia, which have influenced neighboring Byzantium and are considered some of the best examples of book illuminations of the Middle Ages.

Professor Der Nersessian's communication with a number of scholars is very lively. Today as ever before, her interest in the work of younger scholars has remained very keen. Many scholars of all ages come to seek her advice and consult with her on various problems. Others from four continents, unable to visit her in Paris, write regularly. She is often invited to serve as a member of the jury for doctoral dissertations, a duty she has always performed with the greatest pleasure.

The honors bestowed on Professor Der Nersessian are listed at the end of this essay. But one in particular, the Gold Medal of the Society of Antiquaries of London, presented on 23 April 1970, is a rare distinction with which only one other woman has been previously honored. To quote the late Professor Francis Wormald, the Society's president at the time: "An essential criterion has always been that the recipient should have extended considerably the borders of learning."[43] The British Academy recognized Professor Der Nersessian's scholarly merits by electing her on 10 July 1975 a Corresponding Fellow, and in 1978 the French elected her corresponding member of the Académie des Inscriptions et Belles-Lettres.

This solid record of achievement is the image which Professor Sirarpie Der Nersessian, an international scholar at home in several cultures, has created in the course of over fifty years of scholarly activity. In all her research she has studied deeply, never relying on guesswork nor on superficial experiments. Her erudition, her methodology, and her clear judgment have created in each of her studies a model of its genre and thus made all her works definitive. Her investigations have never been confined to a single field; they embrace different aspects of medieval civilization based on her profound knowledge of historical, liturgical, and religious texts, as well as all aspects of material culture. Her work will stand the test of time because it has all the necessary qualities of durable scholarship. Beyond the honors she has received, her lifetime achievement rests on her continuous and indefatigable research in the field of Byzantine and Armenian art and history and in the resulting disclosure of the role played by Armenian civilization in, and its contribution to, the Byzantine world.

Sirarpie Der Nersessian has pioneered Armenian studies in the United States and furthered them not only in the West but also in Armenia. Her long and distinguished scholarly life parallels the growth and development of Armenian and Byzantine scholarship both in the United States and abroad. From their origins as obscure subspecialties of medieval studies, taught in America at only a few institutions, Byzantine and Armenian studies today flourish in the United States at such centers as New York University, Princeton, Columbia, and, above all, Dumbarton Oaks. Perhaps no one individual has contributed more to the development of this field than Sirarpie Der Nersessian.

HONORS

Special Achievement Award from the American Association of University Women, 1948
Honorary Degree, Wilson College, 1948
Honorary Degree, Smith College, 1957
Medal of the Order of Saint Gregory the Illuminator, first class, 1960
Académie des Inscriptions et Belles-Lettres, Prix Schlumberger, 1963
Society of Antiquaries, Gold Medal, 1970
Fellow of the Mediaeval Academy of America

Associate Member of the Société Nationale des Antiquaires de France
Member of the Academy of Sciences of Armenia, Erevan, 1966
Corresponding Fellow of the British Academy, 1975
Corresponding Member of the Académie des Inscriptions et Belles-Lettres, 1978

NOTES

A short biographical account by Agnes A. Abbot is found in *The Wellesley Magazine* (July, 1946), 333-334, "Sirarpie Der Nersessian." On her seventieth birthday, the *Revue des études arméniennes*, 3 (1966), was dedicated to her, as was *Dumbarton Oaks Papers*, 21 (1967), which included a short biographical sketch limited to her years of residence in the United States. In the *Revue des études arméniennes* a portrait photograph and the bibliography of her works are given, but biographical notes are lacking. Two articles honoring her eightieth birthday were published in Armenian, in Erevan. The first is by L. Zakarian, "Sirarpie Ter Nersessian," *Patma'banasirakan Handes* (1976), 237-40; and the second by Levon Aznarian, "Sirarpie Der Nersessian on the Occasion of her Eightieth Birthday," *Lrabar Hasarakakan Gitout'iounneri* (1977), 62-68. Scattered but useful information is found in Wellesley College catalogues, in the annual reports of Dumbarton Oaks, in those of the Walters Art Gallery, in introductions to her books, and in some of the reviews of Professor Der Nersessian's works. Among unpublished sources are the archival material at Dumbarton Oaks and the files of the Walters Art Gallery. Interviews and correspondence with former students, colleagues, and friends of Professor Der Nersessian were conducted between 1975 and 1977.

1. I wish to express my gratitude to former students, colleagues, and friends for all the information they provided: Mrs. Irene Underwood, Dr. Margaret Bouton, Dr. Richard H. Howland, Dr. Barron Hunnicut, Miss Anne Eagles, and Professor Ann Zwinger, all formerly of Wellesley College; as well as to colleagues and friends at Dumbarton Oaks: Dr. John S. Thacher, the late Father Dvornik, and Professors Otto Demus and Ernst Kitzinger. Professor Dr. Levon Khachikian, director of the Matenadaran, was good enough to receive me in Erevan. The Honorable William R. Tyler, former director of Dumbarton Oaks, allowed me to examine some of the institution's archival material, and the staff of the Walters Art Gallery generously opened their files to me. The present director of Dumbarton Oaks, Professor Giles Constable, enabled me to visit the Der Nersessians in December 1977. Above all, my most sincere gratitude goes to Professor Sirarpie and Mrs. Arax Der Nersessian, who welcomed me most kindly and helped me to fill the lacunae in the material I had collected.

2. Francis Wormald, *The Antiquaries Journal*, 50 (1971), 185.

3. B. Bareilles, "Preface to the French edition," in: Maghak'ia Ormanian, *The Church of Armenia* (London, 1912), p. xxii.

4. The Ottoman Empire was the former sultanate with its capital in Constantinople (today Istanbul), which ceased to exist in 1923, when the Republic of Turkey was proclaimed.

5. The second French edition was issued in 1954 in Ante'lias (Lebanon) by the Armenian church of Cilicia. The second British edition came out in 1955 (London, Mowbray), while the first American edition was published in 1954, by H. Toumayan at Brookline, Mass. However, Monsignor Ormanian's major work was the three-volume "Azgapatoum," a history of the Armenian church from the beginning to the present time, recounted together with contemporary national events. The first volume was published in 1912 and the second in 1914, in Constantinople. The third and last volume was published in Jerusalem in 1927.

6. *Manuscrits arméniens illustrés des XIIe, XIIIe, et XIVe siècles de la Bibliothèque des Pères Mekhitharistes de Venise* (Paris, 1937), p. iii.

7. Charles Diehl wrote the preface to *L'illustration du Roman de Barlaam et Joasaph* (Paris, 1937), and Gabriel Millet wrote the one for *Manuscrits arméniens. . . .* (Paris, 1937).

8. Vol. 9 (1929), 137-81.

9. When Sirarpie Der Nersessian first came to Wellesley the faculty of the art department consisted of two Lecturers—Harriet Boyd Hawes, the famous pioneer archaeologist, and herself; two Assistant Professors—William Alexander Campbell and Laurine Elizabeth Mack (later Bongiorno); two Instructors—Agnes Ann Abbot and Helen Bostick Hamilton; one Assistant—Adele Sophie de la Barre (later Robinson). Professor Myrtilla Avery chaired the department and served as director of the Art Museum. For further information about the Wellesley art department, Avery, and Hawes, see Chapters 2-3 and the bibliography at the end of this volume.

10. The college catalogues from 1930/31 through 1945/46 show that she gave thirteen different courses, from "Ancient Art" to "Post-Renaissance and Modern Art."

11. Agnes Abbot, "Sirarpie Der Nersessian," *The Wellesley Magazine* (July 1946), 333-34.

12. The first book was awarded the "Prix Fould" of the Académie des Inscriptions et Belles Lettres, while the second one won the Prix de l'Association des Etudes grecques.

13. Actes du IVᵉ Congrès International des Etudes Byzantines. *Bulletin de l'Institut Archéologique Bulgare*, 10 (1936), 98-106.

14. *Mélanges Nicolas Jorga* (Paris, 1933), pp. 695-725.

15. Florence Converse, *Wellesley College: A Chronicle of the Years 1875-1938* (Wellesley, 1935), pp. 91-93; 251-53. Jean Glasscock, ed. [et al.], *Wellesley College 1875-1975: A Century of Women* (Wellesley, Mass., 1976), p. 143.

16. Abbot, "Sirarpie Der Nersessian," 333-34.

17. Professor William Alexander Campbell held the rank of associate professor; a well-known archaeologist, he was also field director of the Antioch excavations, organized by Professor Charles Rufus Morey of Princeton University. To pursue field work he was always on leave of absence for the second semester until the war broke out, when he was called to active duty. Assistant professors were Laurine Mack (Bongiorno) and Agnes Anne Abbot, who eventually succeeded Der Nersessian as the chairman of the department, and the instructor was Adele de la Barre (Robinson). In years to come there were visiting lecturers invited for one term, such as Dr. Perry Blythe Cott and Professor George Rowley. The new, younger members of the faculty were appointed either for a short term, of one or two semesters to replace an absent professor, or they were appointed for longer periods. Among them were: Arnold Geissbuhler, Richard Hubbard Howland, Margaret Innes Bouton, Anna Jaszi Lesznai, Sara Anderson, Elisabeth Holmes Frisch, John McAndrew, and Phyllis Williams Lehmann.

18. Ann H. Zwinger to Anne Eagles, 28 July 1976. Anne Eagles gave permission to publish this letter.

19. Adele de la Barre Robinson, "Exhibition of Indian Baskets," *College Art Journal* (1, no. 2, 1942), 37-38.

20. Sirarpie Der Nersessian, foreword to the "Exhibition of Chinese Ritual Bronzes and Paintings," *The Art Museum, Wellesley College Bulletin*, 3 (1943), 2.

21. Abbot, "Sirarpie Der Nersessian," 334.

22. An expression of appreciation issued by the Academic Council on 1 June 1961, at the close of Der Nersessian's second term as the "faculty trustee."

23. Vol. 5 (1940-41); vol. 16 (1942-43); vol. 17 (1944-45).

24. Kurt Weitzmann, "Byzantine Art and Scholarship in America," *American Journal of Archaeology*, 51 (1947), 394-418.

25. These projects were known as the "Research Archives" and the "Fontes" (literary sources) respectively.

26. Weitzmann, "Byzantine Art . . .," 394-414.

27. She wrote articles "in Memoriam" to her colleagues and friends: "Alexander Alexandrovich Vasiliev. Biography and Bibliography," *Dumbarton Oaks Papers*, 9-10 (1956), 1-12; "A.M. Friend. In Memoriam," *Dumbarton Oaks Papers*, 12 (1958), 1-2.

28. The themes of the symposia were: "Portraits and Biographies in Byzantine Manuscripts," 1944; "The Relations between Byzantium and Its Neighbors," 1949; "The Cultural

Era of Constantine Porphyrogenitus," 1952; "Byzantine Liturgy and Music," 1954; "The Mosaics and Frescoes of Kariye Djami, Their Cultural and Artistic Background," 1960.

29. She was invited to give a lecture at the symposium of 1967, but because of her sister's illness, her plans had to be altered.

30. Cilicia, in southeastern Asia Minor, also known as Lesser Armenia, was an independent Armenian principality (1080) and kingdom since 1198; it was conquered by the Turks in the fifteenth century.

31. Greater Armenia is the name given in medieval times to the region of the ancient state of Armenia. Today its territories lie in the Soviet Union (S.R. Armenia), Iran, and eastern Turkey.

32. The Walters Art Gallery. *Third Annual Report of the Trustees . . . for the year 1935*, p. 5.

33. The Walters Art Gallery. *Thirty-third Annual Report . . . for the year 1965*, p. 27. Also correspondence between Dorothy Miner and Der Nersessian from 1965 to 1973, Walters Art Gallery.

34. She contributed to the following Armenian journals: *Armenian Quarterly*; *Hayastaneayc' Ekelec'i*, New York; *Pazmaveg*, Venice; *Revue des etudes arméniennes*, Paris; *Handes Amsorya*, Vienna; *Chaghakat*, Istanbul; *Hask*, Antilias (Lebanon); *Sion*, Jerusalem; *Etchmiadzine*; *Patmabanasirakan Handes*, Erevan; *Lraber Hasarakakan Gitout'iounneri*, Erevan.

35. Ernst Kitzinger, "Remarks introducing Miss Der Nersessian's lecture, May 20, 1963." Unpublished archival material, Dumbarton Oaks.

36. Nathan M. Pusey, president of Harvard University in a letter of 18 June 1963 wrote "I have tried to express in conversation some sense of Harvard's indebtedness for the scholarly contribution which you have made to Byzantine studies and to the corporate life of our faculties both at the Library in Washington and in the seminars and conferences here. A good share of responsibility for the distinction of our program in this field derives from your own outstanding work and from the cooperation and encouragement which you have given so generously to your colleagues and to our younger research scholars . . .," while Leonard Carmichael, Secretary of the Smithsonian wrote earlier in May, "The scholarly community of Washington will indeed miss you, but I can certainly say how fortunate we have been to have your wisdom in our midst during the years you have been here. . . ." Unpublished archival material, Dumbarton Oaks.

37. Der Nersessian to Dorothy Miner, 27 November 1964.

38. Der Nersessian to Dorothy Miner, 28 March 1968.

39. Peter Charanis, *Byzantinoslavica*, 32 (1971), 340.

40. Der Nersessian's letters to Dorothy Miner, 1966-68.

41. Haïg Berberian to J. S. Allen, 22 July 1976.

42. An English version of this magnificent work was also published.

43. Wormald, *The Antiquaries Journal*, 50 (1971), 185.

SELECTED BIBLIOGRAPHY OF SIRARPIE DER NERSESSIAN

A complete bibliography of seventy-eight articles and twenty-three book reviews published up to 1973 is given in her book of collected works, *Byzantine and Armenian Studies* (see listing under "Books"). All her major publications are listed here in addition to articles and book reviews that have appeared since 1973.

Books

Manuscrits arméniens illustrés des XII*ͤ*, XIII*ͤ* et XIV*ͤ* siècles de la Bibliothèque des Pères Mékhitaristes de Venise, 2 vols. Paris, E. de Boccard, 1937.

L'illustration du Roman de Barlaam et Joasaph. Préface de Ch. Diehl, Paris, E. de Boccard, 1937.
Armenia and the Byzantine Empire: A Brief Study of Armenian Art and Civilization, Cambridge, Mass., Harvard University Press, 1945.
The Chester Beatty Library: A Catalogue of the Armenian Manuscripts, with an Introduction on the History of Armenian Art, 2 vols. Dublin, Hodges, Figgis and Co., 1958.
Armenian Manuscripts in the Freer Gallery of Art (Freer Gallery of Art Oriental Studies, 6), Washington, 1963.
Aght'amar: Church of the Holy Cross (Harvard Armenian Texts and Studies, I), Cambridge, Mass., Harvard University Press, 1965.
L'art byzantin: Art européen. Publications filmées d'art et d'histoire, Paris, 1965.
The Armenians (Ancient Peoples and Places), London, Thames & Hudson, 1969.
L'illustration des psautiers grecs du Moyen Age. II. Londres Add. 19.352 (Bibliothèque des Cahiers archéologiques V), Paris, Klincksieck, 1970.
Armenian Manuscripts in the Walters Art Gallery, Baltimore, 1973.
Études Byzantines et Arméniennes—Byzantine and Armenian Studies, 2 vols. (Bibl. de la Fondation Calouste Gulbenkian), Louvain, Imprimerie Orientaliste, 1973.
L'art arménien (Flammarion: Orient et Occident), Paris, Arts et Métiers Graphiques, 1977.

Articles

"Francis Dvornik," *Dumbarton Oaks Papers* 27 (1973), 1-2.
"Moskovskiĭ Menologiĭ," *Vizantiia, Iuzhnye Slaviane i drevniaia Rus, Zapadnaia Evropa. Sbornik stateĭ v chest V.N. Lazareva*, Moscow, 1973, pp. 94-111.
"Armenian Manuscripts," *Apollo*, November 1974, 360-65. Published separately with more numerous illustrations as a Walters Art Gallery Picture Book under the title *An Introduction to Armenian Manuscript Illumination*. Selections from the Collection of the Walters Art Gallery, Baltimore, 1974.
"The Church of the Holy Cross: The Paintings," *Aght'amar* (Documenti di architettura armena 8), Milan, 1974, 14-18.
"The Praxapostolos of the Walters Art Gallery," *Gatherings in Honor of Dorothy E. Miner*, Baltimore, 1974, 39-50.
"Program and Iconography of the Frescoes of the Parecclesion." In: Paul A. Underwood, *The Kariye Djami*, vol. 4, New York, 1975, 303-49.
"Deux tympans sculptées arméniens datant de 1321," *Cahiers archéologiques* 25 (1976), 109-22.
"Feuillets dispersés d'un evangile du Vaspurakan," *Handes Amsorya*, 90 (1976), 1-12, col. 89-110 (figs. 1-14) (published in 1977).
"L'illustration du stichéraire du monastère de Koutloumous No. 412," *Cahiers archéologiques* 26 (1977), 137-144.
"La miniature arménienne au XIIIᵉ siècle," *Archéologia* 126 (Jan. 1979), 18-25.

Book Reviews

Ambed (Documenti di architettura armena 4), Milan, 1972, in *Revue des études arméniennes*, N.S. 9 (1972), 464-66.
O. G. Minassian and O. S. Eganian, *Catalogue des manuscrits arméniens du monastère du Saint-Sauveur de Nouvelle Djoulfa (Iran)* (Bibliothèque arménienne de la Fondation C. Gulbenkian, 2), Vienna, 1972, in *Revue des études arméniennes*, N.S. 9 (1972), 461-63.
L. Azarian, *Khatchkars arméniennes*. Album publié par ordre de S. S. Vasken Iᵉʳ, Catholicos-Patriarche de tous les Arméniens, sous les auspices de la Fondation C. Gulbenkian.

Saint-Siège d'Etchmiadzine, 1973, in *Revue des études arméniennes*, N.S. 10 (1973-1974), 375-78.

W. Kleiss and H. Seihoun, *S. Taddei' Vank* (Documenti di architettura armena 4), Milan, 1971, in *Revue des études arméniennes*, N.S. 10 (1973-1974), 370-72.

A. Saginian, *G(h)eghard* (Documenti di architettura armena 6), Milan, 1972, in *Revue des études arméniennes*, N.S. 10 (1973-1974), 366-67.

A. Khatchatrian, *Inscription et histoire des églises arméniennes*. Introduction de A. Alpago-Novello, Milan, 1974. 100 pages ronéotypées, in *Revue des études arméniennes*, N.S. 10 (1973-1974), 419. The author of this book died in 1967, and his work was published seven years later, under the supervision and following the suggestions of Sirarpie Der Nersessian.

A. Guevorkian, *Les métiers et la mode de vie dans les miniatures arméniennes*, Erevan, 1973, in *Revue des études arméniennes*, N.S. 10 (1973-1974), 367-68.

N. Stépanian and A. Tchakmaktchian, *L'art décoratif de l'Arménie médiévale*, Leningrad, 1971, in *Revue des études arméniennes*, N.S. 10 (1973-1974), 368-70.

N. Bogharian, *Grand Catalogue des manuscrits de Saint Jacques (Grand Catalogue of St. James Manuscripts)*, vol. VII (C. Gulbenkian Foundation Armenian Library), Jerusalem, 1974, in *Revue des études arméniennes*, N.S. 11 (1975-1976), 433-34.

H. Oskian, *Catalogues des manuscrits parus dans le "Handes Amsorya,"* Vienna, 1976, in *Revue des études arméniennes*, N.S. 11 (1975-1976), 434-35.

CHAPTER 13
DOROTHY BURR THOMPSON (b. 1900): CLASSICAL ARCHAEOLOGIST

Christine Mitchell Havelock[1]

In 1919 Dorothy Burr began her first year at Bryn Mawr College. The choice was propitious; perhaps no other educational institution at that time in America could have provided to the same degree the stimulation and opportunities she hoped for or indeed demanded. That she selected this particular college, however, is just one more instance of the good fortune and intelligence with which her life and professional career are marked. The biography of Dorothy Burr does not entail deep conflicts, fruitless struggles, and unfulfilled dreams; with perhaps one exception her entry into and participation in academia and archaeology have been remarkably smooth and harmonious.

Dorothy's good fortune began with her parentage and family life. Her home in Philadelphia, where she lived from 1900 to 1917, was one in which intellectual matters were routinely discussed, and women as well as men were expected to participate. Dorothy's mother, Ann Robeson Burr, was a rather prolific author of novels and later of biographies; her daughter remembers that she was inaccessible in the mornings not in order to pay social calls or to attend to household affairs but to seclude herself in the study for solid research and writing. As a young girl, then, Dorothy became aware that the activities of a married woman need not be confined to the care of children and home. Her father, a lawyer, Charles Henry Burr, also played a crucial role in her development by invoking, as perhaps only a father can, his daughter's self-esteem and ambition. It was under his shrewd direction that she chose Bryn Mawr. Yet even earlier, while she was in her teens, he requested that she read and offer critical comment on a manuscript he worked on for years but never completed, about the ideological framework of the United States Constitution. The biographies written by her mother and the examination of the roots of American institutions by her father reveal the antiquarian bias of the Burr household. To them the past, both artistic and intellectual, was of intense interest. From her mother and her mother's family, Dorothy inherited a perceptive eye and a love of art; from her father she learned an appreciation of the power of words and the precision with which they should be employed. These symmetrical and complementary interests in the Burr home undoubtedly shaped and conditioned much of Dorothy's subsequent career.

When still a young girl, Dorothy intended to become either a writer or painter. She could not decide which and considered combining her interests by illustrating her own books. In her thirteenth year, her parents escorted her to Europe—the traditional "Grand Tour"—in which museums and art galleries were the major stops for sightseeing. The work of the old masters thrilled her, and with the optimism of youth she resolved to become another Leonardo da Vinci. For the next few years, before entering Bryn Mawr, she painted steadily, chiefly watercolors but also a few oils. Landscape was her favorite subject, but not any landscape. She favored the scenery of Maine (and later of Greece) with its simple and large forms rather than the tangled and dense lushness of Pennsylvania. She soon realized, however, that her painting was to be a hobby rather than a profession, but for many years she continued to draw and paint, either museum objects or landscapes, in order to augment her memory and knowledge.

At the same time the scholarly and antiquarian world was having a strong impact upon her. As it happened, their next-door neighbor in Philadelphia was the renowned Semitic scholar Morris Jastrow, a professor at the University of Pennsylvania. Jastrow and Dorothy's father visited back and forth as together they examined, to take one example, the text of the code of Hammurabi. By the time Dorothy was eleven years old it is clear that her precocity impressed Jastrow, for he presented her with a Babylonian clay tablet from Ur of the Chaldees in cuneiform writing. Jastrow was a family friend, but he also constituted Dorothy's first encounter with a professional archaeologist; and the tablet was her first material possession from remote antiquity. The incident remained a vivid one in her memory.

When Dorothy was twelve, a second woman in addition to her mother had a significant affect on her intellectual development. Edith Hall Dohan, a Smith College graduate with a doctorate from Bryn Mawr, was lecturing on the Bronze Age town of Gournia in Crete, where she had excavated in the early 1900s. The leader of the expedition had also been a woman, Harriet Boyd Hawes. This intrepid female had discovered the site herself after a long period of search in the roadless terrain of Crete; she hired and paid her own workers and lived in primitive housing near the dig.[2] By 1912 Edith Hall had married and had ceased active excavating, but she held the responsible position of Curator of the Mediterranean section of the University of Pennsylvania Museum. An attractive woman with two children, she lived on a family farm near Philadelphia; her lively narration of the uncovering of the houses and palace of ancient Gournia electrified Dorothy Burr. In those years the archaeological profession was virtually all male; Hawes and Dohan were early pioneers, courageous and independent, perhaps a little romantic about Greece but nonetheless efficient and determined managers.

Until this point Dorothy had not chosen an archaeological career, but it now occurred to her that it was a possible option, well within her reach if she so desired. But she already had been introduced to a study of the past; at the Latin High School in Philadelphia she had, at the age of nine, begun Latin and, at twelve, started elementary Greek. It was her father, with his fascination with the written word, who had arranged with the school special lessons in these ancient languages. During a two-year stay in England from 1917 to 1919, her serious interest in the classics began under English tutors and her mind matured under the influence of the many distinguished people, including scholars, whom she met there.

Dorothy Burr entered Bryn Mawr already predisposed if not committed to archaeology, and with an awakened mind eager to appreciate the special advantages and strengths of this college. The president, M. Carey Thomas, a formidable and energetic woman, had played a leading role in the development and expansion of the American School of Classical Studies in Athens, an institution founded in 1881 for the study and unearthing of Greek antiquity. In particular she had pressed for permanent housing for the school's women students.[3] But, more important, she understood the discipline of archaeology and the training it required both in the library and in the field. Many years later she confessed to Dorothy that she had always wanted to be an archaeologist.

By 1919, the year Dorothy went to Bryn Mawr, Miss Thomas had already brought to the college two outstanding scholars in the ancient field: Mary Swindler and Rhys Carpenter. The philological study of the classics had seemed relatively dull to Dorothy, but the visual manifestations of Greek culture as presented by these teachers immediately gained her interest. Swindler's course on ancient painting, which she took in her second year, proved decisive. Dorothy now chose to be the first Bryn Mawr undergraduate major in Greek and archaeology. But Rhys Carpenter's inspired teaching of Hellenistic sculpture had, in her senior year, the most fundamental effect; and Dorothy's deep and enduring regard for him—she frequently refers to him as her "maestro"—is attested in much of her subsequent research and publication.[4] Carpenter's interests and expertise were manifold, but what she found particularly enticing and congenial were his sensitivity toward sculptural style and his understanding of costume and drapery systems in classical art. Dorothy belonged to a world where dress was important and, as a young woman, she was under intense pressure to keep abreast of current fashion. She resisted its extreme form, but today she does not hesitate to admit that her natural love of clothes led to her initial interest in the stylish appearance of Tanagra and Myrina terra cottas and to her appreciation of the social role of dress.

In her senior year (1922-23) an event attracting international attention removed from her mind any lingering doubts as to her choice of career. The British Egyptologist Howard Carter discovered the Tomb of Tutankhamen. A more dazzling archaeological incident can hardly be imagined, and Dorothy vicariously shared in it by delivering her first public lecture. Carrying with her the *Illustrated London News*, which contained the only available photographs of the tomb, she described the find to a group of adolescent factory girls; their enthusiasm, she happily realized, equaled her own.

Upon graduation in 1923 and with a European Fellowship from Bryn Mawr, Dorothy Burr set off on the long journey by ship to Greece to attend the American School of Classical Studies in Athens. She thus became one of the earlier Fellows of the school from a college that for generations was to send, with the special encouragement of Rhys Carpenter, its top classical majors for graduate study and archaeological experience. The next two years were exhilarating for Dorothy. World War I had somewhat curtailed excavation projects, but now the school was again active at Corinth, Korakou, Zygouries, and Halae as well as on the Acropolis in Athens under the direction of such stellar figures as Carl W. Blegen, Bert H. Hill, William B. Dinsmoor, and a very singular woman, Hetty Goldman.

In the spring of 1924 Blegen needed assistance at his dig at Phlius, a new small site near Nemea in the Peloponnesus. Goldman, who had preceded Dorothy at Bryn Mawr and had received a doctorate from Radcliffe College, was already an extremely competent archaeologist and was also supervising the work at this site.[5] Though a neophyte, Dorothy was asked to join them. Her first assignment was to oversee the excavation of a Byzantine cemetery in pursuit of a temple of Herakles. As the twelfth-century tombs were opened, one by one, it was her duty to pull the earrings, rings, and bracelets off the dead! Phlius was mainly a neolithic site, and the excavators never found a temple. But for Dorothy it was an invaluable experience because she learned some of the fundamental rules of archaeological digging. The keeping of detailed records and precise methods of notetaking were among them. She also realized at this time that for herself one of the greatest pleasures of the work was the opportunity to be outside in the fresh air all day; the brilliant sun and clear atmosphere of Greece, especially during the spring, buoyed her. On the other hand, as she was petite, small-boned, and wiry, by nighttime she was exhausted and required large quantities of sleep. She also now appreciated that the camera is an indispensable part of the archaeologist's equipment; by 1912, as a young girl, she had already learned the rudiments of photography.

Hetty Goldman was in charge of a Harvard dig at Eutresis near Thebes and in the autumn of 1924 she asked Dorothy and another student, Hazel Hansen, to assist her. Dorothy found Goldman a strict disciplinarian and a most exacting and careful director. This archaeological experience was, she recognized, excellent training, and she deeply respected her teacher. Eutresis was a Bronze Age town; digging was slow and by small sections so that stratifications and profiles could be plotted in detail and preserved. During the campaign Dorothy and Goldman occupied a simple house in the village of Parapoungia among the Albanian peasants. The two of them proved to be sympathetic colleagues and later became fast friends. In addition to the daily routine at the site they attended dances and weddings and met the colorful leaders of the village. For the first time Dorothy became aware, through these conservative peasants living in a remote community, of some of the complexities of Greek government and life and of the tensions between Greek villages and cities.

The pottery unearthed at Eutresis had been taken to Thebes, and before departing for the United States Goldman offered Dorothy the chance to stay on and study it. She rented a room on Pindar Street in the town, borrowed Goldman's bed and oil stove, and settled down for a winter of potsherds. Her room was draughty; her food, taken at a nearby restaurant, was usually chilly and greasy. Her work was conducted in a small storage shelter near the Thebes museum that had a tiny fire. Once a week she went to the school in Athens for a bath and lectures. She never considered these living conditions a hardship. Her project, to establish a system for classifying and dating pottery, was an original and challenging one. There were few books to fall back on. The pottery, mainly mere fragments, had to be examined in detail, turned over and over in the hand in order to feel and see the quality of the clay and its color. It was at this time that she realized that the basic fabric of a sherd was at least as important as its decoration. Though working alone, she was never lonely; indeed, she felt privileged to be able to work on unstudied original material. Moreover, she now felt completely at home in the Greek countryside and among Greek peasants who were unfailingly courteous and helpful. Archaeologists of note passed through Thebes that year, and it was a break in her routine—as well as professionally stimulating—to be able to meet and spend time with someone as delightful as the British scholar Humfrey Payne. Though his eye for archaic art was exquisite, he knew no modern Greek; Dorothy ordered his meals for him and introduced him to some special Greek dishes.

When the spring came around again, Dorothy returned to Eutresis for a second campaign. For a brief period, however, she also journeyed over to Prosymna in the Argolid to work with Blegen at the Sanctuary of Hera. Her archaeological experience was further broadened. At Eutresis, they had been looking for the ancient town, so that walls and stratifications were critical. Here at Prosymna they were searching for tombs, which involved another type of digging: long trenches were excavated at right angles to the slopes. Dorothy considered Blegen a wizard at sniffing out a tomb and deciding on the location of a trench. The dig turned out to be rich, and she learned a great deal about Mycenaean pottery and grave offerings. Secretly, moreover, she hoped to direct an excavation of her own, and she had selected as a possible site Dendra near Prosymna. On the Easter weekend of 1925, therefore, she mounted a mule to take a closer look and on the way made the remarkable discovery of a beehive tomb. Unfortunately the American School was unable to take on the clearance of the tomb, which was carried out the next year by Greek and Swedish archaeologists.[6] In July of 1925 Dorothy's father died, and she returned to Philadelphia.

There was now the question of a postgraduate degree, for Dorothy had determined upon an archaeological career. With the idea that she might take her doctorate there she now headed for Harvard, a natural choice in view of her admiration for Hetty Goldman. The program for the Ph.D. degree at Harvard proved unattractive to her, but one course prompted the subject of her thesis, which she was to complete at Bryn Mawr in 1931. In choosing a subject, Dorothy coordinated her two main interests: her love of Hellenistic sculpture and her by now considerable expertise in the clay medium. The Boston Museum of Fine Arts owned an outstanding collection of 117 terra cottas (Figure 23) from Myrina (in Asia Minor), and she proposed to catalogue them and write an historical introduction. The choice was a wise one because, as her father had once counselled, the topic was limited and therefore manageable; she was also working directly with Greek originals. But she suffered keen disappointment when Lacey D. Caskey, Curator of Classical Antiquities, rejected the catalogue for publication by the museum. His criticism of her point of view and writing style—in her opinion not unjustified—was the stiffest she had ever received. In retrospect Dorothy realized that this was a critical event in her career and that it impressed upon her the need to write in a tight austere style best suited to the uses of scholarship. In 1934 she published the catalogue at her own expense in Austria. The book, which was her first, has been cited frequently in studies devoted to Hellenistic terra cottas.

When she had been a student in Athens in 1924, discussions between the Greek government and the American School were just beginning on the possibility of American excavation of the ancient Athenian market place or Agora. Negotiations continued for the next few years, funds were raised in the United States, and the first campaign started auspiciously in 1931. The excavation of the Athenian Agora became the most important and one of the most prolonged enterprises of the American School.[7] In 1932 Dorothy was the first woman to be appointed as a Fellow of the Agora, a post she retained until the war in 1939. Each season, all day long, she supervised digging on the site; once again she was in the open air, and a member of a

Figure 23. Flying Eros. Hellenistic Figurine from Myrina. Boston, Museum of Fine Arts. (*Courtesy Museum of Fine Arts, Boston; Gift by Contribution*)

large and well-outfitted campaign staffed by congenial and familiar col-
leagues. One of them, an Assistant Director of Field Work was Homer A.
Thompson, an attractive and very gifted young Canadian archaeologist.
They worked together on several projects and, it seems inevitably, they fell
in love. Theirs was a meeting of minds and interests, and in 1934 they were
married. Their winter place of residence became Canada, for in 1933
Homer had been appointed Curator of the Classical Collection at the Royal
Ontario Museum in Toronto and Assistant Professor in Fine Arts at the
University of Toronto. Twin daughters, Hope and Hilary, were born in
Philadelphia on 23 May 1935, and a third child, Pamela, in Athens in 1938.
Dorothy's archaeological activity continued. Nursemaids and housekeepers
were easily procured in Athens in those days. In 1936 she identified the quite
unique "Theseum Garden," the potted plantings of laurel bushes around the
Temple of Hephaistos; and she soon found herself an expert on garden lore,
not only in Greece but also in Babylon, Egypt, and Italy. Off-season, with
the children still very young, Dorothy could devote part of her day to the
cataloguing and study of terra cotta figurines found during excavation
in the Agora. Those of Hellenistic origin had become her special responsibility.

World War II inevitably interrupted their lives. By 1940 most of the
Agora staff had secured their records and treasures in bomb shelters and
departed for home. Germany occupied Greece in April of 1941, and in 1942
Homer volunteered for service with the Canadian navy. As his courses in
Greek and Roman art were consequently left without an instructor, his
eminently qualified wife was immediately appointed to replace him. The
present writer remembers Dorothy as a teacher both forthright and demanding; she was self-confident and rather wry and did not attempt to
disguise her preference for Greek as opposed to Roman art. This kind of
personal and open prejudice was stimulating as well as engaging. She had an
intense identification with every object shown on the screen or in the
museum's display case; they were never merely abstract documents of a
remote civilization. She gave the impression of actually having talked with
the subjects of Greek or Roman portraits. If an object seemed to her of
inferior quality she would not hesitate to say so. Her knowledge and love of
the material and of the Greeks themselves, both ancient and modern, were
imparted to her students; yet her lecture style was casual, even matter of
fact. Though she admired the Greek achievement, her viewpoint was not
romantic.

On the cessation of hostilities in Europe, Homer returned to the University of Toronto in 1945. He was asked to assume the Directorship of the
Royal Ontario Museum but declined, and a year later he accepted the Directorship of the Agora excavations, which could now be resumed, and a chair
at the Institute for Advanced Study in Princeton. In 1946 Dorothy was

offered the Acting Directorship of the Royal Ontario Museum for the one year before she and Homer went to Princeton. She accepted the offer although her salary, she recalls, was much less than a man in that office would have received. She took her case determinedly to the president of the university and succeeded in eliciting an appropriate raise. This is the only occasion in her career on which she is aware of having been discriminated against because of her sex. She was unaccustomed to it; she fought on her own behalf, during her husband's absence in Greece, and she triumphed. The unorthodox appointment of a woman to the post stirred considerable local interest.[8] Some members of the museum staff let it be known that they expected Mrs. Thompson to be weak and incompetent; this was a severe test, but she soon learned to exercise authority.

As teacher and museum official Dorothy B. Thompson had reached a kind of professional pinnacle. From 1942 to 1947 she was actively and significantly involved in the community and in academia. She lent her support and planning ability to Greek war-relief enterprises; she arranged a concert of native songs and dances that lifted the morale of Greek immigrants and philhellenes in Toronto. Her university students pressed her to publish her translations of some ancient Greek lyrics. This small volume, *Swans and Amber*, appeared in 1948; it is delightful and unpretentious and succeeds in capturing the spirit of the Greeks that, during the disheartening war and civil war years, so much needed to be kept alive. Between 1944 and 1946, Eric A. Havelock initiated the steps that led to the founding of the Ontario Classical Association and its organ the *Phoenix*. Dorothy B. Thompson and Mary E. White became his close collaborators in both these projects, and when the Ontario Association was converted into the Canadian Association the *Phoenix*, on which Dorothy continued to be a contributing editor, became the major classical journal in Canada. The name of the journal was her personal choice; and in a foreword to the first issue, written in 1945 not long after the bombing of Hiroshima, she records not only the ancient myth of the phoenix but what it can also symbolize to the humanist after the devastation of modern war. At the end of 1947 the Thompsons moved to Princeton, where Homer succeeded to the Institute chair left vacant by Hetty Goldman. As Goldman continued to work at the Institute, an old friend became a neighbor.

For the next five years Dorothy found it necessary to give her main attention to the care of her children. She did not do so without complaint because it entailed staying home in Princeton during the summer digging season. But in 1952 and thereafter her life settles into an enviable pattern. Winters were spent at the Institute in research and writing; as not only the wife of the director of the Agora excavations but, more important, a member of the team preparing materials for publication, Dorothy received privileges and space within the Institute. During the summer both Thompsons flew to Athens to resume their supervision of the Agora excavation. They rented an apartment in the city, and domestic help was found again. Greece, meanwhile, was slowly recovering from the war. Other foreign schools resumed operation, and funding for further excavation of the Agora was forthcoming. In the mid-1950s the American School rebuilt the Stoa of Attalos, a great colonnade of the second century B.C., which served as a museum and also provided storage, offices, and work space for the staff. Thus Dorothy could lay her objects on long tables for close inspection and cataloguing. The days at the Agora were structured and busy; simple lunch was served in the upper gallery of the museum to all staff members, and tea was regularly taken at five o'clock. Archaeological issues and problems could be discussed informally at these times, and the discussions were often enlivened and enlarged by visiting students and scholars, who were received with warm hospitality. In the evenings the Thompsons enjoyed an extended social intercourse with their colleagues in the French, German, or British schools or with dignitaries of the Greek and American governments. Yet travel to other countries, sites, and museums, either alone or with Homer, was also a necessary and regular aspect of Dorothy's life. She was now an internationally known expert; a reputation first gained through her study of the Boston Museum figurines was reinforced by a series of impeccable articles on the Agora terra cottas that began to appear in *Hesperia* in 1952. An amusing episode arising out of her well-deserved reputation involved the chance discovery of a group of ancient terra cottas in a gardener's back yard in Athens. Dark suspicions were aroused. Dorothy, on being asked to identify the objects, pronounced them not Greek, but pre-Columbian. It was understood that her expertise went well beyond the classical Greeks but nevertheless the officials were incredulous. How did American terra cottas end up in Athens, and why were they buried? The mystery was subsequently solved: the servants of a German ambassador had stolen them and, when pursued by the police, had first tried to burn them (but because they were pottery, this made them still more indestructible) and finally, in desperation, had interred them.

While her major preoccupation was with the Agora terra cottas, those from Asia Minor continued to fascinate her because her long-range and most profound concern from the beginning was the whole field of Hellenistic sculpture. The figurines from Athens had naturally led her to a thorough investigation of those from Boeotia in the "Tanagra" style, and she had ultimately concluded that the types originated in Athens after all. She was glad to accept, therefore, Carl W. Blegen's invitation to publish the terra cottas of the Hellenistic period that had been unearthed at Troy by the University of Cincinnati between 1932 and 1938. This impressive book entails, as Blegen acknowledges in the foreword, not only a detailed cata-

logue of Trojan figurines but a "veritable history of Hellenistic terracottas." It appeared in 1963, having required arduous research in Istanbul.

Years before, Dorothy had realized that a full understanding of Hellenistic sculpture and drapery styles had been impeded by the dearth of dated
examples, particularly of the third century B.C., and she had pondered the
need to study a limited body of material for which there existed objective
chronological data. To this end she chose an unusual and little-known
group of objects, Ptolemaic *oinochoai* (small wine jugs) and portraits in
faience, which seemed to furnish ideal material. She began to work on them
in 1955 but soon found that much more than drapery styles was involved.
By taking a small field and putting it under the microscope, she began to see
the chaos of a culturally rich period with its many crosscurrents of influence
and its fluctuations of trends and styles. She envisioned it as a kind of
microcosm containing problems and characteristics paralleled in other great
periods such as the Italian Renaissance. The examples were scattered or had
remained overlooked in many museums in Europe and the Near East. She
travelled widely, collecting facts and photographs, and eventually the
glistening faience led into every aspect of the history, politics, religion, and
art of ancient Alexandria. The book, a major opus, took fifteen years to
finish. This is not surprising in view of the number of projects upon which
she simultaneously worked.

Between 1953 and 1972 Dorothy held six teaching positions as Visiting
Professor, five at major American institutions including her alma mater
Bryn Mawr and one at the University of Sydney, Australia. These teaching
stints were invariably stimulating, but she never yearned for a full-time
academic post. Nevertheless, she maintained an interest in the education of
the young, as is shown by her compilation of a catalogue of visual aids for
Ontario schools in the 1940s; she also directed a film on Greece in the 1950s
for the Archaeological Institute of America, which satisfied her love of
theater. Another project was to set up in 1956 a meeting at the Institute with
Dr. Robert Oppenheimer and a group of archaeologists and chemists to
discuss the possibility of applying the methods of nuclear research to the
study of classical archaeology. The experiment was not much heeded, but it
drew the attention of scholars to the potential use of modern science in this
field.

Homer Thompson retired as director of the Agora excavations in 1967;
he gave up his chair at the Institute in 1977. Dorothy and her husband
continue the pleasant routine of summers in Greece and winters in Princeton preparing further materials for publication in the several series of Agora
reports, books, and booklets. Dorothy's volume, close to completion at this
writing, will contain her final analysis of the Hellenistic figurines introduced in her *Hesperia* articles. Although she is at this writing in her eighty-

first year, her agile mind still reaches beyond the Greek mainland. Archaeologists for a long time have observed the impact of Greek art on that of
Persia; Dorothy hopes to further investigate Persian influence on Greek art,
an original line of inquiry she first explored in an article in 1955. Rooted in
the Myrina studies of her youth is yet another interest: the peasant type, an
almost irresistible subject amply represented in the art of terra cotta sculpture.

Dorothy Burr Thompson's field of concentration—Greek terra cotta
sculpture—is one of the most confused and difficult in the history of art.
Anonymous for the most part, often mass-produced, sometimes bizarre in
style and subject, small and frequently cheap, and usually fragmentary,
they are minor works of art, but works of art they truly are. They require
minute, prolonged, and firsthand study and an intimate knowledge of technique and fabric. Only infinite patience and a sensitive eye can detect
nuances of color, consistency, and modelling. Infinitesimal variations in the
rendering of drapery folds or the construction of an eye or coiffure can be
crucial. All of Dorothy Burr Thompson's scholarly contributions have
originated in the observation of the concrete, material object. Her publications to date on the Agora figurines are exemplary in this regard. The
accuracy and reliability of her descriptions of the individual terra cotta
examples are widely recognized, but she is not content to leave it at that.
The meaning and the function of the object are also important to her.
However, in Greek antiquity a work of art was rarely accompanied by
documentation; imagination and ingenuity must deduce the plausible, and
plausibility is more frequent than certainty. There may be signposts, but
they are very distantly spaced, and between them the Greek archaeologist
has to carve out his or her own road. This is particularly true of Mrs.
Thompson's later work, in which fact and imagination are skillfully paired.
To cite one example, in her article "The House of Simon the Shoemaker" a
few archaeological clues lead to a persuasive and vivid evocation of an
ancient Greek personality who was a friend of Socrates.

Mrs. Thompson's writings reveal a deep knowledge of the clamps and
dowels of field archaeology and of Greek art and artifacts, yet they also
evince wide familiarity with Greek literature and history. She is not a
theoretician like her teacher Carpenter; her primary purpose is first to describe the artifact and then to place it in its cultural context. One is tempted,
perhaps, to remark that her femininity has affected her scholarship: in her
interest in the lives of Egyptian-Ptolemaic queens, her feeling for garden
lore, her concern for drapery detail, and her ability to clinch an argument
by citing contemporary Greek customs, not seldom in the domestic sphere.
From her unsentimental writing we sense that the ancient Greeks were real
people, and sometimes even ordinary people, whose daily lives did not al-

together differ from our own. She can also be an extremely sophisticated analyst of style, as is shown in her article on the famous Bronze Dancer in the Baker collection or on the circular designs of Greek drinking cups. Her use of words is apt—it is the comparative language of the art historian, which is not always to be detected in archaeological writing. As a person she is known for her directness if not bluntness, her single-mindedness and strong opinions. Her self-confidence can be disconcerting, and especially in her younger years she was not always easy to be with. Her peers, and here her husband must be included, admit that she has always been an excessive talker. But it should be added that she can be an attentive listener, too, especially to students, to whom she has never condescended.

"I seem to have been at the right place at the right time," she recently remarked. This was not only true of the time of her arrival at Bryn Mawr under the presidency of M. Carey Thomas and tutelage of Rhys Carpenter, but also of her early years at the American School of Classical Studies in Athens, which by the 1920s, unhesitatingly sent talented young women for training on its various archaeological campaigns. Dorothy Burr's first digs were small ones, but they were nevertheless significant because they could fill in and secure chronologies that more spectacular excavations had left ambiguous or uncertain. Shortly after 1900 archaeology had come of age, and its methods were scientific and exacting; Dorothy began her career at this opportune moment working under and alongside brilliant directors of both sexes and of international repute. Then she happened to be in Athens when the American school procured the enviable rights to the exploration of the Agora, and her appointment as a Fellow was a recognition of the merit she had already earned. Her subsequent marriage to Homer Thompson allowed her to enjoy the normal pleasures of home and family, as well as providing opportunities to advance her career and studies. Archaeological teams of husband and wife are not uncommon and are a solution to the problem of an absentee spouse. But the Thompson team has been unusual in that each was a well-trained and first-rate scholar, and each had "arrived" before their marriage. That Dorothy was accepted as a scholar in her own right is everywhere in evidence, but it is most recently shown by her being granted an honorary degree in 1972 by the College of Wooster. In the same year the Hellenic Society of Great Britain recognized her, though a female, as a *vir clarissimus* ("a most illustrious man").

Both Dorothy and Homer enjoyed good health; and long archaeological days, walks, and journeys could be undertaken together. It is clear that Dorothy always admired her husband; and in many of her publications she acknowledges her genuine gratitude to him for reading her manuscript, for advising her on format, or for stimulating her thinking. She in turn advised and assisted him. It was a good partnership, a noncompetitive one, with interests identical enough to permit fruitful discussion; and yet with recognition of the superiority of the other in a chosen field. They have differed publicly and in print, not to inflict defeat but to illuminate an archaeological problem.

As I have said, the circumstances and rhythm of Dorothy Burr Thompson's life have been unusually fortunate. She considers herself when a child to have been docile, and she was lucky to have been guided by a superior father. She grew up with parents who were cultivated and financially comfortable in a city, Philadelphia, that was a major cultural center in America. Bryn Mawr, a college close to home, was a judicious choice, but it was also a convenient one. Role models—women scholars, teachers and scholarly mothers—were always present to inspire her. Her solitary ventures in pursuit of archaeology were undertaken in a country, Greece, which was uncommonly safe for the unaccompanied woman. Throughout her marriage the seasons in Athens brought her into contact with most of the major scholars of antiquity; the classical library at the American School supplied an excellent supporting service. Foreign museums and international conferences could be attended en route to or from Athens. Intellectual stimulus and research facilities are also provided at the Institute in Princeton. To this very day the rhythmic pattern continues (Figure 24). Both in Athens and in Princeton the Thompsons are surrounded by colleagues and friends and are in close touch with children and grandchildren. Their home in each place is charming and dotted with Greek mementoes and with the paintings of their daughters, who have inherited their mother's profound understanding of art.

"Perhaps the most lasting impression is of her vitality and alertness and her sustaining interest in persons and ideas." This is the testimony of the late Rhys Carpenter, the "maestro" of Dorothy Burr Thompson.[9]

NOTES

The only published biographical source is the article by Liz Gardner, "First-Rate Digger," *Chatelaine*, February (1947), 16. Much of the material of this essay is based upon personal interviews with, and letters from, Mrs. Thompson between 1975 and 1979. She has, in addition, furnished the photograph of herself and her husband. At all times she has been extremely cooperative and helpful, but also stimulating—just as I found her to be when she introduced me to archaeology at the University of Toronto in 1942. For her labors and assistance I extend my deep gratitude. Homer A. Thompson also expressed interest in this project, and I wish to thank him for his comments and suggestions. My husband Eric A. Havelock knew both the Thompsons in Toronto and has been invaluable in providing background to the academic scene in the 1930s and 1940s.

1. I am indebted to Patricia Neils Boulter and Jennifer Neils, both Bryn Mawr graduates, who during a trip in Greece in the summer of 1975, provided me with insights into Bryn Mawr, both past and present. George M.A. Hanfmann of Harvard University shed much light on the archaeological events described in this essay and on some of the personalities involved. Thanks

Figure 24. Dorothy and Homer Thompson, 1975. (*Courtesy Dorothy Burr Thompson*)

are due to Cornelius C. Vermeule and Alice W. Ellis, who both responded most helpfully to questions concerning their stay at Bryn Mawr and at the American School, and to Professor Helen Dow, also a former student of Mrs. Thompson.

2. Details of Harriet B. Hawes' expeditions in Crete can be found in "Memoirs of a Pioneer Excavator in Crete," *Archaeology* 18 (1965), 94-101 and 268-76.

3. On Miss Thomas' role at the American School and on all other matters concerning the activities of the School before World War II see Louis E. Lord, *A History of the American School of Classical Studies at Athens, 1882-1942* (Cambridge, Mass., 1947). See also Edith Finch, *Carey Thomas of Bryn Mawr* (New York, 1947).

4. In the *Bryn Mawr Alumnae Bulletin* 4 (1955), 2. Mrs. Thompson writes perceptively and affectionately about her favorite professor on the occasion of his retirement.

5. Miss Goldman's achievements are celebrated in *A Symposium in Memory of Hetty Goldman, 1881-1972* (Princeton, 1974).

6. See Axel W. Persson, "The Royal Tombs at Dendra," *Skrifter utgivna av Vetenskaps-Societeten i Lund* 15 (1931), 5.

7. For the most recent and comprehensive account of the Agora in Athens: Homer A. Thompson and Richard E. Wycherley, *The Agora of Athens: The History, Shape and Uses of an Ancient City Center* (Princeton, 1972).

8. Reactions to Mrs. Thompson as a person and as a museum official are recorded in the Canadian magazine *Chatelaine* (February 1947), 16.

9. In a letter kindly written to the author dated 23 December 1975.

SELECTED BIBLIOGRAPHY OF DOROTHY BURR THOMPSON

Books:

Terra-cottas from Myrina in the Museum of Fine Arts, Boston. Vienna (1934).
Swans and Amber: Some Early Greek Lyrics Freely Translated and Adapted. Toronto (1948).
Miniature Sculpture from the Athenian Agora. Agora Picture Book No. 3. Princeton (1959).
Garden Lore of Ancient Athens. Agora Picture Book No. 8. Princeton (1963).
Troy: The Terracotta Figurines of the Hellenistic Period, Supplementary Monograph No. 3. Princeton (1963).
An Ancient Shopping Center: The Athenian Agora. Agora Picture Book No. 12. Princeton (1971).
Ptolemaic Oinochoai and Portraits in Faience: Aspects of the Ruler-Cult. Oxford (1973).

Periodical Publications:

"A Primitive Statue from Arcadia." *American Journal of Archaeology* 31 (1927), 169-76.
"Agora Excavations: A Geometric House and a Proto-Attic Votive Deposit." *Hesperia* 2 (1933), 542-640.
"Agora Excavations: The Terracotta Figurines." *Hesperia* 2 (1933), 184-94.
"Terracotta Figurines from the Pnyx and Thesmophorion." *Hesperia* 5 (1936), 170-79.
"The Garden of Hephaistos." *Hesperia* 6 (1937), 396-425.
"*Mater Caelaturae:* Impressions from Ancient Metal Work." *Hesperia* 8 (1939), 285-316.
"Small Objects from the Pnyx I: The Terracotta Figurines." *Hesperia*, Supplement 7 (1943), 112-66.
"The Golden Nikai Reconsidered." *Hesperia* 13 (1944), 173-209.

Review of William A. McDonald, *The Political Meeting Places of the Greeks* (Baltimore, 1943). *American Journal of Archaeology* 48 (1944), 312-14.

"The Phoenix." *Phoenix* 1 (Jan. 1946), 2-3.

Review of Antoine Bon, *Introduction générale à l'histoire de l'art, 1: Préhistoire, Orient méditerranéen* (Rio de Janeiro, 1941). *American Journal of Archaeology* 51 (1947), 462.

Review of Anne Marie and Antoine Bon, *La Grèce ne meurt pas* (Rio de Janeiro, 1944). *American Journal of Archaeology* 51 (1947), 462-63.

"The Charmed Circle." *Archaeology* 1 (1948), 158-64.

Review of Robert C. Trevelyan, *A Translation of the Idylls of Theocritus* (Cambridge, England, 1947). *Phoenix* 2 (1948), 63-64.

Review of Arthur D. Trendall, *Handbook to the Nicholson Museum* (2d ed. Sydney, Australia, n.d.). *American Journal of Archaeology* 53 (1949), 420-21.

"Ostrakina Toreumata." *Hesperia*, Supplement 8 (1949), 365-72.

"A Bronze Dancer from Alexandria." *American Journal of Archaeology* 54 (1950), 371-85.

"Parks and Gardens of the Ancient Empires." *Archaeology* 3 (1950), 101-6.

Review of Gerhard Kleiner, *Tanagrafiguren: Untersuchungen zur hellenistischen Kunst und Geschichte* (Berlin, 1942). *American Journal of Archaeology* 54 (1950), 440-44.

"Ancient Gardens in Greece and Italy." *Archaeology* 4 (1951), 41-47.

Review of Richard E. Wycherley, *How the Greeks Built Cities* (London, 1949), *Phoenix* 5 (1951), 23-24.

"Three Centuries of Hellenistic Terracottas: IA: The Late Fourth Century B.C., the Coroplast's Dump." *Hesperia* 21 (1952), 116-64.

"Three Centuries of Hellenistic Terracottas: IB and IC: The Late Fourth Century B.C., the Hedgehog Well, the Demeter Cistern." *Hesperia* 23 (1954), 72-107.

"New Trees for Old Athens." *Bulletin of the Garden Club of America* (1954).

Review of Agnes N. Stillwell, *Corinth. XV, Part II. The Potters' Quarter, The Terracottas* (Princeton, 1952). *Phoenix* 8 (1954), 71-72.

"Rhys Carpenter: From Poet to Archaeologist." *Bryn Mawr Alumnae Bulletin* (1955), 2.

"A Portrait of Arsinoe Philadelphos." *American Journal of Archaeology* 59 (1955), 199-206.

"The Persian Spoils in Athens." *Aegean War and Near East Studies Presented to Hetty Goldman.* (Locust Valley, New York, 1956), 281-91.

Review of Vassil Micoff, *Le Tombeau antique près de Kazanlǎk* (Sofia, 1954). *American Journal of Archaeology* 60 (1956), 295-96.

"Three Centuries of Hellenistic Terracottas II: The Early Third Century B.C." *Hesperia* 26 (1957), 108-28.

"Foreword to Neutron Activation Study of Mediterranean Potsherds." *American Journal of Archaeology* 61 (1957), 35.

Review of John H. Young and Suzanne Halstead Young, *Terracotta Figurines from Kourion in Cyprus* (Philadelphia, 1955). *American Journal of Archaeology* 62 (1958), 238-40.

Review of Ekrem Akurgal and Ludwig Budde, *Vorläufiger Bericht über die Ausgrabungen in Sinope* (Ankara, 1956). *American Journal of Archaeology* 62 (1958), 446.

Review of Alfred Laumonier, *Exploration archéologique de Délos XXIII, Les figurines de terre cuite* (Paris, 1956). *American Journal of Archaeology* 63 (1959), 209-11.

"Three Centuries of Hellenistic Terracottas: IIB: The Altar Well." *Hesperia* 28 (1959), 127-52.

"The House of Simon the Shoemaker." *Archaeology* 13 (1960), 234-40.

Review of Wilhelmina van Ingen, *Figurines from Seleucia on the Tigris* (Ann Arbor, Michigan, and London, 1939). *American Journal of Archaeology* 44 (1940), 266-67.

"Three Centuries of Hellenistic Terracottas: IIC: The Satyr Cistern." *Hesperia* 31 (1962), 244-62.

"A Clay Model of an Ephebe." *Hesperia* 32 (1963), 88-90.

"Three Centuries of Hellenistic Terracottas: III: The Late Third Century B.C." *Hesperia* 32 (1963), 276-92.

"Three Centuries of Hellenistic Terracottas: IV: The Second Century B.C." *Hesperia* 32 (1963), 301-17.

"Myrina Terracottas." *Enciclopedia dell'arte antica classica e orientale* 5 (Rome, 1963), 306-13.

"A Study of a Clay Impression from a Metal Cup of Hellenistic Date." *Journal of Egyptian Archaeology* 50 (1964), 147-63.

"Glauke and the Goose." *Essays in Memory of Karl Lehmann, Marsyas*, Supplement 1 (Locust Valley, New York, 1964), 314-22.

"A Stamp of the Coroplast Diphilos." *Studi in onore di Luisa Banti* (Rome, 1965), 319-25.

"Three Centuries of Hellenistic Terracottas: V: The Mid-Second Century B.C. VI: The Late Second Century B.C. to 86 B.C." *Hesperia* 34 (1965), 34-71.

Review of Ernie D. S. Bradford, *Ulysses Found* (London, 1963). *Archaeology* 18 (1965), 84.

Review of Simone Mollard-Besques, *Catalogue raisonné des figurines et reliefs en terre-cuite grecs et romains,* II, *Myrina* (Paris, 1963). *American Journal of Archaeology* 69 (1965), 81-82.

"Three Centuries of Hellenistic Terracottas: VII: The Early First Century B.C., A. The Kybele Cistern." *Hesperia* 35 (1966), 1-19.

"Three Centuries of Hellenistic Terracottas: VII: The Early First Century B.C., B. The Mask Cistern. VIII: The Late First Century B.C." *Hesperia* 35 (1966), 252-67.

"The Origin of Tanagras." *American Journal of Archaeology* 70 (1966), 51-63.

"Tanagra Terracottas." *Enciclopedia dell'arte antica classica e orientale* 7 (Rome, 1966), 590-95.

Review of Elfriede M. Abbe, *The Plants of Virgil's Georgics* (Ithaca, 1965). *Phoenix* 20 (1966), 265-66.

"The Cult Significance of the Faience Oinochoai." *Antike Kunst* 10 (1967), 148-49.

Review of Berta Segall, *Tradition und Neuschöpfung in der frühalexandrinischen Kleinkunst* (Berlin, 1966). *American Journal of Archaeology* 71 (1967), 105-6.

Review of Anna A. Peredolskaya, *Attische Tonfiguren aus einem südrussischen Grab* (Olten, Switzerland, 1964). *Archaeology* 20 (1967), 140.

"Mourning Odysseus." *Hesperia* 38 (1969), 242-51.

Review of Doris Pinkwart, *Das Relief des Archelaos von Priene und "Die Musen des Philiskos"* (Kallmünz, 1965). *American Journal of Archaeology* 73 (1969), 384-85.

"Edith H. H. Dohan," *Notable American Women.* Eds. Edward T. James, Janet W. James, and Paul S. Boyer (Cambridge, Mass., 1971), 1, 496-97.

Review of Artur Müller, *The Seven Wonders of the World: Five Thousand Years of Culture and History in the Ancient World* (New York, 1968). *Archaeology* 25 (1972), 318.

Review of Helga Herdejürgen, *Die Tarentinischen Terrakotten des 6. bis 4. Jahrhunderts v. Chr. im Antikenmuseum Basel* (Mainz, 1971). *American Journal of Archaeology* 77 (1973), 246-47.

Review of Erich Boehringer, ed., *Pergamon, Gesammelte Aufsätze* (Berlin, 1972). *American Journal of Archaeology* 78 (1974), 310-12.

Review of Kenneth Heuer, *City of the Stargazers: The Rise and Fall of Ancient Alexandria* (New York, 1972). *Archaeology* 27 (1974), 215.

Review of Christine Mitchell Havelock, *Hellenistic Art: The Art of the Classical World from the Death of Alexander to the Battle of Actium* (Greenwich, Conn., 1971). *Archaeology* 27 (1974), 70-71.

"O Dea Certe." *Antike Kunst* 18 (1975), 82-84.

Review of Bernhard Schmaltz, *Terrakotten aus dem Kabirenheiligtum bei Theben: menschen-ähnliche Figuren, menschliche Figuren and Gerät* (Berlin, 1974). *American Journal of Archaeology* 79 (1975), 382-84.

"A Faience Fellah." *Studies in Classical Art and Archaeology, A Tribute to Peter Heinrich von Blanckenhagen* (Locust Valley, New York, 1979), 175-78.

Review of Eva Töpperwein, *Terrakotten von Pergamon* (Deutsches Archäologisches Institut, *Pergameinische Forschungen*, 3) (Berlin, 1976). *American Journal of Archaeology* 83 (1979), 117-18.

"A Numismatic Commentary on the Ptolemaic Cult Oinochoai," *Greek Numismatics and and Archaeology, Essays in Honor of Margaret Thompson* (Wetteren, Belgium, 1979), 251-55.

CHAPTER 14

DOROTHY EUGENIA MINER (1904-1973): THE VARIED CAREER OF A MEDIEVALIST: SCHOLAR AND KEEPER OF MANUSCRIPTS, LIBRARIAN AND EDITOR AT THE WALTERS ART GALLERY

Claire Richter Sherman[1]

INTRODUCTION

From September 1934 until shortly before her death on 15 May 1973, Dorothy Eugenia Miner played a large role in the development of the Walters Art Gallery to its present position as one of the most distinguished American museums. Miner was one of the original five professional staff members engaged to prepare the great private collection of William T. Walters and his son Henry to become a public museum bequeathed by Henry Walters to the city of Baltimore. With unflagging energy and zest, she performed several full-time jobs simultaneously. Her main title and field of activity centered on her responsibilities as Keeper of Manuscripts and Rare Books, but she was also curator in charge of Islamic and Near Eastern art. She served as reference librarian of the Walters, and in 1934 she became unofficial editor of its publications. In this last capacity, she was from 1938 to 1969 editor of the *Journal of the Walters Art Gallery*. She is perhaps best known for her role in organizing a series of landmark exhibitions. The first was *Early Christian and Byzantine Art*, held in 1947. There followed *Illuminated Books of the Middle Ages and Renaissance* (1949); *The World Encompassed* (1952), on maps and cartography; and *The History of Bookbinding, 525-1950 A.D.* (1957). These are four in a series of exhibitions that were pioneer surveys of American private and public collections in each field.

In addition to these substantial accomplishments at the Walters, Dorothy Miner's activities encompassed other areas. Her published writings number ninety-one items. She also lectured extensively, and as an adjunct member of the art history department at the Johns Hopkins University, taught courses there for many years. Another sphere of her work involved active support of both local and national learned societies.

All these phases of Dorothy Miner's career—curator, editor, librarian, scholar, teacher, and supporter of learned groups—form the subject of this study. Such an artificial separation of her activities obscures the fact that they all went on at the same time. What made the wide range of these accomplishments possible was her quick and lively mind, her extraordinary energy, and her total dedication to completing the task at hand with high professional standards. Yet a study of Dorothy Miner that neglected her personality would be sadly dry and incomplete. To all who sought information and advice, her kindness and warmth were immediately reflected in her engaging smile and her wholehearted interest and attention. No matter how pressing her deadline, she found time to listen and help. Her words, modestly spoken, revealed a keen wit and a gift for plain, succinct expression totally devoid of the pomposity or affectation often encountered in the museum world. Also notable in the sometimes closed atmosphere of rare-book rooms was her generosity in making manuscripts (and information about them) accessible without jeopardizing their safety.

Dorothy Miner's bailiwick, the rare-book room of the Walters, was directly accessible to visitors when the museum was open. Curious members of the public interrupted her work from time to time with questions that she answered irrespective of the person's age or station in life. Within the charming but cluttered space containing the Walters' manuscripts and rare books, a variety of activities were conducted by Miner and her knowledgeable assistants. Some days a seminar for visiting students or groups was held; at other times, distinguished scholars were examining manuscripts. When problems or questions arose, Miner quickly supplied the necessary materials from shelves or table tops piled high with books, catalogues, and photographs. As Dorothy Miner searched the room, visitors watched with a mixture of fear and awe her quick ascents and descents of the movable ladders that led to books and manuscripts kept in the upper reaches of the balcony. Unforgettable, too, were her deft movements as she displayed with quickness and enthusiasm particular pages or features of a book (Figure 25). At the same time, her careful treatment of manuscripts provided instruction for students and visitors on the proper handling of these precious objects.

EARLY LIFE

Dorothy Miner's professional achievements were fostered by a family background that encouraged hard work and valued intellectual attainment.[2] She and her twin brother Dwight were born in New York City on 4 November 1904 to Roy Waldo Miner and the former Anna Elizabeth Carroll. A second son, Roy, was born two years later. Her father came from an old New England family. Roy Waldo Miner graduated first from Williams

Figure 25. Dorothy Miner in the Rare Book Room of the Walters Art Gallery, Baltimore, 1966. (*Courtesy Walters Art Gallery*)

College and then from the General Theological Seminary in New York. He decided, however, not to pursue a religious calling and instead elected to continue his studies in biology. At this time, he met the young woman who was to become his wife. Anna Elizabeth Carroll had come to New York to work from her home town after also deciding not to continue in a religious vocation. Her family had emigrated from Ireland in the eighteenth century and settled in the Adirondack area of New York state. After the Civil War her father moved to Wilkes-Barre, Pennsylvania. They were married on 15 September 1903.

While he carried on his graduate studies at Columbia University, Roy Waldo Miner taught Latin and biology at the Berkeley School from 1900 to 1904 to support himself and later his family. During the next year he served as headmaster of the Kelvin School. In 1905 he joined the American Museum of Natural History as an assistant curator of invertebrate zoology, rising in 1922 to become curator of marine life, a post he held until his retirement. Roy Miner's interest in marine biology led him to study sea life in various environments. During the summer, his family would sometimes accompany him to the Wood's Hole Oceanographic Institution on the southern tip of Massachusetts. In addition to his studies and museum duties Dr. Miner wrote books on various aspects of marine biology. He also was an innovator in his approaches to exhibition design, including the use of new materials like motion pictures of underwater life.[3] Although she was not to follow her father's field of study, Dorothy Miner was introduced to the museum milieu at an early age, especially to the challenges and satisfactions of mounting unusual and visually exciting exhibitions.

Roy Waldo Miner is remembered by family and friends as a dynamic personality and charming man who exerted a strong influence on his children. Mrs. Miner was completely devoted to her family. A woman of persistence and determination, she had a rare sweetness of character which her daughter inherited. Mrs. Miner was a gifted and delightful hostess. Friends of her children especially cherish the memories of her warm hospitality. In those early days, and later, when the family circle widened to include Dwight's wife Marie and Roy's wife Nancy, an evening with the Miners was filled with stimulating talk and vigorous discussion, enlivened by the wit and humor which were Miner attributes.

The family lived in the Morningside Heights area, where Columbia University is located, until they moved to Yonkers after World War I. Dorothy and her twin Dwight enjoyed a close relationship, complete with their own language. Dwight Miner, who died on 1 August 1978, became a greatly admired professor of American history and chairman of the history department at Columbia. Dorothy was also close to her younger brother Roy, who followed his scientist father by choosing chemistry as his field.

Although a museum curator's salary was modest, the Miner children were sent to private schools. From the first through the sixth grade, Dorothy Miner attended the Graham School for Girls run at the time by her paternal uncle and his wife. The Graham School was a long-established institution, then located at 42 Riverside Drive.[4] For junior and senior high school, she attended the Horace Mann School for Girls, located at Broadway and 120th Street. Both the Horace Mann School for Boys, which the Miner sons attended beginning in elementary school, and its female counterpart offered a high quality of academic preparation for college. Several strands of Dorothy Miner's development were strengthened by the faculty and courses offered at Horace Mann. For one thing, her early exposure to the classics at home was reinforced by the excellent Latin teachers at the school. Her facility in drawing (inherited from her father)—as well as her interest in art—probably received encouragement from the art teacher, Belle Boas. Boas, a pioneer in the field of art education, went on to teach the subject at Columbia Teacher's College. Boas later encountered her protegee in Baltimore, when she became director of education at the Baltimore Museum from 1943 to 1954. A magnetic personality, Boas was greatly admired by Miner's class at Horace Mann, as shown in their dedication to her of their yearbook, *The Horace Mannikin, Class of 1922*. As an art editor of this publication, as well as of the *Record Board*, Dorothy Miner must have worked closely with Boas. The linoleum cuts that Miner produced for the yearbook show that her childhood interest in medieval subjects and themes continued to inspire her imagination. Miner's artistic interests extended also to executing posters for special occasions, as well as to her scenic direction of the senior play, *Aucassin and Nicolette*. Boas served as faculty advisor for this play, along with Helen Bartlett Baker, the English teacher who secured a scholarship for Miner so that she could join a group of students on a trip to Europe during the summer before her senior year at Horace Mann. The "class chart" of the yearbook predicted that the arts would be Miner's "public occupation" and prophetically assigned her as a personal motto: "Success reflects effort."

In September 1922 Dorothy Miner entered Barnard College. She had a distinguished academic career there. Not only was she elected to Phi Beta Kappa, but upon her graduation in 1926, she was the first recipient of the Barnard International Fellowship. In 1976, she received the Medalie Award given each year by the fiftieth-anniversary class to a member outstanding both in character and in accomplishments within a given field. She was the first person to receive this award posthumously. A year later a scholarship in her memory was established by her Barnard class (1926).

Miner majored both in English and in classics. She also took a number of courses in history and in architecture. Among the English faculty, she was particularly influenced by Charles Sears Baldwin, a specialist in Chaucer, and by Minor White Latham, active in the field of medieval drama. Dean Virginia Gildersleeve's emphasis on the responsibilities of educated women also made a deep impression. Altogether, Dorothy Miner's studies at Barnard in English, history, and the classics provided a firm foundation for her later specialization in manuscript studies.[5]

Miner lived at home during her years at Barnard. In spite of her increased family responsibilities following her mother's death in 1924, she took an active role in extracurricular activities. Members of the class of 1926 still remember her outstanding work on the Greek games, a combined intellectual, dramatic, and athletic annual event of great importance in Barnard life. Her first post was as freshman chairman of costumes for the Greek games. In this job, her artistic abilities came to the fore, as well as her practical sense of knowing how to make things from scratch with whatever means were at hand. Her friend Madeleine Hooke Rice recalls "the Dottie who dyed Greek Games Costumes until her hands seem to have acquired the tints of a permanent rainbow."[6] Professor Rice also remembers that although she was Miner's sophomore rival, a spirit of cooperation prevailed, characteristic of her friend's generosity. Her performance was so impressive that the next year Miner was made sophomore chairman of the Greek games.

In addition to the Greek games, she took part in other kinds of undergraduate activities. She served as vice-president of the Undergraduate Association in 1925/26 and took an important role in the reform of the honor system.[7] The junior class named her its most versatile member, perhaps because of her various dramatic accomplishments, from medieval miracle plays to writing the lyrics for the junior show. As art editor of the class yearbook, the *Mortarboard*, her charming drawings show even more clearly than the *Horace Mannikin* linoleum cuts her droll sense of humor, her interest in calligraphy, and her continued fondness for medieval lore and costume.

As the first Barnard International Fellow, Miner studied for about eighteen months from the fall of 1926 to the end of 1927 at Bedford College of the University of London. Her field was medieval literature. It was during her stay in England that she decided to return to the United States to study art history. The particular channel for her interest in this subject may have been the illustrations accompanying the texts of the medieval manuscripts she was studying in connection with her literary or historical research. Or perhaps her European travels decisively stimulated her interest in the fine arts. During this time in England, she met Helen Lowenthal, who became a lifelong friend and travelling companion.

Dorothy Miner began her graduate studies in art history at Columbia as a Carnegie Fellow in February 1928. Although the Department of Fine Arts and Archaeology had long granted advanced degrees in archaeology, graduate instruction in art history was just beginning in the late 1920s.[8] As an undergraduate at Barnard, she had already taken several courses in Italian and northern Renaissance painting with Professor Haring after the Fine Arts department was organized in 1923.[9] She expanded her knowledge of the field to include Chinese art, which she studied with George Rowley; Italian Renaissance sculpture, with Marion Lawrence, and medieval art, with Emerson Swift. Most closely related to her future specialty was the seminar on early Christian and medieval illuminated manuscripts given in 1928/29 by Meyer Schapiro, just beginning his teaching career at Columbia. This subject, taught only at a few universities in the United States, had recently developed as a special area of study. The seminal figure in the field was Professor Charles Rufus Morey of Princeton, who also served as a visiting professor during this period at Harvard, Columbia, and New York University. Miner's doctoral dissertation topic, growing out of her work with Professor Schapiro, concerned an illustrated Carolingian Apocalypse manuscript in Trier dating from about 800. Professor Schapiro, an inspiring teacher and brilliant scholar, must have stimulated his students' enthusiasm for this field.

During 1929/30, Miner went abroad as a Carnegie Fellow to study Apocalypse and related manuscripts in various European libraries, museums, and monastic collections. On one journey, she walked for nine miles from the railway station to a small Italian town, where the local populace found the presence "of this solitary-American female" in their midst a fascinating puzzle.[10] Again, her travels led to encounters with fellow students who became colleagues and devoted friends. At the Cabinet des Manuscrits of the Bibliothèque Nationale, she met Eleanor Spencer, then working on her Radcliffe doctoral dissertation on a fifteenth-century French illuminator, Maître François. Spencer also settled in Baltimore in the 1930s, where she became the head of the art department at Goucher College. Their mutual love of manuscripts became the basis for a lifelong friendship.

The full force of the Great Depression had struck when Miner returned to Columbia for another year of study on a President's fellowship. In 1931/32, she was appointed as assistant in the art history department at Barnard, a post equivalent to that of a teaching fellow. Although at this point the preparation of her dissertation was quite advanced, she never completed it. The subsequent shift of her professional activity to the museum world made the doctorate less important than if she had continued in academic life.

The turning point in her career came in 1933, when she secured a position as assistant at the Morgan Library to help with the catalogue of an exhibition of illuminated manuscripts held at the New York Public Library, for which Charles Rufus Morey wrote the introduction. It was the first exhibition held in the United States devoted entirely to illuminated manuscripts. In charge of this display of the manuscript treasures of the Morgan Library was its formidable and colorful director, Belle da Costa Greene.[11] Miner had apparently met Belle Greene through a friend of her father, Bashford Dean. Dean was an icthyologist who was also a noted collector of armor and curator of the armor collections at the Metropolitan Museum.[12] Dean advised Miner, whose interest in armor arose from her long fascination with medieval life, to ask Greene for permission to consult a famous Morgan manuscript, the Shah Abbas Bible, notable for its depictions of armor. From the time of her employment at the Morgan Library, Belle Greene took Miner under her wing and fostered her career and interests with the devotion of a mother. In turn, Miner returned her mentor's affection and would never tolerate an unkind word directed against her. Although how Miner got the Morgan Library job remains unclear, Belle Greene certainly recommended her for the Walters position in 1934. As a member of the advisory committee of the Walters, Belle Greene took a great interest in the new museum and made frequent trips to Baltimore to attend meetings of this group. She also generously supported the Walters' reference library by gifts of books and donations of funds. The friendship between Dorothy Miner and Belle Greene continued to flourish. Greene may have been disappointed when her protegee was not chosen to succeed her as director of the Morgan Library upon her retirement in 1948. Despite contrasting personalities, they shared deep interests. Miner's friends report that she admired Belle Greene's quick brain, her very individual personal style, and her pungent wit. She also valued Greene's ability to distinguish in both books and people authentic from specious qualities. Miner's most lasting tribute was the magnificent book of essays honoring Belle Greene that she organized and edited.[13] Unfortunately, the volume was not published until four years after Greene's death in 1950, although Miner was able to indicate to her the preliminary plans. Ironically, this pattern of the incomplete memorial volume was repeated shortly before Dorothy Miner's own death, when the staff of the Walters Gallery revealed to her the main outlines of *Gatherings in Honor of Dorothy E. Miner*.

Dorothy Miner was almost thirty and a strikingly lovely woman (Figure 26) when she moved to Baltimore in September 1934 as one of the original five professional staff of the Walters Gallery. Baltimore, and the Walters Art Gallery, were to become the center of her life until her death almost thirty-nine years later.

LANDMARK EXHIBITIONS

When at the beginning of September 1934, Dorothy Miner and the four other staff members began work at the Walters, they faced a tremendous

Figure 26. Dorothy Miner, ca. 1933. (*Courtesy the late Dwight Miner*)

task.[14] The collection of Henry Walters (1848-1931) and that of his father William T. Walters (1820-1894) comprises more than twenty thousand items. Historically it embraces works from ancient Egypt, Greece, and the Near East, as well as those produced in nineteenth-century Europe and America. The collection contains objects in all media, from monumental sculpture to precious jewelry. Until the new wing opened in 1974, it was housed in a Renaissance-style building especially designed as a private gallery on Mt. Vernon Place and built between 1905 and 1906.[15] Before the staff arrived, the administrator of the Walters, C. Morgan Marshall, had already supervised certain structural changes in the building, such as the installation of air-conditioning.

An advisory committee of persons prominent in the art and museum worlds helped the administrator, who was not an art historian, to decide policies of the new public museum.[16] The staff had just two months to ready the Gallery for its opening to the public. As the collection was then largely disorganized, unremitting work—much of it plain physical labor—was necessary. Large parts of the collection still remained in packing cases or were scattered about Henry Walters' adjoining house and the gallery. Unlike the curators of the oldest American museums, the professional staff of the Walters were academically trained art historians. Because they were so few in number and limited in practical experience, from the beginning the aid of outside experts with specialized knowledge in various subjects was enlisted. Excitement was great when hitherto unknown objects were brought to light. Visitors would be shown these new finds, and also previously published works that had not been easily accessible to the public during Henry Walters' lifetime. Naturally, scholars were fascinated by the great new treasure trove gradually being unveiled at the Walters. Dorothy Miner used to say, "Every day is Christmas at the Walters."

The Walters staff encouraged and facilitated scholars' study of objects from the collections. During the 1930s, close ties were maintained with Princeton's art history department, particularly noted for its medievalists. Its chairman, Charles Rufus Morey, has already been mentioned as an early and influential scholar who fostered the study of illuminated manuscripts.[17] Among other specialists in this field at Princeton at that time were Ernest T. DeWald, Albert M. Friend, Jr., and Donald Drew Egbert. Soon they were joined by the distinguished refugee scholars Kurt Weitzmann, Erwin Panofsky, and Hanns Swarzenski, active also at the Institute for Advanced Study. According to Hanns Swarzenski, Dorothy Miner used to telephone to announce the discovery of a new object and ask one or more of these experts to come down and take a look. Lively discussions took place in the Gallery about the date, localization, and attributions of these recently discovered objects. Miner joined in the debates, vigorously disputing the pros and cons of the various arguments advanced. In this exciting first phase of the Walters' existence, Dorothy Miner was, according to Hanns Swarzenski, a "radiating force" in creating a network of scholars involved in studying the Gallery's collections.

Although small exhibitions were held frequently at the Walters in the 1930s and the early 1940s, the famous series of exhibitions already mentioned did not begin until the end of World War II permitted a resumption of artistic activities and exchanges. According to her friends and colleagues, preparing and putting on exhibitions was the part of her work at the Walters that Dorothy Miner enjoyed most. Especially delightful to her was determining which objects should be included. This process involved visits to collections and meeting and sharing enthusiasms with curators and librarians. After returning to the Walters, she examined and assimilated her notes. Then she began the requests for loans. Somehow time flew by in writing the copy for the catalogue entries, securing the proper photographs, preparing the labels, and planning the installation. Often Miner worked through the night before an opening. Sometimes her assistant Irene Butterbaugh, seated on the floor of the exhibition space, typed the labels and set them in place at the last moment. The objects in Dorothy Miner's care always received special attention, as she made every effort to display their finest features.

The famous exhibitions associated with Miner were organized by the Walters. Because the Gallery lacked suitable exhibition space, they were installed at the Baltimore Museum of Art in conjunction with the Peabody Institute or with Evergreen House of the Johns Hopkins University. A notable feature of these exhibitions was the remarkable degree of cooperation between these various Baltimore institutions. All these exhibitions, including those with objects borrowed from overseas, surveyed often for the first time the extent of American holdings in these fields. As a result, the catalogues of all these shows, still in print today, remain acknowledged and standard reference books.

The History of Bookbinding has been chosen to illustrate Dorothy Miner's approach to organizing a comprehensive exhibition in a hitherto unexplored field. By way of contrast, the exhibition commemorating the five-hundredth anniversary of the introduction of printing in France, entitled *The First University Press*, will serve as an example of her ability to put on small, imaginative shows based only on the Walters holdings.

Among the most enthusiastically received of the large exhibitions, *The History of Bookbinding, 525-1950 A.D.* was held at the Baltimore Museum between 12 November 1957 and 12 January 1958. Like an earlier show on *Illuminated Books of the Middle Ages and the Renaissance*, the exhibition and catalogue were the product of Miner's own work.[18] She did not wish, however, to be credited as author, as she believed that the Walters Gallery deserved the honor. Miner wanted the bookbinding exhibition, which she had long envisioned, to become "something of a landmark in the scholarship of the subject."[19]

Except for certain crucial bindings lent by the governments of Tunisia and Morocco, Miner decided to limit the scope of the exhibition to American private and public collections. In view of the lack of any previous publication of these holdings this goal was a useful and necessary one. Even this narrowed focus did not eliminate difficulties in her preliminary research. Because American collecting in this field was based on the importance of the edition of the volume, and not primarily on its binding, Miner noted: "This fact meant, of course, that our selection necessarily involved much hunting of shelves, and that many a fine specimen must certainly have been missed."[20] Her own expertise in the highly specialized area of bookbinding arose from her interest in all aspects of book design. Furthermore, the Walters collection of manuscripts and printed books possessed bindings of unusual interest and value, which undoubtedly spurred her to acquire a knowledge of the history and development of the craft.

Miner's visits to private and public collections were obviously preceded by careful advance preparation. A tightly crammed schedule of work did not interfere with her sense of excitement at examining and discussing the various bindings she saw during the course of her trip. Her gift of communicating with people comes across both from her letters of thanks and from the responses of the curators and librarians who shared their treasures with her. On the occasion of her visit to the Houghton Library at Harvard —which lent forty-five bindings to the exhibition—her absorption in her work caused unexpected difficulties. So engrossed was Miner in her research that she neglected to leave the building at closing time and for a while was locked inside it.[21]

A summary glance at the catalogue reveals the comprehensiveness of Miner's goals in presenting a history of bookbinding. Forty-eight lenders provided 718 bindings for the exhibition. The correspondence relating to the show provides some idea of the scope of the undertaking. Her crowded itinerary and the very specialized vocabulary used in describing book bindings probably suggested the design of a special printed form for lenders that aided the donors in describing and evaluating the bindings for insurance purposes. Miner also took these forms with her on her research trips in order to assure uniformity and accuracy of detail in recording information for the catalogue entries. Indeed, her precise descriptions of the individual bindings offer another example of her considerable skills in concise writing and of her firm command of the technical processes of a particular craft.

The preparation of the exhibition gave Dorothy Miner an opportunity to develop her knowledge of a particular field, which she applied in her later acquisitions for the Walters. The show also provided the prospective donors with an occasion for reexamining and reappraising their collections. For example, both Frederick Goff, then chief of the Rare Book division of the Library of Congress, and Karl Kup, director of the Spencer collection of the New York Public Library at that time, held special "teaser exhibitions" of book bindings in their collections. Their purpose was to help Miner better choose during her whirlwind visits which loans she wanted.[22]

Both the exhibition itself and the accompanying catalogue received resounding critical acclaim. The installation of the exhibition by Mabel Kaji and Margaret Powell of the Baltimore Museum following Miner's design was considered unusually handsome. Particularly outstanding was the alcove containing the first section of the show: twenty-five "treasure bindings" in ivory, precious metals, and textiles. Other highlights included Coptic bindings from the Morgan Library, important sections on the Near East, and loans from Tunisia of the Islamic bindings of Kairouan of the ninth to eleventh centuries. From a multivolume Koran loaned by the Moroccan government came several thirteenth-century bindings, the first dated examples of gold tooling on leather. Despite occasional criticism of weaknesses here and there, the experts enthusiastically praised the over-all quality and achievement of the exhibition.[23]

The catalogue won equally high marks for its usefulness as a reference work. The foreword shows Dorothy Miner's ability to reduce a complex body of material to a clear and graceful synthesis intelligible to the nonspecialist. The fourteen main sections, and many of the subsections, are introduced by short paragraphs summarizing the historical significance or particular function of each group of bindings. All 718 entries have a short running title and are identified as to lender and, wherever known, their provenance. If the binding remains attached to the text, the contents of the latter are identified. The descriptions of the bindings themselves are models of precision in respect to their colors, designs, techniques, and materials employed, as well as other niceties of the craft. Both the selected bibliography and individual bibliographical references are very valuable features in a field where no over-all recent compilations existed. The index is admirably organized under various headings, including early monastic provenances, owners, binders, and cities in which the bindings were produced. Another important feature is the excellent quality of the 106 pages of plates, which facilitates comparisons of many unfamiliar works.

In view of the enormous task Miner had set herself, the short time available for realizing the project, and the difficulties of identifying and assembling the materials, the bookbinding exhibition and catalogue were outstanding achievements. The breadth of her vision and scholarship, combined with extraordinary precision in recording details, produced a lasting synthesis and overview of the field.

Dorothy Miner's small exhibitions at the Walters showed the same wide range of interests and a developed imagination in choosing contents and subjects. All were based upon sound scholarship and an ability to synthesize diverse strands of intellectual and social history in the comprehensive labels she wrote describing the objects. Many exhibitions involved illuminated manuscripts and early printed books in the Walters collections. In a different vein, Miner used the Walters' recently acquired collection of 172 monumental brass rubbings as the focus of an exhibition of medieval costume from the eleventh through the sixteenth centuries, entitled *Medieval Parade*. Her descriptions of costume and of the armor of the rubbings are extremely evocative and show how her early interest in medieval lore and life continued in full force.[24]

Among the most delightful of these small exhibitions was the one held from 31 October to 7 December 1970 entitled *The First University Press*. In a lecture delivered on 2 November 1970 in connection with the show, Miner explained the occasion in this way:

> It is always fun to celebrate anniversaries—so we have seized upon the fact that just exactly 500 years ago—probably in October—the first book to be printed in France came off the printing press. It was a very small press set up in the library of the Sorbonne at the University of Paris—and its purpose was simply to make more readily available copies of the texts needed by the scholars and the students at the University of the life-blood of their teaching and learning.[25]

Although, as she explained in the lecture, the Walters (and other American collections) did not possess any of the original volumes printed at the Sorbonne, she believed that the Gallery had enough early books printed in Paris to mark the occasion. The exhibition was housed in two small galleries and included both manuscripts and printed books illustrating eight main topics. The earliest group of six Walters manuscripts showed how carefully the University of Paris controlled and supervised the texts needed for courses. This section of this exhibition illustrated Dorothy Miner's lifelong interest in the process of replicating texts, as well as her keen awareness of the precise audience for and the changing functions of books within the social and intellectual contexts of historical periods. Other parts of the exhibition were devoted to different types of books put out by early Paris printers, various types of bindings, and the emergence of Renaissance tastes in print-types and texts of the first half of the sixteenth century.

In a letter to her old friend Eleanor Spencer, Miner commented on the information contained in the labels she wrote for the show. "I have given much chattier information on the labels—a favorite device by which insignificant things can *reflect* significance."[26] For example, in the label describing the Walters' edition of Robert Gaguin's *Compendium de origine et gestis Francorum* ("Compendium on the Origins and Deeds of the French"), Miner managed to compress a great deal of information about the biography of the author and the history of the text.

To evoke the appearance of Paris in the fifteenth and sixteenth centuries, Miner placed at the entrance two visual introductions to the exhibition. The first was a blow-up of the Jean Fouquet miniature from the Etienne Chevalier Hours belonging to the Robert Lehman collection, now in the Metropolitan Museum in New York.[27] The miniature gives a view "from the Quai des Grands Augustins over to the Ile de la Cité with wonderful renderings of Notre Dame, and the walls of the Palais, and the Spire of little St. Michel, and the Pont St. Michel, with the booksellers' shops, etc." The second visual reference was a "large wall-map, reproduced from the unique plan of Paris now in Basle which gives the city of Henry II's time, with a good many street and church names."[28] Miner cut up details of the large map, which she herself hand-tinted. She placed them next to the label, giving wherever possible contemporary information on the location of the specific printer's shop. These kinds of imaginative details were visually handsome in themselves. They also reinforced the verbal information in the exhibitions. Typical of Dorothy Miner's verve and flair, these visual touches combined with her strong sense of history to make a modest exhibition a personal, as well as an intellectual and artistic, statement.

EDITORIAL CONTRIBUTIONS

A snapshot in the yearbook of the Horace Mann School for Girls shows Dorothy Miner engrossed in her editorial and art work for this publication. Her work as an editor continued throughout her professional career to form an extremely valuable part of her contribution to scholarship, if a less visible one than her role in organizing exhibitions. Her efforts again involved various Walters publications. From 1934 to 1968 she engaged in every aspect of publication from finding authors for articles, designing layouts, and dealing with printers to reading proof and making indexes.[29] Miner did not regard any of these jobs as tedious or beneath her. Rather, they were seen as part of a larger goal, in which the final product came up to her high standards within the limitations set by budgets and deadlines.

One of her prime accomplishments as an editor was the *Journal of the Walters Art Gallery*. She originated the idea for its publication and set its policy until 1969. The first issue, which appeared in 1938, was applauded for the high quality of its contents, photographs, and design, and it was regarded as a model for other museum publications. Miner was well suited to finding the best scholarly authorities to write for the *Journal*. As a natural consequence of her policy of encouraging scholars to visit the Walters and facilitating their access to objects that interested them, she was able to ask them to write up their findings.

Miner was extremely skillful in getting people to improve their writings for all the Walters publications that she edited. She did not accept copy as submitted, if it did not meet her standards. Instead, she tactfully made suggestions on the organization and expression of an author's ideas to avoid wounding his or her feelings. Sometimes she actually sat down with an author to indicate how and in what order an object needed to be described. Here, Miner's exceptional skill in this basic part of art-historical writing came to the fore. On some occasions she reworked articles until they measured up to her standards. Her editing was aimed at the general intelligent reader and so avoided abstruse abbreviations or references. Miner was very conscientious about checking details, including chapters and verses of Biblical citations. When necessary, she consulted major sources of articles in order to make sure that she understood the basic concepts involved. Although careful of details, she did not become obsessed by them. She was also realistic about the degree of comprehensiveness in an index when faced by a rapidly impending deadline. For Miner, her work as an editor served as a learning experience in which she acquainted herself with problems and works of art outside her own field. She seems always to have remembered in detail arguments advanced in studies she had edited.

In addition to the *Journal* and the annual reports of the Walters Gallery, for which Dorothy Miner was responsible, a new publication was introduced after World War II had ended and Gallery programs expanded. In 1948, Dorothy Kent Hill became editor until 1970 of the *Bulletin of the Walters Art Gallery*, a useful guide of the Gallery's activities. Two years later, Dorothy Miner designed the first Christmas catalogue of objects for sale from the Walters collection. Miner and her assistant Irene Butterbaugh photographed the objects at the latter's home because the official photographers were engaged in other pressing tasks. Various domestic props in the Butterbaugh house served as suitable backgrounds for setting off various objects. In 1960, Miner designed *Dragons and Animals: A Walters Art Gallery Coloring Book*. It has been described as the first book of its kind to use medieval woodcuts for children to color and was widely copied. Both Miner's long love of medieval lore and her interest in getting children involved in enjoying art are shown in *Dragons and Animals*.

Among the major catalogues of the Walters collections edited by Dorothy Miner were the *Catalogue of Egyptian Sculpture* by George Steindorff (1946); *A Catalogue of the Work of William Henry Rinehart, Maryland Sculptor, 1825-74*, by Marvin C. Ross and Anna W. Rutledge (1948); *American Works of Art in the Walters Art Gallery*, by Edward S. King and Marvin C. Ross (1956); and *Russian Art, Icons and Decorative Arts from the Origin to the Twentieth Century*, by Philippe Verdier (1959). These were followed by *Arts of the Migration Period in the Walters Art Gallery*, by Marvin C. Ross and Philippe Verdier (1961); *Catalogue of Painted Enamels of the Renaissance*, by Philippe Verdier (1967); and *Armenian Manuscripts in the Walters Art Gallery*, by Sirarpie der Nersessian (1973).[30] Miner also edited the catalogues of the famous exhibitions organized by the Walters after World War II, some of which have already been mentioned. Two others in the series were *The International Style: The Arts in Europe around 1400*, by Philippe Verdier (1962), for which Miner contributed the section on manuscripts; and *2000 Years of Calligraphy*, which she edited and co-authored with Victor I. Carlson and P. W. Filby (1965).

A final and notable example of Miner's work as an editor deserves particular attention. *Studies in Art and Literature for Belle da Costa Greene*, published in 1954 by the Princeton University Press, must be one of the most monumental memorial volumes ever issued. It runs to 480 pages of text written by fifty-one separate authors. The contents range from all aspects of the history of art and manuscript studies to printed books, bibliography, literature and autograph manuscripts, and bookbinding. A generation after these works were written by outstanding authorities in their fields, they are still regarded as important contributions to scholarship.

Every phase of the volume took tremendous effort and time. Miner's editorial labors alone—approaching contributors, encouraging them to produce articles of the highest quality, and guiding them gently but firmly—are simply awesome. Equally staggering were the administrative aspects of the enterprise. Miner formed an advisory committee on the publication, which she chaired. She also undertook to find substantial financial support for the book. She enlisted four sponsors and seventy-five donors, who were kept informed on the progress of the volume. After elaborate negotiations with the press when publication was at last in sight, Miner concerned herself with distribution and sales of the book. Together with her assistant Irene Butterbaugh, she assembled offprints for authors from press overruns.

Too often the backstage, unglamorous work of the scholarly editor is taken for granted, although it demands many exacting skills and unlimited reserves of patience and fortitude. Miner's achievements as editor of the Walters publications and the Greene volume deserve recognition in terms of both professional and personal commitment.

PUBLICATIONS

In addition to her work as curator, librarian, and editor, Dorothy Miner has left a significant body of writings, a worthy scholarly heritage in itself. The subjects of her bibliography of ninety-one items collected in *Gatherings in Honor of Dorothy E. Miner* mainly concern works from the Walters collection. They include the fifteen catalogues which she edited, wrote herself, or coauthored. Aside from one book about a Walters manuscript written with Grace Frank, her other writings are published lectures or articles for periodicals. Of this group, twenty-six are short notices in the *Bulletin of the Walters Art Gallery*. Her "non-Walters" pieces mostly pertain to her favorite subjects—medieval manuscripts and printed books. These include book reviews, contributions to "festschriften," and articles describing university, and other, collections of manuscripts.

Dorothy Miner's scholarship is enhanced by her considerable gifts as a writer. In both scholarly and popular pieces, she has a rare facility to compress clearly into a few paragraphs a great deal of solid, factual information. Her writing is graced by a pungent wit, a gift for singling out the telling detail, and the ability to organize and focus a discussion. One of her particularly striking talents has been noted more than once: an uncanny skill in describing an object with the utmost precision, while at the same time making its physical and aesthetic character come alive.

Miner's innate response to a manuscript as a concrete, physical object was intensified by her continuous exposure to the magnificent Walters collection of manuscripts. In a mysterious but palpable way they would "speak to her" and yield some of their secrets. In a discussion of vellum as the material on which manuscripts are written, she describes how final stages in its preparation can reveal regional preferences: "Medieval Italy liked her vellum shiny and crackling; Germany and Italy preferred it suede-like and thick; France made it so thin it was semitransparent." She concludes: "One can almost tell the general region or origin of a book by one's fingertips, so much does the texture of the vellum vary, particularly in the centuries before the Renaissance."[31]

Her constant study of the Walters manuscripts probably stimulated another constant theme of her scholarship: her awareness of the interrelationship of all the elements of book design to form a coherent aesthetic structure. The continued presence of the manuscripts in her care, as well as her strong literary and historical background, led her to avoid the separation—as scholars have done until recently—of texts from miniatures, or miniatures from ornament. Miner's insistence on the manuscript as an integrated physical structure anticipates, although without any methodological emphasis, the program for the type of manuscript studies called codicology, later outlined independently by her friend the late L. M. J. Delaissé.[32] The following passage gives a good idea of Miner's views on book design:

> The book with pages was the stimulus to everything that we think of when we discuss book design. It was the delimited field of the two opposing pages seen at a time —instead of the constantly shifting area of the scroll—that spurred the sense of fitness of the scribe to consider proportions of his script, of his length of line, of his margins, in relation to the two pages in view; it challenged the illustrator to unify his picture with the script-block; it stimulated ornamental treatment. The same urge affected the craftsman entrusted with the binding of the book. The book with pages required a stout pair of covers to protect it, and the rectangular boards invited ornaments.[33]

Some of Miner's finest writings occur in published lectures for general audiences. In an article on the Book of Kells, her description and analysis of the abstract qualities of the various types of ornament in the manuscript are brilliantly interwoven with her discussion of its essential design structure and its dynamic aesthetic. With an eloquence rarely found in the literature on illuminated manuscripts, Miner finds the secret of the fascination of the ornament in the Book of Kells in the "dynamically conceived design." One feels the vividness of her response to the physical character of the manuscript summarized in this masterful sentence:

This unrivalled abundance and diversity, this restlessness of endlessly evolving spiral and lacertine, this infinity of forms within forms, of human and animal shapes that are mere allusions to something experienced, scarcely recognized before they are snatched into the realm of the impossible and their bodies stretched and twisted and woven as by some inevitability into the masterplan of the pattern—all of these and more derived their main force from the character of the compositions of which they are but incidents.[34]

Miner's earliest articles show that she was equally at home in the field of scholarly writing. Drawing on her research for her doctoral dissertation in her first published writing of 1933, her review of Wilhelm Neuss's book on early Apocalypse manuscripts contains a masterful summation of the strengths and weaknesses of that volume, as well as a command of the complex literature on the subject.[35] Three years later, she wrote an exemplary piece on "A Late Reichenau Evangeliary" in the Walters.[36] Thorough examination and analysis of the paleographic and textual characteristics of the manuscript and its affiliated works are combined with knowledge of previous scholarship and a keen stylistic analysis of the miniatures.

Proverbes en Rimes ("Proverbs in Rhymes"), written with Grace Frank and published in 1937 by the Johns Hopkins University Press, was an unusual and innovative project for manuscript studies of this period. The subject is a late fifteenth-century manuscript (W. 313) in the Walters Gallery containing a collection of proverbs written in verse, each one accompanied by an illustration. Grace Frank, a specialist in medieval French, transcribed the edition of the text and discussed the literary background of the genre. Miner dealt with the illustrations in Walters 313 and in related manuscripts. Both women worked on "borderline" problems. One unconventional aspect of the project is the choice of a secular manuscript of only average quality. At that time, art historians usually studied the illuminations of de luxe manuscripts executed for aristocratic or learned patrons. Also unusual in *Proverbes en Rimes* is the authors' study of the relationship between the text and the accompanying images of the manuscript. Only recently, stimulated by codicology and semiotics, has this kind of approach to manuscript studies been pursued methodically. To be sure, on pages 9-26 of the introduction Miner discusses more usual questions of styles, the various hands responsible for the illustrations, and the relationship of these illustrations to later manuscripts of the same text and their derivation from a common model. Yet Miner concerns herself with the general function of the text in terms of its didactic purpose and literal character.

The preface provides an interesting analysis of the relationship of the Walters manuscript to Renaissance emblem books in regard to the employment of word-picture reinforcement.[37] Miner's discussion of the intellectual and social history of the manuscript adds immeasurably to the dimensions of *Proverbes en Rimes*. Her sketch of its middle-class, urban patrons of limited education is linked to the use of paper as a cheap material for "inexpensive, amusing books, not for display but to be read and enjoyed."[38] Miner's knowledge of the economics of book production, as well as of the functions and audiences for different types of texts, is an extremely important feature of all her writing on manuscripts. In combination with her emphasis on the integrated physical structure of manuscripts, this historical framework again anticipates the scope of later codicological studies.

In *Proverbes en Rimes*, Miner confronts another set of problems that predominates in her later writings: the study of the process of copying or reproducing designs of visual material. One facet of her interest lay in the problem of artists' model books. Model books are collections of motifs, figures, and other representational forms kept by individual artists or workshops as sources for diverse kinds of visual representations used in illustrating and decorating different types of texts. In the published form of a lecture given at the Library of Congress in 1952 when it acquired the Giant Bible of Mainz, Miner discusses current theories of model books in relationship to the decoration of this manuscript.[39] She begins with a spellbinding tour de force of imagining the mental and technical processes followed by the master scribe entrusted with the writing of the book. After an equally memorable description of the borders of five folios at the beginning of the manuscript, she focuses on the similarities between the human and animal forms in these borders and those of fifteenth-century playing cards. These cards were widely disseminated as they are "considered to be the very first examples of copper-engraved prints."[40] Miner concludes that the question is not whether the borders of the Giant Bible depended on the playing cards, or vice versa, but that both have "in common the same model-book and even, in specific cases, the same pricked patterns."[41]

In 1961/62, Dorothy Miner spent a year as a fellow of the Institute for Advanced Study in Princeton to continue her work on model books and related problems. As the acknowledged authority in this field, she was invited by Professor Ernst Kitzinger, then director of studies at Dumbarton Oaks, to conduct a colloquium on the subject in 1962. Although her projected work on means of transmitting visual forms in medieval manuscripts did not materialize, two studies—one dating from the 1960s and the other from the early 1970s—give some clues as to the kinds of information she was collecting. The earlier of these is concerned with pouncing,[42] a stage in the process of copying a drawing or motif by putting a blank sheet beneath it and making a series of small holes or pricks around the outlines of the object to be transferred. The design is transferred to its destination by "pouncing" it with a small bag of powdered charcoal or color.[43] Miner discovered that pouncing of selected motives went back to the second third of the eleventh century. She traces the practice to a group of related manuscripts from the abbey of Saint Germain-des-Prés in Paris. She believes not only that these examples are the earliest cases of European pouncing yet detected but also that they disprove the hypothesis that pricking was used only for transferring embroidery patterns. In this study, Miner shows that, unlike the practice in the earlier period of pouncing, pricking was used for whole scenes or entire designs in the fourteenth and fifteenth centuries, when book production became more systematized.[44] A second study dating from 1972 concerns the relationship between preparatory drawings bound with a Walters manuscript (W. 148) and finished illuminations in a manuscript of Oxford's Bodleian Library.[45] Among other things, the article contains further evidence of Miner's marvelous sensitivity to the physical features of a book—minute holes and creases that would have escaped the notice of all but the keenest eye. Miner concludes that the drawings in the Walters manuscript were based on the finished miniatures of the Bodleian manuscript, from which they were selectively copied. She attributes them to the Master of (the Bodleian's) Douce MS 185. Both studies are representative examples of her knowledge of the complex manner in which visual representations were transmitted in medieval book production.

Among her later writings on manuscripts, two articles in the *Journal of the Walters Art Gallery* show Dorothy Miner in top form. They are devoted to a discussion of manuscripts acquired since 1934 by the Walters under her guidance.[46] The first one deals with manuscripts "from the eastern Mediterranean region and central Europe dating from the tenth through the sixteenth century."[47] With the greatest ease she covers a wide range of periods and geographical areas, to say nothing of a broad assortment of artistic styles, patrons, and texts. Whether describing the binding of an Ethiopic codex, the parade pages of a tenth-century Gospel book, or a rare Byzantine monastic Psalter, she provides comprehensive discussions of their provenance, textual and liturgical significance, and affiliations with other manuscripts and distinctive art-historical features. Her sensitivity to the physical features of a manuscript tells her that a Bohemian Missal (W. 756) was used exclusively for the observance of the Eucharist. Only the pages pertaining to this rite are worn; the rest remain in a pristine condition. In the second part of the study, Miner discusses manuscripts from France, Flanders, and Italy. She relates the latest developments in art-historical scholarship to the styles of the Boucicaut Master (W. 770) or the Florentine artist Zanobi Strozzi (W. 767). Miner was even more excited by what she herself called "manuscript sleuthing," finding other fragments of partial manuscripts, discovering their original owners, and their relationship to affiliated scriptoria and ateliers.[48] Her undiminished enthusiasm for the solution of every kind of puzzle associated with a manuscript—textual, art-historical, paleographic—emerges clearly. Among the most lively and engaging of these mysteries is her narration of the Walters acquisition of additional fragments of a French sacramentary of the twelfth century (W. 28).[49] The excitement of the "hunt" and subsequent purchase of forty-five leaves is vividly told, and the account of the physical condition of these fragments sympathetically and sensitively described. Masterfully presented, too, is the reconstruction of the volume on liturgical lines and the extraction of information about its original patron from the evidence of the binding.

A final example of Dorothy Miner's writing does not concern manuscripts but is also linked with the Walters collection. "The Publishing Ventures of a Victorian Connoisseur—A Sidelight on W. T. Walters," analyses the content and design of the various publications sponsored by the elder Walters.[50] This essay also offers many other fascinating insights, including interesting nuggets about American art collecting and the state of nineteenth-century Western scholarship on Oriental porcelains. Her account of American book design of the nineteenth century is in itself a valuable contribution. In this study, her skill at biography comes to the fore. Although sometimes contained in footnotes, her writing on William Walters' advisors and friends provides skillful synopses of characters and careers obviously based on extensive research. Her particular accounts of both William and Henry Walters offer acute insights into their personalities as individuals and as collectors, whether of Percheron horses or of Oriental porcelains. Perhaps the most interesting part of this study is the section on the Bushell publication on Oriental porcelains, including a marvelous description of its 116 color lithographs by Louis Prang.[51] Here Miner gracefully interweaves human interest, the history of scholarship, and an appreciation of the techniques of color lithography. The article closes with a catalogue of the publications sponsored by William T. Walters, written with an exemplary precision. In a way, this study sums up Miner's appreciation of the two Walters, based on her profound knowledge and love of their benefactions.

Although Dorothy Miner's writings do not include the kind of broad, synthetic works of scholarship so highly esteemed by academic art historians, they do have a remarkable scope and resonance. In many respects, they anticipate new approaches to manuscript studies developed relatively recently. Furthermore, her continued exposure and sensitive response to the works in her care give her writings a liveliness and eloquence often conspicuously absent in purely academic scholarship.

PROFESSIONAL ACTIVITIES

The impressive and varied array of Dorothy Miner's accomplishments at the Walters did not prevent her from engaging in a wide range of extra-Gallery activities. She genuinely enjoyed working with others for good causes, cultural and civic. To her, membership in a group meant active support and participation. In turn, her contributions were recognized, valued, and honored.

Dorothy Miner was an active member of various learned societies. She belonged to the Mediaeval Academy of America and served as a member of the council. She was also a charter member of the Renaissance Society of America and representative on the council. She belonged to the College Art Association of America and was a director from 1958 to 1961.

Among groups with which she was associated, many represented different phases of her interest in book design. Miner was a member of the Hroswitha Club, founded in New York in 1944. The Club was "named after the tenth-century canoness of the Abbey of Gandersheim, Saxony, the most remarkable poet, dramatist, and historian of her time in Germany."[52] Comprised of wealthy book collectors, bibliophiles, and scholars, the Hroswitha Club was formed as a feminine, if not feminist, counterpart to the Grolier Club, which only recently has admitted women to membership. She was also an honorary Fellow of the Pierpont Morgan Library, honorary member of the Société de la Reliure Originale and of the Society of Scribes and Illuminators, and member of the Bibliographical Society of America and the Cambridge Bibliographical Society.

Certain aspects of Dorothy Miner's work as a lecturer and teacher—particularly as an adjunct faculty member in the art history department at Johns Hopkins—have been mentioned. In 1962, she taught a seminar on manuscripts at the New York University summer session in Brussels as adjunct professor. She was very much in demand as a speaker, both locally and nationally. She spoke easily, at times with only a few notes. She brought works of art to life for her audiences, occasionally overestimating her listeners' attention span because of her own enthusiasm for the subject. Dorothy Miner was the first woman to be named Rosenbach Fellow in Bibliography at the University of Pennsylvania in 1955. Unfortunately, the lectures she gave in Philadelphia remain unpublished. She was also the first woman to deliver, in 1969/70, the Kraus Lectures in Medieval Illuminated Manuscripts at the Beinecke Library of Yale University.

Miner was a devoted and effective member of advisory committees of several academic institutions. At Columbia University, she served as a member of the advisory council of the Department of Art History and Archaeology beginning in 1960 and was on the visiting committee from 1969 until her death. Her service as a member of the art gallery advisory council of Notre Dame University was honored by a memorial exhibition entitled *Medieval Art 1060-1550*. Held at the art gallery of Notre Dame in the spring of 1974, the show featured works of art belonging to fellow members of the advisory council and was supplemented by loans from the Pierpont Morgan Library and the Walters Art Gallery. The catalogue's foreword, written by the Rev. Anthony J. Lauck, C.S.C., director of the art gallery, pays warm tribute to the human and professional contributions of Dorothy Miner to the activities of the Notre Dame gallery.

Miner was particularly active in her adopted city of Baltimore as member and supporter of a wide group of associations including the Baltimore Museum of Art, the Peale Museum, Baltimore Heritage, Inc., and the Hamilton Street Club. She received in 1957 a doctor of laws degree from Goucher College and in 1972 an honorary doctor of art degree from the Maryland Institute College of Art. Of particular importance to her was the Evergreen House Foundation of the Johns Hopkins University, to which the late Robert W. and Alice Garrett had bequeathed their estate and collections of art and rare books. Beginning in 1951, Miner served as a trustee of the Evergreen House Foundation and as president of the board from 1965 to 1968. According to Elizabeth Baer, former librarian of Evergreen House and Dorothy Miner's close friend, she devoted a great deal of time and energy to her work at Evergreen, particularly to the scholarship committee.

Both Dorothy Miner and Elizabeth Baer were co-founders of the Baltimore Bibliophiles, known as the BBs. The BBs came into being "on a hot starlit night" as a "booklovers' club—a club to gather together the rare souls who find pleasure not only in the reading but especially in the handling of books, people who enjoy as amateur or professionals the arts that go into the designing and illustrating, printing and covering of a fine book, whether made today or five hundred years ago."[53] The monthly meetings of the BBs include men and women with the most diverse interests in books. On these occasions, speakers—often members, but also distinguished guests from all over the United States and from abroad—speak on an astonishing range of topics—from Sherlock Holmes to the Nuremberg Chronicle. Paper-making, the development of juvenile literature, bookbinding, calligraphy, and book illustration were among the subjects that engaged the attention of the BBs at their meetings at Evergreen House and during their trips to various library and museum collections. The *camaraderie* that comes from sharing deep interests is obvious in the BBs' published history. As a generous and suitable gesture, the BBs honored the memory of its co-founder by publishing as a "keepsake" Dorothy Miner's lecture entitled "Anastaise and Her Sisters: Women Artists of the Middle Ages."[54] Delivered in connection with the exhibition, *Old Mistresses—Women Artists of the Past*, held in 1972 at the Walters, Miner's lecture considers the role of medieval women as artists, particularly as illuminators of manuscripts, with both seriousness and grace. The publication of Dorothy Miner's talk by the BBs is a testimonial to her treatment of the subject and to her work with the group. It is appropriate that this study is cited as a pioneer treatment of the field in the growing literature on women artists.

CONCLUSION

When after several months of illness Dorothy Miner died on 15 May 1973, many moving tributes to her were received by the Walters and by her family from people whose lives she had touched by her thoughtful and generous acts. Shortly before her death, she saw in typescript form the impressive volume of nineteen essays written by colleagues and friends originally intended to be presented to her on 4 November 1973, the date of her sixty-ninth birthday. In her honor, the trustees of the Walters Art Gallery bought a fourteenth-century Italian embroidered altar hanging made for Jean Grandisson, bishop of Exeter, which she had admired. A memorial fund established by Dorothy Miner's friends was used in 1978 to buy a manuscript to fill a gap in the Gallery's collection, an early thirteenth-century English text, the *Historia Anglorum* ("History of the English") by Henry of Huntingdon.[55]

The range of the studies in *Gatherings in Honor of Dorothy E. Miner*, as well as the exceptional quality of the tributes to her in the volume, again bears witness to the formative role the Walters' collections played in her development as a scholar. The essays cover the fields in which during almost thirty-nine years at the Walters she had become a well-known expert: medieval manuscripts, printed books, and bookbinding. But they also deal with various kinds of decorative arts in the Walters collections in which she took a strong interest. Two studies are concerned with phases of Islamic art, in which Miner as curator in charge of the Gallery's twenty-three-hundred objects in this area, had become an authority. Without much previous training, she developed expertise in such specialties as Mogul miniatures, Sassanian silver, and Islamic ceramics. In many cases, the essays in *Gatherings* show the results of "many of the ideas avidly discussed [by Dorothy Miner] with colleagues, often over a period of many years. . . ."[56]

Dorothy Miner is, however, best known for her work in manuscript studies. When the Gallery opened in 1934, the Walters collection numbered 728 manuscripts, the second largest collection in the United States after the Pierpont Morgan Library. The range of the Walters manuscripts provided an opportunity for her to expand her knowledge from her original area of expertise in the early medieval period to all phases and schools of medieval illumination. By her conservation, as well as by her encouragement of the study and publications of the Walters manuscripts, Miner notably fulfilled her responsibilities as curator. A milestone in making the Walters collections known to a wide scholarly and general audience was the 1949 seminal exhibition of *Illuminated Books of the Middle Ages and Renaissance*, apparently the first ever held to show the holdings of American private and public collections in this field. Although funds for acquisitions were limited, Miner added fifty-four Western, Near Eastern, and Greek manuscripts to the collections. Among her most notable editions was the multivolume Antiphonary of Beaupré, a North French Manuscript dating from 1290, "containing the musical service for the year."[57] The Antiphonary was presented to the Walters in 1957 by the Hearst Foundation, after Miner had written a letter inquiring about the disposition of the manuscript. The opening pages of the Antiphonary (Figure 27) give some idea of the volume's magnificent decoration, illustration, and writing. It was entirely fitting that the inscription of the Antiphonary became the model for the dedication page of *Gatherings in Honor of Dorothy E. Miner*.

Dorothy Miner's ties with the Walters offered her exceptional opportunities for intellectual and professional growth, while the Gallery benefited enormously from her devotion. As she never married, the Walters was really the center of her life. She thoroughly enjoyed the vigorous and varied activity afforded by the museum setting. The visits of students and scholars constantly offered informal opportunities for teaching and learning about the collections. Perhaps if greater financial resources for more staff support —and more time off—had been available, she might have completed her work on model books and other means of visual reproduction in medieval manuscripts. In view of Dorothy Miner's many responsibilities, the range of her accomplishments reflects the optimum achievements possible in the "active" professional circumstances of the museum milieu, which does not always present the extended opportunities for research available in academic life. When the handsome new wing of the Walters opened in November 1974—the realization of a long-sought dream—many people regretted deeply that Dorothy Miner did not live to see this milestone achieved. The lasting imprint of her scholarship at the Walters, however, remains alive and is greatly enhanced by memories of her warm, generous, and witty personality.

NOTES

There is no complete biography. For Dorothy Miner's early career, see Madeleine Hooke Rice, "Dorothy Miner," *Barnard College Alumnae Monthly* (March 1938), 9-10. For her work at the Walters, see Weldon Wallace, "Life is Thing of the Past for Manuscript Keeper," *Baltimore Sun*, 23 June 1957. For short biographical accounts, see *Who's Who in American Art* (1973);

Figure 27. *Antiphonary of Beaupré*, ca. 1290. Baltimore, Walters Art Gallery, MS. W. 759, Vol. I, fols. 1v-2. *(Courtesy Walters Art Gallery)*

obituary notices in the *Baltimore Sun* of 16 May 1973 and the *New York Times* of 17 May 1973; "Dorothy E. Miner," *Library of Congress Information Bulletin*, 32 (25 May 1973), 186-87; and "Obituary Note: Dorothy Eugenia Miner," *AB Bookman's Weekly*, 51 (11 June 1973), 2192 and 2194. Tributes are contained in James H. Bready, "Dorothy E. Miner, Scholar: An Appreciation," *AB Bookman's Weekly*, 51 (11 June 1973), 2194 and 2196; "Dorothy E. Miner," *Bulletin of the Walters Art Gallery*, 25 (October 1973), n.p.; Lilian M. C. Randall, "Editors' Foreword," in *Gatherings in Honor of Dorothy E. Miner* (Baltimore, 1974), pp. xi-xii; "Walters Honors Librarian," *Baltimore Sun*, 19 May 1974; *Gesta*, 13/1 (1974), 3; Anthony J. Lauck, *Medieval Art 1060-1550, Dorothy Miner Memorial* (Notre Dame, Indiana, 1974), p. 3 (catalogue of a memorial exhibition at the Art Gallery, University of Notre Dame); Marion Lawrence, Review of *Gatherings in Honor of Dorothy E. Miner, Barnard Alumnae* (Winter 1975), 11; and Richard H. Randall, Jr., "In Memoriam: Dorothy E. Miner," *Journal of the Walters Art Gallery*, 35 (1977), v-vii. See also *Who's Who of American Women* (1974-75) and a short notice by the author in Supplement to *Notable American Women*, eds. Barbara Sicherman and Carol Hurd Green (Cambridge, Mass., 1980). Information about Dorothy Miner's activities can be found in the Annual Reports and the *Bulletin of the Walters Art Gallery*. Correspondence and papers are preserved at the Walters Art Gallery, Baltimore, Maryland. The Barnard College alumnae office maintains a collection of class yearbooks. Interviews with the family, friends, and colleagues of Dorothy E. Miner were conducted between 1975 and 1977.

1. I wish to thank the friends, colleagues, and family of Dorothy E. Miner who so generously responded to my requests for information about her life and work both in letters and in interviews. I am especially grateful to Dorothy Miner's brother and her niece, the late Dwight C. Miner and Dorothy M. Miner, for sharing so much family history with me. Catherine Baldwin Woodbridge kindly lent me the copy of the 1922 Yearbook of the Horace Mann School for Girls and spoke to me of Dorothy Miner's experiences there. Madeleine Hooke Rice was an unfailing and indispensable source of information about Dorothy Miner's family and career at Barnard. On the early days of the Walters Art Gallery, I am indebted to Edward S. King, Eleanor P. Spencer, and Hanns Swarzenski. For their discussion of the Walters Bookbinding exhibition and other aspects of Dorothy Miner's career, I am grateful to Frederick Goff and Karl Kup. Ursula E. McCracken, former editor of publications at the Walters, provided me with the essential information on Miner's work as an editor. Lilian M. C. Randall, Sandra Hindman, and Meyer Schapiro were very helpful in discussing Dorothy Miner's contributions to manuscript studies. Elizabeth Baer enthusiastically explained the history and character of the Baltimore Bibliophiles. At the Walters, two of Dorothy Miner's former assistants, Irene Butterbaugh and Sarah Vogelhut, gave me many valuable insights into her working habits and research methods. Reminiscences of Dorothy Miner derive from my relationship with her from 1960 to 1973 as student and friend. I am obliged to the administration of the Walters Art Gallery for allowing me to consult the papers and correspondence of Dorothy Miner deposited there.

2. The following account of Miner's family history and early life is based on interviews with her twin brother, the late Dwight C. Miner, her niece, Dorothy M. Miner, and her lifelong friend, Madeleine Hooke Rice.

3. Obituary of Dr. Roy Waldo Miner, *New York Times*, 14 December 1955.

4. For a brief description of the Graham School as the oldest private school for girls in New York City (established in 1816), see Porter E. Sargent, *The Best Private Schools of the United States and Canada* (Boston, 1915), p. 123.

5. For further details of the faculty and administration mentioned here, see Alice D. Miller and Susan Myers, *Barnard College: The First Fifty Years* (New York, 1939).

6. "Dorothy Miner," *Barnard College Alumnae Monthly* (March 1938), 10. For a detailed

account of the components and administration of the Greek Games, see Mary P. O'Donnell and Lelia M. Finan, *Greek Games: An Organization for Festivals* (New York, 1932). See also Miller and Myers, *Barnard College*, 91-94, and Marian C. White, *A History of Barnard College* (New York, 1954), pp. 57-59.

7. White, *Barnard College*, 106.

8. See William B. Dinsmoor, "The Department of Fine Arts and Archaeology," in *A History of the Faculty of Philosophy, Columbia University* (New York, 1957), pp. 252-59.

9. Miller and Myers, *Barnard College*, 126.

10. Rice, "Dorothy Miner," 9.

11. According to Dorothy Miner ("Illuminated Books of the Middle Ages and Renaissance," *Print*, 6/3 [1949], 30), the first exhibition in the United States in which manuscripts were shown along with books of all periods was the *Arts of the Book* show organized by William Ivins in 1924 at the Metropolitan Museum. For Miner's article on Belle da Costa Greene, which she coauthored with Anne L. Haight, see *Notable American Women*, eds. Edward T. James, Janet W. James, and Paul S. Boyer, II (Cambridge, Mass., 1971), pp. 83-85.

12. For a lively account of Bashford Dean's personality and character, see Calvin Tomkins, *Merchants and Masterpieces: The Story of the Metropolitan Museum of Art* (New York, 1970), pp. 149-64.

13. Discussed at length later in this chapter.

14. The other four (with their subsequent titles) were Dorothy Kent Hill, Curator of Ancient Art; Marvin Chauncey Ross, Curator of Medieval and Subsequent Decorative Arts; Edward S. King, Curator of European Painting and Far Eastern Art; and George Heard Hamilton, Curator of Modern Painting and American Art.

15. For a judicious discussion of the Walters collection, see René Brimo, *L'Évolution du goût aux Etats-Unis d'après l'histoire des collections* (Paris, 1938), especially pp. 53 and 87-89. For more complete coverage, see *Apollo*, 94 (Dec. 1966) and 100 (Nov. 1974), on the new wing.

16. The original advisory committee consisted of Francis Henry Taylor, chairman, director of the Worcester Art Museum; Belle da Costa Greene, director of the Pierpont Morgan Library; Tenney Frank, professor of classics at the Johns Hopkins University; Henri Marceau, assistant director of the Philadelphia Museum of Art; and George L. Stout, director of technical research, the Fogg Museum of Art, Harvard University. The advisory committee was disbanded in 1950.

17. For an evaluation of Morey's role, see Rensselaer W. Lee, "Art History at Princeton," *Princeton Alumni Weekly*, 64/3 (8 October 1963), 6-8 and 13. George H. Forsyth, Jr. kindly brought this article to my attention.

18. Miner noted that Howard Nixon wrote some of the entries in the British section of the catalogue *The History of Bookbinding, 525-1950 A.D.* (Baltimore, 1957), p. xi.

19. Miner to the librarian of the College of William and Mary, 26 September 1957. Unless otherwise noted, all letters are found at the Walters Art Gallery.

20. *Bookbinding*, viii.

21. Miner to William A. Jackson, 2 July 1957.

22. *Bookbinding*, x.

23. Reviews of the exhibition include those by Frederick B. Adams, Jr., *Burlington Magazine*, 100 (1958), 22-25; Samuel A. Ives, *Library Quarterly*, 28 (1958), 369-71; and Howard M. Nixon, *Book Collector*, 7 (1958), 419-26.

24. "Brasses, Rubbings and Costumes," *Bulletin of the Walters Art Gallery*, 7/4 (Jan. 1955). This journal is not paginated.

25. "Paris University Book Production before Printing," unpublished lecture given at the Walters Art Gallery, 2 November 1970. See also Miner's article, "The First University Press," *Bulletin of the Walters Art Gallery*, 23/2 (Nov. 1970).

26. Miner to Eleanor P. Spencer, 3 November 1970.

27. For a reproduction of this miniature illustrating the Vespers of the Holy Ghost, see Paul Wescher, *Jean Fouquet and His Time* (New York, 1947), pl. 14.

28. Miner to Spencer, 3 November 1970.

29. The information in this section on Dorothy Miner's working methods as an editor derives from an interview with Ursula E. McCracken, former editor of publications at the Walters.

30. Der Nersessian dedicated the catalogue to Dorothy Miner, who died before the catalogue was published. The two women were friends and colleagues for forty years. See also Chapter 12 of this volume for Jelisaveta S. Allen's essay on Sirarpie Der Nersessian.

31. "Illuminated Books of the Middle Ages and Renaissance," *Print*, 6/3 (1949), 33.

32. For a discussion of the background of codicology, see Albert Gruijs, "Codicology or the Archaeology of the Book? A False Dilemma," *Quaerendo*, 2/2 (1972), 87-108. See also L. M. J. Delaissé, "The Importance of Books of Hours for the History of the Medieval Book," in *Gatherings in Honor of Dorothy E. Miner* (Baltimore, 1974), pp. 203-26.

33. *Bookbinding*, vii.

34. "The Book of Kells," *Library of Congress Quarterly Journal of Acquisitions*, 8/4 (1951), 7.

35. Review of Wilhelm Neuss, *Die Apokalypse des Hl. Johannes in der altspanischen und altchristlichen Bibel-Illustration. Das Problem der Beatus-Handschriften, Art Bulletin*, 15 (1933), 388-91.

36. "A Late Reichenau Evangeliary in the Walters Art Gallery Library," *Art Bulletin*, 18 (1936), 168-85. An evangeliary contains parts of the Gospels used in the liturgy.

37. *Proverbes en Rimes* (Baltimore, 1937), pp. 5-6.

38. Ibid., 10.

39. *The Giant Bible of Mainz, 500th Anniversary* (Washington, D.C., Library of Congress, 1952).

40. Ibid., 16.

41. Ibid., 25. For a study dedicated to Dorothy Miner and in part influenced by her lecture on the Giant Bible of Mainz, see Anne H. Van Buren and Sheila Edmunds, "Playing Cards and Manuscripts: Some Widely Disseminated Fifteenth-Century Model Sheets," *Art Bulletin*, 56 (1974), 12-30.

42. "More About Medieval Pouncing," *Homage to a Bookman—Studies in Honor of H. P. Kraus* (New York, 1967), pp. 87-107.

43. Ibid., 87.

44. Ibid., 96-103.

45. "Preparatory Sketches by the Master of Bodleian Douce MS 185," *Kunsthistorische Forschungen Otto Pächt zu Ehren* (Salzburg, 1972), pp. 118-28.

46. "Since De Ricci—Western Illuminated Manuscripts Acquired Since 1934. A Report in Two Parts, Part I," *Journal of the Walters Art Gallery*, 29-30 (1966-67), 69-103; and Part II, Ibid., 31-32 (1968-69), 41-117.

47. "Since De Ricci, Part II," 41-48.

48. "Manuscript Sleuthing," *Bulletin of the Walters Art Gallery*, 3/2 (Nov. 1950).

49. "Since De Ricci, Part II," 41. A sacramentary is an early liturgical book containing the rites and prayers relating to the sacraments.

50. "The Publishing Ventures of a Victorian Connoisseur—A Sidelight on W. T. Walters," *Papers of the Bibliographical Society of America*, 57 (1963), 271-311.

51. Ibid., 300-06.

52. *Hroswitha of Gandersheim: Her Life, Times, and Works*, ed. Anne L. Haight (New York, 1965), p. ix.

53. *The Baltimore Bibliophiles 1954-1959* (Baltimore, 1960), p. 5. For a continuation of the history of this group, see *The Baltimore Bibliophiles 1954-1974* (Baltimore, 1974).

54. The lecture was published in two editions (Baltimore, 1974)—one of 250 for the BBs; one of 500 as a gift to the Walters Art Gallery in memory of Dorothy Miner. See also Ann Sutherland Harris and Linda Nochlin, *Women Artists 1550-1950* (New York, 1976), p. 17.

55. For a description of the manuscript, see Lilian M. C. Randall, "Dorothy Miner Memorial Purchase, *Historia Anglorum* by Henry of Huntingdon," *Bulletin of the Walters Art Gallery*, 31/2 (Nov. 1978).

56. Ursula E. McCracken, "Gatherings in Honor of Dorothy E. Miner," *Bulletin of the Walters Art Gallery*, 26/8 (May 1974).

57. "The Antiphonary of Beaupré," *Bulletin of the Walters Art Gallery*, 9/8 (May 1957). See also idem, "Since De Ricci, Part II," 63-68.

SELECTED BIBLIOGRAPHY OF DOROTHY EUGENIA MINER

A complete bibliography is found in *Gatherings in Honor of Dorothy E. Miner*. Edited by Ursula E. McCracken, Lilian M. C. Randall, and Richard H. Randall, Jr. Baltimore, 1974.

Books and Exhibition Catalogues

Proverbes en Rimes. Baltimore, 1937. With Grace Frank.
Early Christian and Byzantine Art. Baltimore, 1947. With Marvin C. Ross.
Illuminated Books of the Middle Ages and Renaissance. Baltimore, 1949.
The World Encompassed. Baltimore, 1952. With Elizabeth Baer and Lloyd A. Brown.
The History of Bookbinding, 525-1950 A.D. Baltimore, 1957.
Dragons and Other Animals: A Walters Art Gallery Coloring Book, Baltimore, 1960.
The International Style: The Arts in Europe around 1400. Baltimore, 1962. With Philippe Verdier.
Memorable Objects. Baltimore, 1964. With Richard H. Randall, Jr.
2000 Years of Calligraphy. Baltimore, 1965; reprinted in 1972. With Victor I. Carlson and P. W. Filby.

Works Edited

Journal of the Walters Art Gallery, 1-30 (1938-1969).
Dionysiac Sarcophagi in Baltimore, by Karl Lehmann-Hartleben and Erling C. Olsen. Baltimore, 1942.
Catalogue of Egyptian Sculpture in the Walters Art Gallery, by George Steindorff. Baltimore, 1946.
A Catalogue of the Work of William Henry Rinehart, Maryland Sculptor, 1825-1874, by Marvin C. Ross and Anna W. Rutledge. Baltimore, 1948.
Studies in Art and Literature for Belle da Costa Greene. Princeton, 1954.
American Works of Art in the Walters Art Gallery, by Edward S. King and Marvin C. Ross. Baltimore, 1956.
Russian Art, Icons and Decorative Arts from the Origin to the 20th Century, by Philippe Verdier. Baltimore, 1959.
Arts of the Migration Period in the Walters Art Gallery, by Marvin C. Ross and Philippe Verdier. Baltimore, 1961.
The Art of Reuben Kramer, by Theodore L. Low. Baltimore, 1963.
Catalogue of Painted Enamels of the Renaissance, by Philippe Verdier. Baltimore, 1967.
Armenian Manuscripts in the Walters Art Gallery, by Sirarpie Der Nersessian. Baltimore, 1973.

Articles and Published Lectures

"The Collection of Manuscripts and Rare Books in the Walters Art Gallery." *Annual Papers of the Bibliographical Society of America*, 30 (1936), 104-09.

"A Late Reichenau Evangeliary in the Walters Art Gallery Library." *Art Bulletin*, 18 (1936), 168-85.

"A Carving in Lapis Lazuli." *Journal of the Walters Art Gallery*, 7-8 (1944-45), 83-103. With Emma J. Edelstein.

"From Manuscript to Printed Book." *Baltimore Museum of Art News*, 10 (Dec. 1946), 4-6.

"Heroic Scale in Miniature." *Art News*, 47 (Feb. 1949), 20-23.

"Illuminated Books of the Middle Ages and Renaissance." *Print*, 6/3 (1949), 29-52.

"An Introductory Note to the Exhibition of Illuminated Books." *Baltimore Museum of Art News*, 13 (Jan. 1949), 2-5.

"The Manuscripts in the Grenville Kane Collection." *Princeton University Library Chronicle*, 11 (1949), 37-44.

"Masterpieces of the Scribes." *American Institute of Graphics Art Journal*, 2 (May 1949), 20-21.

"A Medieval Indulgence." *Bulletin of the Walters Art Gallery*, 2/8 (May 1950), n.p.

"Manuscript Sleuthing." *Bulletin of the Walters Art Gallery*, 3/2 (Nov. 1950), n.p.

"The Book of Kells." *Library of Congress Quarterly Journal of Current Acquisitions*, 8/4 (1951), 3-8.

"The Islamic Collection in the Walters Art Gallery." *Bulletin of the Near East Society*, 4/9 (1951), 5-6, 10.

"Accessions to the Islamic Collection." *Bulletin of the Walters Art Gallery*, 4/5 (Feb. 1952), n.p.

"Manuscript Exhibition." *Bulletin of the Walters Art Gallery*, 4/6 (March 1952), n.p.

The Giant Bible of Mainz, 500th Anniversary. Washington, D.C., Library of Congress, 1952.

"Two Great Bibles." *Library Journal*, 77 (1952), 1335-42.

"World Encompassed." *Baltimore Museum of Art News*, 16 (1952), 1-6.

"The New Purple Gospel Manuscript." *Bulletin of the Walters Art Gallery*, 5/3 (Dec. 1952), n.p.

"Dutch Illuminated Manuscripts in the Walters Art Gallery." *Connoisseur Year Book* (1955), 66-77.

"Illuminated Manuscripts at Harvard." *College Art Journal*, 14/3 (1955), 229-35.

"Brasses, Rubbings and Costume." *Bulletin of the Walters Art Gallety*, 7/4 (Jan. 1955), n.p.

"The Antiphonary of Beaupré." *Bulletin of the Walters Art Gallery*, 9/8 (May 1957), n.p.

"The Development of Medieval Illumination as Related to the Evolution of Book Design." *Catholic Life Annual*, 1 (1958), 3-20.

"A Sheet of Fifteenth-Century Playing Cards." *Bulletin of the Walters Art Gallery*, 11/6 (March 1959), n.p.

"An American Collection of Manuscripts." *Times Literary Supplement* (19 June 1959), 376.

"A New Renaissance Manuscript." *Bulletin of the Walters Art Gallery*, 12/6 (March 1960), n.p.

"Islamic Arms and Armor." *Bulletin of the Walters Art Gallery*, 14/6 (March 1962), n.p.

"The Publishing Ventures of a Victorian Connoisseur—A Sidelight on W. T. Walters." *Papers of the Bibliographical Society of America*, 57 (1963), 271-311.

"The Illuminated Books of Armenia and Byzantium." *Bulletin of the Walters Art Gallery*, 16/3 (Dec. 1963), n.p.

"Gold Bracelet, Ornamented with Doves." *Burlington Magazine*, 107 (1965), 227-28.

"The Little Round Madonna." *Bulletin of the Walters Art Gallery*, 18/3 (Dec. 1965), n.p.

"The Conradin Bible—A Masterpiece of Italian Illumination." *Apollo*, 84 (1966), 470-75.

"Madonna and Child Writing." *Art News*, 64/10 (1966), 40-43.

"Since De Ricci—Western Illuminated Manuscripts Acquired Since 1934. A Report in Two Parts, Part I." *Journal of the Walters Art Gallery*, 29-30 (1966-67), 69-103.

"The Book of Eastern Christendom—American Collections of Near Eastern Manuscripts." *Gazette of the Grolier Club*, n. s./3 (Feb. 1967), 14-22.

"More about Medieval Pouncing." *Homage to a Bookman—Studies in Honor of H. P. Kraus.* New York, 1967, pp. 87-107.

"The Rare Book Collection at the Walters Art Gallery." *Maryland Libraries*, 33/2 (1967), 7-11.

"Early Bookbindings (Walters Art Gallery)." *Burlington Magazine*, 110 (1968), 462-64.

"Since De Ricci—Western Illuminated Manuscripts Acquired Since 1934. A Report in Two Parts, Part II." *Journal of the Walters Art Gallery*, 31-32 (1968-69), 41-117.

"Masterpieces of Illuminated Manuscripts." *Bulletin of the Walters Art Gallery*, 21/4 (Jan. 1969), n.p.

"The First University Press." *Bulletin of the Walters Art Gallery*, 23/2 (Nov. 1970), n.p.

"Belle da Costa Greene." *Notable American Women*, eds. Edward T. James, Janet W. James, and Paul S. Boyer. Cambridge, Mass., 1971, II, pp. 83-85. With Anne L. Haight.

"The Gutman Missal and its Puzzles." Baltimore Museum of Art, *Annual* 4 (1972) (*Studies in Honor of Gertrude Rosenthal*, Part II), 25-31.

"Lecture on Himmerod and its Manuscripts." *Bulletin of the Walters Art Gallery*, 24/8 (May 1972), n.p.

"Preparatory Sketches by the Master of Bodleian Douce MS 185." *Kunsthistorische Forschungen Otto Pächt zu Ehren.* Salzburg, 1972, pp. 118-28.

"The Collecting of Islamic Manuscripts in America." *Acts of the Seventh International Congress of Bibliophiles*, 1974, pp. 69-79.

Anastaise and Her Sisters: Women Artists of the Middle Ages. Baltimore, 1974.

Reviews

Review of Wilhelm Neuss, *Die Apokalypse des Hl. Johannes in der altspanischen und altchristlichen Bibel-Illustration. Das Problem der Beatus-Handschriften. Art Bulletin*, 15 (1933), 388-91.

Review of Donald Drew Egbert, *The Tickhill Psalter and Related Manuscripts—A School of Manuscript Illumination in England during the Early Fourteenth Century. American Journal of Archaeology*, 47 (1943), 513-18.

Review of Karl Kup, *The Christmas Story in Medieval and Renaissance Manuscripts from the Spencer Collection. The Print Collector's Newsletter*, 1/5 (1970), 116-17.

Review of François Bucher, *The Pamplona Bibles. American Notes and Queries*, 10/1 (Sept. 1971), 12-15.

CHAPTER 15
AGNES MONGAN
(b. 1905): CONNOISSEUR
OF OLD MASTER
DRAWINGS
Diane DeGrazia Bohlin

Agnes Mongan's name has been associated with the Fogg Art Museum at Harvard University for over forty years. As its director from 1969 to 1971 she became one of the first women to head a major art museum in the United States. When she retired from that position, John Canaday wrote, "Whoever the director has been, Agnes Mongan has personified the ideal of uncompromising scholarship directed by wit and sensibility that has given the Fogg, at its best, its special character."[1] Prior to her appointment as director of the Fogg, Mongan had served as a lecturer in Harvard's Department of Fine Arts, where she was an influential teacher and an enthusiastic mentor to young art historians. Her major contribution to the arts, however, grew from her role as curator of drawings at the Fogg. As coauthor of the first catalogue of drawings of a collection in an American Museum,[2] she was a leader in this country in the study of old master drawings, an academic discipline that emerged between the World Wars. Throughout her life she has encouraged the collecting of drawings, and her contribution as a connoisseur of the objects she loves will be a lasting one.

Agnes Mongan grew up in a familial environment where intellectual achievement was recognized and encouraged. Her comfortable Irish ancestors with literary interests arrived in America at the beginning of the nineteenth century. The O'Briens, her mother's family, settled in Charlestown, Massachusetts. Her father's family had lived in Somerville, where she was born, since the early years of the nineteenth century. Her mother, one of a large family, had been brought up in the shadow of the Bunker Hill Monument. She was a school teacher, as were the majority of her female siblings. In 1901 when she married Charles Edward Mongan, she exchanged this career for that of housewife and mother. Charles Mongan's ancestors were also well educated, mainly in religious schools. A priest in the family had founded the first Catholic churches in the Somerville area where the family settled. After his graduation from Harvard Medical School, Charles Mongan pursued postgraduate study in London and at Trinity College, Dublin. He was trained as an obstetrician and gynecologist. However, when he returned to this country, he chose to practice general medicine in Somerville. He served as president of the Massachusetts Medical Society and the Massachusetts Society for Gynecology and Obstetrics.

In 1905, Agnes Mongan, the second of four children, was born in Somerville, less than a mile from Harvard Yard. Her childhood was extraordinarily rich in experiences by standards of the period, although she did not realize it at the time. Every evening music filled the household as Agnes and her sister Betty played for four hands at the piano. During the summer Mrs. Mongan read each night to the children for an hour from such works as *Silas Marner*, *Tanglewood Tales*, and other classics. During spring vacations the family traveled, once to see the famous historical sites in Massachusetts, once to the New England mountains to fish. After 1915 they spent summers in Maine. Each summer, Mrs. Mongan assigned the children different projects that involved finding and identifying different kinds of flowers, mushrooms, or trees of the area.

Agnes Mongan remembers the goal her father had set for his four children to have both the best education this country could provide and a year's stay in Europe. Dr. Mongan wanted them to benefit as he had from similar experiences that had stimulated his love of learning. Charles, the eldest, went to M.I.T. for his first two degrees. Then he spent many years in Zurich, where he received his doctor of science degree. He is a noted physicist and mathematician. Agnes' younger brother John received the A.B. and M.B.A. degrees from Harvard. After extensive travel in this country, he settled in Paris, where he worked for over thirty years as a businessman. Agnes and Elizabeth (Betty) attended Bryn Mawr College. Elizabeth became the curator of the Rosenwald Collection, the great private graphic arts collection in Jenkintown, Pennsylvania, and the first curator of graphic arts at the National Gallery of Art.[3]

Earlier in life than most people, Agnes Mongan knew what she wanted to do. When she was about thirteen, her father asked her about her goals. She answered, "I'd like to know something about that," indicating the Oriental rugs, eighteenth-century American furniture, and old silver that filled the house.[4] She had been attending Somerville High School, but her father decided that she would get the strongest foundation for a career by enrolling in Bryn Mawr, which he considered the best women's school for liberal arts study in this country. In preparation for Bryn Mawr, Agnes entered the Cambridge School for Girls, where she gained the required instruction in classics, literature, and languages. By the fall of 1923, when Agnes Mongan enrolled in Bryn Mawr, she already had a background in Latin, French, and some Italian. By adding German to her other languages at college, she rounded out her linguistic skills.

At Bryn Mawr Agnes Mongan chose a dual major in the history of art and in English,[5] a wise decision for a scholar and lecturer who would come to depend on her solid background in language and literature for developing her ideas. In 1923 there were only two teachers of the history of art at Bryn Mawr, Professor Georgiana Goddard King, founder of the department, and George Rowley, an instructor in Oriental art. In May, Edward Stauffer King was appointed to the faculty and taught northern Renaissance art.[6] Although Agnes Mongan took courses from both men, Miss King was the principal professor in the department and Agnes Mongan's strongest influence.[7] She acknowledged her gratitude by dedicating *Drawings in the Fogg Museum of Art* to the memory of Georgiana Goddard King and by editing King's posthumously published book, the *Heart of Spain*. In the preface to the latter, she articulated the feelings of King's students: "To them as long as they live she will inevitably be more than a name and a memory, for what she conjured to life in them remains a beat in their sensibilities, a balance in their judgment and a light behind their eyes."[8] This love of art and the enthusiasm for its study was the legacy Georgiana Goddard King left to Agnes Mongan.

Agnes Mongan was a dedicated, ambitious student, determined to prepare herself for a career in art history. One classmate remembers her as "one of the best students in Georgiana King's course in Italian Renaissance painting."[9] Mongan herself considers her preparation in English invaluable, attributing "her comparative ease in forming her thoughts in writing to courses in English she took at Bryn Mawr," especially to one teacher, Miss Donnelly.[10] In her published works, her lectures, and her correspondence, she has always expressed her ideas logically, meticulously, and with precision. She admires this quality in others and deplores the lack of training in languages and literature in students entering graduate school today.[11]

Not everyone believed that Agnes Mongan would achieve her goal to pursue a career in art history. Mongan related that Georgiana Goddard King herself thought, "when I was ill in my junior or senior year, that I wasn't strong enough to go on in fine arts. The college sent me home in the spring vacation. My father, who was a doctor, promptly sent me back and said they didn't have any idea of what I could do. I think he was right."[12] Perhaps it is her personal determination, aided by the incentive of a supportive father, that has made Agnes Mongan so successful in her chosen field. In addition, she had the ability to devote endless energy in one direction, first to the study of Italian art and later to the area of old master drawings.[13]

After her graduation from college in 1927, Mongan spent her year abroad studying Italian art with the Smith College seminar conducted by Ruth and

Clarence Kennedy. This program had been given once previously in the year 1925/26 and was to be given only once or twice again. Later, a summer program on a much reduced scale continued. The course allowed graduate students the opportunity to examine closely works of art in their original location. The five women taking the course that year met outside the doors of the Florence Baptistery on 15 September at nine in the morning to begin a year of intense study of Italian painting and sculpture of the trecento and quattrocento in museums and private collections.[14] They spent five months in Florence and central Italy, three months in Paris, and the remainder of the year traveling in central Europe and northern Italy. During the day, when the normal accessibility and natural lighting did not otherwise permit a thorough study, the women examined paintings with the aid of a binocular microscope, an automobile headlamp, and a stepladder. In the evening, they discussed the works studied during the day. At the end of the course, the students were examined by a committee of six people. For three hours questions were posed in Italian or English, but they were allowed to answer in English. The students also completed a six-hour written examination and a thesis on a particular subject. Mongan chose as her topic the Italian pictures in the Musée Jacquemart-André in Paris. This extraordinary year, with its extensive research and travel,[15] prepared Agnes Mongan in the careful and complete study of objects in the original, emphasizing their present condition and past history, their conservation and their attributions. This firsthand knowledge of Italian art provided a strong basis for Agnes Mongan's future achievements in connoisseurship.

In August 1928 Agnes Mongan returned to Massachusetts lighter by twenty-five pounds and exhausted from the strenuous year abroad. Consequently, she decided at this point not to pursue a doctorate but instead to finish the requirements for her A.M. from Smith College. Because she wished to live at home instead of at the college, she was allowed to attend Professor Arthur Pope's course in the theory of design at Harvard in order to fulfill the remaining requirement for her degree at Smith.[16] At the same time she attended two important Harvard courses, Paul Sachs' museum seminar and Edward Waldo Forbes' course on the history of technique, the latter affectionately referred to as the "egg and plaster course."

Three weeks after the beginning of the first semester, an opportunity that changed the course of her career presented itself to Mongan. Phyllis Bache, another student from the Smith year abroad, decided to give up her new job cataloguing the drawings in the Fogg Art Museum under Paul Sachs in order to study for her doctorate. After Bache told her of this decision, Agnes Mongan asked Sachs if she could take over the cataloguing. Mongan got the job, which was, as she put it, "her first and, as it turned out, her only post."[17] Mongan enjoys telling this story because the year before— once in Florence and again in Paris—Phyllis Bache had given up her attractive apartments and Agnes Mongan, recognizing her good luck, quickly moved into them. This pattern was repeated in 1928 when Phyllis Bache became the catalyst for her opportunity to work with one of the most esteemed connoisseurs in the country. Agnes Mongan's later achievements were the result of her own tenacity of purpose and dedication to her profession, but the fortuitous occurrence of the job opening at the Fogg set her on the particular path that would bring her success in the field of old master drawings rather than in another art historical discipline.

Agnes Mongan has acknowledged many times that she owes the development of her career and interest in drawings to Paul Sachs. A 1900 Harvard graduate, Sachs joined the prosperous family banking business, but he never neglected his first love, the collecting of prints and drawings. In 1915 Edward Waldo Forbes, director of the Fogg, persuaded Sachs, who had briefly taught at Wellesley, to leave the banking world for good to become the associate director of the museum. Together they ran the Fogg until their joint retirement in 1944. In the tradition of the gentleman collector, Sachs had a catholic taste in his purchases, and one overriding factor in any and all of his acquisitions was the need for and appreciation of quality. At the time of his death, he had given or bequeathed to the Fogg more than three thousand objects, of which five hundred were drawings and 2,012 were prints.[18] In the early part of the century, Sachs began collecting prints because he felt that with a "modest fortune and a discerning eye" one could gather together a fine collection. Even before the first war, however, his taste turned toward drawings, and as Mongan has pointed out, he was the "pacesetter in the United States in this field."[19]

The appreciation of drawings as individual works of art, rather than as preparatory for the major arts of painting and sculpture, dates back to the seventeenth century in Europe when wealthy patrons of the church and aristocracy collected these sheets of paper and kept them in albums for their enjoyment. The practice of collecting drawings in this country did not take hold seriously until the early twentieth century and was dependent on the writings of Bernard Berenson and the teaching of Paul Sachs. Almost all the great drawing collections in private hands in this country—e.g., the Winslow Ames, Robert Lehman, Lessing J. Rosenwald, Charles A. Loeser, and Grenville Winthrop collections—were amassed between the World Wars. At this time, when the collecting of drawings in the United States increased, some of the best objects from Europe entered American private and public collections. As there were no longer a vast number of paintings on the market as was true before World War I and during the 1920s and because one could obtain a drawing by a master at a fraction of the cost of one of his paintings, American collectors turned to drawings. Private collectors were extremely active in picking up the plums being sold piecemeal from European collections. The enthusiasm, encouragement, and advice in forming these collections came initially from Paul Sachs; but the knowledge and study of these newly acquired objects and the continued momentum begun by Paul Sachs were carried on mainly by Agnes Mongan. From the moment she took the job as research assistant to Sachs in 1928, she devoted her professional life to master drawings.

In the following decades, Agnes Mongan became one of the leading connoisseurs of master drawings, and she played a principal role in the history of connoisseurship in this country. Her work continues the tradition of research and training in connoisseurship at Harvard begun by the writings of Bernard Berenson. As defined by Berenson, one of her formative influences, connoisseurship is "the comparison of works of art with a view to determining their reciprocal relationship."[20] The connoisseur bases his or her studies on the work of art itself rather than on the documents or traditions surrounding it. The connoisseur attempts to attribute a work to an individual, a period, or a school by its stylistic characteristics and what it has in common with other works by the same hand or hands. As he did with Agnes Mongan, Berenson influenced most of the connoisseurs of the twentieth century by his publications on the subject. He awoke in them a sense of the need to come in contact with the original work of art.

One of Agnes Mongan's accomplishments in connoisseurship was her discovery of the so-called left-handed artist. A left-handed person herself, she has been able to note the different methods and directions of hatching used by these draughtsmen. Moreover, with her constant travel and knowledge of most of the drawing collections of the world, Agnes Mongan had given herself the broad base necessary for comparing drawings by the same hand or school. The connoisseur must also compare the drawings of an artist with drawings by his contemporaries in order to assess the artistic value of the sheet studied. With her well-trained eye and inherent sensitivity to drawings, Mongan has been able to determine the differences in quality among the drawings of draughtsmen of the same period. This developed trait is especially important for a museum person who must take part in the decisions to purchase works of art. The judgments of museum curators may influence the prices of works set in the art market, but they should have no monetary stake in the outcome.

When Mongan undertook the task of cataloguing the drawings in the Fogg Art Museum, she began her career of scholarly examination of the sheets in the museum, punctuated by frequent travel to Europe to acquaint herself with drawings in other collections and to advise on the purchase of further drawings for the Fogg and Sachs collections. In 1929 she spent from June to November in England, France, and Italy. For purposes of comparative study, she was armed with photographs of every drawing in the Fogg as well as with letters of introduction from Paul Sachs in order to gain entry into private collections. Mongan was thus preparing herself for the cataloguing of the Fogg collection, which she successfully completed in 1940 with the publication of the renowned *Drawings in the Fogg Museum of Art*. On these frequent trips abroad her visual perception as a connoisseur was continually being sharpened by her acquaintance with as many originals as possible.

Coauthored by Paul Sachs and Agnes Mongan, *Drawings in the Fogg Museum of Art* was the first comprehensive catalogue of a drawing collection in this country. The research and writing for the book took place in the museums and private collections of Europe and in Mongan's third-floor office of the Fogg, where she was surrounded by books, photographs, and drawings. Her cataloguing of the Fogg collection consisted not merely of a listing of the objects but of a thorough examination and study of them. Although Paul Sachs coauthored *Drawings in the Fogg Museum of Art*, it was indeed Agnes Mongan who researched it and wrote most of it.[21] Moreover, she chose its format, which served as a prototype for other catalogues, and designed its layout, even choosing the colors for the cover. A typical entry in the catalogue consists of the following specifics: a biography of the artist, a description of the drawing, a detailed account of the medium, the subject, provenance, collections, bibliography, and exhibitions of the drawing, and a perceptive analysis of the work, all meticulously organized. Its format of separating plate and text volumes facilitated comparing photographs of the objects with the catalogue entries. Before the appearance of this catalogue, there were no American and few European drawing collections so published, and the quality of the latter varied. The Louvre published its first volume in 1907, the British Museum in 1915, the Albertina in 1926, Windsor Castle in 1935, and the Ashmolean in 1938. Consequently, the Fogg volumes proved to be a model not only for cataloguing collections in the United States but also for European collections as well. The most successful examples of drawing catalogues published after these volumes and probably influenced by them are the British Museum Italian volumes begun in 1950, the Yale catalogue of 1970, and the recently published Christ Church and Princeton catalogues, dated 1976 and 1977 respectively.[22]

Although the writing of the Fogg catalogue took ten years, Agnes Mongan did not confine herself to this one task. She published numerous articles on single sheets in the museum collection. Many of these articles read like catalogue entries, reporting specifics such as medium, size, and especially provenance. Indeed, the history of the drawing and its social ambience seems to have especially fascinated her. During the 1930s Mongan also published exhibition reviews as well as articles on drawings in other collections in the United States. She was rapidly establishing her reputation as an authority in the field. In all of Mongan's catalogues, articles, reviews, and lectures, she has, as in *Drawings in the Fogg Museum of Art*, been thorough and precise in compiling and reporting every aspect of her subject, always basing the discussion on accurate scholarship. Her flair for cataloguing may in part derive from the example set by her mother when she aided the children in classifying flora on summer vacations in Maine.

Under the tutelage of Paul Sachs, Agnes Mongan developed a network of professional and social contacts during this early period at the Fogg. She was ushered into some of the most exclusive and inaccessible private collections in the world. In 1929, carrying a letter of introduction from Sachs, she first met Bernard Berenson. The meeting is described briefly in Nicky Mariano's book on "B.B.": "Sent by Paul Sachs they [Agnes and Betty Mongan] turned up one day, very late for lunch and rather flushed. B.B. liked them both from the first moment and very quickly made them feel at their ease with him."[23] The friendship lasted until Berenson's death in 1959. The meeting with Berenson must have been a dream fulfilled for Agnes Mongan, his publications having formed a basis for her methodology in connoisseurship from the time she was at Bryn Mawr. In the following years, Mongan aided him in the revision of his book on Lorenzo Lotto and on the *Drawings of the Florentine Painters*. She was also instrumental in successfully convincing Harvard to accept the gift of Berenson's home I Tatti for the university.[24]

In 1935 Gordon Bailey Washburn, then the director of the Albright Art Gallery in Buffalo, decided to organize a show of old master drawings as his first exhibition there. Washburn, who had been in Paul Sachs' museum course, admired Sachs' connoisseurship of drawings. He asked Agnes Mongan to help him with the exhibition, and together they selected the drawings while Mongan wrote the catalogue entries. *Master Drawings Selected from the Museums and Private Collections of America*, one of the first exhibitions of its kind in this country, was the first large and important drawing show in which Mongan was involved. It was extremely popular, perhaps because it pointed up the outstanding selection of master drawings collected in this country in the twentieth century. The fully illustrated exhibition catalogue, with brief catalogue notes, did much to familiarize the public with the beauty of old master drawings. The exhibition, which included only drawings of major importance from all schools and periods, was a model for drawing exhibitions at the Crocker Art Gallery in 1939 and at Smith College in 1941. Not until the 1960s, however, did drawing exhibitions of this scale and importance reappear.[25] They have since become frequent additions to museum schedules, obviously well-received by informed visitors. Mongan had helped create these new audiences by her participation in this kind of exhibition.

During the 1930s, Agnes Mongan also took part in an exciting adventure tinged with overtones of espionage and intrigue. With the crash of 1929 many European private collectors were hit hard by the depression and needed to relinquish their treasures in order to pay debts. At this time, one drawing collection that was to appear privately on the market almost in its entirety was that of the Albertina Graphische Sammlung, one of the greatest print and drawing cabinets in the world. The Austrian parliament had returned it to its former owner, the Hapsburg Archduke Albrecht, who immediately planned to sell it to pay political debts. His liaison, the London dealer Gus Mayer, offered the Albertina drawings to the Boston Museum of Fine Arts (the M.F.A.) in 1935. At that time, when Paul Sachs was a trustee of the M.F.A., he worked out a plan that would divide the collection between the M.F.A. and the Fogg. Because of her drawing expertise, the young Agnes Mongan was abroad from September to November 1936 to take part in the long negotiations to buy the Albertina collection. This episode was one of the most exciting events in her life. Secret meetings in Paris and Vienna followed, but by December of that year the story had become public, and the Austrian government declared the Albertina collection national property, a decision Mongan feels should have been made originally.[26]

The 1930s also saw the beginning of Mongan's particular interest in French drawings, which had practical value because the Fogg had more drawings from France than any other country in its collections. Her first publication in this field was a study of Degas portraits in various collections.[27] The article, which appeared in 1932, dealt not only with the compositions, techniques, and physical aspects of the drawings but also with the histories of the persons portrayed. Emphasizing the psychological penetration of the artist, Mongan herself penetrated beyond the masks of the sitters to evoke an understanding of their ambience. This aspect of her scholarship is always apparent. With full attention to timeless aesthetic qualities, she attempts to place each drawing in its historical context, analyzing the artist's circumstances during its production. Mongan's interest in French drawings and history is part of her fascination with French culture. She once stated, "Delicacy, grace, precision and elegance have ever been the distinguishing marks of the French School."[28] These qualities are also characteristics of Mongan's personality and taste.

As a young scholar in the 1930s, Agnes Mongan was forever busy with research, travels, and exhibitions for the Fogg Museum, advising on purchases of additional drawings for the Fogg and Sachs collections and aiding students with an interest in drawings. Besides her regular duties at the museum, she found time in the winters of 1935 and 1936 to become a lecturer in modern art at the Boston Center for Adult Education. She was also one of the organizers of the Institute of Contemporary Art in Boston and later involved with the activities of the Museum of Modern Art. As her main concern has been with old master drawings, this little-known interest in contemporary art adds another dimension to her career.

In 1940, Agnes Mongan received the first of many official recognitions for her achievements. At the age of thirty-six, Smith College awarded her an honorary L.H.D.

The war years slowed down many activities in this country and kept Agnes Mongan from traveling, but it did not prevent her from taking full advantage of the domestic resources available to her. While participating in the war effort,[29] she catalogued the immense Winthrop bequest of 1943 and organized successful teaching exhibitions at the Fogg. Delving into the growing collections of the museum, she produced shows that she believed were of topical interest related to the war. One of these was *North Africa Interpreted by European Artists*. It was also during this period that her qualities as a teacher became more apparent. Always encouraging her students, she depended on them to aid in the research for the exhibitions. Moreover, she became immersed in the Fogg image of the teaching museum. Although the Fogg is open to the public, she has always believed its primary function is the development of scholars and museum professionals. To this end, she has given freely of her time to all students with a serious interest in drawings, encouraging them, helping them in their projects, and editing and promoting their first publications. Her teaching was always done essentially on the individual level.

The Winthrop Bequest of 1943 afforded Mongan the opportunity to catalogue and publish an immense amount of material. She had already devoted an exhibition to the gifts from Grenville Winthrop in 1942, which consisted entirely of French art of the nineteenth century.[30] A Harvard alumnus, Grenville Winthrop bequeathed a staggering amount of objects of the finest quality to the Fogg Museum. Among these were five hundred watercolors and drawings, mostly from the nineteenth-century French school. Agnes Mongan had already written articles on Daumier and Degas; the Winthrop collection would enable her to devote years to the research of works by other French artists. It also presented an extraordinary opportunity to study the artist with whom she is most often associated: Jean Auguste-Dominique Ingres. No fewer than thirty-five drawings by Ingres entered the Fogg from the Winthrop collection. Her interest in that artist had been primed earlier by her study of Ingres drawings in the collection of Paul Sachs, who shared her taste for them.[31] The grace, delicacy, elegance, and precision she admired in French art were strikingly embodied in drawings by Ingres.

The Winthrop Bequest had opened a new era in scholarship of French art for Mongan that has continued to develop in many directions. Her area of specialty, originally Italian and French drawings of the sixteenth to the eighteenth centuries, was now extended to include French drawings of the nineteenth century. In recognition of her expertise in this area, she was asked to assist in the cataloguing of the French paintings in the Frick Collection. Mongan relates that she actually became an "Ingriste" in the 1940s while working on the French paintings at the Frick.[32] Her involvement with the catalogue began as early as 1942, and in 1945 and 1946 she spent much of her time in New York at the Frick preparing her entries. The first volume of the catalogue appeared in 1949, and Mongan also assisted with the catalogue of acquisitions of French art contained in the volume published in 1955.[33]

For Agnes Mongan's efforts in the field of French art and culture she received in 1947 a Palme académique (Ordre des Palmes Académiques) from the French government. In 1949 she was again recognized by France for "promoting knowledge of French culture in America."

Although Paul Sachs retired as associate director of the Fogg Museum in 1944, he remained curator of drawings until 1947. It was in that year that Agnes Mongan was named to the position. She acknowledged her debt to Paul Sachs in 1949 by organizing an exhibition honoring his seventieth birthday. Not surprisingly, it included seventy drawings of the highest quality from American collections, an appropriate recognition of Sachs' decisive influence in this field. In 1950 Mongan expanded the catalogue of the exhibition into an important illustrated volume of one hundred drawings.[34] Now that Paul Sachs had retired from his official position of pre-eminence, Agnes Mongan took over and remains in the leading role of principal American drawing connoisseur, the "grande dame" of drawings. It was in the late 1940s that she earned her now famous cognomen "la folle du Fogg," a nickname she accepts with relish.[35] The title indicates her continuing association with the Fogg and her unswerving dedication to its principles.

The decade of the 1950s, when Agnes Mongan was in her late forties and early fifties (Figure 28), saw the addition of administrative duties and committee work to her career as a scholar and curator. In 1951 she was appointed assistant director of the Fogg Museum of Art, a position she held in conjunction with her curatorial post in drawings. The year before, she took the summer off to become Art Historian in Residence at the American Academy in Rome. Awarded a Fulbright grant, she was working on a book of saints and symbols. Although she was assistant director during this period, she in fact appropriated many of the tasks usually associated with the director of a museum and actually shared this position unofficially and amiably with John Coolidge, the official director.[36] She attended the museum meetings, escorted important foreign visitors, and directed many of the activities involved in cultivating donors and friends of the museum. Finally, in 1964, her title was changed to the more appropriate one of associate director.

In spite of the fact that Agnes Mongan had assisted Harvard professors in teaching graduates and undergraduates in the history and connoisseurship of drawings, had published as much as many of them, and was not the only person at the Fogg without a Ph.D., her name did not appear in the *Harvard College Catalogue* as a lecturer in fine arts until 1954. Even then it came at the end of a long list of other teachers.[37] Other institutions, as well

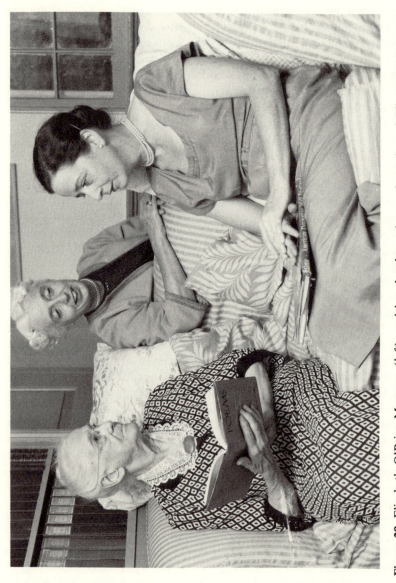

Figure 28. Elizabeth O'Brien Mongan, (*left*); and her daughters Agnes, (*center*); and Elizabeth Mongan, (*right*); ca. 1954. (*Courtesy Gordon N. Converse, Chief Photographer, The Christian Science Monitor*)

as several foreign governments recognized her achievements. In 1954 she was awarded an honorary Litt.D. degree from Wheaton College, and in that year she lectured in Brazil on old master drawings and advised on their conservation as a guest of the Brazilian government. In 1958 she chaired a special exhibition of *French Drawings from American Collections* that traveled to Paris and Rotterdam, and she was chosen as curator of the exhibition. One cannot overemphasize the importance of this exhibition as a milestone in the collecting of drawings in America. It showed Europeans that after less than half a century of serious collecting in this field, this country could boast a number of private and public collections of a quality higher than many in Europe.

In 1960, rather than lose her to another institution, Harvard appointed Agnes Mongan the Martin A. Ryerson Lecturer in the Fine Arts. Although she was given the rank and privileges commensurate with those of full professor, she was never allowed to carry that title. This appointment gave formal recognition to a teaching situation that had been underway for many years. During this period she taught seminars on her specialties: one in French drawings from the sixteenth to the nineteenth centuries in 1960; a seminar on Watteau, Ingres, and Degas in 1961; Venetian drawings in 1962 and 1963; and nineteenth-century French drawings in 1965/66 and 1967/68.[38]

In 1964/65 Agnes Mongan's name appeared for the first time in the *Harvard College Catalogue* as the teacher of the Seminar on Art Museum Problems, although she had already been alternating with John Coolidge in giving this course. This is the well-known museum course Paul Sachs had initiated at Harvard in 1921 for museum directors and curators. At the Fogg he taught the course until 1949. Over the years the seminar provided valuable instruction in many practical problems of the museum world for several generations of Harvard graduate students who went on to become directors and curators of major museums in the United States.

Agnes Mongan taught the course somewhat differently from her predecessors.[39] Sachs had treated the seminar rather informally, inviting visiting foreign collectors and scholars to talk to the students, as well as taking them to various public and private collections. It was an introduction not only to the operation of museums but also to the important personalities who ran them. Mongan continued this tradition, inviting notables to speak to her classes and taking students on tours of private collections as far afield from Cambridge as possible in the limited time available. In addition, the students were given the problem of studying the origins, collections, and purposes of at least one large and one small museum. As a term project, the class would organize its own exhibition, doing everything connected with it in order to understand the broad range of activities needed to put on a show.[40] Also, Mongan varied the emphasis of each class as it evolved. One seminar worked mainly on learning about the physical spaces of museums, and that year several famous architects spoke to the class. Another seminar organized and built its own fictional museum using a set amount of funds, with each student acting in a different position at the museum. Every year her ingenuity enabled her to present a different set of museum problems.

In the 1960s Agnes Mongan produced and collaborated on several major drawing exhibitions held at the Fogg. The most important of these was the 1967 *Ingres Centennial Exhibition*, which she organized around the Ingres drawings in the Fogg, the largest collection of his works in the country. In connection with the centennial she participated in a colloquium in Montauban, France, Ingres' home town. The catalogue of the exhibition itself, which she coauthored with Hans Naef, is a model of careful and meticulous analysis of the subjects, techniques, compositions, and historical ambience of each drawing. In addition, Mongan encouraged the paper conservator Marjorie Cohn to include a detailed section on the conservation of each drawing. From her year in Europe under the Kennedys, Mongan had acquired a keen sense of the importance of conservation. This interest was later nurtured by the proximity of the excellent conservation department at the Fogg set up by Edward Waldo Forbes. After the publication of the Ingres catalogue, conservation notes have been included in other Fogg exhibition catalogues.

In 1968 John Coolidge retired as director of the Fogg Museum of Art, a position he had held since 1948. Coolidge's natural successor was Agnes Mongan, who that year was named acting director and in 1969 was appointed director of the museum. She held this post two brief years until her retirement in 1971. If one feels this reward for forty years of distinguished service was long in coming, one should recall that 1948 was the only previous year in which the job was open. At that time (particularly at Harvard), as a woman Agnes Mongan would have been excluded from consideration for this position. When Mongan took on the job of running the Fogg without a co-director, times were not favorable for American museums. Private funding was at a minimum, and many of the old donors were now gone. Moreover, the country and the universities were preoccupied with the escalating conflict in Viet Nam. In spite of these difficulties, Mongan carried on the administration according to traditional practice.

When Agnes Mongan retired as director of the Fogg in 1971, she retained her title of curator of drawings and continued in that post until 1975. The 1970s have been a decade during which Mongan has reaped the harvest of her hard years of labor. In 1971 she was awarded the Merito della Repubblica Italiana by the Italian government "for her help with the restoration of art following the floods of Florence and her years of work fostering Italian culture."[41] In 1971/72 she was appointed visiting director of the Timken Art Gallery in San Diego. In the spring of 1976 she served as Edith Kreeger Wolf Distinguished Professor at Northwestern University. In the fall of 1976 she was named Bingham Professor at the University of Louisville, and in the spring of 1977 visiting professor at the University of Texas.

She was appointed Kress Professor at the National Gallery of Art for the term 1977-78, the first woman to hold that position. In the spring of 1979 she was visiting professor of fine arts at the University of California at Santa Barbara. Mongan's activity has not slowed down, but perhaps has increased as she has become a septuagenarian. Some of her students have complained goodnaturedly that her physical activities and her energetic pace are difficult to follow. She continues to travel at every opportunity, driving herself at the high speed at which she is known to drive her car, seldom relaxing, always undertaking further projects.

One of the greatest rewards of this decade must have been the party given in her honor when she retired as director of the Fogg. On 17 May 1971 the "Evening in Honor of Agnes Mongan" began at 6:30 at the Harvard Faculty Club[42] when eighty friends of Mongan and the Fogg dined on melon and prosciutto, roast ribs of beef, and other delights. Following dinner the guests were treated to a concert of "Chamber Music of the Baroque Era in France" at Sanders Theatre. Later they attended a reception at the Fogg, where Mongan, wearing an orchid corsage, greeted friends assembled to view an exhibition mounted as a tribute to her forty-two years of association with the museum. The objects displayed, mostly drawings, were chosen to reflect Mongan's taste or her special objects of research.[43] As always, they represented the highest level of quality, the goal for which Agnes Mongan strove during her years at the Fogg. The festivities, reflecting the formality and tradition of Fogg functions, could not have been better organized had Agnes Mongan arranged them herself.

When Agnes Mongan was curator of drawings and director of the Fogg, purchase funds were minimal, but she was able to acquire by gift and purchase many works that consistently reflect her sense of connoisseurship. In publishing some of her new acquisitions, she indicated her pride in and love of the objects entering the collection. In making most of the purchases, Mongan had the support of many loyal donors whom she had encouraged in the formation of their drawing collections. One of these sheets was Poussin's *Infant Bacchus Entrusted to the Nymphs*, a drawing for the painting in the Fogg, given in 1958 by Mr. and Mrs. Donald S. Stralem, about which Agnes Mongan wrote an enthusiastic article on its discovery and subsequent purchase.[44] In 1955 with the help of Mrs. Charles W. Phinney she added three Ingres drawings to the collection. John Newberry donated Watteau's *Three Views of a Drummer* in 1964. The Friends of the Fogg, the organization Mongan encouraged while at the museum, helped with several purchases, notably with a drawing by Piet Mondrian in 1957 and one by Claude Lorrain in 1967. She successfully obtained the Hendrick Goltzius *Allegorical Composition of the Artist's Motto: "Eer Boven Golt"* with the help of an anonymous donor who sent her a check when he learned of her desire to purchase the drawing.

Agnes Mongan's friendship with various Fogg supporters cannot be overestimated. She became acquainted with most of the drawing collectors in this country (as well as Europe) and obtained help from many of them in acquiring works for the Fogg even when the bulk of their collections was promised elsewhere. One example must be Robert Lehman who, at Mongan's instigation, gave the money to purchase a Cochin drawing in honor of Paul Sachs' eightieth birthday in 1959. Disappointments sometimes occurred when donors promised the Fogg their collections with Agnes Mongan's encouragement but died prematurely before wills were changed or when circumstances altered. Yet, there were also instances of unexpected gifts such as that of part of the estate of Mrs. Mary Harris Phinney. Loyalty by donors will become more noticeable in the future as drawings whose purchase Mongan advised return as bequests to the Fogg. Further evidence of appreciation by collectors is shown by the endowment by Mrs. Edwin H. Land of a fellowship in art history at the Fogg Museum in Agnes Mongan's name.[45]

Agnes Mongan has also had a strong influence on her students. They have seen in her a selfless person willing to give of her time and energy to direct a student in the beginning of his or her career. In taking on the role of mentor to the young, Agnes Mongan did not neglect the social side of her position. As assistant, associate, and then director of the Fogg, this has been the most visible aspect of Mongan's activity. She has worked on numerous committees and boards, organized and overseen the social functions of openings and dinners at the Fogg, and traveled abroad to museum meetings and functions. Discussing the Fogg and its activities, she has served as its "ambassador" whether dining with diplomats and collectors or squiring prominent persons about the museum.

Although Agnes Mongan's professional life has been devoted to the care and study of drawings, she has had rich outside interests in her private life. One of them is her house in Rockport, Massachusetts, which she shares with her sister Betty. She lovingly tends to her flower garden whenever her peripatetic life allows her the time to enjoy the tranquility of the country. She enjoys English literature and history, two of her first loves.

Agnes Mongan became a success in the male-dominated atmosphere of Harvard University because of her determination and hard work. She never allowed chauvinism to deter her from performing her job on the highest level. Her accomplishments brought her recognition as one of the finest authorities in her field. Although other women might have given up careers because tradition prevented them from joining the faculty club or having their names appear in college handbooks as professors of their subjects, Mongan accepted the conditions as they were and distinguished herself in spite of them.

Her love of quality in works of art permeates Mongan's responses to quality in other aspects of life. Her lifestyle has the sense of a twentieth-century Renaissance woman. She personifies dignity and tradition while she

Figure 29. Agnes Mongan, by Rick Stafford, 1979. (*Courtesy Rick Stafford*)

is aware and appreciative of the changing lifestyles of the present (Figure 29). With a singleness of purpose, the incentive for hard work and preparation, the ambition and desire for success, and a dedication to principles, she has obtained recognition in her field, the respect of her colleagues, and the adoration of her students. In her life and in her work Mongan has followed the ideal set down in the catalogue of *Drawings in the Fogg Museum of Art* by maintaining "an alliance of the functions of the art historian and the connoisseur, a combination of accurate scholarship with an instinct for quality."[46] Like Ingres, who once called himself a "conserver of good doctrines,"[47] Agnes Mongan has organized and clarified principles—the good doctrines of art-historical research. Her life and work reflect the motto she has taken as her own, "Chance favors the prepared mind."[48]

NOTES

Important articles consulted for this essay were Alice Whiting Ellis, "Career in Art,' *Bryn Mawr Alumnae Bulletin*, 23, 1 (Fall 1952) 6 − 7 +; John Canaday, "Fogg Bids Agnes Mongan, Au Revoir," *The New York Times* (19 May 1971); Roberta Faul, "Careers in American Museums: Agnes Mongan," *Museum News*, 54,1 (Sept./Oct. 1975), 30-33; Sara Landsdell, "Liberated Museum Pioneer," *The Courier-Journal and Times* (5 December 1976); and Janet Baker-Carr, "A Conversation with Agnes Mongan, Art Historian, Teacher, Editor, Museum Director," *Harvard Magazine* (July/Aug. 1978), 50-54. Also consulted were the *Harvard College Catalogue*, issues from 1921 on; *Bryn Mawr College Calendar*, issues from 1923 to 1928; *Bryn Mawr Alumnae Bulletin*, issues from 1927 on; *Smith College Alumnae Quarterly*, issues from 1929 on; and the *Fogg Art Museum Newsletter*, issues from 1963 on. (It should be noted here that the Fogg Art Museum is known also as the Fogg Museum of Art and the Fogg Museum. Its official name is the William Hayes Fogg Museum of Art, Harvard University, Cambridge, Mass. For consistency in the notes and in the bibliography of Agnes Mongan's work, the title given to the museum is the Fogg Art Museum.) Shorter newspaper articles and unpublished letters, memoranda and photographs were found in the Smith Archives and the Fogg Archives, including the pamphlet *Evening in Honor of Agnes Mongan* (17 May 1971). Interviews with Agnes Mongan and her professional colleagues, students, and friends were conducted from January through October 1977.

1. John Canaday, "Fogg Bids Agnes Mongan Au Revoir," *New York Times* (19 May 1971).
2. Agnes Mongan and Paul Sachs, *Drawings in the Fogg Museum of Art* (Cambridge, 1940).
3. Elizabeth Mongan is a noted authority on prints, as is her sister on drawings. Consequently, the two women are often referred to as "the Mongan sisters, A and B" (Agnes and Betty). In his book *Recollections of a Collector*, Lessing J. Rosenwald acknowledged his debt to Elizabeth Mongan for her advice as his curator for thirty years. Lessing J. Rosenwald, *Recollections of a Collector* (Alverthorpe Gallery, Jenkintown, Pennsylvania, 1976), pp. 36-37.
4. Roberta Faul, "Careers in American Museums: Agnes Mongan," *Museum News*, 54, 1 (Sept./Oct. 1975), 31.
5. *Bryn Mawr College Calendar*, 20, 3 (May 1927), 41. Agnes Mongan relates that she had an early interest not only in art history but also in English history and literature, nurtured by her mother. Conversation with Agnes Mongan (Sept./Oct. 1977).

6. Ibid., 17, 3 (May 1924) 126; 18, 3 (May 1925) 118; 19, 3 (May 1926) 117; and conversation with Agnes Mongan (Sept./Oct. 1977).

7. For a biography of Georgiana Goddard King see the essay in this volume by Susanna Saunders.

8. Georgiana Goddard King, *Heart of Spain* (Cambridge, 1941), p. v.

9. Elizabeth N. Potter to the author, 8 December 1976.

10. Alice Whiting Ellis, "Career in Art," *Bryn Mawr Alumnae Bulletin*, 23, 1 (Fall 1952), 6; and conversation with Agnes Mongan (Sept./Oct. 1977).

11. Conversation with Agnes Mongan (Sept./Oct. 1977).

12. Agnes Mongan to Susanna Saunders, 19 August 1975.

13. This does not imply that Agnes Mongan did not have other interests throughout her career. She always had many friends and with them pursued a full and varied social life that included traveling, music, dancing, swimming, and other activities.

14. There were two women from Bryn Mawr, two from Smith College and one from Mount Holyoke. They were Dora Shipley, Phyllis Bache, Dorothy Graves, and Belle-mead Pritchard. Conversation with Agnes Mongan (Sept./Oct. 1977).

15. Information about the Kennedy seminars comes from the *Bulletin of Smith College*, 1, 8 (June 1927), n.p.; from Ellis, "Career in Art," 6; and conversation with Agnes Mongan (Sept./Oct. 1977).

16. See Faul, "Careers in American Museums," 31, for the conditions surrounding Agnes Mongan's fulfillment of the M.A. degree at Smith College.

17. Fogg Art Museum, *Memorial Exhibition of Works of Art from the Collection of Paul J. Sachs* (Cambridge and New York, 1965-66), p. 13.

18. *Fogg Newsletter*, 3, 2 (Oct. 1965), n.p. Information on Paul Sachs is found in the introduction to Fogg Art Museum, *Memorial Exhibition*. Several interesting facts are added to his biography by Colin Eisler, "*Kunstgeschichte* American Style: A Study in Migration," in *The Intellectual Migration*, ed. by Bernard Bailyn and Donald H. Fleming (Cambridge, 1969), pp. 590-91. See also Ada V. Ciniglio, "Paul J. Sachs," *Museum News*, 55, I (Sept./Oct. 1976), 48-51 and 68-71.

19. Fogg Art Museum, *Memorial Exhibition*, p. 11.

20. Bernard Berenson, "Rudiments of Connoisseurship," *The Study and Criticism of Italian Art* (London, 1902), p. 122.

21. Conversation with the late Jakob Rosenberg and confirmed by other colleagues (Feb. 1977).

22. The first Louvre series of catalogues, encompassing French and northern drawings, is found as Paris, Musée National du Louvre, Cabinet des Dessins, *Catalogue Raisoné* (Paris, 1907-). The new Louvre series is found under the title *Inventaire Général des Dessins Italiens du Musée du Louvre*, begun in 1972. The early British Museum volumes began with Arthur M. Hind, *Catalogue of Drawings by Dutch and Flemish Artists Preserved in the Department of Prints and Drawings* (London, 1915-1932). The Italian volumes, by various authors are entitled *Italian Drawings in the Department of Prints and Drawings in the British Museum* (London, 1950-). The Albertina volumes, by various authors, are catalogued as *Beschreibender Katalog der Handzeichnungen in der Graphischen Sammlung Albertina*, 6 vols. (Vienna, 1926-1941). The first Windsor Castle volume was Kenneth McKenzie Clark, *A Catalogue of the Drawings of Leonardo da Vinci in the Collection of His Majesty the King at Windsor Castle* (Cambridge, 1935). The Ashmolean catalogue is K.T. Parker, *Catalogue of the Collection of Drawings in the Ashmolean Museum* (Oxford, 1938). For the recent drawing catalogues see E. Haverkamp Begemann and Anne Marie S. Logan, *European Drawings and Watercolors in the Yale University Art Gallery, 1500-1900* (New Haven, 1970); James Byam Shaw, *Drawings by Old Masters at Christ Church, Oxford* (Oxford, 1976); and Felton Gibbons, *Catalogue of Italian Drawings in the Art Museum, Princeton University* (Princeton, 1977).

23. Nicky Mariano, *Forty Years with Berenson* (New York, 1966), p. 213. Agnes Mongan relates that the cause of their tardy arrival was the breakdown of their hired car. Conversation with Agnes Mongan (Sept./Oct. 1977).

24. Ibid., pp. 297 and 317.

25. The reappearance of these exhibitions may have been due to the initiation of the publication of a journal on drawings, *Master Drawings*, the first issue of which appeared in 1963. It was not, however, the first journal devoted to drawings. That was *Old Master Drawings*, which was published in London in the years 1926-1940, the period when an interest in old master drawings was being awakened in this country. For the earlier exhibitions see Crocker Art Gallery, *Old Master Drawings from the E.B. Crocker Collection* (Sacramento, 1939) and Smith College Museum of Art, *Italian Drawings 1330-1780* (Northampton, Mass., 1941).

26. Faul, "Careers in American Museums," 33, and conversation with Agnes Mongan (Sept./Oct. 1977).

27. "Portrait Studies by Degas in American Collections," *Fogg Art Museum Bulletin*, 1 (May 1932), 61-68.

28. Buffalo Fine Arts Academy, *Master Drawings Selected from the Museums and Private Collections of America* (Buffalo and New York, 1935), n.p.

29. Even before the war Mongan was part of the American Defense Harvard Group which helped monitor newspapers and radio programs for propaganda. She also assisted Paul Sachs in making lists of key monuments in Europe that should be saved from allied bombing. Conversation with Agnes Mongan (Sept./Oct. 1977).

30. Fogg Art Museum, *Paintings, Prints, Drawings: French Art of the Nineteenth Century* (Cambridge, 1942).

31. Mongan and Sachs, viii.

32. Conversation with Agnes Mongan (Sept./Oct. 1977).

33. The Frick Collection, *An Illustrated Catalogue of the Works of Art in the Collection of Henry Clay Frick* (Pittsburgh and New York, 1949-1956), 12 vols.

34. Fogg Art Museum, *Seventy Master Drawings: A Loan Exhibition Arranged in Honor of Professor Paul J. Sachs on the Occasion of His Seventieth Birthday* (Cambridge, 1948-1949), and *One Hundred Master Drawings* (Cambridge, 1949).

35. Jean Seznec gave her this nickname and also called the Mongan sisters the "Beaux-Arts Belles." Conversation with Agnes Mongan (Sept./Oct. 1977).

36. Conversation with John Coolidge (February 1977).

37. *Harvard College Catalogue* (November 1954). Paul Sachs, for example, who never obtained a Ph.D., was a full professor in the Department of Fine Arts at Harvard.

38. See the *Harvard College Catalogue* for these years.

39. Sachs taught the course from 1918 to 1940 (from 1940 with Jakob Rosenberg); Jakob Rosenberg taught it after 1950; Charles Kuhn from 1955, assisted by John Coolidge; and after 1960 John Coolidge taught the course. See the *Harvard College Catalogue* for these years.

40. Exhibitions by one person had been organized in the early years of the seminar, but as the exhibitions became more complicated there was a need to form a committee to prepare them. Conversation with Agnes Mongan (Sept./Oct. 1977).

41. *Harvard Gazette* (19 March 1971), n.p.

42. In earlier days as a woman Agnes Mongan was not invited to join the Harvard Faculty Club.

43. Memoranda concerning the preparation of this evening are found in the Fogg Archives. See also the pamphlet of the exhibition *An Evening in Honor of Agnes Mongan* (17 May 1971).

44. Agnes Mongan, "The Infant Bacchus Entrusted to the Nymphs," *Fogg Museum Annual Report* (1958-59), 29-37.

45. American Association of Museums, *Aviso* (n.d.) found in the Fogg Archives.

46. Mongan and Sachs, p. vii.

47. Agnes Mongan, "Ingres and the Antique," *Journal of the Warburg and Courtauld Institutes*, 10 (1947), 10-11.

48. Conversation with Eunice Williams (February 1977). The motto comes from Louis Pasteur, who used it in a speech in 1854 when he became professor and dean of the Faculté des Sciences at Lille. In relating a scientific discovery he said that it was made "by chance you will say, but chance only favours the mind which is prepared." See René Vallery-Radot, *The Life of Pasteur* (New York, 1960), p. 76.

BIBLIOGRAPHY OF AGNES MONGAN*

Books:

Agnes Mongan and Paul J. Sachs. *Drawings in the Fogg Museum of Art.* 2 vols. Cambridge, 1940.

Georgiana Goddard King. *Heart of Spain.* Ed. by Agnes Mongan. Cambridge (1941).

Ingres, 24 Drawings. New York (1947).

One Hundred Master Drawings. Ed. by Agnes Mongan. Cambridge (1949).

New York. The Frick Collection. *An Illustrated Catalogue of the Works of Art in the Collection of Henry Clay Frick.* Contributions by Agnes Mongan. 12 vols. Pittsburgh and New York, 1949-1956.

French Drawings, 13th Century to 1919. Vol. 3 of *Great Drawings of All Times.* New York (1962).

European Paintings in the Timken Art Gallery. By Agnes Mongan and Elizabeth Mongan. San Diego (1969).

Exhibition Catalogues:

Buffalo. Buffalo Fine Arts Academy. *Master Drawings Selected from the Museums and Private Collections of America.* Introduction by Agnes Mongan. Buffalo and New York (1935).

Cambridge. Fogg Art Museum. *Paintings, Prints, Drawings: French Art of the Nineteenth Century.* Cambridge (1942).

_____. *French Romanticism of the Eighteen-Thirties.* Cambridge (1943).

_____. *North Africa Interpreted by European Artists.* Cambridge (1943).

_____. *Exhibition Washington, Lafayette, Franklin: Portraits, Books, Manuscripts, Prints, Memorabilia.* Preface by Agnes Mongan and Mary Wadsworth. Cambridge (1944).

_____. *Paintings and Drawings of the Pre-Raphaelites and Their Circle.* Consultant to the exhibition and introduction by Agnes Mongan. Cambridge (1946).

_____. *Seventy Master Drawings: A Loan Exhibition Arranged in Honor of Paul J. Sachs on the Occasion of His Seventieth Birthday.* Cambridge (1949).

_____. *Twentieth-Century Drawings from the Collection of Mr. and Mrs. Richard Davis.* By Agnes Mongan and Helen Willard. Cambridge (1951).

Detroit. Detroit Institute of Arts. *French Drawings of Five Centuries, from the Collection of the Fogg Museum of Art.* Detroit (1951).

New York. Knoedler Galleries. "Ingres in American Collections." *A Loan Exhibition of Painting and Drawing by Ingres from the Ingres Museum at Montauban.* Essay by Agnes Mongan. New York (1952).

Cambridge. Fogg Art Museum. *Drawings and Oil Sketches by P.P. Rubens from American Collections.* Cambridge (1956).

Lawrence, Kansas. University Museum of Art. *Austrian Rococo 18th-Century Prints and Drawings.* Introduction by Agnes Mongan. Lawrence (1956).

*Compiled by Dorothy Wilson.

Cambridge. Fogg Art Museum. *Drawings from the Collection of Curtis O. Baer*. Cambridge (1958).

Rotterdam. Museum Boymans. *Von Clouet tot Matisse*. Introduction by Agnes Mongan. Rotterdam (1958).

Cambridge. Fogg Art Museum. *Modigliani Drawings from the Collection of Stefa and Leon Brillouin*. Cambridge (1959).

New York. Metropolitan Museum of Art. *French Drawings from American Collections: Clouet to Matisse*. Introduction by Agnes Mongan. New York (1959).

Cambridge. Fogg Art Museum. *Andrew Wyeth: Dry Brush and Pencil Drawings*. Cambridge (1963).

New York. Charles Slatkin Galleries. *Toulouse-Lautrec, 1864-1901: Portraits and Figure Studies, The Early Years*. New York (1964-1965).

Cambridge. Fogg Art Museum. *Memorial Exhibition: Works of Art from the Collection of Paul J. Sachs 1878-1965*. By Agnes Mongan and Mary Lee Bennett. Cambridge (1965-1967).

_____. *Ingres Centennial Exhibition 1867-1967*. By Agnes Mongan and Hans Naef. Cambridge (1967).

Oberlin. Allen Memorial Art Museum. *Ingres and His Circle*. Essay by Agnes Mongan. Oberlin (1967).

Cambridge. Fogg Art Museum. *Selections from the Drawing Collection of David Daniels*. By Agnes Mongan and Mary Lee Bennett. Cambridge (1968).

_____. *Tiepolo: A Bicentenary Exhibition*. Foreword by Agnes Mongan. Cambridge (1970).

_____. *Edward Waldo Forbes: Yankee Visionary*. Introduction by Agnes Mongan. Cambridge (1971).

_____. *Modern Painting, Drawing, and Sculpture, Collected by Louis and Joseph Pulitzer, Jr.* Vol. 2, pp. 333-35, and vol. 3, 374-76, by Agnes Mongan. Cambridge (1971).

Cambridge. Busch-Reisinger Museum. *Margaret Fisher: Drawings, Water-colors, Gouaches*. Cambridge (1973).

Cambridge. Fogg Art Museum. *Benjamin Rowland, Jr. Memorial Exhibition*. Cambridge (1973).

Waterville, Maine. Colby College. *American Painters of the Impressionist Period Rediscovered*. Essay by Agnes Mongan. Waterville (1975).

Cambridge. Fogg Art Museum. *Harvard Honors Lafayette*. By Agnes Mongan and Louise Todd Ambler. Cambridge (1975-1976).

Alice Stallknecht. *A New England Town: A Portrait*. Contributions by Agnes Mongan. The Municipal Art Gallery. Los Angeles (1977).

Elizabeth Mongan. *Daumier in Retrospect, 1808-1879*. Introduction by Agnes Mongan. Los Angeles County Museum of Art. Los Angeles (1979).

Articles:

"A Sheet of Studies by Veronese." *Old Master Drawings*, 6 (September 1931), 21-25.

"Portrait Studies by Degas in American Collections." *Fogg Museum Bulletin*, 1 (May 1932), 61-68.

"Federigo Baroccio." *Old Master Drawings*, 7, 25 (June 1932), 5-6.

"Drawings in the Platt Collection." *American Magazine of Art*, 25 (July 1932), 47-54.

"Loeser Collection of Drawings." *Fogg Museum Bulletin*, 2 (March 1933), 21-24.

"Fogg Drawings and Prints of the Eighteenth Century." *Fogg Museum Bulletin*, 3 (March 1934), 5-9.

"Drawings in the Fogg Art Museum." *Fogg Museum Bulletin*, 5, 3 (Summer 1936), 47.

"Degas: Master Observer Seen in Philadelphia." *Art News*, 35, 7 (14 November 1936), 11-13.

"Gift of Old Master Drawings." *Fogg Museum Bulletin*, 6 (March 1937), 21-34.

"Six Aquarelles Inédites de Daumier." *Gazette des Beaux-Arts*, 17 (April 1937), 245-53.
"Six Rediscovered Satires by Daumier." *Art News*, 35 (August 1937), 11-12.
"Degas as Seen in American Collections." *Burlington Magazine*, 72 (June 1938), 290-302.
"Jacopo Bellini." *Old Master Drawings*, 13,50 (September 1938), 24-25.
"Some Notes on the Drawings in the Fogg Museum." *Fogg Museum Bulletin*, 8 (November 1938), 3-4.
"Notes on Canaletto Drawings in the Fogg Art Museum." *Old Master Drawings*, 3, 51 (December 1938), 34-36.
"Jordaens Drawing." *Burlington Magazine*, 75 (December 1939), 245-46.
"Pietà by Simon Marmion." *Fogg Museum Bulletin*, 9 (March 1942), 114-20.
"Winthrop Bequest." *Fogg Museum Bulletin*, 10 (November 1943), 53-57.
"Winthrop Collection: Before and After Impressionism." *Art News*, 42, 16 (1 January 1944), 22-23, 31.
"What Makes a Museum Modern?" *Art News*, 43, 9 (1-13 August 1944), 12-13, 22-23.
"Drawings by Ingres in the Winthrop Collection." *Gazette des Beaux Arts*, 26 (December 1944), 387-412.
"Cradle for Museum Men." *Art News*, 44, 7 (15 May 1945), 24-25, 31.
"New Clouets Come to Cambridge." *Art News*, 45, 1 (March 1946), 24-25, 69-70.
"A Group of Newly Discovered 16th-Century French Portrait Drawings." *Harvard Library Bulletin*, 1, 2 (Spring 1947), 161-62, and 1, 3 (Autumn 1947), 397-98.
"Ingres and the Antique." *Journal of the Warburg and Courtauld Institutes*, 10 (1947), 1-13.
"Drawings—Forgeries." *Magazine of Art*, 41 (May 1948), 188-89.
"Supplement to 'Six Unpublished Water-colors by Daumier.'" *Gazette des Beaux-Arts*, 36 (July and September 1949), 132, 176.
"Notes on the History of Drawing." *Journal of the American Association of University Women*, 24 (January 1951), 81-86.
"Find the Artist." *Art News*, 50, 1 (March 1951), 20-23, 61.
"An Architectural Fantasy of Giovanni Battista Piranesi." *Arte Veneta*, 5 (1951), 176.
"Master Copyists All." *Vogue* (1 September 1951), 184-85.
"Portrait of a Genius: Leonardo." *New York Times Sunday Magazine* (13 April 1952), 12-13.
"An Album of Water-colors by Oudry." *Fogg Museum Annual Report* (1953-54), 10.
"A Drawing by Rigaud." *Bulletin of the California Palace of the Legion of Honor*, 11 (February 1954), 1-6.
"Chardin and French Eighteenth-Century Painting." *Minneapolis Institute of Arts Bulletin*, 43 (October 1954), 52-55.
"'A Study of a Nude Figure' by Paul Cézanne." *Fogg Museum Annual Report* (1954-55), 15-16.
"Three Drawings by Ingres." *Art Quarterly*, 18 (Summer 1955), 180-85.
"Notes on Collection of Graphic Arts in Rio de Janeiro." *Art Quarterly*, 18 (Autumn 1955), 283-93.
"Venetian Drawings in America." *Venezia e l'Europa: Atti del XVIII Congresso Internazionale di Storia dell'Arte* (Venice 1955), 303-5.
"Deutsche Handzeichnungen Meisterwerke aus fünf Jahrhunderten." *Kunstchronik*, 9, 6 (June 1956), 149-52.
"Ingres et Madame Moitessier." *Bulletin du Musée Ingres*, 2 (July 1957), 3-8.
"Fogg Art Museum Collection of Drawings." *Harvard Library Bulletin*, 13 (Spring 1958), 196-209.
"'The Infant Bacchus Entrusted to the Nymphs' by Poussin." *Fogg Museum Annual Report* (1958-59), 29-37.
"Unpublished Preparatory Drawing for Portrait of Princesse de Broglie." *Bulletin du Musée Ingres*, 5 (1958) 6-7.
"Bernard Berenson." *Encyclopedia Britannica* (1958).

"Ingres." *Enciclopedia Universelle dell'Arte* (1959).

"De Clouet à Matisse. Les Américains Collectionneurs de Dessins Français." *Le Jardin des Arts*, 51 (January 1959), 185-90.

"Ingres." *Encyclopedia of World Art* (1963).

"Water-colors from Delacroix's North African Journey in American Collections." *Hommage à Jean Alazard, Souvenirs et Mélanges* (Paris 1963), 187-94.

"Forsyth Wickes, Newport, R.I." *Great Private Collections*. Edited by Douglas Cooper (New York, 1963), 148-57.

"Souvenirs of Delacroix's Journey to Morocco in American Collections." *Master Drawings*, 1, 2 (Summer 1963), 20-31.

"European Landscape Drawings, 1400-1900." *Daedalus*, 10 (Summer 1963), 581-635.

"The Drawings of Andrew Wyeth." *American Artist*, 27 (September 1963), 28-33.

"'Three Views of a Drummer' by Antoine Watteau." *Fogg Art Museum, Acquisitions* (1964), 42-48.

"A Portrait Drawing by Ingres (Madame Moitessier)." *Worcester Art Museum News* (1965), 1-3.

"Study for a Portrait at Worcester Museum." *Bulletin du Musée Ingres* 17 (July 1965), 3-8.

"Andrew Wyeth." *Encyclopedia Americana* (1968).

"Mondrian's Flowers." *Altena Festschrift* (Amsterdam, 1968), 228-31.

"Foreword." *Fogg Art Museum, Acquisitions* (1968), 5-8; (1969-70), 5-8.

"Ingres as a Great Portrait Draughtsman." *Colloque Ingres, Montauban* (1969), 134-50.

"Renoir." *The Economist* (Tokyo, 1970).

"Some Drawings by Francesco Lorenzi." *Studi di Storia dell'Arte* (1971), 347-52.

"'Cranberry Harvest' by Eastman Johnson." *San Diego Union* (19 November 1972).

"Ingres." *Encyclopedia Britannica* (1973).

"Some Drawings by David from his Roman Album I." *Etudes d'Art Français Offertes à Charles Sterling* (Paris, 1975), 319-26.

"'Heavenly Twins,'" *Apollo*, 107 (June 1978), 477-79.

Reviews:

"Italian Drawings of 1330-1780: An Exhibition at Smith College Museum of Art." *Art Bulletin*, 24 (March 1942), 92-94.

"*Raphael's Drawings* by Ulrich Middeldorf." *Art Bulletin*, 28 (September 1946), 204-5.

"*European Master Drawings in the U.S.A.* by Hans Tietze." *Art Bulletin*, 31, 3 (September 1949), 237-38.

"*The Medici* by Ferdinand Schevill." *The New York Times* (1949).

"*The Drawings of Antonio Canaletto at Windsor Castle*, by K.T. Parker, and *The Drawings of Domenichino at Windsor Castle*, by J. Pope Hennessy." *Art Bulletin*, 33 (March 1951), 63-65.

"*Painting in Florence and Siena after the Black Death* by Millard Meiss." *Renaissance News*, 5, 1 (Spring 1952), 13-15.

"Review of Exhibition 'De Clouet à Matisse.'" *La Revue des Arts* 8, 5 (Sept./Oct. 1958), 237-40.

"*Portraits by Degas*, by Jean S. Boggs." *Canadian Art*, 20 (May/June 1963), 191-92.

"A Subtle Court Painter of Peter Mellen's *Jean Clouet*." *Apollo*, 96 (December 1972), 560-62.

EPILOGUE

From 1820 to 1979, the contributions of women to the interpretation of the visual arts present a rich and varied record of achievement, one shaped by the changing social and cultural roles of women in European and American society. During the period 1820 to 1890, when women were largely excluded from participation in public life, they nevertheless exercised important influence on the field as published authors, the only professional avenue open to them. Generally self-educated and struggling to forge independent identities for themselves, these women writers were widely read by general audiences in popular and more specialized journals. Women also had a substantial part in articulating new attitudes toward art and in creating a receptive climate for changing aesthetic taste in their guidebooks describing monuments and collections, as well as in reviews and essays and biographies of artists. Translations and popular histories of art by women were significant in diffusing new ideas and critical attitudes to a wide readership. In a more scholarly vein, women contributed to the growing art-historical literature in such genres as monographs on individual artists, collections of documents, iconography, and architectural history and criticism.

Women's prominence in the field as writers did not attract the opposition encountered by females attempting to enter such exclusively male bastions as law and medicine. In fact, two seemingly negative aspects of women's confinement to the domestic sphere promoted their emergence in large numbers as interpreters of the visual arts. Aesthetic cultivation was permissible as an extension of female amateurism in the arts and was related to the larger concept of women as guardians of culture. By the 1890s, women began to enter the two main institutional branches of art history: museums and colleges and universities. In the United States, women's colleges fostered study of the visual arts as an extension of the female amateur and guardian-of-culture traditions. American women were thus able to gain access both to undergraduate and graduate study in the emerging disciplines of archaeology and art history. Around 1890, in Germany and Austria, women gradually entered the universities where art history had been first defined as an academic discipline. In another important development, American women began at this time to work in professional capacities in libraries and museums, although they were clustered mostly on junior levels and limited to less prestigious fields. Women's employment in American higher education was largely confined to women's colleges, even when they attained equivalent educational credentials in the same institutions as men. In German universities, however, women could not teach until after World War I.

In this later period, 1890 to 1930, women outside academic or museum establishments continued to produce writings of the highest caliber as art critics and historians. These writings continued to address broad, educated audiences, while women scholars with institutional affiliations began to specialize in publications of narrower, more professional interest. Women took leading roles in bringing art into the lives of large segments of the public by running educational programs in settlement houses, museums, and schools. Social change in women's roles during this period permitted extended activity as facilitators of research, editors, and art administrators. Women also made prime contributions to the new discipline of archaeology in the field, as well as in museums and colleges. One consequence of professional status was a difficult choice for women between marriage and career—one that did not come up while women remained outside established institutions. It also seemed to follow that newly won professional status inhibited women employed in museums or academe from continuing to press for social and political reform of women's condition, as many female nineteenth-century writers on the arts had done. In short, between 1890 and 1930, women entered the mainstream of the art historical professions, but on unequal terms with their male colleagues. By 1917, women made up almost 50 percent of the fledgling College Art Association of America—a figure that holds true today.

Women's roles as guardians and preservers of culture took on new dimensions during the crises of the 1930s created by the rise of Hitlerism and the effects of the Great Depression. Women made heroic efforts in the face of personal disasters to attain lives of dignity and professional achievement while preserving old and creating new institutions for scholarly and community endeavor. Often under extremely difficult circumstances, women continued to function as scholars, museum curators, librarians, and facilitators of research. Women art critics and museum curators and directors once again exercised powerful influence on taste as champions and interpreters of the then unpopular or controversial causes of American art and European modernism.

From this historical record, it has become apparent that women's contributions as interpreters of the visual arts have been affected by their social and cultural roles, including the range of educational and professional opportunities open to them. Yet, as most women have adopted the methodology of mainstream art history since attaining professional status, an attempt to define feminine characteristics in their work is not historically valid. In the earlier period when women remained outside art historical institutions, some of their work showed feminist characteristics, often linked to their activity for political and social reform of women's condition. As soon as women gained entrance to established art-historical and other institutions, their adherence to generally recognized standards of scholarship makes it difficult to maintain that women's research or publications show definable feminine characteristics. Some areas in which women's writings have excelled, such as travel writing, interior design, landscape gardening, decorative arts, crafts, and textiles, do reflect social and cultural attitudes related to the traditions of women as guardians of culture and amateurs of the arts. That these genres or fields have not been highly regarded in the prevailing judgment of art historians again reflects underlying social and aesthetic biases that are just now undergoing fresh scrutiny.

This last consideration of disdain for certain fields seems directly related to the neglect of women in current art-historiographic literature. Is it not possible that the lingering association of the interpretation of the visual arts with the tradition of female amateurism has inspired a particular dislike of those fields that have been historically identified with women? A further extension of this hypothesis would also explain the desire to create a record of accomplishment in the field free of any traces of feminine involvement. Surely the explanation that women have not earned a place in the annals of art-historical achievement because they have not been theorists is unconvincing on several grounds. First, the absence of a comprehensive history of the field makes such an assumption untenable. Second, such an exclusive criterion would eliminate most men included in art-historiographic chronicles. Finally, such a narrow point of view reveals the present conservatism of academic art history, particularly its tendency to focus on specialized problems of research without reference to larger cultural issues affecting the profession.

Another facet of neglect of women's contributions as interpreters of the visual arts is that many women discussed in this book were either unaffiliated or were employed by less prestigious institutions than those in which research is the most important consideration. Those women who did succeed in penetrating the most exclusive educational or museum establishments accepted their inferior status; some worked with great distinction as facilitators of research; others in fields that did not command the highest professional esteem or recognition.

In the last decade, the women's movement has brought attention to the existing inequities in the present status of women as interpreters of the visual arts as part of a larger consciousness about women's historical and contemporary roles in society. As Romanticism did in the nineteenth century, the women's movement has provided a sense of women's individual identity and history that has encouraged creative intellectual and artistic endeavors. The women's movement has also helped to build networks of support of the kind that have traditionally given women a sense of community. The seminal conference on women in the arts held at the Corcoran Gallery in Washington, D.C., in April 1972 proved an important rallying point for review of the inequities prevailing in all areas related to American women's professional activities in the visual arts. Earlier that year, the Women's Caucus of the College Art Association, now the Women's Caucus for Art, had been launched. This nationwide association, with many state chapters, now has some 2,800 members. Although critics, librarians, educators, and art historians belong to this group, women artists predominate. In fact, women artists have successfully organized local art centers in which they can show their work, act as pressure groups for increased opportunities for exhibition of members' works in museums, and serve other social and educational functions in promoting professional activities.

The women's movement has brought new attention to topics previously neglected in the existing accounts of art history. The primary example is the intense study of past and present women artists. Thus far this new field of interest has produced at least half a dozen books on the subject and in 1976 a pioneer survey exhibition and catalogue, *Women Artists 1550-1950*, organized and written by Ann Sutherland Harris and Linda Nochlin. In American colleges and universities, many courses on "Women and Art" reflect the new interest in women artists and attract students in studio and art history courses on the undergraduate level, who are predominantly female. Undergraduate women majors in art history are 79 percent of the total enrollment and 67 percent of those on the doctoral level. Some idea of the scope of these new programs emerges in the new edition (1980) of *Women's Studies and the Arts*, edited by Elsa H. Fine, with Lola Gellman and Judy Loeb. Critical studies of women artists and the psychological, social, and sexual aspects of their creativity have also flourished. This literature, as well as other relevant issues, is considered in two review essays in *Signs: Journal of Women in Culture and Society*. The first was written by Gloria F. Orenstein (Winter 1975); the second, by H. Diane Russell (Spring 1980).

Feminist scholarship has also made significant contributions to studies of the imagery of women, particularly from the perspective of women's traditional social and cultural roles as perceived by male artists. One topic explored by feminist art historians but hitherto avoided in academic scholarship is an examination of the conventions and cultural implications of erotic art. Another much needed reevaluation is occurring in the area of the so-called "minor arts." An outstanding example of a feminist perspective combined with the methods of social history is the study by Anthea Callen of *Women Artists of the Arts and Crafts Movement, 1870-1914.*

Although these developments in feminist scholarship have brought new life to the increasingly conservative discipline of academic art history, the slowness of change also reflects the unequal status of women in college and university teaching. As Diane Russell points out in her *Signs* essay, very little research on women artists and allied subjects figures in the latest listings of doctoral dissertations. The present state of academic scholarship is surely one reason for this phenomenon. Second, graduate students, whose future rests on pleasing their teachers and publishing orthodox scholarship, cannot be expected to occupy an avant-garde position. Younger women faculty who are not yet tenured must exercise caution in avoiding controversial research for fear of ruining their chances for a permanent appointment in a rapidly shrinking job market. Of course, women graduate students will not find too many tenured female professors to encourage women's studies in the arts. The latest statistics (1978) show that only 17 percent of tenured faculty in American art history departments that grant doctorates are women. This figure is disproportionately low when one considers that in the 1960s, 30 percent of the doctorates in the field were awarded to women; by 1970/71 this figure had risen to 48 percent, and in 1978, to 56 percent. At the moment, academic art history seems like a discouraging environment for promoting innovative scholarship concerned with feminist issues. It does not hold very auspicious employment prospects either for the many women contenders for positions in institutions facing declining enrollments.

The available statistics for American art museums are almost ten years old and thus do not show the effect of the women's movement on hiring practices. The figures quoted in *Museums U.S.A.* for 1971/72 indicate, however, that women still had trouble in achieving senior positions. This was true particularly of the largest institutions, and especially of museums run by the federal government. Women are becoming curators in major fields in greater numbers. There are also more women directors of art museums, although generally of smaller or more specialized institutions. In 1978, when she was named director of the Philadelphia Museum, Jean Sutherland Boggs—formerly director of the National Gallery of Canada and later a professor at Harvard—became the first woman to head a major American art museum.

The women's movement has had important repercussions in allowing freer choices in lifestyles. Marriage and children no longer mean that women have to abandon their careers. Also common is the phenomenon of the commuting couple, with each spouse employed in a different location. Yet, particularly when child care is involved, the practical difficulties of combining family responsibilities with full-time professional activity remain substantial. In general, social attitudes toward women's roles in the family and workplace have changed, but at a slower pace than the realities of professional life demand.

Although it is difficult to predict accurately what the future holds for women professionals in the visual arts, certain patterns emerge from the historical record sketched in this book. If women wish to reach their full creative potential as interpreters of the visual arts, several paths lie open. The simplest is to accept the status quo, with its continuing disadvantages for women. For those who want to see women take their places as leaders in the profession, either within or outside established institutions, they can choose to support social, legal, and political equality for women. For those who want and are able to exert leadership as creative outsiders, alternative social networks and publications have an important contribution to make. For other women, who wish to bring about reforms within existing institutions, forging alliances with like-minded women on a personal and social basis is essential. If women wish to attain a sense of their identities as individuals and examine the value of their professional endeavors, they need to understand their own history. To this end, the present volume has attempted to show that as interpreters of the visual arts women have indeed found "a field for their efforts."

C.R.S.

SELECTED BIBLIOGRAPHY
Compiled by Claire Richter Sherman

General Background on Art History, Museums, and Archaeology
Women's Education
Education in the Visual Arts at Women's Colleges
Women's Relationship to Art, Culture, and the Professions
Published Biographical Sources on Selected Women Interpreters of the Visual Arts

GENERAL BACKGROUND OF ART HISTORY, MUSEUMS, AND ARCHAEOLOGY

Ackerman, James S., and Carpenter, Rhys. *Art and Archaeology*. Englewood Cliffs, N.J., 1963.
Alexander, Edward P. *Museums in Motion: An Introduction to the History and Functions of Museums*. Nashville, Tenn., 1979.
"Archaeology: Research and Discoveries." In *Encyclopedia of World Art*, 1, New York, 1959.
Brimo, René. *L'Évolution du goût aux États-Unis d'après l'histoire des collections*. Paris, 1938.
Burt, Nathaniel. *Palaces for the People: A Social History of the American Art Museum*. Boston, 1977.
Eisler, Colin. "*Kunstgeschichte* American Style: A Study in Migration." In *The Intellectual Migration: Europe and America 1930-1960*. Edited by Bernard Bailyn and Donald Fleming, pp. 544-629. Cambridge, Mass., 1969.
Fox, Daniel M. *Engines of Culture: Philanthropy and Art Museums*. Madison, Wis., 1963.
Hawkes, Jacquetta, ed. *The World of the Past*. 2 vols. New York, 1963.
Hiss, Priscilla, and Fansler, Roberta. *Research in Fine Arts in the Colleges and Universities of the United States*. New York, 1934.
Kenyon, Kathleen. *Beginning in Archaeology*. London, 1952.
Kleinbauer, W. Eugene. *Modern Perspectives in Western Art History: An Anthology of 20th-Century Writings on the Visual Arts*. New York, 1971.
Kultermann, Udo. *Geschichte der Kunstgeschichte*. Vienna, 1966.
MacKendrick, Paul. *The Greek Stones Speak: The Story of Archaeology in Greek Lands*. New York, 1962.

_____. *The Mute Stones Speak: The Story of Archaeology in Italy*. New York, 1976.

Meyer, Karl E. *The Art Museum: Power, Money, Ethics*. New York, 1979.

Panofsky, Erwin. "Three Decades of Art History in the United States: Impressions of a Transplanted European." In *Meaning in the Visual Arts*, pp. 321-46. Garden City, N.Y., 1955.

Salerno, Luigi. "Historiography." In *Encyclopedia of World Art*, 10, New York, 1965.

Waetzoldt, Wilhelm. *Deutscher Kunsthistoriker*. 2 vols. Leipzig, 1921.

Wortham, John D. *The Genesis of British Egyptology 1549-1906*. Norman, Okla., 1971.

WOMEN'S EDUCATION

Baker, Liva. *I'm Radcliffe! Fly Me!: The Seven Sisters and the Failure of Women's Education*. New York, 1976.

Boas, Louise S. *Women's Education Begins: The Rise of the Women's Colleges*. Norton, Mass., 1935.

Charrier, Edmée. *L'Évolution intellectuelle féminine*. Paris, 1937.

Conway, Jill K. "Perspectives on the History of Women's Education in the United States." *History of Education Quarterly*, 14 (Spring 1974), 1-12.

Ellsworth, Edward W. *Liberators of the Female Mind: The Shirreff Sisters, Educational Reform, and the Women's Movement*. Westport, Conn., 1979.

Jex-Blake, Sophia. *A Visit to Some American Schools and Colleges*. London, 1867; reprint ed., Westport, Conn., 1976.

Newcomer, Mabel. *A Century of Higher Education for American Women*. New York, 1959.

Simmons, Adele. "Education and Ideology in Nineteenth-Century America: The Response of Educational Institutions to the Changing Role of Women." In *Liberating Women's History: Theoretical and Critical Essays*. Edited by Berenice A. Carroll, pp. 115-26. Urbana, Ill., 1976.

Stock, Phyllis. *Better than Rubies: A History of Women's Education*. New York, 1978.

Wein, Roberta. "Women's Colleges and Domesticity, 1875-1918." *History of Education Quarterly*, 14 (Spring 1974), 31-47.

Woody, Thomas. *A History of Women's Education in the United States*. 2 vols. New York, 1929.

EDUCATION IN THE VISUAL ARTS AT WOMEN'S COLLEGES

These sources are mainly institutional histories of women's colleges. More detailed information can be found in the annual reports of the presidents and descriptions of the courses of instruction of these colleges.

Barnard College

Miller, Alice D., and Myers, Susan. *Barnard College: The First Fifty Years*. New York, 1939.

White, Marian C. *A History of Barnard College*. New York, 1954.

See also Dinsmoor, William B. "The Department of Fine Arts and Archaeology." In *A History of the Faculty of Philosophy, Columbia University*, pp. 252-69. New York, 1957.

Bennington College

Jones, Barbara. *Bennington College: The Development of an Educational Idea*. New York, 1946.

Bryn Mawr College

Finch, Edith. *Carey Thomas of Bryn Mawr*. New York, 1947.
Meigs, Cornelia. *What Makes a College? A History of Bryn Mawr*. New York, 1956.

Goucher College

Knipp, Anna H., and Thomas, Thaddeus P. *The History of Goucher College*. Baltimore, 1938.

Mount Holyoke College

Cole, Arthur C. *A Hundred Years of Mount Holyoke College: The Evolution of an Educational Ideal*. New Haven, Conn., 1940.

Radcliffe College

Howells, Dorothy E. *A Century to Celebrate Radcliffe College, 1879-1979*. Cambridge, Mass., 1978.
See also Chase, George C. "The Fine Arts, 1874-1929." In *The Development of Harvard University Since the Inauguration of President Eliot, 1869-1929*. Edited by Samuel E. Morison, pp. 130-45. Cambridge, Mass., 1930.

Sarah Lawrence College

Warner, Constance. *A New Design for Women's Education*. New York, 1940.

Smith College

Seelye, Laurens C. *The Early History of Smith College 1871-1910*. Boston, 1923.
_____. "Music and Art as College Studies." *Educational Review*, 27 (Jan. 1904), 104-06.
Thorp, Margaret F. *Neilson of Smith*. New York, 1956.

Vassar College

Letters from Old-Time Vassar Written by a Student in 1869-70. Poughkeepsie, N.Y., 1915.
Norris, Mary H. *The Golden Age of Vassar*. Poughkeepsie, N.Y., 1915.
Plum, Dorothy, A., and Dowell, George B., comps. *The Magnificent Enterprise: A Chronicle of Vassar College*. Poughkeepsie, N.Y., 1961.
Taylor, James M., and Haight, Elizabeth H. *Vassar*. New York, 1915.
Vassar College Art Gallery. Poughkeepsie, N.Y., 1939.

Wellesley College

Abbot, Agnes A. "The Department of Art at Wellesley College." *AJ*, 21/4 (Summer 1962), 264-65.
Avery, Myrtilla. "Methods of Teaching Art at Wellesley College." *Parnassus*, 3/4 (April 1931), 31.
Converse, Florence. *Wellesley College: A Chronicle of the Years 1875-1938*. Wellesley, Mass., 1939.
Der Nersessian, Sirarpie. "The Direct Approach in the Study of Art History." *College Art Journal*, 1/3 (March 1942), 54-60.
Glasscock, Jean, et al., eds. *Wellesley College 1875-1975: A Century of Women*. Wellesley, Mass., 1975.

WOMEN'S RELATIONSHIP TO ART, CULTURE, AND THE PROFESSIONS

Bernard, Jessie. *Academic Women*. University Park, Pa., 1964.

Callen, Anthea. *Women Artists of the Arts and Crafts Movement 1870-1914*. New York, 1979.

Cole, Doris. *From Tipi to Skyscraper: A History of Women in Architecture*. Boston, 1973.

Conrad, Susan P. *Perish the Thought: Intellectual Women in Romantic America 1830-1860*. New York, 1976.

Deegan, Mary Jo. "Women and Sociology: 1890-1930." *Journal of the History of Sociology*, 1/1 (Fall 1978), 11-32.

Delamont, Sara, and Duffin, Lorna, eds. *The Nineteenth-Century Woman: Her Cultural and Physical World*. London, 1978.

Douglas, Ann. *The Feminization of American Culture*. New York, 1977.

Fine, Elsa H. *Women and Art: A History of Women Painters and Sculptors from the Renaissance to the 20th Century*. Montclair, N.J., 1978.

_____; Gellman, Lola B.; and Loeb, Judy, eds. *Women's Studies and the Arts*. New York, 1980.

Garrison, Dee. *Apostles of Culture: The Public Librarian and American Society 1876-1920*. New York, 1979.

_____. "The Tender Technicians: The Feminization of Public Librarianship, 1876-1905." In *Clio's Consciousness Raised: New Perspectives on the History of Women*. Edited by Mary Hartman and Lois W. Banner, pp. 158-78. New York, 1974.

Greer, Germaine. *The Obstacle Race: The Fortunes of Women Painters and Their Work*. New York, 1979.

Harris, Ann S., and Nochlin, Linda. *Women Artists 1550-1950*. New York, 1976.

Harris, Barbara J. *Beyond Her Sphere: Women and the Professions in American History*. Westport, Conn., 1978.

Hess, Thomas B., and Baker, Elizabeth C., eds. *Art and Sexual Politics*. New York, 1973.

Hubbard, Ruth; Henifin, Mary Sue; and Fried, Barbara, eds. *Women Look at Biology Looking at Women*. Boston, 1979.

Loeb, Judy, ed. *Feminist Collage: Educating Women in the Visual Arts*. New York, 1979.

Lurie, Nancy O. "Women in Early American Anthropology." In *Pioneers of American Anthropology*. Edited by June Helm, pp. 29-81. Seattle and London, 1966.

Marzolf, Marion. *Up from the Footnote: A History of Women Journalists*. New York, 1977.

Moers, Ellen. *Literary Women: The Great Writers*. Garden City, N.Y., 1977.

Orenstein, Gloria F. "Review Essay: Art History." *Signs: Journal of Women in Culture and Society*, 1/2 (Winter 1975), 505-25.

Rosaldo, Michelle Z., and Lamphere, Louise, eds. *Woman, Culture, and Society*. Stanford, Calif., 1974.

Russell, H. Diane. "Review Essay: Art History." *Signs: Journal of Women in Culture and Society*, 5/3 (Spring 1980), 468-80.

Sklar, Kathryn K. "American Female Historians in Context 1770-1930." *Feminist Studies*, 3, 1-2 (Fall 1975), 171-84.

Strachey, Ray. *The Cause: A Short History of the Women's Movement in Great Britain*. London, 1928; reprint ed., London, 1978.

Torre, Susana, ed. *Women in American Architecture: A Historic and Contemporary Perspective*. New York, 1977.

Vicinus, Martha, ed. *Suffer and Be Still: Women in the Victorian Age*. Bloomington, Ind., 1973.

_____, ed. *A Widening Sphere: Changing Roles of Victorian Women*. Bloomington, Ind., 1977.

Walsh, Mary R. *"Doctors Wanted: No Women Need Apply": Sexual Barriers in the Medical Profession 1835-1975.* New Haven, Conn., 1977.

Walton, Ronald G. *Women in Social Work.* London and Boston, 1975.

Welter, Barbara. "She Hath Done What She Could: Protestant Women's Missionary Careers in Nineteenth-Century America." *American Quarterly*, 30/5 (1978), 624-38.

Woolf, Virginia. *A Room of One's Own.* London, 1929.

_____. *Three Guineas.* New York, 1938.

Wright, Gwendolyn. "On the Fringe of the Profession: Women in American Architecture." In *The Architect: Chapters in the History of the Profession.* Edited by Spiro Kostof, pp. 280-308. New York, 1977.

PUBLISHED BIOGRAPHICAL SOURCES ON SELECTED WOMEN INTERPRETERS OF THE VISUAL ARTS

The reader is referred to the list of abbreviations that follows the Introductory Note at the beginning of this book. Maiden names of subjects are identified by enclosing parentheses. If the title of a periodical article simply repeats a subject's name, it is omitted. No titles are given for entries in biographical dictionaries or encyclopedias; authors for such entries are also omitted unless they are of special interest in the context of this book.

Addams, Jane, 1860–1935

Addams, Jane. *Twenty Years at Hull-House.* New York, 1910.

Davis, Allen F. *American Heroine: The Life and Legend of Jane Addams.* New York, 1973.

_____, and McCree, Mary L., eds. *Eighty Years at Hull-House.* Chicago, 1969.

Linn, James W. *Jane Addams: A Biography.* New York, 1935.

NAW.

Ameisenowa, Zofja, 1897-1967

Mayer, L. A. *Bibliography of Jewish Art.* Edited by Otto Kurz. Jerusalem, 1967.

Schmidt, Gerhard. *Wiener Jahrbuch für Kunstgeschichte*, 24 (1971), 7-9: obituary.

Avery, Myrtilla, 1868–1959

Wellesley College Magazine (June 1937), 365-67: appreciation.

Der Nersessian, Sirarpie. *College Art Journal*, 19/3 (Spring 1960), 255: obituary.

NY Times, 5 April 1959: obituary.

"Portrait on Ivory of Myrtilla Avery by Artemis Tavshanjian." *Wellesley College Bulletin, The Art Museum*, 2/3 (May 1939), n.p.

Ayzac, Félicie D', 1801–1891

Dictionnaire de biographie française, 4. Paris, 1948.

Prache, Anne. "Félicie d'Ayzac, Une des premières historiennes de la symbolique chrétienne." *GBA*, 72 (Oct. 1968), 145-50.

Bell, Gertrude, 1868–1926

Bell, Gertrude. *The Letters of Gertrude Bell.* Edited by Lady Bell. 2 vols. London, 1927.

Burgoyne, Elizabeth. *Gertrude Bell from her Personal Papers*, I, 1889-1914; II, 1914-1926. London, 1958-61.

DNB, 1922-30.

Winstone, Harry V.F. *Gertrude Bell.* London, 1978.

Bennett, Gwendolyn, b. 1902

Afro-American Artists: A Bio-bibliographical Directory. Compiled and edited by Theresa D. Cederholm. Boston, 1973.

O'Connor, Francis V., ed. *Art for the Millions: Essays from the 1930s by Artists and Administrators of the WPA Federal Art Project.* Greenwich, Conn., 1973, pp. 213-15 and 270.

Berenson, Mary (Smith) Costelloe, 1864–1945

Brown, David Alan. *Berenson and the Connoisseurship of Italian Painting: A Handbook to the Exhibition.* National Gallery of Art, Washington, D.C., 1979.

Mariano, Nicky. *Forty Years with Berenson.* New York, 1966.

Samuels, Ernest. *Bernard Berenson: The Making of a Connoisseur.* Cambridge, Mass., 1979.

Secrest, Meryle. *Being Bernard Berenson: A Biography.* New York, 1979.

Strachey, Barbara. *Remarkable Relations: The Story of the Pearsall Smith Family.* London, 1980.

Berger, Florence (Paull), 1871–1967

AAA, 23 (1926), 460.

Bulletin of the Wadsworth Atheneum (Spring-Fall 1968), 16.

Carlson, Barbara. "Knick-knacks Recall Career in Museums." *Hartford Courant*, 10 June 1966.

Hartford Sunday Courant, 30 April 1967: obituary.

Whitehill, Walter M. *Museum of Fine Arts, Boston: A Centennial History.* Cambridge, Mass., 1970; I, 393-94.

Bing, Gertrud, 1892–1964

Gombrich, Ernst H. *Jahrbuch der Hamburger Kunstsammlungen*, 10 (1965), 7-12: obituary.

Heise, Carl G. *Kunstchronik*, 17 (Jan. 1964), 258-59: obituary.

Momigliano, Arnaldo. *Rivista storica italiana*, 76 (1964), 856-58: obituary.

Times of London, 6 July 1964: obituary.

Warburg Institute, London University. London, 1965: memoirs and bibliography.

Breeskin, Adelyn (Dohme), b. 1896

Berman, Avis. *Feminist Art Journal* (Summer 1977), 9-14: profile.

———. "Perseverance of Vision." *Baltimore Sunday Sun*, 30 October 1977.

CA, 33-36.

WWAA, 1978.

Brown, Alice Van Vechten, 1862–1949

Abbot, Agnes A. "The Department of Art at Wellesley College." *AJ*, 21/4 (Summer 1962), 264-65.

Avery, Myrtilla. *Wellesley Alumnae Magazine*, 14/5 (June 1930), 326-28: appreciation.

———. "Portrait on Ivory of Alice Van Vechten Brown." *Wellesley College Bulletin, The Art Museum*, 2/2 (June 1937), 2-3.

NAW.

Scudder, Vida D. *Wellesley Alumnae Magazine*, 34/4 (April 1950), 297-98: obituary.

Callcott, Maria (Dundas) Graham, Lady, 1785–1842

DNB.

Gotch, Rosamund B. *Maria, Lady Callcott.* London, 1937.

Haskell, Francis. *Rediscoveries in Art: Some Aspects of Taste, Fashion and Collecting in England and France*. London, 1976, pp. 47-49.

Cary, Elisabeth Luther, 1867–1936

DAB, 11/2 (Supp. 2), 1958, 99-100: by Elizabeth McCausland.
NAW.

Chézy, Wilhelmine Von (Von Klencke), 1783–1856

Chézy, Wilhelmine von. *Unvergessenes; Denkwürdigkeiten aus dem Leben von Helmina von Chézy*. Leipzig, 1858.
LDF.
Neue Deutsche Biographie, 3. Berlin, 1957.

Claflin, Agnes (Rindge), 1900–1977

Askew, Pamela. "Memoir." *Gallery* (Friends of the Vassar Art Gallery), 3/1 (Autumn 1977), n.p.
NY Times, 14 June 1977: obituary.
Vassar Art Gallery. *An Exhibition in Memory of Agnes Rindge Claflin*, 30 April-4 June 1978. Poughkeepsie, N.Y., 1978: appreciations.
WWAW, 1958-59.

Coffey, Katherine, 1900–1972

Barnard Alumnae, 61/3 (Spring 1972), 29: obituary.
Craft Horizons, 32 (June 1972), 6: obituary.
"Museum Director." *Barnard College Alumnae Monthly* (Dec. 1949), 4.
WWAW, 1970-71.

Coor, Gertrude (Achenbach), 1915–1962

Lee, Rensselaer W. *AJ*, 22/4 (Summer 1963), 246: obituary.
NY Times, 10 Sept. 1962: obituary.

Crick-Kuntziger, Marthe, 1891-1963

Calberg, Marguerite. *Revue belge d'archéologie et d'histoire de l'art*, 36 (1967), 183-85: obituary.

Devigne, Marguerite, 1884–1965?

Sulzberger, Suzanne. *Revue belge d'archéologie et d'histoire de l'art*, 35 (1966), 234-35: obituary.

Dohan, Edith (Hall), 1877–1943

Hall, Edith (later Dohan). "Memoirs of an Archaeologist in Crete." Edited by Katharine Page. *Archaeology*, 31/2 (March-April 1978), 5-11.
NAW: by Dorothy Burr Thompson.

Eastlake, Elizabeth (Rigby), Lady, 1809–1893

Denvir, Bernard. "The Eastlakes." *QR*, 295 (Jan. 1957), 85-97.
DNB, 22 (Supp.).

Eastlake, Elizabeth, Lady. *Journals and Correspondence.* 2 vols. Edited by Charles Eastlake
    Smith. London, 1895.
Gould, Cecil. "The Eastlakes." *Apollo,* 101 (May 1975), 350-53.
Lochhead, Marion. *Elizabeth Rigby, Lady Eastlake.* London, 1961.
Robertson, David. *Sir Charles Eastlake and the Victorian Art World.* Princeton, N.J., 1978.

Edwards, Amelia Ann Blandford, 1831–1892

British Authors of the Nineteenth Century. Edited by Stanley J. Kunitz and Howard Haycraft.
    New York, 1936.
DNB, 22 (Supp.).
Who Was Who in Egyptology. Compiled by Warren R. Dawson and Eric P. Uphill. London,
    1972.
Winslow, William C. *The Queen of Egyptology, Amelia B. Edwards* [Boston, 1892?].
Wortham, John D. *The Rise of British Egyptology 1549–1906.* Norman, Okla., 1971, pp.
    106-09.

Ellet, Elizabeth Fries (Lummis), 1812?–1877

Conrad, Susan P. *Perish the Thought: Intellectual Women in Romantic America 1830-60.* New
    York, 1976, pp. 116-22.
NAW.
Phillips, Elizabeth. In *American Women Writers: A Critical Reference Guide from Colonial
    Times to the Present,* edited by Lina Mainiero, I, 581-83. New York, 1979.

Esdaile, Katharine Ada (McDowall), 1881–1950

AR, 108 (Nov. 1950), 327: obituary.
BM, 92 (Nov. 1950), 329: obituary.
DNB, 1941-50.

Force, Juliana (Rieser), 1876–1948

Berman, Avis. *Museum News,* 55/2 (Nov.-Dec. 1976), 45-49 and 59-62: profile.
CB, 1941.
Friedman, B. H. *Gertrude Vanderbilt Whitney.* New York, 1978.
NAW.
Whitney Museum of American Art. *Juliana Force and American Art.* Memorial Exhibition,
    23 Sept.-30 Oct. 1949. New York, 1949.

Gardner, Helen, 1878–1946

NAW.

Goldman, Hetty, 1881–1972

Institute for Advanced Study. *A Symposium in Memory of Hetty Goldman 1881-1972.* Prince-
    ton, N.J., 1974.
NAW (Supp.).
NCAB, 56 (1975).
NY Times, 6 May 1972: obituary.
Who Was Who in America, 1969-73.

Gothein, Marie Luise, 1863–1931

Gothein, Percy. "Aus dem florentiner Tagebuch." *Castrum Peregrini*, 6 (1952), 5-23.
Salin, Edgar. *Ruperto-Carola* 34 (Dec. 1963), 81-85: memoir.

Greene, Belle da Costa, 1883–1950

Bühler, Curt. *Speculum*, 32 (July 1957), 642-44: obituary.
NAW: by Dorothy Miner and Anne L. Haight.
Miner, Dorothy. *Studies in Art and Literature for Belle da Costa Greene*. Edited by Dorothy
    Miner, pp. ix-xiii. Princeton, N.J., 1954.
Secrest, Meryle. *Being Bernard Berenson: A Biography*. New York, 1979.
Wroth, Lawrence C. "A Tribute to the Library and Its First Director." In *The First Quarter
    Century of the Pierpont Morgan Library. A Retrospective Exhibition in Honor of Belle
    da Costa Greene*, 5 April-23 July 1949. New York, 1949, pp. 9-19, 26-29.

Hawes, Harriet Ann (Boyd), 1871–1945

Boyd, Harriet (later Hawes). "Memoirs of a Pioneer Archaeologist in Crete." *Archaeology* 18
    (Summer and Winter 1965), 94-101 and 268-76.
DAB (Supp. 3), 1941-45: by Phyllis W. Lehmann.
Lehmann, Phyllis W. "Introductory Remarks." In *A Land Called Crete: A Symposium in
    Memory of Harriet Boyd Hawes* (Smith College Studies in History, 45). Northampton,
    Mass., 1968, pp. 11-14.
NAW.

Heaton, Mary Margaret (Keymer), 1836–1883

DNB.
Modern English Biography. Compiled by Frederic Boase. London, 1897.
Monkhouse, Cosmo. *The Academy*, 23 (9 June 1883), 408-09: obituary.

Hill, Dorothy Kent, b. 1907

Dictionary of American Scholars, 1978.
Randall, Richard H., Jr. In *Journal of the Walters Art Gallery, Essays in Honor of Dorothy
    Kent Hill*, 36 (1977), v-vi: profile.
Who's Who, 1974.
WWAA, 1978.

Johnson, Ellen H., b. 1910

CA, 37-40.
Gorney, Jay. "Oberlin's Tribute to Ellen Johnson." *Art News*, 74 (April 1975), 33-34.
WWAA, 1978.
Young, C. H. *Oberlin College Bulletin*, 34/2 (1976-77), 74-77: appreciation.

Jones, Lois Mailou, b. 1905

Afro-American Artists: A Bio-bibliographical Directory. Compiled and edited by Theresa D.
    Cederholm. Boston, 1973.
Fine, Elsa H. *The Afro-American Artist: A Search for Identity*. New York, 1973, pp. 136-39.
Lewis, Samella S. *Art: African American*. New York, 1978, pp. 97-100.
WWAA, 1978.

Kennedy, Ruth (Wedgwood), 1896–1968

Lee, Rensselaer W. *AJ* (Fall 1969), 100-01: obituary.
Sheard, Wendy S. *Antiquity in the Renaissance: In Honor of Phyllis Williams Lehmann*, 6 April-6 June 1978. Exhibition catalogue, Smith College Museum of Art. Northampton, Mass., 1978; n.p.: memoir by Phyllis W. Lehmann.

Kenyon, Kathleen, 1906–1978

CA, 21-24.
International Authors and Writers Who's Who, 1977.
International Who's Who, 1977-78.
Moorey, P.R.S. "Kathleen Kenyon and Palestinian Archaeology." *Palestinian Exploration Quarterly* (Jan.-June 1979), 3-10: appreciation.
Rittenhouse, Mignon. *Seven Women Explorers*. New York, 1964, pp. 102-07.
Washington Post, 25 Aug. 1978: obituary.
Who's Who, 1974.

Kuh, Katharine, b. 1904

"Interpreter Kuh." *Newsweek*, 391 (25 Feb. 1952), 60.
WWAA, 1978.
WWAW, 1958-59.

Lawrence, Marion, 1901-1978

College Art Association Newsletter, Sept. 1978, 12: obituary.
Heuser, Mary. *American Journal of Archaeology*, 82 (Fall 1978), 575: obituary.
WWAA, 1976.
WWAW, 1958-59.

Lee, Vernon, pseud. See Paget, Violet

Lehmann, Phyllis Williams, b. 1912

Dictionary of American Scholars, 1978.
Sheard, Wendy S. *Antiquity in the Renaissance: In Honor of Phyllis Williams Lehmann*, 6 April-6 June 1978. Exhibition catalogue, Smith College Museum of Art. Northampton, Mass., 1978; n.p.: appreciation.
Who's Who in America, 1976-77.

Levy, Florence Nightingale, 1870–1947

NAW.
NY Times, 17 Nov. 1947: obituary.
Woman's Who's Who of America, 1914-15.

McCausland, Elizabeth, 1899–1965

NY Times, 17 May 1965: obituary.
Publisher's Weekly, 21 June 1965, 80: obituary.

McMahon, Audrey, b. 1900?

McKinzie, Richard D. *The New Deal for Artists*. Princeton, N.J., 1973.

O'Connor, Francis V., ed. *Art for the Millions: Essays from the 1930s by Artists and Administrators of the WPA Federal Art Project.* Greenwich, Conn., 1973.

The Gallery Association of New York State; Park, Marlene, and Markowitz, Gerald E. *New Deal for Art: The Government Art Projects of the 1930s with Examples from New York City and State.* Hamilton, N.Y., 1977.

Masson, Georgina, b. 1912

CA 11-12 (see Johnson, Marion Georgina Wikeley).
Writer's Directory, 1976.

Mechlin, Leila, 1874–1949

NAW.
NY Times, 8 May 1949: obituary.
Who Was Who in America, 2 (1950).
Woman's Who's Who of America, 1914-15.

Merrifield, Mary Philadelphia, 1804/05-1889

Modern English Biography. Compiled by Frederic Boase. London, 1897.

Sewter, A. C. "Introduction," to Merrifield, Mary Philadelphia, *The Art of Fresco Painting.* London, 1846; reprint ed., London, 1952, pp. vii-x.

Miller, Dorothy Canning, b. 1904

Gruen, John. "Dorothy Miller in the Company of American Art." *Art News*, 75/9 (Nov. 1976), 54-58.

Lynes, Russell. *Good Old Modern: An Intimate Portrait of the Museum of Modern Art.* New York, 1973.

WWAA, 1978.

Moholy-Nagy, Sibyl, 1903-1971

Architectural Forum, 134 (June 1971), 29: obituary.
Banham, Reyner. *AR*, 150 (June 1971), 64: obituary.
NY Times, 9 Jan. 1971: obituary.

Stephens, Suzanne. "Voices of Consequence: Four Architectural Critics." In *Women in American Architecture: A Historic and Contemporary Perspective.* Edited by Susana Torre, pp. 40-41. New York, 1977.

Morgan, Sydney (Owenson), Lady, 1783?-1859

British Authors in the Nineteenth Century. Edited by Stanley J. Kunitz and Howard Haycraft. New York, 1936.

DNB.

Fitzpatrick, William J. *Lady Morgan: Her Career, Literary and Personal.* London, 1860.

Morgan, Lady. *Lady Morgan's Memoirs: Autobiography, Diaries, and Correspondence.* 2 vols. Edited by W. H. Dixon. London, 1862; reprint ed., New York, 1975.

_____. *Lady Morgan in France.* Edited by Elizabeth Suddaby and P. J. Yarrow. Newcastle Upon Tyne, 1971.

Stevenson, Lionel. *The Wild Irish Girl: The Life of Sydney Owenson, Lady Morgan (1776-1859).* 1st ed., 1939; reissued, New York, 1969.

Morley, Grace McCann, b. 1900

"Twenty Years of Grace." *Time*, 65 (28 Feb. 1955), 58-59.
WWAA, 1978.

Morris, Frances, 1865/66-1955

AAA, 23 (1926), 477.
Breck, Joseph. "Resignation of Miss Frances Morris." *Bulletin of the Metropolitan Museum of Art*, 24 (Jan.-Dec. 1929), 266.
Howe, Winifred E. *History of the Metropolitan Museum of Art*. New York, 1945. II, 146, 148, 187, and 202.
NY Times, 27 Jan. 1955: obituary.

Murray, Margaret Alice, 1863-1963

Murray, Margaret. "Centenary." *Antiquity*, 37 (June 1963), 92-95.
―――. *My First Hundred Years*. London, 1963. Reviewed by Jacquetta Hawkes, *Antiquity*, 37 (June 1963), 311-13.
Who Was Who in Egyptology. Compiled by Warren R. Dawson and Eric P. Uphill. London, 1972.

Paget, Violet, 1856-1935 (pseud. Vernon Lee)

DNB, 1931-40.
Gunn, Peter. *Vernon Lee: Violet Paget, 1856-1935*. London, 1964; reprint ed., New York, 1975.
Samuels, Ernest. *Bernard Berenson: The Making of a Connoisseur*. Cambridge, Mass., 1979, pp. 277-92.
Wellek, René. "Vernon Lee, Bernard Berenson, and Aesthetics." In *Friendship's Garland: Essays Presented to Mario Praz on his Seventieth Birthday*. Edited by Vittorio Gabrieli, II, 233-51. Rome, 1966.

Peter, Sarah (Worthington) King, 1800-1877

Callen, Anthea. *Women Artists of the Arts and Crafts Movement 1870-1914*. New York, 1979.
DAB, 7.
King, Margaret. *Memoirs of the Life of Mrs. Sarah Peter*. 2 vols. Cincinnati, 1889.
McAllister, Anna S. *In Winter We Flourish: Life and Letters of Sarah Worthington King Peter 1800-1877*. New York, 1939.

Quinton, Cornelia Bentley (Sage), 1876–1936

Buffalo Evening News, 18 May 1936: obituary.
Trucco, Terry. "Where Are the Women Museum Directors?" *Art News*, 77 (Feb. 1977), 52-55.
WWAA, 1936-37; 1938-39: obituary.
Woman's Who's Who of America, 1914-15.

Rebay, Hilla; Hilla Rebay von Ehrenwiesen, Baroness, 1890–1967

Davis, John H. *The Guggenheims: An American Epic*. New York, 1978.
Day, Douglas. "Guggenheim Gold." *Newsweek*, 87 (3 May 1976), 80-83.
Solomon R. Guggenheim Museum. *Acquisitions of the 1930's and 1940's: A Selection of Paintings, Watercolors and Drawings in Tribute to Baroness Hilla Von Rebay, 1890-1967*. New York, 1968.

Lomask, Milton. *Seed Money: The Guggenheim Story*. New York, 1964.
NAW, (Supp.).

Richter, Louise (Schwab), 1852-1938

Lexikon deutscher Frauen der Feder. Edited by Sophie Pataky. Berlin, 1898; reprint ed., Berne, 1971.
Supplement to Allibone's Critical Dictionary of English Literature and British and American Authors. Compiled by John Kirk. Philadelphia, 1902.
Who Was Who, 1929-1940.
Who Was Who Among English and European Authors, 1931-1949. Detroit, 1978.

Rindge, Agnes. See Claflin, Agnes (Rindge)

Rosenau, Helen, b. 1900

Mayer, L. A. *Bibliography of Jewish Art*. Edited by Otto Kurz. Jerusalem, 1967.
Who's Who in Art, 1977.

Rosenthal, Gertrude, b. 1903

Baltimore Museum of Art. *Annual 3, Studies in Honor of Gertrude Rosenthal*, Part 1 (1968), 1-3: appreciation by Charles Parkhurst; and *Annual 4, Studies in Honor of Gertrude Rosenthal*, Part 2 (1972), 11-13: appreciation by Adelyn D. Breeskin.
WWAA, 1978.

Saarinen, Aline (Bernstein) Louchheim, 1914-1972

Architectural Forum, 90 (July 1972), 90: obituary.
CA, 37.
CB, 1956.
Marzolf, Marion. *Up from the Footnote: A History of Women Journalists*. New York, 1977, pp. 169-70.
NAW (Supp.).
NY Times, 15 July 1972: obituary.

Sage, Cornelia Bentley: See Quinton, Cornelia Bentley (Sage)

Savage, Augusta, 1892-1962

Afro-American Artists: A Bio-bibliographical Directory. Compiled and edited by Theresa D. Cederholm. Boston, 1973.
Bearden, Romare, and Henderson, Harry. *Six Black Masters of American Art*. New York, 1972, pp. 76-98: biography.
CB, 1941; 1962.
Lewis, Samella S. *Art: African American*. New York, 1978, pp. 84-86.
NAW (Supp.).

Schapire, Rosa, 1874-1954

Leicestershire Museums and Art Gallery. *The Expressionist Revolution in German Art, 1871-1933*. Catalogue by Barry Herbert and Alisdair Hinshelwood. Leicester, 1978, p. 113: biography.
Wietek, Gerhard. *Gemalte Künstler Post: Karten und Briefe deutscher Künstler aus dem 20. Jahrhundert*. Munich, 1977.

_____. *Jahrbuch der Hamburger Kunstsammlungen*, 9 (1964), 115-59: biography and bibliography.

Schlegel, Dorothea (Mendelssohn) Veit von, 1763–1839

Deibel, Franz. *Dorothea Schlegel als Schriftstellerin im Zusammenhang mit der romantischen Schule*. Berlin, 1905.
Deutsches Literatur-Lexikon. Edited by Wilhelm Kosch. Berne, 1956.
LDF.
Meyer, Bertha. *Salon Sketches: Biographical Studies of Berlin Salons of the Emancipation*. New York, 1938, pp. 21-47.

Schopenhauer, Johanna Henriette (Trosiener), 1766–1838

Deutsches Literatur-Lexikon. Edited by Wilhelm Kosch. Berne, 1956.
Frost, Laura. *Johanna Schopenhauer: Ein Frauenleben aus der klassischen Zeit*. Berlin, 1905.
LDF.
Schopenhauer, Johanna. *Ihr glücklichen Augen: Jugenderrinerungen, Tagebucher, Briefe*. Edited by Rolf Weber. Berlin, 1978.
_____. *Youthful Life and Pictures of Travel, Being the Autobiography of Madame Schopenhauer*. 2 vols. Edited by Adèle Schopenhauer. London, 1847.

Schreiber, Lady Charlotte (Bertie) Guest, 1812–1895

British Authors of the Nineteenth Century. Edited by Stanley J. Kunitz and Howard Haycraft. New York, 1936.
Herrmann, Frank. *The English as Collectors: A Documentary Chrestomathy*. London, 1972, pp. 329-43.
Phillips, David R. *Lady Charlotte Guest and The Mabinogion: Some Notes on the Work and Its Translator, with Extracts from Her Journals*. Carmarthen, 1921.
Schreiber, Lady Charlotte. *Journals*. Edited by Montague Guest. 2 vols. London, 1911.
_____. *Lady Charlotte Guest, Extracts from her Journal, 1833-1852*; and *Extracts from her Journal, 1853-1891*. Edited by the Earl of Bessborough. London, 1950-1952.

Spencer, Eleanor Patterson, b. 1895

Gartrell, Eugenia R. *Goucher Alumnae Quarterly*, 40/4 (Summer 1962), 20: appreciation.
Goucher Library News, 24 (May 1979), n.p.: notice.
WWAA, 1976.
WWAW, 1958-59.

Staël, Madame de. Staël-Holstein, Anne Louise Germaine (Necker), Baroness of, 1766–1817

Biographie universelle ancienne et moderne, 40. Edited by J. F. Michaud. Paris, 1854; reprint ed., Graz, 1969.
Blennerhasset, Lady Charlotte. *Madame de Staël: Her Friends and Her Influence in Politics and Literature*. 3 vols. London, 1889.
European Authors 1000-1900. Edited by Stanley J. Kunitz and Vineta Colby. New York, 1967.
Herold, J. Christopher. *Mistress to an Age: A Life of Madame de Staël*. New York, 1958.
Moers, Ellen. *Literary Women: The Great Writers*. Garden City, N.Y., 1977, pp. 264-319 and 466-68.

Starke, Mariana, 1762?–1838

DNB.
Haskell, Francis. *Rediscoveries in Art: Some Aspects of Taste, Fashion and Collecting in England and France.* London, 1976, pp. 107-08.

Starr, Ellen Gates, 1859–1940

Callen, Anthea. *Women Artists of the Arts and Crafts Movement 1870–1914.* New York, 1979, pp. 198-99 and 226.
Davis, Allen F., and McCree, Mary L., eds. *Eighty Years at Hull-House.* Chicago, 1969.
NAW.

Steinitz, Kate (Trauman), 1889–1975

CA, Permanent Series, 2.
Los Angeles Times, 27 April 1975: obituary.
Wilson Library Bulletin, 44 (Jan. 1970), 512-37: memoirs and bibliography.
Wilson Library Bulletin, 49 (June 1975), 717: obituary.

Steinweg, Klara, 1902–1972

Hueck, Irene. *BM* (June 1973), 397: obituary.
Mitteilungen des kunsthistorischen Institutes in Florenz, Klara Steinweg in Memoriam, 17/2-3 (June 1973), n.p. and 199-200: obituary and bibliography.

Stevenson, Sara (Yorke), 1847–1921

DAB, 9.
A Tribute from the Civic Club of Philadelphia. Edited by Frances A. Wister. Philadelphia, 1922, pp. 1-64: biography and bibliography.
Warner, Langdon. *Pennsylvania Museum Bulletin*, 70 (Feb. 1922), 3-4: obituary.
Who Was Who in America, 1897-1942.
Woman's Who's Who of America, 1914-15.

Strong, Eugénie (Sellers), 1860–1943

DNB, 1941-50.
Sprigge, Sylvia. *Berenson: A Biography.* London, 1960, pp. 176-81.
Thomson, Gladys S. *Mrs. Arthur Strong: A Memoir.* London, 1949.

Sullivan, Mary Josephine (Quinn), 1877–1939

Goodyear, A. Conger. *The Museum of Modern Art: The First Ten Years.* New York, 1943.
Lynes, Russell. *Good Old Modern: An Intimate Portrait of the Museum of Modern Art.* New York, 1973.
NAW.
NY Times, 6 Dec. 1939: obituary.

Swindler, Mary Hamilton, 1884–1967

"In Honor of Mary Hamilton Swindler." *American Journal of Archaeology*, 54/4 (Oct. 1950), 292-93: tribute and bibliography by Dorothy Burr Thompson.
American Journal of Archaeology, 71/2 (April 1967), 115: obituary.

Brendel, Otto J. "Symposium for Mary Hamilton Swindler." *Classical Journal*, 45 (Nov. 1949), 96-98.
NAW (Supp.).
NCAB, 54, 1973.
NY Times, 18 Jan. 1967: obituary.

Townsend, Gertrude, 1892-1979

AAA, 23 (1926), 484.
Whitehill, Walter M. *Museum of Fine Arts, Boston: A Centennial History*. Cambridge, Mass., 1970; II, 566-69 and 711-12.

Toynbee, Jocelyn Mary Catherine, b. 1897

CA, 37.
International Authors and Writers Who's Who, 1977.
Who's Who, 1979.

Twining, Louisa, 1820-1911

LDF.
Twining, Louisa. *Recollections of Life and Work*. London, 1893: autobiography.
Young, Agnes F., and Ashton, E. T. *British Social Work in the Nineteenth Century*. London, 1956, pp. 55-58 and 142-44.

Underhill, Gertrude, 1874-1954

AAA, 23 (1926), 484.
Milliken, William M. *Bulletin of the Cleveland Museum of Art*, 34/4 (April 1947), 63-64: appreciation.
_____. *Bulletin of the Cleveland Museum of Art*, 41/6 (June 1954), 115-16: obituary.

Van Deman, Esther Boise, 1862-1937

American Academy in Rome. *Fotografia archeologica 1865-1914*. Edited by Karin Bull-Simonsen Einaudi. Rome [1978?], 12-18.
DAB, 11/2 (Supp. 2), 1958: by Marion E. Blake.
MacKendrick, Paul. *The Mute Stones Speak: The Story of Archaeology in Italy*. New York, 1976, pp. 317-21.
NAW.

Varnhagen Von Ense, Rahel (Levin), 1771-1833

Arendt, Hannah. *Rahel Varnhagen: The Life of a Jewish Woman*. New York, 1974.
Key, Ellen. *Rahel Varnhagen: A Portrait*. New York and London, 1913; reprint ed., Westport, Conn., 1976.
LDF.
Starr-Guilloton, Doris. "Rahel Varnhagen und die Frauenfrage in der deutschen Romantik: Eine Untersuchung ihrer Briefe und Tagebuchnotizen." *Monatshefte*, 69/4 (Winter 1977), 391-403.
Varnhagen, Rahel. *Briefwechsel*. 4 vols. Edited by Friedhelm Kemp. Munich, 1966-68.

Vavalà, Evelyn Sandberg, 1888-1961

Pope-Hennessy, John. *BM*, 103 (Nov. 1961), 466-69: obituary.

Waters, Clara (Erskine) Clement, 1834–1916

Boston Transcript, 21 Feb. 1916: obituary.
NAW.
A Woman of the Century. Edited by Frances E. Willard and Mary A. Livermore. Buffalo, 1893; reprint ed., Detroit, 1967.

Weibel, Adele (Coulin), 1880–1963

Ferry, Eleanor. *Bulletin of the Detroit Institute of Arts*, 42/4 (Summer 1963), 76: obituary.
Scheyer, Ernst. *Art Quarterly*, 26/2 (Summer 1963), 247-48: obituary.

Wescher, Herta (Kauert), 1899-1971

Bauhaus and Bauhaus People: Personal Opinions and Recollections of Former Bauhaus Members and their Contemporaries. Edited by Eckhard Neumann. New York and London, 1970, p. 63: biography.
NY Times, 5 March 1971: obituary.

Wharton, Edith Newbold (Jones), 1862–1937

Lewis, R. W. B. *Edith Wharton: A Biography*. New York, 1975.
NAW.
Sutton, Denys. "The Sharp Eye of Edith Wharton." *Apollo*, 103 (Jan. 1976), 2-12.
Wharton, Edith. *A Backward Glance*. New York, 1934.

Winser, Beatrice, 1869–1947

NAW: by Katherine Coffey.
NY Times, 27 April 1947: tribute; 16 Sept. 1947: obituary; 18 Sept. 1947: editorial.
Who Was Who in America, 1950.

Wischnitzer, Rachel (Bernstein), b. 1885

Encyclopaedia Judaica, 1971.
Mayer, L. A. *Bibliography of Jewish Art*. Edited by Otto Kurz. Jerusalem, 1967.
New Standard Jewish Encyclopedia, 1977.
Who's Who in World Jewry, 1978.
Wischnitzer, Rachel. "From My Archives." *Journal of Jewish Art*, 6 (1979), 6-15: memoir; 158-65: bibliography, edited by Rochelle Weinstein.

INDEX

NOTES ON CONTRIBUTORS

Jelisaveta Stanojevich Allen is an art historian and the Bibliographer at Dumbarton Oaks Center for Byzantine Studies, where she is editor of the series *Dumbarton Oaks Bibliographies based on Byzantinische Zeitschrift.*

Diane DeGrazia Bohlin is Curator of Italian Drawings at the National Gallery of Art, Washington. Her principal field of study encompasses Italian prints and drawings of the sixteenth and seventeenth centuries, focusing primarily on those of Parma and Bologna. She has published on the drawings of Guercino and Bertoia and is the author of the volume *Prints and Related Drawings by the Carracci Family, a Catalogue Raisonné.*

Larissa Bonfante is Professor and Head of the Department of Classics at New York University. She is a specialist in Etruscan studies and ancient dress, the author of *Etruscan Dress*, and co-editor, with Helga von Heintze, of *In Memoriam Otto J. Brendel: Essays in Archaeology and the Humanities.*

Ingrid E. M. Edlund is an Assistant Professor in the Department of Classics at the University of Texas at Austin and Associate Director of the University of Texas Excavations at Metaponto. Her special field of research is Etruscan art and archaeology and the history and archaeology of Early Rome. She has published studies on Etruscan terra-cotta sculptures from Poggio Civitate, the Olcott collection of Iron Age and Etruscan Vases at Columbia University, and the historical sources for Early Rome. She is currently working on the publication of the University of Texas excavations at Metaponto and a monograph on Dionysios of Halikarnassos.

Colin Eisler is Robert Lehman Professor at the New York University Institute of Fine Arts, where he has taught for more than twenty years. Working with the Metropolitan Museum of Art, the Grey Art Gallery, the Jewish Museum, the Drawing Center, and the Israel Museum, he combines connoisseurship and exhibition planning with art history. His fields include Renaissance art of Western Europe, prints, drawings, and photography. *The Master of the Unicorn: The Life and Work of Jean Duvet* (New York, Abaris Books, 1979) is his most recent publication.

Christine Mitchell Havelock is Professor of Art and Curator of the Classical Collection at Vassar College. Earlier she was also Assistant to the President and the Director of Women's Studies at Vassar. Her several published articles reveal her special interest in archaizing revivals and their causes in Greek art, the round sculptures from the Mausoleum at Halicarnassos, and the impact of Greek sculpture and painting on the ancient spectator. She is the author of the book *Hellenistic Art.*

Adele M. Holcomb is an art historian who is Associate Professor and Chairperson of the Department of Fine Art at Bishop's University, Lennox-ville, Québec. She has written on the symbolism of Romantic landscape painting, on Turner, J. S. Cotman, Anna Jameson, and other aspects of nineteenth-century art history and criticism for such journals as the *Art Quarterly*, *Gazette des Beaux-Arts*, and the *Warburg Journal*. Her *John Sell Cotman* was published in 1978 by British Museum Publications. Presently she is working on a book on Anna Jameson and Victorian Art Criticism.

Madlyn Millner Kahr is Professor of Art History and Criticism at the University of California, San Diego. She is the author of a number of articles, mainly concerned with sixteenth- and seventeenth-century European painting or with iconographic problems, which have been published in scholarly journals in the United States and abroad, and of the books *Velasquez: The Art of Painting* (New York, 1976) and *Dutch Painting in the Seventeenth Century* (New York, 1978).

Cynthia D. Kinnard is Assistant Professor of English at Indiana University, where she teaches literature, women's studies, and American studies. Her dissertation was on Mariana G. Van Rensselaer, and she is presently at work on a book on antifeminism in America, from colonial times to the present.

Anna Marguerite McCann is an archaeological consultant to the Department of Education at the Metropolitan Museum of Art and was formerly a Senior Research Fellow in the Department of Greek and Roman art. She is also a lecturer at the Natural History Museum in New York and Director of the Cosa Port excavations in Italy. She has taught art history and Greek and Roman archaeology at Swarthmore College, the University of Missouri, the University of California at Berkeley, New York University and the New School for Social Research, New York City. She is the author of numerous articles on underwater archaeology and Roman sculpture. Her most recent book is on the *Roman Sarcophagi in the Metropolitan Museum of Art.*

Claire Richter Sherman is an independent research scholar. A medievalist, she has taught at the University of Michigan, American University, and the University of Virginia. She is the author of *The Portraits of Charles V of France (1338-1380)* and of various studies of manuscripts from the library of this bibliophile king published in scholarly journals. She is working on a book about illustrations of Aristotle's *Ethics* and *Politics* in French manuscripts.

Susanna Terrell Saunders has taught the history of art at the Maryland College of Art and Design and lectured at several museums in the Washington area. Most recently she was Assistant Director of the Hull Gallery in Washington, D.C. She is a graduate of Bryn Mawr College with an M.A. in the history of art.

Corlette Rossiter Walker is Lecturer in Art History at the University of California at Santa Barbara. Her principal research interests are in late eighteenth-century European art and American art of the nineteenth century. In 1976 she organized and directed an exhibition and catalogue, *William Blake in the Art of His Time.* She is at present at work on a book on British and American artists attached to exploratory expeditions in the eighteenth and nineteenth centuries.